TAKE YOUR WRITING TO A HI...
CLIMBING THE 3 G'S OF CRITICAL THINKING

STEP 3: GENERATE (Create an idea of your own.)

- Merge the new idea into your own thought base.
- Incorporate the idea smoothly into your writing.
- Give credit where required.
- Write a draft.
- Revise and edit.

STEP 2: GRAPPLE (React to the new idea.)

- Be curious.
- Wrestle with the implications.
- Ask questions.
- Evaluate the idea with common sense and logic.
- Respond with integrity.

STEP 1: GRASP (Understand the idea you have encountered.)

- Figure out what point is being made.
- Adopt the author's view.
- Separate fact from opinion.
- Frame the idea in your own words.
- Look up unfamiliar words.

FIFTEENTH EDITION

Readings for Writers

Jo Ray McCuen-Metherell
Anthony C. Winkler

CENGAGE
Learning·

Australia • Brazil • Japan • Korea • Mexico • Singapore • Spain • United Kingdom • United States

CENGAGE
Learning®

Readings for Writers
Fifteenth Edition

Jo Ray McCuen-Metherell,

Anthony C. Winkler

Product Director:
Monica Eckman

Product Team Manager:
Christopher Bennem

Product Manager: Kate Derrick

Content Developers:
Leslie Taggart, Karen Mauk

Associate Content Developer:
Rachel Smith

Product Assistant: Katie Walsh

Media Developer:
Janine Tangney

Marketing Manager:
Erin Parkins

Content Project Manager:
Dan Saabye

Vice President, Director of
Advanced and Elective Product
Programs: Alison Zetterquist

Content Developer, Advanced
and Elective Product Programs:
Ashley Bargende

Senior Media Developer,
Advanced and Elective Product
Programs: Philip Lanza

Art Director: Marissa Falco

Manufacturing Planner: Betsy
Donaghey

IP Analyst: Ann Hoffman

IP Project Manager: Farah Fard

Production Service: S4 Carlisle

Compositor: S4 Carlisle

Text Designer: Diane Beasley

Cover Designer: Gary Ragaglia

Cover Image: Boat Studio, 1874,
oil on canvas by Claude Monet
(1840–1926)/De Agostini
Picture Library/The Bridgeman
Art Library

For product information and technology assistance, contact us at
Cengage Learning Customer & Sales Support, 1-888-915-3276

For permission to use material from this text or product,
submit all requests online at **www.cengage.com/permissions.**
Further permissions questions can be emailed to
permissionrequest@cengage.com.

Library of Congress Control Number: 2014940406

ISBN-13: 978-1-305-11313-8

Cengage Learning
20 Channel Center Street
Boston, MA 02210
USA

Cengage Learning is a leading provider of customized learning solutions
with office locations around the globe, including Singapore, the United
Kingdom, Australia, Mexico, Brazil, and Japan. Locate your local office at
www.cengage.com/global.

Cengage Learning products are represented in Canada by Nelson
Education, Ltd.

To learn more about Cengage Learning Solutions, visit **www.cengage.com**.
To find online supplements and other instructional support, please visit
www.cengagebrain.com.

Printed in the United States of America
Print Number: 01   Print Year: 2014

This edition is dedicated to the students who will use it. Our hope is that as they encounter new ideas, they will absorb them into their intellectual horizons, realizing that ideas are the foundation of all good writing.

Jo Ray Metherell and Anthony C. Winkler

About the Cover

Claude Monet's *Studio Boat* (1874) represents an actual fishing boat the artist turned into a studio where he could retreat and paint. It is easy to imagine how the artist could lounge outside the little hut attached to the boat and observe the blue water and the luxuriant vegetation as the boat drifted along. Then, when he felt creativity prodding, he could retreat into the private studio to reflect and plan what to transfer to canvas. Similarly, every writer must retreat into his or her mind and the private world housed there. The students who use this book will learn to explore ideas as if they were drifting along and observing their environment until they must retreat into the hut of the mind to think critically and decide on what ideas to transfer onto paper.

Studio Boat (1874) by Claude Monet
Oil on canvas

Contents

7 Developing Good Paragraphs   141

14 Division/Classification   316

15 Causal Analysis   338

PART FOUR
Special Writing Projects   441

Thematic Table of Contents

Issues for Critical Thinking and Debate

In Print and Online in *MindTap for Readings for Writers* 15th Edition

Readings, images, and videos in blue are accompanied by questions.

The American Dream (Chapter 3)

IN PRINT AND MINDTAP

- *The Death of Horatio Alger* / Paul Krugman
- *By Our Own Bootstraps* / W. Michael Cox and Richard Alm
- *Long Live the American Dream* / Shikha Dalmia

ONLY IN MINDTAP

- *Deer Hunting with Jesus: Dispatches from America's Class War* / Jack Estes
- *Farewell, Buffalo* / Julia Burke
- *Crumbling American Dreams* / Robert D. Putnam
- *The American Dream* / Martin C. Jischke
- *The American Dream* / Richard Todd
- *Niall Ferguson on the End of the American Dream* / Niall Ferguson

Terrorism (Chapter 8)

IN PRINT AND MINDTAP

- *Terrorism: America in Fear* / Jeffrey Metherell (Student Corner essay)
- *Image Gallery*

ONLY IN MINDTAP

- *My Accidental Jihad* / Krista Bremer
- *The Real War* / Thomas L. Friedman
- *Violence in the Name of Allah?* (video)
- *How America Made ISIS* / Tom Engelhardt
- *American Extremist Reveals His Quest to Join ISIS* / Richard Engel, James Novogrod and Michele Neubert

Immigration (Chapter 12)

IN PRINT AND MINDTAP

- *Immigrants in America / Dave Herman (Student Corner essay)*
- *Image Gallery*

ONLY IN MINDTAP

- *Illegal Immigrants Are Bolstering Social Security with Billions / Eduardo Porter*
- *Wide-open Spaces / Bill Bryson*
- *Immigration Protest (video)*
- *Three Cheers for Pluralism Over Separatism / Thomas Friedman*
- *My Immigration Story / Raul Ramos y Sanchez (Website)*
- *"Making" in America, Changing the World: An Immigrant Maker's Story / Doug Rand and Bess Evans*

Online Dating (Chapter 13)

IN PRINT AND MINDTAP

- *"OMGILY2!!" Online Dating Is at Your Own Risk / Kindra M. Neuman (Student Corner essay)*
- *Image Gallery*

ONLY IN MINDTAP

- *The Truth about Online Dating / Robert Epstein*
- *Evaluating Internet Dating / Tim Daughtry*
- *Looking for Love (video)*
- *A Million First Dates: How Online Romance is Threatening Monogamy / Dan Slater*
- *Playing the Numbers in Digital Dating / Leah Reich*

Racism (Chapter 14)

IN PRINT AND MINDTAP

- *Color of Their Skin AND Content of Their Character / Carrie Moore (Student Corner essay)*
- *Image Gallery*

ONLY IN MINDTAP

- *Warriors Don't Cry / Melba Patillo Beals*
- *Incidents with White People / Sarah L. and A. Elizabeth Delany*
- *Protesters in Support of Darren Wilson (video)*
- *Black Dog Syndrome / Katy Waldman*
- *When Slang Becomes a Slur / Geoffrey Nunberg*

The Status of Women (Chapter 15)

IN PRINT AND MINDTAP

- *"Woman" Is a Noun* / *Paula Rewa (Student Corner essay)*
- *Image Gallery*

ONLY IN MINDTAP

- *The New Feminism* / *Kate Gubata*
- *The Farce of Feminism* / *Rebecca E. Rubins*
- *Hillary and Her Campaign for Women (video)*
- *The Gender Wage Gap Lie* / *Hanna Rosin*

Homelessness (Chapter 16)

IN PRINT AND MINDTAP

- *People Out on a Limb* / *Antoinette Poodt (Student Corner essay)*
- *Image Gallery*

ONLY IN MINDTAP

- *Homeless* / *Anna Quindlen*
- *The Homeless Lack a Political Voice, But Not American Ideals* / *Matt Lynch*
- *Good Night Moon Project (website)*
- *Citizen Crusaders for the Homeless (video)*
- *Rethink Homelessness Campaign* / *Impacthomelessness.org (video)*

The New Technology (Chapter 17)

IN PRINT AND MINDTAP

- *Thoughts about the Internet* / *Charlie Sorensen (Student Corner essay)*
- *Image Gallery*

ONLY IN MINDTAP

- *No Technology? No Problem* / *Eric Brende*
- *Beware the Apps!* / *Lacreta Scott*
- *Digital Detox (video)*
- *Too Much Technology Is Bad for the Brain* / *Steve Nelson*
- *The Problem with Easy Technology* / *Tim Wu*

Preface

Do textbooks have a tendency to gain weight as they age? This might seem a preposterous question to ask about an inanimate object made of cellulose, cardboard, paper and glue. But *Readings for Writers* is a spectacularly different book from others like it, having sold over a million copies and been used by hundreds of thousands of students as their basic freshman composition reader. Chances are good that it was your English teacher's first composition reader many years ago. It is also an incontrovertible fact that over the years it has grown bigger and fatter. It made its debut as a freshman composition text in 1974 at a girth of 530 pages. Now on the verge of its fifteenth edition, it weighs in at a colossal 820 pages—a gain of 290 pages. The time had come, we decided, to put the porker on a strict diet.

There are practical reasons for doing so. An inescapable fact about textbooks is they have a distressing tendency to not only get fatter with age but to get more expensive with every added page.

Over the years, Readings for Writers has kept pace with the themes, times and technology, some of which have perished and disappeared. For example, we have bounded from slow research in library carrels to instant research on the Internet. Although many of the issues we debated decades ago remain unresolved, we have moved on to more current topics such as terrorism and online dating. Nonetheless, we continue to teach writing as a skill that combines clarity and precision. Best of all, we immerse students in a mixture of classical masterpieces as well as progressive prize winners, which we encourage them to use as intellectual models. Moreover, realizing that indeed "one picture is worth a thousand words," we have taken the Art Gallery and distributed its images throughout the Part 2 chapters.

Readings for Writers provides a taste of all kinds of brilliant writing—literary classics, poems, speeches, narratives, and philosophy. Here William Shakespeare and Abraham Lincoln mingle with Martin Luther King and Maya Angelou. The aristocrat Sir Arthur Grimble mixes with common laborer Rick Bragg. We respect and challenge each one of them. All of the anthologized material is brought together and ordered under the headings of either *advice* or *examples,* giving students, as well as instructors, an idea of the practical emphasis of each selection. It is this unique structure, range of readings, and multifaceted appeal to every conceivable taste that have endowed *Readings for Writers* with its remarkable longevity.

New to This Edition—Online and in Print

The most significant change in this fifteenth edition is that the book is now online as well as in print.

MindTap for *Readings for Writers*, 15th Edition

The new **MindTap for Readings for Writers** allows you to personalize your teaching through a Learning Path built with key student objectives and the syllabus in mind. The MindTap includes an ebook exactly like the print book, plus multimedia "Issues for Critical Thinking and Debate" casebooks for each Part 2 chapter designed for students to analyze, evaluate, and synthesize sources and ideas. Chapter 3 on synthesis is also accompanied by a range of readings on the American dream that expand the print book's selections. Autogradable vocabulary activities for each reading help ensure that students have grasped essential meanings as they read.

The course is as flexible as you want it to be: you can add your own activities, PowerPoints, videos, and Google docs or simply select from the available content, and you can rearrange the parts to suit the needs of the course. Analytics and reports provide a snapshot of class progress, time in course, engagement and completion rates.

The Insite App in MindTap provides students with an easy way to upload papers for peer review, teacher comments, and if desired, an originality check. You can comment on student papers using prepopulated comments or write your own; create your own library of comments that can then be reused; or respond to student papers in a video, which is especially useful in an online course to personalize your interaction with students. The Aplia App has a variety of grammar activities that you can assign if the class needs them, and these activities are autogradable.

Writing on Social Networks

In print and online, we've added material to take advantage of students' eagerness to write to friends and acquaintances on social networking sites:

- A new section in Chapter 2 on "Writing on the Social Networks" provides recommendations for becoming a better writer while writing for online communities and websites.
- A new feature in Part 2 chapters called "To the Point" asks students to write tweets on particular topics as a way to encourage them to be pithy within the 140-character count limit of Twitter posts.

Writing about Images

We've responded to reviewers' suggestions by moving the images previously located in the Image Gallery to each Part 2 chapter in a new section titled "Image Gallery for Critical Thinking and Debate." The images—13 of them new to this edition—are accompanied there by analysis questions and writing suggestions. The readings on that issue can now be found in the MindTap online, expanded with multimedia and links to other readings for an even richer immersion in the issue.

A New Issue

The issue now addressed in Chapter 10's images (in the print book) and readings and media (in the MindTap) is bullying.

Vocabulary in Print and Online

Vocabulary words are now highlighted where they appear in a reading so that students can focus on them in context. In the MindTap, vocabulary activities for each word provide ways for students to work with words so they become part of their own usable lexicon.

New Readings

Nine new readings offer fresh perspectives on topics as diverse as bullying, Middle East ideologies, soldiers with PTSD, and the value of construction work. Two new student essays round out the new readings in the fifteenth edition, one on drugs in America and the other on bullying.

A Beautiful New Four-Color Design

A new four-color design throughout helps students pick out important information on the page and generally makes for a more aesthetically pleasing reading experience.

Unchanged in This Edition

For longtime users of *Readings for Writers,* let us reassure you that the basic structure and intent of the book remain unchanged.

- In Part I, Chapter 3, "Synthesis: Incorporating Outside Sources," gets students ample practice and instruction in effectively synthesizing outside sources. Numerous models and exercises as well as an extensive synthesis essay assignment engage students with a range of source materials. This chapter introduces students to the concepts and skills they will need to do well on the synthesis question of the AP® exam. Along with the rhetoric chapter in Part I and the argumentation chapter in Part II, these three chapters cover the concepts that students need for the three AP® essays on the exam.
- The unique labeling system that identifies the intended function of every anthologized piece as either giving **advice** about some fundamental principle of writing or as serving as **examples** of it.
- The included works offer a broad sweep of topics, styles, and arguments.
- The popular "Student Corner" showcases the essays of real students, along with their commentary on how they learned to write and the personal tips they offer composition students.
- The "Punctuation Workshop" drills students in the use of the most common punctuation marks, such as the comma, semicolon, dash, and colon.
- The "Rhetorical Thumbnail" sketches out the major considerations that went into writing the selections.

AP® and Advanced Placement Program® are trademarks registered and/or owned by the College Board, which was not involved in the production of, and does not endorse, this product.

- Quirky little prompts send students to the popular Editing Booth with its checklist of fundamental rules for editing.
- Each anthologized piece is still followed by questions about the Facts, Strategies, and Issues explored, and is bolstered by suggestions for writing.
- Each chapter still ends with Chapter Writing Assignments and Writing Assignments for a Specific Audience.

All of the changes in this fifteenth edition have one unmistakable aim: to make *Readings for Writers* even easier and more practical to use than before. Combining the advice of its anthologized experts with the authors' commentary, *Readings for Writers* can still be used unaccompanied by any other book.

Ancillaries

- **The Heinle Original Film Series in Literature DVD**—This DVD includes three short films. The first film, Eudora Welty's *A Worn Path,* includes an interview with Eudora Welty conducted by Pulitzer Prize–winning playwright Beth Henley. The second film, John Updike's *A&P,* includes an interview with John Updike conducted by Pulitzer Prize–winning writer Donald Murray. The final film, Raymond Carver's *Cathedral,* includes an interview with Raymond Carver's widow, Tess Gallagher, conducted by Carver scholars William Stull and Maureen P. Carroll.
- **Online Instructor's Manual**—Explore different literary interpretations and prepare for class more quickly and effectively with our online instructor's manual, which provides possible answers to the questions posed at the end of the readings and the Image Gallery images.
- **Resources for Writers**—Resources for Writers offers a variety of online activities for students to practice and refine their understanding of key concepts via interactive grammar and proofreading exercises, anti-plagiarism tutorials, writing and research modules, multimedia activities, and downloadable grammar podcasts.
- **"Salvation" by Langston Hughes (DVD): The Wadsworth Original Film Series in Literature**—Based on a chapter from Langston Hughes's autobiography, *The Big Sea, Salvation* stars Lou Beatty, Jr., and Ella Joyce. The video also includes interviews with Alice Walker and Arnold Rampersad, the foremost authority on Langston Hughes.
- *Fast Track to a 5*: *Preparing for the* AP® *English Language and Composition Examination*—This test-preparation guide includes an introduction on taking the exam, a vocabulary of literary terms, detailed preparation guidelines for each type of question found on the exam, and two complete practice exams. Written by Steve Olsen and Eveline Bailey, both of La Porte High School, La Porte, Texas.

Please contact your National Geographic/Cengage sales representative for more information, to evaluate examination copies of any of these teacher or student resources, or for product demonstrations.

The Journey Ahead

Learning to write well is comparable to taking a journey. Students travel from topic to topic—picking up tips and techniques as they go, meeting new writers whose art they can study and perhaps try to imitate. If there were a metaphorical equivalent for this book, it would be a field trip, where students learn by observing and by practicing what they have learned. Along the way, we send students to some editing workshops and guide their steps along various road signs, indicating the directions they are to follow. Think of this book, then, not merely as a text with the usual implications of dryness that the word suggests, but as a road map that will rush students off to far-flung destinations and then take them back to their own backyards as better writers than when they began.

Acknowledgments

A textbook is always a collaborative work. Many people—including editors, proofreaders, fact checkers, and various supporting personnel—contribute their skills and insights into making a book of this sort what it finally becomes. We thank them all for sharing their minds and talents with us and for making themselves available to us any time we needed them. Specifically, we would like to thank our editor, Karen Mauk, for encouraging us to keep to our time line and for her careful attention to detail, which often included helping us find material we needed and keeping us organized. We also wish to thank the following strong advisors at Cengage Learning: Kate Derrick, Product Manager; Leslie Taggart, Senior Content Developer; Dan Saaybe, Content Project Manager; Stacey Purviance, Marketing Director; Erin Parkins, Marketing Manager; Kathleen Walsh, Product Assistant; and Rachel Smith, Assistant Content Developer.

We would like to also gratefully acknowledge those reviewers who helped shape this fifteenth edition:

Belinda Adams, *Navarro College*

John Bennett, *Lake Land College*

Patricia Cain, *Pasadena Memorial High School*

Anthony Cavaluzzi, *SUNY Adirondack*

Susan Dawson, *University of Louisville*

Erwin Ford, *Albany State University*

Jane Gamber, *Hutchinson Community College*

Pat Herb, *North Central State College*

Terri Hilgendorf, *Lewis and Clark Community College*

Amelia Keel, *Lone Star College — Kingwood*

Howard Kerner, *Polk State College*

Laura La Flair, *Belmont Abbey College*

Christine Long, *Bellbrook High School*

Julie Long, *College of the Albemarle*

Alexis Moore, *Xavier University of Louisiana*

Jamie Pickering, *Paradise Valley High School*

Andrew Preslar, *Lamar State College – Orange*
Maria Rankin-Brown, *Pacific Union College*
Paula Rash, *Caldwell Community College & Technical Institute*
LeJeanna Raymond, *Richard Bland College*
Donald Richardson, *Phoenix College*
Nancy Risch, *Caldwell Community College & Technical Institute*
Nina Scaringello, *Suffolk County Community College*
Jennifer Schoch, *Southwestern Middle/High School*
Jasna Shannon, *Coker College*
James Suderman, *Northwest Florida State College*
Jason Thibodeaux, *Westminster Christian Academy*
Amy Towne, *Florida Gulf Coast University*
Victor Uszerowicz, *Miami-Dade College*
Bradley Waltman, *College of Southern Nevada*
Lewis Whitaker, *University of Connecticut*

We would also like to thank reviewers of previous editions:

Roseanna Almaee, *Darton College*
Daniel Bartlett, *Lamar University*
David Beveridge, *Butte College*
Shelley Bingham, *Darton College*
Rob Blain, *Houston Community College*
Gricelle Cano, *Houston Community College, Southeast*
Helen Ceraldi, *North Lake Community College*
Constance Christophersen, *Homestead High School*
Linda Cohen, *Bridgewater State University*
Eric Decker, *John Marshall High School*
Jane Gamber, *Hutchinson Community College*
Amy Habberstad, *South Anchorage High School*
Mark Howland, *Tabor Academy*
Ferdinand Hunter, *Gateway Community College*
Erica Lara, *Southwest Texas Junior College*
Christine Long, *Bellbrook High School*
Julie Long, *College of the Albemarle*
Caroline Mains, *Palo Alto College*
Deborah Manson, *Georgia Perimeter College*
Shawn Miller, *Francis Marion University*
Vicki Moulson, *College of the Albemarle*
Maureen O'Bryan, *Effingham County High School*

Erika Olsen, *NHTI*
Jamie Pickering, *Pinnacle High School*
Maria Rankin-Brown, *Pacific Union College*
Suzanna Riordan, *Baruch College*
Jill Silos, *Hesser College*
Tina Smith, *West High School*
Michael Sollars, *Texas Southern University*
Valerie Stevenson, *Patrick Henry High School*
Mary Ann Sullivan, *Hesser College*
Andrew Tomko, *Bergen Community College*
Kamana Tshibengabo, *Georgia Perimeter College, Newton*
Victor Uszerowicz, *Miami-Dade College*
Bradley Waltman, *Community College of Southern Nevada*
Bradley Waltman, *Darton College*
Mark Weber, *Buffalo State College*
Lewis Whitaker, *Georgia Perimeter College*
John Williamson, *Highlands High School*
Theodore Worozbyt, *Georgia Perimeter College, Newton*
Anita Wyman, *Hillsborough Community College*
Diana Yeager, *Hillsborough Community College*

Finally, we thank the members of our Advanced Placement advisory board, who offered valuable input:

Patricia Bond, *Shonomish High School*
John Brassil, *Mt. Ararat High School*
Patricia Cain, *Pasadena Memorial High School*
Debbie Engler, *Llano High School*
Steve Klinge, *Archmere Academy*
Joanne Krajeck, *Canton South High School*
Tania K. Lyon, *Mankato West High School*
Jason P. Thibodeaux, *Westminster Christian Academy*

Jo Ray McCuen-Metherell and
Anthony C. Winkler

PART ONE

From Reading to Writing

A veteran English teacher once remarked to us that she had known readers who were not writers, but she had never known writers who were not readers. Neither have we. All writers begin as eager readers and continue to read throughout their lives. Their lifelong pleasure in reading wanes only in the presence of the greater pleasure they take in writing.

You may not be a writer in the sense of making a living from what you write, and you may not even write every day. But like it or not, you read every day, even if it is nothing more than the sign on a passing bus or the words on a billboard. Unless you live in a cave or on a desert island, modern life compels you to read.

All of us begin life as nonreaders. Reading is a skill that is learned in childhood and shapes our intellectual growth in ways that are still not completely understood. And even though we might have learned to read under peculiarly similar or different conditions, we all more or less share a similar reading history.

It began with the delight we felt when we first were taught to read. And once we were able to read on our own, many of us found ourselves swept away into magical worlds. Books took us on exotic journeys to places that existed only on the page and in our heads. We were visited by cats wearing hats, by talking rabbits, and by children who never grow old. We walked down yellow brick roads, sailed a balloon to the moon, and traveled with a crusty pirate in search of buried treasure on a remote island. Reading had planted in our heads a delightful high-definition TV called *imagination*, and never were colors brighter or images sharper.

But as we grew older, a curious thing happened: Reading became associated with schoolwork as we were forced to read textbooks we disliked on subjects we hated. The very act of opening a book became a labor. Soon we were watching television to relax and reading only when we had to because of schoolwork. For many, reading changed from fun to drudgery. A lucky few retained a deep love of reading and will continue throughout their lives to read for fun. Speaking for them, the famous eighteenth-century British historian Edward Gibbon wrote in his *Memoirs*: "My early and invincible love of reading, I would not exchange for the treasures of India."

If you wish to write, you should develop the habit of reading. The skill of writing well is essentially a kind of mimicry, and the more writers we read, the more examples

1

we can choose to imitate. And although reading voraciously is no guarantee that you will write well, your writing is likely to get better if you continue to be an avid reader.

The first part of this book—*Reading and Writing*—covers the preliminary topics of a writing course. Chapter 1 covers critical reading and introduces us to one of America's most prolific writers, himself an avid reader who devoured hundreds of books each year. Chapter 2 examines the role of rhetoric, an ancient discipline that is much misunderstood today. Chapter 3 illumines the weighty skill of synthesis—that is, imbedding other writers' ideas into your own work, Chapter 4 covers the writer's voice, while Chapters 5, 6, and 7 deal first with the nuts and bolts of choosing a thesis topic and organizing a paper, and then with the indispensable craft of paragraph writing.

Among the lessons Part One teaches is this: Writing is not an isolated skill that exists apart from the intellect of the individual. It is, instead, ingrained in the whole person. Read widely and your writing is likely to get better as your judgment of good writing matures. You are also likely to rediscover pleasures you once derived from memorable storybooks—pleasures that have no box office charge, no crowds, and require no hardware more elaborate than a library card. ●

CHAPTER 1

Reading Critically

Kinds of Reading

There are at least four different kinds of reading. ***Casual reading*** is the most common. Everyone does it. The casual reader glances at magazines, newspaper headlines, letters, email messages, and roadside signs. Casual readers read not because they want to, but because they must. Many people, if not most, fall into this category.

Reading for pleasure—whether mystery novels, romances, or tales of adventure— is the second common kind of reading. Reading of this kind is relaxed and uncritical. Many readers do it at bedtime to help them fall asleep. Pleasure readers don't worry about grasping the writer's full meaning as long as they get the gist of it and are transported by the writing to an imaginary world.

Reading for information, the third kind of reading, is practiced by information seekers who use reading as a tool. This type of reading is usually done at work or at school. Doing a job well or completing an assignment on schedule is the primary purpose of reading for information. This type of reading requires attention, understanding, and memorization.

Finally, there is ***critical reading***—the kind of reading you must do for your college classes and the kind we shall emphasize throughout this book. Critical reading is active reading. You engage in a kind of mental dialogue with the writer. The writer says so-and-so is the case and you reply, "Maybe so, but what about this?" You annotate the margins of the book you're reading with your reactions and comments. You not only try to understand the author's main point, but you also try to deduce any consequences of it. Teachers and parents are forever muttering that students can't read well—that they know what the words say, but they don't know what the words mean. Energetic curriculum creators, abhorring this vacuum in students' minds, recently jumped into the fray and designed freshman composition courses that would encourage students to read critically. So what is critical reading? One way to explain it is to say what it is not. Critical reading is not gullibility—accepting as truth anything you read.

1. **Analysis.** First, students are encouraged to analyze their reading so as to see how ideas are composed, how they are connected to other ideas, and how they are often based on biases and prejudices. In research, it means to gather numerous sources

that support a point. For instance, a student writing a paper on the results of online dating will need to explore journals, books, and Internet sources to see what marriage counselors, psychologists, and ordinary people have reported about online romances and what opinions they have offered on the subject.

2. **Synthesis.** Next, students are encouraged to *synthesize*, which means to absorb or blend the ideas analyzed and forge something new and original—belonging to them alone and reflecting the student's mind. In other words, the critical reader will form his own opinion after studying the opinions of other thinkers. This reaching out for new data from new sources can send students on highly exotic adventures. However, the best part about synthesis is that it tampers down the students' arrogance by demonstrating that on most knotty subjects, more than a single opinion exists. For instance, on the subject of online dating, a student will find through research that while online dating is growing at an amazing speed, with thousands of single men and women placing their profiles on the Internet, the results are not consistent. Some couples are finding a harmonious and lasting relationship, but others discover only sexual chaos and even dangerous liaisons. A student reading on the subject must take into account various attitudes or findings, not just one.

3. **Evaluation.** The final step in critical thinking is to *evaluate*. This step is extremely important because what it does is give students the power to assess and grade the material read. After probing ideas that are for or against a point of view, the student finally must take sides. Is online dating the best answer to finding a mate, or is it hazardous? The student's conclusion might well be that more study on the subject is needed before anyone can state with certainty that marriages arranged through the computer are either good or bad. As one teacher lectured to her class: "Blessed are they who walk in the middle of the road, for they shall avoid extremes."

Throughout this book, we shall encourage you to read critically and to form an educated opinion on various controversies. Should the retirement age be raised to 70, or should it remain at 65? Should the United States continue to spend billions of dollars on foreign aid, or should we use the money to solve our own problems? Should we create a path to citizenship for illegal aliens or should we have them deported? These are topics on which writers disagree, and critical reading will offer you the chance to place your own weight on the seesaw. In a way, this is a complete reversal of teacher–student roles because critical reading requires that students think on their own. Now, not all college professors approve of critical thinking. In fact, some few consider it dangerous because they worry that it invites students to pass judgment on whether they should accept or reject all ideas they confront—even time-honored truths. A few critics believe that within critical thinking lie the germs of revolution, as in the French and American Revolution, Tiananmen Square, Kent State, the 1963 march on Washington, and the Tea Party movement. Fear mongering professors worry that students will ask questions such as these: "Is this class important?" "Does anyone see an inconsistency in this university's policy?" "Why should I conform?" "Shouldn't I be allowed to think on my own and make my own rules?"

This book considers critical reading a boon, not a bane. One of our goals is to have all students using this book learn how to solve problems by shining the beam of analysis on them—to take the facts and compare them with other facts in order to extract (synthesize) the truth. We believe that you are qualified to see the historical and cultural contexts of what you read. With experience, you will realize that you cannot allow your personal experience to judge everything you read, but you must see facts in the appropriate context in which they appear. For instance, if a Libertarian insists that the local fire and police departments should be run by a private owner, you have to understand that Libertarians believe, for better or for worse, that the less the government is involved in our lives, the more we shall flourish. Conversely, if some cultural progressive insists that the government must take care of all of the poor and the weak, you have to understand that progressives encourage government spending, especially on the dispossessed. Regardless of where a writer stands on an issue, you will become a better writer yourself if you read critically. The following guidelines will help you form the correct approach to reading critically.

Steps to Critical Reading

1. **Read actively.** Determine the author's main point as well as any secondary effects that stem from it. Ask yourself whether you agree or disagree with the author's opinions. If you disagree, make a note in the margin saying why. If the author makes a mistake of logic or fact, make a note on the page where it occurred.

2. **Demystify the writer.** Many of us have the tendency to regard writers as godlike and to take everything they say as gospel. But writers are only human and are just as likely to make mistakes as anyone else. Reading critically begins with kicking the writer off the throne of public esteem and regarding the writer's work as you would any other human production—which is to say, prone to error.

3. **Understand what you read.** Reread difficult passages, looking up in a dictionary all the unfamiliar words. You cannot form an opinion about what you have read unless you understand what the author is saying. Some students find it helpful to summarize aloud any difficult ideas they encounter. Reread any difficult chapter or essay whose meaning you didn't completely comprehend. A difficult-to-understand point usually seems clearer the second time around. For example, Tolstoy's massive novel *War and Peace*, on first reading, seems like a tangled plot cluttered by an overwhelming mass of scenes and characters. On second reading, however, the plot will seem clearer and the scenes and characters more understandable.

4. **Imagine an opposing point of view for all opinions.** If the writer says that the Arab punishment of cutting off the hands of a thief is more humane than the American system of imprisonment, reverse the argument and see what happens. In other words, look for reasons that support the other side. For example, if an essayist is passionately against the use of dogs in medical research, try to see the opposing point of view—namely, the benefits of such research to the lives of millions who suffer from terrible diseases. A little digging will reveal that insulin, the use of which has prolonged the lives of millions of diabetics, was discovered through research on dogs. The argument boils down to this question: Does a puppy have the same worth as a human baby?

5. **Look for biases and hidden assumptions.** For example, an atheist arguing for abortion will not attribute a soul to the unborn fetus; a devout Catholic will. To ferret

out possible biases and hidden assumptions, check the author's age, sex, education, and ethnic background. These and other personal biographical facts might have influenced the opinions expressed in the work, but you cannot know to what extent unless you know something about the author. (That is the rationale behind the use of biographical headnotes, which accompany the readings in this book.)

6. **Separate emotion from fact.** Talented writers frequently color an issue with emotionally charged language, thus casting their opinions in the best possible light. For example, a condemned murderer may be described in sympathetic language that draws attention away from his or her horrifying crime. Be alert to sloganeering, to bumper-sticker philosophizing about complex issues. To the neutral observer, few issues are as simple as black and white. Abortion is a more complex issue than either side presents. Capital punishment is not simply a matter of vengeance versus mercy. The tendency in public debate is to demonize the opposition and reduce issues to emotional slogans. As a critical reader, you must evaluate an argument by applying logic and reason and not be swayed by the emotionality of either side.

7. **If the issue is new to you, look up the facts.** If you are reading about an unfamiliar issue, be willing to fill in the gaps in your knowledge with research. For example, if you are reading an editorial that proposes raising home insurance rates for families taking care of foster children, you will want to know why. Is it because foster children do more property damage than other children? Is it because natural parents are apt to file lawsuits against foster parents? You can find answers to these questions by asking representatives of the affected parties: The State Department of Social Services, typical insurance agencies, foster parents associations, the county welfare directors association, any children's lobby, and others. To make a critical judgment, you must know and carefully weigh the facts.

8. **Use insights from one subject to illuminate or correct another.** Be prepared to apply what you already know to whatever you read. History can inform psychology; literature can provide insights into geography. For example, if a writer in psychology argues that most oppressed people develop a defeatist air that gives them a subconscious desire to be subjugated and makes them prey to tyrants, your knowledge of American history should tell you otherwise. As proof that oppressed people often fight oppression unto death, you can point to the Battle of Fallen Timbers in 1794, to the Battle of Tippecanoe in 1811, and to the Black Hawk War of 1832—conflicts in which the Indians fought desperately to retain their territories rather than go meekly to the reservations. In other words, you can use what you have learned from history to refute a falsehood from psychology.

9. **Evaluate the evidence.** Critical readers do not accept evidence at face value. They question its source, its verifiability, its appropriateness. Here are some practical tips for evaluating evidence:

   • **Verify a questionable opinion by cross-checking with other sources.** For example, if a medical writer argues that heavy smoking tends to cause serious bladder diseases in males, check the medical journals for confirmation of this view. Diligent research often turns up a consensus of opinion among the experts in any field.

- **Check the date of the evidence.** In science especially, evidence varies from year to year. Before 1976, no one really knew exactly how the immune system worked. Then Susumu Tonegawa, a geneticist at the Massachusetts Institute of Technology, discovered how our bodies rearrange genetic material and manufacture diverse types of antibodies to protect us from foreign substances. In 1976, when he first started his research, the evidence would say that how these specific antibodies came about was a mystery, but that evidence would be inaccurate ten years later.

- **Use common sense in evaluating evidence.** For example, if a writer argues that a child's handwriting can accurately predict his or her life as an adult, your own experience with human nature should lead you to reject this conclusion as speculative. No convincing evidence exists to corroborate it.

10. **Ponder the values behind a claim.** In writing the Declaration of Independence, Thomas Jefferson based his arguments on the value that "all men are created equal." On the other hand, Karl Marx based the arguments of his *Communist Manifesto* on the value that the laborer is society's greatest good. Critical reading means thinking about the values implicit in an argument. For instance, to argue that murderers should be hanged in public to satisfy society's need for revenge is to value revenge over human dignity. On the other hand, to argue that democracy can exist only with free speech is to value freedom of speech.

11. **Recognize logical fallacies.** Logic is not interested in the truth or falsehood of a claim. It is only interested in the method used to reach certain conclusions. Consider this train of thought: "All Italians are musical. Luigi is Italian, therefore Luigi must be musical." It is perfectly logical, but we know that it is not true because the major premise "All Italians are musical" is not true. As with any people, there will be some Italians who can't sing a note. In other words, sometimes a claim is supported by evidence, and sometimes it is not. Being logical does not guarantee being right, but avoiding logical fallacies is a requirement of critical thinking. The following logical flaws are among the ones most commonly used in a wide range of arguments: the *ad hominem* attack (attacking the person instead of the point of view or the argument); the *ad populum* appeal (the use of simplistic popular slogans to convince); the *false analogy* (comparing situations that have no bearing on each other); *begging the question* (arguing in circles); *ignoring the question* (focusing on matters that are beside the point); *either/or reasoning* (seeing the problem as all black or all white, with no shades of gray); *hasty generalization* (the mistake of inadequate sampling); and *non sequitur* (drawing a conclusion that is not connected to the evidence given). For a more detailed discussion of logical fallacies, turn to Chapter 16.

12. **Don't be seduced by bogus claims.** Arguments are often based on unsubstantiated statements. For example, a writer may warn that "Recent studies show women becoming increasingly hostile to men." Or, another writer might announce, "Statistics have shown beyond doubt that most well-educated males oppose gun control." You should always remain skeptical of these and similar claims when they are unaccompanied by hard-headed evidence. A proper claim will always be documented with verifiable evidence.

13. **Annotate your reading.** Many of us have the tendency to become lazy readers. We sit back with a book and almost immediately lapse into a daze. One way to avoid being a lazy reader is to annotate your reading—to write notes in the margins as you read. Many students are reluctant to scribble in the margins of a book because they hope to resell it at the end of the term. But this is a penny-wise-and-pound-foolish outlook. Instead of aiming to resell the book, your focus should be on getting the most out of it. Annotating is one way to do that. Indeed, to make notes in the margins of books is, in a way, to interact with the reading—almost like chatting with the author. If you can't bring yourself to write directly on the printed page of this book, we suggest you make notes on a separate sheet as you read. Here are some suggestions for annotating your reading:

- **Write down your immediate impression of the essay.**
   a. Did the subject interest you?
   b. Did the reading leave you inspired, worried, angry, amused, or better informed?
   c. Did the reading remind you of something in your own experience? (Cite the experience.)
   d. Did you agree or disagree with the author? (Note specific passages.)
   e. Did the reading give you any new ideas?

- **Note the author's style, especially the words or expressions used.**
   a. What specific passages really made you think?
   b. Where did the writer use an especially apt expression or image? What was it? What made it so good?
   c. Where, if any place, did the author write "over your head"?
   d. What kind of audience did the author seem to address? Did it include you or did you feel left out?

- **Make marginal notes that express your response to the author's ideas.**
   a. Supplement the author's idea or example with one of your own.
   b. Underline passages that seem essential to the author's point.
   c. Write any questions you might want to ask the author if he or she were sitting next to you.
   d. Write down any sudden insight you experienced.
   e. Write why you disagree with the author.
   f. Write a marginal explanation of any allusion made by the writer. For example, in the fourth paragraph of this chapter, we wrote, "We were visited by cats wearing hats, by talking rabbits, and by children who never grow old." Did you understand these three allusions? The first is a reference to *The Cat in the Hat* by Dr. Seuss; the second, to *Alice in Wonderland;* the third, to *Peter Pan.*

14. **Finally, be sure you understand the writer's opening context.** The writing may be part of an ongoing debate that began before you arrived and will continue after

you've left. Some essays begin by plunging right into an ongoing discussion, taking for granted that the reader is familiar with the opening context. The effect can be mystifying, like hearing an answer but not knowing the question.

Here are the principles of critical reading applied to a brief essay by CBS News commentator Andy Rooney. The annotations in the margins raise questions that we think any reasonable critical reader would ask. At the end of the essay, we provide the answers.

1. What is the opening context of this article?

1   I would choose to have written Fowler's *Modern English Usage.*

2. Who is Fowler?

2   My book, known far and wide and for all time as Rooney's *Modern English Usage* and comparable in sales to the Bible, would have assured my fame and fortune. Even more than that, if I'd had the kind of command of the language it would take to have written it, I would never again be uncertain about whether to use further or farther, hung or hanged, dived or dove. When I felt lousy and wanted to write about it, I'd know whether to say I felt nauseous or nauseated.

3. What is his book about?

3   If I was the intellectual guru of grammar, as author of that tome, I would issue updated decrees on usage such as an end to the pretentious subjunctive. Not if I were.

4. What do we learn about Fowler's book in this paragraph?

4   I would split infinitives at will when I damn well felt like it, secure in my knowledge that I was setting the standard for when to and when not to. Challenged by some petty grammarian quoting a high school English textbook, I would quote myself and say, as Fowler does, "Those upon whom the fear of infinitive-splitting sits heavy should remember that to give conclusive evidence, by distortions, of misconceiving the nature of the split infinitive is far more damaging to their literary pretensions than an actual lapse could be, for it exhibits them as deaf to the normal rhythm of English sentences."

5. What is Rooney doing here?

5   Never again would I suffer indecision over matters like whether it was necessary for me to use an "of" after "apropos." I would not be looking up "arcane" eight or ten times a year. I would not use "like" when I meant "such as."

6. What does this quotation tell us about Fowler?

6   The fine difference between sophisticated bits of usage such as syllepsis and zeugma would be clear in my mind. ("She ate an omelet and her heart out" is either syllepsis or zeugma. I am unclear which.)

7. What do these terms mean?

7   Having produced the best book on English usage ever written, I would berate the editors of the newly issued *New York Times Manual of Style and Usage* for their insistence that the President of the United States be referred to as merely president except when used as a title immediately preceding his name. In my book he's The President. Corporate chief executives are plain president.

8. What is the best book ever written on English usage?

8   I would conduct a nationwide poll to choose a satisfactory gender neutral replacement for both "he," "she," "him," and "her." This would relieve writers of the cumbersome but socially correct necessity of "he or she," "him or her," or the grammatically incorrect "they" or "their" with a singular precedent. ("Someone left their keys.")

9. What does this paragraph mean?

10. What is the significance of either "I nor me"?

9   Eventually, I'd expect Oliver Stone to buy the movie rights to Rooney's *Modern English Usage*. His film would prove it was neither I nor me who murdered the English language.

● ANSWERS TO CRITICAL READING QUESTIONS ON ANDY ROONEY

1. If you do not know the opening context of this essay, you're likely to miss the writer's intent—although you could probably reconstruct it from his essay. Rooney's essay initially appeared in the 2000 annual awards issue of the *Journal of the Screenwriters' Guild* as part of a feature called *A Writer's Fantasy—What I Wish I Had Written.* Various writers, Rooney among them, were asked to select the one work they wish they had written and say why.

2. Henry Watson Fowler (1858–1933) was an English lexicographer and philologist—someone who studies linguistics—who, in collaboration with his younger brother Frank, published in 1906 *The King's English,* a witty book on English usage and misusage. After the death of his brother, Fowler completed the classic Rooney wished he had written, *A Dictionary of Modern English Usage* (1926). Fowler was known for being definitive and blunt in his grammatical and literary opinions.

   He wrote, "Anyone who wishes to become a good writer should endeavor, before he allows himself to be tempted by the more showy qualities, to be direct, simple, brief, vigorous, and lucid"—certainly good advice for anyone who writes.

3. Many people consider *A Dictionary of Modern English Usage* to be the definitive book on English usage and grammar. Grammarians often consult it to settle arguments over the fine points of acceptable usage.

4. We learn in this paragraph that Fowler's book sold as well as the Bible and that its popularity ensured fame and fortune to its writer.

5. He's mocking the rule of the subjunctive, which many people think is an ugly Latin holdover.

6. It gives us a glimpse of the sometimes starchy writing style of Fowler, who is capable of going from clarity and plainness to a scholastic denseness in a single page.

7. These are examples of the kind of arcane topics that Fowler deals with in his book. *Syllepsis* refers to the use of a word in the same grammatical relationship with two other words while disagreeing in case, gender, number, or sense with one of them. An example is "Neither she nor they are coming," where *are* agrees with *they* but not with *she*. Syllepsis is also a figure of speech in which a single word is linked to two others but in different senses, as in this use of *write:* "I write with enthusiasm and a pen." *Zeugma* refers to the linking of one word to two, one of which it does not grammatically fit, as in this use of *were:* "The seeds were devoured but the banana uneaten."

8. Obviously Fowler's, in Rooney's opinion.

9. Rooney is referring here to the quest for a nonsexist, third-person pronoun so that a sentence like "A doctor should take care of his patients" can be written without the sexist bias implicit in the use of "his." In 1858, Charles Crozat Converse, of Erie, Pennsylvania, proposed the use of *thon,* a shortened form of *that one,* as a neutral, third-person pronoun—"A doctor should take care of thon patients"—but the word never caught on.

10. Again, Rooney is spoofing another fusty rule from English grammar—namely, that the verb "to be" takes no object. Rigorous practice of this rule is responsible for the snooty construction one hears over the telephone occasionally: "It is I" or "This is he."

 For tips on how to revise your work, exit on page 422 to the **Editing Booth!**

CHAPTER 2

Rhetoric: The Art of Persuasion

Road Map to Rhetoric

Rhetoric is the art of putting one's case in the strongest and best possible way. All of the strategies of communicating in speech and writing that we use daily in an attempt to sway each other come under its heading, with practical effects so lasting and widespread that we take them for granted. For instance, when we open a popular cookbook, we expect it to be written clearly, with ordinary words framed into speakable sentences. We do not expect it to be dense and wordy like a piece of legislation. Because of rhetoric, cookbooks are not written like legal contracts; insurance policies do not read like a comic's jokes; and love letters do not sound like State of the Union speeches.

Yet, there is no law requiring that this should be so. It is merely the effect of rhetoric—a combination of audience expectation and writers' desire to please—that operates like a force of nature. No doubt there are badly written cookbooks, but few are either published or read; flippant insurance companies go bankrupt; and pompous lovers have trouble finding mates. This desire of writers to please—to communicate with their audiences—is the basic law of rhetoric.

Grammar and Rhetoric

In the minds of some students, grammar and rhetoric are often confused, but they are significantly different. Grammar tells a writer how words should be used and sentences framed. Just as drivers obey the rules of the road, writers follow the rules of grammar. They know that they should not begin a sentence with "one" and then suddenly switch to "you," as in "One must try to do well or you will be embarrassed." That is called a shift in point of view and, like most grammatical lapses, tends to muddy meaning.

The Importance of Good Grammar

In an ideal world, grammar would be strictly neutral and mechanical and would imply nothing about anyone's inner self or social standing. In our grubby world, grammar is often the self-serving weapon of the language snob. Some people passionately believe that anyone who says or writes *ain't* instead of *isn't* would not be a suitable guest for tea. Yet as a wise orator from ancient times once remarked, "Nobody ever praises a speaker for his grammar; they only laugh at him if his grammar is bad." Grammar, in short, is a bit like tact: When it is absent we notice it; when it is present we don't.

There are basically two schools of grammar: prescriptive grammar and descriptive grammar. Prescriptive grammar begins with the assumption that the rules of grammar are etched in granite and have the universal application of gravity. People must be taught how to speak and write properly—for their own good and the good of the language. Descriptive grammar, on the other hand, makes no such assumptions. It begins by asking, How do certain people express themselves? How do they say this or that? Without making any value judgments on the usage based on some supposed universal standard of right and wrong, the descriptive grammarian infers the grammar rules that a community of writers and speakers observe. It says, under these conditions people use *ain't*. But since that is what they do, even though it's not what we do, we can still be good neighbors. People not in the prescriptive or descriptive camp fall somewhere between these two extreme positions.

The importance of good grammar, however, in our view, should be based on its useful function of helping us communicate and not on its misuse as a benchmark to sort people into social classes. In some countries, having a certain accent and using a bookish formal grammar are essential for social advancement and acceptance. In the United States, there are pockets of the population that think this way about grammar, but this belief is by no means common or universal.

Everyone knows what grammar is in general, but not everyone agrees that a particular construction is right or wrong. English grammar is in this muddle because its principles were founded by Latin grammarians who tried to superimpose the rules of that dead language on the emerging infant of English. This led to the formulation of some silly rules. Take, for example, the so-called split infinitive rule. Many instructors, editors, and institutions would damn as incorrect this popular phrase used in the introduction of *Star Trek* episodes: "to boldly go where no man has gone before." This is regarded as wrong because it puts the adverb *boldly* between the infinitive *to go*. In other words, it splits the infinitive as if it were a banana. According to the orthodox view, this should read "to go boldly" or "boldly to go." Why is this splitting wrong? Because since the infinitive in Latin is a single word that cannot be split, its equivalent in English, even though it consists of two words, should likewise never be split. On the basis of that silly line of reasoning was sculpted a rule of grammar that has bedeviled generations of writers and speakers.

However we arrived at our present state of confusion, the fact is that grammar is undeniably important because the world at large will judge you by your use or nonuse of it. The hard fact is that if you are applying for a job with a company sensitive about its image, you are less likely to be hired if your English is ungrammatical. Like it or not, the way you write and talk reveals your inner person as definitively as the way you dress or act. This concept of the inner man dates back to ancient Greece where, as the story goes, a rich merchant had taken his son to a philosopher who he hoped would accept the boy as a student. The philosopher glanced at the boy who was standing four feet away in broad daylight, and said, "Speak, so I can see you." We do not have on record what followed. But if there had been two boys, one of whom replied something like, "I ain't getting your point," and the other, "I don't quite understand what you mean," which boy do you think would have been chosen?

■ Letting the Habits of Literate Writers Be the Final Referee

Call it being snobbish and promoting class distinctions, but the truth is that if you want to achieve top-level jobs, you will have a better shot at doing so if you follow the grammar of people considered literate—those who write editorials in magazines like *Time*, *Harper's*, and *The New Yorker*, or in newspapers that influence public thinking, such as *The New York Times*, *The Wall Street Journal*, and *The Washington Post*. What we would like students to do is follow the grammatical rules observed by the best writers when they write unselfconsciously and regularly. All good writers make an occasional grammatical goof, and when someone corrects them, they are grateful. The most important rules to follow are those whose violations will stigmatize you as a person who uses substandard English. Here are some of the most grating errors committed by thousands of writers:

1. **Double negatives: Wrong:** He had hardly no clothes to wear in cold weather. **Right:** He had hardly any clothes to wear in cold weather. **Wrong:** I don't know nothing about baseball. **Right:** I don't know anything about baseball.

2. **Nonstandard verbs: Wrong:** Pete **knowed** the name of each bird. **Right:** Pete knew the name of each bird. **Wrong:** Melanie should've **wrote** an apology. **Right:** Melanie should've **written** an apology.

3. **Double comparatives: Wrong:** If you climb over the fence, you'll get there **more faster. Right:** If you climb over the fence, you'll get there **faster**.

4. **Adjective instead of adverb: Wrong:** That was a **real** stupid answer. **Right:** That was a **really** stupid answer. **Wrong:** She types good without looking at the keyboard. **Right:** She types **well** without looking at the keyboard.

5. **Incorrect pronoun: Wrong:** The coach never chooses him or **I. Right:** The coach never chooses him or me. **Wrong: Her** and **me** might get married. **Right: She** and **I** might get married.

6. **Subject-verb disagreement: Wrong:** They **was** always late. **Right:** They **were** always late. **Wrong:** That **don't** matter in the least. **Right:** That **doesn't** matter in the least.

These and numerous other grammatical errors we could have listed belong to the category of mistakes that literate writers never knowingly make. By the way, literate writers will instantly notice when another writer makes such errors, but not making these errors is simply taken for granted. Don't expect to garner special kudos if you avoid them. The rules we hope you will learn and obey are those that help you avoid being stigmatized as "illiterate." If you think your knowledge of correct grammar is weak, then we suggest you purchase a compact grammar handbook, such as *Grammar Matters* or *The Least You Should Know About Grammar*, to review or brush up on the rules.

● EXERCISES

1. Write a paragraph in which you express your views about the rules of grammar with which you are familiar. Do you consider their observance important, or do you see them as a way of segregating people?

2. Write a paragraph in which you describe your reaction to people who seem to disregard grammatical rules. Does their lack of grammatical sense affect your attitude toward them, or is it irrelevant to your attitude?

The Importance of Rhetoric

While grammar speaks in terms of rules, rhetoric speaks only in terms of effectiveness—and effectiveness is a relative judgment. If you are writing to a child, for example, you must use simple words and short sentences if you wish to be understood. However, simple words and short sentences may be entirely inappropriate in a paper explaining a complex process to an audience of specialists. When you know the rules of grammar, it is easy to compare two versions of a writing assignment and say if one is more conventionally grammatical than the other. It is far harder to say whether one version is more effectively written than the other.

Judging the effectiveness of a work is, in fact, the chief business of rhetoric. For example, consider this student paragraph:

> During high school, my favorite English course was English literature. Literature was not only interesting, but it was also fun. Learning about writers and poets of the past was enjoyable because of the teachers I had and the activities they scheduled. Teachers made past literature interesting because they could relate the writers back to the time in which they lived. This way I learned not only about English writers but also about English history.

Grammatically, this paragraph is correct; rhetorically, it is empty. It cries out for examples and supporting details. Which writers and poets did the student find so interesting? What activities did the teacher schedule to make them seem so? Without such details, the paragraph is shallow and monotonous.

Here is a paragraph on the same subject, written by a student with a strong sense of rhetoric:

> Picture a shy small-town girl of eighteen, attending college for the first time in a large city. She is terrified of the huge campus with its crowds of bustling students, but she is magnetically drawn to a course entitled "Survey of English Literature," for this awkward girl has always been an avid reader. College for me, this alien creature on campus, was the sudden revelation of a magical new world. I now could read the great English literary masterpieces—Milton's *Paradise Lost*, Shakespeare's *Othello*, Jane Austen's *Pride and Prejudice*. Then I could discuss them in class under the watchful eye of my professor, who encouraged me to dig for ideas and interpret them on my own. As the teacher asked questions, and the students responded to them, I received exciting flashes of insight into the human condition: I understood the loneliness of Jude the Obscure, the hardness of life in *Oliver Twist*, and the extravagant beauty of nature as detailed by the Romantic poets. English literature also led me into the mazy paths of history. I learned about the greed for political power as I read about the War of the Roses. I saw how the Magna Carta,

so reluctantly signed by King John, influenced our present democracy. And Chaucer's tales convinced me that the pageantry of people has not changed much since medieval times. English literature educated me without my being aware of the act of acquiring knowledge. I learned through falling in love with English literature.

The second paragraph is rhetorically more effective than the first because it tells us in richer detail exactly how the author was affected by her English classes.

Audience and Purpose

To write well, you must bear in mind two truths about writing: It has an audience and it is done for a purpose. Many students think that the audience of their writing is a single instructor whose tastes must be satisfied, but this viewpoint is too narrow. The instructor is your audience only in a symbolic sense. The instructor's real job is to be a stand-in for the educated reader. In this capacity, the instructor represents universal standards of today's writing. An English instructor knows writing, good and bad, and can tell you what is good about your work and what is not so good. In this capacity, your instructor can be compared to the working editor of a newspaper, and you, to a reporter.

Purpose, on the other hand, refers to what you hope to accomplish with your writing—the influence you intend your work to exert on your reader. Contrary to what you might think, earning a grade is not the purpose of an essay. That might be its result, but it cannot be its purpose. A freelance writer who sits down to do an article has expectations of earning money for the effort, but that is not the writer's primary purpose. Instead, purpose refers to the intention—be it grand or simple—the writer had in mind when pen first touched paper. If you are writing an essay about the funniest summer vacation you have ever had, your purpose is to amuse. If you are writing an essay about how amino acids are necessary for life, your purpose is to inform. If you are writing an essay urging mandatory jail terms for sellers of child pornography, your purpose is to persuade.

It follows from this discussion that you must understand the audience and purpose of an assignment if you are to have a context for judging the effectiveness of your words and sentences. Context hints at what might work and what might flop; it warns of perils and points to possible breakthroughs. Anyone knows that a love letter should not be written in the dense sentences of a bank report and that a note of sympathy to a grieving friend should not tell jokes—anyone, that is, who thinks about the audience and the purpose of the written words. As the English writer W. Somerset Maugham put it, "To write good prose is an affair of good manners." Like good manners, good prose is always appropriate. It fits the audience; it suits the purpose. This fitting and suiting of one's writing to audience and purpose are among the chief concerns of rhetoric.

The Internal Reader/Editor

The basic aim of any instruction in rhetoric is to teach you how to distinguish between what is appropriate and inappropriate for different audiences and purposes. You develop a sixth sense of what you should say in an essay for an English instructor, a note addressed to your mother, or an ad seeking a new roommate. We call this sixth sense the internal reader/editor. One writer defined it this way: ". . . as it is for any writer, there are two characters in my head: the Writer (me) and a Reader/Editor (also me), who represents anyone who reads what I write. These two talk to each other."

Your internal reader/editor is your sense for judging aptness and effectiveness in writing. This sense improves with practice and exposure to assignments intended for different audiences and purposes. Whether you are penning an essay for a psychology instructor or a letter to a creditor asking for more time to repay a debt, the same internal reader/editor judges the rhetorical and grammatical appropriateness of what you have written.

By the time you are old enough to read this book, your internal reader/editor is already in place and functioning with some sophistication. For example, your reader/editor surely knows that obscenities have no place in an essay, that "ain't" is not appropriate in a formal exam paper, and that a wealth of personal jokes and anecdotes do not belong in an objective paper on science.

Levels of English

Virtually all writing can be divided into three levels of English: formal, informal, and technical. Each has its place in the various assignments you will be asked to do. It is your internal reader/editor who must decide on the appropriateness of each for a specific assignment.

Formal English is characterized by full, complex sentences and the use of standard and consistent grammar. It states ideas in an orderly fashion and with an educated vocabulary. It avoids the "I" point of view and does not use contractions such as "can't," "don't," "he'd," or "wouldn't." Here is an example of formal English:

> As the sun rose higher that morning, swarms of canoes, or *canoas* as they were called in the Arawak language, were pushed out to sea through the surf breaking over the glistening white sands of Long Bay. They were all full of excited, painted Indians carrying balls of cotton thread, spears and vividly colored parrots to trade with the vessels lying a short distance off-shore. The Indian craft, probably painted as colorfully as their occupants, must have given the atmosphere of a festive regatta, and trading was brisk and lasted all day until nightfall.
>
> —D. J. R. Walker, *Columbus and the Golden World of the Island Arawaks*

The aim of formal writing is to make a case or present an argument impartially rather than to relate the writer's own views on a subject. The writer takes special care to eliminate the "I" reference and to remain discreetly in the background. Examples are either generalized or in the third person, but never personal. Note the following differences:

Generalized: "All of the participants agreed to publish their notes on the laboratory experiment."

Third person: "Murdoch, the director of the experiment, came to a different conclusion."

Personal: "I was delighted with the results of the study because it promised hope for diabetes patients."

In formal English, the personal example would be disallowed because it seems too biased or emotional and therefore unscientific. In formal writing, the facts are allowed to speak for themselves; the writer's task is to present them with objectivity.

Formal English is the staple of college writing. You should use it in research papers, scholarly papers, written examinations, and serious letters. Unless instructed to do otherwise, you should also use it in your essays.

Informal English is based on the familiar grammatical patterns and constructions of everyday speech. You should use it in journalistic writing and in personal letters, diaries, and light essays. The following student essay is a typical example:

> I drive a truck for a living, and every other week I'm assigned to a senior driver called Harry. Now, Harry is the dirtiest person I've ever met. Let's start with the fact that he never takes a bath or shower. Sitting in the closed cab of a diesel truck on a hot August day with Harry is like being shut up in a rendering plant; in fact, the smell he emanates has, on many occasions, made my eyes water and my stomach turn. I always thought Harry was just dark-complexioned until it rained one day and his arms started to streak—I mean, this guy is a self-inflicted mud slide. In fact, I could've sworn that once or twice I saw Harry scratch his head and a cloud of dust whirled up above him.

This point of view is unabashedly personal and relaxed. The "I" point of view is mixed with contractions, such as "I've," "I'm," and "could've." However, in many fields, the strict standards for using formal over informal English are easing. Even some scientific journals today allow the investigator to use the "I" pronoun, especially if the writer was heavily involved in the research. Consider this paragraph about a revolution in Nepal, reprinted from an article in *National Geographic*:

> From the teahouse I can see the police station, a broken concrete shell daubed with Maoist graffiti. The police have fled from here, as they have from most of rural Nepal, and the village is now the front line, the first community I've seen that is openly controlled by the rebels. When photographer Jonas Bendiksen and I arrived in Babiyachour, we noticed a few Maoist soldiers buying aluminum plates and sacks of rice for hundreds of new recruits training on a hill above the village. One of the highest ranking Maoists, Comrade Diwakar, was said to have arrived for their "graduation." We sent our letters of introduction up the hillside, asking to meet him. Nobody seemed in a hurry to respond.

In brief: Use formal English in most papers you submit to your teacher. Use informal English in your personal writing and in those special circumstances where you are free to express yourself in your own individualistic style.

Technical English is formal English that uses the vocabulary of a specialized field. It is written most often by engineers, technicians, and scientists. It commonly suffers from wordiness, overuse of abstract nouns, misuse of the passive voice, and improper subordination. Nevertheless, some technical writers are experts at their craft. Here is an example of technical writing:

Using a style set to change line spacing for an entire document

1. Go to the **Home** tab, in the **Styles** group, and click **Change Styles**.
2. Point to **Style Set** and point to the various style sets. Using the live preview, notice how the line spacing changes from one style set to the next.
3. When you see spacing that you like, click the name of the style set.

The level of English you should use in any specific essay will depend on its audience and purpose; that is a judgment your internal reader/editor must make. Let us take an example. Your English teacher asks you to write an essay on the most unforgettable date you've ever had. One student wrote this paragraph:

> My most unforgettable date was with Carolyn, whom I took to a drive-in movie. I chose the drive-in movie as the site of our date because Carolyn was nearly a foot taller than I, and I was embarrassed to be seen out in the open with her. What I did not expect was that my car would break down and I would not only have to get out and try to fix it, but that we would end up walking home side by side like Mutt and Jeff.

The tale that followed was a funny one about the writer's mishaps at the drive-in with Carolyn. He wrote the paragraph and the essay in an informal style because that is exactly what this assignment called for.

If, however, your sociology teacher asks you to write an essay on dating as a courtship ritual in America, you must write a formal essay. Instead of saying what happened to you personally on a date, you must say what is likely to happen on a date. Instead of airing your personal views, you must express the researched ideas and opinions of others. You should not use the pronoun "I" to refer to yourself, nor attempt to impose your personality on the material. This does not mean you should have no opinions of your own—quite the opposite—but you should base your expressed opinions on grounds more substantial than personal experience or unsupported belief. Here is an example of a student paper that follows the rules of objectivity:

> Dating is a universal courtship experience in the life of most American adolescents. The ritual goes back to the earliest chaperoned drawing-room meetings between eligible couples and has evolved to the present-day social outing. But the greatest impact on the ritual, so far as its American practice goes, has been the introduction and popularization of the automobile.

The writer supported her thesis—that the automobile has had a drastic impact on the dating ritual in America—throughout the paper and amply supported it with statistics, facts, and the testimony of experts. Her examples are also generalized rather than personal. Instead of writing that so-and-so happened to me on a date, she wrote that so-and-so is likely to happen to an American couple dating.

All writers will similarly adapt their language to suit the audience and purpose of their writing, using the principles that spring from common sense and the ancient discipline of rhetoric. While much of this adapting may be done unconsciously, it still must be done by all who sincerely wish to communicate with an audience.

Writing as a Process

Learning to write well cannot be mastered by rote, the way you might absorb facts about the anatomy of a fish or the chemistry of a nebula. It involves learning a process, and that is always harder to do than memorizing a set of facts. The parts of a bicycle can be memorized from a manual, but no one can learn to ride a bicycle merely by reading a book about it. *Scribendo disces scribere*, says the Latin proverb: "You learn to write by writing." Here, then, are some truths about the writing process uncovered by laboratory research:

- **Composing is a difficult, back-and-forth process.** Many writers compose in a halting, lurching way. A writer will pen a few sentences, pause to go back and revise them, compose several new sentences, and then pause again to reread and further edit before continuing with the paragraph. "In their thinking and writing," says one researcher, "writers 'go back' in order to push thought forward."

  Any professional writer will recognize the truth of this observation, but often it comes as a revelation to students who tend to worry when their own compositions emerge by similar fits and starts. Be assured that this back-and-forth movement is a healthy and normal part of composing. The research even suggests that writers who accept the halting, stumbling nature of composing actually have an easier time with this necessary process of "waiting, looking, and discovering" than those who fight against it. Because of this circularity in composing, writing is often described as a recursive process, meaning that results are achieved by a roundabout rather than a straight-line path. Often it is necessary to retrace one's trail, to go back to the beginning of a work, or to revise earlier sentences and paragraphs before writing new ones. If you find yourself doing something similar in your own writing, be heartened by this truth: That is how the vast majority of writers work. You are merely going through the normal cycle of composing.

- **The topic can make a difference in your writing.** Professional or amateur, few writers are entirely free to choose their own topics. Most are assigned topics by employers, professors, or circumstances. Yet, when choice does exist, the lesson from common sense and research is that you should always pick the topic you like best. The fact is that most people write better when they write about a subject that appeals to them. It is no mystery why this should be so. We all try harder when we are engaged in a labor of love—whether building our dream house or writing an essay. Unfortunately, in a classroom setting, many students are content to settle for a topic that seems simplest to research or easiest to write about, regardless of whether they find it appealing. This is a mistake. When you write for your own enjoyment, you will behave more like an experienced writer than when you force yourself to write about a subject you find boring.

- **Your writing will not automatically improve with each essay.** Writing does not automatically get better with every paper. It is realistic to compare writing to, say, archery. The first arrow might hit the bull's-eye, while the tenth might entirely miss the target. An archer's overall accuracy will gradually improve with practice, but never to the point of absolute certainty for any one arrow. In practical terms, this simply means that you shouldn't brood if you find a later essay turning out worse than an earlier one. Your overall writing skills are bound to improve with experience, even if the improvement isn't reflected in any single essay.

The gist of this chapter may be summed up thus: You can learn to write well, and rhetoric can teach you how. Writing well means doing more than simply scribbling down the first idea that pops into your head. It involves thinking about your audience and purpose and choosing between this level of language and that. It means developing a rhetorical sense about what techniques are likely to work for a particular assignment. All of these skills can be learned from a study of rhetoric.

Writing about Visual Images

Visual images range from works of art found only in museums to photographs published in daily newspapers. They include television images, line drawings, sketches, computer graphics, and a bewitching gallery of exotic scenes and pictures of beautiful people from advertising. So widespread and influential are visual images that many instructors use them as essay topics. This book, for example, contains images in every chapter of Part 2 that you will be asked to interpret or evaluate in the context of the various readings they are meant to illustrate.

If you've never done this kind of writing before, don't worry. Writing about an image is not that different from writing about a pig, a poem, or an adventure. Here are some techniques for writing about artwork, news photographs, cartoons, and advertising images.

Writing about Artwork   You do not have to be an art critic to write about a work of art, and you do not have to try to write like one. As in all kinds of writing, it is better for a writer to write from an honest self than to pretend to be someone else. In other words, be yourself always, whether you're writing about a real plum or one in a still-life painting. Here are some steps you can take to write about a work of art:

- **Study the work carefully.** Is it realistic or is it an abstract work with a distorted and imaginary vision? If it is a realistic work—say, a painting of a rural scene—take note of the colors and the way the paint is applied. An artist, by using drab colors and bold strokes of the brush, can suggest a negative feeling about a scene. On the other hand, a scene can be idealized with the use of bright colors and fine brushstrokes. After studying the work carefully, sum up in a single sentence your overall impression of it. This single sentence will be your thesis.

- **Pay attention to the title of the work.** Many expressionist painters create images that are purely imaginary and have no equivalent in reality. It often takes a title to help us understand what the images mean. Figure 2.1 is a dramatic example of the importance

■ **FIGURE 2.1** *The Pillars of Society, 1926, by George Grosz.*

How admirable are these pillars of society?

of titles. The painting shows a sinister assembly of men, two of whom have half a skull crammed with what looks like excrement and miscellaneous garbage. In the background are an ugly priest and a Nazi soldier with a bloody sword. It is only after we know the title of the painting, *The Pillars of Society*, that we grasp who these revolting men are meant to be—the emerging Nazi rulers whom the artist was satirizing.

- **Use the Internet to research background about the artist and the work.** For example, before writing the paragraph about *The Pillars of Society*, we entered the name of the artist George Grosz and the title of his painting in the search engine Google, which gave us the information we needed about the work and its creator.

- **Check your response to the work of art against the responses of art critics.** We all have a unique eye. If beauty is in the eye of the beholder, so is much of art. Some modernists argue that one reaction to a work of art is as valid as another. Traditionalists take just the opposite point of view, arguing that it is possible for one reaction to be "right" and another "wrong." Most likely the truth lies somewhere in between. It is possible for an interpretation of an artwork to be so farfetched and unprovable as to come entirely from the viewer's mind rather than from the artwork itself. It is also possible for two contrary interpretations of the same artwork to exist side by side, one no more "right" than the other. In situations like this one, art critics can be helpful. They have the experience and background in evaluating artistic works that enable them to spot what is unique about an artwork and what is imitative.

- **Support your opinions or interpretations of the artwork.** Any opinion you have about an artwork should be supported by details drawn from the work itself. If you say that the portrait of a certain person reflects an air of gloom, you should say why you think that. In support of this opinion, you can point to background colors, a grim facial expression, or perhaps the way the figure slumps.

- **Say how the work made you feel.** Artwork is meant to appeal both to the mind and to the heart. Don't be afraid to express how the work made you feel or to say why you think it affected you as it did. That kind of admission will help a reader better understand your opinions of the work. It is also perfectly allowable to use "I" in an essay interpreting a visual image. As a matter of fact, writing on such a personal topic without the use of "I" would be very difficult to do. You are, after all, expected to say how the work affected you and how you feel about it. You should not necessarily feel any obligation to like the artwork just because you're writing an essay about it. You may find that you heartily dislike the work. In such a case, what you have to do is to say why. If you did like the work, you should also say why.

In review, here are the steps involved in writing about artwork:

1. State your overall impression of the work in a single sentence.
2. Ground your opinions and impressions of the artwork in details drawn from it.
3. Say how the work affected you.

WRITING ASSIGNMENT

Find and make a copy of a work of art you like. Write three paragraphs about it, interpreting the work of art and saying what about it you especially appreciate. Include a copy of the work of art with your essay.

Writing about News Photographs   *News photographs*, a staple of newspapers and magazines, range from the serene to the horrific. In the hands of a good photographer, the camera can seem to totally capture a subject. That uncanny ability to seemingly x-ray the human soul, coupled with the spontaneity missing in more formal artworks such as paintings, has made photography into a universal language. A photograph of people leaping to their death from a burning skyscraper is globally understandable and universally wrenching, no matter what language we speak. Here are some tips on how to approach writing about a news photo:

- **Begin by researching and describing the context of the photograph.** When was it taken and by whom? Under what circumstances was it shot? Knowing its context puts a photograph in historical perspective and affects your interpretation of it.

- **Describe the news photograph by clearly stating its details.** Sum up, as well as you can, the importance of the scene depicted. Figure 2.2, for example, catches a spectacular moment in mountain rescuing.

Andreas Strauss/Getty Images

■ **FIGURE 2.2**

A helicopter rescues a man lost in the French Alps.

In review, here are the steps involved in writing about news photos:

1. Establish the context of the photograph, when and where it was taken, and why.
2. Describe the photo in detail.
3. Compose a thesis for the photo.
4. Develop evidence from the photo and its context to support your thesis.

● WRITING ASSIGNMENT

Write a couple of paragraphs about a news photograph, explaining its context and giving your interpretation of it. Include a copy of the photo with your written work.

Writing about Cartoons Nothing captures the spirit of an age better than a collection of its best cartoons. They seem to sum up in shorthand the idiosyncrasies of the time. The political cartoon, particularly the caricature—which is a cartoon that exaggerates physical appearance—is actually a good measure of how a particular person is regarded at a particular time. To get an idea of how Teddy Roosevelt was perceived in his day, for example, you need only go to the collection of cartoons that depict him. Here are some tips for writing about cartoons:

- **Make sure you understand the message of the cartoon.** Some cartoons, of course, are merely intended to amuse and have no particular message. Many cartoons mix sugar (humor) with medicine (a message). Look at Figure 2.3, for example. It is re-printed from a French Canadian newspaper. Here, we see a young boy with his pants at half mast, revealing the top of his buttocks, which forms a clear "Y." To the left, preceding the image, are the words (in French) "GENERATION." In its January 22, 2008 edition, the Quebec City paper *Le Soleil* introduced the cartoon by grouping generations by age groups, as follows:

  —The Silent Generation, people born before 1945

  —The Baby Boomers, people born between 1945 and 1961

  —Generation X, people born between 1962 and 1976

  —Generation Y, people born between 1977 and 1989

Why do we call the last group "generation Y"? The cartoon gives the answer with eloquent satire. At the same time, it subtly asks the reader to ponder why kids would ever want to follow a dress code meant to shock the elderly and other people with less inhibition than the kids who decided to popularize this fashion in the Western part of the world.

Another example of this subtlety is in a cartoon that depicts an English teacher standing angrily in front of her class. Behind her on the chalkboard is scrawled, "Home-work due today." In front of the teacher stands a young boy who is saying, "I did my homework, but the dog pressed Control-Alt-Delete." What makes this line funny is that it is the computer-age equivalent of "The dog ate my homework."

- **Be aware of the topsy-turvy world of cartoons.** Many cartoons spoof the accepted and habitual views of society, often by turning the world upside down. For example, one cartoon shows the seats of a movie theater filled with an audience of winged bugs waiting for the feature to begin. On the screen is the name of the upcoming movie: *Return of the Killer Windshield*. Another—one of our favorites—shows a horrible monster scrambling to get dressed. Looking at his watch worriedly, he is complain-ing to his wife that he's late and should have already been in a certain boy's closet.

GÉNÉRATION

■ **FIGURE 2.3**
Cartoon lampooning the current fad of boys wearing low-riding pants.

The caption of the cartoon? "Monster jobs." The humor of both cartoons comes mainly from the inversion of normalcy, giving us an unusual slant on a familiar situation.

- **State what lesson the cartoon teaches.** Many cartoons teach a lesson. Sometimes the lesson is obvious, as in an old cartoon that shows two males stranded on a tiny tropical island. One fellow looks at the other and suggests that perhaps they should form some simple form of government—reminding the viewer that setting up governments is part of the human instinct for politics. Sometimes the lesson is less obvious. For example, a cartoon featuring two forlorn-looking people standing side by side in the aisle of a library and looking at two different books, one entitled *Self-Improvement*, the other *Self-Involvement*, is teaching a subtle lesson about narcissism. In any case, part of your interpretation of the cartoon is to say what lesson it teaches—if it, indeed, teaches any. Study the cartoon until you get its meaning.

In review, here are the steps involved in writing about cartoons:

1. Make sure you understand the message of the cartoon, if it has one.
2. Be aware of the topsy-turvy world of cartoons.
3. Study the lesson of the cartoon.

WRITING ASSIGNMENT

Write a few paragraphs about any cartoon that you particularly like. Be sure to include a copy of the cartoon with your work.

Writing about Advertisements Advertising images, although sometimes bewitching, often have an air of unreality. They glamorize persons, settings, and objects. Or they can make products seem to have an exaggerated influence on the world. See Figure 2.4, which asks us to believe that taking an Altoids mint can snap your mind into immediate attention.

Many of the graphic messages in advertisements are either exaggerated or outright lies. We know that it is impossible for anyone to turn a rainy day into a sunny one just by swallowing a pill, that all our worries will not vanish if we take a certain laxative, and that rubbing our faces with a cream will not make wrinkles disappear overnight. Buying a certain mattress will not turn an insomniac into another Rip Van Winkle, nor will driving a new car make you into an overnight sensation with the opposite sex.

Anyone who writes about advertising images has to exercise both common sense and logic. Common sense will enable you to see through the pitch. Logic will help you to sift through the exaggerated claims made by the hype. Writing about an advertising image requires you to take the following steps:

- **Be sure you know the audience at whom the ad is aimed and the product that is being advertised.** An ad directed at women—for a perfume, for example—often comes with a feminized image. On the other hand, masculine images are typically found in a beer advertisement aimed mainly at men. Strange as it may seem, a few advertisements have been oblique rather than blunt in their hype of a product. Probably the most famous example of this is the advertising campaign for a certain Japanese car. The ads show scenes of pastures and mountain brooks—to the accompaniment of philosophical babble that has little to do with owning a car. Ask yourself what the product is, who uses it, and what it does. Sum up this information in a single sentence and you have your thesis.

- **Pay attention to the language that accompanies the image.** Advertising copy is often written in fragments rather than whole sentences. For example, an ad for a trip to Wales uses the following copy: "Suggested itinerary: London-Nirvana-London. It's a stopover in serenity. A side trip to paradise. Where the wonders of nature and the comforts of home live side by side. Wales. Just two hours from London." One sentence and five fragments make up this copy. Notice any poetic touch used to highlight the image. For example, the most successful advertising slogan of all time consists of two rhyming words: "Think Mink." Advertising copy is also often openly romantic, as in this example: "Somewhere she went from the girl of your dreams to the love of your life. A diamond is forever."

- **Notice any inversion of reality.** Advertisers are notorious for turning reality on its head. If a product is bad for you, the advertising may surround it with an aura of health and well-being. For example, cigarette advertisements used to always show

■ **FIGURE 2.4**

Altoid ad with its popular slogan.

smokers as specimens of perfect, robust health. The typical image associated with Marlboro cigarettes was a rugged cowboy shown on the range herding cattle and occasionally pausing for a "healthful" smoke. While those ads have faded from view, they have been replaced by commercials touting creams to cure pimples, baldness, or erectile dysfunction. Can anyone not envy the male who has taken Cialis or Viagra before strolling through a spring meadow planning to make love to his beloved "when the time is right"?

- **Watch out for buzzwords or euphemisms.** A buzzword is a slogan or saying that is associated with the product. The slogan of a certain underarm deodorant was, "Strong enough for a man. But made for a woman." A euphemism is a gentler way of saying something. For example, saying "he passed away" is a euphemism for "he died." Advertisers often combine images with euphemisms as part of their pitch. For example, an advertisement for insurance will talk about sparing your family the heartbreak of final decisions—meaning, finding a place to bury you and a way to pay for it. Personal-hygiene products for women are always euphemistic in their claims. Sometimes, even an image can be euphemistic, as is often the case in some advertisements for laxatives.

- **Use logic to evaluate the extravagant claims of an advertising image.** It is no exaggeration to say that advertisements often tell outright lies. Ad people would probably claim that they do not lie, but merely stress the positives about their product. Yet, anyone with common sense can't help but wonder what to make of a claim like "*X* toothpaste is used by two out of three dentists." How many dentists were surveyed to come to this conclusion? It might have been three. And what does this claim mean: "Degree antiperspirant deodorant is body-heat activated. Your body heat turns it on." And when an insect repellent advertises that it makes you "invisible to bugs," is that claim meant literally or figuratively?

- **Mention any humor associated with image.** An ad for Toshiba copy machines features a speaking copier: "I print eighty pages per minute and sit near the men's room. She types eighty words per minute and gets the corner office. Is there no balance in the universe?" To discuss this particular image, you would have to touch on the humor of the talking copier.

In review, here are the steps involved in writing about advertisements:

1. Be sure you know what's being advertised and to whom.
2. Pay attention to the language that accompanies the image.
3. Notice any inversion of reality.
4. Watch out for buzzwords or euphemisms.
5. Use logic to evaluate the extravagant claims of an advertising image.
6. Mention any humor associated with the image.

● WRITING ASSIGNMENT

Write two paragraphs on a magazine or newspaper ad that you particularly dislike. Include a copy of the ad with your work.

Writing on the Social Networks An essay is a formal piece of college writing, whereas a blog, text, email, or Facebook posting is an informal discussion online of particular topics and interests. In the last decade, informal online writing has exploded into a worldwide obsession. People—old as well as young—everywhere sit, walk, and drive while typing on their phones, tablets, or laptops. A wife in Los Angeles is texting her husband in Dubai. A business executive in Brussels is using his laptop to compose a group email to five colleagues in Chicago. The famous 2011 "Arab Spring" revolution in Egypt began with messages sent via social networks and ended by overthrowing the ruling president, Hosni Mubarak.

This book focuses on the formal essay, yet most students spend large chunks of time writing online, which means texting, blogging, tweeting, or emailing. Since this kind of writing is here to stay, we propose you practice getting good at it. Most of the chapters in this book will help you become a better blogger or emailer because writing well is the bedrock of all communication. For instance, the need to make a clear point and support it (see Chapter 5) is as necessary to blogging or emailing as it is to writing a formal essay.

It is no secret that some academics worry about the writing skills of students addicted to texting and blogging without the discipline of traditional sentence structure, spelling, or punctuation. Teachers shake their heads when they see passages like the following appear in college papers:

> @TEOTD (at the end of the day) , most of my classmates prefer listening to rap lyrics by artists like Jayz, Ice Cube, or Kanye West than reading the secretive lines of classical poets. The way I see it, rappers tell it like it iswhereas GOK (God only knows) what Robert Browning, T/S. Eliot, or Emily Dickinson is trying to say. %-)

Our aim is not to demean texting and blogging, given that their popularity is swelling, not shrinking. We believe they are here to stay, so we suggest you use them to build your writing skills, not turn you into an illiterate scribbler. Instead of having a cavalier outlook on the rules of correct grammar and punctuation, practice these rules when you are "thumbing" your way in a text or placing a post on your Facebook wall. In sum, use your contributions to the social networks as training to become a better writer. Adhering to the following pointers will help:

- **Reread your message before pressing "Send" or "Submit."** Even when no acronyms are involved, the grammar used by cell phone typists is often so poor that a reader can barely follow the train of thought. Here is an example from a student's Facebook post:

  > Love all the latest hand creams advertised on the Net a scientist from Cambridge claims he has created age-pacific anti-aging cream a Jewish entrepreneur at the mall has some oil on sale from the Dead Sea its suppose to moisterize your hands best of all some Zhairdresser in Palm Springs is promoting a cream with magic compositions detracted from the honeycomb of bees.

  A second glance at this carelessly pecked out passage would surely make the writer realize that some punctuation and word analysis could lead to this improved version:

  > I love all the latest hand creams advertised on the Internet. A scientist from Cambridge claims he has created age-specific anti-aging cream. A Jewish entrepreneur at the mall has some oil on sale from the Dead Sea. It's supposed to moisturize your hands. Best of all, some hairdresser in Palm Springs is promoting a cream with magic ingredients extracted from the honeycomb of bees.

Remember that once you press that "Send" button, you cannot retrieve what you have mailed. It is destined to remain in cyberspace. Also, beware of your smartphone's uncanny ability to finish words that you start. We have seen messages mangled by being sent before double checking. One student meant to text this: "I love *to sit and read,*" but his phone typed, "I love *to spit and rebel.*" Another texter thought she was writing "I stepped into the hot *shower,*" but she actually typed, "I stepped into the hot *snow.*" A quick second glance would have prompted corrections. Spelling and grammatical errors are commonplace in the rapid finger pecking of electronic mailers, but we think that the diligent practice of reviewing even your most informal texts will help mold you into a better writer.

- **Think through what you want to say.** Before you write, make a mental topic outline of the points you want to make. For instance, if you are writing to remind your roommate to take care of the house chores while you are on vacation, you might make this mental list: (1) Walk the dog; (2) Take out the garbage; (3) Bring in the mail. If you are writing about a sensitive matter, it is doubly important to make a mental note of what you plan to cover in your text, especially if your purpose is tactful disapproval.

- **Don't send an email or text when you are seething with anger.** Words spewed out in a fit of fury tend to cause serious regrets later when the emotional explosion has died away. It is better NOT to send a scathing rebuke than to feel remorse gnawing at you after having sent it. The truth is that emotional turmoil tends to block your ability to be logical and clear, which are two traits of good writing.

- **Slow down the speed at which you peck away at your keyboard either with your thumbs or fingers.** Composing sentences at blitz speed doesn't save you time in the long run if you write incoherently and illegibly. Stick to a comfortable speed that saves you from retyping or backspacing.

- **Write the way you speak.** That does not mean you should feel free to be vulgar or crass. It means you should write naturally and let your authentic voice sound out from your writing. If you tend to be a "cusser," delete the bad words as you type.

- **Use graphics when they would enlighten your point,** but use them sparingly lest they act like an avalanche rather than a ray of light. People are visual, but you must be selective and choose only graphics that will make an impact on your reader and enhance your point.

- **Avoid acronyms entirely.** In the intimacy of close friendships, you may use secret codes as you like—abbreviating or codifying to your heart's content as in these popular examples:
  - ATAIC (As far as I am concerned)
  - ANFSCD (And now for something completely different)

- LOL (Laughing out loud)
- NVNG (Nothing ventured, nothing gained)

However, in the extended classroom atmosphere, these kinds of acronyms are regarded as a plague upon the land. Do not use them at all—lest they permanently endanger your ability to communicate with anyone except members of your own tight-knit community.

- **Use tweets to practice clarity, conciseness, and brevity.** Our book encourages clarity and vividness in everyday writing, but sadly we have found only one social network that champions our point of view—Twitter. Because a tweet is limited to 140 characters or less, it can train users to be precise and focused in expressing their opinions. Given that the blogosphere sets the tone for heated emotional written outbursts, writers who write at such a hysterical pitch are like opera singers stuck on a high-C note. Their writing too often devolves into half-baked ideas or murky expressions. Punctuation gets lost in the process or becomes irrelevant. We think tweets are not only a practical way of telling the world what you think, but they force you to do so without the wasteful blah blah blah that accompanies many blogs. Sprinkled throughout Part Two of this book, you will find writing assignments under the heading "**To the Point.**" The purpose of these assignments is to teach you how to prune deadwood from your messages, using the restraint of Twitter's 140-character limit. Pithy Anglo-Saxon verbs must replace torturous Latin ones—such as "spit" instead of "expectorate." One strong adjective is better than several limp ones—such as "gleaming" instead of "shining and well-polished." Words that repeat one another must be deleted—such as "outcome' instead of "final outcome."* As in most aspects of writing, practice makes perfect. Here are four examples of opinions expressed in forceful tweets:

> In 2013, I heard Maestro James Levine interviewed following his spinal injury. His determination to conduct the New York Met despite intense pain was stirring.

> Philip Seymour Hoffman is dead from a drug overdose. We all have our demons, so who are you to call him selfish? Don't spit nasty comments into the wind lest they come back and hit you in the face.

> I'm mad as hell because our City Council refuses to construct bicycle lanes in our town.

> Are you sure you want to wear that to work? Register online to download "Dress Code Policy" from White Paper. It's free.

> Study tweets you admire and try to imitate their author's style. This is the same kind of exercise as scrutinizing the writing of a famous author you admire.

---

* For more on how to prune deadwood, see p. 426.

In review, here are the steps involved in writing for the social networks:

1. Review your message before sending it.
2. Don't text while angry.
3. Make a mental note of what you wish to say.
4. Avoid typing too fast.
5. Write the way you speak.
6. Use graphics to light up your point.
7. Don't use acronyms or abbreviations.
8. Practice writing tweets to achieve clarity, conciseness, and brevity.

WRITING ASSIGNMENTS

1. Write an essay in which you defend the social networks as a useful force in our society. Use examples to prove that a social network has saved lives, has started a needed revolution, or has kept a family together.

2. Write an essay in which you point out the dangers involved when students become addicted to Facebook, Twitter, YouTube, email, or other aspects of the social networks.

To the Point

Write a tweet in response to one of the following comments:

"Football has become far too violent and should be regulated more strictly to protect players from serious injuries."

"The average student cannot afford the current cost of textbooks."

"In our courts of law, marijuana should be treated like smoking or drinking."

"The Muslim hijab makes an attractive fashion statement."

Exercises for Understanding Rhetoric

1. After studying the following passages, suggest the purpose of each and the audience for which it is intended. Give specific examples of language suitable to that audience.

    a. At first, our Greg was a model child. Healthy, happy, unfailingly sweet-tempered, he was a total joy as a baby. When he was one year old, he thought that everything mother and father wanted him to do was wonderful. His second birthday passed, and he remained cooperative and adorable. Aha, I thought, the "terrible twos" that everyone complains about must result from inadequate attention and discipline.

    Then, Greg turned two and three-quarters. Suddenly we had an obnoxious monster in the house. His favorite word was "No!" and he used it constantly. At the simplest request, he would stamp his feet and cry. It was a battle getting him to put on clothing he had previously worn happily. Favorite foods were thrown on the floor. It became almost impossible to take him shopping because he would lie down in the store and refuse to move. There was constant tension in the house, and my husband and I became irritable, too. We felt as if we were living on the slopes of a volcano, and we found ourselves giving in to Greg too much in order to avoid the threatened eruptions.

b. Others will debate the controversial issues, national and international, which divide men's minds. But serene, calm, aloof, you stand as the nation's war guardians, as its lifeguards from the raging tides of international conflict, as its gladiators in the arena of battle. For a century and a half you have defended, guarded, and protected its hallowed traditions of liberty and freedom, of right and justice.

Let civilian voices argue the merits or demerits of our processes of government: whether our strength is being sapped by deficit financing indulged in too long; by federal paternalism grown too mighty; by power groups grown too arrogant; by politics grown too corrupt; by crime grown too rampant; by morals grown too low; by taxes grown too high; by extremists grown too violent; whether our personal liberties are as firm and complete as they should be.

These great national problems are not for your professional participation or military solution. Your guidepost stands out like a tenfold beacon in the night: duty, honor, country.

c. To give Eleanor her due, any suspicion as to the slightest inclination on her part toward Mr. Slope was a wrong to her. She had no more idea of marrying Mr. Slope than she had of marrying the bishop, and the idea that Mr. Slope would present himself as a suitor had never occurred to her. Indeed, to give her her due again, she had never thought about suitors since her husband's death. But nevertheless it was true that she had overcome all that repugnance to the man which was so strongly felt for him by the rest of the Grantly faction. She had forgiven him his sermon. She had forgiven him his low church tendencies, his Sabbath schools, and puritanical observances. She had forgiven his pharisaical arrogance, and even his greasy face and oily vulgar manners. Having agreed to overlook such offences as these, why should she not in time be taught to regard Mr. Slope as a suitor?

d. Earthquakes are often accompanied by a roaring noise that comes from the bowels of the earth. This phenomenon was known to early geographers. Pliny wrote that earthquakes are "preceded or accompanied by a terrible sound." Vaults supporting the ground give way and it seems as though the earth heaves deep sighs. The sound was attributed to the gods and called *theophany*.

The eruptions of volcanoes are also accompanied by loud noises. The sound produced by Krakatoa in the East Indies during the eruption of 1883 was so loud it was heard as far away as Japan, 3,000 miles away, the farthest distance traveled by sound recorded in modern annals.

e. I beg you to excuse a father who dares to approach you in the interests of his son.

I wish to mention first that my son is twenty-two years old, has studied for four years at the Zurich Polytechnic and last summer brilliantly passed his diploma examinations in mathematics and physics. Since then he has tried unsuccessfully to find a position as assistant, which would enable him to continue his education in theoretical and experimental physics. Everybody who is able to judge praises his talent, and in any case I can assure you that he is exceedingly assiduous and industrious and is attached to his science with a great love.

f. Letters written by a potential customer asking suppliers for free materials, information, or routine services are among the easiest to write. The customer will usually receive what he or she is asking for since it is to the supplier's advantage to provide it. The potential customer need only be clear and courteous. In writing routine request letters, give all the information the supplier will need in order to be really helpful, keep your request as brief as possible without omitting important details, and express your wishes courteously and tactfully.

2. Write two one-page essays explaining the reasons you wish to pursue a certain career. Address the first to the personnel manager of an organization that might hire you and the second to your father. Contrast the language and phrasing of each essay and explain the differences between them.

3. Both of the following letters refuse credit to a potential customer. How does the second differ in purpose from the first?

a. Please accept our regrets that we cannot offer you a 60-day credit for the meeting of your organization here at Pine Lodge in July of 2009. When you held your meeting here last year, we had the embarrassing experience of having to wait six months before you made full payment on your bill. I am sure that you will understand that we cannot take chances on such bad credit risks.

b. Thank you for choosing Pine Lodge again for your 2009 meeting. We consider it a pleasure to have you, although we must ask you to send us a 25% deposit and to make a full settlement when you check out. This is now our standard arrangement with organizations similar to yours. If these arrangements are satisfactory, we shall do our best to make sure that your group is extended every courtesy and service during its stay.

4. A restaurant owner has sent the following memorandum to the waiters and waitresses working for him. Rewrite the memo to create a more positive tone, without destroying its purpose.

To: All waiters and waitresses. I've had it with you lazy clowns! This month's profits fell 20% below last year's at this same time. Now, any fool can tell that the problem is your sloppy service to the customers, your excessive breaking of china and glassware, and your horsing around instead of paying attention to such details as keeping the food warm, setting the tables properly, and getting the customer's order straight. So, I'm warning you: either start doing your job right, or you'll find yourselves fired.

5. Assuming an educated audience, label the purpose of each of the following passages: (1) to inspire, (2) to get action, (3) to amuse, or (4) to inform.

a. Please send us either a check within the next week or an explanation if some problem has arisen. We are eager to cooperate with you.

b. Conscience is a sacred sanctuary where God alone may enter as judge.

c. In great straits, and when hope is small, the boldest counsels are the safest.

d. Men seldom make passes at girls who wear glasses.

e. The more one comes to know men, the more one admires the dog.

f. "Gavelkind" is the custom of having all of the sons of an estate holder share equally in the estate upon the death of the father. Most of the lands in England were held in gavelkind tenure prior to the Norman Conquest.

g. Seek not the favor of the multitude; it is seldom got by honest and lawful means. But seek the testimony of few; and number not voices, but weigh them.

h. Botticelli isn't a wine, you dunce! Botticelli is a cheese.

i. The Indus River is approximately 1,900 miles long. It rises in the Kailas range of Tibet, flows west across Kashmir, India, and then moves southwest to the Arabian Sea.

j. Flaming manifestoes and prophecies of doom are no longer much help, and a search for scapegoats can only make matters worse. The time for sensations and manifestoes is about over. Now we need rigorous analysis, united effort, and very hard work.

6. Label each of the following passages according to its level of English: formal, informal, or technical. In each case, describe the characteristics that identify the level of writing.

a. Sometimes I wish I were a mountain stream. If I were a mountain stream, I'd flow down a beautiful, green, woodsy, snow-capped mountain. I'd be fed by the cool, melting snow, and I'd shimmer and glisten as the sun warmed my flowing presence. Being a mountain stream, I'd attract only a few select people—those with enough courage and stamina to climb through thickets, across ravines, and up steep paths to my cool, ethereal banks. Those special people could enjoy sitting on my banks to search my clear depths for the solitude, serenity, and peace they're longing to find.

b. The bony remains of Peking Man all came from a single limestone cave at Chou-k'ou-tien. The bones consist of fifteen crania, six facial bones, twelve mandibles, a miscellaneous collection of postcranial bones, and 147 teeth. Studies of the physical characters of these bones by Davidson Black and Franz Weidenreich disclose that Peking Man was still in an early stage of human development, comparable to the *Homo erectus* of Java.

   The limbs were highly developed and quite modern, indicating that he stood upright and walked on two feet, but the cranium is characterized by low vault, heavy bony features, thick wall, and small cranial capacity (914–1,225 cc., with an average of 1,043 cc., as against Java Man's 860 cc. and modern man's 1,350 cc.).—John T. Meskill.

c. Unlike in nature, where the root feeds the plant, in art, the pinnacle makes possible the base. Drama did not begin with a lot of hacks gradually evolving into Aeschylus and Sophocles; the novel did not start with a slew of James Micheners and Leon Urises building up to Dickens and Joyce. Richardson, Fielding, Sterne, and Smollett started things on a pretty high level; it is they who made the Jacqueline Susanns possible, not the other way around. Public funds for the dissemination of culture are necessary, but unless the most difficult and demanding creations on the individual level are subsidized, no amount of grants to public television to put on *The Adams Chronicles* will prevent culture and art from withering away or becoming debased, which is the same thing. —John Simon.

7. Remember your last significant writing assignment and answer the following questions:

   a. Who was your audience?

   b. What was your purpose?

   c. What level of English did you use?

8. Assuming that the choice of topic affects the quality of your writing, choose the topic that most interests you from the following list. In two or three sentences, state why the topic appeals to you. Describe the audience for whom you would like to write about your chosen topic.

   a. The future of working women

   b. Care for the elderly

   c. The cost of owning a house

   d. The pleasures associated with a particular hobby

   e. Preserving our environment

   f. Some aspect of working with computers

   g. Handicapped children

   h. Some aspect of primitive civilization

   i. A favorite painter, sculptor, dancer, or musician

   j. Business ethics

   k. Political reform

 *Stumped by wordiness? Exit on pages 426–429 at the **Editing Booth!***

▨ Advice

What—and How—to Write When You Have No Time to Write

DONALD MURRAY

Rhetorical Thumbnail

Purpose:	provide some practical tips about the daily business of writing
Audience:	college students and others who write frequently
Language:	a blend of formal and informal English; frequent use of contractions
Strategy:	cites his own experience with writing deadlines and schedules

Donald Murray (1924–2006) was a Pulitzer Prize–winning journalist who made it part of his life's work to teach others how to write. He wrote a much-read weekly column for *The Boston Globe* as well as feature articles for a variety of magazines. Many teachers of composition rely on Murray's books for teaching strategies. Among his most influential books are *Shoptalk: Learning to Write with Writers* (1990); *Expecting the Unexpected: Teaching Myself and Others to Read and Write* (1989); *The Craft of Revision* (2007); and *Crafting a Life in Essay, Story, Poem* (1996). Murray was Professor Emeritus of English at the University of New Hampshire.

Murray, who was known for his practical approach to writing, dispenses some sensible advice, which he summarizes into "ten little habits of mind and craft." While his ideas apply particularly to the full-time writer, they are also practical enough to help the student.

• • •

1   The less time I have for writing, the more important it is that I write. Writing gives me a necessary calm, what Robert Frost called "a momentary stay against confusion." Writing slows down the rush of life, forcing awareness and reflection. As writing increases my awareness, language clarifies that vision. What is vague and general becomes concrete and specific as I find the words. These words connect with other words in phrase and sentence, placing the immediate experience in the context of my life. I read the story of my life by writing it. I also receive the gift of concentration and escape the swirling problems of my life as I follow paragraph and page toward meaning.

2   I write fragments in slivers of time, always with interruptions, and yet, when I look back, I am surprised that the writing caught on the fly has produced a lifetime of productivity. I have come to realize that very little published writing is produced during **sustained** periods of composition without interruption. You have to arrange a life in which part of your mind is writing all the time; that's when the seeds of writing are sown and then cultivated. The writing is harvested in short periods of time between the busy chores that crowd the day.

3   Graham Greene said, "If one wants to write, one simply has to organize one's life in a mass of little habits." Here are ten little habits of mind and craft that I realize, looking back, made me a productive writer—without long writing days free of interruption.

1. Don't wait for an idea.

4   If you know what you want to say, you've probably said it before, or it's not worth saying. Writing is thinking, and thought begins not with a conclusion but with an itch, a hint, a clue, a question, a doubt, a wonder, a problem, an answer without a question, an image that refuses to be forgotten. Such fragments are caught on the wing, when I think my mind is somewhere else.

5   My four-year-old grandson told his mother, "I know Grandpa is a writer because he's always writing in his wallet." It is not a wallet, but a container for the 3" × 5" cards that are always in my shirt pocket with three pens. In a shoulder case that is not far from me night and day is the spiral **daybook** in which I talk

to myself, capturing and playing with fragments of language that may become a draft.

2. Listen to your own difference.

6   People who want to write look at what is being published, but the writers who are published have looked within themselves, found their own vision of the world, heard their own voices. Sandra Cisneros said, "Write about what makes you different."

7   As I look back, I realize that what made me strange to my family, classmates and teachers, friends and neighbors, colleagues and editors, is what has produced the writing that has been read. In the wonderful way of art, what is most personal, **eccentric**, individual, becomes most universal. When I have tried to become someone else I have failed; when I have been myself I have succeeded.

3. Avoid long writing sessions.

8   Most people believe, as I once did, that it is necessary to have long, uninterrupted days in which to write. But there are no such days. Life intrudes. I try to follow the counsel of Horace, Pliny, and so many others through the centuries: *nulla dies sine linea*—never a day without a line.

9   How long does it take me to write? My weekly columns take 71 years of living and about forty-five minutes of writing. I write in bursts of twenty minutes, five, fifteen, thirty, sixty; ninety minutes is the maximum amount of writing time that is effective for me.

10   And how much writing do I produce? I've finished a book averaging 300 words a day. These days I try to average 500 words a day. The important thing is not the time or the words, but the habit, that dailiness of the writing.

4. Break long writing projects into brief daily tasks.

11   Books are written a page at a time, and I find it helpful—essential—to break a book into units that can be finished in a short morning's writing: lead for Ch. 3, scene in court, description of experiment, interview with source, column on writing time.

5. Write in the morning.

12   Most writers write in the early morning before the world intrudes. They harvest the product of their subconscious. Each hour of the day becomes less efficient as the writer is not only interrupted, but increasingly aware of all the professional and family concerns that crowd the mind. An 800-word column I can write in 45 minutes in the morning takes me three hours in the afternoon.

6. Know tomorrow's task today.

13   I set myself a single writing task and know what it is the night before. I don't know what I am going to write, but I assign the writing problem to my subconscious at the end of the morning writing session or before I go to bed, and part of my mind works on it as I go about my living.

7. Seek instructive failure.

14   Effective writing is the product of instructive failure. You try to say what you cannot yet say, but in the attempt you discover—draft by draft—what you

have to say and how you can say it. Failure is essential. Failure occurs when the words race ahead of thought, producing insights that may be developed through revision. The writer should seek to fail, not to say what has been said before, but what has not yet been said and is worth saying.

8. Focus on what works.

15   Once failure has revealed what you want to say, you should develop the topic by concentrating on what works, rather than focusing on correcting errors. Most errors will not occur if you develop what works and, at the end of the drafting process, you can solve any problems that remain. I revise mostly by layering, writing over—and over—what has been written.

9. Keep score.

16   As you write, it is important to **suspend** critical judgment until after a draft is finished. It's helpful to count words—or pages or hours—so that you can tell yourself that you have written without **assessing** how well you have written until the piece is finished.

10. Let it go.

17   Hardest of all is to let it go. The draft never equals the dream. The draft will expose your private thoughts and feelings to the world, but when you are published, what you most feared would appear foolish, your readers often find most profound. You have given words to their private thoughts and feelings.

18   Writing produces writing. When writing you are more aware of the world and your own reaction to it. As a writer, you relive your life hundreds of times, and when you are in your seventies, as I am, you'll come to your writing desk and discover you have even more to say than you imagined when you were 7 years old and dreaming of a writing life.

Donald Murray, "What—and How—to Write When You Have No Time to Write." From THE WRITER (September 1996). Reprinted by permission of The Poynter Institute.

▦ Examples

I Have a Dream

MARTIN LUTHER KING, JR.

Rhetorical Thumbnail

Purpose: to draw the attention of American society to the oppressed condition of black people

Audience: the English-speaking world, particularly America

Language: elevated, semi-poetic English

Strategy: uses language with powerful moral overtones

Martin Luther King, Jr. (1929–1968), American clergyman and black civil rights leader, was born in Atlanta and educated at Morehouse College, Crozer Theological Seminary, and Boston University (Ph.D., 1955). Dr. King, a lifelong advocate of nonviolent resistance to segregation, led a boycott by blacks in Montgomery, Alabama (1955–1956), of the city's segregated bus system and organized a massive march on Washington, D.C., in 1963, during which he delivered his famous "I Have a Dream" speech. In 1964, he was awarded the Nobel Peace Prize. Dr. King was assassinated on April 4, 1968, on a motel balcony in Memphis, Tennessee, where he had journeyed in support of the city's striking sanitation workers.

In August 1963, more than 200,000 blacks and whites gathered peacefully in Washington, D.C., to focus attention on black demands for civil rights. The marchers gathered at the Lincoln Memorial, where Dr. King delivered this impassioned speech.

• • •

1 Five score years ago, a great American, in whose symbolic shadow we stand today, signed the Emancipation Proclamation. This **momentous** decree came as a great beacon light of hope to millions of Negro slaves who had been seared in the flames of withering injustice. It came as a joyous daybreak to end the long night of their captivity.

2 But one hundred years later, the Negro still is not free. One hundred years later, the life of the Negro is still sadly crippled by the **manacles** of segregation and the chains of discrimination.

3 One hundred years later, the Negro lives on a lonely island of poverty in the midst of a vast ocean of material prosperity. One hundred years later, the Negro is still **languished** in the corners of American society and finds himself an exile in his own land. So we have come here today to dramatize a shameful condition.

4 In a sense we have come to our nation's capital to cash a check. When the architects of our republic wrote the magnificent words of the Constitution and the Declaration of Independence, they were signing a promissory note to which every American was to fall heir. This note was a promise that all men, yes, black men as well as white men, would be granted the **unalienable** rights of life, liberty, and the pursuit of happiness.

5 It is obvious today that America has defaulted on this promissory note insofar as her citizens of color are concerned. Instead of honoring this sacred obligation, America has given the Negro people a bad check, which has come back marked "insufficient funds."

6 But we refuse to believe that the bank of justice is bankrupt. We refuse to believe that there are insufficient funds in the great vaults of opportunity of this nation. So we have come to cash this check—a check that will give us upon demand the riches of freedom and the security of justice.

7 We have also come to this **hallowed** spot to remind America of the fierce urgency of now. This is no time to engage in the luxury of cooling off or to take the tranquilizing drug of **gradualism**. Now is the time to make real the promises of democracy. Now is the time to rise from the dark and desolate valley of segregation

to the sunlit path of racial justice. Now is the time to lift our nation from the quick-sands of racial injustice to the solid rock of brotherhood. Now is the time to make justice a reality for all of God's children.

8   It would be fatal for the nation to overlook the urgency of the movement and to underestimate the determination of the Negro. This sweltering summer of the Negro's legitimate discontent will not pass until there is an **invigorating** autumn of freedom and equality. 1963 is not an end but a beginning. Those who hope that the Negro needed to blow off steam and will now be content will have a rude awakening if the nation returns to business as usual.

9   There will be neither rest nor tranquility in America until the Negro is granted his citizenship rights. The whirlwinds of revolt will continue to shake the founda-tions of our nation until the bright day of justice emerges.

10   But there is something that I must say to my people who stand on the warm threshold which leads into the palace of justice. In the process of gaining our right-ful place we must not be guilty of wrongful deeds.

11   Let us not seek to satisfy our thirst for freedom by drinking from the cup of bitterness and hatred. We must forever conduct our struggle on the high plane of dignity and discipline. We must not allow our creative protest to **degenerate** into physical violence. Again and again we must rise to the majestic heights of meeting physical force with soul force.

12   The marvelous new **militancy** which has engulfed the Negro community must not lead us to a distrust of all white people, for many of our white brothers, as evi-denced by their presence here today, have come to realize that their destiny is tied up with our destiny and they have come to realize that their freedom is **inextricably** bound to our freedom. This offense we share mounted to storm the battlements of injustice must be carried forth by a biracial army. We cannot walk alone.

13   And as we walk, we must make the pledge that we shall always march ahead. We cannot turn back. There are those who are asking the devotees of civil rights, "When will you be satisfied?" We can never be satisfied as long as the Negro is the victim of the unspeakable horrors of police brutality.

14   We can never be satisfied as long as our bodies, heavy with the fatigue of travel, cannot gain lodging in the motels of the highways and the hotels of the cit-ies. We cannot be satisfied as long as the Negro's basic mobility is from a smaller ghetto to a larger one.

15   We can never be satisfied as long as our children are stripped of their self-hood and robbed of their dignity by signs stating "for whites only." We cannot be satisfied as long as a Negro in Mississippi cannot vote and a Negro in New York believes he has nothing for which to vote. No, we are not satisfied, and we will not be satisfied until justice rolls down like waters and righteousness like a mighty stream.

16   I am not unmindful that some of you have come here out of excessive tri-als and **tribulation**. Some of you have come fresh from narrow jail cells. Some of you have come from areas where your quest for freedom left you battered by the storms of persecution and staggered by the winds of police brutality. You have been the veterans of creative suffering. Continue to work with the faith that un-earned suffering is **redemptive**.

17   Go back to Mississippi; go back to Alabama; go back to South Carolina; go back to Georgia; go back to Louisiana; go back to the slums and ghettos of the Northern cities, knowing that somehow this situation can, and will be changed. Let us not wallow in the valley of despair.

18   So I say to you, my friends, that even though we must face the difficulties of today and tomorrow, I still have a dream. It is a dream deeply rooted in the American dream that one day this nation will rise up and live out the true meaning of its creed—we hold these truths to be self evident, that all men are created equal.

19   I have a dream that one day on the red hills of Georgia, sons of former slaves and sons of former slave-owners will be able to sit down together at the table of brotherhood.

20   I have a dream that one day, even the state of Mississippi, a state **sweltering** with the heat of injustice, sweltering with the heat of oppression, will be transformed into an oasis of freedom and justice.

21   I have a dream my four little children will one day live in a nation where they will not be judged by the color of their skin but by the content of their character. I have a dream today!

22   I have a dream that one day, down in Alabama, with its vicious racists, with its governor having his lips dripping with the words of **interposition** and **nullification**, that one day, right there in Alabama, little black boys and black girls will be able to join hands with little white boys and white girls as sisters and brothers. I have a dream today!

23   I have a dream that one day every valley shall be **exalted**, every hill and mountain shall be made low, the rough places shall be made plain, and the crooked places shall be made straight and the glory of the Lord will be revealed and all flesh shall see it together.

24   This is our hope. This is the faith that I go back to the South with.

25   With this faith we will be able to hew out of the mountain of despair a stone of hope. With this faith we will be able to transform the jangling discords of our nation into a beautiful symphony of brotherhood.

26   With this faith we will be able to work together, to pray together, to struggle together, to go to jail together, to stand up for freedom together, knowing that we will be free one day. This will be the day when all of God's children will be able to sing with new meaning—"my country 'tis of thee; sweet land of liberty; of thee I sing; land where my fathers died, land of the pilgrim's pride; from every mountain side, let freedom ring"—and if America is to be a great nation, this must become true.

27   So let freedom ring from the **prodigious** hilltops of New Hampshire.

28   Let freedom ring from the mighty mountains of New York.

29   Let freedom ring from the heightening Alleghenies of Pennsylvania.

30   Let freedom ring from the snow-capped Rockies of Colorado.

31   Let freedom ring from the **curvaceous** slopes of California.

32   But not only that.

33   Let freedom ring from Stone Mountain of Georgia.

34   Let freedom ring from Lookout Mountain of Tennessee.

35   Let freedom ring from every hill and molehill of Mississippi, from every mountainside, let freedom ring.

36   And when we allow freedom to ring, when we let it ring from every village and hamlet, from every state and city, we will be able to speed up that day when all of God's children—black men and white men, Jews and Gentiles, Catholics and Protestants—will be able to join hands and to sing in the words of the old Negro spiritual, "Free at last, free at last; thank God Almighty, we are free at last."

● THE FACTS

1. The speech begins "Five score years ago . . ." Why was this beginning especially appropriate?
2. What grievances of black Americans does Dr. King summarize in paragraphs 2 and 3 of this speech?
3. What does Dr. King caution his listeners against in paragraph 11?
4. What attitude toward white people does the speaker urge upon his audience?
5. Although Dr. King speaks out mainly against injustices committed against blacks in the South, he is also critical of the North. What can be inferred from this speech about the living conditions of blacks in the North during the early 1960s?

● THE STRATEGIES

1. One critic of this speech has written that its purpose was to intensify the values of the black movement. What characteristic of its style can you point to that might be said to have served this purpose?
2. Paragraphs 4 through 6 of the speech are linked through the use of an extended analogy. What is this analogy?
3. What common rhetorical device does the speech frequently use to emphasize its points?
4. It is often said that speakers and writers use paragraphs differently. How are the paragraphs of this speech especially adapted for oral delivery? What is the most obvious difference between these paragraphs and those a writer might use?
5. What is the function of the brief paragraph 32?

● THE ISSUES

1. "Black" is a term widely used in the United States to designate people whose skin color may range from dark brown to sepia; however, what definition of blackness does our society seem implicitly to use?
2. In your opinion, what is the basis of racial prejudice?
3. Will the United States ever have a female black president? Defend your answer.
4. Does prejudice in the United States against black men exceed or equal the prejudice against black women? Explain the difference, if there is one, and justify your answer.

5. What stereotypes do you hold about people of other races? Write them down along with an explanation of how you arrived at them. Share them with your classmates.

● SUGGESTIONS FOR WRITING

1. Write an essay analyzing the extensive use of metaphors in this speech. Comment on their effectiveness, bearing in mind the audience for whom the speech was intended.

2. Write an essay analyzing the oral style of this speech. Point out specific techniques of phrasing, sentence construction, paragraphing, and so on, that identify this composition as a speech. Suggest how a writer might have phrased some passages if this work had been written to be read rather than heard.

Letter to Horace Greeley

ABRAHAM LINCOLN

Rhetorical Thumbnail

Purpose:	to explain the writer's political determination to preserve the Union
Audience:	not just Greeley, but all Americans
Language:	old-fashioned formal English
Strategy:	uses repetition to make emphatically clear that the writer's overwhelming aim is preservation of the Union.

Abraham Lincoln (1809–1865) is ranked by many historians as among the best U.S. presidents ever. Born in a log cabin and reared to work on frontier farms, Lincoln was often poor and given little formal schooling. Before entering the political arena, he worked as a mill manager, grocery store keeper, surveyor, postmaster, and lawyer. His political career began in 1834 with his election to the Illinois state legislature. In 1860, after many debates with his opponents, Lincoln was elected the sixteenth president of the United States.

The letter that follows was written during the turmoil of the Civil War and stands as a classic statement of Lincoln's constitutional responsibilities. Horace Greeley, editor of the influential New York Tribune, *had written an editorial implying that Lincoln's administration lacked direction and resolve. Lincoln's response reveals his unshakable commitment to preserving the Union.*

● ● ●

Executive Mansion,
Washington, August 22, 1862.
Hon. Horace Greeley:
Dear Sir,

1   I have just read yours of the 19th. addressed to myself through the New-York Tribune. If there be in it any statements, or assumptions of fact, which I may know

to be erroneous, I do not, now and here, **controvert** them. If there be in it any **inferences** which I may believe to be falsely drawn, I do not now and here, argue against them. If there be **perceptable** [sic] in it an impatient and dictatorial tone, I waive it in deference to an old friend, whose heart I have always supposed to be right.

2   As to the policy I "seem to be pursuing" as you say, I have not meant to leave any one in doubt.

3   I would save the Union. I would save it the shortest way under the Constitution. The sooner the national authority can be restored; the nearer the Union will be "the Union as it was." If there be those who would not save the Union, unless they could at the same time save slavery, I do not agree with them. If there be those who would not save the Union unless they could at the same time destroy slavery, I do not agree with them. My **paramount** object in this struggle is to save the Union, and is not either to save or to destroy slavery. If I could save the Union without freeing any slave I would do it, and if I could save it by freeing all the slaves I would do it; and if I could save it by freeing some and leaving others alone I would also do that. What I do about slavery, and the colored race, I do because I believe it helps to save the Union; and what I **forbear**, I forbear because I do not believe it would help to save the Union. I shall do less whenever I shall believe what I am doing hurts the cause, and I shall do more whenever I shall believe doing more will help the cause. I shall try to correct errors when shown to be errors; and I shall adopt new views so fast as they shall appear to be true views.

4   I have here stated my purpose according to my view of official duty; and I intend no modification of my oft-expressed personal wish that all men everywhere could be free.

Yours,

A. Lincoln.

● THE FACTS

1. What was Lincoln's motivation for writing this letter?
2. What attitude does Lincoln show in addressing Greeley? What is the tone of the letter?
3. How does Lincoln imply that he detects an impatient edge to Greeley's letter? What is Lincoln's reaction to this tone?
4. In paragraph 2, Lincoln states that he did not intend to leave anyone in doubt about his policies. Were you left in doubt about Lincoln's policies after reading this letter? Explain your answer.
5. What does the date of the letter add to your understanding of its content?

● THE STRATEGIES

1. What do you think Lincoln achieved when he used the words "I waive it in deference to an old friend, whose heart I have always supposed to be right"?
2. What is the thesis of the letter? State it in one clear sentence with your own words.
3. What is the most obvious rhetorical strategy used in the letter? Provide examples of the strategy. How effective is it?

4. What tactic had Greeley used to criticize Lincoln's administration? Does his approach seem fair or backhanded? Give reasons for your answer.

5. What is the purpose of the final paragraph of Lincoln's letter? Is this paragraph necessary? Why or why not?

● THE ISSUES

1. How do you react to Lincoln's view that keeping the Union intact was more important than freeing the slaves? How would that opinion be regarded today?

2. In the final paragraph of his letter, Lincoln refers to his "official duty." What is his official duty? Do you think that today the "official duty" of U.S. presidents has changed? What, in your opinion, is the president's primary duty while in office?

3. With your advantage of being able to look back at U.S. history, what is your attitude toward Lincoln's view of slavery?

4. What attitude does Lincoln hold toward errors and toward new views? Do you support his attitude or do you believe he is too wishy-washy?

5. What do you think of Lincoln's statement to Greeley that he does not plan to refute any of Greeley's wrong ideas or conclusions and that he will overlook Greeley's impatient voice and dictatorial posture? What advantage, if any, does Lincoln's response present?

● SUGGESTIONS FOR WRITING

1. Choosing one of your political points of view with which someone you know strongly disagrees, write a letter meant to justify your opinion with reason and evidence.

2. Write a paragraph or two analyzing the tone of Lincoln's letter.

▥ Chapter Writing Assignments

1. Select any two paragraphs, one from an article in *Reader's Digest* and another from an article in *The New Yorker*. Analyze the differences in the language (diction, phrasing, sentence style, and paragraph length) and speculate on the intended audience of each magazine.

2. Write an essay on the meaning and practice of rhetoric as exemplified in this chapter.

▥ Writing Assignments for a Specific Audience

1. To an audience of African American readers, write an essay arguing for or against the idea that race relations in America have gotten better since Dr. King delivered his "I Have a Dream" speech.

2. Write an essay aimed at an audience of eighth graders explaining to them what they can expect to encounter later in high school and college writing courses.

Pointer from a Pro

WRITE OFTEN

No one presumes to give a dance recital without having first mastered the rudiments of dance, to perform Mozart before playing scales, or to enter a weight-lifting contest without first hoisting weights. Yet, because we've been reading since age five, we blithely assume we can read; because we scrawled our signature when six, we glibly aspire to write.

—Nicholas Delbanco, "From Echoes Emerge Original Voices."
Writers on Writing, p. 47.

All students who are serious about wanting to write well should welcome each opportunity to set ideas on paper because the more you write with a desire to improve your writing, the better you will become in honing your craft.

Real-Life Student Writing

Email from Samoa

The following excerpt is from an actual email written by one student to another. The sender, Mark, is writing from the South Pacific island of Samoa, where he had arrived two months before as a Peace Corps volunteer. He was on the island only a month when he and another volunteer fell afoul of local authorities and were expelled from the Peace Corps—in their opinion, unfairly. To appeal their expulsion would have required a trip to Washington, D.C., which neither could afford. Instead of returning home as his friend did, Mark decided to stay on the island for as long as he could. He took a job teaching English at a local school while he applied for his visa, which would allow him to remain in Samoa for at least another year. Mark sent this email to his friend, Adam. The two had been classmates in a cross-cultural program in British and American studies.

• • •

From: Mark Smith
Sent: Wednesday, January 15, 2009 4:14 PM
To: Adam Johnson
Subject: Hey What's Up

So things got a little out of hand last night. My friend Taui fire danced at this club last night and we made quite an event of the whole thing.

I guess I got a little wasted and then found myself in the Peace Corps office and for the first time in weeks I had access to email and just figured I should send something, anything. I guess my typing fluency was a bit shattered with the excessive alcohol abuse.

I still haven't heard about this work permit. My stamp on my passport runs out soon. Tomorrow actually. I probably should have prepared better for this, but I didn't. I just went to the immigration office. Maybe they'll deport me. It's hard to say.

This school year ends in a couple of weeks, and after that I've got a couple of months off to do absolutely nothing I don't feel like doing. I'll have no money, so I can't really go anywhere, but I've got plenty of free places to stay in Samoa.

If I get my work permit I'm going to buy a spear for spear fishing. Basically, you just put on your snorkel gear and carry around this 4-pronged spear with a rubber band on the end of it that wraps around your wrist. It'll be a fun thing to do when I take my boat out every day.

My Samoan language skills are going to hell. I haven't been learning that much because I don't want to spend my precious time (that is, maybe my last month or so here) learning new words that I'll never ever use again. It's more fun to swim in the ocean, drink recklessly, and use the language I'm used to.

But if I stay I'll get my butt back in gear.

A new Peace Corps group just showed up. They've heard many stories about me and my fellow, fallen comrade.

They're scared. When we arrived I was told by some friends the only way to get kicked out was to ride up to the Country director's house with a spliff in your mouth on a motorcycle naked with no helmet.

That was true for a while there; now, with the new administration, they're cracking down on this wild summer camp in Samoa called the Peace Corps. I'm not really too bothered by it. I'm still doing it my own way without that childish organization.

Anyway . . .

Post me some literature if you've got any—writing of any sort. I'm reading like a madman, and writing even more. I've started my book. I like where it's going so far. It's time to stop talking about being a writer and actually piece this thing together.

If people like us aren't going to do it, who will?

Well, let me know what you're doing back home?

You've quit the carpet cleaning job, right? What sort of job does a guy with a degree in British and American cultures get?

Well, take care man. Give me a buzz too if you get a phone card and some time.

Rock on, Mark

Oh yeah, for Halloween I grew a moustache. It was absolutely repulsive.

CHAPTER 3

Synthesis: Incorporating Outside Sources

▓ Road Map to Synthesis

Synthesis is the act of putting together different parts or elements to form a new complete whole. An ancient Greek word, its modern revival is credited to psychologist Benjamin Bloom whose ideas, although first put forward in the 1950s, are still in use *today*. Learning, Bloom argued, involved gaining mastery over a particular body of knowledge until one could *synthesize* its parts into a whole of one's own. It's as if learning is a ladder and students need to climb one particular rung at a time. This idea is often referred to as "Bloom's hierarchy of cognition" or "Bloom's taxonomy of learning." (See Figure 3.1 on p. 52.)

Bloom's taxonomy has been presented in many different ways. For our purposes, however, the process of synthesis can be expressed in three essential steps:

Step 1. Comprehend the ideas presented; gain a basic understanding of them.

Step 2. Analyze and evaluate the ideas; ask questions; wrestle with the information to find where you agree or disagree; begin to formulate your own thoughts and responses.

Step 3. Integrate all of the above into a formal response of your own.

As simplified in the preceding text, this three-step process is what critical reading and writing are all about.

For our discussion of paraphrase, summary, and quotation, we'll refer to Abraham Lincoln's Gettysburg Address, reproduced in full in the following section.

Gettysburg Address

ABRAHAM LINCOLN

Address delivered at the dedication of the Soldiers' National Cemetery at Gettysburg, Pennsylvania, November 19, 1863.

• • •

1 Four score and seven years ago our fathers brought forth upon this continent, a new nation, conceived in Liberty, and dedicated to the proposition that all men are created equal.

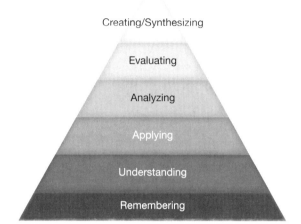

Creating/Synthesizing

Evaluating

Analyzing

Applying

Understanding

Remembering

■ **FIGURE 3.1** *Adapted from Bloom's Taxonomy 1956, as revised by Anderson and Krathwohl 2001.*

2   Now we are engaged in a great civil war, testing whether that nation, or any nation so conceived and so dedicated, can long endure. We are met on a great battlefield of that war. We have come to dedicate a portion of that field, as a final resting place for those who here gave their lives that that nation might live. It is altogether fitting and proper that we should do this.

3   But, in a larger sense, we can not dedicate—we can not consecrate—we can not hallow—this ground. The brave men, living and dead, who struggled here, have consecrated it, far above our poor power to add or detract. The world will little note nor long remember what we say here, but it can never forget what they did here. It is for us the living, rather, to be dedicated here to the unfinished work which they who fought here have thus far so nobly advanced. It is rather for us to be here dedicated to the great task remaining before us—that from these honored dead we take increased devotion to that cause for which they gave the last full measure of devotion—that we here highly resolve that these dead shall not have died in vain—that this nation, under God, shall have a new birth of freedom—and that government of the people, by the people, and for the people, shall not perish from the earth.

Paraphrase

To paraphrase means to put a specific passage in your own words. The passage being paraphrased can be as short as a phrase or as long as a paragraph, but is typically a sentence or a few sentences. However, when you paraphrase, you must be careful to use your own language, not the author's:

> **Original:** "But, in a larger sense, we can not dedicate—we can not consecrate—we can not hallow—this ground. The brave men, living and dead, who struggled here, have consecrated it, far above our poor power to add or detract."

Paraphrase: We can't make this ground holy because the struggle and sacrifice of the soldiers who died here have already made it holy—far beyond our feeble abilities to do so.

In addition you must always properly acknowledge the source when incorporating its paraphrase into your writing:

make this ground holy, because the struggle and sacrifice of the soldiers who died here have already made it holy—far beyond our feeble abilities to do so (58).

EXERCISES

Only ten sentences long, the Gettysburg Address, although brief, is rich in meaning. Working your way through the entire speech one sentence at a time, paraphrase each sentence. As in the discussion examples earlier, first write the original sentence, using quotation marks. Then, write your paraphrase of that sentence. As necessary, use a dictionary or other outside references for words or concepts you do not understand.

1. Evaluate the Gettysburg Address in relation to its audience and purpose (to review these concepts, see p. 16). You may use a source or sources of your own choosing. Write a paragraph that argues your point of view and that incorporates at least one paraphrase of the address.

Summary

To summarize is to shorten or condense another's work. You can summarize almost anything, short or long: a poem, an article, a speech, an entire book, or even an author's life's work. While a *paraphrase* restates a work on the sentence level—and somewhat mirrors the language of the original—a *summary* crystallizes a writer's or speaker's main idea.

When you summarize, you must be careful to use your own language (never the author's exact wording) and to document the source properly. Here are possible summaries of Lincoln's entire speech:

Lincoln told the crowd that the best way to honor the soldiers who died at Gettysburg would be to save the union and win the war (58).

Note that if we summarize an entire book, citing pages is not required:

David Copperfield charts the eponymous hero's quest from the vulnerability of childhood to the struggles and triumphs of the adult.

Both paraphrase and summary are important critical reading and research skills. To review critical reading skills, see Chapter 1. For more on paraphrase and summary as part of research and note-taking, see Part Four.

● EXERCISES

1. Summarize your favorite novel in one sentence, conveying the essence of its plot, themes, and/or style. Write two different one-sentence summaries: one using diction appropriate for a college course, and another using diction appropriate for a book jacket.

2. What is the most interesting or significant book-length work of nonfiction you have ever read? How would you describe it to an interested reader? How would you condense its main argument down to the essentials? Conveying as much information about the book's main argument as possible, summarize a favorite book-length work of nonfiction in one to three sentences. Use diction appropriate for a book review in a current periodical.

Quotations

A quotation reproduces an author's writing word for word as in this example:

> Faced with the enormous losses at the battle of Gettysburg—and indeed with the enormous loss of life over the course of the war thus far—Lincoln did not shrink from noting the inadequacy of dedicating the National Cemetery on that November day: "We can not dedicate—we can not consecrate—we can not hallow—this ground. The brave men, living and dead, who struggled here, have consecrated it, far above our poor power to add or detract" (58).

Quotation is especially effective when the original text is so striking or eloquent that conveying the mere sense of the words would fall flat.

When incorporating a quotation, always use quotation marks; be careful to preserve the punctuation, spelling, and capitalization of the original; and always use appropriate documentation. For details and exceptions consult a style manual appropriate to your field of study (or ask your instructor which style manual he or she recommends).

● EXERCISES

1. Choose some aspect of the Gettysburg Address that interests you. Bolster your understanding of the speech's historical and cultural context by consulting at least two outside sources. Then, develop a clear position and write a three-paragraph essay that incorporates at least one quotation from the Gettysburg Address and one paraphrase and one summary, either of the address itself or of an outside source.

2. Write a three-paragraph book review that evaluates and describes its style and content. Incorporate at least one paraphrase, one summary, and one quotation from the book itself. Use diction appropriate for a contemporary periodical, take a strong point of view, and strive to engage the reader.

3. Choose a contemporary topic that interests you and write a one- to three-paragraph letter to the editor (brevity is essential; the *New York Times,* for example, allows only 150 words per letter). Take a clear position and defend it logically, incorporating at least two outside sources. Acknowledge the sources in the text of your letter and also create a separate list of sources with complete documentation. Make your writing clear, concise, and persuasive.

Guidelines for Effectively Synthesizing Outside Sources

First, allow space for your thoughts. Every writer is occasionally overwhelmed by the swarm of experts milling around a topic. One way to avoid being intimidated is to set aside some space for your opinions even if you haven't yet come to any conclusions about the topic. Making space for your entry into the argument will at least legitimize it.

Second, initiate a dialogue with the material. Listen to yourself and the material even if you don't know where you stand in the discussion and need a road map to be open to discovery. Critical reading and writing should be a voyage of discovery, not a rigid steamrolling of pre-assumed dogma.

Third, think, revise, rewrite. A first reading of any text is unlikely to floor you with comprehension for your topic or miraculously enable you to analyze, evaluate, and synthesize it for your own purposes. For many, writing itself unlocks the deepest level of engagement on any topic. So don't just rush through a paper and hand it in. Give yourself time to think and rewrite if you want to truly figure out what you have to say and find the best way to say it.

Repeat all of the above. Writing is a recursive, not a linear process. This means, as we say in Chapter 2, that writing is a back-and-forth process. You often find yourself going back to push forward. But most writers will tell you that they revisit any and all of the preceding steps listed, in every possible sequence, before they achieve a final draft with which they can be satisfied.

In fact, many of the most common weaknesses in student writing stem from a failure to fully engage with the preceding fundamental processes. We began this chapter by discussing how the ability to successfully synthesize and integrate outside sources is both a writing and a critical-thinking skill. Integrating outside sources into your writing requires that you harness both critical-thinking and writing skills. The more you engage with the source materials and with the writing process, the clearer and the more interesting your writing will be.

Commenting on her essay "Body Modification—Think about It!" (pp. 209–213), student writer Shelley Taylor offers some excellent advice about these processes to her fellow writers:

> Before I actually begin writing, I do a lot of reflective thinking and organizing in my mind. I decide what information I am going to include and try to get a rough idea of the order and format I want to use. I usually sketch out an outline that I can follow. After I have finished, I read through my work several times to do further editing.
>
> While working on this piece, I used the Internet to look up a few sites and articles on my subject to get an idea about current research, others' opinions, etc. I searched my memory for incidents in my own experience . . . that were relevant to the issue. Finally, I synthesized and integrated all of this information to formulate my own thoughts, feelings, and insights.

(214)

To review approaches to critical reading, the writing process, and working with visual imagery, see Chapters 1 and 2.

Guidelines for Improving Your Use of Outside Sources

Whether you are using a quotation, paraphrase, or summary, outside sources have essentially two functions in your writing:

1. to support your argument
2. to enliven your writing

But these two functions can be effectively carried out in various ways, depending on what you want to say and how you want to say it. As in other writing tasks, different kinds of writing that incorporate outside sources often require different strategies to be effective. You need to be clear on the purpose of your writing. Are you writing a personal essay *or* a researched argument? Are you writing for a newspaper, a popular magazine, *or* an academic journal? Should your diction be formal or informal, humorous or serious? For your writing to be effective, it depends on the ebb and flow of details, opinions, and synthesized emphasis.

That said, a few guidelines apply.

Always keep your argument in the foreground. In any kind of writing, your argument—also termed your thesis—drives content. Your argument drives the essay forward; your argument drives the writing. (This is even true in a narrative essay, in which "argument" becomes "story.") The outside source is used to support your argument not replace it. A research paper—even one in which most of the information comes from outside—must be filtered and focused through your point of view. It is always up to you, the writer, to shape the material.

Weave the sources into your argument. One of the most common criticisms of student writing is that outside information is inserted willy-nilly with little to no connection to the writer's argument. As discussed earlier, this kind of weak relationship between source and writing can often be traced to a shallowness in understanding the source and/or a shallowness in thinking through your argument. Moreover, even when you know what you want to say and how you want to use the outside information to support it, successfully weaving outside sources into your argument takes study and practice. An apt metaphor here might be a casserole. What if, instead of a delicious mix of sauce, chopped meat, minced vegetables, and carefully chosen spices, someone handed you a bowl with an uncooked hunk of meat, unchopped vegetables, and a salt shaker? Doubtless you would be perplexed. Surely, the reader tackling the "uncooked" essay feels the same way.

Consider form as well as function. First strive to make your writing clear, then strive to make it lively. And by "lively" we mean all of the nuances that make someone's writing a pleasure to read. Once you've achieved clarity, you can turn your attention to greater elegance of style. That said, as you'll notice in the examples that follow, what makes a particular piece of writing well written and pleasurable, and what makes the writer's incorporation of an outside source particularly effective, is often as individual as the piece itself. But a few generalizations apply. Good writing often has variation, but not too much. Shifts in tone and diction, variation in wording, and shifts in pace as appropriate often help keep things lively. Too much variation and it's a mess. Too little and the writing is dull and boring. Good writers find the right balance. Good writers know how to use humor (when that's their aim). Good writers know how to make us go silent. They know how to place emphasis and draw the reader's attention where they want it to go. Learning what works to create readable writing is a matter of study and practice.

Writers at Work: Strategies for Incorporating Outside Sources

One of the best ways to improve your writing is by studying how experienced writers work. What kinds of strategies do these writers employ? How do they use quotation, paraphrase, and summary (either separately or in combination) to build persuasive arguments and to enliven their writing?

Writers at Work: Using Paraphrase and Summary

Paraphrase and summary are the real workhorses for integrating outside sources into your writing. Because any paraphrase or summary of another text is itself a synthesis, using paraphrase and summary in your writing keeps you—your thoughts, your responses, your unique point of view—in the driver's seat. By paraphrasing a phrase, sentence, or passage or by summarizing an entire book, chapter, article, or idea (however long or short), you've already begun your own process of understanding, analyzing, evaluating, and synthesizing the information.

While paraphrase and summary are in some ways alike, each has a different function. Paraphrase, to recap, restates a specific phrase, sentence, or passage in your own words. It is especially useful when the original writing *isn't* memorable and uses obscure language that requires simplifying. Paraphrase is often a useful way to introduce or conclude a quotation.

Summary gives you the greatest degree of flexibility to adapt outside sources to your argument. Because you can summarize anything from a passage to an entire series of books, summary puts you fully in charge of the breadth of scope or level of detail with which you want to discuss a particular idea. Consider these examples of summary:

> The famous storm scene in *David Copperfield* brings to an end the story of David's boyhood friend and hero, Steerforth.

> *David Copperfield* charts the eponymous hero's quest from the vulnerability of childhood to the struggles and triumphs of the adult.

> Dickens's later novels show a repeated obsession with double lives and duplicity.

> Throughout his long career—from the orphaned Oliver Twist of his second novel to the pitiful street urchin Jo in the mature *Bleak House* to Pip's coming-of-age-struggles in the later *Great Expectations*—Dickens returned again and again to the child's struggle against a brutal and seemingly uncaring universe.

A quotation, by contrast, restricts you not just to the original author's words but also to the pace and scope of the original idea. A paraphrase frees you somewhat but, because it operates at the sentence level, it doesn't allow the same freedom to zoom in or out as a summary. Whether you want to provide a broad sweeping overview or home in sharply on a microscopic detail, the summary puts you in charge. Summary also gives you far more room than either quotation or paraphrase to present an outside idea through the lens of your own interpretation.

Let's consider, then, the following passages to see how some of the writers in this book have used paraphrase and summary to support their ideas and enliven their writing.

Student writer Shelley Taylor's sweeping summary of the history of tattoos gives breadth and depth to her initial observations about the current craze for body modification:

> Actually, through history, people from various cultures have decorated their bodies with piercings and tattoos. In 1992, a 4,000-year-old body of a tattooed man was found in an Austrian glacier. From 4000 to 2000 BC, Egyptians identified tattooing with fertility and nobility. Body piercing has been used as a symbol of royalty and courage, as well as other lauded attributes. In some societies, body piercing and tattoos have long been used in initiation rites and as socialization symbols.
>
> (209)

Notice that she doesn't document each of these details because she's summarizing from what can legitimately be thought of as common knowledge. (This information can, however, go into a bibliography.)

One of the most humorous and most effective uses of paraphrase is the one with which Bill Bryson closes his argument (highlighted next). Having begun his essay "Wide-open Spaces" (online only) by telling us "Daniel Boone was an idiot," Bryson leaves us in suspense about what this could possibly mean until the next-to-last paragraph:

> Of course, Americans have always tended to see these things in a different way. Daniel Boone famously is supposed to have looked out his cabin window one day, seen a wisp of smoke rising from a homesteader's dwelling on a distant mountain, **and announced his intention to move on, complaining bitterly that the neighborhood was getting too crowded.**
>
> Which is why I say Daniel Boone was an idiot. I just hate to see the rest of my country going the same way.

Bryson paraphrases the famous Boone saying ("Too many people! Too crowded, too crowded! I want some elbow room!") to knock this beloved American icon down a peg— and get us to rethink our mythical view of ourselves as Boone-like independent spirits, while bringing his essay to its witty conclusion.

Writers at Work: Using Quotation

Like paraphrases and summaries, quotations can be used to provide evidence. A classic use of quotation for this purpose is when a writer quotes an expert authority to support his or her argument. And, of course, quotations can be used in other ways simply to deliver information. But quotations differ from summaries and paraphrases in that they can be especially useful at providing stylistic flair. Because quotations reproduce another person's speech and writing word for word, they are a flexible and effective way to add emphasis to a particular thought, land a punch, bring your paragraph, section, or entire essay to a walloping conclusion. For this reason, quotations can be particularly effective at or toward the end of a paragraph. But opening and mid-paragraph placements can, of course, also be used effectively.

Quotations are also uniquely suited to writing situations where you want to add depth or breadth to an argument, where you turn to someone else's mullings on your particular topic to allow the reader to dwell more deeply. For this purpose, writers will often use quotations from famous authors, philosophers, artists, or other respected public figures. We expect William Shakespeare or Albert Einstein, for example, to have something to say that is uniquely insightful about the human condition. One final note: Use quotations sparingly. By their very nature, quotations are never in your voice. Consider the following examples of effective use of quotation.

Student writer Shelley Taylor brings "Body Modification—Think About It!" to a well-punched end with a classic, end-placed quotation:

> Remember that this decision [to get a tattoo or body piercing] will most likely affect the rest of your life. That makes it extremely important, wouldn't you say? Whether you are a teenager, a young adult, or a middle-aged person who has always dreamed of doing something fun and outrageous, don't forget to look at all sides of this issue. It will be well worth the trouble. At the risk of being unoriginal, I would like to end with a quotation from one of those very wise anonymous writers for *The College Chalkboard* Web site: **"Ponder before you pierce, and think before you ink."** I couldn't have said it better myself.
>
> (213)

Readers will likely walk away from this essay with "think before you ink" bouncing around their brains for a few hours at least. The quotation is effective at bringing Taylor's essay to its conclusion because of placement (end of paragraph), because it's funny and memorable (especially with its use of rhyme and alliteration), and because it's an apt and clever summing up of her overall thesis, already nicely clarified in the title and well developed in the overall flow of her argument.

In "Illegal Immigrants Are Bolstering Social Security—with Billions" (online only), Eduardo Porter uses expert opinion to support and provide evidence for his point of view:

> Illegal immigration, Marcel Suárez-Orozco, codirector of immigration studies at New York University, noted sardonically, could provide **"the fastest way to shore up the long-term finances of Social Security."**

His expert, as we would expect in an essay on a current social issue, is someone with recognized professional standing in the field being discussed. Note, too, that Porter uses this quotation (one of only two in a 15-paragraph article) to cap an argument he's been building over several paragraphs, having first described a single immigrant's typical workday, wages, and contribution to Social Security and then filled in the big picture with a paragraph or so of convincing statistics.

An "expert" quotation can also be from someone who speaks not as a noted authority *on* a particular subject but as someone who *is* the subject. In "Body Image" (online only), health professional Cindy Maynard speaks about teenage body image primarily from her own position as a health expert. But she includes a paragraph in which teenagers speak for themselves:

> Some sports can contribute to a negative body image. The need to make weight for a sport like wrestling or boxing can cause disordered eating. But other boys say sports make them feel better about themselves. Jon, a 15-year-old, states, **"Guys are in competition, especially in the weight room. They say, 'I can bench 215 lbs.' and the other guy says, 'Well, I can bench 230 lbs.' If you're stronger, you're better."** Daniel, age 16, shares, **"Guys are into having the perfect body. But if you feel good about your body, you automatically feel good about yourself."**

By doing so, Maynard brings a different kind of expertise to her article. She shifts from a professional to a personal point of view and from her own "expert" voice to the boys' personal voices, and she lets her teenage readers know that she's not just an expert talking *at* them; she's willing to listen.

Alfred Lubrano makes a similar shift in voice, but in a different direction, in the deeply personal "Bricklayer's Boy" (pp. 347–352). Over the essay's 28 paragraphs, there are only two brief uses of outside sources. In this one, toward the essay's conclusion, he quotes an expert in men's issues, on the subject of father–son class divides:

> When we see each other these days, my father still asks how the money is. Sometimes he reads my stories; usually he likes them, although he recently criticized one piece as being a bit sentimental: "Too schmaltzy," he said. Some psychologists say that the blue-white-collar gap between fathers and sons leads to alienation, but I tend to agree with Dr. Al Baraff, a clinical psychologist and director of the MenCenter in Washington, DC. **"The core of the relationship is based on emotional and hereditary traits," Baraff says. "Class [distinctions] just get added on. If it's a healthful relationship from when you're a kid, there's a respect back and forth that'll continue."**
>
> (351)

By bringing in Dr. Baraff's perspective, Lubrano shifts from the truth of his own story to a proposed truth about all such father–son relationships; he shifts from talking about his experience as the white-collar son of a blue-collar man to a society-wide observation about all such relationships. Quoting an expert makes this shift effective and economical.

In narrative nonfiction, quotation can also become dialogue to great effect. Partway through the excerpt from *Warriors Don't Cry* (online only), Melba Patillo Beals talks about what it was like to be invited to the Clinton governor's mansion 30 years after a previous Arkansas governor fostered a climate of violence and hatred to keep Beals and a handful of other young African Americans out of Arkansas high schools:

> During all the fancy ceremonies, some of Arkansas's highest officials and businessmen came from far and wide to welcome us. And perhaps the most astounding evidence that things have indeed changed for the better was the attitude of Governor Bill Clinton.
>
> "Call me Bill," he said, extending his hand, looking me in the eye. "You'll come on up to the house and sit a while." He flashed that charming grin of his. A few minutes of conversation assured me that his warm invitation was genuine. He is, after all, a man my brother refers to as "good people," based on their working relationship over the years.

Here the use of quotation as dialogue provides a powerful means of showing—not just telling—how much times had changed.

Chapter Writing Assignment: Writing a Synthesis Essay

This assignment asks you to write an essay synthesizing at least three outside sources in support of your argument.

The essay topic is described next. You will find three readings on the pages that follow. Suggestions for additional reading can be found on pages 70–71. Links to more readings, questions, and media on the topic of the American Dream can be found by visiting the *MindTap for Readings for Writers*, 15e online.

Essay prompts can be found on pages 69–70.

Income Disparity, Social Mobility, and the American Dream

Introduction

The "American Dream" has been dismissed as a cliché and upheld as the glue that holds our nation together. It has been variously described throughout our nation's history. In the past decade, a number of studies have documented a rising gap between the incomes of the wealthiest Americans and all other wage earners, alongside a decrease in America's much-touted tradition of social mobility. These findings have many policymakers, journalists, researchers, and ordinary people wondering about our long-held notions of social mobility and the American Dream. The following readings present a number of viewpoints on this topic.

Directions

First, read and annotate each source critically and carefully. Pay attention to the different points of view they each express, the different ways they each express them, and the rhetorical context for each source.

Then, using one of the prompts on pages 69–70, write an essay that synthesizes at the sources in support of your argument.

Make sure to acknowledge sources properly. Strive to make your argument as clear and persuasive as possible, and to make your writing effective and readable.

Sources

1. Magazine article, "The Death of Horatio Alger." Paul Krugman, "The Death of Horatio Alger," *The Nation,* January 5, 2004, 16.

2. Book excerpt, "By Our Own Bootstraps." From W. Michael Cox and Richard Alm, "Chapter 4: By Our Own Bootstraps," *Myths of Rich and Poor: Why We're Better Off Than We Think* (New York: Basic, 1999), 69, 87–89.

3. Online commentary, "Long Live the American Dream." Shikha Dalmia, "Long Live the American Dream," Reason.com, March 1, 2011; originally published at TheDaily.com, February 24, 2011.

The Death of Horatio Alger

PAUL KRUGMAN

In the following Nation *article, Paul Krugman discusses the impact of rising inequality on the American Dream. Krugman won the Nobel Prize in Economics in 2008; he is a professor of economics at Princeton and a regular columnist for the* New York Times. *He also served on the Council of Economic Advisers for the Reagan administration.*

• • •

1   The other day I found myself reading a leftist rag that made outrageous claims about America. It said that we are becoming a society in which the poor tend to stay poor, no matter how hard they work; in which sons are much more likely to inherit the socioeconomic status of their father than they were a generation ago.

2   The name of the leftist rag? *Business Week*, which published an article titled "Waking Up from the American Dream." The article summarizes recent research showing that social mobility in the United States (which was never as high as legend had it) has declined considerably over the past few decades. If you put that research together with other research that shows a drastic increase in income and wealth inequality, you reach an uncomfortable conclusion: America looks more and more like a class-ridden society.

3   And guess what? Our political leaders are doing everything they can to fortify class inequality, while denouncing anyone who complains—or even points out what is happening—as a practitioner of "class warfare."

4   Let's talk first about the facts on income distribution. Thirty years ago we were a relatively middle-class nation. It had not always been thus: Gilded Age America was a highly unequal society, and it stayed that way through the 1920s. During the 1930s and '40s, however, America experienced what the economic historians Claudia Goldin and Robert Margo have dubbed the Great Compression: a drastic narrowing of income gaps, probably as a result of New Deal policies. And the new economic order persisted for more than a generation: Strong unions; taxes on inherited wealth, corporate profits and high incomes; close public scrutiny of corporate management—all helped to keep income gaps relatively small. The economy was hardly egalitarian, but a generation ago the gross inequalities of the 1920s seemed very distant.

5   Now they're back. According to estimates by the economists Thomas Piketty and Emmanuel Saez—confirmed by data from the Congressional Budget Office—between 1973 and 2000 the average real income of the bottom 90 percent of American taxpayers actually fell by 7 percent. Meanwhile, the income of the top 1 percent rose by 148 percent, the income of the top 0.1 percent rose by 343 percent, and the income of the top 0.01 percent rose 599 percent. (Those numbers exclude capital gains, so they're not an artifact of the stock market bubble.) The distribution of income in the United States has gone right back to Gilded Age levels of inequality.

6   Never mind, say the apologists, who churn out papers with titles like that of a 2001 Heritage Foundation piece, "Income Mobility and the Fallacy of Class-Warfare Arguments." America, they say, isn't a caste society—people with high incomes this year may have low incomes next year and vice versa, and the route to wealth is open to all. That's where those commies at *Business Week* come in: As they point out (and as economists and sociologists have been pointing out for some time), America actually is more of a caste society than we like to think. And the caste lines have lately become a lot more rigid.

7   The myth of income mobility has always exceeded the reality. As a general rule, once they've reached their 30s, people don't move up and down the income ladder very much. Conservatives often cite studies like a 1992 report by Glenn Hubbard, a Treasury official under the elder Bush who later became chief economic adviser to the younger Bush, that purport to show large numbers of Americans moving from low-wage to high-wage jobs during their working lives. But what these studies measure, as the economist Kevin Murphy put it, is mainly "the guy who works in the college bookstore and has a real job by his early 30s." Serious studies that exclude this sort of pseudo-mobility show that inequality in average incomes over long periods isn't much smaller than inequality in annual incomes.

8   It is true, however, that America was once a place of substantial intergenerational mobility: Sons often did much better than their fathers. A classic 1978 survey found that among adult men whose fathers were in the bottom 25 percent of the population as ranked by social and economic status, 23 percent had made it into the top 25 percent. In other words, during the first thirty years or so after World War II, the American dream of upward mobility was a real experience for many people.

9   Now for the shocker. The *Business Week* piece cites a new survey of today's adult men, which finds that this number has dropped to only 10 percent. That is, over the past generation upward mobility has fallen drastically. Very few children of the lower class are making their way to even moderate affluence. This goes along with other studies indicating that rags-to-riches stories have become vanishingly rare, and that the correlation between fathers' and sons' incomes has risen in recent decades. In modern America, it seems, you're quite likely to stay in the social and economic class into which you were born.

10   *Business Week* attributes this to the "Wal-Martization" of the economy, the proliferation of dead-end, low-wage jobs and the disappearance of jobs that provide entry to the middle class. That's surely part of the explanation. But public policy plays a role—and will, if present trends continue, play an even bigger role in the future.

11   Put it this way: Suppose that you actually liked a caste society, and you were seeking ways to use your control of the government to further entrench the advantages of the haves against the have-nots. What would you do?

12   One thing you would definitely do is get rid of the estate tax, so that large fortunes can be passed on to the next generation. More broadly, you would seek to reduce tax rates both on corporate profits and on unearned income such as dividends and capital gains, so that those with large accumulated or inherited wealth could more easily accumulate even more. You'd also try to create tax shelters mainly useful for the rich. And more broadly still, you'd try to reduce tax rates on people with high incomes, shifting the burden to the payroll tax and other revenue sources that bear most heavily on people with lower incomes.

13   Meanwhile, on the spending side, you'd cut back on healthcare for the poor, on the quality of public education, and on state aid for higher education. This would make it more difficult for people with low incomes to climb out of their difficulties and acquire the education essential to upward mobility in the modern economy.

14   And just to close off as many routes to upward mobility as possible, you'd do everything possible to break the power of unions, and you'd privatize government functions so that well-paid civil servants could be replaced with poorly paid private employees.

15   It all sounds sort of familiar, doesn't it?

16   Where is this taking us? Thomas Piketty, whose work with Saez has transformed our understanding of income distribution, warns that current policies will eventually create "a class of renters in the U.S., whereby a small group of wealthy but untalented children controls vast segments of the U.S. economy and penniless, talented children simply can't compete." If he's right—and I fear that he is—we will end up suffering not only from injustice, but from a vast waste of human potential.

17   Goodbye, Horatio Alger. And goodbye, American Dream.

"The Death of Horatio Alger" by Paul Krugman. THE NATION, January 5, 2004, p. 16.

By Our Own Bootstraps

W. MICHAEL COX AND RICHARD ALM

This excerpt from W. Michael Cox and Richard Alm's classic Myths of Rich and Poor: Why We're Better Off Than We Think *articulates their belief in the importance of opportunity versus equality in striving for the American Dream. Cox is Director of the William J. O'Neil Center for Global Markets and Freedom at Southern Methodist University and the former chief economist for the Federal Reserve Bank of Dallas. Alm is a business reporter with the Dallas Morning News.*

• • •

1   "Land of Opportunity." Anywhere in the world, those three words bring to mind just one place: the United States of America.

2   Opportunity defines our heritage. The American saga entails waves of immigrant farmers, shopkeepers, laborers, and entrepreneurs, all coming to the United
States for the promise of a better life. Some amassed enormous fortunes—the
Rockefellers, the Carnegies, the DuPonts, the Fords, the Vanderbilts, to name
just a few. Even today America's opportunity is always on display. Bill Gates in
computer software, Ross Perot in data processing, Bill Cosby and Oprah Winfrey
in entertainment, Warren Buffett in investing, Sam Walton in retailing, Michael
Jordan in sports, and Mary Kay Ash in cosmetics could head a list of the many
thousands who catapulted from society's lower or middle ranks to the top. Many
millions more, descendants of those who arrived with little more than the clothes
on their backs and a few bucks in their pockets, took advantage of an open economic system to improve their lot in life through talent and hard work. . . .

3   That's what the American Dream, a dream of opportunity, is all about. . . .

4   [But] judging from the public debate, at least some Americans would prefer a
more equal distribution of income to a less equal one, perhaps on moral grounds,
perhaps as a part of an ideal of civic virtue. There's no *economic* reason, however,
to prefer one pattern of income distribution over another. In fact, the income statistics do little but confirm what's obvious: America isn't an egalitarian society. It
wasn't designed to be. Socialism, a failed and receding system, sought to impose
an artificial equality. Capitalism, a successful and expanding system, doesn't fight
a fundamental fact of human nature—we vary greatly in capabilities, motivation,
interests, and preferences. Some of us are driven to get ahead. Some of us are
just plain lazy. Some of us are willing to work hard so we can afford a lifestyle rich
in material goods. Some of us work just hard enough to provide a roof overhead,
food, clothes, and a few amenities. It shouldn't come as a surprise that our incomes vary greatly.

5   Income inequality isn't an aberration. Quite the opposite, it's perfectly consistent with the laws that govern a free-enterprise system. In the early 1970s, three
groups of unemployed Canadians, all in their twenties, all with at least 12 years of
schooling, volunteered to participate in a stylized economy where the only employment was making woolen belts on small hand looms. They could work as much or
as little as they liked, earning $2.50 for each belt. After 98 days, the results were
anything but equal: 37.2 percent of the economy's income went to the 20 percent
with the highest earnings. The bottom 20 percent received only 6.6 percent. This
economic microcosm tells us one thing: Even among similar people with identical
work options, some workers will earn more than others.

6   In a modern economy, incomes vary for plenty of reasons having little to do
with fairness or equity. Education and experience, for example, usually yield higher
pay. As industry becomes more sophisticated, the rewards to skilled labor tend to
rise, adding to the number of high-income earners. Location matters. New Yorkers
earn more than Mississippians. Lifestyle choices play a part, too. Simply by having
an additional paycheck, two-income families make more money than those with a
single breadwinner. Longer retirements, however, will add to the number of households with low income, even if many senior citizens live well from their savings.
Demographic changes can twist the distribution of income. As the Baby Boomers
enter their peak earning years, the number of high-income households ought to

rise. Economic forces create ripples in what we earn. The ebb and flow of industries can shift workers to both ends of the income distribution. Layoffs put some Americans into low-income groups, at least temporarily. Companies with new products and new technologies create jobs and, in most cases, share the bounty by offering workers higher pay. In technology industries, bonuses and stock options are becoming more common. Higher rates of return on investments—with, for example, a stock-market boom—will create a windfall for households with money riding on financial markets.

7   In and of itself, moreover, income distribution doesn't say much about the performance of an economy or the opportunities it offers. A widening gap isn't necessarily a sign of failure, nor does a narrowing one guarantee that an economy is functioning well. As a matter of fact, it's quite common to find a widening of income distribution in boom times, when almost everyone's earnings are rising rapidly. All it takes is for one segment of the workforce to become better off faster than others. However, the distribution can narrow in hard times, as companies facing declining demand cut back on jobs, hours, raises, and bonuses. In fact, we often see a compression of incomes in areas where people are sinking into poverty.

8   There's no denying that our system allows some Americans to become much richer than others. We must accept that, even celebrate it. Opportunity, not equality of income, is what made the U.S. economy grow and prosper. It's most important to provide equality of opportunity, not equality of results. There's ample evidence to refute any suggestion that the economy is no longer capable of providing opportunity for the vast majority of Americans. At the end of the twentieth century, upward mobility is alive and well. Even the lower-income households are sharing in the country's progress. What's more, data suggest that the populist view of America as a society torn between haves and have-nots, with rigid class lines, is just plain wrong. We are by no means a caste society.

Long Live the American Dream

SHIKHA DALMIA

Now a senior policy analyst at the Reason Foundation, Shikha Dalmia emigrated to America from New Delhi, India. Her article "Long Live the American Dream" first appeared online at TheDaily.com. Dalmia analyzes her adopted country's particular strengths by means of comparison against fast-growing India and China.

• • •

1   Americans, hit first by outsourcing and then a recession, are becoming deeply pessimistic about their country's ability to maintain its economic leadership in a globalized world. America's Aristophanes, Jon Stewart, commented during a recent interview with Anand Giridhardas, author of *India Calling*: "The American dream is still alive—it's just alive in India." Likewise, 20 percent of Americans in a

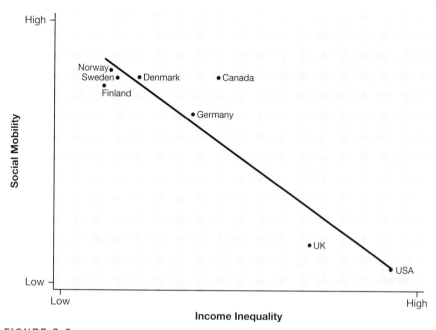

■ FIGURE 3.2

Social mobility is lower in more unequal countries.

December *National Journal* poll believed that the U.S. economy was no longer the strongest. Nearly half picked China instead.

2   But there are at least five reasons why neither India nor China will knock America off its economic perch any time soon, at least not by the only measure that matters: Offering the best life to the most people.

America Wastes No Talent

3   Conventional wisdom holds that America's global competitiveness is driven by geniuses flocking to its shore and producing breathtaking inventions. But America's real genius lies not in tapping genius—but every scrap of talent up and down the scale.

4   A 2005 World Bank study found that the bulk of a people's wealth comes not from tangible capital like raw resources and infrastructure. It comes from intangible wealth: effective government, secure property rights, a functioning judiciary. Such intangible factors put the equivalent of $418,000 at the disposal of every American resident. India and China? $3,738 and $4,208 respectively.

5   America's vast intangible wealth makes everyone more productive and successful. Personal attributes—talent, looks, smarts—matter only on the margins. Having witnessed the life trajectory of many Indian immigrants, what's striking to me is that, with some exceptions, it doesn't matter whether they are the best in their profession in India or just mediocre. Within 10 to 15 years of arriving, they land in a very similar space. They get good jobs, buy homes, have children, send them to decent schools and colleges, and save for their retirement. The differences in their standard of living would have been far greater had they stayed home.

America Does Not Have India's Infrastructure Deficit or China's Civil Society Deficit

6   India's gap with America extends not just to intangible capital but tangible capital as well. Basic facilities in India—roads, water, sewage—remain primitive. For example, a 2010 McKinsey Global Institute report found that India treats 30 percent of raw sewage, whereas the international norm is 100 percent. India provides 105 liters of water per person per day; the minimum standard is 150 liters. It needs to spend twice the slated expenditures over the next 10 years to deliver basic services.

7   China, meanwhile, has a major civil society problem. America has made about $100 trillion in Social Security and Medicare promises to seniors that it can't fund. But American seniors face nothing like the kind of destitution that the Chinese do. China's one-child policy has decimated the natural safety net that old people rely on in traditional societies. And China offers no public safety net to the vast majority of village-born. Worse, many Chinese have invested their nest eggs in various asset bubbles that will wipe out their only means of subsistence if they burst, making the Great Depression look like a beach party.

America Does Not Have Grinding Poverty

8   Despite all the recent hoopla about China becoming the world's second biggest economy and India hoping to follow suit, the reality is that the per capita GDP—even measured by purchasing power parity—in both is pathetic. America's is about $47,000, China's $7,500, and India's $3,290.

9   Worse, both still harbor medieval levels of poverty with 300 million people in each living on less than $1.25 a day. India's IT boom gets big press, but it—along with all the tertiary industries it has spawned—employs 2.3 million people, or 0.2 percent of the population.

10   Neither country is a font of opportunity comparable to America.

American Education Is Superior

11   [The] President . . . claims that America is in an "education arms race" with India and China. Rubbish.

12   Notwithstanding all the horror stories about American kids underperforming on standardized tests compared to Asian kids raised by Tiger moms, things are worse in India and China. India's literacy rate is 66 percent. China puts it at 93 percent—but between 2000 and 2005, China's illiterate population *grew* by 30 million. The same may happen in India, thanks to last year's Right to Education Act whose regulations will cripple India's private school market. The fundamental problem is that both countries put their resources into educating elite kids—and ignoring the rest.

13   College education in both countries, especially in engineering, is also vastly overrated. Harvard researcher Vivek Wadhwa has shown that, contrary to conventional wisdom, not only does America graduate a comparable number of engineers to India and China—American engineers are vastly superior.

14   But unless more Indian and Chinese kids get access to a quality education, their countries won't be able to actualize their human potential, precisely what America does so well.

America Doesn't Have a Culture of Hype

15   An important reason why the gloom-and-doom about America is unjustified is precisely that there is so much gloom-and-doom. Indians and Chinese, by contrast, have drunk their own Kool Aid. Their moribund economies have barely kicked into action and they are entertaining dreams of becoming the next global superpower. This bespeaks a profound megalomania—not to mention lopsided priorities. There is not a culture of hope in these countries, as Giridhardas told Jon Stewart. There is a culture of hype.

16   By contrast, Americans are their own worst critics—always looking for lessons to improve what is working and fix what's not. Alexis de Tocqueville observed that although Americans were the freest and most enlightened men placed in the happiest of conditions, "a sort of cloud habitually covered their features." Why? Because "they were constantly tormented by a vague fear of not having chosen the shortest route that can lead to . . . their wellbeing."

17   Indeed, Americans have a grab-the-bull-by-its-horns quality so that they simply don't hang around hoping for things to get better on their own. If the public school monopoly is failing kids, by golly, then they'll homeschool them themselves. (Public schools are dysfunctional virtually everywhere, but which other country has spawned anything equivalent to America's homeschooling movement?) The government responds ineffectually to the recession, modest by historic standards, and Americans go into panic mode. Grass-roots movements such as the Tea Party emerge to rein in the government. PayPal founder Peter Theil has even given close to a million dollars to the Seasteading Institute to establish new countries on the sea to experiment with new forms of government. This might be wacky but it puts an outside limit on how out-of-whack Americans will let their institutions get before they start fixing them.

18   This American spirit, ultimately, is the biggest reason to believe that the American dream is and will stay alive—in America.

From Reason.com, March 1, 2011; originally published at The Daily.com, February 24, 2011. Reprinted with permission from Shikha Dalmia, Senior Analyst at Reason Foundation.

▨ Chapter Writing Assignments

Choose one of the following prompts and write an essay that synthesizes the three sources in support of your argument. Remember that in addition to using quotations, you can also incorporate sources as paraphrases and summaries.

1. Using the readings and drawing from your own beliefs and experience, write an essay that defends, challenges, or qualifies the claim that anyone can make it in contemporary America if he or she is willing to work hard and persevere.

2. James Truslow, famous historian and originator of the term "American Dream," claimed in the 1930s that the American Dream is "a dream of a social order in which each man and each woman shall be able to attain to their fullest stature of which they are innately capable." To what extent does this ideal depend on individual initiative versus societal support? Write an essay discussing to what extent and in what ways a society is responsible for creating fair opportunities for all its citizens.

3. The Declaration of Independence says "We hold these truths to be self-evident: That all men are created equal, that they are endowed by their creator with certain unalienable rights, that among these are life, liberty and the pursuit of happiness." Cox and Alm state that "America isn't an egalitarian society. It wasn't designed to be." How would you reconcile the tension between these two statements? Drawing from the readings and from your own beliefs and experience, write an essay that defends, challenges, or qualifies Cox and Alm's statement that "America isn't an egalitarian society." As part of this essay, you will also need to conduct outside research to define what is meant by "egalitarian" and synthesize this research into your essay.

4. Considering the various sources from a cultural and historical point of view, develop a position on whether and to what extent the American Dream is about individual material success or about some greater national vision. If the latter, explain what that greater national vision might be. Are these two visions mutually exclusive or complementary? What relation might there be, if any, between the two?

5. Develop a position on what the American Dream means to you, incorporating ideas and evidence from the source materials. Make sure to defend your position by drawing from source materials in support of your argument and taking into account source materials that qualify or challenge your point of view.

6. With your instructor's approval, conduct additional research to bring in at least two additional sources of your own choosing or draw from the list of additional readings that follow. Write your own prompt, in response to your research, and use this prompt to write an essay that synthesizes the readings and your independent research.

● SUGGESTIONS FOR ADDITIONAL READING

James Truslow Adams, "Epilogue: The American Dream." From *The Epic of America* (Boston: Little, 1931), 404–12.

Joe Bageant, *Deer Hunting with Jesus: Dispatches from America's Class War* (New York: Crown, 2007), 62–64, 69–74.

Ronald Bailey, "The Secrets of Intangible Wealth," *The Wall Street Journal Online* (WSJ.com), September 29, 2007.

Aaron Bernstein, "Waking Up from the American Dream," *Business Week,* December 1, 2003.

Chuck Collins, Mike Lapham, and Scott Klinger, *I Didn't Do It Alone: Society's Contribution to Individual Wealth and Success* (United for a Fair Economy, 2004).

Martin C. Jiscke, "The American Dream," *Vital Speeches of the Day* 73, no. 7 (July 2007): 314–15.

David Kamp, "Rethinking the American Dream," *Vanity Fair,* April 2009.

Erich Origen and Gan Golan, *The Adventures of Unemployed Man* (New York: Little, 2010).

Theodore Roosevelt, "New Nationalism," in *Letters and Speeches* (New York: Library of America, 2004).

Katharine W. Seelye, "What Happens to the American Dream in a Recession?" *The New York Times,* May 7, 2009.

Richard Todd, "Who Me, Rich? What It Takes (and What It Means) to Be Wealthy Today: A Look at the Top 1 Percent," *Worth,* September 1997, 70–84.

Louis Uchitelle, "The Richest of the Rich, Proud of a New Gilded Age," *The New York Times,* July 15, 2007.

Richard Wilkinson and Kate Pickett, *The Spirit Level: Why Greater Equality Makes Societies Stronger* (New York: Bloomsbury, 2009).

World Bank, "Where Is the Wealth of Nations? Measuring Capital for the 21st Century" (Washington: World Bank, 2006).

CHAPTER 4

The Writer's Voice

▮ Road Map to Writer's Voice

Most writers do not sit down to write consciously in a certain style. They do, however, try to project a certain voice onto the page. Sometimes the writer assumes this voice deliberately, but often it is chosen for the writer by the psychology of the audience and the material—and by the need and occasion that make the writing necessary.

Here is an example. You are the boss. You sit down to write a memo to your employees, but being the boss goes to your head, and you write:

> Illumination of the overhead fixtures must be extinguished by the final person exiting the premises.

This notice tells the employee reader two things: First, it tells them to turn off the lights before leaving the room; second, it tells the reader that you are the boss and you order they do this. That is not the only kind of notice you could have written. You might, for example, have written this equivalent:

The last person to leave this room must turn out the overhead lights.

This makes the point, but you think it also makes you sound more modest than the first version.

The difference between these two is not one of content, but of tone or style. It is tone of voice when you are composing the memo, for what you tried to do was not write in a certain style but to sound like the boss; to the reader, however, it is your style.

Many writing teachers, with some justification, approach voice and style as if they were always related to the writer's psychology. If you had confidence in your authority as the boss, if you really felt comfortable with your power, you wouldn't think it necessary to sound like God in your every memo. If you must sound like the Almighty in your memos, perhaps it is because you really don't feel at ease with the idea of being the boss. Many similar mishaps of voice or style in student papers can be traced to a psychological uncertainty about the material, to a self-doubting attitude, or even to the writer's feelings about the assignment.

The relationship between feelings and tone is slippery but makes sense. It is only natural that our feelings about a subject or person should spill out onto the page and affect our tone. Here is an example:

Dear Monty,

I'm really sick and tired of your mess. It's embarrassing to walk into our room with a visitor and see your bed unmade, your clothes scattered all over the floor, and your beer cans making sticky rings on the table. I've told you before about this, but now I want you to know that if you don't shape up, I'm moving out.

Bob

Do you hear the angry tone in that note? On the other hand, listen to the difference in the tone of this email:

Hi, Everyone,

I have just returned from my backpacking trip through Europe. You won't believe the wonderful experiences I had. At one point I even lost my passport, but the American consulate was very helpful in getting me a temporary one. I met some exciting new friends, who, like me, were camping out or riding the second-class compartments of the trains. The world is really a great place. Anyway, I'll wait until I see you to fill in the details. I sure missed you a bunch.

Irene

The practical effect of tone on our writing is sometimes plainly evident and sometimes not. We would expect, for example, that if we write a letter to a roommate we're mad at, our tone will reflect that anger. Less evident is the effect a feeling of boredom about an assignment might have on our tone. It is only logical to assume that if we're bored with the topic and think it a waste of our time, our tone will be affected for the worse. That is why instructors always urge students to write about topics they like.

Another piece of traditional advice related to tone is the ancient warning instructors often give to student writers to be themselves—and it is genuinely good advice. Don't try to write in a voice that is not truly your own; don't try to put on airs in your writing. If you do, your tone is bound to be affected by the pretense. You will discover, if you have not already, that you do your best writing when you simply sound like your true self.

These psychological considerations aside, we do know—on a more practical level—that voice in writing is influenced by three factors under the writer's control: (1) vocabulary, (2) syntax, and (3) attitude. Before exploring these factors, let's enjoy a bit of humor as we explore a famous question, answered in a variety of voices.

Why Did the Chicken Cross the Road?

Politician (Self-Righteous)

My fellow conservatives, the chicken crossed to steal a job from a decent, hardworking American. That is what these reckless left-wing chickens do.

Children's Book Writer (Nonsensical)

Did the chicken cross the road? Did he cross it with a toad? Yes, the chicken crossed the road, but why he crossed, I've not been told!

Ernest Hemingway (Straightforward)

To die. In the rain. Alone. From an idée fixe.

Grandpa (overbearing)

In my day, we didn't ask why the chicken crossed the road. Someone told us that the chicken crossed the road, and that was good enough for us.

Karl Marx (philosophical)

It was a historical inevitability.

Sigmund Freud (psychological)

All chickens cross the road for the same reason: sex.

Albert Einstein (ambiguous)

Did the chicken really cross the road or did the road cross under the chicken?

Colonel Sanders (miffed)

Darn! I missed one!

Vocabulary

The English language is a treasure trove of words. It is bursting with synonyms—words that have the same meaning. As you write, you can express the same idea any number of different ways. Often, the choice seems to boil down to expressing yourself either simply or complexly. You can give the facts without frills while remaining quietly in the background or you can mount the pulpit, take on the grandeur of a bishop, and posture.

The second choice is one that we do not recommend. You will do your reader a kindness if you write without putting on airs or pretending to be a know-it-all. Choose your words to inform, not to impress. Faced with the choice between a big, little-known word and a smaller, better-known equivalent, choose the smaller one because more people will understand it. Your overriding aim is to tell your reader what you know about the subject, not to impress. (Yet, oddly enough, sophisticated readers are generally impressed by writing that is plain and to the point.)

Here's an example of a style of writing that even for its day was pompous:

> It is the fate of those who toil at the lower employments of life, to be rather driven by the fear of evil, than attracted by the prospect of good; to be exposed to censure, without hope of praise; to be disgraced by miscarriage, or punished for neglect, where success would have been without applause, and diligence without reward.
>
> —Samuel Johnson, *Preface to the Dictionary of the English Language (1755)*

Johnson was a noted scholar and conversationalist who had a definite flair for spoken and written pompousness. If we replace some of the words with their more common equivalents, the passage takes on a different tone:

It is the lot of those who work at the lower jobs of life, to be rather driven by the fear of evil, than drawn by the likelihood of good; to be open to criticism, without hope of praise; to be shamed by mistakes, or punished for neglect, where success would have been without recognition, and hard work without reward.

Even with the changes in vocabulary, this passage is still hard to follow because it suffers from a second problem—knotty syntax.

Syntax

The arrangement of words in a sentence is known as *syntax*. Because English is so flexible, the same idea can be said in many different ways and in many different kinds of sentences. The considerate writer uses only as many sentences as are needed to get the job done. Most of these sentences will be simple subject-verb-object combinations. For the sake of variety, a few will have a different construction, but mainly, the sentences will be short and easy to read and understand.

In constructing a sentence, your aim should be to express your ideas clearly. It should not be to show off your learning or scholarship. The Johnson passage quoted earlier consists of a single sentence punctuated by commas and semicolons. A little alteration in the syntax—mainly in the use of simpler sentences—makes the ideas in the quotation much easier to understand:

Those who work at the lower jobs of life are driven by the fear of doing wrong, rather than drawn by the likelihood of doing good. They are open to criticism yet have no hope of praise. They are both shamed by their mistakes and punished for their neglect; yet their success wins no recognition, and their hard work no reward.

Now we have a better idea of what Johnson is trying to say. We may agree or disagree with it, but at least we share a common understanding.

Why, then, did Johnson express himself the way he did if he could have written the same idea more clearly? The answer is because of his attitude—the third factor affecting a writer's voice.

Attitude

Your attitude toward yourself and your work is bound to affect your voice. If you regard writing as a means of communication, you will work hard to make your meaning clear. If you regard writing as a reflection of your inner self, you might behave as some people do when they stand in front of a mirror: they preen and strut.

The problem with the Johnson passage is that he does not believe what he says, because he knows it is not true. He is, in fact, pretending to feel a humility and modesty he does not have. It is his attitude toward the work that makes his style so self-inflated and pompous. Here are the next two paragraphs from the preface:

Among these unhappy mortals is the writer of dictionaries; whom mankind have considered, not as the pupil, but the slave of science, the pioneer of literature, doomed only to remove rubbish and clear obstructions from the paths of Learning and Genius, who press forward to conquest and glory, without bestowing a smile on the humble drudge that facilitates their progress. Every other author may aspire to praise; the lexicographer can only hope to escape reproach, and even this negative recompense has been yet granted to very few.

      I have, notwithstanding this discouragement, attempted a dictionary of the English language, which, while it was employed in the cultivation of every species of literature, has itself been hitherto neglected, suffered to spread, under the direction of chance, into wild exuberance, resigned to the tyranny of time and fashion, and exposed to the corruptions of ignorance, and caprices of innovation.

Does Johnson really believe that he is a "drudge," a "slave of science," a garbage man "doomed only to remove rubbish and clear obstructions from the paths of Learning and Genius?" Nothing about the man or his life tells us that he saw himself in such lowly terms. He had just completed, after a massive labor of nine years, a dictionary that defined 43,000 words supported by 114,000 quotations from literature. His was not the first dictionary of the English language, but even today it is ranked as the most important. Part of the problem with his preface is that he uses it to show off his learning and scholarship rather than to communicate facts about his dictionary. His attitude affects his voice.

      Vocabulary, syntax, and attitude—these are all factors the writer can control. They are important in developing the voice you can use in factual writing. Naturally, they're less important in some other kinds of writing—poetry and fiction, for example—that aim to do more than merely communicate an idea. The lessons we are teaching are meant only for factual writing, which is to prose what the camel is to the desert. For that kind of writing, you must strive for clarity and readability if you wish to please your reader.

● EXERCISES

1. How would you characterize the tone of the following paragraph that came from a letter a tenant sent to a landlord?

      If you want your rent this month, you'd better do something about the leaky kitchen faucet. I've told you about this at least five times and still you have done nothing. The dripping at night is driving me mad. I don't know what ever possessed me to rent such a pigsty. But if you don't do something about it, I'm going to go to the city and complain and tell them what a roach-infested dump you're renting to innocent people.

2. Change the voice of the preceding paragraph by rewriting it to reflect a softer tone.

3. How would you characterize the voice in the following excerpts? Describe the vocabulary, syntax, and attitude evident in each passage:

   a. I am twenty years of age today. The past year has been crappy—breaking up with my boyfriend, losing my job mixing blended drinks for a local Dutch Boy drive-in, and flunking a math night class at Sierra Community College. What a bummer!

   b. The Internet is a treasure chest of data, facts, statistics, opinions, speculations, and viewpoints—all that comes under the general heading of information.

   c. In clinical psychiatry and psychoanalytical work there are few such heroes, men and women whose intelligence, compassion, and above all, candor, illuminate their deeds, their words, and the failures they inevitably suffer.

4. Write two brief letters on any event that occurred in your school and in which you took part: one to a parent or an authority figure and the other to your best friend.

5. Write a paragraph or two analyzing the differences in the voices you used in the letters you just wrote.

6. What attitude toward medical doctors does the following paragraph reveal? What kind of person might write such a paragraph?

> If I had cancer, I would not submit to chemotherapy. I watched my mom have chemotherapy, and it made her so nauseated and so weak that she often said, "I can't take this anymore." I can't see why it would be beneficial to put what is obviously a strong poison into any human body. Surely, nature has better ways of curing cancer than chemotherapy. Doctors are just too tunnel-visioned to use natural herbs to help cure cancer. They think that only prescriptions you get through pharmaceutical companies can possibly be effective; yet, I know someone who was cured of breast cancer by drinking a quart of carrot juice every day.

7. Which of the two statements that follow reflects the more rational and objective tone toward a photographic exhibit? Identify the vocabulary that makes the difference.

a. This photographic exhibit is a wonderful gallery of varied portraits—politician, seamstress, drifter, ballet dancer, mother, and much more. Each portrait has been shot against a starkly white background, which seems to allow no place for the subject to hide and therefore suggests a confrontational intimacy between the photographer and the subject. Because of the backlighting involved, each head appears to sprout a halo that contrasts paradoxically with the shadows on the face, lending a beguiling mystery to the facial features in each frame.

b. After staring at this portrait gallery for almost an hour, I decided that it was all meaningless trash. Who wants to waste time looking at this sort of nightmare? This is not art; it is the revelation of a sick mind. All I could see were men and women photographed against a white wall. Some kind of weird circle of light surrounded their heads, but their faces were dark and wrinkled. The ugliness of these faces really bugged me. I felt depressed to think that this Halloween-type exhibit was considered great modern art and was shown at the local museum.

Advice

Tone: The Writer's Voice in the Reader's Mind

MORT CASTLE

Rhetorical Thumbnail

Purpose: to teach the use of tone in writing

Audience: writing students and instructors

Language: snappy, informal English as befitting a writing guru

Strategy: draws details from personal experience to make a convincing case for the meaning of "tone"

Mort Castle (b. 1946) is a dedicated teacher and fiction writer. He has 350 short stories and a dozen books to his credit, including *Cursed Be the Child* (1994), *The Strangers* (1984), and *Moon on the Water* (2000). Castle takes particular pride in the fact that 2,000 of his students, ranging in age from six to ninety-three, have seen their work in print. He is a frequent keynote speaker at writing conferences or workshops. His book, *Writing Horror* (1997), for which he served as editor, has become the "bible" for aspiring horror authors. He is also the executive editor of Thorby Comics, which publishes the popular comic books *Night City, Death Asylum, The Skuler, Blythe: Nightvision, and Johnny Cosmic.*

Novice writers often think that tone is used only in speaking, not in writing. By using numerous examples and taking on a humorous tone, Castle convinces us that tone is a key ingredient in the relationship between reader and writer.

• • •

1   Johnny, the new kid, walks into third grade, casually waves to his teacher, Ms. Cruth, and says, "How's it goin', Butthead?"

2   "We do not talk that way in this class, Johnny," says Ms. Cruth. Opting for educational strategy #101: **neo-traditional** negative reinforcement, but not allowed to hit, she sends Johnny to the corner.

3   The next day, Johnny steps into the classroom, with "Hey, what's up, Ms. Bimbo?"

4   "Corner, Johnny," says Ms. Cruth.

5   The day after, Johnny comes into the classroom. He says, "Good morning, Ms. Cruth."

6   "Go to the corner, Johnny," says Ms. Cruth.

7   "Huh?" Johnny's inquiring mind wants to know. "Why are you sending me to the corner? I did not call you 'Butthead' and I did not call you 'Ms. Bimbo,' and I didn't say one word that might be considered **pejorative!**"

8   "No," says Ms. Cruth, "but I don't like your tone."

9   When we speak to others, our tone of voice is no less important than our actual words. Call your faithful friend, Fido, into the room, for our experiment in tone. Granted, with the difference in the communicative arts as practiced by human being and canine being, the following analogy is not fully **apropos,** yet 'twill serve:

10   Talk to your dog. Though your tone is a warm one, you know, "praise the pup, I love my wonderful companionate animal, etc.," don't use real words of praise. Try: "Fido, you double ugly moron, you stinky poo puppy, you drecky wretched doggy dastard!"

11   Fido wags his tail. All is well. I may not get the words, but I know what you mean.

12   In speaking, stressed sounds, vocal **cadences,** pronunciation, rhythm and pauses, repetition, voice **pitch, timbre,** and volume, etc. help the listener get the message. The "sincere" tone tells the listener "I'm sorry" truly indicates . . . "I am sorry." Yet, with a sneering, sarcastic tone, those same two words can implicitly

say, "I am sorry I did not cause you half the grief, misery, agony, and woe I could have had I only been a trace more imaginative."

13 The "listen up" tone is for when the mechanic needs to hear that this time, damn it, he'd better find the oil leak.

14 The "cooing selected little nothings" tone can be well-suited for the prelude to the proposal moment, whether that be a major commitment proposal or a suggestion of serious messing around.

15 Most kids know the tone that signals, "You'd really better cut it out and this time I mean it!"

16 The **conspiratorial** tone signals it's "true dirt-dishing time."

17 The "ha ha ha ready to happen" tone is for the joke . . .

18 The writer putting words on the page (or computer screen or out there in cyberville) also has a tone of voice. The writer, of course, does not have a speaker's unique tone tools: vocal cords, sinus cavities, lip, tongue, palette, etc. Nor does the writer have a raised eyebrow to provide a hint, nor a smile, nor a broad hand wave. Instead, tone is achieved by choice and arrangement of our prime building blocks: words.

19 The reader hears—and responds to—that tone of voice as he is reading.

20 That voice, that tone, must be suited to the material so that the reader clearly understands what is said, understands on both the literal and the **figurative** levels.

21 "Let us go then, you and I," T. S. Eliot begins "The Love Song of J. Alfred Prufrock." The tone is somber and formal, made more so, perhaps, by the deliberate grammar fluff of the nominative "I" used instead of the objective "me," an error often made by those hoping to sound "educated": the reader is invited to undertake a **desolate** and wearying journey. The tone helps to establish the mood of the poem, gives the reader a feeling. But if Eliot had begun (with or without an apology to The Ramones): "Hey ho! Let's go!"

22 Or had he whined in classic Jerry Lewis style, "Look, would you please come on, already? Aw, just come on, okay?"

23 Or in keeping with contemporary "dirty words currently acceptable on Prime Time Network TV": "Let's haul ass!"

24 Well, we would not exactly be anticipating gloom and soul dread as we walk with J. Alfred, would we?

25 Consider the opening of Edgar Allan Poe's familiar "The Tell-Tale Heart":

26 "True!—nervous—very very dreadfully nervous I had been and am, but why will you say that I am mad?"

27 There's an immediate rush of energy with that very first word and exclamation point: A frantic energy. A crazed madman's energy. You hear the protagonist protesting way, way more than a "bit too much" the idea that he is insane. To use today's **pseudo-artistic** term, the "edgy tone" of the story is established: a barely-in-control-and-soon-to-wig-out tone.

28 The right tone, the proper voice in the reader's mind, lets you say what you want to say the way you want to say it.

29 And the wrong tone . . .

30   In the scene that follows from a deservedly unpublished short story, Mike is visited by his psychopathic brother, Arnold. Mike believes Arnold intends to kill him—and Mike is right.

31   Arnold stepped in. "How are you doing, Mike?" he asked.

32   "I've been doing all right," Mike responded promptly.

33   "That's good," Arnold said.

34   "How about you?" Mike asked.

35   "Well, I guess I have been doing okay," Arnold calmly said.

36   "I'm glad to hear it. It certainly is a snowy day."

37   "I guess everyone talks about the weather but no one does anything about it," Arnold said. "That is my opinion, anyway."

38   "I agree," Mike said.

39   Then Arnold shouted, "It's a perfect day for you to die, you dirty rat!"

40   Except for Arnold's closing outburst, the tone of this passage is **mundane, prosaic,** no more tense (or interesting) than that of an ordinary, everyday conversation you might overhear in the dentist's waiting room. It is totally unsuited for what is meant to be a moment of high drama.

41   Here's another cutting from a different "wrong tone" story. The protagonist is attempting to get up the nerve to stand before an Alcoholics Anonymous meeting and say for the first time: "My name is Sharon and I am an alcoholic." She sits, biting her nails, and then shakily gets to her feet, ". . . flinging her hair back like a galloping filly tossing its mane . . ."

42   Uh-uh. That "mane tossing filly" gives the scene an inappropriate tone. My Girl Friend Flicka. Lighthearted Retro-Range-Romance: Up rides Dale Evans on Buttermilk, meeting her spunky niece from out East, Manda Llewellyn Travis . . . This lighthearted tone and the upbeat optimism one feels make for what most critics would judge a wrong tone.

43   That is not to say, of course, that only the "comic tone" can be employed for comic writing, that the "romantic tone" must be used for romance writing, that a horrific tone must be used for horror writing.

44   Let's spend a tone moment with the late Charles Beaumont, one of my all-time literary heroes and the writer of many classic short short stories that came to typify what is thought of as "Playboy Magazine horror" in the late 1950s and 1960s.

45   Beaumont's short story is called "Free Dirt":

46   It opens:

"No fowl had ever looked so **posthumous.**"

47   Seven words—and the tone is established. "Posthumous" gives the sentence an overly formal, almost pompous tone. "Fowl," rather than chicken, is likewise formal. The voice that reads this sentence inside the reader's mind is wryly **sardonic,** not unlike the voice of the late Alfred Hitchcock. There's humor

here, but it's dark humor, the laughter we can hear as we stand by the gravesite, and it's perfect for a brief and utterly chilling story, a work of "moral fiction" in the best sense: It teaches in a **non-didactic** way.

48   The right tone, then, is the one that allows the writer to speak clearly to the reader. The goal, of course, is the essence of the writer–reader relationship: "I get it," the reader implicitly says.

49   You don't want your home builder cracking up with laughter, telling you that you should be swapping one-liners with Leno, when you demand he put the front door in front, just as the blueprints have it, instead of on the roof—and you don't want your reader snickering, giggling, guffawing, and hoo-ha-ing because your voice in his mind cues him to laugh at your sequel to A Christmas Carol, in which Tiny Tim dies of consumption, Bob Cratchit is run over by a hansom cab, and Scrooge gets murdered by Marley's ghost!

Mort Castle, "The Writers Voice on the Readers Mind" from WRITERS WRITE: THE INTERNET WRITING JOURNAL, September 2000. Copyright 1997–2000 by Writers Write, Inc. Reprinted by permission.

● THE FACTS

1. What kind of student is the author portraying through Johnny? How would you react to having such a student in your class?

2. What was wrong with Johnny's third greeting?

3. What analogy does the author use to illustrate the importance of tone over words in speech? What other analogy can you cite?

4. What elements, not used in writing, can a person use to communicate in speech?

5. What is the only arsenal available to writers to establish tone? Does this limited arsenal curtail good writers? Give examples that support your opinion.

● THE STRATEGIES

1. What rhetorical strategy does the author use to persuade us that his view of tone is correct? Are you convinced? Give reasons for your answer.

2. In what paragraph does the author switch from vocal tone to writing tone? Were you able to follow his shift? If no, why not? If yes, why?

3. Why do you think the author uses the opening line of T. S. Eliot's "J. Alfred Prufrock" as an example of setting a definite tone? Do you think this was a good choice? Why or why not?

4. In paragraph 29, the author does not finish his sentence, but leaves you hanging with ellipsis points. How would you finish this sentence?

5. In what paragraph does the author tell you what the right tone is? What will the reader implicitly say if the author has established the right tone?

⬤ THE ISSUES

1. Are there kinds of writing in which no tone is necessary? If you think there are, give examples of this kind of writing.

2. How can mastery of tone help your writing?

3. How can voice and tone be suited to the material on the figurative level? (See paragraph 20.) Explain this idea by using an example.

4. The author assures us that tone does not always need to match the writing genre. For instance, a comic tone might be used for a romance and a romantic tone for a comedy. Cite an example from literature that mixes tone and genre.

5. What tone would most likely suit the following situations?

   a. A mother writes goodbye to her son leaving for war.

   b. A college student thanks her sorority sisters for giving her a wild bachelorette party the week before her wedding.

   c. A minister encourages his congregation to donate money for some new hymnbooks.

⬤ SUGGESTIONS FOR WRITING

1. Write a letter to one of the following people, using an appropriate tone:
   a. To your boss, announcing that you are quitting the company for a new assignment
   b. To your father, asking for money to pay your car insurance
   c. To your best friend, describing a recent camping trip
   d. To an acquaintance who borrowed money from you and refuses to pay you back

2. Write an essay in which you define tone as you now understand it.

▦ Examples

Salvation

LANGSTON HUGHES

Rhetorical Thumbnail

Purpose:	to pen his autobiography
Audience:	general readers
Language:	standard English
Strategy:	to recollect and re-create an experience with religion as seen through the eyes of the child he used to be.

Langston Hughes (1902–1967) was born in Joplin, Missouri, and educated at Columbia University, New York, and Lincoln University, Pennsylvania. He worked at odd jobs in this country and in France before becoming established as a writer. His lifelong interest was the promotion of black art, history, and causes. In addition to many collections of poetry, Hughes wrote a novel, *Not Without Laughter* (1930), and an autobiography, *The Big Sea* (1940).

In this selection from The Big Sea, *Hughes recounts a dramatic incident from his childhood. The incident is narrated from the perspective of a twelve-year-old boy and demonstrates a skillful writer's use of language to re-create the innocent voice of childhood.*

• • •

1   I was saved from sin when I was going on thirteen. But not really saved. It happened like this. There was a big revival at my Auntie Reed's church. Every night for weeks there had been much preaching, singing, praying, and shouting, and some very hardened sinners had been brought to Christ, and the membership of the church had grown by leaps and bounds. Then just before the revival ended, they held a special meeting for children, "to bring the young lambs to the fold." My aunt spoke of it for days ahead. That night I was escorted to the front row and placed on the mourners' bench with all the other young sinners, who had not yet been brought to Jesus.

2   My aunt told me that when you were saved you saw a light, and something happened to you inside! And Jesus came into your life! And God was with you from then on! She said you could see and hear and feel Jesus in your soul. I believed her. I had heard a great many old people say the same thing and it seemed to me they ought to know. So I sat there calmly in the hot, crowded church, waiting for Jesus to come to me.

3   The preacher preached a wonderful rhythmical sermon, all moans and shouts and lonely cries and dire pictures of hell, and then he sang a song about the ninety and nine safe in the fold, but one little lamb was left out in the cold. Then he said: "Won't you come? Won't you come to Jesus? Young lambs, won't you come?" And he held out his arms to all us young sinners there on the mourners' bench. And the little girls cried. And some of them jumped up and went to Jesus right away. But most of us just sat there.

4   A great many old people came and knelt around us and prayed, old women with jet-black faces and braided hair, old men with work-**gnarled** hands. And the church sang a song about the lower lights are burning, some poor sinners to be saved. And the whole building rocked with prayer and song.

5   Still I keep waiting to see Jesus.

6   Finally all the young people had gone to the altar and were saved, but one boy and me. He was a rounder's son named Westley. Westley and I were surrounded by sisters and deacons praying. It was very hot in the church, and getting late now. Finally Westley said to me in a whisper: "God damn! I'm tired o' sitting here. Let's get up and be saved." So he got up and was saved.

7   Then I was left all alone on the mourners' bench. My aunt came and knelt at my knees and cried, while prayers and songs swirled all around me in the little church. The whole congregation prayed for me alone, in a mighty wail of moans and voices. And I kept waiting serenely for Jesus, waiting, waiting—but he didn't come. I wanted to see him, but nothing happened to me. Nothing! I wanted something to happen to me, but nothing happened.

8   I heard the songs and the minister saying: "Why don't you come? My dear child, why don't you come to Jesus? Jesus is waiting for you. He wants you. Why don't you come? Sister Reed, what is this child's name?"

9   "Langston," my aunt sobbed.

10   "Langston, why don't you come? Why don't you come and be saved? Oh, Lamb of God! Why don't you come?"

11   Now it was really getting late. I began to be ashamed of myself, holding everything up so long. I began to wonder what God thought about Westley, who certainly hadn't seen Jesus either, but who was now sitting proudly on the platform, swinging his knickerbockered legs and grinning down at me, surrounded by deacons and old women on their knees praying. God had not struck Westley dead for taking his name in vain or for lying in the temple. So I decided that maybe to save further trouble, I'd better lie, too, and say that Jesus had come, and get up and be saved.

12   So I got up.

13   Suddenly the whole room broke into a sea of shouting, as they saw me rise. Waves of rejoicing swept the place. Women leaped in the air. My aunt threw her arms around me. The minister took me by the hand and led me to the platform.

14   When things quieted down, in a hushed silence, **punctuated** by a few **ecstatic** "Amens," all the new young lambs were blessed in the name of God. Then joyous singing filled the room.

15   That night, for the last time in my life but one—for I was a big boy twelve years old—I cried. I cried, in bed alone, and couldn't stop. I buried my head under the quilts, but my aunt heard me. She woke up and told my uncle I was crying because the Holy Ghost had come into my life, and because I had seen Jesus. But I was really crying because I couldn't bear to tell her that I had lied, that I had deceived everybody in the church, and I hadn't seen Jesus, and that now I didn't believe there was a Jesus any more, since he didn't come to help me.

● THE FACTS

1. How does Westley's attitude differ from the narrator's? Is Westley more realistic and less gullible, or is he simply more callous and less sensitive than the narrator?

2. The narrator holds out to the last minute and finally submits to being saved. What is his motive for finally giving in?

3. Who has been deceived in the story? The aunt by the narrator? The narrator by the aunt? Both the narrator and the aunt by the minister? Everybody by the demands of religion?

4. What insight does the narrator reach at the end of the story? What has he learned?

5. The story is told as a flashback to Hughes's boyhood. What is his attitude toward the experience as he retells it?

THE STRATEGIES

1. The story is narrated from the point of view of a twelve-year-old boy. What techniques of language are used in the story to create the perspective of a boy? How is the vocabulary appropriate to a boy?

2. In his article "How to Say Nothing in Five Hundred Words," Paul Roberts urges the use of specific details in writing. How does Hughes make use of such details?

3. The description in paragraph 4 is vivid but compressed. How does Hughes achieve this effect?

THE ISSUES

1. Marx wrote that "religion . . . is the opium of the people." What is your view of this sentiment? How does it apply or not apply to this excerpt?

2. The little girls were the first to break down and offer themselves to be saved. The last two holdouts were boys. How do you explain this different reaction of the two sexes?

3. What do you think would likely have happened if the narrator had not gone up to be saved?

4. Religions often use ovine terms (sheep, lamb, flock) to refer to their congregations. What do you think is the origin of this usage? What does this usage imply about the members?

SUGGESTIONS FOR WRITING

1. Describe an experience of your own in which group pressure forced you into doing something you did not believe in.

2. Write a brief biographical sketch of Westley, fantasizing on the kind of man you believe he grew into and the kind of life he eventually led.

3. Defend or challenge the view that to be truly effective, religious belief must be based on emotion.

Parkinson's Disease and the Dream Bear

ANTHONY C. WINKLER

Rhetorical Thumbnail

Purpose: to express what it feels like to suffer from a neurological disease that eventually cripples your ability to walk, to speak, to write, and to remain calm and composed

Audience: any reader curious about the sufferings of fellow human beings

Language: a blend of scientific terms and poetic imagery

Strategy: to reveal how one victim of a cruel disease fights it with a blend of despair and courageous faith

Anthony C. Winkler (b. 1942) is often introduced as "the best writer you've never read." He is the author of several acclaimed novels, ranging from *The Painted Canoe* (1983), which tells the epical story of Zechariah, a stubborn Jamaican fisherman who fights to maintain his dignity in a harsh world that gives him no respect, to the rollicking comedy *The Lunatic* (1987), which one critic called "a brilliantly written and outrageous Jamaican fable." Winkler is the co-author of a highly successful series of college textbooks, written in collaboration with Jo Ray McCuen-Metherell, a retired professor of English. Some of these books on rhetoric and the art of writing have gone through a dozen editions since 1974, the first date of publication. A film scriptwriter, as well as a playwright for the legitimate theater, Winkler had a stage play, *The Burglar,* performed in Jamaica in 1973 and in Toronto in 1974, to audience acclaim. *The Hippopotamus Car* was broadcast in German as a radio play by a station in Cologne. Winkler resides in Atlanta with his wife of forty years, Cathy.

• • •

1   When I turned 50, a dream bear invaded my body and tried to ride **roughshod** over my life. The antics of the bear left me with a profound weariness I had never felt before. It made me shiver and shake like a flu victim, and every now and again it gave me a rabbit punch that would send a drinking glass **hurtling** across the room to shatter on the floor. Wedged in my left armpit was the sensation of a lump the size of a golf ball. By now my doctors suspected that there was something **neurologically** wrong with me, perhaps Parkinson's Disease.

2   Unlike many other diseases, Parkinson's has no tests to identify its presence in a patient. Typically a diagnosis is made by how the patient responds to medication known to work against Parkinsonism. Chief among these is dopamine, a chemical produced by the brain to control movement. One week after I began

taking dopamine, one of my symptoms, micrographia (tiny unreadable handwriting) vanished like magic.

3   Parkinson's Disease is a witch's brew of ills for which there is no cure. It is a relatively "young" disease that gained recognition only in 1817 with the publication of "Essay on the Shaking Palsy" by an English apothecary surgeon, paleontologist, and political activist, James Parkinson (1755–1824). Before the publication of that groundbreaking work, Parkinson's seldom appeared in medical literature, and then only in a passing blur. However, PD is rated as the 14th cause of death by the Center of Disease Control when its interactions with other ailments are taken into account.

4   PD has such a **histrionic** range of symptoms that their medical names sound like a roll call of extinct dinosaurs.

Anosmia	loss of smell
Hypominia	low speech
Micrographia	small handwriting
Sialorrhea	drooling due to poor swallowing
retropulsion	the tendency to fall backwards

This is only a partial listing of the symptoms of PD. Fortunately, these symptoms do not explode like the blast of a shotgun, but instead pick you off **sporadically** like sniper fire.

5   PD makes everything harder to do and longer to accomplish. Eating is a chore. Routine tasks bristle with booby traps. Decrease in **muscular** strength is dramatic and a definite challenge to your **ingenuity**. It is almost an embarrassment to eat steak in a restaurant. You simply don't have the arm strength to slice the meat into chewable chunks without causing the entire complex of booths and tables to vibrate. Every action or reaction that used to be simple suddenly becomes complex. Laced shoes are a nightmare. Using the toilet sometimes engages you in **impromptu** gymnastics floor exercises.

6   From bad to worse is the general prognosis of PD. Occasionally I run into a patient who is in the end stage of the disease. One of the most pathetic sufferers I ever saw was a jockey clad in his racing silks, who had managed to pull himself into a partly upright position so he could mount his pillow like a makeshift saddle. Stuck in bed in an ironic victory freeze of triumph, he was unable to move while his wife wept at his side and fussed with his bed sheets. Another appalling sight I encountered was an end-stage Parkinson's victim whose entire body was buried under a carpet of twitching bumps.

7   What works against this **horripilating** disease which twists the patient— man or woman—into a perpetual forward slouch and makes each scowl as if a crotchety bear with a **morose** outlook has captured his soul? Practically nothing. **Minuscule** improvement in a patient's condition can be expected once PD is the confirmed sentence. Exercise, especially on stationary bikes, seems to forestall the ravages of PD. Mentally counting off steps as you walk appears to lessen the likelihood of a fall.

8   But if you're a believer it's a good time to pray. One morning I woke up with this prayer for mercy on my lips.

> Oh lord, awake me to a gentle rain
> Like a baby's tears on a tender cheek.
> Your majesty I already know and fear.
> Your power and might I've felt before
> In the roll of thunder and storm.
> But now is come a time for tenderness
> That I crave and need and desire
> On the first light of this **fledging** day.

9   "Do not go gentle into that Goodnight" wrote the poet, and that is generally good advice for anyone suffering from PD. One thing about the sick room is that there is always someone sicker than you. To die from the 14th cause of death is better than to die from the 13th.

10   So what to do about the surly bear? Ignore the brute. Or when he begins to **bellow**, give him a good kick in the **butt**.

● THE FACTS

1. What were the first symptoms of the disease noticed by the author? What image does the author use to describe the disease?
2. By what system is Parkinson's usually diagnosed? When did Parkinson's gain recognition? How did the disease acquire its name?
3. Among the partial listing of the Parkinson's Disease symptoms, what does "retropulsion" mean, and why do you think it is listed last?
4. What prognosis does medical science assign to Parkinson's? What examples from the author's own experience support this prognosis?
5. What kinds of therapy does the author offer?

● THE STRATEGIES

1. How does the author manage to express an audible voice in his essay? Does he use the same voice throughout his narrative, or does he express more than one voice? Explain your answer.
2. How does Winkler's description of Parkinson's differ in writing style from other descriptions of diseases you have read in magazines or newspapers? How does this difference affect the general quality of the essay?
3. Why do you think the author likened the medical names for symptoms of Parkinson's to a "roll call of extinct dinosaurs"? Does the comparison work? Give reasons for your answer.
4. Why does Paragraph 8 introduce a prayer which on first thought might be too big a leap from scientific objectivity to a mystical cry for help? Suggest the motivation for such a prayer.

5. How would you describe the voice rendered in the final paragraph? Why does the essay end with this voice? How does it differ from the voice in Paragraph 9? Do you find the ending satisfying? Why or why not?

THE ISSUES

1. How common are neurological diseases today? What are the three best known neurological diseases in our western culture? Do a Google search of "neurological diseases" if you are not acquainted with any disease that attacks the nervous system.

2. If you had been diagnosed with an incurable neurological disease, how would you prepare yourself for the rest of the time allotted to you? Name some ideas on which you would dwell and some activities you would plan. What physical activity do you think you would miss most?

3. What role do you think our government should play in dealing with victims of Parkinson's who are poor and cannot afford decent facilities in which to live, caregivers to provide physical therapy, drivers to take them to medical appointments or special social centers, and people who care enough to make sure these victims are not lost or lonely? Suggest some areas—if any—where the government should step in.

4. How do you think society will eventually find a cure for Parkinson's? Will the funding for such a cure come from wealthy pharmacies, from government funding, from university research, or from some other unexpected source? Try to formulate your opinion on this problem.

5. Do you believe that taxing our citizens is an appropriate way to fund research for diseases that so far have no cure? Or can you suggest a better system of financing this research? Provide examples and evidence for your answer.

SUGGESTIONS FOR WRITING

1. Choose an incurable disease that took the life of someone you loved. Describe the disease and how you dealt with your sorrow, using Winkler's essay as a model.

2. How much time, effort, or money are you willing to invest in finding a cure for some of the big killer diseases of our century? Write an essay stipulating which percentage of taxes you think should be used for education and research connected with curing major diseases. Quote a minimum of three experts to bolster your argument. Integrate these sources into your essay according to the guidelines suggested in Chapter 3 of this book.

Chapter Writing Assignments

1. Contrast the voice of the writer of "Parkinson's Disease and the Dream Bear" with that of the writer of "Salvation."

2. When you write, do you find yourself deliberately altering your voice for a particular audience? In a paragraph or two, describe how you use your writing voice in different contexts.

Writing Assignments for a Specific Audience

1. Assuming an audience of junior high students, write a couple of paragraphs explaining the concept of voice in a writer's work.

2. Write two letters to the editor of your local newspaper complaining about a problem in your neighborhood. In the first letter, try to sound impatient and angry. In the second, let your voice be that of a reasonable but concerned citizen. State which of the two approaches you consider more effective and likely to garner results.

Real-Life Student Writing

A Thank-You Note to an Aunt

The thank-you note continues to flourish even in these days of email and instant communication by telephone. Nothing can replace the personal touch found in a handwritten note. Here, for example, is a student's note thanking her aunt for a graduation present.

• • •

Thank You . . .

Dear Auntie Jo-Jo:

Thanks tons for the $50.00 graduation present. I didn't place it in a savings account because you said to spend it on something personal. Well, I thought you might want to know how prudently I spent the money. I went to T. J. Maxx, my favorite discount store, where I always get amazing deals. Believe it or not, for $50.00 I bought a smart-looking DKNY argyle sweater and a pair of navy corduroy pants. I'm sure my friends think I have been spending profligately at Neiman Marcus. I wish every college student had an adorable aunt like you. You have been far better than Auntie Mame.

Much love,
Trudi

P.S. I painted this card myself; hope you like it.

*Stumped by the passive voice? Exit on pages 428–429 at the **Editing Booth!***

CHAPTER 5

The Writer's Thesis

▤ Road Map to Thesis

The thesis is a single sentence that announces to your reader exactly what you intend to argue, to prove, to refute, to describe, to tell, or to explain. By convention, it is usually the final sentence of the first paragraph. Of course, this is not the only place a thesis can appear. However, the final sentence of the first paragraph has evolved in classroom compositions as the most effective niche for the thesis, especially in the 500-word essay, which students are usually asked to write.

The idea of the thesis is an old one that has survived for the simple reason that it works. Writers generally write better when they know exactly what they have to say, and readers usually are better able to follow a writer's thought development when they know the main point of a written work. For example, consider this thesis statement from an actual student essay:

> Our government must assume the responsibility of caring for the thousands of homeless mentally ill people who are now forced to roam the streets because of changes in governmental policy.

This thesis tells us, in a nutshell, what the student intends to argue. We expect her to show us how changes in governmental policy have caused thousands of the mentally ill to become homeless. We also expect her to argue the moral rightness of helping them.

The thesis, then, is the main point of your essay summed up in a single sentence. In it, you tell the reader where you stand on the issue, what subtopics you intend to cover, and in what order.

Finding Your Thesis

Let us say, for example, your assignment is to write an essay about a sport or recreation you enjoy. You muse and think and finally decide to write about sailing. That is your topic. It is a usable topic because it falls under a general subject. If you had

91

decided to do an essay on the composition of mosaic tile or on the Roman technique of road building, you would have strayed from the subject, because neither is a sport or recreation.

So sailing will be your topic. You think some more and decide to write an essay on the joys of sailing. Note, by the way, that you could have chosen to write about the boredom and work of sailing; you could also have slanted your essay any number of other ways. But you love sailing and think it a wonderful sport, so you decide to sing its praises in your essay. The joy of sailing will be your main point.

Next, you must express this main point in a thesis. One way to do this is to write down the main point on the top of a page either as a sentence or a fragment—sailing is a wonderful sport; sailing is a joy; sailing is a relaxing recreation—and then ask yourself questions about it. Write down the questions as they occur to you. Perhaps you will come up with a list of questions such as these:

Main Point: Sailing is a wonderful sport.

Why do I love sailing as much as I do?

What are the benefits of sailing?

Why is sailing such a popular sport?

Why is sailing so relaxing?

What does sailing teach?

To find your thesis, choose the question that seems most appropriate to your main point, audience, and assignment, and answer it in a single, detailed sentence. This means you must make a decision about whether the instructor wants a personal essay—one heavy with "I" pronouns and emphasizing your own experiences with sailing—or an impersonal essay that presents its ideas in an objective style. For example, you might answer the last question this way:

Sailing is a delightful sport that teaches independence, balance, and navigation.

Now you have a thesis. You also have a sketch of your essay's subtopics. First, you will explain how sailing teaches independence; next, how it teaches balance; finally, how it teaches navigation. You will draw on your personal experiences and anecdotes as a sailor to amplify these points.

Answering a different question will obviously give you another thesis. For example, if your instructor makes it clear that the essay may be based on your own experiences, answering the first question would give you a thesis suitable for a personal essay:

I love the exhilaration, the freedom, and the adventure of sailing.

You now have a thesis that emphasizes your personal views of sailing.

When you do have your thesis, write it on a sticky note and stick it on your computer. It is a promise you make to your reader, and you must be faithful to it in the essay by covering the subtopics in the exact order of occurrence in your thesis. This means, for example, that in writing an essay on the joy of sailing, you must first discuss the exhilaration, and then the freedom, and finally the adventure of sailing. And you should discuss nothing else but these three points.

Key Words in the Thesis

Every thesis contains one or more key words that represent ideas on which the essay will focus. In effect, these key words are ideas that the essay must amplify with definitions, examples, and explanations. Each of the following theses, for example, contains a single key word, which is highlighted:

Pheasant hunting is a tiring sport.

I am a jealous person.

Investing in the stock market is risky.

Most of the time, however, theses will contain several key words:

Good English is clear, appropriate, and vivid.

Studies show that, as children, the real achievers in our society were independent and spirited.

Riding a bicycle to work has several advantages over driving a car.

Islam requires that women learn obedience, self-discipline, and subordination.

Occasionally, the thesis will contain a proposition that is inseparable from its individual words. The essay will have to amplify the whole statement:

Students should be advised against majoring in subjects in which job prospects are limited.

If the United States is to survive, Americans will have to learn to conserve their country's resources.

Characteristics of a Good Thesis

The precision with which you word your thesis will help determine the quality of your essay. At a minimum, a good thesis predicts, controls, and obligates.

The Thesis Predicts A good thesis will contain a discussible idea while also suggesting to the writer a method of developing it. (For more on methods of development, see Part Two of this book.) Some propositions, however, such as the following, are so self-evident that they warrant no further discussion:

A relationship exists between excessive eating and gaining weight.

Rich people usually live in big houses.

In our country, movie stars are greatly admired.

None of these statements contains a discussible idea on which one might enlarge in a whole essay; their wording suggests no method of development. They would, therefore, not make good theses. In contrast, the following thesis not only contains discussible assertions but also predicts a likely method of development:

> Being a student reporter for the local paper means conducting interviews at odd hours and in strange places.

One immediately wonders, at what odd hours and in which strange places? The most obvious method of development for such a thesis is by illustration/exemplification (see Chapter 11). The reader expects more particulars about interviews at odd hours and in strange places, and the writer knows that he or she must find examples of these and work them into the essay. This sentence would make a good thesis.

Consider another example of how a properly worded thesis can predict the development of an essay:

> Because of the computer revolution and the premium it places on educational skills, many people over the age of twenty-one are enrolling in colleges today.

This is a "reason why" thesis, one that predicts the development of the essay primarily by an analysis of cause (see Chapter 15).

Common sense tells us that it is easier to write the essay whose method of development is predicted in the wording of its thesis than the one for which some developmental pattern must be found during the actual writing. Wording the thesis so that it predicts not only what you will say, but the pattern of development in which you will say it, can help you write a better essay.

The Thesis Controls The thesis controls the essay by restricting you to a specific order of topics or by presenting an obvious organizing principle for the essay (for more on patterns of organization, see Chapter 6 and the introduction to Chapter 8). Consider this term paper thesis, for example:

> Today, religion is no longer the uncontested center and ruler of human life, because Protestantism, science, and capitalism have brought about a secularized world.

Implicit in this thesis are a certain number and order of subtopics:

1. A description of medieval society when religion was the center of human existence
2. An explanation of how Protestantism secularized the world
3. An explanation of how science secularized the world
4. An explanation of how capitalism secularized the world

The advantage of this thesis is obvious. You do not have to cast around wondering what you should say next, for you know what your subtopics are and in what order they should occur. Moreover, the wording of the thesis tells you the kind of information you need to look up in the library.

Sometimes a thesis will control an essay by presenting the writer with a ready-made scheme of organization. Consider, for example, this thesis:

> My religious outlook has been shaped by three distinct phases of belief and disbelief in my life.

This thesis requires a chronological organization, with the writer detailing her religious beliefs from the earliest to the present. Note, however, that this thesis is suitable only for a personal essay; you could not write an objective essay on it without some drastic rewording.

Consider, on the other hand, this thesis:

> A winning tennis strategy requires a player to have a grasp of the geometry of the playing surface and to work to cut off the angle of an opponent's shots.

This thesis cries out for an essay organized by a spatial pattern. You could divide the playing surface into three zones—backcourt, midcourt, and net—and show how a player might win by maneuvering within them to cut off the angle of an opponent's shots.

The Thesis Obligates When a writer strays from the thesis, the result is often vague, unfocused writing. If the thesis is "Police officers spend more time controlling traffic and providing information than they spend enforcing the law," then you must prove this point in your essay. You should not rhapsodize about the heroism of the police or complain about police brutality. Likewise, if your thesis is "California college students are more sexually liberated than their New York counterparts," then that is the only point you should discuss. You should not write about the disputed intellectual superiority of New York college students or weave in facts about vegetarianism in California, unless these issues are somehow related to the sexual behavior of college students in New York and California.

However, it follows that in a focused essay the wording of the thesis must obligate the writer to discuss a single issue. Consider this thesis, for example:

> Definitions of obscenity change as society changes, and the courts' decisions on censorship reflect the legal profession's confusion on the issue.

This thesis is pulling in two directions. The first part of it requires a discussion of how definitions of obscenity reflect changes in society, while the second part leads to a discussion of the legal profession's confusion on obscenity. An essay based on this thesis would fall into two mismatched parts. The student should rewrite the thesis until it discusses a single issue. Here is a suggested revision of the thesis, which unifies its two parts and commits the writer to a single idea:

> Because definitions of obscenity change as society changes, the courts have handed down some contradictory decisions on censorship.

Although many students worry about making their theses too restrictive, this fault is found only rarely in the essays of beginners. Far more common is the overly broad thesis that cannot be adequately developed in a brief essay. For example, none of the following actual student theses is restrictive enough to be dealt with in a short paper:

Parachuting is unbelievable!

The war against Iraq was stupid.

Evaluating college teachers is an interesting idea.

Admittedly, these examples are vaguely worded and overly terse, but they are also not restrictive enough to guide a writer's hand. Ambiguous key words like *unbelievable*, *stupid*, and *interesting* need to be replaced. To predict, control, and obligate the course of an essay, a thesis must be unambiguous, structured, and restrictive. Common sense also tells us that the scope of the thesis must be in proportion to the length of the essay. A broad thesis is not suited to a short essay, nor a narrow thesis to a long essay.

Nine Errors to Avoid in Composing a Thesis

1. **A thesis should not be a fragment.** A fragment is a phrase or dependent clause that is punctuated as if it were a complete sentence. Our objection to using a fragment as a thesis, however, is based neither on punctuation nor on grammar, but on the fact that it is usually too limited or sketchy for a writer to elaborate on in an essay. A fragment simply cannot adequately sum up what your essay will cover, which is what the thesis should do. Here is an example:

   Poor: How life is in a racial ghetto.

   Better: Residents of a racial ghetto tend to have a higher death rate, a higher infant mortality rate, and a higher unemployment rate than do residents of the suburbs.

2. **A thesis must not be worded as a question** (usually, the answer to the question could be the thesis). The purpose of the thesis is to spell out the main idea of the essay, which is difficult, if not impossible, to do in a question:

   Poor: Do Americans really need large refrigerators?

   Better: If Americans did their marketing daily, as do most Europeans, they could save energy by using smaller refrigerators.

3. **A thesis should not be too broad.** An overly broad thesis will commit you to write on an idea you may be unable to adequately cover in a short essay. The solution in that case is to rewrite your thesis and begin again. Otherwise, no matter how hard you work, your essay will seem labored and abstract:

   Poor: The literature of mythology contains many resurrection stories.

   Better: One of the oldest resurrection myths is the story of the Egyptian god Osiris.

4. **A thesis should not contain unrelated elements.** The expression of a single and unified purpose should be your overriding aim in drafting your thesis. You are trying to prove one point, make one case, dramatize one situation. Veteran writers can, of course, complete more than one task in an essay, but this is a skill acquired only with much practice. The beginner is better off framing the thesis to commit the essay to making one point or performing one function. One way to do this is to avoid using a compound sentence as a thesis statement.

   A compound sentence is two independent clauses joined by a conjunction. An independent clause is a grammatical construction that can be punctuated to make sense on its own. Two independent clauses automatically imply two different ideas, which may be hard for the writer to keep separate or treat fairly in a single essay without making a muddle of both. Here is an example:

   Poor: All novelists seek the truth, and some novelists are good psychologists.

   Properly punctuated, each clause expresses a different idea and can stand on its own. "All novelists seek the truth" is one idea. "Some novelists are good psychologists" is the other. Writing an essay on this thesis will require the writer to prove two unrelated points.

   Better: In their attempt to probe human nature, many novelists become excellent psychologists.

5. **A thesis should not contain phrases like "I think" or "in my opinion" because they weaken a writer's argument.** Use the thesis to tell your reader plainly where you stand, what you think, or what you intend to prove in the essay. This is no place to be wishy-washy or uncertain, as if you are not quite sure about your opinion or viewpoint. Indeed, if you are not sure about the opinion expressed in your thesis, you should rethink it until you are.

   Poor: In my opinion, smoking should be outlawed because of the adverse health effects of "passive smoking."

   Better: Smoking should be outlawed because of the adverse health effects of "passive smoking."

6. **A thesis should not be expressed in vague language.** With only rare exceptions, it is a general truth that the vague thesis will lead to a vague essay. If the thesis is vaguely worded, it is usually because the writer is uncertain of what to say or has not sufficiently thought through the controlling idea. Should that happen to you, rethink your views on the topic.

   Poor: Religion should not be included in the school curriculum because it can cause trouble.

   Better: Religion should not be included in the school curriculum because it is a highly personal commitment.

7. **A thesis must not be expressed in muddled or incoherent language.** If the thesis is incoherent or muddled, the essay is likely to follow suit. Work on your thesis until it expresses exactly the opinion or viewpoint you intend to cover in the essay.

Poor: The benefits of clarity and easy communication of a unified language compel a state to adopt codes to the effect that make bilingualism possible but preserving a single official language for transacting business and social intercourse.

Better: The benefits of clarity and easy communication offered by a single official language in a state are compelling and persuasive.

8. **A thesis should not be expressed in figurative language.** Figurative language has a place in factual writing, but not in a thesis statement. As we have stressed, the thesis is where you plainly state the main point of your essay. Figurative language tends to weaken this healthy plainness and should, therefore, never be used in a thesis.

Poor: The Amazons of today are trying to purge all the stag words from our language.

Better: Today's feminists are trying to eliminate the use of sex-biased words from public documents and publications.

9. **A thesis must not be nonsensical.** Above all else, your thesis statement must make sense. You cannot defend the indefensible or argue the unarguable, nor should you waste ink on behalf of a thesis that is absurd. For example, consider this sentence:

Poor: A good university education is one that is useful, fulfilling, and doesn't require study.

As a thesis, it is virtually useless, even though it does predict, control, and obligate. The problem is that its proposition is plainly nonsense. We cannot conceive of a good university education that doesn't require study. Only a frivolous essay could be written on such a thesis.

Better: A good university education is one that is useful, fulfilling, and challenging.

We are not suggesting that your theses should always advance narrowly orthodox or boringly conventional ideas, but the ideas they contain should be sensible enough to merit discussion by reasonable people.

The Explicit versus the Implicit Thesis

Anyone who has ever listened to a speaker ramble or read a piece of aimless writing can readily appreciate the usefulness of a thesis statement that sets down clearly the writer's main point. However, not all writers find it necessary to be explicit about their main points. Veteran writers know how to make a main point and stick faithfully to it without broadcasting it in a thesis statement. A conspicuous example of this is the essay "Once More to the Lake," reprinted in Chapter 17. In that essay, the writer sticks to the point without ever expressing it in a single thesis sentence.

As a matter of fact, many veteran writers do not need or use a thesis. Yet they always write with a built-in sense of structure; they do not stray from the point or lose their train of thought. The explicit thesis admittedly has become a requirement of classroom writing, but while it is a useful device for the inexperienced, it can be too simplistic for the professional writer—too much of a formula. Later, as you become a more experienced writer, you, too, might abandon the use of the explicit thesis. But for now, it is a convention that will help you write better essays.

● EXERCISES

1. Formulate a thesis for one of the following topics. Use the step-by-step method outlined in the chapter.

   a. Adolescence

   b. Women and the military

   c. Obligations of parents

   d. The entertainment world

   e. Spectator sports

2. Find a picture that expresses some aspect of today's society, such as students protesting, someone reading a Kindle, a scene from *Dancing with the Stars,* or people attending a church service; then write a thesis that could serve as an appropriate caption.

3. Underline the key words of the following theses:

   a. Memory entails recall, recognition, and revival.

   b. An argument must present both sides of the question being debated.

   c. The Amish people resist public education because they believe that a simple farm life is best and that formal education will corrupt their young people.

   d. A good farmer cooperates with weather, soil, and seed.

   e. Laura in "Flowering Judas" by Katherine Anne Porter is tortured by doubt, guilt, and disappointment.

   f. The racetracks, the ballparks, the fight rings, and the gridirons draw crowds in increasing numbers.

4. Which of the following theses is the best? Support your choice.

   a. Forest fires are enormously destructive because they ravage the land, create problems for flood control, and destroy useful lumber.

   b. Installment buying is of great benefit to the economy, having in mind the consumer to use a product while paying for it and being like forced savings.

   c. Television is a handicap.

5. The following theses are poorly worded. Analyze their weaknesses in terms of the nine errors discussed earlier, and rewrite each to make it clear and effective.

   a. In my opinion, birth control is the most urgent need in today's world.

   b. Just how far should the law go in its tolerance of pornography?

c. How Christian missionaries were sent to the Ivory Coast of Africa to introduce Western civilization.

d. The history of psychology had its inception with Plato and came to full term with Freud.

e. Strip mining is an environmentally destructive solution to the problem of fuel shortage, and the fuel shortage is caused by our government's foreign policy.

f. In the United States, the press is the watchdog of society.

g. Three factors may be singled out as militating against the optimum adjustment that partners in the marriage relationship should experience as money, culture, and education.

h. Homemaking is the most meaningful work a woman can perform.

i. The problem with sound pollution is: How much longer can our ears bear the noise?

j. The noteworthy relaxation of language taboos both in conversation and in print today.

k. My feeling is that educationalists are just as infatuated with jargon as are sociologists.

l. Retirement homes need not be depressing places which commercial activities can bring residents together in shared experiences.

m. The city of New York is in bad shape.

6. From the following pairs of theses, pick out the thesis with the discussible issue. Explain your choice.

a. (1) The Eiffel Tower is located near the center of Paris.

(2) Three spectacular crimes have been committed near the Eiffel Tower in Paris.

b. (1) Michelangelo's *David* symbolizes the best qualities of youthful manhood.

(2) Michelangelo's *David* is carved out of white marble from Carrara.

c. (1) The Model A Ford became popular because it was dependable and uncomplicated.

(2) Close to a million people still own Model A Fords today.

d. (1) In Hemingway's *A Farewell to Arms,* the knee injury suffered by Frederick Henry symbolizes man's wounded spirit.

(2) In Hemingway's novel *A Farewell to Arms,* Frederick Henry is shot in the knee while driving an ambulance truck.

e. (1) The Greek historian Herodotus claimed that the city of Troy was destroyed in 1250 B.C.

(2) Troy was an important city because any fortress built on its site could control all shipping traffic through the Dardanelles.

f. (1) Good grammar is the equivalent of good manners.

(2) According to the rules of grammar, "he don't" is a barbarism.

▣ Advice

The Thesis

SHERIDAN BAKER

Rhetorical Thumbnail

Purpose: to teach about the thesis

Audience: freshman composition students

Language: uses a blend of formal and informal language

Strategy: addresses the reader as *you* with a style that is both simple and refreshingly direct

Sheridan Baker (1918–2000) was Emeritus Professor of English at the University of Michigan and had been a Fulbright lecturer. He edited several works by the eighteenth-century novelist Henry Fielding, including *Joseph Andrews, Shamela,* and *Tom Jones.* Baker's two rhetorics, *The Practical Stylist* (1962) and *The Complete Stylist* (1976) have been widely used in colleges throughout the United States.

In this excerpt from The Complete Stylist, Baker advises the student to state clearly, in a sharp-edged thesis, the controlling purpose of the essay.

• • •

1   You can usually blame a bad essay on a bad beginning. If your essay falls apart, it probably has no primary idea to hold it together. "What's the big idea?" we used to ask. The phrase will serve as a reminder that you must find the "big idea" behind your several smaller thoughts and musings before you start to write. In the beginning were the logos, says the Bible—the idea, the plan, caught in a flash as if in a single word. Find your logos, and you are ready to round out your essay and set it spinning.

2   The big idea behind our ride in the speeding car[1] was that in adolescence, especially, the group can have a very deadly influence on the individual.

3   If you had not focused your big idea in a thesis, you might have begun by picking up thoughts at random, something like this:

> Everyone thinks he is a good driver. There are more accidents caused by young drivers than any other group. Driver education is a good beginning, but further practice is very necessary. People who object to driver education do not realize that modern society, with its suburban pattern of growth, is built around the automobile. The

[1]The example to which the paragraph refers occurred earlier in material that was not printed here.

car becomes a way of life and a status symbol. When a teenager goes too fast he is probably only copying his own father.

4   A little reconsideration, aimed at a good thesis sentence, could turn this into a reasonably good beginning:

> Modern society is built on the automobile. Every child looks forward to the time when he can drive; every teenager, to the day when his father lets him take out the car alone. Soon he is testing his skill at higher and higher speeds, especially with a group of friends along. One final test at extreme speeds usually suffices. The teenager's high-speed ride, if it does not kill him, will probably open his eyes to the deadly dynamics of the group.

5   Thus the central idea, or thesis, is your essay's life and spirit. If your thesis is sufficiently firm and clear, it may tell you immediately how to organize your supporting material and so **obviate** elaborate planning. If you do not find a thesis, your essay will be a tour through the miscellaneous. An essay **replete** with scaffolds and catwalks—"We have just seen this; now let us turn to this"—is an essay in which the **inherent** idea is weak or nonexistent. A purely expository and descriptive essay, one simply about "Cats," for instance, will have to rely on outer scaffolding alone (some orderly progression from Persia to Siam) since it really has no idea at all. It is all subject, all cats, instead of being based on an idea about cats.

The Argumentative Edge
Find Your Thesis

6   The aboutness puts an argumentative edge on the subject. When you have something to say about cats, you have found your underlying idea. You have something to defend, something to fight about: not just "Cats," but "The cat is really man's best friend." Now the hackles on all dog men are rising, and you have an argument on your hands. You have something to prove. You have a thesis.

7   "What's the big idea, Mac?" Let the impudence in that time-honored demand remind you that the best thesis is a kind of **affront** to somebody. No one will be very much interested in listening to you deplete the thesis "The dog is man's best friend." Everyone knows that already. Even the dog lovers will be uninterested, convinced that they know better than you. But the cat . . .

8   So it is with any unpopular idea. The more unpopular the viewpoint and the stronger the push against convention, the stronger the thesis and the more energetic the essay. Compare the energy in "Democracy is good" with that in "Communism is good," for instance. The first is filled with **platitudes**, the second with plutonium. By the same token, if you can find the real energy in "Democracy is good," if you can get down through the sand to where the roots and water are, you will have a real essay, because the opposition against which you generate your energy is the heaviest in the world: boredom. Probably the most energetic thesis of all, the greatest inner organizer, is some tired old truth that you cause to jet with new life, making the old ground green again.

9   To find a thesis and put it into one sentence is to narrow and define your subject to a workable size. Under "Cats" you must deal with all felinity from the jungle up, carefully partitioning the eons and areas, the tigers and tabbies, the sizes and shapes. The minute you proclaim the cat the friend of man, you have pared away whole categories and chapters, and need only think up the arguments sufficient to overwhelm the opposition. So, put an argumentative edge on your subject—and you will have found your thesis.

10   Simple exposition, to be sure, has its uses. You may want to tell someone how to build a doghouse, how to can asparagus, how to follow the outlines of relativity, or even how to write an essay. Performing a few exercises in simple exposition will no doubt sharpen your insight into the problems of finding orderly sequences, of considering how best to lead your readers through the hoops, of writing clearly and accurately. It will also illustrate how much finer and surer an argument is.

11   You will see that picking an argument immediately simplifies the problems so troublesome in straight exposition: the defining, the partitioning, the narrowing of the subject. Actually, you can put an argumentative edge on the flattest of expository subjects. "How to build a doghouse" might become "Building a doghouse is a thorough introduction to the building trades, including architecture and mechanical engineering." "Canning asparagus" might become "An asparagus patch is a course in economics." "Relativity" might become "Relativity is not so inscrutable as many suppose." You have simply assumed that you have a loyal opposition consisting of the uninformed, the scornful, or both. You have given your subject its edge; you have limited and organized it at a single stroke. Pick an argument, then, and you will automatically be defining and narrowing your subject, and all the partitions you don't need will fold up. Instead of dealing with things, subjects, and pieces of subjects, you will be dealing with an idea and its consequences.

Sharpen Your Thesis

12   Come out with your subject pointed. Take a stand, make a judgment of value. Be reasonable, but don't be timid. It is helpful to think of your thesis, your main idea, as a debating question—"Resolved: Old age pensions must go"—taking out the "Resolved" when you actually write the subject down. But your resolution will be even stronger, your essay clearer and tighter, if you can sharpen your thesis even further: "Resolved: Old age pensions must go because—." Fill in that blank and your worries are practically over. The main idea is to put your whole argument into one sentence.

13   Try, for instance: "Old age pensions must go because they are making people irresponsible." I don't know at all if that is true, and neither will you until you write your way into it, considering probabilities and alternatives and objections, and especially the underlying assumptions. In fact, no one, no master sociologist or future historian, can tell absolutely if it is true, so **multiplex** are the causes in human affairs, so endless and tangled the consequences. The basic assumption—that irresponsibility is growing—may be entirely false. No one, I repeat, can tell absolutely. But by the same token, your guess may be as good as another's. At any rate, you are now ready to write. You have found your logos.

14   Now you can put your well-pointed thesis sentence on a card on the wall in front of you to keep from drifting off target. But you will now want to dress it for the public, to burnish it, and make it comely. Suppose you try:

> Old age pensions, perhaps more than anything else, are erod-ing our heritage of personal and familial responsibility.

15   But is this true? Perhaps you had better try something like:

> Despite their many advantages, old age pensions may actually be eroding our heritage of personal and familial responsibility.

16   This is really your thesis, and you can write that down on a scrap of paper too.

Sheridan Baker, THE COMPLETE STYLIST AND HANDBOOK, 3rd ed., © 1984, pp. 22–25. Adapted by permission of Pearson Education, Inc., Upper Saddle River, New Jersey.

Examples

Remarks on the Life of Sacco and on His Own Life and Execution

BARTOLOMEO VANZETTI

Rhetorical Thumbnail

Purpose: to argue for and his and Sacco's innocence

Audience: the court of public opinion in the 1920s

Language: fractured English

Strategy: Vanzetti's strategy was to humanize himself and Sacco; the editors' is to dramatize the power of broken English

Bartolomeo Vanzetti (1888–1927) was born of peasant stock in northern Italy, where he worked as a baker's apprentice. He migrated to the United States in 1908, where he worked as a laborer and became an avowed anarchist. In 1920, along with Nicolo Sacco, another Italian immigrant, Vanzetti was arrested for the murder of a guard during a payroll robbery. While in prison awaiting execution, he wrote his autobiography. Maintaining their innocence to the end, and despite the worldwide public protest mounted in their behalf, Sacco and Vanzetti were executed on August 22, 1927.

These four paragraphs are assembled from Vanzetti's writings and sayings. The first three paragraphs are notes from a speech. Vanzetti intended to deliver them in court before his sentencing, but the judge barred him from doing so. The final paragraph is a transcription from an interview that Vanzetti gave to Philip D. Strong, a reporter for the North American Newspaper Alliance, *in April 1927.*

• • •

1   I have talk a great deal of myself but I even forgot to name Sacco. Sacco too is a worker from his boyhood, a skilled worker lover of work, with a good job and pay, a good and lovely wife, two beautiful children and a neat little home at the verge of a wood, near a brook. Sacco is a heart, a faith, a character, a man; a man lover of nature and of mankind. A man who gave all, who sacrifice all to the cause of Liberty and to his love for mankind; money, rest, **mundane** ambitions, his own wife, his children, himself and his own life. Sacco has never dreamt to steal, never to assassinate. He and I have never brought a morsel of bread to our mouths, from our childhood to today—which has not been gained by the sweat of our brows. Never. His people also are in good position and of good reputation.

2   Oh, yes, I may be more witful, as some have put it, I am a better babbler than he is, but many, many times in hearing his heartful voice ringing a faith **sublime**, in considering his supreme sacrifice, remembering his heroism I felt small small at the presence of his greatness and found myself compelled to fight back from my throat to not weep before him—this man called thief and assassin and doomed. But Sacco's name will live in the hearts of the people and in their gratitude when Katzmann's[1] and your bones will be dispersed by time, when your name, his name, your laws, institutions, and your false god are but a deem rememoring of a cursed past in which man was wolf to the man . . .

3   If it had not been for these thing . . . I might have live out my life talking at street corners to scorning men. I might have die, unmarked, unknown, a failure. Now we are not a failure. This is our career and our triumph. Never in our full life could we hope to do such work for tolerance, for joostice, for man's onderstanding of man as now we do by accident.

4   Our words—our lives—our pains—nothing! The taking of our lives—lives of a good shoemaker and a poor fish-peddler—all! That last moment belongs to us—that agony is our triumph.

[1]Frederick G. Katzmann was the district attorney who prosecuted the case.

● THE FACTS

1. What kind of man does the excerpt make Sacco out to be?
2. What does Vanzetti claim to be better at than Sacco?
3. According to Vanzetti, how might his life have turned out were it not for his trial and conviction?

● THE STRATEGIES

1. The author was an Italian with a frail grasp of the American speech idiom. What is the effect of his grammatical errors on the way he expresses himself?
2. How would you characterize the diction of this excerpt? Is it lofty? Plain?
3. Why do some editors include this excerpt in poetry anthologies? What is poetic about it?

● THE ISSUES

1. Because of his beliefs, Vanzetti was labeled a philosophical anarchist. What is a philosophical anarchist?

2. In the final paragraph, Vanzetti calls his impending execution with Sacco "our triumph." What do you think he meant by that?

3. The Sacco and Vanzetti trial was made famous mainly because of the intense media attention it drew. What restrictions, if any, do you think should be imposed on media coverage of sensational criminals and trials? Why? Justify your answer.

● SUGGESTIONS FOR WRITING

1. Copy this excerpt, correcting its grammatical and spelling errors as you go. Add any words that are necessary to make it grammatical. Write a paragraph on which version you think is more effective—the original or the corrected one—giving your reasons.

2. Without doing any further research into Vanzetti, and using this excerpt as your only evidence, write an impressionistic description of the kind of man you think he was. Be specific in your references to passages in the excerpt.

● RESEARCH PAPER SUGGESTION

Write a research paper on the Sacco-Vanzetti trial. After carefully pondering the evidence and opinions you found, present your own conclusion as to whether the trial was just or unjust. Be sure to evaluate and synthesize your information. Assure that your reader can trace the critical thinking that led to your conclusion.

A Good Man Is Hard To Find

FLANNERY O'CONNOR

Rhetorical Thumbnail

Purpose: to present the author's Catholic worldview

Audience: educated readers

Language: Southern Creole and its many idioms

Strategy: focuses on characterizing the two children as representatives of the Gothic southern character—leading logically (with the underpinnings of Catholic theology) to a gruesome conclusion

Flannery O'Connor (1925–1964) was a Christian humanist writer and a member of the so-called "Southern Renaissance" in American literature. She was born in Savannah, Georgia, and educated at the Woman's College of Georgia and the State University of Iowa. Her best-known stories, written from an orthodox Catholic perspective, are contained in *A Good Man Is Hard to Find and Other Stories* (1953) and *Everything That Rises Must Converge* (1956).

We do not usually think of a story as having a thesis, but we almost always think of a story as having a point. The point of this story—its thesis—is hinted at in its title, from which it proceeds with grim, irresistible logic. Readers should remember that the racist language used in this selection is partly what labeled O'Connor's stories "Southern Grotesque." Moreover, O'Connor wrote at a time when blacks in the South were often treated in a derogatory manner.

• • •

1   The grandmother didn't want to go to Florida. She wanted to visit some of her connections in east Tennessee and she was seizing at every chance to change Bailey's mind. Bailey was the son she lived with, her only boy. He was sitting on the edge of his chair at the table, bent over the orange sports section of the Journal. "Now look here, Bailey," she said, "see here, read this," and she stood with one hand on her thin hip and the other rattling the newspaper at his bald head. "Here this fellow that calls himself The Misfit is loose from the Federal Pen and headed toward Florida and you read here what it says he did to these people. Just you read it. I wouldn't take my children in any direction with a criminal like that aloose in it. I couldn't answer to my conscience if I did."

2   Bailey didn't look up from his reading so she wheeled around then and faced the children's mother, a young woman in slacks, whose face was as broad and innocent as a cabbage and was tied around with a green headkerchief that had two points on the top like a rabbit's ears. She was sitting on the sofa, feeding the baby his apricots out of a jar. "The children have been to Florida before," the old lady said. "You all ought to take them somewhere else for a change so they would see different parts of the world and be broad. They never have been to east Tennessee."

3   The children's mother didn't seem to hear her but the eight-year-old boy, John Wesley, a stocky child with glasses, said, "If you don't want to go to Florida, why dontcha stay at home?" He and the little girl, June Star, were reading the funny papers on the floor.

4   "She wouldn't stay at home to be queen for a day," June Star said without raising her yellow head.

5   "Yes and what would you do if this fellow, The Misfit, caught you?" the grandmother asked.

6   "I'd smack his face," John Wesley said.

7   "She wouldn't stay at home for a million bucks," June Star said. "Afraid she'd miss something. She has to go everywhere we go."

8   "All right, Miss," the grandmother said. "Just remember that the next time you want me to curl your hair."

9   June Star said her hair was naturally curly.

10   The next morning the grandmother was the first one in the car, ready to go. She had her big black valise that looked like the head of a hippopotamus in one corner, and underneath it she was hiding a basket with Pitty Sing, the cat, in it. She didn't intend for the cat to be left alone in the house for three days because he would miss her too much and she was afraid he might brush against one of the gas burners and accidentally **asphyxiate** himself. Her son, Bailey, didn't like to arrive at a motel with a cat.

11   She sat in the middle of the back seat with John Wesley and June Star on either side of her. Bailey and the children's mother and the baby sat in front and they left Atlanta at eight forty-five with the mileage on the car at 55890. The grandmother wrote this down because she thought it would be interesting to say how many miles they had been when they got back. It took them twenty minutes to reach the outskirts of the city.

12   The old lady settled herself comfortably, removing her white cotton gloves and putting them up with her purse on the shelf in front of the back window. The children's mother still had on slacks and still had her head tied up in a green kerchief, but the grandmother had on a navy blue straw sailor hat with a bunch of white violets on the brim and a navy blue dress with a small white dot in the print. Her collars and cuffs were white organdy trimmed with lace and at her neckline she had pinned a purple spray of cloth violets containing a **sachet**. In case of an accident, anyone seeing her dead on the highway would know at once that she was a lady.

13   She said she thought it was going to be a good day for driving, neither too hot nor too cold, and she cautioned Bailey that the speed limit was fifty-five miles an hour and that the patrolmen hid themselves behind billboards and small clumps of trees and sped out after you before you had a chance to slow down. She pointed out interesting details of the scenery: Stone Mountain; the blue granite that in some places came up to both sides of the highway; the brilliant red clay banks slightly streaked with purple; and the various crops that made rows of green lace-work on the ground. The trees were full of silver-white sunlight and the meanest of them sparkled. The children were reading comic magazines and their mother had gone back to sleep.

14   "Let's go through Georgia fast so we won't have to look at it much," John Wesley said.

15   "If I were a little boy," said the grandmother, "I wouldn't talk about my native state that way. Tennessee has the mountains and Georgia has the hills."

16   "Tennessee is just a hillbilly dumping ground," John Wesley said, "and Georgia is a lousy state too."

17   "You said it," June Star said.

18   "In my time," said the grandmother, folding her thin veined fingers, "children were more respectful of their native states and their parents and everything else. People did right then. Oh look at the cute little pickaninny!" she said and pointed to a Negro child standing in the door of a shack. "Wouldn't that make a picture, now?" she asked and they all turned and looked at the little Negro out of the back window. He waved.

19   "He didn't have any britches on," June Star said.

20   "He probably didn't have any," the grandmother explained. "Little niggers in the country don't have things like we do. If I could paint, I'd paint that picture," she said.

21   The children exchanged comic books.

22   The grandmother offered to hold the baby and the children's mother passed him over the front seat to her. She sat him on her knee and bounced him and told him about the things they were passing. She rolled her eyes and screwed up her mouth and stuck her leathery thin face into his smooth **bland** one. Occasionally he gave her a faraway smile. They passed a large cotton field with five or six graves fenced in the middle of it, like a small island. "Look at the graveyard!" the grandmother said, pointing it out. "That was the old family burying ground. That belonged to the plantation."

23   "Where's the plantation?" John Wesley asked.

24   "Gone With the Wind," said the grandmother. "Ha. Ha."

25   When the children finished all the comic books they had brought, they opened the lunch and ate it. The grandmother ate a peanut butter sandwich and an olive and would not let the children throw the box and the paper napkins out the window. When there was nothing else to do they played a game by choosing a cloud and making the other two guess what shape it suggested. John Wesley took one the shape of a cow and June Star guessed a cow and John Wesley said, "no, an automobile," and June Star said he didn't play fair, and they began to slap each other over the grandmother.

26   The grandmother said she would tell them a story if they would keep quiet. When she told a story, she rolled her eyes and waved her head and was very dramatic. She said once when she was a maiden lady she had been courted by a Mr. Edgar Atkins Teagarden from Jasper, Georgia. She said he was a very good-looking man and a gentleman and that he brought her a watermelon every Saturday afternoon with his initials cut in it, E. A. T. Well, one Saturday, she said, Mr. Teagarden brought the watermelon and there was nobody at home and he left it on the front porch and returned in his buggy to Jasper, but she never got the watermelon, she said, because a nigger boy ate it when he saw the initials, E. A. T.! This story tickled John Wesley's funny bone and he giggled and giggled but June Star didn't think it was any good. She said she wouldn't marry a man that just brought her a watermelon on Saturday. The grandmother said she would have done well to marry Mr. Teagarden because he was a gentleman and had bought Coca-Cola stock when it first came out and that he had died only a few years ago, a very wealthy man.

27   They stopped at The Tower for barbecued sandwiches. The Tower was a part stucco and part wood filling station and dance hall set in a clearing outside of Timothy. A fat man named Red Sammy Butts ran it and there were signs stuck here and there on the building and for miles up and down the highway saying, TRY RED SAMMY'S FAMOUS BARBECUE. NONE LIKE FAMOUS RED SAMMY'S! RED SAM! THE FAT BOY WITH THE HAPPY LAUGH! A VETERAN! RED SAMMY'S YOUR MAN!

28   Red Sammy was lying on the bare ground outside The Tower with his head under a truck while a gray monkey about a foot high, chained to a small chinaberry

tree, chattered nearby. The monkey sprang back into the tree and got on the highest limb as soon as he saw the children jump out of the car and run toward him.

29   Inside, The Tower was a long dark room with a counter at one end and tables at the other and dancing space in the middle. They all sat down at a board table next to the nickelodeon and Red Sam's wife, a tall burnt-brown woman with hair and eyes lighter than her skin, came and took their order. The children's mother put a dime in the machine and played "The Tennessee Waltz," and the grandmother said that tune always made her want to dance. She asked Bailey if he would like to dance but he only glared at her. He didn't have a naturally sunny disposition like she did and trips made him nervous. The grandmother's brown eyes were very bright. She swayed her head from side to side and pretended she was dancing in her chair. June Star said play something she could tap to so the children's mother put in another dime and played a fast number and June Star stepped out onto the dance floor and did her tap routine.

30   "Ain't she cute?" Red Sam's wife said, leaning over the counter. "Would you like to come be my little girl?"

31   "No I certainly wouldn't," June Star said. "I wouldn't live in a broken-down place like this for a million bucks!" and she ran back to the table.

32   "Ain't she cute?" the woman repeated, stretching her mouth politely.

33   "Aren't you ashamed?" hissed the grandmother.

34   Red Sam came in and told his wife to quit lounging on the counter and hurry up with these people's order. His khaki trousers reached just to his hip bones and his stomach hung over them like a sack of meal swaying under his shirt. He came over and sat down at a table nearby and let out a combination sigh and yodel. "You can't win," he said. "You can't win," and he wiped his sweating red face off with a gray handkerchief. "These days you don't know who to trust," he said. "Ain't that the truth?"

35   "People are certainly not nice like they used to be," said the grandmother.

36   "Two fellers come in here last week," Red Sammy said, "driving a Chrysler. It was a old beat-up car but it was a good one and these boys looked all right to me. Said they worked at the mill and you know I let them fellers charge the gas they bought? Now why did I do that?"

37   "Because you're a good man!" the grandmother said at once.

38   "Yes'm, I suppose so," Red Sam said as if he were struck with this answer.

39   His wife brought the orders, carrying the five plates all at once without a tray, two in each hand and one balanced on her arm. "It isn't a soul in this green world of God's that you can trust," she said. "And I don't count nobody out of that, not nobody," she repeated, looking at Red Sammy.

40   "Did you read about that criminal, The Misfit, that's escaped?" asked the grandmother.

41   "I wouldn't be a bit surprised if he didn't attact this place right here," said the woman. "If he hears about it being here, I wouldn't be none surprised to see him. If he hears it's two cent in the cash register, I wouldn't be at all surprised if he . . ."

42   "That'll do," Red Sam said, "Go bring these people their Co'-Colas," and the woman went off to get the rest of the order.

43   "A good man is hard to find," Red Sammy said. "Everything is getting terrible. I remember the day you could go off and leave your screen door unlatched. Not no more."

44   He and the grandmother discussed better times. The old lady said that in her opinion Europe was entirely to blame for the way things were now. She said the way Europe acted you would think we were made of money and Red Sam said it was no use talking about it, she was exactly right. The children ran outside into the white sunlight and looked at the monkey in the lacy chinaberry tree. He was busy catching fleas on himself and biting each one carefully between his teeth as if it were a delicacy.

45   They drove off again into the hot afternoon. The grandmother took cat naps and woke up every few minutes with her own snoring. Outside of Toombsboro she woke up and recalled an old plantation that she had visited in this neighborhood once when she was a young lady. She said the house had six white columns across the front and that there was an avenue of oaks leading up to it and two little wooden trellis arbors on each side in front where you sat down with your suitor after a stroll in the garden. She recalled exactly which road to turn off to get to it. She knew that Bailey would not be willing to lose any time looking at an old house, but the more she talked about it, the more she wanted to see it once again and find out if the little twin arbors were still standing. "There was a secret panel in this house," she said craftily, not telling the truth but wishing that she were, "and the story went that all the family silver was hidden in it when Sherman came through but it was never found . . ."

46   "Hey!" John Wesley said. "Let's go see it! We'll find it! We'll poke all the woodwork and find it! Who lives there? Where do you turn off at? Hey Pop, can't we turn off there?"

47   "We never have seen a house with a secret panel!" June Star shrieked. "Let's go to the house with the secret panel! Hey Pop, can't we go see the house with the secret panel!"

48   "It's not far from here, I know," the grandmother said. "It wouldn't take over twenty minutes."

49   Bailey was looking straight ahead. His jaw was as rigid as a horseshoe. "No," he said.

50   The children began to yell and scream that they wanted to see the house with the secret panel. John Wesley kicked the back of the front seat and June Star hung over her mother's shoulder and whined desperately into her ear that they never had any fun even on their vacation, that they could never do what THEY wanted to do. The baby began to scream and John Wesley kicked the back of the seat so hard that his father could feel the blows in his kidney.

51   "All right!" he shouted and drew the car to a stop at the side of the road. "Will you all shut up? Will you all just shut up for one second? If you don't shut up, we won't go anywhere."

52   "It would be very educational for them," the grandmother murmured.

53   "All right," Bailey said, "but get this: This is the only time we're going to stop for anything like this. This is the one and only time."

54   "The dirt road that you have to turn down is about a mile back," the grand-mother directed. "I marked it when we passed."

55   "A dirt road," Bailey groaned.

56   After they had turned around and were headed toward the dirt road, the grandmother recalled other points about the house, the beautiful glass over the front doorway and the candle-lamp in the hall. John Wesley said that the secret panel was probably in the fireplace.

57   "You can't go inside this house," Bailey said. "You don't know who lives there."

58   "While you all talk to the people in front, I'll run around behind and get in a window," John Wesley suggested.

59   "We'll all stay in the car," his mother said.

60   They turned onto the dirt road and the car raced roughly along in a swirl of pink dust. The grandmother recalled the times when there were no paved roads and thirty miles was a day's journey. The dirt road was hilly and there were sudden washes in it and sharp curves on dangerous embankments. All at once they would be on a hill, looking down over the blue tops of trees for miles around, then the next minute, they would be in a red depression with the dust-coated trees looking down on them.

61   "This place had better turn up in a minute," Bailey said, "or I'm going to turn around."

62   The road looked as if no one had traveled on it in months.

63   "It's not much farther," the grandmother said and just as she said it, a hor-rible thought came to her. The thought was so embarrassing that she turned red in the face and her eyes **dilated** and her feet jumped up, upsetting her valise in the corner. The instant the valise moved, the newspaper top she had over the basket under it rose with a snarl and Pitty Sing, the cat, sprang onto Bailey's shoulder.

64   The children were thrown to the floor and their mother, clutching the baby, was thrown out the door onto the ground; the old lady was thrown into the front seat. The car turned over once and landed right-side-up in a gulch off the side of the road. Bailey remained in the driver's seat with the cat—graystriped with a broad white face and an orange nose—clinging to his neck like a caterpillar.

65   As soon as the children saw they could move their arms and legs, they scram-bled out of the car, shouting, "We've had an ACCIDENT!" The grandmother was curled up under the dashboard, hoping she was injured so that Bailey's wrath would not come down on her all at once. The horrible thought she had had before the accident was that the house she had remembered so vividly was not in Geor-gia but in Tennessee.

66   Bailey removed the cat from his neck with both hands and flung it out the window against the side of a pine tree. Then he got out of the car and started looking for the children's mother. She was sitting against the side of the red gut-ted ditch, holding the screaming baby, but she only had a cut down her face and a broken shoulder. "We've had an ACCIDENT!" the children screamed in a frenzy of delight.

67   "But nobody's killed," June Star said with disappointment as the grandmother limped out of the car, her hat still pinned to her head but the broken front brim

standing up at a **jaunty** angle and the violet spray hanging off the side. They all sat down in the ditch, except the children, to recover from the shock. They were all shaking.

68   "Maybe a car will come along," said the children's mother hoarsely.

69   "I believe I have injured an organ," said the grandmother, pressing her side, but no one answered her. Bailey's teeth were clattering. He had on a yellow sport shirt with bright blue parrots designed in it and his face was as yellow as the shirt. The grandmother decided that she would not mention that the house was in Tennessee.

70   The road was about ten feet above and they could see only the tops of the trees on the other side of it. Behind the ditch they were sitting in there were more woods, tall and dark and deep. In a few minutes they saw a car some distance away on top of a hill, coming slowly as if the occupants were watching them. The grandmother stood up and waved both arms dramatically to attract their attention. The car continued to come on slowly, disappeared around a bend and appeared again, moving even slower, on top of the hill they had gone over. It was a big black battered hearselike automobile. There were three men in it.

71   It came to a stop just over them and for some minutes, the driver looked down with a steady expressionless gaze to where they were sitting, and didn't speak. Then he turned his head and muttered something to the other two and they got out. One was a fat boy in black trousers and a red sweat shirt with a silver stallion **embossed** on the front of it. He moved around on the right side of them and stood staring, his mouth partly open in a kind of loose grin. The other had on khaki pants and a blue striped coat and a gray hat pulled down very low, hiding most of his face. He came around slowly on the left side. Neither spoke.

72   The driver got out of the car and stood by the side of it, looking down at them. He was an older man than the other two. His hair was just beginning to gray and he wore silver-rimmed spectacles that gave him a scholarly look. He had a long creased face and didn't have on any shirt or undershirt. He had on blue jeans that were too tight for him and was holding a black hat and a gun. The two boys also had guns.

73   "We've had an ACCIDENT!" the children screamed.

74   The grandmother had the peculiar feeling that the bespectacled man was someone she knew. His face was as familiar to her as if she had known him all her life but she could not recall who he was. He moved away from the car and began to come down the embankment, placing his feet carefully so that he wouldn't slip. He had on tan and white shoes and no socks, and his ankles were red and thin. "Good afternoon," he said. "I see you all had you a little spill."

75   "We turned over twice!" said the grandmother.

76   "Oncet," he corrected. "We seen it happen. Try their car and see will it run, Hiram," he said quietly to the boy with the gray hat.

77   "What you got that gun for?" John Wesley asked. "Whatcha gonna do with that gun?"

78   "Lady," the man said to the children's mother, "would you mind calling them children to sit down by you? Children make me nervous. I want all you all to sit down right together there where you're at."

79   "What are you telling us what to do for?" June Star asked.

80   Behind them the line of woods gaped like a dark open mouth. "Come here," said their mother.

81   "Look here now," Bailey began suddenly, "we're in a predicament! We're in . . ."

82   The grandmother shrieked. She scrambled to her feet and stood staring. "You're The Misfit!" she said, "I recognized you at once!"

83   "Yes'm," the man said, smiling slightly as if he were pleased in spite of himself to be known, "but it would have been better for all of you, lady, if you hadn't of reckernized me."

84   Bailey turned his head sharply and said something to his mother that shocked even the children. The old lady began to cry and The Misfit reddened.

85   "Lady," he said, "don't you get upset. Sometimes a man says things he don't mean. I don't reckon he meant to talk to you thataway."

86   "You wouldn't shoot a lady, would you?" the grandmother said and removed a clean handkerchief from her cuff and began to slap at her eyes with it.

87   The Misfit pointed the toe of his shoe into the ground and made a little hole and then covered it up again. "I would hate to have to," he said.

88   "Listen," the grandmother almost screamed, "I know you're a good man. You don't look a bit like you have common blood. I know you must come from nice people!"

89   "Yes ma'am," he said, "finest people in the world." When he smiled he showed a row of strong white teeth. "God never made a finer woman than my mother and my daddy's heart was pure gold," he said. The boy with the red sweat shirt had come around behind them and was standing with his gun at his hip. The Misfit squatted down on the ground. "Watch them children, Bobby Lee," he said. "You know they make me nervous." He looked at the six of them huddled together in front of him and he seemed to be embarrassed as if he couldn't think of anything to say. "Ain't a cloud in the sky," he remarked, looking up at it. "Don't see no sun but don't see no cloud neither."

90   "Yes, it's a beautiful day," said the grandmother. "Listen," she said, "you shouldn't call yourself The Misfit because I know you're a good man at heart. I can just look at you and tell."

91   "Hush!" Bailey yelled. "Hush! Everybody shut up and let me handle this!" He was squatting in the position of a runner about to sprint forward but he didn't move.

92   "I pre-chate that, lady," The Misfit said and drew a little circle in the ground with the butt of his gun.

93   "It'll take a half a hour to fix this here car," Hiram called, looking over the raised hood of it.

94   "Well, first you and Bobby Lee get him and that little boy to step over yonder with you," The Misfit said, pointing to Bailey and John Wesley. "The boys want to ast you something," he said to Bailey. "Would you mind stepping back in them woods there with them?"

95   "Listen," Bailey began, "we're in a terrible predicament! Nobody realizes what this is," and his voice cracked. His eyes were as blue and intense as the parrots in his shirt and he remained perfectly still.

96   The grandmother reached up to adjust her hat brim as if she were going to the woods with him but it came off in her hand. She stood staring at it and after a second she let it fall on the ground. Hiram pulled Bailey up by the arm as if he were assisting an old man. John Wesley caught hold of his father's hand and Bobby Lee followed. They went off toward the woods and just as they reached the dark edge, Bailey turned and supporting himself against a gray naked pine trunk, he shouted, "I'll be back in a minute, Mamma, wait on me!"

97   "Come back this instant!" his mother shrilled but they all disappeared into the woods.

98   "Bailey Boy!" the grandmother called in a tragic voice but she found she was looking at The Misfit squatting on the ground in front of her. "I just know you're a good man," she said desperately. "You're not a bit common!"

99   "No'm, I ain't a good man," The Misfit said after a second as if he had considered her statement carefully. "But I ain't the worst in the world neither. My daddy said I was a different breed of dog from my brothers and sisters. 'You know,' Daddy said, 'it's some that can live their whole life out without asking about it and it's others has to know why it is, and this boy is one of the latters. He's going to be into everything!'" He put on his black hat and looked up suddenly and then away deep into the woods as if he were embarrassed again. "I'm sorry I don't have on a shirt before you ladies," he said, hunching his shoulders slightly. "We buried our clothes that we had on when we escaped and we're just making do until we can get better. We borrowed these from some folks we met," he explained.

100   "That's perfectly all right," the grandmother said. "Maybe Bailey has an extra shirt in his suitcase."

101   "I'll look and see terrectly," The Misfit said.

102   "Where are they taking him?" the children's mother screamed.

103   "Daddy was a card himself," The Misfit said. "You couldn't put anything over on him. He never got in trouble with the Authorities though. Just had the knack of handling them."

104   "You could be honest too if you'd only try," said the grandmother. "Think how wonderful it would be to settle down and live a comfortable life and not have to think about somebody chasing you all the time."

105   The Misfit kept scratching in the ground with the butt of his gun as if he were thinking about it. "Yes'm, somebody is always after you," he murmured.

106   The grandmother noticed how thin his shoulder blades were just behind his hat because she was standing up looking down on him. "Do you ever pray?" she asked.

107   He shook his head. All she saw was the black hat wiggle between his shoulder blades. "No'm," he said.

108   There was a pistol shot from the woods, followed closely by another. Then silence. The old lady's head jerked around. She could hear the wind move through the tree tops like a long satisfied insuck of breath. "Bailey Boy!" she called.

109   "I was a gospel singer for a while," The Misfit said. "I been most everything. Been in the arm service, both land and sea, at home and abroad, been twicet married, been an undertaker, been with the railroads, plowed Mother Earth, been in

a tornado, seen a man burnt alive oncet," and looked up at the children's mother and the little girl who were sitting close together, their faces white and their eyes glassy; "I even seen a woman flogged," he said.

110   "Pray, pray," the grandmother began, "pray, pray . . ."

111   "I never was a bad boy that I remember of," The Misfit said in an almost dreamy voice, "but somewheres along the line I done something wrong and got sent to the penitentiary. I was buried alive," and he looked up and held her attention to him by a steady stare.

112   "That's when you should have started to pray," she said. "What did you do to get sent to the penitentiary that first time?"

113   "Turn to the right, it was a wall," The Misfit said, looking up again at the cloudless sky. "Turn to the left, it was a wall. Look up it was a ceiling, look down it was a floor. I forget what I done, lady. I set there and set there, trying to remember what it was I done and I ain't recalled it to this day. Oncet in a while, I would think it was coming to me, but it never come."

114   "Maybe they put you in by mistake," the old lady said vaguely.

115   "No'm," he said. "It wasn't no mistake. They had papers on me."

116   "You must have stolen something," she said.

117   The Misfit sneered slightly. "Nobody had nothing I wanted," he said. "It was a head-doctor at the penitentiary said what I had done was kill my daddy but I known that for a lie. My daddy died in nineteen ought nineteen of the epidemic flu and I never had a thing to do with it. He was buried in the Mount Hopewell Baptist churchyard and you can go there and see for yourself."

118   "If you would pray," the old lady said, "Jesus would help you."

119   "That's right," The Misfit said.

120   "Well then, why don't you pray?" she asked trembling with delight suddenly.

121   "I don't want no hep," he said, "I'm doing all right by myself."

122   Bobby Lee and Hiram came **ambling** back from the woods. Bobby Lee was dragging a yellow shirt with bright blue parrots in it.

123   "Throw me that shirt, Bobby Lee," The Misfit said. The shirt came flying at him and landed on his shoulder and he put it on. The grandmother couldn't name what the shirt reminded her of. "No, lady," The Misfit said while he was buttoning it up, "I found out the crime don't matter. You can do one thing or you can do another, kill a man or take a tire off his car, because sooner or later you're going to forget what it was you done and just be punished for it."

124   The children's mother had begun to make heaving noises as if she couldn't get her breath. "Lady," he asked, "would you and that little girl like to step off yonder with Bobby Lee and Hiram and join your husband?"

125   "Yes, thank you," the mother said faintly. Her left arm dangled helplessly and she was holding the baby, who had gone to sleep, in the other.

126   "Hep that lady up, Hiram," The Misfit said as she struggled to climb out of the ditch, "and Bobby Lee, you hold onto that little girl's hand."

127   "I don't want to hold hands with him," June Star said. "He reminds me of a pig."

128   The fat boy blushed and laughed and caught her by the arm and pulled her off into the woods after Hiram and her mother.

129   Alone with The Misfit, the grandmother found that she had lost her voice. There was not a cloud in the sky nor any sun. There was nothing around her but woods. She wanted to tell him that he must pray. She opened and closed her mouth several times before anything came out. Finally she found herself saying, "Jesus, Jesus," meaning, Jesus will help you, but the way she was saying it, it sounded as if she might be cursing.

130   "Yes'm," The Misfit said as if he agreed, "Jesus thrown everything off balance. It was the same case with Him as with me except He hadn't committed any crime and they could prove I had committed one because they had the papers on me. Of course," he said, "they never shown me my papers. That's why I sign myself now. I said long ago, you get you a signature and sign everything you do and keep a copy of it. Then you'll know what you done and you can hold up the crime to the punishment and see do they match and in the end you'll have something to prove you ain't been treated right. I call myself The Misfit," he said, "because I can't make what all I done wrong fit what all I gone through in punishment."

131   There was a piercing scream from the woods, followed closely by a pistol report. "Does it seem right to you, lady, that one is punished a heap and another ain't punished at all?"

132   "Jesus!" the old lady cried. "You've got good blood! I know you wouldn't shoot a lady! I know you come from nice people! Pray! Jesus, you ought not to shoot a lady, I'll give you all the money I've got!"

133   "Lady," The Misfit said, looking beyond her far into the woods, "there never was a body that give the undertaker a tip."

134   There were two more pistol reports and the grandmother raised her head like a **parched** old turkey hen crying for water and called, "Bailey Boy, Bailey Boy!" as if her heart would break.

135   "Jesus was the only One that ever raised the dead," The Misfit continued, "and He shouldn't have done it. He thrown everything off balance. If He did what He said, then it's nothing for you to do but throw away everything and follow Him, and if He didn't, then it's nothing for you to do but enjoy the few minutes you got left the best way you can—by killing somebody or burning down his house or doing some other meanness to him. No pleasure but meanness," he said and his voice had become almost a snarl.

136   "Maybe He didn't raise the dead," the old lady mumbled, not knowing what she was saying and feeling so dizzy that she sank down in the ditch with her legs twisted under her.

137   "I wasn't there so I can't say He didn't," The Misfit said. "I wisht I had of been there," he said, hitting the ground with his fist. "It ain't right I wasn't there because if I had of been there I would of known. Listen lady," he said in a high voice, "if I had of been there I would of known and I wouldn't be like I am now." His voice seemed about to crack and the grandmother's head cleared for an instant. She saw the man's face twisted close to her own as if he were going to cry and she murmured, "Why, you're one of my babies. You're one of my own children!" She reached out and touched him on the shoulder. The Misfit sprang back as if a snake had bitten him and shot her three times through the chest. Then he put his gun down on the ground and took off his glasses and began to clean them.

138   Hiram and Bobby Lee returned from the woods and stood over the ditch, looking down at the grandmother who half sat and half lay in a puddle of blood with her
legs crossed under her like a child's and her face smiling up at the cloudless sky.

139   Without his glasses, The Misfit's eyes were red-rimmed and pale and
defenseless-looking. "Take her off and throw her where you thrown the others," he
said, picking up the cat that was rubbing itself against his leg.

140   "She was a talker, wasn't she?" Bobby Lee said, sliding down the ditch with
a yodel.

141   "She would of been a good woman," The Misfit said, "if it had been somebody there to shoot her every minute of her life."

142   "Some fun!" Bobby Lee said.

143   "Shut up, Bobby Lee," The Misfit said. "It's no real pleasure in life."

● THE FACTS

1. Why didn't the grandmother want to go to Florida? Where did she want to go
   instead?
2. Why does the family turn off onto the lonely dirt road?
3. What caused the accident?
4. For what crime was The Misfit sent to the penitentiary?
5. Why does he call himself "The Misfit"?

● THE STRATEGIES

1. The Misfit is mentioned in the first paragraph. Why does O'Connor introduce
   him so early?
2. What does the initial dialogue between the grandmother and the children
   accomplish?
3. In paragraph 70, The Misfit's automobile is described as "a big black battered
   hearselike automobile." What is O'Connor doing in this description?
4. At a climactic part of the story, the grandmother has a sudden, dramatic recognition of responsibility. When does it occur? Whom does it involve?
5. In paragraph 80, O'Connor writes: "Behind them the line of woods gaped like a
   dark open mouth." What does this description accomplish? What does it signal
   to the reader?

● THE ISSUES

1. The Misfit and his cronies commit cold-blooded murder on a family of six. What
   prerequisite, if any, do you think must exist before a person is capable of murder? If you think there is no prerequisite, do you also think anyone is capable
   of cold-blooded murder? Justify your answer.

2. What punishment would you regard as just and fitting for The Misfit and his henchmen?

3. Some commentators have said that the children are brats, pure and simple, whereas others have argued that they are rather typical. What is your opinion of the children and their behavior?

4. One interpretation argues that The Misfit is the devil and the grandmother a Christian who confronts him. What is your opinion of this interpretation?

5. What do you think the grandmother meant when she said to The Misfit, "Why you're one of my babies. You're one of my own children!" Why do you think The Misfit killed her when she said that?

● SUGGESTIONS FOR WRITING

1. Write an essay analyzing the techniques used by the author to foreshadow the family's fatal encounter with The Misfit. Make specific references to scenes and images and include as many quoted passages as necessary to prove your case.

2. Write an essay interpreting this story. You might begin by asking yourself, "What does the story teach about life?" "Are some people born evil?" "What makes a misfit like the one in the story?" Since the topic of criminal personalities is fraught with questions that are difficult to answer, try to evaluate critically any claims you encounter. Your thesis should contain the main point of the story.

▥ Chapter Writing Assignments

1. Convert one of the following general subjects into a suitable thesis:
   a. college life
   b. the relationship of parents to their offspring
   c. teenage pregnancies
   d. television coverage of crime, war, or natural disasters
   e. finding a meaningful job
   f. youth and age
   g. today's heroes
   h. freedom of speech

2. Select any issue covered in your local news reports, formulate your position on it in a thesis, and then explain and defend your thesis in an essay.

▥ Writing Assignments for a Specific Audience

1. For an audience of junior high students, explain in an essay the concept of a thesis and how you make use of it in your own writing. Hint: Keep your vocabulary simple.

2. Explain to an audience of business executives how the English education you are presently receiving will make you a better employee.

■ Real-Life Student Writing

A Eulogy to a Friend Killed in a Car Wreck

Students sometimes have the unenviable duty of saying a few last words at a funeral or memorial service of friends, relatives, and classmates. Here is a brief eulogy, given by a young man whose best friend was killed in an automobile crash.

• • •

He was my best friend. We went to elementary school together, where we drove our teachers crazy. We grew up in North Hollywood, both loving the Giants, the 49ers, and the Lakers. We never missed a Rose Bowl game on TV. We weathered a thunderstorm in our pup tents in the Sierra Nevadas; we played Blind Man's Bluff in my parent's swimming pool; we TP'd our girlfriends' homes; we learned to play the guitar; and we read a lot of science fiction books together. When I was angry at my parents, Brett would calm me down. When I felt nervous about some final exam, Brett encouraged me.

What evil force is this that has taken Brett away without warning?

Yes, I am angry at the driver who mowed him down; I am angry that God didn't save him. But I am also aware that anger won't bring him back. So, I guess we must all live with the knowledge that Brett was a one-of-a-kind friend—loyal, upbeat, and generous. We'll all remember the good times we had with him. And for those of us who believe in life after death—we look forward to some day meeting him again and hearing him say, "Hey man, how's it goin'?"

*Stumped by noun clusters? Exit on page 431 at the **Editing Booth!***

CHAPTER 6

Organizing Ideas

■ Road Map to Organizing

Writers and the way they work fall mainly into two major camps: the organic and the mechanical. The organic writer writes from the subconscious. Such writers often go to sleep thinking about an assignment and wake up the next morning knowing exactly what they intend to write. The mechanical writer, like a carpenter building a house, works from a blueprint or plan. These writers organize their thoughts before writing and plot out their ideas and topics before committing a single word to paper.

We raise this distinction to point out that organizing is not for everyone. It is a technique better suited to the working habits of the mechanical writer. For the organic writer whose subconscious does most of the work, organizing offers little benefit and might even interfere with the process of composing.

Organizing the Short Essay

Short essays (about 300 words long) are usually written in class under the pressure of a time limit. An instructor may assign you to write three paragraphs on some topic you have been studying in class, or you may be asked to write an informal essay on a topic such as why an uninformed person should or should not vote. Obviously, you cannot spend a great deal of time planning what to say in such an essay. Yet you think some preliminary sketch would be helpful. What can you do?

Make a Jot List A "jot list" is exactly as it sounds like: a list of those points you mean to cover in the essay. You begin your jot list by scribbling down your main point or thesis. In this case, you think it is better for an ignorant voter to abstain than to cast a vote that amounts to a guess. You express this position in a thesis sentence:

> **Thesis:** To vote for someone whose record you don't know is worse than not voting at all.

Then, you add the points you think you ought to cover:

1. If I don't vote, at least the people who know what the candidates stand for will make the decision for me.
2. Uncle John picks candidates by closing his eyes and poking at the ballot with his finger.
3. Voting from ignorance is disrespectful of the democratic process.
4. If I don't know anything about a candidate or an issue, I won't vote. At least that way, I leave the decision up to people who do know.

The jot list has no conventional form. You do not hand it in to your instructor. You can number its entries or arrange them in any other way you please. When you're done writing the essay, you can make a paper plane of the jot list if you like. It is nothing more than a thumbnail sketch of what you want to do.

Sketch out Your Paragraphs   This method of organizing is as simple as a jot list. Sketch out the paragraphs you intend to write. Most in-class essays require no more than five paragraphs—and usually around three. Here's an example. You have been given the essay topic to write on any aspect of modern popular culture. You choose to write about the movies and why you like them.

Begin by writing down a rough draft of your thesis:

> **Thesis:** The most interesting and entertaining products of modern popular culture are movies.

Next, write down the topics of your beginning paragraphs:

> **First paragraph:** interesting movies. *Hotel Rwanda, Sicko, March of the Penguins.* Why these movies are interesting to me.
> **Second paragraph:** entertaining movies. *Wall-E, Steel Magnolias, Sex and the City.* Why I find these movies entertaining.
> **Third paragraph:** Our movies are global influences. They spread our culture and way of life better than literature does.

You don't want to make this list too long because you still have the actual essay to write. But at least you know what topics you have to cover in upcoming paragraphs.

Make a Flowchart   This is a more graphic variation of the jot list. Simply make a plan of your entire essay, using specially shaped boxes for supporting ideas and main points. In the example given (Figure 6.1), the triangular shapes indicate supporting details. The rectangular shapes indicate main points, and the diamond shape indicates where transitions need to be inserted.

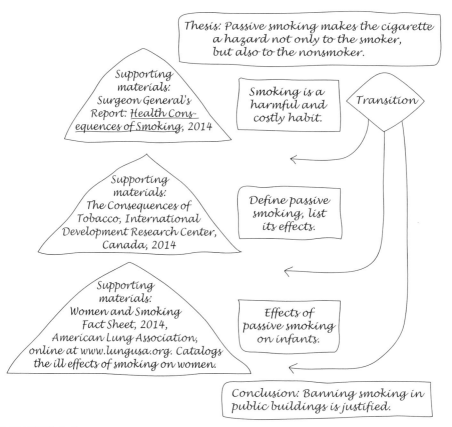

■ FIGURE 6.1

Example of Essay Flowchart.

Organizing the Long Essay

The long essay might be a weekend assignment or a research paper completed over the course of several weeks. You might be expected to write an essay five to ten pages long with appropriate and accurate documentation on a topic such as the following: "Why the Shark Is Such a Successful Predator"; "Art Therapy"; or "Initial Critical Reactions to Henry Miller's Novels." Writing about such subjects will require library and Internet research as well as reading periodicals or books found in the libraries of friends and relatives.

The plan of such an essay should function as a guide not only to its writing but also to the research you need to do before you are ready to write. You should consult the plan both as you do the research—modifying it if necessary as you accumulate more supporting materials and possibly change your mind about what you want to say—and as you do the writing. If you find yourself going off in a different direction from the plan during the actual writing, never mind. Follow the lead of inspiration. When you have finished, go back over the rough draft and compare it with your original plan. Be sure you can justify the switch.

Planning by Listing Supporting Materials

If you have a topic, you can often generate a crude outline of the essay by making a list of the supporting materials you will need for reference. How can you know what supporting materials you need? You find out by asking commonsense questions about the topic. These questions are those that any interested reader would likewise ask.

Here is an example: A student who accompanied her parents on a summer trip to Stonehenge, England, decided to do a paper on the area's mysterious monoliths. Her own tourist pamphlets, bolstered by some preliminary background reading in the college library, led her to this thesis:

> **Thesis:** A visit to Stonehenge, England, taught me that some civilizations of the past have left us some challenging mysteries we can't seem to solve.

These are the questions that naturally occurred to her as she thought about what supporting materials she would need:

- Where is Stonehenge? Give its geographical location.

- What is Stonehenge? Describe the stones so that the reader can visualize their size and arrangement. Try to get across the awesome nature of the stones.

- What was Stonehenge used for? What are the theories of its use?

- Summarize the most popular legends surrounding the history of Stonehenge:
  1. Stonehenge as a sanctuary of the Druids. Look up "Druids" in the encyclopedia. See what role they played in the early history of England (probably Celtic).
  2. The Devil's confrontation with a friar. Find out how this exotic legend got started.
  3. A memorial to the slain knights of King Arthur.
  4. An observatory for tracking the heavens, especially the rising of the moon. This seems to be a realistic explanation. Find out if many sources mention this theory.
- Why is Stonehenge so popular even today? Explain the reasons for its popularity.

These rather straightforward questions gave the writer an idea of the supporting materials she needed to complete the assignment. Asking these questions also resulted in a rough outline of the paper.

Organizing with a Formal Outline

The outline is a summary of what you plan to say in your essay. The outline tells you what you have to do, where you have to go, and when you have gotten there. If you tend to get sidetracked by details or bogged down in vast quantities of information, outlining is a handy way of imposing structure on a long essay.

A convention has evolved for the formal outline, based mainly on the desire to make it readable at a glance. The title of the essay is centered at the top of the page, with the thesis below it. Main ideas are designated by Roman numerals. Sub-ideas branching off the main ideas are indented and designated by capital letters. Examples of these sub-ideas are further indented and designated by Arabic numerals. Indented beneath the examples are supporting details, designated by lowercase letters. In theory, this subdividing could go on forever; in practice, it rarely extends beyond the fourth level. Here is the framework for the formal outline:

Title
  Thesis
    I. Main idea
      A. Sub-idea
        1. Division of sub-idea
          a. Part of division of sub-idea

An outline omits introductory materials, transitions, examples, illustrations, and details; it lists only the major ideas and sub-ideas of the essay. This practice makes sense when you remember that the prime purpose of an outline is to condense the major divisions of a long essay into a form that can be read at a glance. To make the outline as long and complex as the essay itself is self-defeating and pointless labor.

To make an outline, begin with the thesis of your essay and divide it into smaller ideas. It is an axiom of division that nothing can be divided into fewer than two parts. From this, it follows that under every main idea that has been divided, at least two sub-ideas must appear. In other words, for every I there must be at least a II; for every A, at least a B. Consider this example:

Temperatures and Mountain Climbers

  Thesis: Extremes in temperatures can have dangerous effects on mountain climbers.
  I. The dangerous effects of excessive heat
    A. Heat exhaustion
    B. Heat stroke
  II. The dangerous effects of excessive cold
    A. Surface frostbite
    B. Bodily numbness

The logic of division will always produce an outline characterized by symmetry. A by-product of this symmetry is evenness in the treatment of all topics. Notice also that each entry is worded in more or less parallel language. This wording underscores the equal importance of the entries and emphasizes the major divisions in the outline.

Creating the Outline Outlining is systematic thinking about your thesis. You examine the essay as a reader might and try to decide what points you need to present, and in what order, to make the topic understandable. For example, let us suppose you were planning to write an essay on this thesis:

> **Thesis:** Listening is such an important and badly practiced communicative skill that schools should begin offering courses in how to do it better.

The first question a reader is likely to ask is, "Why is listening so important?" The answer should be the development of your first major point.

I. Listening is an important communicative skill.

What do you mean by "listening is badly practiced"? Common sense suggests that this is the second question likely to occur to an interested reader. The answer could be the development of your second major point.

II. Listening is a badly practiced communicative skill.

Fill out these two major headings with some secondary points that serve as answers, and you have completed the first part of your outline.

I. Listening is an important communicative skill.
   A. We spend most of our communicating time listening.
   B. We get most of our political information from radio and television.

II. Listening is a badly practiced communicative skill.
   A. We typically understand only one-half of what we hear.
   B. We typically recall only one-quarter of what we hear.

Following this line of thinking, we can deduce some other questions that common sense tells us are likely to occur to a reader: What do you mean by listening? Are all types of listening alike? Answers to these questions can provide us with two more headings:

III. Listening is an active communicative skill that is divisible into four components.
   A. Receiving entails decoding the message.
   B. Attending entails analyzing the message.
   C. Assigning meaning entails interpreting the message.
   D. Remembering entails information storage and retrieval.

IV. Listening is grouped into five major types.

    A. Appreciative listening involves acceptance.

    B. Discriminative listening involves selection.

    C. Comprehensive listening involves generalizing.

    D. Therapeutic listening involves relaxation.

    E. Critical listening involves judgment.

Think about the purpose of the assignment and the questions your thesis is likely to evoke in a reader and you will likewise discover the logical divisions of your essay.

Guidelines for Outlining You should observe the following guidelines in making your outline:

1. **Don't make the outline too long.** One page of an outline is the basis for five pages of developed writing. Your aim is to produce a model of the essay that you can inspect for flaws at a glance.
2. **Don't clutter the sentences of your outline.** Make your entries brief. The idea is to make the outline instantly readable.
3. **Use parallel wording for subordinate entries whenever possible.** Parallel entries are easier to read than nonparallel ones.
4. **Align the entries properly.** Do not allow the second line of an entry to go farther toward the left margin than the line above it.

If you observe these simple guidelines, the outline that results should be easy to read. You should be able to glance at its major entries and immediately spot any flaws in the structure of the essay.

Outlining by Topic/Outlining by Sentence Some outlines are topic outlines in which the entries are not complete sentences, but fragments that sum up the topic. Other outlines are sentence outlines in which the entries are complete sentences. Your decision on whether to use a topic or a sentence outline depends on how complete a breakdown you need. If your subject is simple and all you need are key words to serve as guideposts so that you will not get sidetracked, or if you merely wish to set down some major trends, categories, or stages, then you should use a topic outline. If your subject is a difficult one or in an area that is new to you, you should use a sentence outline. Consider the following topic outline:

The Future of Our Cities

    Thesis: An assessment of the future of our cities reveals two emerging trends.

    I. The megalopolis

      A. Definition

        1. Cluster

        2. System

    B. Two major organizational problems

        1. Transcendence

        2. Coordination

II. Shift in decision making

    A. Local decisions

        1. Facts not known

        2. Outside agencies

    B. Federal government

        1. Increase in power

        2. Local restrictions

This topic outline is of no value to a person who is not thoroughly familiar with the problems of city government. A student writing a paper based on such a cryptic outline is bound to have difficulty. Now consider the following sentence outline of the same subject:

The Future of Our Cities Thesis: An assessment of the future of our cities reveals two emerging trends.

    I. The megalopolis is replacing the city.

        A. Megalopolis can be defined in two ways.

            1. A megalopolis is a cluster of cities.

            2. A megalopolis is a system of interwoven urban and suburban areas.

        B. Two major organizational problems of the megalopolis will need to be solved.

            1. One problem is how to handle questions that transcend individual metropolitan areas.

            2. Another problem is how to coordinate the numerous activities in the megalopolis.

    II. Decision making is shifting from local control to higher echelons of public and private authority.

        A. The growing scale of the urban world often makes local decisions irrelevant.

            1. Local agencies may not know all of the facts.

            2. National policies may supersede local decisions.

        B. The federal government moves into the picture.

            1. The extent of federal involvement increases as the city grows.

                a. Federal long-range improvement plans are used.

                b. Grant-in-aid programs become necessary.

            2. Federal assistance imposes restrictions.

                a. Federal policies make sure that no discrimination takes place in the areas of housing, employment, and education.

                b. Federal representatives check on local installations to make sure they are up to federal standards.

A good sentence outline supplies all of the basic information you need to write your paper. Without an outline, you run the risk of treating major ideas like details and details like major ideas; furthermore, you may find yourself moving forward, then backtracking, and then moving forward again, resulting in an incoherent paper. Because a careful outline takes into account the relationships among ideas and their degrees of importance, it keeps a novice from producing muddled writing.

We do not wish to mislead you into thinking that every essay you write will be just as easily and neatly outlined as our examples may suggest. In fact, you will most likely find it necessary to revise the outline heavily. You might even end up with three or four scratched-up versions before you are satisfied with the result. As you outline, new ideas will occur to you and clamor to be fitted in somewhere. Old headings will strike you as too obvious to be included. Whether you make a formal outline or simply draw up a sketch of your essay, you are still likely to revise heavily before you are happy with your plan.

EXERCISES

1. Write a paragraph outline for one of the following theses:
   a. Inflation has a deteriorating effect on the purchasing power of the dollar.
   b. The essay exam has several advantages over the objective test.
   c. The first three months of an infant's life are crucial to the development of his or her personality.
2. Create a flowchart for one of the following theses:
   a. Society often uses language to favor one sex over the other.
   b. Economic inflation has political consequences.
   c. Teachers deserve higher salaries.
   d. English should be made the official language of the United States.
3. List the supporting materials you might use for an essay on one of the following topics:
   a. Why people often don't help in a crisis.
   b. Multiple-choice versus essay exams as tools of education.
   c. Comic strips that have social value.
   d. Why modern products are often shoddy.
4. Identify the key words in the following theses, specifying two or three subtopics into which they may be divided:
   a. Strong diplomatic ties with China would have several advantages for the United States.
   b. An electrical blackout in any major city of the United States would have disastrous results.
   c. The words *disinterested, inflammable,* and *fortuitous* are often misunderstood.

5. Delete the entry that destroys the logical order in the following outlines:

   a. *Thesis: Because of their cultural traits, the Dobuans are different from other primitive tribes.*

     I. The location and environment of Dobuan Island make it difficult for the Dobuans to find sufficient food.

     II. The rituals of marriage set the Dobuans apart from other primitive tribes.

     III. The Dobuans' reliance on magic makes them more superstitious than other primitive tribes.

     IV. The fact that the Dobuans value treachery and ill will sets them apart from other primitive tribes.

   b. *Thesis: The purpose of the California missions was to Christianize the Indians and to strengthen Spain's claim to California.*

     I. The mission padres taught the Indians Christian virtues.

     II. The padres were concerned with saving the souls of the Indians.

     III. The missions were constructed in the form of small cities.

     IV. Without its colonists in California, Spain's claim to this territory was weak.

     V. Spain was competing with Russia and England for territory in California.

   c. *Thesis: American political assassins have acted on nonpolitical impulses.*

     I. They are pathetic loners.

     II. Their reality is a fantasy world.

     III. The victim is usually a surrogate parent image.

     IV. The assassin is seeking the same "fame" that the victim has.

     V. European assassinations, unlike ours, have been the result of elaborate plots.

6. Scrutinize the following outline for errors of form as well as content. Correct the errors by producing two improved versions—a sentence outline and a topic outline.

   a. *Thesis: The adult Moses is one of the most commanding and inspirational figures of the Old Testament.*

     I. Moses as a God-intoxicated man.

       A. Moses's faith in God.

       B. He created in the Hebrews a religious faith that was to endure after their life as a nation had died.

         1. The Babylonian and Persian conquests.

         2. The faith endured during the Greek conquest.

         3. The faith endured during the Roman conquest.

         4. Despite their faith, the Hebrews often worshiped foreign gods.

         5. The faith endured during the various diasporas.

     II. Moses was a peerless travel guide.

       A. During the long sojourn in the wilderness, Moses showed endless patience.

         1. Enduring constant grumbling on the part of the tribes.

         2. This period of desert wandering symbolizes the age of innocence of any developing nation.

         3. He settled quarrels with great patience.

    B. His earlier flight in order to escape punishment for having killed an Egyptian made him fully acquainted with the Sinai desert.

       1. He knew where to find water.

       2. He knew how to avoid dangerous enemy territory.

       3. He always followed a magical cloud by day and a pillar of fire by night.

III. Moses was the founder of a complex legal system.

    A. He gave the Hebrews the Torah.

       1. Parts of the Torah dealt with man's relationship to God.

       2. Parts of the Torah dealt with man's relationship to man.

    B. He gave the Hebrews the ordinances.

       1. Some of the ordinances dealt with matters of social justice.

       2. According to one ordinance, a man who knocks out his slave's tooth must let that slave go free.

       3. Others of the ordinances dealt with religious ceremonies.

       4. Some of the ordinances dealt with plans for building a temple.

▌ Advice

Write to Be Understood

JIM STAYLOR

Rhetorical Thumbnail

Purpose: to teach the art of plain writing

Audience: anyone who must write as part of a job

Language: mainly standard English but also gives examples of stuffy writing

Strategy: teaches the rules of clear writing by citing examples tinged with humorous exaggeration

Jim Staylor (b. 1958), a media producer, is a graduate of San Diego State University and California State University at Fullerton. Named a "Top-100 Producer" by *AV, Video, Multimedia* magazine in 2000, Staylor is president of a media production company that serves high-tech, health care, hospitality, defense, restaurant, and retail industries. He is in great demand as a motivational speaker.

Without wasting words or concepts, this essay draws the connection between clarity and organization in writing. Follow its simple rules, and your writing will connect with your reader.

• • •

1　Use clear, direct and simple text to be easily understood. In other words, as a **proponent** of **perspicuity** one should really **espouse eschewing obfuscation** in **typographical emanations**.

2　Good writing (in contrast to the sentence above) is clear, **concise**, **congruent** and compelling. Layout and text design may help organize content and guide the reader to what is important, but ultimately, words and their usage often determine the success or failure of your communications. Six guidelines for clarifying text can help you become more perspicuous in your writing.

Perspicuity is the Goal

3　Perspicuity means being clear of statement or expression; easily understood; or lucid.

4　Titles, headlines, sub-headings, captions and body copy all contain text with the power to confuse or clarify.

5　Find more information about writing well by consulting a few reputable style guides in print or on the Internet.

Clarifying Text

6　According to Hartley (1996)[*], a writer can generally do six things to make text easier to understand.

1. Follow Simple Sentence Structure

7　Sentences with many subordinate clauses and modifying statements are more difficult to understand. Practice the KISS formula; Keep It Simple and Straightforward.

8　Use the fewest possible words to say what you mean.

9　Never say "blah, blah" when all you need is "blah."

2. Use Active vs. Passive Voice

10　The active voice is usually more direct and vigorous than the passive voice. Writing in the active voice results in shorter, stronger sentences. The subject doing the action often holds more interest than the object being acted upon. "The hat which is owned by me was thrown on the roof by Peter who is my brother" is better as "My brother Peter threw my hat on the roof." This has half the words and perhaps twice the impact.

3. Choose Positive Terms

11　Using positive terms makes it easier for readers to grasp concepts and paint mental pictures. Readers would rather know about what is than what is not. Therefore it is generally better to express even negatives in positive form.

Not honest	Dishonest
Not important	Trifling
Did not remember	Forgot
Did not pay attention to	Ignored
Did not have much confidence in	Distrusted

*Hartley, J. (1996) "Text Design." In D.H. Jonassen (ed.) *Handbook of research for educational communication and technology.*

4. Avoid Multiple Negatives

12 Double or triple negatives are often confusing. An example by Harold Evans (1972) compares, "The figures provide no indication that costs would have not been lower if competition had not been restricted," with, "The figures provide no indication that competition would have produced higher costs."

5. Personalize Copy

13 **Personalizing** text or writing in the form of a story helps students recall information. Describing benefits of a medical procedure, for example, comes to life when told from the point of view of a patient receiving treatment as opposed to a clinical step-by-step explanation of the process. "My name is Susie and I'd like to tell you how I discovered I was sick and what my Doctor Steve did about it."

6. Make It Interesting

14 Lively examples and vivid **anecdotes** also help make text interesting and memorable. Be careful to avoid making the details so **seductive** they distract from the main point.

15 These six basic guidelines offer a good start toward good writing. Good Luck.

16 *It's your right to be understood, so write to be understood.*

Jim Staylor, "Write to be Understood," located at http://edweb.sdsu.edu/eet/articles/ writeclearly. Reprinted by permission of San Diego State University and Jim Staylor, http://www .staylor-made.com.

● THE FACTS

1. What kind of writing does the author want his readers to produce? What three adjectives does he use as guiding principles of good writing?

2. According to the author, what is more important than layout and text design? Why?

3. How many rules should be followed to produce easily understood text? To whom does the author give credit for these rules? (See the asterisk at the end of the essay.)

4. What does "KISS" stand for? What will it prevent?

5. Which rules mentioned deal with the avoidance of roundabout writing? Why are these rules important?

● THE STRATEGIES

1. How does the layout or text of this essay help the reader to follow the author's ideas? Do you consider this attempt successful? Explain your answer.

2. How does the author capture the reader's attention at the start of the essay? Do you consider this a helpful strategy? Why or why not?

3. In paragraph 6, what does the reference to Hartley add to the paper? Could it have been left out in order to save space?

4. In numbering the rules of good writing, how is the author keeping his own counsel? Be specific in your answer.

5. What is the author's thesis? State it in one simple sentence. Which, if any of the strategies used in the essay, helped you most to understand the thesis?

● THE ISSUES

1. Do you agree with the author that good writing is "clear, concise, congruent, and compelling"? Have you ever read a book or magazine in which the writing was good and also could not be labeled "clear or concise"? Provide an example from your own reading. Where do you find writing that best fits the author's description of good writing? What is your reaction when you read this style of writing?

2. When, if ever, might you be justified in using the passive rather than active voice in a sentence? Give an example.

3. The author encourages writers to use lively examples and vivid anecdotes to enhance their writing. Why do you think examples and anecdotes are useful writing tools? Cite an instance of you or someone else using an example or an anecdote in writing.

4. What does the author mean when he tells writers never to use "blah, blah" when "blah" will do? What point is he stressing?

5. What strikes you about the italicized remark at the end of Staylor's essay? What is its purpose? Do you consider it a strong ending? Explain your answer.

● SUGGESTIONS FOR WRITING

1. This essay stresses plain writing as one of the keys to being understood. Write a brief essay in which you analyze what happens when a reader confronts unnecessarily complicated sentences or gobbledygook.

2. Choosing one of the following topics, write an essay in which you use a vivid anecdote to liven up your writing:
   a. A job interview that didn't go well.
   b. A date that turned out to be disastrous.
   c. A telephone conversation that made me furious.
   d. What my best friend brings to my life.

▮ Examples

Rules for Aging

ROGER ROSENBLATT

Rhetorical Thumbnail

Purpose: to amuse or entertain

Audience: general educated reader

Language: standard English

Strategy: assumes the voice of a wise counselor giving advice on aging

Roger Rosenblatt (b. 1940) is one of *Time's* most respected editorial writers. His insights into politics and society, as well as his wonderful sense of humor, have delighted his readers for close to two decades. Rosenblatt graduated from Harvard, where he earned a Ph.D. and briefly taught English. He has been featured on television reading his eloquent *Time* essays.

• • •

1   Since older people are as close to perfection as human beings get, I thought it would be generous, from time to time, to use this space to offer guidelines for living to those less old to help them age successfully, or at all. The art of aging requires not doing things more than taking positive action, so this is essentially a list of "nots" and "don'ts."

2   **1.** *It doesn't matter.* Whatever you think matters, doesn't. This guideline is absolutely reliable and **adhering** to it will add decades to your life. It does not matter if you are late for anything; if you're having a bad hair day, or a no-hair day; if your car won't start; if your boss looks at you cockeyed; if your girlfriend or boyfriend looks at you cockeyed; if you are cockeyed; if you don't get the promotion; if you do; if you have spinach in your teeth or if you lose your teeth in your spinach. It doesn't matter.

3   **2.** *Nobody is thinking about you.* Yes, I know. You are certain that your friends are becoming your enemies; that your enemies are acquiring nuclear weapons; that your grocer, garbage man, clergyman, sister-in-law, and dog are all of the opinion that you have put on weight; furthermore, that everyone spends two-thirds of every day commenting on your **disintegration**, **denigrating** your work, plotting your murder. I promise you: Nobody is thinking about you. They are thinking about themselves, just like you.

4   **3.** *Do not go to your left.* Going to one's left, or working on going to one's left, is a basketball term for strengthening one's weakness. A right-handed player will improve his game considerably if he learns to dribble and shoot with his left hand, and to move to his left on the court. But this is true only for basketball, not for living. In life, if you attempt to strengthen a weakness, you will grow weaker. If, on the other hand (the right), you keep playing to your strength, people will not notice that you have weaknesses. Of course, you do not believe me. You will go ahead and take singing lessons or write that novel anyway. Trust me.

5   **4.** *Give honest, frank, and open criticism to nobody, never.* The following situation will present itself to you over and over: There is a friend, a relative, an employee, an employer, a colleague, whose behavior flaws are so evident to everyone but themselves, you just know that a straightforward, no-punches-pulled conversation with them will show them the error of their ways. They will see the light at once, and forever be grateful that only as good and candid a person as you would have sufficient kindness and courage to confront them.

6   Better still: From the moment you inform them about their bad table manners, their poor choices in clothing, their hygiene, their loudness, their deafness, their **paranoia**, they will reform on the spot. Their lives will be redeemed, and they will owe their renewed selves and all future happiness to you—honest, frank, and open you.

7   I implore you: forget about it. When the **muse** of **candor** whispers in your ear, swat it, take a long walk, a cold shower, and clear your head. This guideline relates to guideline number two. Nobody is thinking about you, unless you tell them about their faults. Then you can be sure they are thinking of you. They are thinking of killing you.

8   That's enough wisdom for now. I know younger people will not heed my advice anyway. So the guideline I offer them is: Don't. Go ahead and stay awake worrying what people are thinking about you, work on your weaknesses, and criticize your friends. It doesn't matter.

Excerpt from RULES FOR AGING, copyright © 2000 by Roger Rosenblatt, reprinted by permission of Houghton Mifflin Harcourt Publishing Company.

● THE FACTS

1. How many rules for aging does Rosenblatt offer? What form do these rules follow?
2. The first rule is pronounced with great authority—"It doesn't matter." What is the author telling us with this rule?
3. In what way is rule #2 related to rule #1?
4. What does the author mean by the image of "going to your left"?
5. What is the implication behind rule #4?

● THE STRATEGIES

1. How would you describe the tone of this essay? How does the tone affect the purpose of the essay? Does the essay have a thesis? If so, where is it stated?
2. What is your reaction to the opening sentence of the essay? How did it strike you? Consider such matters as the author's voice, his tone, and his purpose.
3. What is the effect of the "Yes, I know" sentence at the beginning of paragraph 3?
4. Where does the author use parallelism to achieve balance and euphony? Point to specific passages in the essay.
5. Why does the author refer to "the muse of candor" in paragraph 7?

● THE ISSUES

1. What is your personal understanding of the author's statement, "It doesn't matter"? Elaborate on his meaning.
2. Assuming that most human beings are concerned with their own problems more than those of other people, why do they often persist in feeling that their neighbors are plotting against them or making disparaging remarks behind their backs?
3. From the following list of widely admired 20th-century persons, choose one whose contributions you can organize into an essay with a clear thesis. Synthesize any outside sources as taught in Chapter 3.

Mother Teresa	Helen Keller	Mohandas Gandhi
Martin Luther King, Jr.	Albert Einstein	Nelson Mandela

4. Which of Rosenblatt's rules do you think is the most difficult to follow? Why?

5. In giving us rule #3, do you think the author is discouraging forays into new and exciting territories? Might he be keeping older people from trying new hobbies or taking on new responsibilities that might enrich the final years of their lives? Explain your answer.

● SUGGESTIONS FOR WRITING

1. Write an essay in which you propose your own rules for aging. You can be humorous like Rosenblatt or dead serious, but use a clear method of organization.

2. Choose one of the following comments and turn it into your thesis for a brief essay. Use a clear pattern of organization.

   a. Don't let the opinions of others control your life.

   b. Decide how you will react to unsolicited advice.

That Time of Year (Sonnet 73)

WILLIAM SHAKESPEARE

William Shakespeare (1564–1616) is generally acknowledged as the greatest literary genius of the English language. Born in Stratford-upon-Avon, England, he was the son of a prosperous businessman, and probably attended grammar schools in his native town. In 1582, Shakespeare married Anne Hathaway, who was eight years his senior, and who bore him three children. The legacy of his writing includes 36 plays, 154 sonnets, and 5 long poems.

The English or Shakespearean sonnet is composed of three quatrains of four lines each and a concluding couplet of two lines, rhyming abab cdcd efef gg. There is usually a correspondence between the units marked off by the rhymes and the development of the thought. The three quatrains, for instance, may represent three different images or three questions from which a conclusion is drawn in the final couplet. As a result, the sonnet is one of the most tightly organized poetic forms used.

● ● ●

That time of year thou mayst in me behold
When yellow leaves, or none, or few, do hang
Upon those boughs which shake against the cold,
Bare ruined choirs where late the sweet birds sang.
5   In me thou see'st the twilight of such day
As after sunset fadeth in the west,
Which by and by black night doth take away,

Death's second self, that seals up all in rest.
In me thou see'st the glowing of such fire,

10   That on the ashes of his youth doth lie
As the deathbed whereon it must expire,
Consumed with that which it was nourished by.
This thou perceivest, which makes thy love more strong,
To love that well which thou must leave ere long.

THE FACTS

1. What image does the poet focus on in the first quatrain? What relationship does this image have to the speaker?

2. The speaker shifts to another image in the second quatrain. What is it, and what relationship does it bear to him?

3. Yet another image is introduced in the third quatrain. What is the image, and how does it relate to the speaker? What rather complex philosophical paradox is involved?

4. The final couplet states the poet's thesis (or theme). What is that thesis? State it in your own words.

THE STRATEGIES

1. The entire poem is organized around three analogies. State them in three succinct sentences.

2. The three images in the poem are presented in a particular order. Do you see any reason for this order?

3. In lines 3 and 4, what effect do the words "cold,/Bare ruined choirs" have on the rhythm and meter?

4. In line 2, what would be the result of substituting "hang" for "do hang"?

5. What is the antecedent of "this" in line 13?

THE ISSUES

1. What can you deduce from this poem about the speaker and his frame of mind?

2. Someone once said, "Youth is wasted on the young." How might that witticism be applied to this poem?

3. Why should a student whose major is, say, business and who has no interest whatsoever in literature be forced to take classes in which poems such as this one are studied?

4. Shakespeare has been called surprisingly modern in his outlook. What about this poem would seem to justify that observation?

● SUGGESTIONS FOR WRITING

1. In two or three well-developed paragraphs, challenge or defend the claim that too much money is spent on extending the lives of old people.

2. Write an essay about a memorable older person.

▦ Chapter Writing Assignments

1. Write a well-organized essay in which you describe your conflicting attitudes about some aspect of society that puzzles you or to which you have no clear answer.

2. Write a well-organized chronological autobiography.

3. Write an essay detailing the steps you follow when you have to complete a writing assignment.

4. Detail in a tightly organized essay any particular procedure or process (e.g., how to send digital photographs via email) with which you are intimately familiar.

▦ Writing Assignments for a Specific Audience

1. Write an essay of appreciation directed at your favorite teacher—from any grade—telling how he or she affected your life.

2. Write an essay, after doing the necessary research, telling an audience of high-school dropouts the opportunities available to them for continuing their education.

▉ Real-Life Student Writing

Note from a Graduate Student to a Department Secretary

The following note was written by a student named Jennifer, who is in the graduate school program of a well-known Catholic university. Katie is the department secretary of the business school. Jennifer is writing to Katie to ask for her help in getting registered in a statistics class. Notice the polite social remarks Jennifer makes before saying what she really wants. Jeff is Katie's new husband. Bailey is Jennifer's boyfriend.

● ● ●

Hi Katie!

Welcome back from your honeymoon! Hope married life is treating you well. Bailey said he ran into ya'll last night, and Jeff's wig was realistically scary. Wish I could have seen it.

Lucinda sent me to you on an issue I'm having. I keep trying to register for classes in the business school for next quarter, but the system won't let me in! Lucinda said something about how they've changed their criteria. I wonder if I could be using the wrong password. I heard it was due to be changed, but I haven't seen any memo telling us that it had been. Meantime, I need to register for business statistics ASAP! As department secretary, you're my last hope.

Can you help me?

Thanks!
Jennifer

Stumped by the passive voice? Exit on pages 428–429 at the Editing Booth!

CHAPTER 7

Developing Good Paragraphs

Road Map to Paragraphs

From ancient times, the primary use of the paragraph has been to signal the introduction of a new idea or the further development of an old one. Here is an example of a paragraph signaling a new idea:

> In the modern formal bullfight or "corrida de toros" there are usually six bulls that are killed by three different men. Each man kills two bulls. The bulls by law are required to be from four to five years old, free from physical defects, and well armed with sharp-pointed horns. They are inspected by a municipal veterinary surgeon before the fight. The veterinary is supposed to reject bulls that are under age, insufficiently armed or with anything wrong with their eyes, their horns or any apparent disease or visible bodily defects such as lameness.
>
> The men who are to kill them are called matadors and which of the six bulls they are to kill is determined by lot. Each matador, or killer, has a caudrilla, or team, of from five to six men who are paid by him and work under his orders. Three of these men, who aid him on foot with capes and at his orders place the banderillas, three-foot wooden sharps with harpoon points, are called peones or banderilleros. The other two, who are mounted on horses when they appear in the ring, are called picadors.
>
> —Ernest Hemingway, *The Bullfight*

The shift in discussion between the first and second paragraph is obvious: Paragraph 1 is about the bulls; paragraph 2 is about the men who will fight and kill them.

A second use of the paragraph is to add significantly to or elaborate on what has been said in a preceding paragraph. Here is an example:

> The oxen in Africa have carried the heavy load of the advance of European civilization. Wherever new land has been broken they have broken it, panting and pulling knee-deep in the soil before the ploughs, the long whips in the air over them. Where a road has been made they have made it; and they have trudged the

iron and tools through the land, to the yelling and shouting of the drivers, by tracks in the dust and the long grass of the plains, before there ever were any roads. They have been inspanned before daybreak, and have sweated up and down the long hills, and across dungas and riverbeds, through the burning hours of the day. The whips have marked their sides, and you will often see oxen that have had an eye, or both of them, taken away by the long cutting whip-lashes. The waggon-oxen of many Indian and white contractors worked every day, all their lives through, and did not know of the Sabbath.

It is a strange thing that we have done to the oxen. The bull is in a constant stage of fury, rolling his eyes, shovelling up the earth, upset by everything that gets within his range of vision—still he has got a life of his own, fire comes from his nostrils, and new life from his loins; his days are filled with his vital cravings and satisfactions. All of that we have taken away from the oxen, and in reward we have claimed their existence for ourselves. The oxen walk along within our own daily life, pulling hard all the time, creatures without a life, things made for our use. They have moist, limpid, violet eyes, soft muzzles, silky ears, they are patient and dull in all their ways; sometimes they look as if they were thinking about things.

—Isak Dinesen, *Out of Africa*

In the first paragraph the author points out that oxen have played a key role in civilizing the African continent. In the second paragraph she elaborates on the first by reminding us that the oxen's patient subservience has come at a price.

Parts of the Paragraph

A paragraph generally consists of two main parts: a topic sentence and specific details that support it.

The Topic Sentence This is the sentence that tells us what the writer intends to propose, argue, or demonstrate. In the following paragraph, the topic sentence is highlighted.

To all English-speaking peoples the Bible is a national as well as a noble monument, for much of their history is securely rooted and anchored within it. In 17th century England it nurtured the Puritan revolt and paved the way for the Bill of Rights. In 17th and 18th century America it supplied not only the names of our ancestors but the stout precepts by which they lived. They walked by its guidance; their rough places were made plain by their trust in its compassionate promises. It was a lamp to their feet and a light to their path, a pillar of cloud by day and of fire by night. It was the source of the convictions that shaped the building of this country, of the faith that endured the first New England winters and later opened up the Great West. It laid the foundations of our educational system, built our earliest colleges, and dictated the training within our homes. In the words alike of Jefferson and Patrick Henry, John Quincy Adams and Franklin it made better and more useful citizens to their country by reminding a man of his individual responsibility, his own dignity, and his equality with his fellow man. The Bible is, indeed, so imbedded in our American heritage that not to recognize its place there becomes a kind of national apostasy, and not to know and understand it, in these days when we give all for its principles of human worth and human freedom, an act unworthy of us as a people.

—Mary Ellen Chase, *The Bible and the Common Reader*

Implied Topic Sentences Some paragraphs have an implied topic sentence, also known as a controlling idea. Here is an example:

At graveside, the casket is lowered into the earth. This office, once the prerogative of friends of the deceased, is now performed by a patented mechanical lowering device. A "Lifetime Green" artificial grass mat is at the ready to conceal the sere earth, and overhead, to conceal the sky, is a portable Steril Chapel Tent ("resists the intense heat and humidity of summer and the terrific storms of winter . . . available in Silver Grey, Rose or Evergreen"). Now is the time for the ritual scattering of earth over the coffin, as the solemn words "earth to earth, ashes to ashes, dust to dust" are pronounced by the officiating cleric. This can be accomplished "with a mere flick of the wrist with the Gordon Leak-proof Earth Dispenser. No grasping of a handful of dirt, no soiled fingers. Simple, dignified, beautiful, reverent! The modern way!" The Gordon Earth Dispenser (at $5) is of nickel-plated brass construction. It is not only "attractive to the eye and long wearing"; it is also "one of the 'tools' for building better public relations" if presented as "an appropriate noncommercial gift" to the clergyman. It is shaped something like a saltshaker.

—Jessica Mitford, *The American Way of Death*

The controlling idea of this paragraph is that the funeral industry is guilty of vulgar commercialism. The details amply support that point, and the writer's focus is clear even though she uses no topic sentence. A writer does not have to telegraph a paragraph's meaning in an explicit topic sentence so long as all its details are linked by some organizing theme or focus.

Supporting Details

Good paragraphs are filled with supporting facts, instances, examples, and details. They make a point and then adequately support it. They do not circle the subject, nor do they repeat at the same level of generality what the writer has already said. Here are two examples. In both examples, the topic sentence is highlighted. We made up the first example as a dramatic illustration of the repetitive writing often found in bad paragraphs, where the main point is restated over and over at the same level of generality:

Rotten writing is scarcely a new problem. People have always had bad handwriting. Some old manuscripts are difficult to read because they are so badly written. Old letters are also indecipherable. Some writing from the past looks as if a drunken chicken had walked over it. Strain as much as you might, you just can't tell what the writer meant. Inscriptions of various kinds are just as impossible to read.

Has the point of this paragraph—that "rotten writing is scarcely a new problem"—been proved? It has not. The paragraph simply says that people have always written badly but gives no concrete instances or facts to make this assertion believable.

Here, on the other hand, is a paragraph that begins with the same generalization and then proves it with facts and examples drawn from the past:

> Bad handwriting is scarcely a new problem. The original draft of the Declaration of Independence was scribbled over so much that at first glance it is difficult to see its renowned "elegance." Horace Greeley, the venerated 19th-century editor of the *New York Tribune,* had such a terrible handwriting that a note to a reporter, telling him he was fired for gross incompetence, was so indecipherable that for years to come this reporter used it as a letter of recommendation. Robert Frost, one of New England's most celebrated poets, had such bad penmanship, that occasionally it made him seem dyslexic and senseless. It is said that the poet William Butler Yeats couldn't read his own handwriting because it was so illegible. Scholars have spent years trying accurately to transcribe the handwritten manuscripts of famous authors—from David Thoreau to Henry James. The mistakes that keep coming to life in printed page proofs speak of the difficult task involved in reproducing badly written sentences. Usually it takes several eyes to complete the task of transcribing the crabbed and cramped penmanship of important writers.
>
> —Jeffrey O. Sorensen

Paragraphs with a Final Summing-up Sentence Some paragraphs begin and end with a generalization. The first generalization is the topic sentence; the second is a summary. Here is an example:

> A language changes because things happen to people. If we could imagine the impossible—a society in which nothing happened—there would be no changes in language. But except possibly in a cemetery, things are constantly happening to people: they eat, drink, sleep, talk, make love, meet strangers, struggle against natural perils, and fight against one another. They slowly adapt their language to meet the changing conditions of their lives. Although the changes made in one generation may be small, those made in a dozen generations may enormously affect the language. The big and little phases of history, fashions, fads, inventions, the influence of a leader, a war or two, an invasion or two, travel to a foreign land, the demands of business intercourse—may alter a language so much that a Rip Van Winkle who slept two or three hundred years might have trouble making himself understood when he awoke. Even in a relatively quiet society, linguistic change proceeds inexorably.
>
> —J. N. Hook and E. G. Mathews, *Modern American Grammar and Usage*

Topic Sentence Developed over More Than One Paragraph

A single topic sentence can also be developed over the course of two or more paragraphs. This development usually occurs when the topic sentence is too broad or complex to be adequately covered in a single paragraph or when the presentation of supporting details in several paragraphs is more emphatic. In the following example, a topic sentence is developed over two paragraphs. The topic sentence is highlighted:

> There has always been something so fascinating about the mere fact of fatness that men of all nations and of many degrees of wisdom or lack of it have formulated opinions on its state, its origins, and its correction. Shakespeare's characters are at their most eloquent when the topic is obesity. "Make less thy body and hence more thy grace. Leave gormandizing. Know the grave cloth gape for thee thrice wider than for other men." And, of course, to Julius Caesar, the Bard attributed the notion of the harmlessness of fat companions in warning against "the lean and hungry look" of "yon Cassius."
>
> In *Coming Up for Air*, George Orwell has the narrator, himself a fat man, sum it up: "They all think a fat man isn't quite like other men. He goes through life on a light-comedy plane . . . as low farce." Sometimes the situation is just as sad and much less tolerable. When W. D. Howells was consul at Venice, he was told by a tall, lanky man, "If I were as fat as you, I would hang myself." And Osborn in his otherwise lightly satirical picture-essay, *The Vulgarians,* pontificates, "The fat and the fatuous are interchangeable."
>
> —Jean Mayer, *Overweight: Causes, Cost, and Control*

Covering a topic sentence in more than one paragraph allows for a fuller development of the general idea, but it also tempts the writer to stray from the point. Beginning writers will find it safer to use a separate topic sentence for each paragraph.

Position of the Topic Sentence

As the sum of what a paragraph is about, the topic sentence should naturally occupy a prominent position, and in all of our examples so far, the topic sentence has come first. Such a paragraph is said to be organized from the general to the particular: the idea first, followed by the particulars. The reverse of this arrangement is the paragraph organized from the particular to the general: The supporting details come first and the topic sentence last. Here is an example:

> The human population already stands at over 4 billion, and at current growth rates that number will double within thirty-eight years. If the growth rate were to continue unchecked, in fact, the global population would reach about 150 billion within two centuries. Yet nearly two-thirds of the existing inhabitants of the earth are undernourished or malnourished, and they are dying of starvation at the rate of more than 10 million every year. There can be little question that unchecked population growth is the most critical social problem in the modern world, with potential consequences in terms of sheer human misery that are almost unimaginable.
>
> —Ian Robertson, *Sociology*

This arrangement is an uncommon one and somewhat mannered. Before you can cite details in support of an idea, you must first know the idea. Consequently, it has become traditional for writers to first state the general idea of a paragraph and then cite details in support of it—this pattern conforms to the way people usually think. The paragraph in which the topic sentence appears after the supporting details should be used only as a change of pace, not as a matter of course.

Finally, some paragraphs have topic sentences that come not first or last, but second or third. Paragraphs of this kind are usually found in the middle of an essay. The initial sentences are used to ensure a smooth transition from the preceding paragraph, and then the topic sentence makes its appearance. In the following example, the topic sentence is highlighted:

> In our own *way*, we conform as best we can to the rest of nature. The obituary pages tell us of the news that we are dying off, while the birth announcements in finer print, off at the side of the page, inform us of our replacements, but we get no grasp from this of the enormity of scale. There are 3 billion of us on the earth, and all 3 billion must be dead, on schedule, within this lifetime. The vast mortality, involving something over 50 million of us each year, takes place in relative secrecy. We can only really know of the deaths in our households, or among our friends. These, detached in our minds from the rest, we take to be unnatural events, anomalies, outrages. We speak of our own dead in low voices; struck down, we say, as though visible death can only occur for cause, by disease, or violence, avoidably. We send off flowers, grieve, make ceremonies, scatter bones, unaware of the rest of the 3 billion on the same schedule. All that immense mass of flesh and bone and consciousness will disappear by absorption into the earth, without recognition by the transient survivors.
>
> —Lewis Thomas, *Death in the Open*

The first sentence is for transition—to connect this paragraph with the one before. The second sentence is the topic sentence. It contains the assertion that the supporting details prove.

Paragraph Patterns

Paragraphs are often written to conform to certain abstract patterns that are partly rhetorical and partly based on some common operations of thinking. You might, for example, write a paragraph drawing a contrast between two animals, two objects, or two people. Or, you might write a paragraph explaining why an incident occurred or predicting what is likely to happen if something is done or left undone. In the first case, you would develop the paragraph by a pattern of comparison and contrast; in the second, by causal analysis.

In Part Two of this book, we shall focus on how to write paragraphs—even entire essays—by these patterns. We shall explain the paragraph-writing techniques used to compare and contrast, analyze cause, narrate, describe, illustrate, define, classify, and explain process. But for now, we mention these patterns to emphasize this point: No matter what its developmental pattern, any paragraph you write must support its main idea with specific details.

Characteristics of a Well-Designed Paragraph

The characteristics of the well-designed paragraph are unity, coherence, and completeness.

Unity   A paragraph is said to have unity when its sentences stick to the topic and do not stray to secondary issues or deal with irrelevancies. Here's an example of a paragraph that lacks unity:

> (1) A fairy tale is a serious story with a human hero and a happy ending. (2) The hero in a fairy tale is different from the hero in a tragedy in that his progression is from bad to good fortune, rather than the reverse. (3) In the Greek tragedy "Oedipus Rex," for example, the hero goes from highest fortune to lowest misery, but in the end he recognizes his error in judgment and maintains a noble posture despite profound suffering. (4) The audience watching him is purged of pity and fear through what Aristotle labeled a "catharsis." (5) The hero in a fairy tale usually has a miserable beginning. (6) He is either socially obscure or despised as being stupid and lacking in heroic virtues. (7) But in the end, he has surprised everyone by demonstrating his courage, consequently winning fame, riches, and love. (8) We clearly see this bad-to-good-fortune progress in stories like "Cinderella," "Sleeping Beauty," and "The Frog Prince."

The topic sentence of the paragraph promises to give a definition of a fairy tale, but part of the paragraph drifts away from the definition. Sentences 3 and 4 (highlighted) are entirely beside the point. With the fifth sentence, the writer resumes the announced intent of the paragraph—to define a fairy tale.

The possible causes of this fault are several. Some digressions can be traced to a writer's daydreaming; some to boredom with the topic on hand; some to a desire to impress the reader by introducing an interesting but irrelevant point. The cure is not easy to prescribe. The inexperienced writer needs to remember that the purpose of the paragraph is announced in the topic sentence, and it is this purpose that the other sentences of the paragraph must carry out.

Coherence   A paragraph has coherence when its sentences are logically connected. However, sentences are not automatically linked simply because they follow one after another on the page. Four devices can be used to ensure paragraph coherence:

1. Transitional words and phrases
2. Pronoun reference
3. Repeated key terms
4. Parallelism

Transitional words and phrases, which point out the direction of the paragraph, are used to link sentences. Here are examples, highlighted:

> In addition to the academic traditionalism in schools, there are other problems. First, there is the problem of coordinating education with the realities of

the world of work. Second, there is the question of how long the schooling period should be. Despite evidence to the contrary, a case can be made for the notion that we not only overeducate our children, but also take too long to do it.

The highlighted words and phrases add coherence to the passage. They join sentences and consequently ideas in clear and logical relationships. Without the use of transitional words and phrases, the writing would seem choppy and the relationships between sentences unclear.

Coherence can also be achieved by *pronoun reference*. A noun is used in one sentence or clause and a pronoun that refers to it is used in the next sentence or clause. In the following paragraph, the pronouns so used are highlighted:

> Twenty years ago, women were a majority of the population, but they were treated like a minority group. The prejudice against them was so deep-rooted that, paradoxically, most people pretended that it did not exist. Indeed, most women preferred to ignore the situation rather than to rock the boat. They accepted being paid less for doing the same work as men. They were as quick as any male to condemn a woman who ventured outside the limits of the roles men had assigned to females: those of toy and drudge.

Key terms may be repeated throughout the paragraph to link sentences. The key terms in the following paragraph are highlighted:

> Fantasy is not restricted to one sector of the southern California way of life; it is all-pervasive. Los Angeles restaurants and their parking lots are such million-dollar structures because they are palaces of fantasy in which the upward-moving individual comes to act out a self-mythology he or she has learned from a hero of the mass media. Often enough, the establishments of La Cienega Boulevard's Restaurant Row are fantasies of history in their very architecture.

Parallelism is also used to ensure coherence, although not nearly so often as any of the other three devices. The principle behind parallelism is that similar ideas are expressed in structurally similar sentences. Here is a paragraph that uses parallelism to ensure coherence:

> Now, I will not for a moment deny that getting ahead of your neighbor is delightful, but it is not the only delight of which human beings are capable. There are innumerable things which are not competitive. It is possible to enjoy food and drink without having to reflect that you have a better cook and a better wine merchant than your former friends whom you are learning to cold-shoulder. It is possible to be fond of your wife and children without reflecting how much better she dresses than Mrs. So-and-So and how much better they are at athletics than the children of that old stick-in-the-mud Mr. Such-and-Such. There are those who can enjoy music without thinking how cultured the other ladies in their women's club will be thinking them. There are even people who enjoy a fine day in spite of the

fact that the sun shines on everybody. All these simple pleasures are destroyed as soon as competitiveness gets the upper hand.

—Bertrand Russell, *The Unhappy American Way*

The repetition of "It is possible" and "There are" add bridges that smoothly connect one thought with another.

Completeness   A paragraph is complete when it has provided enough details to support its topic sentence. A paragraph is incomplete when the topic sentence is not developed or when it is merely extended through repetition. In either case, the reader is burdened with useless generalizations. The following paragraph is incomplete:

> Withholding tax is a bad way to go about collecting taxes from the people in our country because this system assumes that the American people are incompetent.

This paragraph hints at an argument but then comes to a dead stop. The reader will automatically ask, "In what way or by what means does tax withholding assume that the American people are incompetent?" Without further evidence, the paragraph goes nowhere. Now read the following paragraph:

> Withholding is a bad way to go about collecting tax money, even though the figures may show that it gets results. It is bad because it implies that the individual is incapable of handling his own affairs. The government as much as says, We know that, if left to your own devices, you will fritter away your worldly goods, and tax day will catch you without cash. Or it says, We're not sure you'll come clean in your return, so we will just take the money before it reaches you, and you will be saved the trouble and fuss of being honest. This implication is an unhealthy thing to spread around, being contrary to the old American theory that the individual is a very competent little guy indeed. The whole setup of our democratic government assumes that the citizen is bright, honest, and at least as fundamentally sound as a common stock. If you start treating him as something less than that, you are going to get into deep water. The device of withholding tax money, which is clearly confiscatory, since the individual is not allowed to see, taste, or touch a certain percentage of his wages, tacitly brands him as negligent or unthrifty or immature or incompetent or dishonest, or all of those things at once. There is, furthermore, a bad psychological effect in earning money that you never get your paws on. We believe this effect to be much stronger than the government realizes. At any rate, if the American individual is in truth incapable of paying his tax all by himself, then he should certainly be regarded as incapable of voting all by himself, and the Secretary of the Treasury should accompany him into the booth to show him where to put the X.

—E. B. White, "Withholding"

While the reader may not agree with these ideas, the writer has fulfilled his promise to show why he does not like withholding tax. He has provided clear examples and has moved from the general to the specific, keeping in mind the direction of his topic sentence. His paragraph is complete. Make your own paragraphs complete by providing enough detail to support their topic sentences.

It is an essential part of a writer's job to dig up the details necessary to make an essay complete. One source of such details, of course, is the library. Another is the Internet and its various electronic databases.

Writing Your Own Paragraphs

There is no mystery to writing good paragraphs. Begin with a topic sentence that states your opinion or proposes an idea. Back up this sentence with ample supporting details. Stick to the point of the topic sentence. Insert transitions as necessary to keep the text coherent. That, in a nutshell, is all there is to it.

The problems that arise with paragraph writing are usually problems of content rather than of technique. In other words, the writing is affected by the fact that the writer has not done the necessary research and does not understand the topic. Even gifted writers have difficulty writing on topics about which they know little. Writing does not begin when you first sit down in front of a keyboard. It actually begins when you begin to research your topic. If you are thoroughly grounded in the details of your topic, you'll find that writing paragraphs about it will be surprisingly easy.

● EXERCISES

1. Write a suitable topic sentence for a paragraph that would contain the following supporting details:

   a. (1) Cultivate only the best writers.

      (2) You needn't assume that just because something is in print, it is well-written.

      (3) If you fall into the habit of reading hacks or writers who have only a dulled sense for the right word, then you are not helping yourself to become a writer who is fresh and original.

      (4) Read those authors who appear in *The New Yorker,* who get good reviews in magazines like *Time,* and who haven't faded after writing one book or one play.

   b. (1) In primitive tribes, this concern was limited to members of the tribe. If a man was not a member, one need not worry about whether one was behaving ethically or unethically toward him.

      (2) But as man started reflecting on his own behavior and how it affected others, he slowly began to realize that his social concerns—his ethics—must include all human beings with whom he came in contact.

      (3) Thus, it can be said that a system of ethics evolved in order to ensure that man would be at peace with himself.

   c. (1) Vaccination for German measles has practically eradicated the incidence of birth defects and other complications resulting from that disease.

      (2) The smallpox vaccination has been so effective that the virus lingers only in special labs.

(3) In the last thirty years, vaccines have all but wiped out polio in our country.

(4) While a few people fear that some new and terrible disease will crop up for which no vaccine will be powerful enough, we can rejoice in the fact that at least the major child-killers of the past have been vanquished.

2. Provide four sentences of supporting details for each of the following topic sentences. (Make sure that the details are on a more specific level than the topic sentence.)

   a. Many people treat their pets with a lack of respect.

   b. Buying items "on sale" often means buying lower quality.

   c. The claim that owning a credit card today adds to a student's prestige and is therefore necessary is bogus, and let me tell you why.

   d. A long commute to work can have some advantages.

   e. Today's newspaper cartoons get to the heart of social concerns.

3. Choose one of the following topics and write a paragraph about it based on a controlling idea rather than on a topic sentence:

   a. Summer camp for disabled children

   b. Typical class reunions

   c. Advantages of coming from a poor family or disadvantages of coming from an affluent family

   d. Stereotyping as revealed in movies

   e. Stopping pollution on an individual level

4. Select one sentence from the following pairs that more clearly consists of supporting details:

   a. (1) Much has been written about the afflictions of growing old.

      (2) The worst aspect of growing old is losing hearing and eyesight.

   b. (1) The average outfit for snow skiing costs $1,000.

      (2) Some popular sports are so expensive that few people can afford to compete in them.

   c. (1) In *Little Red Riding Hood,* the wolf pounces on the innocent little girl, devouring her.

      (2) Children's fairytales are filled with horrible violence.

   d. (1) Some women feel more comfortable being treated by a female rather than a male gynecologist.

      (2) For many women who are modest to begin with, to be checked for such problems as uterine or breast cancer is less traumatic when the physician is also female.

   e. (1) Too many cooks today have no idea how to prepare homemade cornbread, meat casseroles from scratch, or freshly cooked garden peas.

      (2) The market of "prepared" or "frozen" foods is replacing food that really tastes good with food that is barely appealing to the gourmet's taste buds.

5. In the following paragraphs, draw a line through any sentence that weakens paragraph unity.

a. I agree with Thomas Jefferson that there is a natural aristocracy among human beings, based on virtue and talent. A natural aristocrat is a person who shows genuine concern for his fellow human beings and has the wisdom as well as ability to help them improve the quality of their lives. He is the kind of person to whom you would entrust your most important concerns because his decisions would be honest rather than self-serving. A natural aristocrat cannot be bought or manipulated. He will not promise what he cannot deliver. But when he makes a promise, he has virtue backed up by talent to fulfill it. Unfortunately, few political leaders today are natural aristocrats, because early in their ambitious careers they become beholden to those powers that helped them up the political ladder.

b. In medieval society, physical strength and animal cunning were the most admired characteristics of human beings, but since the invention of gunpowder, we have come to value other qualities more highly. Now that even a physically weak person can be made strong by carrying a gun, other ingenuities have become the marks of heroic people. Of course, boxing requires physical strength and animal cunning; yet many people today admire good boxers. The qualities most admired today are intellectual acumen, leadership ability, artistic talent, and social adjustment. I find it distressing that we do not prize goodness as much as we should. After all, Lincoln's outstanding feature was goodness. If a person is not good, he is not admirable. The tournament and personal combat have been replaced by the university, the political arena, the stage, and the personality inventory as testing grounds for heroes.

6. Identify the most obvious means used to establish coherence in the following paragraphs:

a. In general, relevancy is a facet of training rather than of education. What is taught at law school is the present law of the land, not the Napoleonic Code or even the archaic laws that have been scratched from the statute books. And at medical school, too, it is modern medical practice that is taught, that which is relevant to conditions today. And the plumber and the carpenter and the electrician and the mason learn only what is relevant to the practice of their respective trades in this day with the tools and materials that are presently available and that conform to the building code.

—Harry Kemelman, *Common Sense in Education*

b. The extent of personal privacy varies, but there are four degrees that can be identified. Sometimes the individual wants to be completely out of the sight and hearing of anyone else, in solitude; alone, he is in the most relaxed state of privacy. In a second situation the individual seeks the intimacy of his confidants—his family, friends, or trusted associates with whom he chooses to share his ideas and emotions. But there are still some things that he does not want to disclose, whether he is with intimates or in public. Either by personal explanation or by social convention, the individual may indicate that he does not wish certain aspects of himself discussed or noticed, at least at that particular moment. When his claim is respected by those around him, he achieves a third degree of privacy, the state of reserve. Finally, an individual sometimes goes out in public to seek privacy, for by joining groups of people who do not recognize him, he achieves anonymity, being seen but not known. Such relaxation on the street, in bars or movies or in the park constitutes still another dimension of the individual's quest for privacy.

—Alan F. Westin, *Privacy*

c. The motor car is, more than any other object, the expression of the nation's character and the nation's dream. In the free billowing fender, in the blinding chromium grills, in the fluid control, in the ever widening front seat, we see the flowering of the America that we know. It is of some interest to scholars and historians that the same autumn that saw the abandonment of the window crank and the adoption of the push button (removing the motorist's last necessity for physical exertion) saw also the registration of sixteen million young men of fighting age. It is of deep interest to me that in the same week Japan joined the Axis, De Soto moved its clutch pedal two inches to the left—and that the announcements caused equal flurries among the people.

—E. B. White, "The Motorcar"

7. Write a provocative introductory paragraph for an essay on one of the following topics:

a. Female soldiers fighting in combat

b. Rationing water or gasoline

c. Automatic capital punishment for terrorists who take hostages

d. Purging our language of all words with a sexist bias ("he" as a general pronoun—chairman, congressman, businessman, insurance man)

e. Job prospects for college seniors

f. One of today's most serious urban problems

8. Write a brief paragraph that would function as a smooth transition from one to the other of the following pairs of paragraphs:

a. (1) The first paragraph lists activities of a male executive that are the same as activities for which the homemaker is chided (long phone conversations, coffee klatches with colleagues, unnecessary fancy luncheons).

(2) The second paragraph indicates the differences between the two sets of activities.

b. (1) The first paragraph provides statistics to demonstrate that thousands of poor people in America live on pet food.

(2) The second paragraph argues that we must do something in order to solve the problem of hunger and malnutrition in America.

c. (1) The first paragraph makes the point that many foreign countries consider Americans wasteful, extravagant, and selfish in their insistence on driving big cars.

(2) The second paragraph holds the automobile industry responsible for shaping America's taste in cars.

▦ Advice

Writing Successful Paragraphs

A. M. TIBBETTS AND CHARLENE TIBBETTS

Rhetorical Thumbnail

Purpose: to teach paragraph writing

Audience: freshman composition students

Language: standard English

Strategy: uses examples to teach mastery of the paragraph

Arnold M. Tibbetts (b. 1927) has taught English at the University of Iowa, Western Illinois University, Vanderbilt University, and the University of Illinois, Urbana. His wife, Charlene Tibbetts (b. 1921), has also taught part-time at the University of Illinois, Urbana. The Tibbettses are coauthors of Strategies of Rhetoric (1969), from which this excerpt was taken.

The proverbial warning "Don't promise more than you can deliver" applies to writing as well as to everyday life. The basis of a good paragraph, say the authors, is a promise that is made in the topic sentence and then carried out in the specific details. In this excerpt, the authors demonstrate with examples how to make and keep your "paragraph promises."

• • •

1 A paragraph is a collection of sentences that helps you fulfill your thesis (theme promise). Itself a small "theme," a paragraph should be clearly written and specific; and it should not wander or make irrelevant remarks. Each paragraph should be related in some way to the theme promise. Here are suggestions for writing successful paragraphs:

1. Get to the Point of Your Paragraph Quickly and Specifically

2 Don't waste time or words in stating your paragraph promise. Consider this good example of getting to the point—the writer is explaining the ancient Romans' technique for conquering their world:

> The technique of expansion was simple. Divide et impera [divide and conquer]: enter into solemn treaty with a neighbouring country, **foment** internal disorder, intervene in support of the weaker side on the pretense that Roman honour was involved, replace the legitimate ruler with a puppet, giving him the status of a subject ally; later, goad him into rebellion, seize and sack the

country, burn down the **temples**, and carry off the captive gods to adorn a triumph. Conquered territories were placed under the control of a provincial governor-general, an ex-commander-in-chief who garrisoned it, levied taxes, set up courts of summary justice, and linked the new frontiers with the old by so called Roman roads—usually built by Greek engineers and native forced labour. Established social and religious practices were permitted so long as they did not threaten Roman administration or offend against the broad-minded Roman standards of good taste. The new province presently became a springboard for further aggression.

—Robert Graves, "It Was a Stable World"

3   Graves makes his promise in the first nine words, in which he mentions the "simple" technique the Romans had for "dividing" and "conquering" in order to expand their empire. Suppose Graves had started his paragraph with these words:

The technique of expansion was interesting. It was based upon a theory about human nature that the Romans practically invented. This theory had to do with how people reacted to certain political and military devices which . . .

4   Do you see what is wrong? Since the beginning sentences are so vague, the paragraph never gets going. The writer can't fulfill a promise because he hasn't made one. Another example of a poor paragraph beginning:

The first step involves part of the golf club head. The club head has removable parts, some of which are metal. You must consider these parts when deciding how to repair the club.

5   Specify the beginning of this paragraph and get to the point quicker:

Your first step in repairing the club head is to remove the metal plate held on by Phillips screws.

6   This solid, specific paragraph beginning gives your reader a clear promise which you can fulfill easily without wasting words. (Observe, by the way, that specifying a writer's stance—as we did in the last example—can help you write clearer paragraph beginnings.)

2. Fulfill Your Reader's Expectation Established by the Paragraph Promise

7 Do this with specific details and examples—explain as fully as you can:

The next thing is to devise a form for your essay. This, which ought to be obvious, is not. I learned it for the first time from an experienced newspaperman. When I was at college I earned extra pocket- and book-money by writing several weekly columns for a newspaper. They were usually **topical**, they were always carefully varied, they tried hard to be witty, and (an essential) they never missed a deadline. But once, when I brought in the product, a copy editor stopped me. He said, "Our readers seem to like your stuff all right; but we think it's a bit amateurish." With due humility I replied, "Well I am an amateur. What should I do with it?" He said, "Your pieces are not coherent; they are only sentences and epigrams strung together; they look like a heap of clothespins in a basket. Every article ought to have a shape. Like this" (and he drew a big letter S on his page) "or this" (he drew a descending line which turned abruptly upward again) "or this" (and he sketched a solid central core with five or six lines pushing outward from it) "or even this" (and he outlined two big arrows coming into collision). I never saw the man again, but I have never ceased to be grateful to him for his wisdom and for his kindness. Every essay must have a shape. You can ask a question in the first paragraph, discussing several different answers to it till you reach one you think is convincing. You can give a curious fact and offer an explanation of it: a man's character (as Hazlitt did with his fives champion), a building, a book, a striking adventure, a peculiar custom. There are many other shapes which essays can take; but the principle laid down by the copy editor was right. Before you start you must have a form in your mind; and it ought to be a form felt in paragraphs or sections, not in words or sentences—so that, if necessary, you could summarize each paragraph in a single line and put the entire essay on a postcard.

—Gilbert Highet, "How to Write an Essay"

8   Highet makes a promise in the first three sentences, and in the remaining sentences he specifically fulfills it.

3. Avoid Fragmentary Paragraphs

9   A fragmentary paragraph does not develop its topic or fulfill its promise. A series of fragmentary paragraphs jumps from idea to idea in a jerky and unconvincing fashion:

> My freshman rhetoric class is similar in some ways to my senior English class in high school, but it is also very different.
>
> In my English class we usually had daily homework assignments that were discussed during the class period. If we were studying grammar, the assignments were to correct grammatical errors in the text. If we were studying literature, we were supposed to read the material and understand its ideas.
>
> In rhetoric class, we do basically the same things, except that in the readings we are assigned, we look much deeper into the purpose of the author.
>
> In my English class . . .

10   Fragmentary paragraphs are often the result of a weak writer's stance.

4. Avoid Irrelevancies in Your Paragraphs

11   The italicized sentence does not fit the development of this paragraph:

> We need a better working atmosphere at Restik Tool Company. The workers must feel that they are a working team instead of just individuals. If the men felt they were part of a team, they would not misuse the special machine tools, which now need to be resharpened twice as often as they used to be. Management's attitude toward the union could be improved too. The team effort is also being damaged by introduction of new products before their bugs have been worked out. Just when the men are getting used to one routine, a new one is installed, and their carefully created team effort is seriously damaged.

12   As with the fragmentary paragraph, the problem of irrelevancies in a paragraph is often the result of a vague writer's stance. The preceding paragraph does not seem to be written for any particular reader.

Examples

Paragraph with the Topic Sentence at the Beginning
From the Lessons of the Past

EDITH HAMILTON

Edith Hamilton (1867–1963) was an American classicist, educator, and writer. Her writing career began after retirement, and at the age of eighty, she started giving public addresses and lectures. When she was ninety, she was made an honorary citizen of Greece. Among her books are *The Greek Way* (1942), *The Roman Way* (1932), and *Witness to the Truth: Christ and His Interpreters* (1948).

Basic to all the Greek achievement was freedom. The Athenians were the only free people in the world. In the great empires of antiquity—Egypt, Babylon, Assyria, Persia—splendid though they were, with riches beyond **reckoning** and immense power, freedom was unknown. The idea of it never dawned in any of them. It was born in Greece, a poor little country, but with it able to remain unconquered no matter what manpower and what wealth were **arrayed** against her. At **Marathon** and at **Salamis** overwhelming numbers of Persians had been defeated by small Greek forces. It had been proved that one free man was superior to many **submissively** obedient subjects of a **tyrant**. Athens was the leader in that amazing victory, and to the Athenians freedom was their dearest possession. **Demosthenes** said that they would not think it worth their while to live if they could not do so as free men, and years later a great teacher said, "Athenians, if you deprive them of their liberty, will die."

Excerpt from THE LESSONS OF THE PAST by Edith Hamilton.

● THE FACTS

1. Were you convinced of the truth of the topic sentence after reading the paragraph? If so, what convinced you?
2. In what way are free men superior to those who are submissively obedient to a tyrant?

● THE STRATEGIES

1. What is the topic sentence of the paragraph?
2. Who is the "great teacher" alluded to?

● THE ISSUES

1. Hamilton writes that freedom was basic to the Greek achievement. What does freedom mean to you in a political context?
2. According to Hamilton, it has "been proved that one free man [is] superior to many submissively obedient subjects." Why do you think this is so?

Paragraph with the Topic Sentence at the End
Man against Darkness

W. T. STACE

Walter Terrence Stace (1886–1967) was an English naturalist and philosopher known for his ability to translate complex theories into terms that appealed to a general reader. An authority on Hegel, Stace was the author of numerous books, among them *A Critical History of Greek Philosophy* (1920) and *The Philosophy of Hegel* (1924).

The picture of a meaningless world, and a meaningless human life, is, I think, the basic theme of much modern art and literature. Certainly it is the basic theme of modern philosophy. According to the most characteristic philosophies of the modern period from Hume in the eighteenth century to the so-called **positivists** of today, the world is just what it is, and that is the end of all inquiry. There is no reason for its being what it is. Everything might just as well have been quite different, and there would have been no reason for that either. When you have stated what things are, what things the world contains, there is nothing more which could be said, even by an **omniscient** being. To ask any question about why things are thus, or what purpose their being so serves, is to ask a senseless question, because they serve no purpose at all. For instance, there is for modern philosophy no such thing as the ancient problem of evil. For this once-famous question pre-supposes that pain and misery, though they seem so inexplicable and irrational to us, must ultimately **subserve** some rational purpose, must have their places in the cosmic plan. But this is nonsense. There is no such overruling rationality in the universe. Belief in the ultimate irrationality of everything is the quintessence of what is called the modern mind.

MAN AGAINST DARKNESS AND OTHER ESSAYS, by W. T. Stace, © 1967. Reprinted by permission of the University of Pittsburgh Press.

● THE FACTS

1. What is the basic theme of much modern art and literature?
2. How do the most characteristic philosophies of the modern era view the world?
3. Why is there no such thing in modern philosophy as the ancient problem of evil?

● THE STRATEGIES

1. Stace is known for expressing complex ideas with clarity. In this example, how does he make clear the complex views of modern philosophy?
2. From which point of view is this paragraph mainly written? How can you tell?
3. "Begging the question" is the logical name given to an argument that assumes as proven the very thing that is in dispute. Is the attitude of modern philosophy toward evil an example of begging the question? Why or why not?

● THE ISSUES

1. What is your opinion of modern philosophy, as Stace summarizes it, that ascribes everything to irrationality? How does this philosophy square with your own beliefs?
2. From your knowledge of various belief systems, what is the most common belief about the origin of evil?
3. What imaginable purpose can evil possibly serve? If evil did not exist, would it have to be invented? Supply evidence for your claim.

■ Chapter Writing Assignments

1. Select one of the following topics and develop it into a unified, coherent, and complete paragraph:

   a. Carelessness can do more harm than lack of knowledge.

   b. Today the prevailing mood of our economy is one of ___ (fill in the words you think apply).

   c. The Global Positioning System (GPS) Is one of the most useful modern inventions.

   d. Kissing is an odd, over-romanticized act.

   e. A female bus driver may face some challenges that a male driver will not.

   f. Buying a research paper from a commercial source is unethical.

2. List the particular details that you would use to write a convincing paragraph on the following topic sentences:

   a. Sarcastic people are unpleasant to be around.

   b. I like the security of dating the same person. Or: I like the freedom of dating different people.

   c. Many of today's popular rappers have unfairly received bad press and a bad name.

   d. Hiring experts in computer technology from India is good for the U.S. economy.

or

   Hiring experts in computer technology from India is bad for the U.S. economy.

   e. Common sense is ___ (define it).

■ Writing Assignments for a Specific Audience

1. Write an essay aimed at an audience of unemployed fishermen in Louisiana, arguing that the government should not have to bear the financial responsibility for accidental oil spills.

or

   Write an essay aimed at an audience of environmentalists, arguing for the importance of paying for oil spill cleanups in order to preserve the natural habitats of fish and fowl.

2. Write a blog in which you respond to the person who posted this blog: "Anyone who is stupid enough to invest in a Ponzi scheme like Bernie Madoff's deserves to lose every penny invested. I don't feel sorry for such a greedy idiot."

Real-Life Student Writing

Letter of Application to an Honors Program

Students who apply to gain entrance to colleges, honors programs, and graduate schools, or for scholarship grants, are usually required to submit a personal essay telling about their goals, motivation, special interests, and the like. The following essay was written as part of an application to a community college honors program. If the tone seems a tad formal and stiff, remember the student was under pressure to look perfect.

• • •

The Assignment In a brief essay, state your educational goals and why you want to be in the Honors Program.

Some day I want to be a labor lawyer like my father and his father before him. To achieve this goal will require dedication and focus. I realize that I will have to give up the more frivolous activities of fraternity life, such as beer busts, poker games, and hanging out. I have already tried to get into the habit of getting top grades not only to gain entrance to a good law school, but also because I would really like to know the details of important historical events, such as how Lincoln won the Civil War, what the Watergate Scandal was all about, and why labor unions have become so weak. I also want to read a few more Shakespeare plays and even learn to read and write in French. My short-term educational goal is to receive a B.A. in history with a minor in business administration. Two reasons drive me to join the Honors Program: First, in honors classes I shall be surrounded by students who are highly motivated and serious about their studies. Consequently, it seems to me that the classroom debates and discussions would be on a more challenging level than in regular classes. Second, I know that the top universities in the country give preference to honor students in their acceptance rankings. While some of my college friends think honors programs are elitist, I think they stimulate students to value learning and scholarship. Thank you for considering my application.

Phil Anderson

*Stumped by the passive voice? Exit on pages 428–429 at the **Editing Booth!***

Patterns of Development

Chances are good you have already heard of the rhetorical patterns or perhaps even practiced them in another class. Part Two of this book is devoted to teaching all eight rhetorical patterns, as well as argumentation.

Behind the rhetorical patterns in composition is this simple idea: To write about a subject, you must first have thought about it, and this systematic thinking can be translated into an idealized pattern for writing. For example, you might choose to tell a story about your subject (narration); to describe it (description); to say how it happened (process analysis); to give examples of it (illustration and exemplification); to define it (definition); to compare it to something else (comparison and contrast); to break it down into its constituent parts (division and classification); or to list its known causes or effects (causal analysis). Superimposing one of these eight abstract modes or patterns on your subject will make it easier to write about.

Each of these rhetorical patterns is a composite of specific writing and organizing techniques that can be isolated and taught. All narrations are alike, whether they tell a story about aliens from Mars or about facing up to a bully. All descriptions draw on common organizing and focusing techniques, no matter what they describe. If you are writing a comparison and contrast, for example, you know that you must alternate between the compared items and that you must insert suitable transitions so your reader can follow this movement. If you are defining, you know that there are specific techniques to be used in a definition. Knowing that a subject is to be approached a certain way also endows a writer's purpose with a refreshing narrowness, for what is especially bedeviling to the writer is not necessarily the complexity of a subject, but the infinity of possible approaches suggested by the blank sheet of paper.

The advice that instructors often give beginning writers is to "Narrow your subject." Writing by rhetorical patterns allows you to limit and narrow your approach to a subject. When you say, "I'm going to divide and classify this subject," you have an abstract pattern in mind that you can follow. When you say, "I'm going to analyze cause," you also have an abstract pattern to follow. In either case, you are not left dangling between "What shall I say?" and "How shall I say it?" You know how to say it in the abstract. What's left is the application of the ideal pattern to your particular subject.

Here is an example—the subject of "guilt" as developed in the eight most widely used rhetorical patterns. Notice how the writer's focus shifts with the use of each new pattern.

Patterns of Development for the Subject "Guilt"

1. Narration

I was seven years old when I first became aware of the terrible power of guilt. For piling our toys into the toy box, Mother had rewarded my brother and me with five shiny pennies each. If I had had ten pennies instead of just five, I could have bought a gingerbread man with raisin eyes and sugar-frosted hair. The image danced in my head all day, until, finally, I crept into my brother's room and stole his five pennies. The next morning, as my brother and I were dressing to go to school, I hid all ten pennies in the pocket of my coat, cramming one of my father's handkerchiefs on top of them. As my brother and I lined up in front of Mother to be kissed goodbye, she looked at my bulging pocket with amazement. "What on earth do you have in your pocket?" she asked. "It's nothing," I said as offhandedly as I could. "It's nothing at all." Bewildered, but too busy to investigate any further, Mother kissed me good-bye. I ran out the door and down our gravel path as fast as my feet could carry me. But the farther from home I got, the more miserable I became. The shiny pennies in my pocket felt oppressively like one-ton boulders. And I was haunted by the idea that I had become a thief. Forgotten was the gingerbread man, for whose sake I had stolen my brother's pennies. Finally, unable to bear my horrible feeling of guilt, I ran back home to blurt out my crime to my mother.

2. Description

Never before had Pedro experienced such a depth of despair and such a sense of isolation. He began to avoid those nearest to him, returning their friendly greetings with rough and indifferent replies. Often he sat in his room staring vacantly into space with hollow eyes. His hands were cold and clammy most of the time, yet his forehead burned hot with a mysterious fever. Terrible nightmares haunted his sleep, causing him to rise out of bed in the middle of the night, overcome with terror. When strangers at the store asked him a simple question such as "Where is the thread?" or "Have you any molasses?" he would read silent accusations in their eyes and his hands would tremble. He had become a man tormented by guilt.

3. Process Analysis

Do you know the most effective way to handle a friend turned a debtor? Make the person feel guilty. Let us say that you lent your friend Tom $500 to buy a motorcycle, but he refuses to repay the loan. Your first step is to place him in a category of bogus moral superiority. Say, "Tom, you have always been a person of honor. Why do you refuse to pay what you owe me?" If that doesn't work, your second step is to take the behavior personally, indicating that it is causing you emotional pain. Say, "I can't tell you how disappointed I am that you are treating me worse than a total stranger. You would pay back your bank, your credit cards, but you ignore me, your best friend, who needs the money." Unless your present debtor and former friend is a sociopath, he will feel bad about hurting you. Finally, you can threaten to cut off the relationship, making the threat look as if it were the debtor's doing. Say, "Look,

Tom, unless I get the money you owe me within a week, I will take your refusal to repay me as a sign that you don't care any more about our friendship." With that, you have really turned up the guilt barometer. Indeed, inducing guilt can be a powerful tool in the process of debt collection.

4. Illustration/Exemplification

Seneca once said, "Every guilty person is his own hangman." The truth of this observation can be illustrated by the lives of countless villains. One such is Macbeth, from Shakespeare's tragedy of the same name. At the instigation of his wife, Macbeth kills the king of Scotland and usurps his throne—an act of treachery for which Macbeth and his wife suffer torments of guilt. Lady Macbeth develops an obsession that her hands are stained with blood, and she wanders somnambulistically through the castle trying vainly to cleanse them. Before he murders the king, Macbeth hallucinates a dagger floating in the air. Later, after his assassins murder Banquo, Macbeth is tormented by hallucinations of Banquo's ghost. Eventually, Lady Macbeth commits suicide. Macbeth is killed during a rebellion of his noblemen, which is brought about—in the main—by the excesses to which his guilt has driven him.

5. Definition

Guilt is the remorse that comes from an awareness of having done something wrong. The origin of guilt is psychological. From childhood, we have all been conditioned by family and society to act within defined standards of reasonableness and decency. Gradually, over a period of years, these standards are internalized and modified to become the core of what is called "conscience." When we do something that violates these internalized standards, we feel guilty. If we have been brought up in a religious environment, we feel an added measure of guilt when we break what we think is a divine commandment. Whenever we don't play according to our internalized rules, we feel miserable, and this misery is what guilt is all about.

6. Comparison and Contrast

Although the two words may seem to share some connotations, *guilt* is not a synonym for *blame*. Guilt must be felt; blame must be assessed. *Guilt* implies self-reproach that comes from an internal consciousness of wrong. *Blame* hints at fault that has been externally assessed. A man may suffer guilt yet be entirely exonerated of blame; conversely, he may be blamed and yet feel no guilt. In short, while guilt is a feeling, blame is a judgment—and that is the chief distinction between the two.

7. Division and Classification

The Bible identifies three kinds of guilt: guilt of the unpardonable sin, redeemable guilt, and guilt of innocence. First, the guilt of the unpardonable sin belongs to any being who has become so steeped in evil that a change for good is no longer possible. Lucifer is said to have committed this sin by which he cut himself off eternally from Yahweh, the source of all good. Second, redeemable guilt is guilt that can be erased because it belongs to one whose heart is not incorrigibly corrupt, but which has weakened temporarily under the pressure of temptation. King David, for instance, murdered Uriah in order to marry Bathsheba, Uriah's wife. But despite this sin, David was a noble king with a thirst for righteousness; he was redeemable. Finally, the guilt of innocence is the guilt that Jesus bore when he decided to be crucified for the collective wrong of mankind even though he was, of all men, most innocent. In other words, Jesus died as if he were guilty, when in fact his character was free from any trace of evil.

8. Causal Analysis

Guilt is caused by the failure of the will. The human mind, according to Freudian theory, is delicately balanced between the drive for instant gratification that comes from the id, and the desire for regulation and postponement that originates in the superego, which is sometimes identified with what we call the conscience. The function of the will is to mediate between these two desires. When the individual succumbs to temptation, the forces of the id have triumphed over the repression of the superego. But the superego fights back by torment-ing the self with regret—in short, by evoking feelings of guilt. The stricter the superego, or conscience, the harsher the toll in guilt and the greater the person suffers. Whoever allows the will to fail must therefore pay for the gratification of the libido's urges in the coin of guilt.

These eight rhetorical modes allow us to teach idealized writing forms and tech-niques. You will not always use them, and you will most likely use them less and less consciously as your writing skills mature. But, in the beginning, you will find it easier to approach a writing assignment from the viewpoint of a specific mode rather than to invent a wholly original form for every essay.

CHAPTER 8

Narration

Road Map to Narration

What Narration Does

To narrate means to tell a story. It does not necessarily have to be a made-up story. Narration, in fact, is a relating of events in some climactic sequence. Whether the events you relate are imaginary or real, the narrative technique is more or less the same. On page 164, the paragraph on guilt in item 1 is an example of narration.

If there is a rhetorical mode that can be said to be inborn in some people, it is narration. Most of us think we can tell a good story, and almost all of us have tried our hand at storytelling.

Granted, our stories may have been oral and told on the front porch to family and friends, but a story and the techniques for telling one orally or in writing are essentially the same.

When to Use Narration

The most widespread use of narration occurs in fiction, whether in the short story or novel. Narration is also used in essays, minutes of business meetings, reports of scientific experiments, news releases, and case histories. Brief narratives, called anecdotes, are often used to effectively enliven or illustrate a point. Use narration whenever you need to relate an experience or present information in dramatic or purposeful sequence.

How to Write a Narrative

Narratives differ in content, length, and point, but the techniques they all use are remarkably similar. To write an engaging narrative, you need to do the following:

Have a Point The point of a story is what gives it movement—a beginning, a middle, and an end. If your story has no point, it will also seem to have no movement, to go nowhere, to become bogged down and stagnant. Good storytellers always begin with a point in mind. They want to show how absentminded Uncle Mickey has become; they wish to prove that "haste makes waste." From this beginning, the story should proceed without pause or slip. Sometimes a storyteller will even begin by revealing the point of the story, an admission that is often helpful to both writer and reader. A classic example of a story that begins by revealing its point is George Orwell's "Shooting an Elephant:"

> One day something happened which in a roundabout way was enlightening. It was a tiny incident in itself, but it gave me a better glimpse than I had had before of the real nature of imperialism—the real motives for which despotic governments act.

This introduction tells us what to expect. As we read on, we expect Orwell to deliver what he has advertised.

Have a point and stick to it—that age-old advice often given by writing teachers definitely applies to narration.

Pace the Story Fiction tells lies about time—it has to. Real time is not always action-packed, does not always carry us to the dizzying brink or make us feel the throb of life. In fact, time is usually humdrum and dull in real life. But no reader wants a story to trudge through uneventful hours. What the reader wants is for the dull and humdrum to disappear in the puff of a sentence, and for the focus of the story always to be on time—that is, eventful and exciting. The technique of doing this is known as pacing.

All storytellers pace their materials to focus only on eventful periods and to ignore all inconsequential stretches in between. In the following example, taken from a story entitled "We're Poor," an entire season disappears in a single paragraph:

> I didn't go back to school that fall. My mother said it was because I was sick. I did have a cold the week that school opened; I had been playing in the gutters and had got my feet wet, because there were holes in my shoes . . . As long as I had to stay in the house anyway, they were all right. I stayed cooped up in the house, without any companionship . . .

In "We're Poor," the author, Floyd Dell, learns from a Christmas experience that his family is poor. The story consequently spends a good deal of time and attention on that climactic Christmas Eve during which the narrator makes this discovery, but the inconsequential months of the preceding fall are quickly dismissed in a paragraph.

Tell the Story from a Consistent Point of View The point of view of a story is the angle from which it is told. This angle can be personal and intimate, referring to the narrator with the pronoun "I," or it can be from an omniscient point of view. In this view, the narrator is like a video camera sweeping over the scene and pausing briefly to focus on selected characters—describing how they look, what they say, and how they feel. Often this omniscient observer will select one central character, setting the person in relief so that he or she will catch the reader's intense and undivided attention. In any case, the writer must always stay in character when telling a story and must always remain consistent to the viewpoint from which he or she is telling it.

Here is an example of the omniscient point of view in a narrative. Telling the story of a troubled teacher–student relationship as an omniscient narrator, Joyce Carol Oates moves skillfully from character to character as if seeing everything clearly and truthfully. About the main female character, the narrator observes:

> Sister Irene was a tall, deft woman in her early thirties. What one could see of her face made a striking impression—serious, hard gray eyes, a long slender nose, a face waxen with thought. Seen at the right time, from the right angle, she was almost handsome. In her past teaching positions she had drawn a little upon the fact of her being young and brilliant and also a nun, but she was beginning to grow out of that.

A little further into the story, the narrator moves from Sister Irene to the male lead character, a student, seeing him just as clearly as she sees Sister Irene:

> About two weeks after the semester began, Sister Irene noticed a new student in her class. He was slight and fair-haired, and his face was blank, but not blank by accident, blank on purpose, suppressed and restricted into a dumbness that looked hysterical.

The story continues to develop both characters, the teacher and the student. Although Sister Irene is the central consciousness of the story, Allen Weinstein, the student, becomes a crucial part of the total narrative conflict—with the author recording faithfully all he does, says, and feels, just as she also records the comings and goings of Sister Irene. In fact, in this story, the narrator records even the actions and words of minor characters, which makes her a typical omniscient narrator.

Now consider the following excerpt from a vivid childhood memory by Beryl Markham in "Praise God for the Blood of the Bull":

> I lean for a moment on my spear peering outward at what is nothing, and then turn toward my thorn tree.
>
> "Are you here, Lakwani?" Arap Maina's voice is cool as water on shaded rocks.
>
> "I am here, Maina." He is tall and naked and very dark beside me. His *shuka* is tied around his left forearm to allow his body freedom to run.
>
> "You are alone, and you have suffered, my child."
>
> "I am all right, Maina, but I fear for Buller. I think he may die."
>
> Arap Maina kneels on the earth and runs his hand over Buller's body.
>
> *"He has been seriously and perhaps mortally wounded, Lakwani, but do not permit your mind to be too obsessed with any imaginary deficiencies or self-recriminations on your part. I conjecture that your lance has rescued him from a certain death, and God will recompense you for that . . ."*

If the final paragraph sounds bizarre to you in the context of the excerpt, it should. We have altered the dialogue (and added italics to clearly distinguish it from Markham's words) to dramatize what we mean by a lapse in consistency. In the final paragraph, Maina suddenly and inexplicably shifts from the simple speech of a native African to the pompous, long-winded speech of a British magistrate. A character in a narrative must always speak more or less the same way throughout and cannot lurch from one style of talk to another, as we have made Maina do. Make your characters consistent and your narrative will seem believable.

Insert Appropriate Details Details are indispensable to narrative writing and can make the difference between boredom and delight in a reader. No one can teach you the art of including captivating details, but common sense tells us that you are more likely to include the right details if you write your narratives about what you truly know. Here, for example, in Beryl Markham's description of a warthog, we get the feeling that the writer has had personal experience with the animal:

> I know animals more gallant than the African warthog, but none more coura-
> geous. He is the peasant of the plains—the drab and dowdy digger in the earth. He
> is the uncomely but intrepid defender of family, home, and bourgeois convention,
> and he will fight anything of any size that intrudes upon his smug existence. Even
> his weapons are plebeian—curved tusks, sharp, deadly, but not beautiful, used inel-
> egantly for rooting as well as for fighting.

If you cannot write about what you know, the next best thing is to know about what you write. The advice to always research your subject before writing about it cannot be given too strongly. Even veteran fiction writers do not simply plunge into their narratives without doing the spadework necessary to make their scenes authentic. Although personal experience is probably the best basis for a narrative, adequate and detailed research can be every bit as good.

Warming Up to Write a Narrative

1. **Choose one of the most interesting people whom you know well and sketch out a conflict you have had with him or her.** List the events that led up to the conflict and also indicate how it was resolved. Before actually narrating the conflict, delete from your list all items that would slow down your narrative with tedious or irrelevant material. Next, jot down the theme of your narrative—that is, the point it made or the lesson you learned about life and human relationships.

2. **Try to recall five moments in your life that somehow defined who you are.** It could be the time you lost an important contest, stood up to a bully, or first realized the importance of parents. List each moment as it occurs to you. Now, select from the list the moment that could best be turned into a good narration. Don't forget to write down how the moment defined who you are today.

3. **What is the most exciting and unusual experience you've ever had?** Try to recall it with a richness of detail. Jot down on a notepad, without paying any attention to sequence, all the incidents and events that made up the experience. Write down everything that you remember about it. Later, after thinking about your list, take the out-of-sequence memories and try to assemble them in some climactic order. If this is not the way you usually work, how did this method of recalling an experience and writing about it work for you?

Examples

My Name Is Margaret

MAYA ANGELOU

Rhetorical Thumbnail

Purpose: to portray what life was like in the southern racist society

Audience: general educated reader

Language: Southern English, especially in the dialogue

Strategy: sketches an example of how the prejudice of the day suffocated everyone in the stereotypes of race

---

Maya Angelou (1928–2014) was a novelist, poet, playwright, actress, composer, and singer. Her varied accomplishments threw her into the public limelight, where she was greatly admired as a speaker and reader of her own works. She is best known for her single-minded devotion to the cause of tolerance. Many of her novels recount incidents in which her characters must fight ardently to maintain their identity in a world of prejudice. Among her best-known works are *I Know Why the Caged Bird Sings* (1970), from which the selection that follows is taken, *Gather Together in My Name* (1974), *Singin' and Swingin' and Gettin' Merry Like Christmas* (1976), *Heart of a Woman* (1981), and *All God's Children Need Traveling Shoes* (1986). Angelou also wrote volumes of poetry, including *Oh Pray My Wings Are Gonna Fit Me Well* (1975) and *I Shall Not Be Moved* (1990). She became a role model for aspiring female writers of various minority backgrounds.

A black author, admired for her stories dealing with affronts to a black person's pride and sense of dignity, tells of an incident in which a white woman attempts to change the name of the author, who was then working for her.

• • •

1   Recently a white woman from Texas, who would quickly describe herself as a liberal, asked me about my hometown. When I told her that in Stamps my grandmother had owned the only Negro general merchandise store since the turn of the century, she exclaimed, "Why, you were a **debutante**." Ridiculous and even **ludicrous**. But Negro girls in small Southern towns, whether poverty-stricken or just munching along on a few of life's necessities, were given as extensive and irrelevant preparations for adulthood as rich white girls shown in magazines. Admittedly the training was not the same. While white girls learned to waltz and sit gracefully with a tea cup balanced on their knees, we were lagging behind, learning the mid-Victorian values with very little money to indulge them. (Come and see Edna Lomax spending the money she made picking cotton on five balls of ecru

tatting thread. Her fingers are bound to snag the work and she'll have to repeat the stitches time and time again. But she knows that when she buys the thread.)

2   We were required to embroider and I had trunkfuls of colorful dishtowels, pillowcases, runners and handkerchiefs to my credit. I mastered the art of crocheting and tatting, and there was a lifetime's supply of dainty doilies that would never be used in **sacheted** dresser drawers. It went without saying that all girls could iron and wash, but the finer touches around the home, like setting a table with real silver, baking roasts and cooking vegetables without meat, had to be learned elsewhere. Usually at the source of those habits. During my tenth year, a white woman's kitchen became my finishing school.

3   Mrs. Viola Cullinan was a plump woman who lived in a three-bedroom house somewhere behind the post office. She was singularly unattractive until she smiled, and then the lines around her eyes and mouth which made her look perpetually dirty disappeared, and her face looked like the mask of an impish elf. She usually rested her smile until late afternoon when her women friends dropped in and Miss Glory, the cook, served them cold drinks on the closed-in porch.

4   The exactness of her house was inhuman. This glass went here and only here. That cup had its place and it was an act of **impudent** rebellion to place it anywhere else. At twelve o'clock the table was set. At 12:15 Mrs. Cullinan sat down to dinner (whether her husband had arrived or not). At 12:16 Miss Glory brought out the food.

5   It took me a week to learn the difference between a salad plate, a bread plate and a dessert plate.

6   Mrs. Cullinan kept up the tradition of her wealthy parents. She was from Virginia. Miss Glory, who was a descendant of slaves that had worked for the Cullinans, told me her history. She had married beneath her (according to Miss Glory). Her husband's family hadn't had their money very long and what they had "didn't 'mount to much."

7   As ugly as she was, I thought privately, she was lucky to get a husband above or beneath her station. But Miss Glory wouldn't let me say a thing against her mistress. She was very patient with me, however, over the housework. She explained the dishware, silverware and servants' bells. The large round bowl in which soup was served wasn't a soup bowl, it was a tureen. There were goblets, sherbet glasses, ice-cream glasses, wine glasses, green glass coffee cups with matching saucers, and water glasses. I had a glass to drink from, and it sat with Miss Glory's on a separate shelf from the others. Soup spoons, gravy boat, butter knives, salad forks and carving platter were additions to my vocabulary and in fact almost represented a new language. I was fascinated with the novelty, with the fluttering Mrs. Cullinan and her Alice-in-Wonderland house.

8   Her husband remains, in my memory, undefined. I lumped him with all the other white men that I had ever seen and tried not to see.

9   On our way home one evening, Miss Glory told me that Mrs. Cullinan couldn't have children. She said that she was too delicate-boned. It was hard to imagine bones at all under those layers of fat. Miss Glory went on to say that the doctor had taken out all her lady organs. I reasoned that a pig's organs included the lungs, heart and liver, so if Mrs. Cullinan was walking around without those

essentials, it explained why she drank alcohol out of unmarked bottles. She was keeping herself embalmed.

10   When I spoke to Bailey about it, he agreed that I was right, but he also informed me that Mr. Cullinan had two daughters by a colored lady and that I knew them very well. He added that the girls were the spitting image of their father. I was unable to remember what he looked like, although I had just left him a few hours before, but I thought of the Coleman girls. They were very light-skinned and certainly didn't look very much like their mother (no one ever mentioned Mr. Coleman).

11   My pity for Mrs. Cullinan preceded me the next morning like the Cheshire cat's smile. Those girls, who could have been her daughters, were beautiful. They didn't have to straighten their hair. Even when they were caught in the rain, their braids still hung down straight like tamed snakes. Their mouths were pouty little cupid's bows. Mrs. Cullinan didn't know what she missed. Or maybe she did. Poor Mrs. Cullinan.

12   For weeks after, I arrived early, left late and tried very hard to make up for her **barrenness**. If she had had her own children, she wouldn't have had to ask me to run a thousand errands from her back door to the back door of her friends. Poor old Mrs. Cullinan.

13   Then one evening Miss Glory told me to serve the ladies on the porch. After I set the tray down and turned toward the kitchen, one of the women asked, "What's your name, girl?" It was the speckled-faced one. Mrs. Cullinan said, "She doesn't talk much. Her name's Margaret."

14   "Is she dumb?"

15   "No. As I understand it, she can talk when she wants to but she's usually quiet as a little mouse. Aren't you, Margaret?"

16   I smiled at her. Poor thing. No organs and couldn't even pronounce my name correctly.

17   "She's a sweet little thing, though."

18   "Well, that may be, but the name's too long. I'd never bother myself. I'd call her Mary if I was you."

19   I fumed into the kitchen. That horrible woman would never have the chance to call me Mary because if I was starving I'd never work for her. I decided I wouldn't pee on her if her heart was on fire. Giggles drifted in off the porch and into Miss Glory's pots. I wondered what they could be laughing about.

20   White folks were so strange. Could they be talking about me? Everybody knew that they stuck together better than the Negroes did. It was possible that Mrs. Cullinan had friends in St. Louis who heard about a girl from Stamps being in court and wrote to tell her. Maybe she knew about Mr. Freeman.

21   My lunch was in my mouth a second time and I went outside and relieved myself on the bed of four-o'clocks. Miss Glory thought I might be coming down with something and told me to go on home, that Momma would give me some herb tea, and she'd explain to her mistress.

22   I realized how foolish I was being before I reached the pond. Of course Mrs. Cullinan didn't know. Otherwise she wouldn't have given me two nice dresses that Momma cut down, and she certainly wouldn't have called me a "sweet little thing." My stomach felt fine, and I didn't mention anything to Momma.

23   That evening I decided to write a poem on being white, fat, old and without children. It was going to be a tragic **ballad**. I would have to watch her carefully to capture the essence of her loneliness and pain.

24   The very next day, she called me by the wrong name. Miss Glory and I were washing up the lunch dishes when Mrs. Cullinan came to the doorway. "Mary?"

25   Miss Glory asked, "Who?"

26   Mrs. Cullinan, sagging a little, knew and I knew. "I want Mary to go down to Mrs. Randall's and take her some soup. She's not been feeling well for a few days."

27   Miss Glory's face was a wonder to see. "You mean Margaret, ma'am. Her name's Margaret."

28   "That's too long. She's Mary from now on. Heat that soup from last night and put it in the china tureen and, Mary, I want you to carry it carefully."

29   Every person I knew had a hellish horror of being "called out of his name." It was a dangerous practice to call a Negro anything that could be loosely construed as insulting because of the centuries of their having been called niggers, jigs, dinges, blackbirds, crows, boots and spooks.

30   Miss Glory had a fleeting second of feeling sorry for me. Then as she handed me the hot tureen she said, "Don't mind, don't pay that no mind. Sticks and stones may break your bones, but words . . . You know, I been working for her for twenty years."

31   She held the back door open for me. "Twenty years. I wasn't much older than you. My name used to be Hallelujah. That's what Ma named me, but my mistress give me 'Glory,' and it stuck. I likes it better too."

32   I was in the little path that ran behind the houses when Miss Glory shouted, "It's shorter too."

33   For a few seconds it was a tossup over whether I would laugh (imagine being named Hallelujah) or cry (imagine letting some white woman rename you for her convenience). My anger saved me from either outburst. I had to quit the job, but the problem was going to be how to do it. Momma wouldn't allow me to quit for just any reason.

34   "She's a peach. That woman is a real peach." Mrs. Randall's maid was talking as she took the soup from me, and I wondered what her name used to be and what she answered to now.

35   For a week I looked into Mrs. Cullinan's face as she called me Mary. She ignored my coming late and leaving early. Miss Glory was a little annoyed because I had begun to leave egg yolk on the dishes and wasn't putting much heart in polishing the silver. I hoped that she would complain to our boss, but she didn't.

36   Then Bailey solved my dilemma. He had me describe the contents of the cupboard and the particular plates she liked best. Her favorite piece was a casserole shaped like a fish and the green glass coffee cups. I kept his instructions in mind, so on the next day when Miss Glory was hanging out clothes and I had again been told to serve the old biddies on the porch, I dropped the empty serving tray. When I heard Mrs. Cullinan scream, "Mary!" I picked up the casserole and two of the green glass cups in readiness. As she rounded the kitchen door I let them fall on the tiled floor.

37   I could never absolutely describe to Bailey what happened next, because each time I got to the part where she fell on the floor and screwed up her ugly face

to cry, we burst out laughing. She actually wobbled around on the floor and picked up **shards** of the cups and cried, "Oh, Momma. Oh, dear Gawd. It's Momma's china from Virginia. Oh, Momma, I sorry."

38   Miss Glory came running in from the yard and the women from the porch crowded around. Miss Glory was almost as broken up as her mistress. "You mean to say she broke our Virginia dishes? What we gone do?"

39   Miss Cullinan cried louder, "That clumsy nigger. Clumsy little black nigger."

40   Old speckled-face leaned down and asked, "Who did it, Viola? Was it Mary? Who did it?"

41   Everything was happening so fast I can't remember whether her action preceded her words, but I know that Mrs. Cullinan said, "Her name's Margaret, goddamn it, her name's Margaret." And she threw a wedge of the broken plate at me. It could have been the hysteria which put her aim off, but the flying **crockery** caught Miss Glory right over the ear and she started screaming.

42   I left the front door wide open so all the neighbors could hear.

43   Mrs. Cullinan was right about one thing. My name wasn't Mary.

● THE FACTS

1. In their preparations for adulthood, what did both white girls and black girls have in common?

2. Where did black girls learn to set the table and cook?

3. What kind of housekeeper was Mrs. Viola Cullinan? How does the narrator view her habits?

4. Why does the narrator feel pity for Mrs. Cullinan?

5. Why did the narrator get furious at Mrs. Cullinan? What did the narrator do to vent her anger?

● THE STRATEGIES

1. From whose point of view is this story told? How does the point of view affect the narration? How is the narration paced?

2. The narrator calls Mrs. Cullinan's house an "Alice-in-Wonderland house." What kind of image does this label conjure up? Where else in the story does the narrator use an image from Lewis Carroll's *Adventures of Alice in Wonderland*? To what purpose?

3. Although the tale about Margaret's name is essentially a serious matter, there are nevertheless some humorous elements in the narrative. What humorous incidents can you point out? Refer to specific passages.

4. What examples of figurative language does the narrator use in paragraph 11? How effective are they?

5. Why does the narrator never explain who Bailey and Mr. Freeman are? From the context of the story, who do you think they are?

THE ISSUES

1. The narrator is extremely sensitive about her name. Why is this so? How do you feel about your own name? Does it bother you when someone mispronounces or misspells it?

2. The narrator leaves the ending wide open. What do you think will happen to Margaret following this incident?

3. What does Margaret's decision to write a poem about Mrs. Cullinan indicate?

4. What is the relationship between Miss Glory and Mrs. Cullinan?

5. Describe Miss Glory. Do you think Margaret will ever be like her?

6. What do you think of Miss Glory's attempt to calm down Margaret after Mrs. Cullinan called her "Mary" from the doorway? (See paragraphs 30–32.) How does her reaction differ from Bailey's? Which reaction seems more appropriate to you?

SUGGESTIONS FOR WRITING

1. Narrate an incident in which you reacted to someone who treated you with arrogance or meanness. Make your narrative come to life by using dialogue and vivid details.

2. Narrate an incident from your youth that taught you a lesson in tolerance concerning race, religion, sex, social status, or some other aspect of society. Pace the narration properly and use vivid details.

Shame

DICK GREGORY

Rhetorical Thumbnail

Purpose: to inform about his early life

Audience: general reader

Language: simple language, particularly the dialogue, of a child

Strategy: re-creates from the "I" point of view the recollected experience of being shamed in school

Dick Gregory (b. 1932) is a political activist, comedian, and writer. He attended Southern Illinois University, where he was named Outstanding Athlete in 1953. Gregory has been much admired for his interest in social issues such as world famine and for his outstanding ability as a standup comedian. In 1966, he ran for Mayor of Chicago, and in 1968, he was the presidential candidate of the Freedom and Peace Party. Gregory has written several books, including *From the Back of the Bus* (1962), *What's Happening?* (1965),

The Shadow That Scares Me (1968), *Dick Gregory's Bible Tales* (1974), and his autobiography, *Up from Nigger* (1976). Gregory was one of the first black comedians to break the "color barrier" and perform for white audiences. His popularity is based on his ability to satirize race relations without being derogatory.

Even if you have never felt the poverty described by the narrator in the story that follows, you can probably remember someone from your childhood or adolescence who somehow represented all the romance and beauty for which you longed. Ponder the details that make the narrator's experience so heartbreaking.

• • •

1   I never learned hate at home, or shame. I had to go to school for that. I was about seven years old when I got my first big lesson. I was in love with a little girl named Helene Tucker, a light-complected little girl with pigtails and nice manners. She was always clean and she was smart in school. I think I went to school mostly to look at her. I brushed my hair and even got me a little old handkerchief. It was a lady's handkerchief, but I didn't want Helene to see me wipe my nose on my hand. The pipes were frozen again, there was no water in the house, but I washed my socks and shirt every night. I'd get a pot, and go over to Mr. Ben's grocery store, and stick my pot down into his soda machine. Scoop out some chopped ice. By evening the ice melted to water for washing. I got sick a lot that winter because the fire would go out at night before the clothes were dry. In the morning I'd put them on, wet or dry, because they were the only clothes I had.

2   Everybody's got a Helene Tucker, a symbol of everything you want. I loved her for her goodness, her cleanliness, her popularity. She'd walk down my street and my brothers and sisters would yell, "Here comes Helene," and I'd rub my tennis sneakers on the back of my pants and wish my hair wasn't so nappy and the white folks' shirt fit me better. I'd run out on the street. If I knew my place and didn't come too close, she'd wink at me and say hello. That was a good feeling. Sometimes I'd follow her all the way home, and shovel the snow off her walk and try to make friends with her Momma and her aunts. I'd drop money on her stoop late at night on my way back from shining shoes in the taverns. And she had a Daddy, and he had a good job. He was a paper hanger.

3   I guess I would have gotten over Helene by summertime, but something happened in that classroom that made her face hang in front of me for the next twenty-two years. When I played the drums in high school it was for Helene and when I broke track records in college it was for Helene and when I started standing behind microphones and heard applause I wished Helene could hear it, too. It wasn't until I was twenty-nine years old and married and making money that I really got her out of my system. Helene was sitting in that classroom when I learned to be ashamed of myself.

4   It was on a Thursday. I was sitting in the back of the room, in a seat with a chalk circle drawn around it. The idiot's seat, the troublemaker's seat.

5   The teacher thought I was stupid. Couldn't spell, couldn't read, couldn't do arithmetic. Just stupid. Teachers were never interested in finding out that you

couldn't concentrate because you were so hungry, because you hadn't had any breakfast. All you could think about was noontime, would it ever come? Maybe you could sneak into the cloakroom and steal a bit of some kid's lunch out of a coat pocket. A bit of something. Paste. You can't really make a meal out of paste, or put it on bread for a sandwich, but sometimes I'd scoop a few spoonfuls out of the paste jar in the back of the room. Pregnant people get strange tastes. I was pregnant with poverty. Pregnant with dirt and pregnant with smells that made people turn away, pregnant with cold and pregnant with shoes that were never bought for me, pregnant with five other people in my bed and no Daddy in the next room, and pregnant with hunger. Paste doesn't taste too bad when you're hungry.

6   The teacher thought I was a troublemaker. All she saw from the front of the room was a little black boy who squirmed in his idiot's seat and made noises and poked the kids around him. I guess she couldn't see a kid who made noises because he wanted someone to know he was there.

7   It was on a Thursday, the day before the Negro payday. The eagle always flew on Friday. The teacher was asking each student how much his father would give to the Community Chest. On Friday night, each kid would get the money from his father, and on Monday he would bring it to the school. I decided I was going to buy me a Daddy right then. I had money in my pocket from shining shoes and selling papers and whatever Helene Tucker pledged for her Daddy I was going to top it. And I'd hand the money right in. I wasn't going to wait until Monday to buy me a Daddy.

8   I was shaking, scared to death. The teacher opened her book and started calling our names alphabetically.

9   "Helene Tucker?"

10   "My Daddy said he'd give two dollars and fifty cents."

11   "That's very nice, Helene. Very, very nice indeed."

12   That made me feel pretty good. It wouldn't take too much to top that. I had almost three dollars in dimes and quarters in my pocket. I stuck my hand in my pocket and held onto the money, waiting for her to call my name. But the teacher closed her book after she called everybody else in the class.

13   I stood up and raised my hand.

14   "What is it now?"

15   "You forgot me."

16   She turned toward the blackboard. "I don't have time to be playing with you, Richard."

17   "My Daddy said he'd . . ."

18   "Sit down, Richard, you're disturbing the class."

19   "My Daddy said he'd give . . . fifteen dollars."

20   She turned around and looked mad. "We are collecting this money for you and your kind, Richard Gregory. If your Daddy can give fifteen dollars you have no business being on relief."

21   "I got it right now, I got it right now, my Daddy gave it to me to turn in today, my Daddy said . . ."

22   "And furthermore," she said, looking right at me, her nostrils getting big and her lips getting thin and her eyes opening wide, "we know you don't have a Daddy."

23   Helene Tucker turned around, her eyes full of tears. She felt sorry for me. Then I couldn't see her too well because I was crying, too.

24   "Sit down, Richard."

25   And I always thought the teacher kind of liked me. She always picked me to wash the blackboard on Friday, after school. That was a big thrill, it made me feel important. If I didn't wash it, come Monday the school might not function right.

26   "Where are you going, Richard?"

27   I walked out of school that day, and for a long time I didn't go back very often. There was shame there.

28   Now there was shame everywhere. It seemed like the whole world had been inside that classroom, everyone had heard what the teacher had said, everyone had turned around and felt sorry for me. There was shame in going to the Worthy Boys Annual Christmas Dinner for you and your kind, because everybody knew what a worthy boy was. Why couldn't they just call it the Boys Annual Dinner, why'd they have to give it a name? There was shame in wearing the brown and orange and white plaid **mackinaw** the welfare gave to 3,000 boys. Why'd it have to be the same for everybody so when you walked down the street the people could see you were on relief? It was a nice warm mackinaw and it had a hood, and my Momma beat me and called me a little rat when she found out I stuffed it in the bottom of a pail full of garbage way over on Cottage Street. There was shame in running over to Mister Ben's at the end of the day and asking for his rotten peaches, there was shame in asking Mrs. Simmons for a spoonful of sugar, there was shame in running out to meet the relief truck. I hated that truck, full of food for you and your kind. I ran into the house and hid when it came. And then I started to sneak through alleys, to take the long way home so people going into White's Eat Shop wouldn't see me. Yeah, the whole world heard the teacher that day, we all know you don't have a Daddy.

● THE FACTS

1. Where did the narrator learn shame?

2. What did the narrator do for Helene Tucker? How important was she in his life?

3. According to the narrator, why could he not do well in school? What did the teachers think?

4. What event at school caused shame to control the narrator's life for a long time? Summarize what happened.

5. What did the author dislike about the Worthy Boys Annual Christmas Dinner?

● THE STRATEGIES

1. The narration begins in paragraph 3, following two paragraphs of commentary about Helene Tucker, a girl on whom the narrator had a crush. What is the purpose of the preliminary paragraphs?

2. What dominant impression is always in the background of the narration? Why?

3. Beginning with paragraph 9, the narrator adds conversation to the narration. What is the effect of this technique?

4. What is the main theme (lesson about life) revealed in this story? Is it implied or stated?

5. In paragraph 5, what is the purpose of repeating the word "pregnant"? What does the author mean?

● THE ISSUES

1. Do you agree with the narrator's comment that "everybody's got a Helene Tucker"? What does Helene Tucker symbolize? Give an example of a Helene Tucker from your own experience.

2. The teacher thought the narrator was a troublemaker. Was he really, or was there another reason for drawing attention to himself?

3. Why did the teacher humiliate the narrator when he announced that his father would donate fifteen dollars? Do you think the teacher should have handled the situation differently? If so, how should she have reacted?

4. The narrator states that he thought the teacher liked him because she always picked him to clean the blackboard on Friday. Why do you think she picked him?

5. Did the narrator do the right thing by not going back to the school often after the shame incident? What kept him away? Do you empathize or do you think the narrator was oversensitive?

● SUGGESTIONS FOR WRITING

1. Write about an incident in which you or someone you love experienced shame. Use the techniques of pacing, using vivid details and making a point.

2. Write an essay in which you examine the psychological effects of poverty on children in elementary school.

Image Gallery for Critical Thinking and Debate: Terrorism

The September 11, 2001, suicide bombing of the World Trade Center in New York and the Pentagon in Washington, D.C., was, to most of the horrified Western world, an act of unspeakable wickedness and evil. To some in the Islamic world, it was a deed of heroic martyrdom done in the name of God and one that guaranteed heaven to the self-sacrificing souls responsible for it. After the attack, as the rescuers sifted through the physical rubble, and the talking heads on television combed through the shreds of whys and whats, the irreconcilable divide between the terrorists and us became sharply clear. While we mourned for the victims and prayed for their families, elsewhere in the world some people rejoiced at our sorrow. Even now, when we think about the murderers' cold-bloodedness, their diabolical planning, and their fanatical sacrifice, many of us cannot comprehend the depth of the hate that drove them to invest so much time and energy into slaughtering so many innocents.

Why do they hate us so? We're used to being admired—our material wealth and lifestyle the envy of the world. Our history has repeatedly shown us to be a generous people, donating billions of dollars to help less-fortunate nations in the grip of war, famine, pestilence, or economic ruin. When we have won wars, we have always tried to help our former enemies rebuild rather than occupy their territories. Yet there are millions of people—some Islamic, some not—who hate us with such passion that they are willing, even eager, to sacrifice themselves in murderous and indiscriminate attacks aimed at our destruction. Al-Qaeda, the terrorist organization headed by Osama bin Laden until his assassination in 2011, even now reportedly continues to train assassins and saboteurs, all willing to blow themselves up in an attempt to hurt us. What stuns most Americans is that these people believe that their terroristic attacks are the will of God. Few of us associate God with mass slaughter; even fewer can comprehend the belief that the rewards of paradise will be lavished on such murderers.

Our image gallery concentrates on three aspects of terrorism the United States has endured since the Twin Towers crumbled and evaporated. First, we present a sinister aspect of the Koran, holy book to all Muslim believers and motivating force for Muslim terrorists to kill any infidel unwilling to bow to Allah's Word. Second is a photo of the havoc caused by Adam Lanza, a mentally troubled malcontent, who on December 14, 2012, shot to death 20 children and 7 adults at the Sandy Hook Elementary School in Newton, Colorado. Last is a portrait of Dzokhar Tsarnaev, the younger of the two brothers with ties to Chechen terrorists, who exploded two pressure cooker bombs, twelve minutes apart, near the finish line of the Boston Marathon on April 15, 2013. This act of terrorism killed 3 and wounded an estimated 264 participants or spectators, causing ripple effects of fear around the world.

An essay by a college student contributes thoughts about terrorism in general and how September 11 now lives in infamy as a date of treachery heaped on our country.

A "To the Point" assignment rounds out the issue.

Study the following three images dealing with terrorism. Then choose the image that most appeals to you. Answer the questions and do the writing assignment.

For readings, questions, and media on the issue of terrorism, visit the *MindTap for Readings for Writers*, 15e online.

MOHAMMED ABED/AFP /Getty Images

Studying the Image

1. What underlying contradiction do you see in this image? What feelings does it evoke from you?

2. What is the effect of the mask worn by the terrorist? Why is the mask black? Would a red mask have a different effect? Explain your answer.

3. What stereotype of terrorism does the photo suggest?

4. How do you think a law-abiding, devout Muslim would feel about this photo? How would you react if you were a moderate Muslim, not interested in ideology or fundamentalism in religion?

Writing Assignment

Write an essay in which you point out the perils of a religious sect that calls for the elimination of innocent citizens believed to be "infidels."

Andrew Sullivan/ZUMA Wire/ZUMAPRESS. com/Alamy Limited

Studying the Image

1. Stated in one declarative statement, what is the dominant impression you get from this scene reflecting one of the early responses to Adam Lanza's horrific act?

2. What feeling do you see expressed in the woman's eyes and face? What are the details that convey this feeling? What do you conclude about the little boy clinging to his mother? What are the thoughts roaming through his mind?

3. What do the police cars tell us about the situation?

4. What is your reaction to the two little girls walking along together? What relationship do you think they have? What is the irony of the older girl's T-shirt having a large heart printed on it?

Writing Assignment

Using the declarative statement you used to answer Question #1 above as your topic sentence, write a well-developed paragraph describing the scene depicted in this photo. Choose details that support your topic sentence, keeping the paragraph unified by not straying from your topic sentence.

AP Images /Robin Young

Studying the Image

1. How old do you judge Dzhokhar to be in this photo? What details point to his approximate age? What comes to your mind as you study the portrait, especially the facial expression? What does the rose pinned to his shoulder add to the portrait?

2. How do you react to knowing that this young man would someday help his older brother detonate bombs on a crowded street where thousands of innocent onlookers were applauding the athletes nearing the finish line of the Boston Marathon? What do you think were the strongest forces that shaped Dzhokhar's outlook on life? If necessary, do a little research to learn about the Tsarnaev family and their affiliations or beliefs.

3. On January 30, 2014, U.S. Attorney General Eric Holder announced that the Federal Government is seeking the death penalty for Dzhokhar Tsarnaev. What is your view of this penalty? Is it fair or unfair?

4. If you were sympathetic to the Chechen or Russian cause, how would you assess Dzhokhar's act? Would it change your judgment of his complicity? Explain your answer.

Writing Assignment

After researching the case of Tamarlan and Dzhokhar Tsarnaev, the two Chechen brothers who conspired to commit the act of terrorism on April 15, 2013, in Boston, narrate how they accomplished their crime by following what is now known about their footsteps on the day of April 15, 2013, and the next two days as the law pursued Dzhokhar. Give credit to any outside sources you used to document your narration.

*Stumped by deadwood? Exit on pages 424–427 at the **Editing Booth!***

Punctuation Workshop

The Period (.)

These are the rules for using periods:

1. Put a period at the end of a sentence:

> **WRONG:** We made a dash for the bus we almost missed it. (This is a run-on sentence.)

> **RIGHT:** We made a dash for the bus. We almost missed it.

> **WRONG:** I never knew my grandfather, he died when I was three years old. (This is called a comma splice.)

> **RIGHT:** I never knew my grandfather. He died when I was three years old.

2. Put a period after most abbreviations:

Mr.	A.D.	Dr.	Wed.	sq. ft.
Ms.	etc.	Jan.	P.M.	lbs.

Exceptions: mph, FM, TV, VCR, NBC, NATO, IRS, DMV

> Dictionaries sometimes give you an option: U.S.A. or USA. When in doubt, consult your dictionary or instructor.

Student Corner

Terrorism: America in Fear

Jeffrey Metherell

University of Idaho

On December 7, 1941, the U.S. naval base in Pearl Harbor was brutally and successfully attacked by the Japanese Imperial Navy. That this assault occurred while negotiations were still taking place between Japan and the U.S. and, even more ironic, that a formal declaration of war did not reach the U.S. until the next day, prompted a huge American outcry. It also elicited a harsh statement from President Franklin Roosevelt, in which he predicted that December 7 would be "a date that will live in infamy." And so it has. "Remember Pearl Harbor" became the rallying cry, and the attack became synonymous with all that is cowardly and underhanded. But then, the calendar reached September 11, 2001, and the events of that awful day eclipsed the events of December 7, 1941. Suddenly, treachery had a new anniversary, and 9/11 is now the date that lives in infamy!

There are some eerie similarities between the two attacks. Obviously, both were devastating shocks to the U.S. Both occurred on American soil (greatly adding to the jolt factor). Beyond the material damage (battle-ships lost and buildings destroyed) the death tolls were approximately the same—2,402 at Pearl Harbor and 2,977 innocent victims from the 9/11 attack. Both attacks promptly plunged our country into war. The aftermath of both attacks included a barrage of hate crimes, ethnic stereotyping, and racial persecution. And although it can be argued that in both events the primary damage inflicted was widespread fear, this is where a distinc-tion can be made. Whereas following Pearl Harbor, we Americans knew who the enemy was, what it looked like, and, for the most part, where it resided, we can make none of these assumptions following 9/11. And that is why in the years after December 7, 1941, we were "America at war," whereas since 9/11, we have become "America in fear."

No fear is stronger or deeper than fear of the unknown. We fight a faceless and nameless enemy, who could literally be living and working in our neighborhood. It could be a group of zealous students enrolled at the local community college; it could be one disgruntled loner who has converted to Islam; or it could even be a bus driver whose soft-spoken ways fool everyone. Terrorists do not jump out of dark alleys, wearing Jihad turbans or gang masks. There are no parades of enemy soldiers with smartly pressed uniforms and unfurled banners marching in unison while showcasing their numbers and weaponry. There is no Geneva Convention or rules of engagement or any form of chivalry. Furthermore, we are not fighting against a "bully" country that has an unquenchable thirst for power, territory, or conquests. Instead, we are fighting against an ideology—a religious fervor that derives from the maniacal twisting and creative interpretation of an ancient document. Herein we find another similarity between the kamikaze pilots of WWII and the suicide bombers of Al Qaeda. Nothing struck more fear to the souls of U.S. naval men than a kamikaze pilot's willingness to explode his plane on the deck of a ship, sacrificing himself for his emperor, who was commonly believed to be a god, descendant from the sun goddess Amaterasu. The kamikaze pilots were proud to be martyrs for the "holy" emperor of Japan, just as the members of Al Qaeda are proud to be martyrs for the glorious cause of obliterating "the infidels" who disgrace Allah and his prophet. The kamikaze pilots were driven by the heroism of dying for their godlike emperor, but the Muslim terrorists had an additional motivation—the reward at death of immediately entering the gates of Paradise to live with the 72 pure and erotic virgins who would be their companions throughout eternity. The unrelenting passion with which both the kamikaze pilots and the Muslim terrorists acted highlights the extremism which martyrdom can embrace—with one added chilling difference: The terrorism since 9/11 does not limit itself to targeting purely military assets and personnel. In fact, civilians are usually the target as fear is ultimately and primarily the objective.

It has been 70 years since the attack on Pearl Harbor. That time segment basically constitutes a generation. December 7, 1941, is mostly a historical memory—conjuring up little visceral reaction. It's been more than a decade since 9/11, and the same can certainly not be said about that date. The horror of that infamous day still pervades our thoughts, and the pallor of fear still envelopes our country. We are America in fear.

How I Write

By personality, I tend to be a "scribble-outside-of-the-lines" type of individual. Now this doesn't mean that I necessarily denounce all rules and regulations. But, I do recognize that my forte is creativity as opposed to order. How does this apply to my writing? Well, let's just say that it's a question of focus. If I focus primarily on the methodology of writing something, I find myself feeling rather hedged in and constricted. I am much more effective if I let the creative juices percolate and apply the rules at some point later. My older sister, who teaches elementary school, tells me that she encourages young students, when they write, to start out with a "sloppy copy." I find this suggestion to be as useful as the one that dark chocolate is actually good for you. I needed to hear the latter only once! I live by the "sloppy copy" (in fact, usually more than one). Generally speaking, if the creative juices aren't flowing, then neither is the ink. In sum, I break the classic rules of writing in a blatant and unapologetic fashion. I encourage creative thinking on the subject; then I transfer those thoughts to paper, and begin sewing it all together—making sure to observe the aforementioned methodology. It's backward. But, it works for me.

My Writing Tip

I realize that I run the risk of sounding like Dr. Phil, but my strongest advice is, "Be yourself!" In other words, if you are by nature a creative, "scribble-out-of-the-lines" kind of person, then be that person even when you write. Don't let the rules of writing and proper methodology keep you from writing! Use the rules to help shape what you write or to transform it from random to orderly and logical.

To the Point

Respond with a tweet to the following blog: "There are really only two causes always present when terrorism occurs: a sense of perceived injustice and the belief that violence will effectively cure it." (http:// terrorism.about.com/od/causes/)

▥ Chapter Writing Assignments

1. Write an essay in which you narrate an incident that proves one of the following:

    a. People are often bigoted.

    b. Having good neighbors is important.

    c. Pets are often astoundingly loyal.

    d. Difficulties can be stepping stones to success.

▥ Writing Assignments for a Specific Audience

1. Write a diary entry, listing chronologically the major events of your day. Treat your diary as a confidential, intimate friend to whom you can trust your innermost feelings.

2. Write to your parents, narrating an incident that happened recently and somehow impacted your attitude toward other people.

 Pointer from a Pro

BE CONCISE

A college class was told they had to write a short story in as few words as possible. The instructions were that the story had to contain the following three items:

1. Religion

2. Sexuality

3. Mystery

Below is the one A+ short story in the class.

"Good God, I'm pregnant! I wonder who did it."

—from Popcorntom@aol.com

(Retrieved Nov. 20, 2010)

We could not resist including this pointer because its humorous hyperbole draws immediate attention to brevity and terseness.

CHAPTER 9

Description

▉ Road Map to Description

What Description Does

A description is a word picture. It is the writer's attempt to capture with words the essence and flavor of a scene, person, or thing. No matter what you have heard to the contrary, a sharply drawn description can be every bit as moving as a picture. Focus and concentration contribute more to a vivid description than either the size of the writer's vocabulary or the heedless splattering of adjectives on a page. Here is an example of what we mean. The author Charles Reade, in this excerpt from *The Cloister and the Hearth,* is describing a medieval inn partly through the eyes, but mainly through the nose, of a weary traveler:

> In one corner was a travelling family, a large one; thence flowed into the common stock the peculiar sickly smell of neglected brats. Garlic filled up the interstices of the air. And all this with closed window, and intense heat of the central furnace, and the breath of at least forty persons.
>
> They had just supped.
>
> Now Gerard, like most artists, had sensitive organs, and the potent effluvia struck dismay into him. But the rain lashed him outside, and the light and the fire tempted him in.
>
> He could not force his way all at once through the palpable perfumes, but he returned to the light again and again like a singed moth. At last he discovered that the various smells did not entirely mix, no fiend being there to stir them around. Odor of family predominated in two corners; stewed rustic reigned supreme in the center; and garlic in the noisy group by the window. He found, too, by hasty analysis, that of these the garlic described the smallest aerial orbit, and the scent of reeking rustic darted farthest—a flavor as if ancient goats, or the fathers of all foxes, had been drawn through a river, and were here dried by Nebuchadnezzar.

The predominant characteristic of this vivid description is its focus. Instead of trying to give us a sweeping view of the dingy inn, the writer zooms in on how bad it smells.

The stink of the inn is the dominant impression of this description, and the writer's every word, image, and metaphor aim only to serve up this stench to our nostrils.

When to Use Description

Next to narration, description is probably the most widely used of all the rhetorical modes. In letters, journal entries, reports, and memos, we describe places we have visited, people we have met, and adventures that we have had. Over the course of any given week, it is likely that we have painted a word picture, if not in writing, then certainly in speech.

How to Write a Description

There are some well-known techniques of description that all writers use. We recommend you practice them in your own writing.

Focus on a Dominant Impression Vivid descriptions invariably focus on a single, dominant impression and unremittingly deliver it. Nothing distracts from the dominant impression; every word and image is devoted to rendering it keener and sharper. By dominant impression, we mean a feature of the scene that is characteristic of it. Not all scenes have strikingly characteristic features, and writers must often absorb the atmosphere of a place before they can sum it up in a dominant impression. Some scenes, however, will give off a dominant impression that leaps out at you. For example, a freeway at rush hour is anything but a scene of placidity; usually it is a tangled skein of cars jockeying for position or trying to nose from one lane into another. To describe a freeway scene at rush hour, you should word your dominant impression to take in the antics of the drivers, the fumes of the cars, the background grind and roar of traffic. You might write, as your dominant impression, "The San Diego Freeway at rush hour is a bedlam of traffic noise, choking fumes, and aggressive drivers." Then you would support that dominant impression with specific images and details.

Here is a description of the Spanish night that uses this technique:

> The Spanish night is so deep and pompous as quite to brow-beat the noisier light of day. The buildings, which always look clear-cut and newly built, become, against the dark stress of evening, brilliantly crisp and more brittle than glass. A long line of white buildings will tower up to threaten you with its proud, wave-like bulwarks. At every corner, behind the dark trees that are deep, still areas of water, there will rise up another of those strutting waves out of the depth. In its turn it will draw up, holding itself to full height before it launches a leonine assault on your puny presence. Then it will hold itself back from you before the superior strength of the next glittering wave that you meet, as you walk through the brittle moonlight. In this way the slowest progress through a town will be running the gauntlet of a whole pack of hungry shadows.

> —Sacheverell Sitwell, *Southern Baroque Art*

The paragraph vividly captures the sights and sensations associated with *nightfall* over a Spanish town. At its core is a single, overwhelming impression of night "so deep and pompous as quite to browbeat the noisier light of day." All of the details in the paragraph support this dominant impression.

The dominant impression of your description should be the heart of the person, place, or scene you are attempting to describe. If you are describing an elderly aunt who is dull, use her dullness as your dominant impression. If you are writing a description of a Christmas shopping scene, word your dominant impression to show the frazzled and weary shoppers, the harried salesclerks, the dazzling Christmas lights.

However, you should not account for every speck in the scene you are describing in your dominant impression. For example, among the streaming throngs in the department store at Christmas, there are bound to be a few souls who are calm and composed and seemingly immune to the shopping frenzy. Because these lucky few are not at all representative of the overall scene, you should leave them out lest they water down the description. Similarly, if your sister is mainly a bundle of nerves, that is how you should paint her on the page, even if you have glimpsed her in rare moments of serenity.

Use Images in Your Descriptions Most of us know the basics of imagery, especially the simile and the metaphor. We know that the simile is an image based on an explicit comparison. For example, in *The King of the Birds,* Flannery O'Connor describes the crest of a peabiddy with this simile: "This looks at first like a bug's antennae and later like the head feathers of an Indian." We also know that the metaphor is an image based on an indirect comparison with no obvious linking word such as "as" or "like" used to cement it. For example, in *Once More to the Lake,* E. B. White uses metaphors to describe a thunderstorm: "Then the kettle drum, then the snare, then the bass drum and cymbals, then crackling light against the dark, and the gods grinning and licking their chops in the hills." This is how a thunderstorm seems to the writer—it makes noises like many drums and flashes wicked lights against the hills that look like gods licking their chops. Even though the writer omits the "like" that might have made the comparison explicit, we still get the picture.

In addition to these basic images, which every writer occasionally uses, there are some hard-won lessons about descriptive imagery that can be imparted. The first is this: Vivid images do not miraculously drip off the pen but are usually the result of the writer reworking the material repeatedly. If nothing original or fresh occurs to you after you've sat at your desk for a scant few minutes trying to write a description, all it means is that you did not sit long enough or work hard enough. Reread what you have written. Try to picture in your mind the person, place, or thing you are struggling to describe. Cut a word here; replace another there; persistently scratch away at what you have written and you'll soon be astonished at how much better it gets.

The second lesson about writing vivid images is summed up in the adage "Less is more." Overdoing a descriptive passage is not only possible, it is very likely. If you are unhappy with a description you have written, instead of stuffing it with more adjectives, try taking some out. Here is an example of a bloated and overdone description, from

Delina Delaney by Amanda McKittrick Ros. The speaker is trying his utmost to describe his feelings as he says goodbye to his sweetheart:

> I am just in time to hear the toll of a parting bell strike its heavy weight of appalling softness against the weakest fibers of a heart of love, arousing and tickling its dormant action, thrusting the dart of evident separation deeper into its tubes of tenderness, and fanning the flame, already inextinguishable, into volumes of blaze.

This is wretched stuff, of course. One can see the writer huffing and puffing at the pen as she tries desperately to infuse her hero's words with passion. She fails awfully from too much effort.

Appeal to All of Your Reader's Senses Most of us are so unabashedly visual that we are tempted to deliver only looks in our descriptions. There is usually much more to a scene than its looks; you could also write about how it sounds, smells, or feels. The best descriptions draw on all kinds of images and appeal to as many senses as are appropriate. Here is an example from Elspeth Huxley's *The Flame Trees of Thika*. The writer is describing a World War I troop train as it leaves an African station at night carrying soldiers to the front:

> The men began to sing the jingle then that was so popular then—"Marching to Tabora"; and the shouts and cheers, the whistles, the hissing and chugging of the engine, filled the station as a kettle fills with steam. Everything seemed to bubble over; men waved from windows; Dick gave a hunting cry; the red hair of Pioneer Mary flared under a lamp; the guard jumped into his moving van; and we watched the rear light of the last coach vanish, and heard the chugging die away. A plume of sparks, a long coil of dancing fireflies, spread across the black ancient shoulder of the crater Menegai; and gradually the vast digesting dark of Africa swallowed up all traces of that audacious grub, the hurrying train.

This description is a mixture of appeals to our senses of sight and hearing. The men sing and cheer, and the engine chugs and hisses. We see Pioneer Mary's red hair and the sparks from the train's engine. We are regaled with a clever simile, "filled the station as a kettle fills with steam," and treated to a riveting image, "the vast digesting dark of Africa swallowed up all traces of that audacious grub, the hurrying train." Did the author really just sit down and calmly mine this rich descriptive vein without effort? We do not know, but most likely not. If her experience is at all typical, she hit this mother lode of imagery only after persistent and labored digging.

Warming Up to Write a Description

1. Train yourself to be observant. Withdraw to your room or some other familiar place with a notepad and pencil or your laptop and place yourself at an angle where you have a sweeping view. Jot down or type the details of what the place looks like. After you have absorbed the details, formulate a dominant impression of the place and

write it down or type it on your laptop. An example might be, "My room always makes me feel cozy because it is filled with mementos from my childhood." Or, "The Hometown Buffet, a restaurant five blocks away from where I live, is a spot where one can breathe in all kinds of smells, hear all kinds of noises, and observe all kinds of people." Next, write only those details that support the dominant impression.

2. Drive through your town or neighborhood, focusing on eyesores that you think the local authorities should correct. Examples might be a huge refuse bin sitting outside a popular coffee house, withered flowers in a planter at the side of a real estate office, or broken-down cars and car parts littering someone's front yard. Take notes that describe the eyesore with sensory details of sight, sound, smell, and touch.

3. Rewrite these undescriptive and dull sentences to make them vivid. Use figurative language whenever possible.

   a. The convalescent hospital smelled unappetizing.

   b. His face bore many signs indicating his old age.

   c. The protesters were quite loud and active.

   d. The snow falling on the creek is lovely.

   As an added exercise, complete the following sentences to make them vividly descriptive:

   e. The squirrels chased each other up and down the trees as if . . .

   f. Jasmine's eyes were so deeply green, they looked like . . .

   g. The suitcase fell off the rack of our car and crashed on the highway, causing . . .

   h. A cold wind blew from the north, shaking up the trees and bending their trunks back and forth so that from a distance the aspen grove looked like . . .

Examples

The Libido for the Ugly

H. L. MENCKEN

Rhetorical Thumbnail

Purpose: to describe the repellent ugliness of an area surrounding Pittsburgh

Audience: magazine readers

Language: oratorical English

Strategy: takes the perspective of a passenger on a train traveling through the Pittsburgh countryside

Henry Louis Mencken (1880–1956) was an editor, author, and critic. He began his journalism career at the *Baltimore Morning Herald* and later became editor of the *Baltimore Evening Herald.* From 1906 until his death, he was on the staff of the *Baltimore Sun* (or *Evening Sun*). In 1924, with George Jean Nathan, Mencken founded the *American Mercury* and served as its editor from 1925 to 1933. Mencken's writing was chiefly devoted to lambasting the smug, conventional attitudes of the middle class. Among his numerous works is *The American Language,* a monumental study of the American idiom, first published in 1919.

Few writers have such an eye for colorful detail as the incomparable Mencken, at his best when he's railing against physical ugliness or storming against a tradition he dislikes. In the essay that follows, Mencken turns his literary wrath against the ugliness of the industrial heartland of America in the 1920s.

• • •

1   On a Winter day some years ago, coming out of Pittsburgh on one of the expresses of the Pennsylvania Railroad, I rolled eastward for an hour through the coal and steel towns of Westmoreland county. It was familiar ground; boy and man, I had been through it often before. But somehow I had never quite sensed its appalling desolation. Here was the very heart of industrial America, the center of its most **lucrative** and characteristic activity, the boast and pride of the richest and grandest nation ever seen on earth—and here was a scene so dreadfully hideous, so intolerably bleak and forlorn that it reduced the whole **aspiration** of man to a **macabre** and depressing joke. Here was wealth beyond computation, almost beyond imagination—and here were human habitations so abominable that they would have disgraced a race of alley cats.

2   I am not speaking of mere filth. One expects steel towns to be dirty. What I allude to is the unbroken and agonizing ugliness, the sheer revolting monstrousness, of every house in sight. From East Liberty to Greensburg, a distance of twenty-five miles, there was not one in sight from the train that did not insult and **lacerate** the eye. Some were so bad, and they were among the most pretentious—churches, stores, warehouses, and the like—that they were downright startling; one blinked before them as one blinks before a man with his face shot away. A few linger in memory, horrible even there: a crazy little church just west of Jeannette, set like a **dormer-window** on the side of a bare, leprous hill; the headquarters of the Veterans of Foreign Wars at another forlorn town; a steel stadium like a huge rat-trap somewhere further down the line. But most of all I recall the general effect—of hideousness without a break. There was not a single decent house within eye-range from the Pittsburgh suburbs to the Greensburg yards. There was not one that was not misshapen, and there was not one that was not shabby.

3   The country itself is not uncomely, despite the grime of the endless mills. It is, in form, a narrow river valley, with deep gullies running up into the hills. It is thickly settled, but not noticeably overcrowded. There is still plenty of room for building, even in the larger towns, and there are very few solid blocks. Nearly every house, big and little, has space on all four sides. Obviously, if there were architects of any professional sense or dignity in the region, they would have perfected

a chalet to hug the hillsides—a chalet with a high-pitched roof, to throw off the heavy winter snows, but still essentially a low and clinging building, wider than it was tall. But what have they done? They have taken as their model a brick set on end. This they have converted into a thing of dingy **clapboards**, with a narrow, low-pitched roof. And the whole they have set upon thin, preposterous brick piers. By the hundreds and thousands these abominable houses cover the bare hillsides, like gravestones in some gigantic and decaying cemetery. On their deep sides they are three, four and even five stories high; on their low sides they bury themselves swinishly in the mud. Not a fifth of them are perpendicular. They lean this way and that, hanging on to their bases precariously. And one and all they are streaked in grime, with dead and **eczematous** patches of paint peeping through the streaks.

4   Now and then there is a house of brick. But what brick! When it is new it is the color of a fried egg. When it has taken on the **patina** of the mills it is the color of an egg long past all hope or caring. Was it necessary to adopt that shocking color? No more than it was necessary to set all of the houses on end. Red brick, even in a steel town, ages with some dignity. Let it become downright black, and it is still sightly, especially if its trimmings are of white stone, with soot in the depths and the high spots washed by the rain. But in Westmoreland they prefer that **uremic** yellow, and so they have the most loathsome towns and villages ever seen by mortal eye.

5   I award this championship only after laborious research and incessant prayer. I have seen, I believe, all of the most unlovely towns of the world; they are all to be found in the United States. I have seen the mill towns of decomposing New England and the desert towns of Utah, Arizona and Texas. I am familiar with the back streets of Newark, Brooklyn and Chicago, and have made scientific explorations to Camden, N.J., and Newport News, Va. Safe in a Pullman, I have whirled through the gloomy, God-forsaken villages of Iowa and Kansas, and the **malarious** tide-water hamlets of Georgia. I have been to Bridgeport, Conn., and to Los Angeles. But nowhere on this earth, at home or abroad, have I seen anything to compare to the villages that huddle along the line of the Pennsylvania from the Pittsburgh yards to Greensburg. They are incomparable in color, and they are incomparable in design. It is as if some titanic and **aberrant** genius, uncompromisingly **inimical** to man, had devoted all the ingenuity of Hell to the making of them. They show **grotesqueries** of ugliness that, in retrospect, become almost diabolical. One cannot imagine mere human beings concocting such dreadful things, and one can scarcely imagine human beings bearing life in them.

6   Are they so frightful because the valley is full of foreigners—dull, **insensate** brutes, with no love of beauty in them? Then why didn't these foreigners set up similar abominations in the countries that they came from? You will, in fact, find nothing of the sort in Europe—save perhaps in the more putrid parts of England. There is scarcely an ugly village on the whole Continent. The peasants, however poor, somehow manage to make themselves graceful and charming habitations, even in Spain. But in the American village and small town the pull is always toward ugliness, and in that Westmoreland valley it has been yielded to with an eagerness bordering upon passion. It is incredible that mere ignorance should have achieved such masterpieces of horror.

7 On certain levels of the American race, indeed, there seems to be a positive **libido** for the ugly, as on other and less Christian levels there is a libido for the beautiful. It is impossible to put down the wallpaper that defaces the average American home of the lower middle class to mere **inadvertence**, or to the obscene humor of the manufacturers. Such ghastly designs, it must be obvious, give a genuine delight to a certain type of mind. They meet, in some unfathomable way, its obscure and unintelligible demands. They caress it as "The Palms" caresses it, or the art of the movie, or jazz. The taste for them is as **enigmatical** and yet as common as the taste for **dogmatic** theology and the poetry of Edgar A. Guest.

8 Thus I suspect (though confessedly without knowing) that the vast majority of the honest folk of Westmoreland county, and especially the 100% Americans among them, actually admire the houses they live in, and are proud of them. For the same money they could get vastly better ones, but they prefer what they have got. Certainly there was no pressure upon the Veterans of Foreign Wars to choose the dreadful edifice that bears their banner, for there are plenty of vacant buildings along the track-side, and some of them are appreciably better. They might, indeed, have built a better one of their own. But they chose that clapboarded horror with their eyes open, and having chosen it, they let it mellow into its present shocking depravity. They like it as it is: beside it, the **Parthenon** would no doubt offend them. In precisely the same way the authors of the rat-trap stadium that I have mentioned made a deliberate choice. After painfully designing and erecting it, they made it perfect in their own sight by putting a completely impossible pent-house, painted a staring yellow, on top of it. The effect is that of a fat woman with a black eye. It is that of a Presbyterian grinning. But they like it.

9 Here is something that the psychologists have so far neglected: the love of ugliness for its own sake, the lust to make the world intolerable. Its habitat is the United States. Out of the melting pot emerges a race which hates beauty as it hates truth. The **etiology** of this madness deserves a great deal more study than it has got. There must be causes behind it; it arises and flourishes in obedience to biological laws, and not as a mere act of God. What, precisely, are the terms of those laws? And why do they run stronger in America than elsewhere? Let some honest **Privat Dozent** in **pathological** sociology apply himself to the problem.

● THE FACTS

1. What area of the country does this essay describe?
2. What is the principal occupation of the region?
3. Mencken not only criticizes the architecture of the region, he also suggests an alternative. What sort of architecture does he think is suited to this region?
4. On what does Mencken blame the ugliness he describes?
5. What are Mencken's views of the villages in Europe? In his view, how do they compare with American towns?

● THE STRATEGIES

1. A good description focuses on and develops a dominant impression. Examine the second paragraph. What is the dominant impression here?

2. Examine the third paragraph. What dominant impression does Mencken focus on in his description of the buildings?

3. With what aspect of the ugliness does paragraph 4 deal?

4. "I have seen, I believe, all of the most unlovely towns of the world; they are all to be found in the United States." Why does he say *unlovely* rather than *ugly*? Which is more effective? Why?

5. "And one and all they are streaked in grime, with dead and eczematous patches of paint peeping through the streaks." What comparison is implied in this metaphor?

● THE ISSUES

1. One of the most vigilant civic groups in the United States today is the environmentalists—men and women determined to preserve historical buildings, wilderness areas, seacoasts, and public parks. What importance do you attribute to the efforts of these people? What do you think would happen if they no longer cared?

2. Mencken seems to feel that although architectural ugliness on any scale is lamentable, it is especially insulting when the edifice is pretentious. Do you agree with Mencken's view? Why or why not?

3. What stretch of highway in the United States is charmingly beautiful and stands in total contrast to Mencken's description of the houses in Westmoreland County? Describe this stretch in detail, focusing on architectural characteristics.

4. Do you agree with Mencken that Americans are psychologically obsessed with ugliness? If you agree, try to find reasons for this obsession. If you disagree, prove that Mencken is wrong by citing instances in which typical Americans have promoted beauty and good taste.

5. If you were to oversee a development of beautiful homes, what aesthetic requirements would you insist on? Describe the development in concrete terms.

● SUGGESTIONS FOR WRITING

1. Write an essay describing the town or city where you live.

2. Write an analysis of Mencken's diction in this essay, paying particular attention to his use of adjectives.

Hell

JAMES JOYCE

Rhetorical Thumbnail

Purpose: to describe hell in the most vivid and concrete terms imaginable

Audience: educated novel readers

Language: standard English

Strategy: uses biblical and other theological references to paint a graphic word picture of hell

---

James Joyce (1882–1941) is considered by many to be among the most significant novelists of the twentieth century. He was born in Dublin, Ireland, and educated at University College, Dublin. Joyce, a writer who pushed language to its outer limit of comprehensibility, wrote poetry, short stories, and novels. His major novels include *A Portrait of the Artist as a Young Man* (1916), *Ulysses* (written between 1914 and 1921 and published in the United States in 1933), and *Finnegan's Wake* (1939).

Joyce, in this selection from A Portrait of the Artist as a Young Man, *shows us the wreathing fires of hell and persuades us to smell its stench of brimstone and sin. The description that follows is so graphic, so detailed, and so filled with such shuddering imagery, that we almost believe that someone has returned from this dreadful place to tell the tale.*

• • •

1 Hell is a **strait** and dark and foulsmelling prison, an abode of demons and lost souls, filled with fire and smoke. The straitness of this prisonhouse is expressly designed by God to punish those who refused to be bound by His laws. In earthly prisons the poor captive has at least some liberty of movement, were it only within the four walls of his cell or in the gloomy yard of his prison. Not so in hell. There, by reason of the great number of the damned, the prisoners are heaped together in their awful prison, the walls of which are said to be four thousand miles thick: and the damned are so utterly bound and helpless that, as a blessed saint, saint Anselm, writes in his book on **similitudes**, they are not even able to remove from the eye a worm that gnaws it.

2   —They lie in exterior darkness. For, remember, the fire of hell gives forth no light. As, at the command of God, the fire of the Babylonian furnace lost its heat but not its light so, at the command of God, the fire of hell, while retaining the intensity of its heat, burns eternally in darkness. It is a never-ending storm of darkness, dark flames and dark smoke of burning brimstone, amid which the bodies

are heaped one upon another without even a glimpse of air. Of all the plagues with which the land of the Pharaohs was smitten one plague alone, that of darkness, was called horrible. What name, then, shall we give to the darkness of hell which is to last not for three days alone but for all eternity?

3   —The horror of this strait and dark prison is increased by its awful stench. All the filth of the world, all the **offal** and scum of the world, we are told, shall run there as to a vast reeking sewer when the terrible **conflagration** of the last day has purged the world. The brimstone too which burns there in such **prodigious** quantity fills all hell with its intolerable stench; and the bodies of the damned themselves exhale such a **pestilential** odour that as saint Bonaventure says, one of them alone would suffice to infect the whole world. The very air of this world, that pure element, becomes foul and unbreathable when it has been long enclosed. Consider then what must be the foulness of the air of hell. Imagine some foul and putrid corpse that has lain rotting and decomposing in the grave, a jellylike mass of liquid corruption. Imagine such a corpse a prey to flames, devoured by the fire of burning brimstone and giving off dense choking fumes of nauseous loathsome decomposition. And then imagine this sickening stench, multiplied a millionfold and a millionfold again from the millions upon millions of **fetid** carcasses massed together in the reeking darkness, a huge and rotting human fungus. Imagine all this and you will have some idea of the horror of the stench of hell.

4   —But this stench is not, horrible though it is, the greatest physical torment to which the damned are subjected. The torment of fire is the greatest torment to which the tyrant has ever subjected his fellow creatures. Place your finger for a moment in the flame of a candle and you will feel the pain of fire. But our earthly fire was created by God for the benefit of man, to maintain in him the spark of life and to help him in the useful arts, whereas the fire of hell is of another quality and was created by God to torture and punish the unrepentant sinner. Our earthly fire also consumes more or less rapidly according as the object which it attacks is more or less combustible so that human ingenuity has even succeeded in inventing chemical preparations to check or frustrate its action. But the sulphurous brimstone which burns in hell is a substance which is specially designed to burn forever and for ever with unspeakable fury. Moreover our earthly fire destroys at the same time as it burns so that the more intense it is the shorter is its duration: but the fire of hell has this property that it preserves that which it burns and though it rages with incredible intensity it rages for ever.

5   —Our earthly fire again, no matter how fierce or widespread it may be, is always of a limited extent: but the lake of fire in hell is boundless, shoreless and bottomless. It is on record that the devil himself, when asked the question by a certain soldier, was obliged to confess that if a whole mountain were thrown into the burning ocean of hell it would be burned up in an instant like a piece of wax. And this terrible fire will not afflict the bodies of the damned only from without but each lost soul will be a hell unto itself, the boundless fire raging in its very vitals. O, how terrible is the lot of those wretched beings! The blood seethes and boils in the veins, the brains are boiling in the skull, the heart in the breast glowing and

bursting, the bowels a redhot mass of burning pulp, the tender eyes flaming like molten balls.

6   And yet what I have said as to the strength and quality and boundlessness of this fire is as nothing when compared to its intensity, an intensity which it has as being the instrument chosen by divine design for the punishment of soul and body alike. It is a fire which proceeds directly from the ire of God, working not of its own activity but as an instrument of divine vengeance. As the waters of baptism cleanse the soul with the body so do the fires of punishment torture the spirit with the flesh. Every sense of the flesh is tortured and every faculty of the soul therewith: the eyes with impenetrable utter darkness, the nose with **noisome** odours, the ears with yells and howls and **execrations**, the taste with foul matter, leprous corruption, nameless suffocating filth, the touch with redhot goads and spikes, with cruel tongues of flame. And through the several torments of the senses the immortal soul is tortured eternally in its very essence amid the leagues upon leagues of glowing fires kindled in the abyss by the offended majesty of the Omnipotent God and fanned into everlasting and ever increasing fury by the breath of the anger of the Godhead.

7   Consider finally that the torment of this infernal prison is increased by the company of the damned themselves. Evil company on earth is so noxious that even the plants, as if by instinct, withdraw from the company of whatsoever is deadly or hurtful to them. In hell all laws are overturned: there is no thought of family or country, of ties, of relationships. The damned howl and scream at one another, their torture and rage intensified by the presence of beings tortured and raging like themselves. All sense of humanity is forgotten. The yells of the suffering sinners fill the remotest corners of the vast abyss. The mouths of the damned are full of blasphemies against God and of hatred for their fellow sufferers and of curses against those souls which were their accomplices in sin. In olden times it was the custom to punish the **parricide**, the man who had raised his murderous hand against his father, by casting him into the depths of the sea in a sack in which were placed a cock, a monkey and a serpent. The intention of those lawgivers who framed such a law, which seems cruel in our times, was to punish the criminal by the company of hateful and hurtful beasts. But what is the fury of those dumb beasts compared with the fury of execration which bursts from the parched lips and aching throats of the damned in hell when they behold in their companions in misery those who aided and abetted them in sin, those whose words sowed the first seeds of evil thinking and evil living in their minds, those whose immodest suggestions led them on to sin, those whose eyes tempted and **allured** them from the path of virtue. They turn upon those accomplices and **upbraid** them and curse them. But they are helpless and hopeless: it is too late now for repentance.

● THE FACTS

1. How thick are the walls of hell?
2. What peculiar characteristics does the fire of hell have?
3. What is the greatest physical torment that the damned of hell suffer?
4. What is the source of the fire in hell?
5. How were parricides punished in olden times?

● THE STRATEGIES

1. Examine carefully this description of hell. What is its overall structure? How are its paragraphs deployed?
2. Examine paragraph 4. How is it developed? What is its purpose?
3. What is the purpose of mentioning the "earthly prisons" in paragraph 1?
4. Examine paragraph 5. How is this paragraph structured? What technique does the writer use to make his description so vivid?
5. In the novel *A Portrait of the Artist as a Young Man,* the preacher delivers this description of hell in a sermon. Identify at least one technique that the preacher uses to involve his listeners in the description.

● THE ISSUES

1. For the most part, modern minds have rejected the medieval view of a physical hell, where the damned suffer such tortures as heat, cold, foul smell, laceration, and persecution from demons. What, if anything, has replaced this notion of hell?
2. In your view, why do many people believe in paradise and hell? What disadvantage or advantage does the lack of belief in these places provide?
3. What effect do you think this sermon on hell might have on young boys listening to it? What is your opinion of the technique used?
4. Is torture as a means of punishment ever justified in a civilized society? Why or why not?
5. A portion of Dante's hell was reserved for those who encouraged others to sin. Where in this excerpt does Joyce express a similar idea? Why do both Dante and Joyce call down a harsh judgment on those who aid and abet evil?

● SUGGESTIONS FOR WRITING

1. Write an essay on hell as it is described here, arguing for or against a belief in its existence.
2. Write a brief description of heaven following the example of this selection.

Image Gallery for Critical Thinking and Debate: Self-Image

Everywhere we look, we see people who are enormously obese. We also see men and women who look as if they were advertising for a circus—with spiked green hair, tattoos up and down their bodies, and piercings that disfigure their noses, ears, and lips—that is, people so obsessed with their looks that they draw attention to themselves by looking bizarre. A totally different group worship at the shrine of glamour as portrayed by their idols in popular magazines and on the cinema or television screen. You can observe them sweating away on exercise machines, dieting on tofu, or paying out their hard-earned money to hire a trainer who will show them exactly how to build up their abs and shoulders. In fact, we are told that average Americans are exposed to 1,500 ads every day and spend dozens of hours per week watching television commercials that promise to transform them into male or female icons of an adulating public. Well, you might think that the media would try to reflect the average look when selling products, but not so. The majority of women models are much thinner and sleeker than the average woman in our cities or suburbs. Similarly, the men are more muscular and well-toned than the men we see walking the aisles of the supermarket or shopping malls.

Since the media glorifies these exotic images and exhibits them on electronic screens, on paper, and on billboards everywhere, young people grow up thinking that if they don't look according to these models, they must be losers. Advertisements create enormous anxiety about weight and body contours in adolescents, who are already insecure about their place in society. Some college graduates have actually postponed looking for jobs until they could achieve the "right weight" or "good muscle tone." This mass mirage sells huge amounts of products, but it also creates low self-esteem and severe depression.

Changing one's look has become a multi-billion-dollar business. In the last decade, huge companies have been built on the new psychology of first impressions that places a higher premium on physical attractiveness than on talent or personality. "Extreme makeover" programs that pool the resources of various plastic surgeons, cosmetic dentists, and personal trainers to transform ugly ducklings into sleek swans proliferate on television. This endless parade of comely flesh would give any alien observer watching from afar the mistaken impression that most Americans are attractive and physically fit instead of chronically overweight and sick. One is tempted to wonder if all of this pressure to live up to a certain standard of beauty does not lead to self-destruction rather than self-improvement.

Our Image Gallery sheds the spotlight on two kinds of people—those who want to create their own extraordinary self-image, and those who are incapable of creating the self-image advertised in the media, so they have given up. Our first page features a cartoon that points out how some people manipulate their looks artificially in order to look more ideal. The second page presents images of two celebrities who would rather look weird than ordinary. One image is that of Mike Tyson with his famous facial tattoo; the other is Lady Gaga whose imagination for outrageous costumes seems to be infinite. The third page reveals four people who are morbidly obese, a problem that is causing anxiety among medical doctors and health officials in our country. Nothing is definitively resolved here, nor would one expect it to be. How we see ourselves is even a more complex phenomenon than how others see us. In the end, the only solution may come from that old adage: Be yourself—whether you're fat, thin, in between, or truly an out-and-out hunk or hottie.

The student essay warns students to think twice before submitting to tattoos or piercings since these kinds of body alterations are difficult to remove should the fad fade and become absurd rather than avant garde.

A "To the Point" assignment rounds out the issue.

Study the following three pairs of images dealing with self-image. Then choose the image that most appeals to you. Answer the questions and do the writing assignment.

For readings, questions, and media on the issue of self-image, visit the *MindTap for Readings for Writers*, 15e online.

Toos, Andrew/CSL, CartoonStock Ltd

"No, your eyes are perfect, but fake glasses would sure make you look smarter."

Studying the Image

1. What does the doctor's comment tell us about what some people believe will overhaul human character and personality traits? Do you agree with this belief?

2. What do you think is the best method for forming a desirable human trait? How much success has this method had? Provide an example or two.

3. What role does sincerity play in personality formation? For instance, if you pretend to be friendly with your classmates, but in reality you find them inferior, will gestures like a pat on their shoulders or a condescending smile win you real friends?

4. What connection, if any, lies between appearance and self-image among today's teenagers? For instance, what vision of themselves are they trying to deliver when boys shave their heads except for a bright green mohawk growing across the top of their heads? Or when girls wear platform shoes that are so thick that onlookers gawk to see if the girl will wobble and plunge to the ground?

Writing Assignment

Write an essay in which you argue for or against allowing teenagers to choose their own styles of appearance. Support your argument with common sense, logic, and evidence from the experience of society.

Mike Tyson

Lady Gaga

Studying the Image

1. Describe in detail Mike Tyson's face and Lady Gaga's costume. Make your description vivid enough so that any person not familiar with these two celebrities could envision their looks.

2. Several years ago, HULIQ News issued the following headline: "Mike Tyson's Facial Tattoo Is Newest Craze for Singles on the Prowl." Why do you think Mike Tyson ordered this tattoo for his face? What is your evaluation of the artistic merits of Tyson's tattoo? Tattoos have now been around for some time. What future do you predict for tattoos? Are they a permanent art form, or are they headed for extinction?

3. Lady Gaga has been a polarizing figure since she became famous in the entertaining world. Her fans adore her, whereas her detractors scream that she is crazy. Since both Tyson and Gaga exude an image that some fans consider exotic, do you think they owe it to their followers to reveal a more traditional self-image, or is the outrage they cause a normal aspect of innovative personal style? Explain your attitude.

4. How important is it for young people to have the kind of self-image that gives them a sense of self-worth? Which aspects of one's background contribute most to the self-image one bares?

5. Do famous people like movie stars, athletes, or political leaders have a responsibility to portray a self-image of decency for young people to emulate? Or do you think that every human being should be free to act on his or her instincts and ambitions? Supply a rationale for your opinion.

Writing Assignment

Focusing on your self-image as you perceive it, write an essay in which you trace the major forces that contributed to who you are at this point in life. Give some specific examples to clarify your claims.

Obesity in public places: three people on a bench, and a young male strolling in black shorts.

Morales/Age Fotostock

Bo Zaunders/CORBIS

Studying the Image

1. What is the visual and emotional impact on you by either the people on the bench or the young man strolling along in public? How would you describe them to a close friend?

2. What is our culture's attitude toward obese people? Analyze some of the effects of attitudes you have experienced—especially comments made by insensitive young people.

3. What role do motion pictures or fashion magazines play in forming the ideal female or male image? What happens when certain individuals cannot measure up to the image?

4. In the lower grades of school, overweight kids are often bullied by being labeled "fatso," "lard ass," or "balloon butt." What can be done to stop this kind of bullying? If you were a parent of an obese child, what measures would you take to curb your child's appetite and to improve his or her self-image? Suggest a practical plan.

5. What are the main reasons why so many Americans continue to be obese despite the recent TV emphasis on losing weight through special diets, supplements, exercise, and psychological counseling? Has our society done enough to reverse the trend? Who should be most responsible for preventing obesity?

Writing Assignment

Write an essay describing an ideal male or female body. Then, suggest a plan for maintaining the kind of body you personally admire. If you use outside sources, integrate them into your writing and assign proper credit.

Stumped by ready-made phrases? Exit
*on page 425 to the **Editing Booth!***

Punctuation Workshop

The Comma (,)

1. **Put a comma before** *and, but, for, or, nor, yet,* **and** *so* **when they connect two independent clauses:** He played the guitar, and his brother played the saxophone.

2. **Put a comma between more than two items in a series:** Isaac ordered a salami sandwich, a salad, and ice cream.

   > **TREAT AN ADDRESS OR DATE AS ITEMS IN A SERIES:** He was born March 5, 1951, in Stoneham, Massachusetts.

   > **OMIT COMMAS IF ONLY THE MONTH AND YEAR ARE USED IN A DATE:** The revolution began in May 1980.

3. **Use a comma after an introductory expression or an afterthought:** Well, that certainly was stressful.

4. **Use a comma after a dependent clause that begins a sentence:** While she was skating across the pond, she fell and broke her ankle.

5. **Put commas around the name of a person spoken to:** Be careful, Professor Gomez, not to slip.

6. **Put a comma around any expression that interrupts the flow of the sentence:** The poor, however, can't live only on food stamps.

7. **Put commas around material that is not essential to meaning:** Joseph Pendecost, who is a tile expert, will lecture on artistic kitchens.

   > **BUT IF THE CLAUSE IS ESSENTIAL TO MEANING, NO COMMAS ARE NEEDED:** The man who is a tile expert will lecture on artistic kitchens. (No other man will lecture except the tile expert.)

8. **Use commas to separate a speaker from dialogue:** "Forget him," the mother said.

9. **Use commas as necessary to prevent misreading:**

   > **Woman:** without her, man is nothing.
   > **Woman,** without her man, is nothing.

Student Corner

Body Modification—Think about It!

Shelley Taylor

State University of New York, Oswego

Not long ago I heard a rumor that Barbie, that icon of glamour and favorite doll of girls from several generations, is getting a butterfly tattoo for her 40th birthday—or is it her 45th? Well, no matter, she hasn't aged a day in her life. She has to keep up with the latest fashion statements. After all, her future and reputation are at stake.

Almost everywhere you look these days you can see people with some sort of body alterations. The vast majority of these alterations are body piercings and tattoos. On a walk through a school campus or a shopping mall, for instance, you are bound to see ears adorned by multiple earrings, jeweled drops cascading down eyebrows, and glittering nose studs. There are yin yang symbols etched on ankles, cartoon characters inked on arms, and roses and names of loved ones permanently stamped on wrists (some other pictures aren't quite as "nice.") These are just examples of things you can *see*; many other body parts, including tongues, belly buttons (well, I guess you *can* see those), and genitals, are routinely pierced, and tattoos can appear practically anywhere.

Actually, throughout history, people from various cultures have decorated their bodies with piercings and tattoos. In 1992, a 4,000-year-old body of a tattooed man was found in an Austrian glacier. From 4000 to 2000 B.C., Egyptians identified tattooing with fertility and nobility. Body piercing has been used as a symbol of royalty and courage, as well as other lauded attributes. In some societies, body piercing and tattoos have long been used in initiation rites and as socialization symbols.

Piercing is performed without anesthesia by either a spring-loaded ear-piercing gun or piercing needles, ranging in diameter from six to eighteen gauge. A tattoo is created by an electric needle, which injects colored pigment into small, deep holes made in the skin. Far too often, however, cruder and less-sanitary methods are used. Even under the best conditions, the process is painful. The discomfort of getting a tattoo has been compared to that of hair removal by electrolysis.

So, why is body alteration so popular? Why do people do this to them-selves? The reason most often cited is that individuals feel a need to ex-press themselves in a creative way. They want to tell the world "who they are" (or who they wish they were). The vast majority of body piercings and tattoos are performed on adolescents, many of whom consider what they wear and how they look to be as important as food and water. Modifying their bodies is their way of being non-traditional and "different."

Interestingly enough, however, being different is the last thing they re-ally want to do. If their peers, especially those who comprise the "in crowd," are doing something, they feel that they need to do it, too. They want to share a common identity, to belong to the group, to fit in. The media plays a big role in all of this. Models, sports idols, members of their favorite music groups, all endorsed by magazines, television, and movies, show off their body piercings and tattoos proudly, as the latest and "coolest" thing.

Teens *do* strive to be different from their parents and anyone in the older generation. Body alterations are one way for them to say, "I'm grow-ing up and making decisions on my own." This becomes, in a way, a rite of passage, declaring that they are changing and becoming mature. They are seeking their own place in society and a sense of empowerment. They are celebrating their growth toward and into adulthood.

Many would argue that changing their appearance is a relatively harm-less way for adolescents to meet the need to search for their identities and to explore less traditional paths. After all, purple hair, hole-filled jeans, and sparkling navel jewels can hardly be compared with drugs and violence. Dress styles come and go, just as they have for centuries, and continue to make the world more interesting and less boring, if nothing else.

The very fact that fads pass so quickly, however, should give one pause when he or she is considering body alterations. While hair color and apparel can be changed easily, a piercing or a tattoo is a physical change that is harder to discard. Body piercing can be relatively tempo-rary in the long run, unless certain types of infection or scarring occur, but its immediate implications can have far-reaching results. A tattoo, how-ever, is permanent. It is not something a person can just take off and throw away when it is no longer in style or desirable. Obviously, this fact points out the utter foolishness of having the name of a boyfriend or girl-friend (or even a spouse) adorning some part of your body forever. What a way to complicate your future!

The question of appearance is an important one. Whether we like it or not, we cannot disregard how we are perceived by others. This factor makes a huge difference in our lives. It takes only ten to fifteen seconds for someone to create a first impression that can affect his or her life for years to come. Nowhere is this truer than in the job market. A prospective employer will take note of your appearance, before giving you a chance to answer a single question or tell about your qualifications. Tattoos and body piercings do not project the type of image that is valued in the conservative business community. Consequently, those who choose to have these body alterations will probably have fewer job opportunities than those who decide not to.

Health is a major issue that must be considered. There are potential health risks involved with the initial process of body piercing and tattoo-ing. Take the tongue, for instance. Tongues swell to twice their normal size when first punctured. This often interferes with eating and effective breathing. Infections, blood clots, drooling, and damaged taste buds and nerves can also develop. Even broken teeth, choking, or impeded speech are possible. Other piercings can cause problems as well. Pierced navels take up to 12 months to heal and are painful, especially when irritated by waistbands. Nipple piercing may cause infection, an allergic reaction to the ring, or scarred milk ducts, which permanently interfere with breast-feeding. The cartilage in the upper ear heals slowly and may become infected. Piercing can cause permanent scarring and keloid formation. An allergic reaction to metal can result in contact dermatitis.

This is just the beginning. Even more serious side effects can occur. Piercing can be responsible for endocarditis, urethral rupture, and a serious infection of the penis foreskin that can result in disability or death. Piercings and tattoos present the risk of chronic infection, hepatitis B and C, tetanus, and theoretically HIV, especially when proper sterilization and safety procedures are not followed. Black henna tattoos can cause significant rashes and allergies, which can lead to kidney failure and even death. These are especially dangerous to young children.

This brings me to another point. It is illegal for commercial tattoo and body-piercing businesses to administer body modification to a person younger than eighteen years of age unless a parent or guardian signs a consent form. An unfortunate response to this law is the practice of "home-made" tattoos and piercings. Adolescents are getting these body altera-tions from friends or other amateurs who make their own tools with the use of pens, erasers, and paper clips and perform the procedures under unsanitary conditions. Very young children are being influenced to "be cool" like the older kids they look up to and want to emulate, often with tragic consequences. Not long ago, in an elementary school in Fort Worth, Texas, ten third-graders tried to give themselves tattoos using razor blades.

Literally, then, body modification can be a matter of life and death. This is true in another way, which some may not be aware of. As I alluded to before, this practice can represent symbols of group identity. This is often associated with gangs. Members of gangs apply tags or marks to show that they belong to their particular group. Middle-school students (grades five to eight) acquire most of these tags as a part of gang initia-tion. Specific color and clothing combinations and tattoos are examples of such tagging. Tattoos are usually applied by fellow gang members.

I worked for a short time in a detention facility for adjudicated youth, ages twelve to eighteen, who had each been convicted of at least one crime. As part of our training, we attended a seminar given by a law officer who had spent years studying gang operations and working with individual gang members. He informed us that graffiti, artwork, specific colors, styles of clothing, music, and dances were all part of the messages that gangs send to their own members and to those who belong to rival gangs.

They establish territory and warn other groups of violent repercus-sions if this territory is not respected. Even dance moves and hand signals have significant meaning. He told of a rock music performer who was murdered by the "Bloods" because he did the "Crip Walk" (or was it the other way around?) and made "disrespectful" signs with his fingers while on a public stage. Immediately I thought of the thousands of kids who are permanently marked with gang tattoos and the danger in which this places them. It is a known fact that prisoners with these tattoos are in fear for their lives while they are incarcerated with other criminals who have come out of rival gangs.

This fear of gang reprisal, along with the tendency of employers and law officials to associate tattoo markings with crime-related activities, has caused many to try to get their tattoos removed. Often these people are gang members who want out. Yet of the ten million Americans who have tattoos, almost half want their tattoos removed—for a variety of reasons. Clinics that offer tattoo removal are springing up everywhere, not only in the U.S., but in other countries as well, especially those in Central and South America. The demand is still more than can be accommodated at this time. Tattoo removal is expensive and is also a very long and painful process. Laser treatments cost thousands of dollars each and have been likened to hot bacon grease streaming down the skin. After multiple sessions, there is still a shadow on the skin while the laser-transmitted pigment enters the lymph system. Other methods of removal involve cutting the skin off with a scalpel or sanding the tattoo off with a wire brush. Many times, total success is not achieved.

So how do you decide what is right for you? Just be sure to consider everything very carefully. As you can see, there is a lot to think about. Take your time. Don't rush out and do something drastic without asking a lot of questions. Are you doing this for yourself or because you want to be like your friends? After all, it is your body. Are the benefits worth all of the risks involved? Are there career plans to consider? How do you think you will want to look in ten years or so? That reminds me—if you decide to go ahead with this, don't gain weight. A cute little frog tattooed onto a size-four stomach can look pretty scary after it has stretched and grown, twenty, thirty, or more pounds later.

Remember that this decision will most likely affect the rest of your life. That makes it extremely important, wouldn't you say? Whether you are a teenager, a young adult, or a middle-aged person who has always dreamed of doing something fun and outrageous, don't forget to look at all sides of this issue. It will be well worth the trouble. At the risk of being unoriginal, I would like to end with a quotation from one of those very wise anonymous writers for *The College Chalkboard* Web site: "Ponder before you pierce, and think before you ink." I couldn't have said it better myself.

How I Write

Before I actually begin writing, I do a lot of reflective thinking and organizing in my mind. I decide what information I am going to include and try to get a rough idea of the order and format I want to use. I usually sketch out an outline that I can follow. When actually writing the piece, I sit down at the computer and start typing, referring constantly to my outline. I edit and make changes as I go along until I am satisfied with the result. After I have finished, I read through my work several times to do further editing.

My Writing Tips

- Start your writing with something that will capture the attention of your reader—such as an interesting story or illustration, an amazing fact, or a dynamic statement.
- Be imaginative, descriptive, and creative.
- Avoid using redundant words and phrases in your writing.
- Make sure that your grammar and spelling are correct and that your ideas are presented as clearly as possible.
- Be sincere. Always be present in your work. Anyone can write down a bunch of facts, but your own insights and personality can make the words come to life.
- Leave your reader with something to think about. (I personally think the intro-duction and conclusion are the crucial parts of an essay.)

 **To the Point**

Answer the following tweet, pretending it was addressed to you:
"You're about the biggest loser in the class. You should tattoo a weepy face on your mom's back."

■ Chapter Writing Assignments

1. Write an essay in which you describe one of the following places:

   a. The most peaceful place you know

   b. The most disturbing place you have ever been to

   c. The most boring place you know

2. Write an essay describing a particularly vivid dream. Begin by thinking of and writing down a dominant impression for the scenes you saw in your dream. Using that dominant impression as your thesis, write a description that is supported by specific details.

■ Writing Assignments for a Specific Audience

1. Write a diary entry, describing the major events of your day. Treat your diary as a confidential, intimate friend to whom you can trust your innermost feelings.

2. Write to a family member, describing to them your college living quarters, or a letter to a friend, describing your favorite spot on campus.

 Pointer from a Pro

WRITE ABOUT THE FAMILIAR

I write about the things that disturb me, the things that won't let me alone, the things that are eating slowly into my brain at three in the morning, the things that unbalanced my world. Sometimes these are things I've seen. Sometimes they're only sentences, sometimes scenes, sometimes complete narratives. I carry these things around inside my head until I'm compelled to write them down to get rid of them. I sit down and begin.

—Roxana Robinson, "If You Invent the Story, You're the First to See How It Ends." *Writers on Writing.*

The point is that when you feel passionate about your writing, your ideas will glisten; whereas when you feel indifferent, your writing will tend to be dreary like your attitude.

CHAPTER 10

Process Analysis

■ Road Map to Process Analysis

What Process Analysis Does

An essay that gives instructions on how to do something or describes how something was done is developed by process analysis. Many best-sellers have been written in this mode, all bearing such telltale how-to titles as *How to Make a Million in Real Estate* or *How to Learn Spanish the Easy Way.* Historians such as Will Durant use process analysis to tell us how Spartan warriors were trained, how Christianity became the dominant religion of Western civilization, and how the Battle of Normandy was won. Like narration, process analysis presents information in chronological order, commonly in the form of instructions. Here, a student explains the process of cooking vegetables in a microwave oven:

> If you follow these seven easy steps, you will have the pleasure of eating veg-etables cooked *al dente,* the way they are done in the finest restaurants where nouvelle cuisine is the rage:
>
> First, choose three vegetables that normally take approximately the same time to cook (for instance, carrots, broccoli, and summer squash). For aesthetic purposes it is a good idea to choose vegetables of different colors.
>
> Second, slice the vegetables into bite-size pieces or slices, depending on which is easier.
>
> Third, arrange the pieces in alternating circles on a ceramic quiche plate.
>
> Fourth, add butter, salt, and pepper to taste.
>
> Fifth, pour one-half cup of water over the vegetables.
>
> Sixth, place a piece of plastic wrap over the plate and seal the sides.
>
> Last, cook the vegetables in the microwave oven for four minutes on "high." The vegetables will be crisply delicious and ready to serve the most discriminating of palates. Best of all, the vitamins will be preserved.

Although process analysis is a simple rhetorical mode and is fairly straightforward to write, it is often done badly and with irksome consequences. Anyone who has ever struggled to understand an inept manual meant to explain some necessary but practical chore can attest to the importance of clear process writing.

When to Use Process Analysis

Although found in all kinds of writing, process explanations are common in science and technology, where they vary from instructions on how to perform a simple test for acidity to how to diagnose a high-risk pregnancy with ultrasound. Many of your classes will require you to write various process explanations: A political-science teacher may ask you to describe how a bill is passed in Congress; a geology teacher, how glaciers are formed; a botany teacher, how flowers are reproduced. Process explanations can range from a historical blow-by-blow account of Custer's Last Stand to an anthropological explanation of how ancient tribes buried their dead.

How to Write a Process Analysis

The first and most important step in writing a process essay is to select an appropriate subject. Decide whether your overall purpose is to give instructions or to inform. If you intend, say, to instruct readers in how to organize a volunteer team to nab graffiti writers or how to study for the SAT, your purpose is to give instructions. On the other hand, if you want to list the circumstances that led to the collapse of the dot-com companies in 2001 or the sequence of events that led to the resignation of President Richard Nixon, your purpose is to inform. In writing either kind of essay, you must know and be able to cite appropriate details.

State Your Purpose in a Clear Thesis The second step in writing your process essay is to begin with a thesis that plainly states your overall aim. "It is possible for you to acquire a competitive spirit" is an example of a thesis that leaves your reader in the dark and is singularly unhelpful to you, the writer. On the other hand, the thesis "You can acquire a competitive spirit by practicing five personality traits" establishes an agenda for the writer and tells the reader what to expect—a recital and description of the five traits. Similarly, "I want to inform you how juveniles are imprisoned," tells your reader practically nothing. Contrast it with this more helpful thesis: "Juveniles face four legal steps before they can be imprisoned."

A convenient and simple way to make the steps of your explanation stand out is to number them 1, 2, 3, etc. For example, in an explanation to a non-swimmer of *how* to become drownproof, the logical sequence of steps is as follows:

1. Take a deep breath.
2. Float vertically in the water.
3. Lift the arms to shoulder height and give scissor kicks while flapping the arms down in a winging motion.
4. Raise the head out of the water and exhale.

This sequence of steps is the only one that works, so your explanation must cover it accurately.

Organize the Sequence of Steps Logically Next, you should arrange the steps in the most logical order. Essays that cover simple how-to tasks, such as changing a tire or baking a cake are best organized chronologically. On the other hand, essays on broader topics, such as how to build self-esteem in a child, how to make a marriage work, or how Stalin rose to power, are best organized in order of importance.

Regardless of which arrangement you use, you should single out and explain each step clearly. It often helps to sketch out the steps exactly as they will occur in your chosen order. For example, let us say that your parents won a court case against a landlord for discriminating against them because of their ethnic origin. Using your familiarity with their case, combined with further research, you decide to write a paper on how to file an antidiscrimination housing suit. Here are your steps, outlined chronologically:

1. File the complaint with the local Fair Housing Council.
2. Explain your reasons for filing to the investigator who hears your complaint.
3. If the investigation uncovers evidence of discrimination, state or federal authorities will formally accuse the landlord of discrimination. (If your case has no merit, the matter will probably fizzle out here.)
4. Choose between appearing before an administrative hearing officer or hiring an attorney to file a lawsuit in civil court.
5. Either the case will be solved through a settlement or the state will impose a punitive fine to compensate for damages.

Once you have outlined these steps clearly, all you have to do is flesh out the essay with necessary facts and details.

Explain Everything The devil is said to be in the details, and that is clearly the case in process essays. Always assume that your reader is uninformed about your subject. Explain everything. Don't be vague, as maddeningly unhelpful manuals often are. If your essay is giving specific directions about how to do something, simply address the reader directly, as in a command: "Next, [you] fold the paper along the dotted line. . . . Then, [you] write your personal number in the upper left-hand corner," and so on.

It also helps to carefully signal the succession of described steps with words such as "first," "second," "next," "then," and "finally." Within each step, using words such as "before," "after," and "while" can help the reader keep track of the discussion. It might even be helpful to mention a previous step before going on to the next. For example, in a process essay about how juveniles are imprisoned, the first step might be for the police to bring the youth to a screening office. If so, you might introduce the second step this way, "If after the screening has taken place the case still cannot be informally resolved, the second step is to arrange a date for a court hearing."

As we said, process essays are usually straightforward and relatively simple to write. Most require no poetic or metaphoric language—a manual so written would drive consumers over the brink—and generally demand nothing more of a writer than a sensible grasp of facts and the ability to explain them in understandable sequence.

Warming Up to Write a Process Analysis

1. Choosing one of the following how-to processes, write down in chronological order or in order of importance the steps involved in completing the task. Do not omit a step.
   a. How to trim a Christmas tree
   b. How to intelligently read a newspaper

    c. How to make your college professors like you

    d. How to get ready for a long-distance bicycle race

    e. How to ask for a dinner date, or how to turn down a dinner date

2. Choosing one of the following how-it-happened processes, write down the major steps that led up to it. If needed, look up the topic on the Internet.

    a. How a friend of yours got hooked on an illegal drug such as cocaine or ecstasy

    b. How a serious accident that involved you or a loved one occurred

    c. How Saddam Hussein was finally caught, detained, and executed

    d. The stages of AIDS

3. From each group, choose the best topic for a process essay.

    a. 1. How to fly a commercial airplane

       2. How to wash a car

       3. How to write a novel

       4. How to speak Chinese

    b. 1. How the world came into being

       2. How your great-grandfather became a millionaire

       3. The stages of international economic bankruptcy

       4. How the United Nations functions

Examples

My Strangled Speech

DAN SLATER

Rhetorical Thumbnail

Purpose: to list the steps involved in overcoming a serious stuttering problem and thereby inspire other stutterers to work on curing their problem

Audience: anyone who has suffered from stuttering, who knows someone with a stutter, or who is interested in the causes of stuttering

Language: formal English that includes some scientific terminology

Strategy: describes vividly what stuttering is and then describes methodically the steps taken by the author to overcome what he considers a personal humiliation and shame

Dan Slater (b. 1977) is a lawyer who has successfully combined a legal career with freelance writing. He graduated from Colgate University with a B.A. in international relations. During his university studies, he also studied abroad In Madrid and in London. Later he attended Brooklyn Law School and earned a J.D., which led to a position with Kay Scholer LLP as a litigation associate representing corporate and individual clients in commercial and Intellectual property matters. Since 2009, Slater has contributed numerous essays to prestigious periodicals, such as *The New York Times, The Washington Post, New York* magazine, *GQ* magazine, and *American Lawyer* magazine. The following essay was reprinted from *The Washington Post.*

This essay reveals in aching details the agony suffered by stutterers. From the time he was four years old, the author blocked on words, and even today, he does not feel completely free from the dreadful fear of stumbling on some hard consonant and turning himself into an object of ridicule in the eyes of his audience. As you read, try to identify with the stutterer's humiliation and his enormous battle with fear. Try to understand the origin of the impediment and follow the steps the author took throughout his life to correct this handicap so that he could express himself unhesitatingly and smoothly in public.

• • •

1   What that I remember most about my stutter is not the **stupefying** vocal paralysis, the pursed eyes, or the daily ordeal of gagging on my own speech, sounds **ricocheting** off the back of my teeth like pennies trying to escape a piggy bank. Those were merely the mechanics of stuttering, the realities to which one who stutters adjusts his expectations of life. Rather, what was most **pervasive** about my stutter is the strange role it played in determining how I felt about others, about you.

2   My stutter became a barometer of how much confidence I felt in your presence. Did I perceive you as friendly, patient, kind? Or as brash and aggressive? How genuine was your smile? Did you admire my talents, or were you wary of my more unseemly traits? In this way I divided the world into two types of people: those around whom I stuttered and those around whom I might not.

3   The onset of my stutter occurred under typical circumstances: I was 4; I had a father who carried a stutter into adulthood; and, at the time, my parents were engaged in a bitter, **protracted**, Reagan-era divorce that seemed destined for mutually assured destruction.

4   My mother chronicled my speech problems in her diaries from the period. Sept. 26, 1981: "Daniel has been biting his finger-nails for the past several weeks; along with stuttering up." July 8, 1982: "After phone call (with his father) Danny stuttering quite a bit, blocking on words."

5   In fact, my father and I had different stutters. His was what speech therapists consider the more traditional kind, in which the first syllable of a word gets repeated. "Bus" might sound like "aba-aba-abus." Mine was a blockage, a less extreme version of what King George VI, portrayed by Colin Firth, must deal with in the new movie *The King's Speech.*

6   My vocal cords would strangle certain sounds. Hard consonants—K's, D's, hard C's, and hard G's—gave me hell. A year of speech therapy in childhood

helped me develop a set of tools for defeating the impediment, or at least concealing it well enough to fool most of the people most of the time. Like many other stutterers, I evolved a verbal **dexterity**. Embarking on a sentence was like taking a handoff and running through the line of scrimmage:

7   I'd look five or 10 words upfield, and if I saw a mean word, such as "camping," I'd stiff-arm it and cut back hard in search of a less-resistant path, opting perhaps for something more literal: "I want to sleep in the woods this weekend."

8   But the strategies of substitution and **circumlocution** were never foolproof. The stuttering rat always lurks. When I was 14 years old, I wanted to ask a girl to the high school dance. Unfortunately, her name was Kim. I sweated it out for a few days, waiting for gumption to arrive. When I finally called Kim's house, her mother answered.

9   "Yeah hi, I was wondering if ahhh . . . if ahhh . . . if . . ."

10   I needed to bust through that K. But all I could do was pant, breathless, as the K clung to the roof of my mouth like a cat in a tree.

11   I breathed deeply and said at once: "Yeah hi I was wondering if Kim was there."

12   "Kim?" her mother said with a laugh. "Are you sure?"

13   Another deep breath: "Oh yeah I'm sure Kim."

14   When Kim took the phone, she told me her mom thought it was funny that I'd forgotten whom I'd called. I laughed along with them, of course, because it was preferable to forget the name of a girl you liked than to be thought an idiot.

15   More than 3 million Americans stutter, about 1 percent of the population. Stuttering afflicts four times as many males as females. Five percent of preschool children stutter as a normal developmental trend and outgrow it without therapy. While no single cause has been identified, stuttering is thought to result from a combination of genetics (about 60 percent of those who stutter have a family member who stutters), neurophysiology, and family dynamics, such as a legacy of high achievement (and the persistent pressures to perform that typically accompany it).

16   Stuttering, like other **enigmatic** ailments, has a checkered past. Beginning more than 2,000 years ago, one ridiculous theory followed another. Aristotle, who may have stuttered, believed the stutterer's tongue was too thick and therefore '"too sluggish to keep pace with the imagination." Galen, the Greek doctor, claimed the stutterer's tongue was too wet; the Roman physician Celsus suggested gargling and massages to strengthen a weak tongue. Such **quackery** reached its logical climax in the 19th century, when Johann Friedrich Dieffenbach, the Prussian plastic surgeon, decided that people stuttered because their tongues were too unwieldy. In several cases he cut the organ down to size.

17   It wasn't until the early 20th century that serious steps were taken to understand and treat stuttering. Therapists tended to focus on the adolescent context in which stuttering evolves. Albert Murphy, a speech pathologist at Boston University, promoted a psychogenic theory, suggesting that the roots of stuttering "lie in disturbed interpersonal relationships and the stutterer's fractured self-image."

18   This theory is at the heart of *The King's Speech.* Screenwriter David Seidler, a stutterer, focused on the trust-building process through which an Australian speech therapist coaxes out of King George his earliest memories. In the breakthrough scene, the king recounts his childhood torments inflicted by his older brother, Edward, the sting of ridicule, and his mistreatment at the hands of the royal nanny.

19   The psychogenic theory can be a seductive one—My parents screwed me up!—but it has largely fallen out of fashion, replaced by physiological diagnoses that call for techniques such as breathing exercises and delayed auditory feedback, which uses hearing-aid-like devices that play the stutterer's speech back to him.

20   For a stutterer, every speech hang-up carves a little more confidence out of him, leaving behind an ever-deepening sinkhole of shame and self-hatred. A child who stutters might excel at science, be a good reader, throw a perfect spiral pass, or demonstrate loyal friendship. But in his mind he only stutters, and that is all that matters. Every stuttering incident intensifies that feedback loop of failure inside his head—"Everyone thinks I'm an idiot"—making the next speech attempt even more difficult.

21   Yet small victories—even one fluent sentence—can be equally emboldening, because the stutterer is a powerful believer. "I'll keep trying to speak," he thinks, "because tomorrow I might just be able to." The trick, for me, was switching that internal soundtrack from "Oh no, here we go again" to "Breathe, relax, and let it ride."

22   When I was 8, my mother took me to a speech therapist. He was a big-hearted, supremely patient man with whom I spent many afternoons discussing my favorite things: football, movies, and my baseball card collection. He taught me the "air-flow" technique developed by Martin Schwartz, a professor at New York University Medical Center. Schwartz believed that stuttering is caused when the vocal cords clamp shut. To release them, the stutterer is instructed to sigh, **inaudibly**, just before speaking. Like a roller coaster, my speech therapist would tell me, the words get a free ride on the airflow.

23   After a year of therapy, I wasn't completely fluent, but I left with new confidence and a toolkit for dealing with my stutter. One of those tools entailed practicing fluency through imitation, whether quoting songs or spouting movie lines with my brother.

24   This was all about changing the feedback loop of failure: Psychologically, I could slide into a different character, no longer expecting to loathe the sound of my own voice. Physiologically, imitation provided new feedbacks to my breathing and voice mechanisms: a different pitch, a different **articulation**, and a different rate of speaking to which I could peg my own speech.

25   However, just as the word-switching technique was never foolproof, neither was imitation. When I was 16, the stuttering rat emerged again.

26   In a class about the legal system, I was assigned to be the prosecutor in a mock murder trial. I would have to write and deliver an opening statement. *A Few Good Men,* a movie about a military trial, had recently been released on video.

I loved the way Kevin Bacon strutted before the jury, so self-assured and confident of his case against the defendants. So I practiced in his speaking style. I even wrote the last sentence of his **monologue** into my own statement.

27   The next morning, when I stepped to the podium, I tried to relax and breathe. But a straitjacket of stress shut me down; the muscles in my throat and chest choked off the air. Thanks to pure stubbornness, I persisted, blocking on every fifth word of a 500-word speech. By the time I reached the Kevin Bacon line—"These are the facts of the case and they are undisputed"—I couldn't move sentences with a dolly.

28   A couple of days later, the teacher stopped me in the hallway and said, "Dan, I had no idea. It was so courageous of you to try." She was a sweet woman, but it was the last thing I wanted to hear. The recognition of one's stutter can be as humiliating as the stutter itself. I'd been found out.

29   During college I ditched a couple of class presentations and made it through a couple of others. In law school I spoke fluently before groups on several occasions but declined an offer to be in the mock trial club. During six years in journalism, including a stint at *The Wall Street Journal,* I've found radio interviews to be much easier than videotaped segments.

30   I'm 33 now. I believe I'm mostly cured of my stutter. Yet when I recently visited a speech therapist in New York and spoke with him, he disagreed. He said that none of my speech during our meeting had indicated **disfluency**. But when I confessed that I switch words several times per day and think quite often about my stutter, he said: "A lot of energy goes into hiding it, to hoping no one finds out. You're thinking about it a lot. We would not call this a mark of success." Think about it a lot? But of course.

31   For all the empathy that can make a good speech therapist effective, perhaps there's one thing a non-stutterer can never understand: If we go to therapy, we think about it. If we don't go to therapy, we think about it. It's always there. Either it defines us or we find ways of accommodating it, working toward a state of peaceful coexistence, pushing on with the Kims and the Katies.

"Stuttering, even if not as severe as in 'The King's Speech,' can be shameful" by Dan Slater appeared in THE WASHINGTON POST, December 20, 2010. Reprinted with permission from the author.

● THE FACTS

1. What, according to the author, was the most persistent aspect of his stuttering? Why is this puzzling? How do you explain this irony?

2. From the author's comments, what can one deduce about the typical circumstances under which stuttering starts? If this is the case, what behavior should parents avoid as they rear their children?

3. Which words were particularly conducive to stuttering? How did the author sidestep these words? What do you think this technique required?

4. What important coping mechanism did Professor Martin Schwartz teach the author? Describe the technique in your own words. How effective do you consider this technique? What are its advantages?

5. On what basis did the speech therapist in New York (see paragraph 30) imply that the author was still not cured of his stutter? Do you agree with his implication? Was the therapist wise to offer his comments? Explain your answer.

● THE STRATEGIES

1. How does the title of the essay connect with its content? Is the connection clear as the reader proceeds through the essay? Describe your reaction to the title.

2. What historical reference does the author use in paragraph 5? What does this reference contribute to the purpose of the essay? If you don't recognize the reference, look it up on the Internet.

3. What strategy does the author use to illumine the extreme anxiety felt by a stutterer trying to get a date with a girl? What advantage does this strategy have?

4. How many major steps were involved in the author's search for a cure to his stutter? List them in the order of their occurrence. In your opinion, which step was the most successful? What additional step, if any, can you suggest?

5. Paragraphs 15–19 provide an overview of the history of stuttering therapy, including some statistics. What, if anything, does this information contribute to the essay? How helpful was it to your understanding of the author's impediment? Explain your answers.

● THE ISSUES

1. What is the most important psychological insight provided by the author? What information can sensitive readers absorb and use in their relationships with people who have speech problems? Describe situations in which you felt unsure about how to handle a conversation with someone suffering from a speech impediment. Discuss some helpful ways to handle such a quandary.

2. According to the author, stuttering cannot be traced to a single cause but possibly to a combination of genetics, neurophysiology, and family dynamics. How would a cure be hastened if science could discover a single cause for this troublesome impediment? How serious do you consider stuttering as an impediment to a person's career? Explain your answer.

3. Do you agree with the author that the psychogenic theory of stuttering can be a seductive one? (See paragraph 19.) Make a case for or against this theory, based on your own experience or that of people you know.

4. What was wrong with the attitude of the teacher who spoke to the author after he had delivered his opening statement as the prosecutor in a mock murder trial? After all, she obviously revealed empathy and admiration. Analyze her comment in light of the author's reaction. What alternative response would you suggest?

5. What is the thesis of this essay? Where is it stated? What are the most striking ideas about stuttering you gained from this essay? State what help the essay provided in your future relationship with people who have speech impediments.

● SUGGESTIONS FOR WRITING

1. After researching the Internet, write a report on today's prevalent opinions of expert speech therapists concerning the status of stuttering. Be sure to refer to valid and respected sources.

2. Using Slater's essay as a model, write an essay in which you mark out the steps you used to deal with some learning difficulty you faced in the past or are facing now.

Hunting Octopus in the Gilbert Islands

SIR ARTHUR GRIMBLE

Rhetorical Thumbnail

Audience: readers and listeners of popular material

Language: standard English

Purpose: amuse and entertain

Strategy: uses conversational English as befitting a radio broadcast

Sir Arthur Grimble (1888–1956) was a British colonial government official and writer. After receiving an education from Magdalene College at Cambridge, he joined the colonial service in the Pacific and was posted to the Gilbert and Ellice Islands, where he remained in various positions from 1914 until 1933. From 1933 to 1948, he worked as administrator and then governor of the Windward Islands, retiring from the colonial service in 1948. In retirement, Grimble developed a talent for narrating his island experiences on radio for the British Broadcasting Corporation. The result was a series of talks that became so popular they were published under the title of *A Pattern of Islands* (1952), from which the following excerpt was taken.

Grimble relates an amusing story of watching two young boys hunting just off a reef in the Gilbert Islands. His curiosity about what the boys were doing got him into a predicament from which he could not escape without taking part in their sport. In the course of telling this riveting story, Grimble gives us a process explanation of how the Gilbertese hunt and kill octopus.

● ● ●

1 The Gilbertese happen to value certain parts of the octopus as food, and their method of fighting it is coolly based upon the one fact that its arms never change their grip. They hunt for it in pairs. One man acts as the bait, his partner as the killer. First, they swim eyes-under at low tide just off the reef, and search the crannies of the submarine cliff for sight of any tentacle that may flicker out for a catch.

When they have placed their **quarry**, they land on the reef for the next stage. The human bait starts the real game. He dives and tempts the lurking brute by swimming a few strokes in front of its cranny, at first a little beyond striking range. Then he turns and makes straight for the cranny, to give himself into the embrace of those waiting arms. Sometimes nothing happens. The beast will not always respond to the lure. But usually it strikes.

2   The partner on the reef above stares down through the **pellucid** water, waiting for his moment. His teeth are his only weapon. His killing efficiency depends on his avoiding every one of those strangling arms. He must wait until his partner's body has been drawn right up to the entrance of the cleft. The monster inside is groping then with its horny mouth against the victim's flesh, and sees nothing beyond it. That point is reached in a matter of no more than thirty seconds after the decoy has plunged. The killer dives, lays hold of his **pinioned** friend at arm's length, and jerks him away from the cleft; the octopus is torn from the anchorage of its **proximal** suckers, and clamps itself the more fiercely to its prey. In the same second, the human bait gives a kick which brings him, with quarry **annexed**, to the surface. He turns on his back, still holding his breath for better buoyancy, and this exposes the body of the beast for the kill. The killer closes in, grasps the evil head from behind, and wrenches it away from its meal. Turning the face up towards himself, he plunges his teeth between the bulging eyes, and bites down and in with all his strength. That is the end of it. It dies on the instant; the suckers release their hold; the arms fall away; the two fishers paddle with whoops of delighted laughter to the reef, where they string the catch to a pole before going to rout out the next one.

3   Any two boys of seventeen, any day of the week, will go out and get you half a dozen octopus like that for the mere fun of it. Here lies the whole point of this story. The hunt is, in the most literal sense, nothing but child's play to the Gilbertese.

4   As I was standing one day at the end of a jetty in Tarawa lagoon, I saw two boys from the near village shouldering a string of octopus slung on a pole between them. I started to wade out in their direction, but before I hailed them they had stopped, planted the carrying-pole upright in a fissure and, leaving it there, swum off the edge for a while with faces submerged evidently searching for something under water. I had been only a few months at Tarawa, and that was my first near view of an octopus hunt. I watched every stage of it from the dive of the human bait to the landing of the dead catch. When it was over, I went up to them. I could hardly believe that in those few seconds, with no more than a frivolous-looking splash or two on the surface, they could have found, caught and killed the creature they were now stringing up before my eyes. They explained the amusing simplicity of the thing.

5   "There's only one trick the decoy-man must never forget," they said, "and that's not difficult to remember. If he is not wearing the water-spectacles of the Men of Matang,1 he must cover his eyes with a hand as he comes close to the *kika* (octopus), or the sucker might blind him." It appeared that the ultimate fate of the eyes was not the thing to worry about; the immediate point was that the sudden pain of a sucker clamping itself to an eyeball might cause the bait to expel

his breath and inhale sea-water; that would spoil his buoyancy, and he would fail then to give his friend the best chance of a kill.

6   Then they began whispering together. I knew in a curdling flash what they were saying to each other. Before they turned to speak to me again, a horrified conviction was upon me. My damnable curiosity had led me into a trap from which there was no escape. They were going to propose that I should take a turn at being the bait myself, just to see how delightfully easy it was.

7   And that is what they did. It did not even occur to them that I might not leap at the offer. I was already known as a young Man of Matang who liked swimming, and fishing, and laughing with the villagers; I had just shown an interest in this particular form of hunting; naturally, I should enjoy the fun of it as much as they did. Without even waiting for my answer, they gleefully ducked off the edge of the reef to look for another octopus—a fine fat one—mine. Left standing there alone, I had another of those visions . . .

8   It was dusk in the village. The fishers were home, I saw the cooking-fires glowing orange-red between the brown lodges. There was laughter and shouted talk as the women prepared the evening meal. But the laughter was hard with scorn. "What?" they were saying, "Afraid of a kika? The young Man of Matang? Why, even the boys are not afraid of a kika!" A curtain went down and rose again on the Residency; the Old Man was talking: "A leader? You? The man who funked a schoolboy game? We don't leave your sort in charge of Districts." The scene flashed to my uncles: "Returned empty," they said. "We always knew you hadn't got it in you. Returned empty . . ."

9   Of course it was all overdrawn, but one fact was beyond doubt; the Gilbertese reserved all their most **ribald** humour for physical cowardice. No man gets himself passed for a leader anywhere by becoming the butt of that kind of wit. I decided I would rather face the octopus.

10   I was dressed in khaki slacks, canvas shoes and a short-sleeved singlet. I took off the shoes and made up my mind to shed the **singlet** if told to do so; but I was wildly determined to stick to my trousers throughout. Dead or alive, said a voice within me, an official minus his pants is a preposterous object, and I felt I could not face that extra horror. However, nobody asked me to remove anything.

11   I hope I did not look as yellow as I felt when I stood to take the plunge; I have never been so sick with **funk** before or since. "Remember, one hand for your eyes," said someone from a thousand miles off, and I dived.

12   I do not suppose it is really true that the eyes of an octopus shine in the dark; besides, it was clear daylight only six feet down in the **limpid** water; but I could have sworn the brute's eyes burned at me as I turned in towards his cranny. That dark glow—whatever may have been its origin—was the last thing I saw as I blacked out with my left hand and rose into his clutches. Then, I remember chiefly a dreadful sliminess with a **herculean** power behind it. Something whipped round my left forearm and the back of my neck, binding the two together. In the same flash, another something slapped itself high on my forehead, and I felt it crawling down inside the back of my singlet. My impulse was to tear at it with my right hand, but I felt the whole of that arm pinioned to my ribs. In most emergencies the mind works with crystal-clear impersonality. This was not even an emergency, for I knew myself perfectly safe. But my boyhood's nightmare was upon me. When

I felt the swift **constriction** of those disgusting arms jerk my head and shoulders in towards the reef, my mind went blank of every thought save the beastliness of contact with that squat head. A mouth began to nuzzle below my throat, at the junction of the collar-bones. I forgot there was anyone to save me. Yet something still directed me to hold my breath.

13   I was awakened from my cowardly trance by a quick, strong pull on my shoulders, back from the cranny. The cables around me tightened painfully, but I knew I was adrift from the reef. I gave a kick, rose to the surface and turned on my back with the brute sticking out of my chest like a tumour. My mouth was smothered by some flabby moving horror. The suckers felt like hot rings pulling at my skin. It was only two seconds, I suppose, from then to the attack of my deliverer, but it seemed like a century of nausea.

14   My friend came up between me and the reef. He pounced, pulled, bit down, and the thing was over—for everyone but me. At the sudden relaxation of the tentacles, I let out a great breath, sank, and drew in the next under water. It took the united help of both boys to get me, coughing, heaving and pretending to join in their delighted laughter, back to the reef. I had to submit there to a kind of war-dance round me, in which the dead beast was slung whizzing past my head from one to the other. I had a chance to observe then that it was not by any stretch of fancy a giant, but just plain average. That took the bulge out of my budding self-esteem. I left hurriedly for the cover of the jetty, and was sick.

"Hunting Octopus in the Gilbert Islands" from A PATTERNS OF ISLANDS, by Sir Arthur Grimble. Copyright (c) 1952. Reprinted with permission from Eland Publishing Ltd.

⬤ THE FACTS

1. What two roles in hunting octopus do the hunting partners separately play?
2. What weapon do the Gilbertese use to kill the octopus?
3. What danger does the decoy man face in the octopus hunt?
4. Why did the author consent to take part in the sport of octopus hunting?
5. After the hunt was over, what did the author do?

⬤ THE STRATEGIES

1. What do you think is the most prominent feature of the style of this piece?
2. What can you infer about Grimble's attitude toward octopuses from the words he uses to describe them?
3. In describing the reaction (see, particularly, paragraph 8) that might follow his refusal to take part in the octopus hunt, what simple device does Grimble use to make the scene humorous?
4. In paragraph 13, Grimble writes that he was awakened from his "cowardly trance." What is your opinion of this characterization? What effect does it and other self-deprecatory remarks have on the tone of the story?
5. This process explanation of how the Gilbertese hunt octopus consists of two major parts. What are they, and how effective do you find them?

● THE ISSUES

1. In spite of the deprecating remarks Grimble makes about his lack of courage, what picture of him emerges from this tale?

2. How does the portrait that Grimble draws of the octopus match your own knowledge of that creature?

3. Had Grimble not been a colonial official assigned to the Gilbert Islands, what do you think his reaction would have been to the invitation from the boys to join the octopus hunt?

4. Based on this story, what can you infer about the Gilbertese and their culture?

5. Imagine yourself in Grimble's place. What would you have done when the Gilbertese boys invited you to take part in the octopus hunt?

● SUGGESTIONS FOR WRITING

1. Write a process essay depicting the steps involved in any sporting event you've experienced.

2. Write an essay showing how you got entangled in doing something you did not really want to do.

Image Gallery for Critical Thinking and Debate: Bullying

If you think bullying is a modern virus, only recently attacking society through cyberspace where the big and tough crush the small and weak, think again. Remember fairy tales like "Snow White," Cinderella," or "Hansel and Gretel." The immovable force in these archetypal stories is a bully—that is, a blustering or quarrelsome person who threatens anyone who tries to lessen his or her rule. Perhaps observing nature is a good place to start understanding the process of bullying. For example, if you have ever watched a covey of mountain blue jays, you have noticed that as soon as two or three smaller birds swoop down on the peanuts offered by some charitable bird watcher, the biggest bird in the flock will charge these weaklings with his powerful wings until they drop their treasure and fly to hide in the nearest fir tree. That's a bully for you. Animals like lions or elephants usually bully for food or power, but why do human beings bully? The quick answer is that they bully because they have scarred personalities; however, the more nuanced answer is that they have not found fulfillment in their environment. Most psychologists admit that they have not had much luck in figuring out exactly why bullies operate in the cruel ways they do. Light is flickering at the end of the tunnel, though, because scientists are beginning to conduct exact studies of the bullying personality. For instance, at Brunel University in the United Kingdom, researcher Ian Rivers found that bullying inevitably reflected certain social attitudes that manifested themselves in the school environment. Based on 666 students (ages 12 to 16 from 14 schools) this study is a valuable beginning. Some facts have been firmly established. For instance, it was found that human bullies pick on people—especially the young and unprotected—who don't fit into their social scheme. Good examples in western culture are gays, non-athletes, and loners who reveal the need to be off by themselves rather than team up in a group. Another set of victims are those who do not fit the looks mold. They may be too fat or too short or physically disabled, so they are shunned and even persecuted. In sum, every society develops certain standards of behavior, attitude, and even looks, and those who don't meet those standards are singled out for bullying.

Although bullying is an ancient issue, societal changes and technological advances have caused the problem to evolve and become more dangerous. In addition to the age-old schoolyard bullies, we now have to face up to cyber bullies, who are the most dangerous of all because they can use deviously clever ways to raze their victims. So, not only does the frail and bookish ninth grader face some muscle-pumping fighter who punches him in the face until he sees stars and his nose spurts with blood, but the pubescent teenage girl is described on Facebook as "creepy ugly"—a label that causes her already teetering self-esteem to crash and collapse. After repeated taunts, she kills herself by slashing her wrists. In other words, this situation has become a battleground of warring factions, and communities need to step up to the table in order to negotiate a peace settlement.

Some people think that the only way to cure bullies is to give them a dose of their own medicine, even if that means "to beat the crap out of them." Others take a more charitable attitude by pitying bullies for their poor self-image, which causes them to feel better about themselves only when they bring down someone else. We believe that anyone who has been branded by a bully is in a position to offer a reason for this abuse and even a cure. Our image gallery gives students the chance to ponder the ramifications of bullying as they study the images on the pages that follow. The first image is a poster, which some campuses have used as a powerful deterrent to school yard bullying. It may well trigger in the viewer some additional ideas for ways to make sure that students defend those who are weak against the cruelty of tyrants on the prowl for victims to destroy. The second image is a photo of Tyler Clementi, who was bullied to the point of suicide. The final image is that of a young girl, so intimidated by two of her peers that she looks as if she is crying out for someone to save her from complete destruction.

The student essay, written by a college freshman, upholds the belief that in an exceptional democracy like ours, bullies have no place because they disrespect their fellow human beings.

"To the Point" rounds out the issue.

Study the following three images dealing with bullying. Then choose the image that most appeals to you. Answer the questions and do the writing assignment.

For readings, questions, and media on the issue of self-image, visit the MindTap for *Readings for Writers*, 15e online.

Najiah Feanny/Corbis

Studying the Image

1. What is the expanded message to anyone reading this sign? Express the message in your own words.

2. Where would you place this sign so it would be most effective on a school campus?

3. Do you consider it important for kids to grow up in an environment that does not tolerate bullying? Or do you think bullying allows young people to face the rough treatment they will inevitably encounter as they mature?

4. What guidance, if any, did you receive from your parents about treating the vulnerable kids in your family circle, neighborhood, or school? How did this guidance affect your view of bullies?

Writing Assignment

1. Write an essay in which you narrate an incident of bullying that you observed and which disturbed you. Be sure to describe the incident as it occurred and what consequences resulted.

Studying the Image

1. What does the inscription "Tyler Clementi, Assistant Councertmaster's Chair, Ridgewood Symphony Orchestra" tell us about Clementi? What is a concertmaster?

2. On September 22, 2010, Tyler Clementi jumped off New York's George Washington Bridge to his death. A student at Rutgers University, he had a passion for playing the violin and was gay. After two of his dormitory roommates photographed and posted a sexual encounter Clementi had with another male, Clementi became suicidal and left a note on Facebook, stating that he was going to jump off the GW Bridge. What is your reaction to this information—even if you never knew Tyler Clementi or saw him in person?

3. Why do young males often make fun of those in their circle who seem artistic or overly refined and lack the rough and tumble ways of the typical football hero? What is your reaction to this kind of discrimination?

4. Why do women often dislike other women whom they perceive as acting like swaggering men rather than like traditionally feminine women? How can society get rid of overt acts of cruelty to anyone whose sexual orientation is nonconformist?

Writing Assignment

In no more than 500 words, write the guidelines you would establish to assure that your campus adheres to the "No Bully Zone" philosophy and that classmates do not exhibit unfair or phobic behavior against gay people or any other persecuted minority on your campus.

© O Driscoll Imaging/Shutterstock.com

Studying the Image

1. Look at how these three girls are dressed. From what social background do you guess them to come?

2. What do you feel like saying to the girls doing the bullying? How would you tell the bullied girl to act in response?

3. If this scene took place on a school campus and you saw it happening, what obligation, if any, would you have concerning the event? Should you report it? Should you ignore it? Should you speak up in defense of the one being bullied?

4. What are the personality traits that might well develop later in her life if the young girl being bullied continuously feels that she is an object of scorn and contempt?

Writing Assignment

Write down a list of ten rules you would post in a public place, such as the library or the student union, setting the standard for the way students should treat their fellow classmates in order to exclude bullying from all relationships on campus.

Punctuation Workshop

The Semicolon (;)

1. **Put a semicolon between two closely related independent clauses not joined by** *and, but, for, or, nor, yet,* **and** *so:*

   > The bakery was closed on Sunday; we settled for crackers.
   >
   > Oatmeal contains antioxidants; it is good for the heart.
   >
   > The scout lifted his binoculars; a yellow object was floating in the water.
   >
   > Some grapes are seedless; others are not.

2. **Put a semicolon in front of** *however, therefore, nevertheless, then,* **and** *therefore* **when these adverbial conjunctions connect two independent clauses:**

   > I love email; however, I don't want just anyone to have access to my email address.
   >
   > Most people have bad habits they constantly try to break; therefore, psychologists keep getting new patients.
   >
   > The gate gave a tired squeak; then, it suddenly flew open.

   Notice that a semicolon precedes the adverbial conjunction, but a comma follows it. Actually, you can write acceptably without ever using semicolons because a period can always be used instead.

3. Use semicolons to separate items in a series already separated by commas:

   > Her garden consists of flowers, common and exotic; vegetables, native as well as imported; and species of herbs found nowhere else on the island.

Student Corner

Bullied

Gunnar Neuman

Walla Walla University, Washington

Throughout our nation, kids are being bullied every day. In other words, someone weak and powerless is being hurt by someone stronger and more powerful. What many of us don't realize is that anyone can be bullied because there are always people with authority who use their position to oppress someone lower on the authority ladder. It is troublesome to think of friends or loved ones being bullied, but do we truly understand the pain and trauma inflicted on individuals who are bullied unless we have been bullied ourselves? Yes, when we see photos on YouTube or TV news programs featuring a young boy or girl who has committed suicide because he or she could no longer bear the humiliation of being belittled, ridiculed, and shamed on campus or on Facebook, we shudder at such cruelty. But I am here to tell you that bullying is more common than we imagine, and if you search your past, you will doubtless bump up against a scene in which you were bullied.

We live in the United States of America, a nation forged to function "under God." We pride ourselves in being the land of parity and equal opportunity for all. If this is true, then why do we constantly dig ourselves a deeper hole of agony by treating people unfairly? We need to see that every day in this beautiful country of ours some form of bullying occurs. At dusk, an elderly gentleman struggling to find his car in a parking lot is knocked to the ground by some ruffian. A shy elementary school girl is told by her classmate that she is "butt ugly" and should stay away from school. A hod carrier on his first day on the job is called a "stupid idiot" by the foreman because the new laborer misjudged a brick wall by one inch. From personal experience I can testify that being bullied is one of the most painful emotions to battle. I love athletics like ice hockey, but when I began the sport, there was always someone more skilled than I who would throw a nasty remark at me to make me feel clumsy and slow. Following some of the worst mockery, I would sit in my room at home, asking myself, "Do I mean anything to anyone? Do I deserve this harsh treatment?" The truth is that these feelings of low self-esteem can gnaw away at your gut and can cause pain down the road as you remember them and ponder if they are valid. This kind of suffering is not what I want to see when I imagine the future of our world. Some philosophers believe that pain and suffering are part of the human condition and therefore bullying, like war, must occur; however, I see a much better future for all of us if we decide to get rid of bullying once and for all.

Bullying is no longer restricted to the school yard. In fact, one of the most vicious places where bullying is prospering is on the Internet. "Cyber bullying" is what they call it. Now, instead of bullying someone face to face, one can torture that person through emails, blogs, tweets, or other media outlets. Nearly 43 percent of kids who have been bullied were bullied online, while only 1 in 10 victims will inform a parent or trusted adult of the abuse. Ironically, much of the time the parents remain unaware that their child is being bullied at all. According to a 2013 study cited by the Department of Health and Human Services (DHHS) "29.3 percent of middle school students have experienced bullying in the classroom; 29 percent experienced it in hallways or locker areas; 23.4 percent were bullied in the cafeteria; 19.5 percent were bullied during gym class; and 12.2 percent of bullied kids couldn't even escape the torture in the bathroom."

What is often difficult for many people to understand is that even parents can be bullies. Children look to their parents for guidance. In my own life, I looked to my parents for basic instruction on how to live. They were there to tell me that happiness can be achieved only through hard work and by demonstrating love for myself and my neighbor. They taught me to be kind to those around me and to accept others for who they were, not for who I fantasized they should be. Unfortunately this is not the upbringing most kids receive today.

Since bullying is common in our society, we might wonder, "Why would any person choose to torture and harass another person? Where does the urge to bully originate?" One answer to consider is that bullying begins when a child suffers abuse from a parent. When parents indiscriminately yell at their offspring, beat them for some perceived minor disobedience, and generally treat them with cruelty, they are bullying. It is a well-known fact that children who experience child abuse are far more likely to become bullies themselves and even to evolve into criminals than children who have been brought up with respect and love from their parents. I believe this is a significant truth and should not be treated lightly. Let's face it, if child abuse were reduced significantly within our society, the problem of bullying would also decrease exponentially and fade away.

So what is the key to freeing ourselves of the evil of bullying? One answer is to value those around us and treat them with the respect we expect to receive in return. To become the kind of person who sees worth in all colleagues may take patience and hard work, but it will pay off in the end. Do we want a country where breaking news constantly features the evil acts of bullies? I shall leave the answer for you to give. Personally, I think we can do better. The moment we put an end to bullying, that is when we take a giant step toward the equality our citizens brag about.

How I Write

Writing has always been easier for me than speaking because when I write, I can ponder the point I want to make. When I am assigned an essay to write, I create an outline of what I want to cover and then I make sure to order my points so the reader can follow my reasoning. I try not only to bolster my arguments with facts or evidence, but also to use my imagination in order to keep my readers' attention without causing them to fall asleep from boredom. While spoken words may fly out of one's mouth thoughtlessly and at random, a sentence can be carefully carved out to persuade with logic. I try to combine a vivid style and solid content because I believe that blend leads to good writing.

My Writing Tip

If I were to offer one writing tip only, I would say, "Be yourself." Don't try to steal the imagination of another writer; instead, create a personal world you have discovered on your own. Use the critical thinking skills your teachers have taught you and make sure your arguments are based on solid evidence. No one wants to read sentences packed with vapid words that lead nowhere. By the way, use your personal experience to light up your message and to make it believable.

 **To the Point**

Respond to the following tweet: "Being different shouldn't mean being bullied."

■ Chapter Writing Assignments

Write a process analysis about one of the following topics:

1. How to cook your favorite dish
2. How you celebrate a favorite holiday
3. How you reconciled two friends who were not speaking to each other
4. How you study for a big test

■ Writing Assignments for a Specific Audience

1. Describe to your parents your typical workday so they will not feel that you are wasting too much time.
2. Explain to an audience of business executives how the English education you are currently receiving will make you a better employee.

Pointer from a Pro

BE SINCERE

I hold that man as hateful
As the gates of hell
Who says one thing, while another in his heart
Lies hidden well

—Homer (ca. 850 B.C.)

Trying to be on paper something you are not in real life will hamper you as a writer. Granted, sincerity is difficult to prove because we can't see into the hearts and minds of others; yet, phonies usually reveal themselves in their exaggerations or contradictions. If you want to write well, you should continually ask yourself, "Do I really mean that? Or am I just saying it to look good?"

CHAPTER 11

Illustration/ Exemplification

Road Map to Illustration/Exemplification

What Illustration/Exemplification Does

To *illustrate* means to give examples that clarify what you are trying to say. Short or long, illustrations are especially useful for embodying abstract ideas or sharpening ambiguous generalizations. They might consist of one item or a list of items that exemplify something, as in this paragraph, which illustrates what the author means by the "Discipline of Nature or of Reality":

> A child, in growing up, may meet and learn from three different kinds of discipline. The first and most important is what we might call the Discipline of Nature or of Reality. When he is trying to do something real, if he does the wrong thing or doesn't do the right one, he doesn't get the result he wants. If he doesn't pile one block right on top of another, or tries to build on a slanting surface, his tower falls down. If he hits the wrong key, he hears the wrong note. If he doesn't hit the nail squarely on the head, it bends, and he has to pull it out and start with another. If he doesn't measure properly when he is trying to build, it won't open, close, fit, stand up, fly, float, whistle, or do whatever he wants it to do. If he closes his eyes when he swings, he misses the ball. A child meets this kind of discipline every time he tries to do something, which is why it is so important in school to give children more chances to do things, instead of just reading or listening to someone talk (or pretending to) . . .
>
> —John Holt, *Kinds of Discipline*

On the other hand, an illustration might consist of one extended example rather than a list. Here is an example:

> Even the shrewdest of men cannot always judge what is useful and what is not. There never was a man so ingeniously practical as Thomas Alva Edison, surely the greatest inventor who ever lived, and we can take him as our example.

In 1896 he patented his first invention. It was a device to record votes mechanically. By using it, congressmen could press a button and all their votes would be instantly recorded and totaled. There was no question but that the invention worked; it remained only to sell it. A congressman whom Edison consulted, however, told him, with mingled amusement and horror, that there wasn't a chance of the invention's being accepted, however unfailingly it might work.

A slow vote, it seemed, was sometimes a political necessity. Some congressmen might have their opinions changed in the course of a slow vote where a quick vote might, in a moment of emotion, commit Congress to something undesirable.

Edison, chagrined, learned his lesson. After that, he decided never to invent anything unless he was sure that it would be needed and wanted and not merely because it worked.

—Isaac Asimov, *Of What Use?*

When to Use Illustration

The illustration is typically used to support an assertion or point. On every page, in almost every paragraph, writers who wish to communicate their meaning must back up their assertions with appropriate examples. It is not enough to generalize that such and such is the case, as you might do in a casual chat. To make your assertions believable, you must back them up with specific instances. Illustration is often practiced in combination with other modes of development, such as definition, description, classification, causal analysis, and so forth. In the following paragraph, for instance, two examples are used to define "romantic recognition":

Romantic recognition. Two examples will do. When we were flying from Erivan, the capital of Armenia, to Sukhum, on the Black Sea, a Soviet scientist, who spoke English, tapped me on the shoulder and then pointed to a fearsome rock face, an immeasurable slab bound in the iron of eternal winter. "That," he announced, "is where Prometheus was chained." And then all my secret terror—for a journey among the mountains of the Caucasus in a Russian plane is to my unheroic soul an ordeal—gave way for a moment to wonder and delight, as if an illuminated fountain had shot up in the dark. And then, years earlier, in the autumn of 1914, when we were on a route march in Surrey, I happened to be keeping step with the company commander, an intelligent Regular lent to us for a month or two. We were passing a little old woman who was watching us from an open carriage, drawn up near the entrance to a mansion. "Do you know who that is?" the captain asked; and of course I didn't. "It's the Empress Eugenie," he told me; and young and loutish as I was in those days, nevertheless there flared about me then, most delightfully, all the splendor and idiocy of the Second Empire, and I knew that we, every man Jack of us, were in history, and knew it once and for all.

—J. B. Priestly, *Romantic Recognition*

Here, an illustration is used to help describe the humility of John Masefield, the English poet:

> This quality of his can best be illustrated by his behavior that night. When the time came for him to read his poems, he would not stand up in any position of pre-eminence but sheltered himself behind the sofa, in the shade of an old lamp, and from there he delivered passages from "The Everlasting Mercy," "Dauber," "The Tragedy of Nan," and "Pompey the Great." He talked, too, melodiously, and with the ghost of a question mark after each of his sentences as though he were saying, "Is that right? Who am I to lay down the law?" And when it was all over, and we began to discuss what he had said, all talking at the top of our voices, very superficially, no doubt, but certainly with a great deal of enthusiasm, it was with a sudden shock that I realized that Masefield had retired into his shell, and was sitting on the floor, almost in the dark, reading a volume of poems by a young and quite unknown writer.
>
> —Beverley Nichols, *Twenty-Five*

Illustration is especially effective as support for a persuasive argument. For example, the bland assertion that animal experimentation is necessary to the advancement of science will persuade more forcefully when coupled with an example of how an infant's life was saved by a surgical procedure learned in practice on laboratory animals.

An illustration can also be visual: a picture, chart, map, line drawing, graph, or spreadsheet. Such visual illustrations are used widely in scientific and technical writing.

How to Use Illustration

1. **An illustration must be real and specific.** It must not consist simply of a restatement of what you've already said. Here is an example of a paragraph whose "illustration" is merely a rewording of a preceding statement:

   Before being sold to the American colonies, many slaves had acquired a knowledge of Wolof and Mandingo, the creolized English that had come into use along the Guinea coast as a trade language. For example, many slaves were conversant in both of these languages.

   Although the writer uses "for example," what follows is not an authentic illustration but only further commentary. Here is an improvement:

   Before being sold to the American colonies, many slaves had acquired a knowledge of Wolof and Mandingo, the creolized English that had come into use along the Guinea coast as a trade language. For example, when a runaway slave who could speak no English was arrested in Pennsylvania in 1731, his white interrogators had no difficulty in finding another Wolof-speaking slave to act as an interpreter.

   The illustration now supports the assertion that many slaves came to America already knowing creolized English.

2. **An illustration should be clearly introduced and contextually linked to the point it is intended to support.** If you reread the preceding paragraphs in this section, you will notice that the writers generally use some introductory phrases such as "take him as our example," "two examples will do," or "for example." Such phrases are needed when the context of the paragraph does not alert the reader that an illustration is to follow. On the other hand, if it is clear from the context that an illustration is to follow, no introductory phrase is necessary:

While viruses and bacteria cause most of the common diseases suffered by people who live in the developed world, protozoa are the major cause of disease in undeveloped tropical zones. Of these diseases, the most widespread are malaria, amoebic dysentery, and African sleeping sickness.

The first sentence makes it plain that malaria, amoebic dysentery, and African sleeping sickness are examples of diseases caused by protozoa in the tropical zones.

Beware, however, of plunging too abruptly into an illustration:

The idea that art does not exist among the lower animals is a primitive notion. The bower birds of Australia decorate their bowers with shells, colored glass, and shining objects. Some paint their walls with fruit pulp, wet powdered charcoal, or paste of chewed-up grass mixed with saliva. One kind of bower bird even makes a paintbrush from a wad of bark to apply the paint.

Notice how this passage is improved with a transition:

The idea that art does not exist among the lower animals is a primitive notion. **A perfect illustration of art in the animal kingdom is the art of the amazing bower birds of Australia.** These birds decorate their bowers with shells, colored glass, and shining objects. Some paint their walls with fruit pulp, wet powdered charcoal, or paste of chewed-up grass mixed with saliva. One kind of bower bird even makes a paintbrush from a wad of bark to apply the paint.

Some illustrations need to be followed by commentary that interprets them for the reader. Here is an example:

In 1796, Edward Jenner observed that people who came down with cowpox were protected against the far more serious infection of smallpox; therefore, he decided to infect people with cowpox to keep them from getting smallpox. In 1881, Louis Pasteur accidentally left a culture of chicken cholera out on a shelf. Two weeks later, having returned from a vacation, he injected the culture into some laboratory animals and found to his surprise that the animals, instead of getting cholera, had become immune to the disease. These two experiences illustrate the beginnings of genetic engineering, a science that is now on the verge of splicing out from a virulent microbe the genes that cause disease. Millions of seriously ill people hope to be cured from deadly viruses through the miracles of genetic engineering.

The last two sentences of the paragraph interpret by telling us that the examples cited were illustrations of early genetic engineering. Whether you should use an introductory phrase or a concluding phrase, or simply embed your illustration within the context of the paragraph, is mainly a matter of common sense. Use phrases to introduce your illustrations only if they are necessary. In every case, you should ask yourself whether you have made your point clearly enough to be instantly understood. If the answer is no, then you should add whatever sentence or phrase is necessary to complete your illustration.

3. **An illustration should always be relevant to the point you are making.** If it is not, you should leave it out. Again, much of this judgment is a matter of common sense. But sometimes we get paragraphs that read like this:

> My stepfather is a stodgy person. For example, he contributes money every year to the Audubon fund. He serves as an usher in church and is a Scoutmaster for my half-brother's troop. He is active in a club that devotes its time to restoring old buildings in our town.

> Not being instances of "stodginess," the examples given do not support the writer's assertion. It is better to avoid illustrations entirely than to cite irrelevant ones that do not support your point.

Warming Up to Write an Illustration

1. Following are five different theses that could well be developed through examples. Sketch out three examples for two theses of your choice. Be sure that each example supports the thesis.

   a. If you shop wisely, you can save large amounts of money.

   b. My mom and dad hear and see things differently.

   c. Sometimes imperfections are beautiful.

   d. Not being covered by medical insurance can be disastrous.

   e. My boyfriend (or girlfriend or spouse) always thinks of romantic things to do.

2. Answer the following questions by listing an example that clarifies the answer to the question.

   a. What makes a snowy landscape beautiful?

   b. What are some typical elements of authority against which teenagers rebel?

   c. Why do most people admire firefighters?

   d. What makes our national parks so valuable?

   e. What are the worst aspects of homelessness?

3. Provide an appropriate example to illustrate each of the following facts.

   a. Being a dentist requires ultimate patience.

   b. The President of the United States is not always a role model.

   c. Email is one of the great inventions of the last decade.

   d. Modern medicine has created miracle cures.

   e. Saying good-bye can be heart wrenching.

■ Examples

The Myth of the Latin Woman: I Just Met a Girl Named Maria

JUDITH ORTIZ COFER

Rhetorical Thumbnail

Purpose: to demonstrate the painful effects of thoughtless stereotyping

Audience: educated readers with a curiosity about people

Language: standard English with a few Spanish expressions thrown in to highlight the author's background

Strategy: uses vivid examples to point out the foolishness of seeing people in terms of ethnic types rather than as individual Americans

Judith Ortiz Cofer (b. 1952) is an American poet and novelist whose writings form a bridge between her childhood in tropical Puerto Rico and her adult life in New Jersey. As a result of this twofold background, Cofer never felt fully grounded in either the Latino or the mainstream U.S. culture. In Puerto Rico she was accused of sounding like a *gringa* whereas in New Jersey she was teased about her "Spanish accent." This constant feeling of being wrenched by two cultures has added strains of sensitivity to Cofer's stories about a *Latina* overcoming her sense of alienation. In the process, she has become an inspiration to other young women who have faced the challenge of feeling like outcasts in society. Cofer is the author of a novel *The Line of the Sun* (1989); a collection of essays and poetry, *Silent Dancing* (1990); and two books of poetry, *Terms of Survival* (1987) and *Reaching for the Mainland* (1987). Among her most recent works is *A Love Story Beginning in Spanish: Poems* (2005). The essay is taken from her collection *The Latin Deli: Prose and Poetry* (1993).

Because every social snub has its standards of beauty, behavior, and achievement, it does not take much for newcomers to feel unwelcome or ostracized when they have been stereotyped as foreigners. Children, of course, are the most vulnerable victims of social snubbing. If they are overweight, handicapped, or slow in learning, they can quickly become the victims of bullies, who delight in tormenting the alien or weak. As you read this essay, try to think what it would be like if you were transposed to a place whose language you did not speak and whose traditions you did not observe. Use your imagination to formulate a plan that would help build up your self confidence and resolve to triumph in a hostile milieu.

• • •

1   On a bus trip to London from Oxford University where I was earning some graduate credits one summer, a young man, obviously fresh from a pub, spotted me and as if struck by inspiration went down on his knees in the aisle. With both hands over his heart he broke into an Irish tenor's rendition of "Maria" from *West Side Story*. My politely amused fellow passengers gave his lovely voice the round of gentle applause it deserved. Though I was not quite as amused, I managed my version of an English smile: no show of teeth, no extreme contortions of the facial muscles—I was at this time of my life practicing reserve and cool. Oh, that British control, how I coveted it. But "Maria" had followed me to London, reminding me of a prime fact of my life: you can leave the island, master the English language, and travel as far as you can, but if you are a Latina, especially one like me who so obviously belongs to Rita Moreno's gene pool, the island travels with you.

2   This is sometimes a very good thing—it may win you that extra minute of someone's attention. But with some people, the same things can make *you* an island—not a tropical paradise but an Alcatraz, a place nobody wants to visit. As a Puerto Rican girl living in the United States and wanting like most children to "belong," I resented the stereotype that my Hispanic appearance called forth from many people I met.

3   Growing up in a large urban center in New Jersey during the 1960s, I suffered from what I think of as "cultural schizophrenia." Our life was designed by my parents as a **microcosm** of their *casas* on the island. We spoke in Spanish, ate Puerto Rican food bought at the *bodega,* and practiced strict Catholicism at a church that allotted us a one-hour slot each week for mass, performed in Spanish by a Chinese priest trained as a missionary for Latin America.

4   As a girl I was kept under strict **surveillance** by my parents, since my virtue and modesty were, by their cultural equation, the same as their honor. As a teenager I was lectured constantly on how to behave as a proper *senorita*. But it was a conflicting message I received, since the Puerto Rican mothers also encouraged their daughters to look and act like women and to dress in clothes our Anglo friends and their mothers found too "mature" and flashy. The difference was, and is, cultural; yet I often felt humiliated when I appeared at an American friend's party wearing a dress more suitable to a semi-formal than to a play-room birthday celebration. At Puerto Rican festivities, neither the music nor the colors we wore could be too loud.

5   I remember Career Day in our high school, when teachers told us to come dressed as if for a job interview. It quickly became obvious that to the Puerto Rican girls "dressing up" meant wearing their mother's ornate jewelry and clothing, more appropriate (by mainstream standards) for the company Christmas party than as daily office attire. That morning I had agonized in front of my closet, trying to figure out what a "career girl" would wear. I knew how to dress for school (at the Catholic school I attended, we all wore uniforms), I knew how to dress for Sunday mass, and I knew what dresses to wear for parties at my relatives' homes. Though I do not recall the precise details of my Career Day outfit, it must have been a **composite** of these choices. But I remember a comment my friend (an Italian American) made in later years that **coalesced** my impressions of that day. She said that at the business school she was attending, the Puerto Rican girls always

stood out for wearing "everything at once." She meant, of course, too much jewelry, too many accessories. On that day at school we were simply made the negative models by the nuns, who were themselves not credible fashion experts to any of us. But it was painfully obvious to me that to the others, in their tailored skirts and silk blouses, we must have seemed "hopeless" and "vulgar." Though I now know that most adolescents feel out of step much of the time, I also know that for the Puerto Rican girls of my generation that sense was intensified. The way our teachers and classmates looked at us that day in school was just a taste of the cultural clash that awaited us in the real world, where prospective employers and men on the street would often misinterpret our tight skirts and jingling bracelets as a "come-on."

6   Mixed cultural signals have perpetuated certain stereotypes—for example, that of the Hispanic woman as the "hot tamale" or sexual fire-brand. It is a one-dimensional view that the media have found easy to promote. In their special vocabulary, advertisers have designated "sizzling" and "smoldering" as the adjectives of choice for describing not only the foods but also the women of Latin America. From conversations in my house I recall hearing about the harassment that Puerto Rican women endured in factories where the "boss-men" talked to them as if sexual **innuendo** was all they understood, and worse, often gave them the choice of submitting to their advances or being fired.

7   It is custom, however, not **chromosomes**, that leads us to choose scarlet over pale pink. As young girls, it was our mothers who influenced our decisions about clothes and colors—mothers who had grown up on a tropical island where the natural environment was a riot of primary colors, where showing your skin was one way to keep cool as well as to look sexy. Most important of all, on the island, women perhaps felt freer to dress and move more provocatively since, in most cases, they were protected by the traditions, mores, and laws of a Spanish/Catholic system of morality and machismo whose main rule was: *You may look at my sister, but if you touch her I will kill you.* The extended family and church structure could provide a young woman with a circle of safety in her small pueblo on the island; if a man "wronged" a girl, everyone would close in to save her family honor.

8   My mother has told me about dressing in her best party clothes on Saturday nights and going to the town's plaza to promenade with her girlfriends in front of the boys they liked. The males were thus given an opportunity to admire the women and to express their admiration in the form of *piropos:* erotically charged street poems they composed on the spot. (I have myself been subjected to a few *piropos* while visiting the island, and they can be outrageous, although custom dictates that they must never cross into obscenity.) This ritual, as I understand it, also entails a show of studied indifference on the woman's part; if she is "decent," she must not acknowledge the man's impassioned words. So I do understand how things can be lost in translation. When a Puerto Rican girl dressed in her idea of what is attractive meets a man from the mainstream culture who has been trained to react to certain types of clothing as a sexual signal, a clash is likely to take place. I remember the boy who took me to my first formal dance leaning over to plant a sloppy, over-eager kiss painfully on my mouth; when I didn't respond with sufficient passion, he remarked resentfully: "I thought you Latin

girls were supposed to mature early," as if I were expected to *ripen* like a fruit or vegetable, not just grow into womanhood like other girls.

9   It is surprising to my professional friends that even today some people, including those who should know better, still put others "in their place." It happened to me most recently during a stay at a classy metropolitan hotel favored by young professional couples for weddings. Late one evening after the theater, as I walked toward my room with a colleague (a woman with whom I was coordinating an arts program), a middle-aged man in a tuxedo, with a young girl in satin and lace on his arm, stepped directly into our path. With his champagne glass extended toward me, he exclaimed "Evita!"

10   Our way blocked, my companion and I listened as the man half-recited, half-bellowed "Don't Cry for Me, Argentina." When he finished, the young girl said: "How about a round of applause for my daddy?" We complied, hoping this would bring the silly spectacle to a close. I was becoming aware that our little group was attracting the attention of the other guests. "Daddy" must have perceived this too, and he once more barred the way as we tried to walk past him. He began to shout-sing a ditty to the tune of "La Bamba"—except the lyrics were about a girl named Maria whose exploits rhymed with her name and gonorrhea. The girl kept saying "Oh, Daddy" and looking at me with pleading eyes. She wanted me to laugh along with the others. My companion and I stood silently waiting for the man to end his offensive song. When he finished, I looked not at him but at his daughter. I advised her calmly never to ask her father what he had done in the army. Then I walked between them and to my room. My friend complimented me on my cool handling of the situation, but I confessed that I had really wanted to push the jerk into the swimming pool. This same man—probably a corporate executive, well-educated, even worldly by most standards—would not have been likely to regale an Anglo woman with a dirty song in public. He might have checked his impulse by assuming that she could be somebody's wife or mother, or at least *somebody* who might take offense. But, to him, I was just an Evita or a Maria: merely a character in his cartoon-populated universe.

11   Another **facet** of the myth of the Latin woman in the United States is the menial, the domestic—Maria the housemaid or counter-girl. It's true that work as domestics, as waitresses, and in factories is all that's available to women with little English and few skills. But the myth of the Hispanic menial—the funny maid, mispronouncing words and cooking up a spicy storm in a shiny California kitchen—has been perpetuated by the media in the same way that "Mammy" from *Gone with the Wind* became America's idea of the black woman for generations. Since I do not wear my diplomas around my neck for all to see, I have on occasion been sent to that "kitchen" where some think I obviously belong.

12   One incident has stayed with me, though I recognize it as a minor offense. My first public poetry reading took place in Miami, at a restaurant where a luncheon was being held before the event. I was nervous and excited as I walked in with notebook in hand. An older woman motioned me to her table, and thinking (foolish me) that she wanted me to autograph a copy of my newly published slender volume of verse, I went over. She ordered a cup of coffee from me, assuming that I was the waitress. (Easy enough to mistake my poems for menus, I suppose.)

I know it wasn't an intentional act of cruelty. Yet of all the good things that happened later, I remember that scene most clearly, because it reminded me of what I had to overcome before anyone would take me seriously. In retrospect I understand that my anger gave my reading fire. In fact, I have almost always taken any doubt in my abilities as a challenge, the result most often being the satisfaction of winning a convert, of seeing the cold, appraising eyes warm to my words, the body language change, the smile that indicates I have opened some avenue for communication. So that day as I read, I looked directly at that woman. Her lowered eyes told me she was embarrassed at her **faux pas**, and when I willed her to look up at me, she graciously allowed me to punish her with my full attention. We shook hands at the end of the reading and I never saw her again. She has probably forgotten the entire incident, but maybe not.

13   Yet I am one of the lucky ones. There are thousands of Latinas without the privilege of an education or the entrees into society that I have. For them life is a constant struggle against the misconceptions perpetuated by the myth of the Latina. My goal is to try to replace the old stereotypes with a much more interesting set of realities. Every time I give a reading, I hope the stories I tell, the dreams and fears I examine in my work, can achieve some universal truth that will get my audience past the particulars of my skin color, my accent, or my clothes.

14   I once wrote a poem in which I called all Latinas "God's brown daughters." This poem is really a prayer of sorts, offered upward, but also, through the human-to-human channel of art, outward. It is a prayer for communication and for respect. In it, Latin women pray "in Spanish to an Anglo God/with a Jewish heritage," and they are "fervently hoping/that if not omnipotent,/at least He be bilingual."

Judith Ortiz Cofer: "The Myth of the Latin Woman: I Just Met a Girl Named Maria" from The Latin Deli: Prose and Poetry. © 1993 by Judith Ortiz Cofer. Reprinted by permission of The University of Georgia Press.

● THE FACTS

1. What is the meaning of "myth" as used in the title of this essay? What other term might be appropriate? Where did the word originate? What connotations surround it?

2. When the author tried to imitate the British people, what traits did she practice on the bus ride from Oxford to London? What is your reaction to her version of the English smile?

3. Why did the author agonize over what to wear on Career Day at her high school? What would you wear for Career Day if it were held this week? Describe your clothing and accessories in detail. What is the general look you would want to achieve?

4. Why did Puerto Rican girls wear bright colors and clothing that left bear skin showing? What kept Puerto Rican boys from disrespectful behavior toward girls who dressed provocatively?

5. What happened at the author's first public poetry reading to highlight the problem of stereotyping Latinas? Think of a similar example you have witnessed.

THE STRATEGIES

1. The author could have written an essay in which she defined *stereotype* and then eloquently attacked people who hurt others by treating them as if they were carbon copies of their cultural kind. She could have limited herself to abstract logic and persuasion, but instead, the author simply offers several concrete examples of when she was treated as a typical Latina and not as the talented individual she is. What advantage, if any, does the author's approach have? What is your reaction to her personal story?

2. What is the schizophrenia experienced early on by the author? Explain it in your own words. Do you think young people from mainstream cultures could experience a similar kind of schizophrenia? Support your claim.

3. What is the grammatical antecedent of "This" at the beginning of paragraph 2? How is this indefinite pronoun clarified? Do you consider the strategy effective? Explain your answer.

4. What is your judgment of the middle-aged man who sang "Don't Cry for Me, Argentina," followed by some shouted song with obscene lyrics? If you had been in the narrator's place, how would you have handled the situation? What seemed to be the main motivation of the narrator's approach?

5. Why does the author save the anecdote about the menial, the domestic until the last? Evaluate how this strategy supports the thesis of the essay.

THE ISSUES

1. According to the author, if you look like Rita Moreno, "the island travels with you" (see paragraph 1). What is the significance of this observation? Are there gene pools other than the Hispanic one that tend to define people in our country? Give examples of how the gene pool works—for good or bad.

2. Do you agree with the author that mothers can send conflicting messages to their daughters? If so, what are some of these messages you have personally observed in the environment in which you grew up? What were the consequences? Give specific examples.

3. In the essay, little is said of the father's influence. What influence, if any, do fathers have in forming the image of girls in our society? Describe the effect of that influence as you have experienced or observed it personally.

4. In many ways, most immigrants feel alienated from their new homeland. Why is this so? What could our society do to make the transition from one culture to the other easier for immigrants? Suggest specific programs or attitudes.

5. Building on the author's intimation in paragraph 2 that moving to a new cultural environment can be "a very good thing," what are some examples of the good that can accrue to immigrants who have moved to a new country? Consider such matters as being bilingual; understanding various attitudes toward religion, etiquette, or the opposite sex; not being afraid to travel; and being open to many wide-ranging traditions rather than just those revered in our country.

● SUGGESTIONS FOR WRITING

1. Write an essay in which you imagine yourself a student transported to a country such as France, Russia, China, or Mexico to live. Using your imagination and common sense, cite some vivid examples of the difficulties you might encounter and how you would resolve them.

2. Write an essay about some famous American—male or female—who was brought up in a foreign country but became an admired U.S. citizen. Examples to consider are Alexander Hamilton, Albert Einstein, Father Edward Flanagan, Felix Frankfurter, Mikhail Baryshnikov, Vladimir Nabakov, Kahil Gibran, Sammy Sosa, Hakeem Olajuwan, Mary Antin, Gloria Estafan, Madeleine Albright, and Ruby Keeler. Check the Internet for other suitable candidates.

"Mirror, Mirror, on the Wall . . ."

JOHN LEO

Rhetorical Thumbnail

Purpose: to acquaint us with standards of beauty

Audience: educated magazine readers

Language: informal journalistic English

Strategy: to establish through the use of examples from history that beauty is a relative concept

John Leo (b. 1935), associate editor of *Time,* was born in Hoboken, New Jersey, and educated at the University of Toronto. He has been associated with *Commonweal,* The *New York Times,* the *Village Voice,* and more recently as editor and columnist for *U.S. News and World Report.*

In the following brief essay from Time, *Leo discusses and gives examples of the relativity of beauty. He amuses us with examples that show how the standards of beauty have changed over the years.*

● ● ●

1 The poet may insist that beauty is in the eye of the beholder; the historian might argue that societies create the image of female perfection that they want. There has always been plenty of evidence to support both views. Martin Luther thought long, beautiful hair was essential. Edmund Burke recommended delicate, fragile women. Goethe insisted on "the proper breadth of the pelvis and the necessary fullness of the breasts." Hottentot men look for sharply projecting buttocks. Rubens favored a full posterior, and Papuans require a big nose. The Mangaians of Polynesia care nothing of fat or thin and never seem to notice face, breasts or

buttocks. To the tribesmen, the only standard of sexiness is well-shaped female genitals.

2   An anthropologized world now knows that notions of what is most attractive do vary with each age and culture. One era's flower is another's **frump**. Primitive man, understandably concerned with fertility, idealized ample women. One of the earliest surviving sculptures, the Stone Age Venus of Willendorf, depicts a squat woman whose vital statistics—in inches—would amount to 96–89–96. This **adipose** standard stubbornly recurs in later eras. A 14th-century treatise on beauty calls for "narrow shoulders, small breasts, large belly, broad hips, fat thighs, short legs and a small head." Some Oriental cultures today are turned on by what Simone de Beauvoir calls the "unnecessary, **gratuitous** blooming" of wrap-around fat.

3   The Greeks were so concerned with working out precise proportions for beauty that the sculptor Praxiteles insisted that the female navel be exactly midway between the breasts and genitals. The dark-haired Greeks considered fair-haired women exotic, perhaps the start of the notion that blondes have more fun. They also offered early evidence of the rewards that go to magnificent mammaries. When Phryne, Praxiteles' famous model and mistress, was on trial for treason, the orator defending her pulled aside her veil, baring her legendary breasts. The awed judges acquitted her on the spot.

4   Romans favored more independent, articulate women than the Greeks. Still, there were limits. Juvenal complains of ladies who "discourse on poets and poetry, comparing Vergil with Homer . . . Wives shouldn't read all the classics—there ought to be some things women don't understand."

5   In ancient Egypt, women spent hours primping: fixing hair, applying lipstick, eye shadow and fingernail polish, grinding away body and genital hair with pumice stones. It worked: Nefertiti could make the cover of *Vogue* any month she wanted. For Cleopatra, the most famous bombshell of the ancient world, eroticism was plain hard work. Not a natural beauty, she labored diligently to learn **coquettishness** and flattery and reportedly polished her **amatory** techniques by practicing on slaves.

6   If Cleopatra had to work so hard at being desirable, can the average woman do less? Apparently not. In the long history of images of beauty, one staple is the male tendency to spot new flaws in women, and the female tendency to work and suffer to remedy them. In the Middle Ages, large women rubbed themselves with cow dung dissolved in wine. When whiter skin was demanded, women applied leeches to take the red out. Breasts have been strapped down, **cantilevered** up, pushed together or apart, oiled and siliconed and, in 16th-century Venice, fitted with wool or hair padding for a sexy "duck breast" look, curving from bodice to groin. In the long run, argues feminist Elizabeth Gould Davis, flat-chested women are evolutionary losers. Says she: "The female of the species owes her modern mammary magnificence to male sexual preference."

7   Still, a well-endowed woman can suddenly find herself out of favor when cultural winds change. The flapper era in America is one example. So is Europe's Romantic Age, which favored the wan, cadaverous look. In the 1820s, women sometimes drank vinegar or stayed up all night to look pale and interesting. Fragility was all. Wrote Keats: "God! she is like a milkwhite lamb that bleats/For man's protection."

8   Victorians took this ideal of the shy, clinging vine, **decorously** desexed it, and assigned it to the wife. According to one well-known Victorian doctor, it was a "vile **aspersion**" to suggest that women were capable of sexual impulses. Inevitably that straitlaced era controlled women's shapes by severe compression of the waistline, without accenting breasts or hips.

9   Those womanly curves reasserted themselves at the turn of the century. During the hourglass craze, Lillie Langtry seemed perfection **incarnate** at 38–18–38. Since then, the ideal woman in Western culture has gradually slimmed down. Psyche, the White Rock girl,[1] was 5 ft. 4 in. tall and weighed in at a hippy 140 lbs. when she first appeared on beverage bottles in 1893. Now, sans **cellulite**, she is 4 in. taller and 22 lbs. lighter.

10   In psychological terms, the current slim-hipped look amounts to a rebellion against male domination: waist-trimming corsets are associated with male control of the female body, and narrow hips with a reluctance to bear children. Says Madge Garland, a former editor of *British Vogue*: "The natural shape of the female body has not been revealed and free as it is today for 1,500 years." W. H. Auden once complained that for most of Western history, the sexy beautiful women have seemed "fictionalized," set apart from real life. In the age of the natural look, a beauty now has to seem as though she just strolled in from the beach at Malibu. Like Cheryl Tiegs.

John Leo, "Mirror, Mirror, On the Wall" From Time Magazine, March 6, 1978. Copyright John Leo.

◉ THE FACTS

1. What kinds of women did primitive man idealize?
2. What was the Greeks' standard of beauty?
3. According to feminist Elizabeth Gould Davis, to what do women owe their "modern mammary magnificence"?
4. What kind of feminine beauty was favored during Europe's Romantic Age?
5. What does the modern, slim-hipped look signify in psychological terms?

◉ THE STRATEGIES

1. What notion do most of the examples in this essay support? Where is this notion stated?
2. Much of the detail about beauty is given not in full-blown examples, but in sketchy references to the opinions of famous people. What are such references called?
3. In paragraph 3, what does the anecdote about Phryne exemplify?
4. The author quotes Goethe, Simone de Beauvoir, Juvenal, Elizabeth Gould-Davis, John Keats, Madge Garland, and W. H. Auden. What effect does all this opinion sampling have on the tone of the essay?

[1]Psyche has been the emblem of White Rock–brand soft drinks and mixes since the nineteenth century.

5. In paragraph 6, the author writes: "In the long history of images of beauty, one staple is the male tendency to spot new flaws in women, and the female tendency to work and suffer to remedy them." How does the author proceed to support and document this view?

THE ISSUES

1. Paragraph 2 alludes to an "anthropologized world." How would you define this world? What significance lies in this label?

2. What, for you, constitutes a beautiful female? A beautiful male? Refer to specific examples from history, from the current scene, or from your personal encounters.

3. How do you feel about the present emphasis on an athletic female body? Is it justified, or does it diminish some other innately feminine characteristic? Give reasons for your answer.

4. Even if you agree with the poet that beauty is in the eye of the beholder, argue that true beauty must follow certain standards. Suggest what these standards might be when applied to, say, a painting or a sculpture.

5. In paragraph 8, the author describes the typical Victorian wife as a woman who must never be perceived as having sexual impulses. How does the typical Victorian wife compare with the women we observe in the movies or on TV today? Give examples to support your view.

SUGGESTIONS FOR WRITING

1. Write an essay that specifies your idea of human beauty. Give convincing examples to illustrate your point.

2. Write an essay in which you argue that human beauty is in the eye of the beholder.

Image Gallery for Critical Thinking and Debate: Drugs and Society

Ours is a society awash in a transcontinental tidal surge of drugs. We awake to the kick of caffeine, soothe our nerves with tobacco, ease our tension headaches with aspirin, wind down the day with alcohol, and swallow an antihistamine to help us sleep—all perfectly legal, respectable, and even expected.

But there is a dark side to this epidemic of drug use. Over 400,000 of us perish annually from the effects of tobacco. Some 23 million of us regularly take illegal drugs, ranging from marijuana to cocaine to heroin. A causal relationship exists between drug addiction and criminal wrongdoing. Here are some current statistics to ponder: According to the U.S. Department of Justice (Bureau of Justice Statistics), currently 600,000 people in the United States are addicted to heroin, a considerable increase since the notorious drug era of the 1980s. The annual number of marijuana initiates has reached 2.3 million. Methamphetamine use is increasing and so are the so-called "club drugs" such as Ketamine, Quaaludes, Xanax, MDMa, and LSD, used by glamorous young adults who become models for ordinary youngsters to imitate.

One of the most alarming trends is the use of illegal tobacco and alcohol among youth. Children who use these substances increase their chances of lifelong dependency problems and catastrophic health crises. Every day, 3,000 children begin smoking cigarettes regularly. As a result, one third of these youngsters will have their lives shortened. The Substance Abuse and Mental Health Services Administration has declared that half of all high school students use illicit drugs by the time they graduate. What do these statistics portend about the future? Here is the grim forecast: 1. Maternal drug abuse will contribute to birth defects. 2. Chronic drug abuse will lead to sexually transmitted diseases. 3. Underage use of tobacco and alcohol will lead to premature deaths. 4. Drug use will add to the burdens of the work place by decreasing productivity.

Then there are the nightmares faced by our correctional facilities. The largest percentage of arrests (75.1%) are for drug-related causes. Drug offenders continue to crowd our nation's jails and prisons. The increase in drug offenders accounts for nearly three-fourths of the growth in federal prison inmates. Drug trafficking is also on the increase, generating violent crimes that have been well documented in newspaper headlines exposing the terror inflicted by drug cartels from Mexico, Columbia, and Guatemala. Unfortunately, illegal drugs remain readily available—often through gangs like the Crips, Bloods, and Dominican or Jamaican "posses." In sum, the problem has not disappeared, but is spreading.

The political response to the spreading tide of illegal drugs has been predictable: Conservatives urge heightened efforts at the interdiction of illegal drugs, mandatory drug testing, stiffer prison terms for pushers, and a crackdown on recreational users. Liberals and libertarians advocate an agenda of education and rehabilitation and, probably the most controversial measure of all, the legalization of drug use. as well as the legalization of marijuana sales in some states.

Our image gallery begins with the thought-provoking issue of whether or not we should legalize marijuana despite the problems that exist beyond the benefits of what marijuana can do for certain illnesses when it is made available as medication. Our first image shows medical clinic advertising for patients with a welcome sign and the assurance that a doctor will be there to consult with patients. The second image is an attempt to remind students that along with the buzz they might get from taking social drugs, they must also take heed of the inevitable violence, corruption, and other dangers that accompany the cartels that push drugs and get young people addicted and thus incapacitated for work or other valuable contributions to their society. Third is a poignant photo of two young boys fooling around with the old-fashioned drug of cigarette smoking. Will they or won't they pay the consequences of becoming heavy smokers?

Our student essay proves to be up to date in its suggestion that it may be time to reconsider the legality of placing certain drugs on the market where they can be controlled properly.

"To the Point" rounds out the issue.

Study the following three images dealing with drugs and society. Then choose the image that most appeals to you. Answer the questions and do the writing assignment.

For readings, questions, and media on the issue of drugs and society, visit the *MindTap for Readings for Writers*, 15e online.

Mike Nelson/epa/Corbis

Studying the Image

1. How would you describe the reaction of the passersby to the sign advertising medical marijuana? Considering the polarizing attitudes that prevail in our society despite the fact that the state of Colorado has passed a law legalizing the use of marijuana, what emotions seem absent? What might this attitude indicate?

2. When you read the words, "Walk-ins welcome," what popular businesses along strip malls or near shopping areas come to mind? What tone do these words convey? What is the purpose of such a tone?

3. What do the words "The doctor is in" add to this sign? Why is no specific name mentioned, such as "Ernest W. Smith, M.D."? Speculate on what kinds of patients would walk into this clinic.

4. Do you consider marijuana for medical purposes the same as herbal supplements or prescription pain medication? Or do you think it still belongs in the category of street drugs? Support your opinion with verifiable evidence.

Writing Assignment

Argue the case for or against legalizing the use of marijuana in all 50 states of the United States. Regardless of which side you take, find at least three expert opinions to support your argument. Use MLA format to document your sources.

Fernando Castillo/LatinContent/Getty Images

Studying the Image

1. What is your reaction to this image of a conflict between law enforcement and crime? Do you feel any sympathy for the people caught in this perilous setting? Or do you think they were motivated strictly by greed and thus deserve to be caught?

2. Recently, several world leaders and numerous columnists or TV pundits have spoken out in favor of decriminalizing the use of drugs the way it happened in the case of smoking and drinking. They believe, for instance, that drug addicts belong in rehab, not in prison, and that making certain drugs legal would prevent crime and illness. What is your reaction to this view? What, if any, new problems might we face if we voted for such a stance?

3. Most people know of someone in their social circle who had to face rehab due to addiction. What is the major reason drug addiction continues to grow in our country? How can we prevent drug addiction from ruining so many lives?

4. How difficult is it to overcome alcohol or drug addiction? Provide an example of someone you know who has remained sober for at least five years following addiction. Describe how the person fought and conquered his/her addiction.

Writing Assignment

Write an essay in which you argue for the protection of children whose parents are addicted to drugs and therefore neglect their offspring. What role, if any, should the government play in this matter? What remedial action do you recommend? Spending some time doing research on the Internet and studying what experts have to say about children and drug abuse may be helpful in completing the assignment.

Mary Kate Denny / PhotoEdit

Studying the Image

1. With so much public information in the media about the dangers of smoking, what do you think motivates young kids to smoke regardless of the warnings?

2. As you study the expressions on the faces of both boys, what is the boy in the red plaid shirt thinking? What is the boy in the blue shirt saying?

3. What role do grownups play in the upsurge or prevention of youthful smoking?

4. Smoking in public places, such as restaurants, college campuses, and office buildings, has been noticeably curtailed in the last four decades. But statistics indicate that smoking among adolescents is on the rise. What reason underlies this increase despite the anti-smoking environmental regulations?

Writing Assignment

Various commercials and ad campaigns have tried to persuade children not to start smoking, but with only marginal success. Write an essay in which you illustrate how smoking has injured the health of someone famous or someone dear to you. Use your essay as an appeal to young people not to smoke.

Punctuation Workshop

The Dash (—)

Not to be confused with a hyphen, the dash is a flexible punctuation mark.

1. **Use a dash to announce an abrupt break or change in thought:**

   > All of us need redemption—or is it acceptance?

   > Light reveals the world to us—a world often tarnished.

   > Let me tell you about kayaking—no, I mean canoeing.

2. **Use a dash to set off parenthetical elements you want to emphasize.**

   > The new Pope—with the help of the Vatican—repeatedly emphasizes religious liberty.

   > Strong personal feelings—love, admiration, fear—are often easier to admit in a letter rather than face to face.

3. **Use a dash to emphasize a list.**

   > Tortured, undecided, fearful—my father embodied all of these character traits.

   > Do not overuse dashes as easy substitutes for commas, periods, or other punctuation marks.

Student Corner

Solving the Drug Problem in the United States

Jordan Dubini

Walla Walla University, Washington

Today the United States is facing many conflicts: a war on terror, a war on solving the healthcare crisis, a war on keeping the country fiscally sound, and a war on drugs. One war that has plagued our country longer than any other is the war on drugs. It has claimed countless lives, and is a burgeoning problem not only in the United States, but throughout the entire world. Although pundits in academic halls and on television have debated for years how to solve this deepening crisis, they have reached no sound conclusion; thus the problem persists. The only way this problem will be solved is if the government changes the way narcotics are regulated, because the deaths from tainted drugs and dangerous drug cartels are just too high and can no longer be tolerated by a humanitarian citizenry. A change as drastic as the decriminalization of narcotics needs to be undertaken.

Certain popular narcotics are illegal, and thus create the need to smuggle, distribute, and sell them on the black market. This illegal route is rampant throughout the United States and is the cause of multiple deaths. The Drug Enforcement Administration (DEA) maintains a list of drugs and other substances that are considered controlled substances under the Controlled Substances Act. The Controlled Substances Act is divided into five schedules. According to the DEA's Office of Diversion Control's website, "Substances are placed in their respective schedules based on whether they have a currently accepted medical use in treatment in the United States, their relative abuse potential, and likelihood of causing dependence when abused." For example, heroin and marijuana are placed in Schedule I, while oxycodone and morphine are placed in Schedule II.

One widely discussed solution is the decriminalization of the use of drugs, and the subsequent legalization of the sale of said drugs. The argument is made that decriminalization and legalization would greatly reduce the activity of dangerous drug cartels, as well as create a safe system of selling narcotics. The federal government could amend the

Controlled Substances Act in a way that would allow the sale of narcotics through a system that would be tightly regulated and would vary, depending on how each drug were scheduled. This would in turn create a society in which those who wish to purchase and use certain narcotics would be able to do so, knowing that the drug had been safely regulated by the FDA and was not tainted. This new approach would also help crush the drug cartels that claim countless lives by their clandestine distribution of drugs to any hungry user.

Opposition to this idea is concentrated and strong. Those against this change argue that it would lead to a higher rate of drug abuse, and would claim even more lives. But, perhaps this would not be the case. Take alcohol as an example. It is legal and well regulated. There are those people who consume safe amounts, and those who abuse alcohol by consuming amounts that are dangerous to their health and potentially lethal. This would be the same way with narcotics. There are those who would use drugs sensibly and those who would abuse them. However, a new system of regulation would create safer drugs for those who wish to use them and would thereby save lives.

For any change in our drug laws to happen, our society would have to set off a strong movement with solid evidence to support that movement. Whatever the change is, the goal should be to save lives. Illegal drugs have claimed too many lives in the United States, and the number is continually growing. The decriminalization of drugs would be an excellent way to make sure that the drugs on the streets are safe for those who wish to use them. In turn, the war on drugs would crumble, and lives would be saved.

Work Cited

"Controlled Substance Schedules." *Resources*, N.p., n.d. Web. 30 March, 2014. http://www.deadiversion.usdoj.gov/schedules/.

How I Write

I have a unique writing method. It usually starts with me staring with a blank document on my computer screen while I gather my thoughts. I figure out my thesis, and then I just start writing. I keep going until I feel that I have typed in all the information needed to prove my point. Then I go back and move sentences around, add evidence, and proofread. This method allows me to write my stream of consciousness and not worry about what the paper looks like when I write the initial draft. I can clean it up later.

My Writing Tip

Getting a paper back that has stupid little mistakes in it is just terrible. That's why I suggest that you always double-check your work, no matter how perfect you think it is. You will always detect a missing comma, or a misplaced word. I suggest that after you have finished a paper, you let it percolate overnight. Then you can come back with a fresh pair of eyes and find those mistakes that pester countless writers every day. Go even further and have a friend take a look at your paper. An impartial reader may find mistakes you did not notice because you were so involved or biased. Hopefully, that friend will give you some good feedback to improve your writing.

To the Point

Tweet your response to this comment found on someone's Facebook page: "Cannabis is cool and helps you concentrate when you study for math or chemistry. Why keep knocking it instead of legalizing it everywhere?"

■ Chapter Writing Assignments

1. Write an essay in which you provide illustrations from history, physics, biology, psychology, or literature to prove one of the following maxims:

   a. "Every man is the architect of his own fortune." (Seneca)

   b. "The injury of prodigality leads to this, that he who will not economize will have to agonize." (Confucius)

   c. "The foundation of every state is the education of its youth." (Diogenes)

d. "The pull of gravity exerts far more influence than one might think." (Anonymous)

e. "Satire is the guerrilla weapon of political warfare." (Horace Greeley)

2. Choose one of the following terms and write an essay giving examples of it.

a. romance

b. tyranny

c. education

d. humility

e. prejudice

f. law

Writing Assignments for a Specific Audience

1. Addressing yourself to a group of eighth graders, write an essay about avoiding drugs, using examples from your own experience, that of acquaintances and friends, or of experts.

2. Give examples to back up this statement: "Freedom usually comes at a high price."

 Pointer from a Pro

BE CLEAR

First clarity; then, clarity; and last, clarity.

—Anatole France

(when asked what he considered the most important ingredient of good writing) Poetry and metaphysics may contain clusters of mystery or obscurity, but most important ideas can be expressed in clear language. Clarity in writing is like fresh air. Lack of clarity is like dense smoke. Which would you rather breathe?

CHAPTER 12

Definition

◼ Road Map to Definition

What Definition Does

Definition means spelling out exactly what a word or phrase means. Articles, essays, and entire books have been written for the sole purpose of defining some abstract or disputed word, term, or phrase. Here is an example of a paragraph that defines *plot*.

> Let us define a plot. We have defined a story as a narrative of events arranged in their time-sequence. A plot is also a narrative of events, the emphasis falling on causality. "The king died and then the queen died," is a story. "The king died, and then the queen died of grief," is a plot. The time sequence is preserved, but the sense of causality overshadows it. Or again: "The queen died, no one knew why, until it was discovered that it was through grief at the death of the king." This is a plot with a mystery in it, a form capable of high development. It suspends the time sequence, it moves as far away from the story as its limitations will allow. Consider the death of the queen. If it is a story we say, "and then?" If it is a plot we ask, "why?" That is the fundamental difference between these two aspects of the novel. A plot cannot be told to a gaping audience of cavemen or to a tyrannical sultan or to their modern descendant the movie-public. They can only be kept awake by "and then-and then." They can only supply curiosity. But a plot demands intelligence and memory also.
>
> —E. M. Forster, *"Aspects of the Novel"*

In the preceding paragraph, the author not only defines *plot*, he distinguishes it from *story*. When he is done, we get a sense not only of what a plot is, but of what it is not.

When to Use Definition

What do words and phrases mean? Especially for abstract words and phrases, the answer is not always simple. It would be easy enough to explain to a Martian what the word *pencil* means because, as a last resort, we can produce one and wave it under the creature's antennas. But how do we explain the meaning of *love* to this alien? Or the meaning of *human rights*? Or even the meaning of *sovereignty*? None of these words overlays an object or thing to which we can point. Each is an idea or concept and, therefore, definable only by experience or words. The problem is that it is difficult, if not impossible, to find two people who have had such an identical experience with *love* or *human rights* or *sovereignty* that they will instantly agree on a common meaning. This is where words rush in to fill the gap.

Definitions are especially useful, then, if your essay hinges on one of these disputed abstractions. If you were writing an essay on *love,* for example, you could not take it for granted that your reader knows what you mean by that word. You would have to define it. You would have to write your definition in such a way as to make it instantly clear to your particular audience.

How to Use Definition

1. **Begin your definition by saying what the term means.** The traditional method is to first place the term in a general class and then show how it differs from others found there. Known as a *lexical definition,* this is the method of defining used by dictionaries. Here is an example:

   A *library* is a repository for artistic and literary materials.

   Repository is identified as the general class to which *library* belongs, but a specialization in artistic and literary materials distinguishes it from other repositories.

   Here are some more examples of lexical definitions:

   A *motor scooter* is a two-wheeled vehicle with small wheels and a low-powered gasoline engine geared to the rear wheel.

   An *oligarchy* is government by the few, especially a small group of people, such as one family.

   Education is the process of systematic instruction in order to impart *knowledge* or skill.

   Mercy is the kind and compassionate treatment of an offender.

   This is a useful and preliminary way of saying what a term means. First show where the term belongs, then distinguish it from others in that same class. Consciously and unconsciously, we practice this method of defining every day.

2. **Expand your definition, if necessary, with an etymological analysis of the term.** The *etymology* of a word is an explanation of its roots, of what it originally meant, and is often useful in shedding light on how the current meaning of a word evolved. Here is an example of an etymological analysis that helps us to understand the meaning of the word *bible:*

   In the derivation of our word *Bible* lies its definition. It comes from the Greek word *biblion,*[1] which in its plural *biblia* signifies "little books." The Bible is actually a collection of little books, of every sort and description, written over a long period of time, the very earliest dating, in part at least, as far back as 1200 B.C. or perhaps even earlier; the latest as late as A.D. 150. In its rich and manifold nature it might be

   _____

   [1]*Biblos* was the name given to the inner bark of the papyrus, and the word *biblion* meant a papyrus roll, upon which the Bible was originally copied.

called a *library* of Hebrew literature; in its slow production over a period of many centuries it might be termed a survey of that literature to be understood as we understand a *survey* of English literature, in which we become familiar with types of English prose and poetry from Anglo-Saxon times to our own.

—Mary Ellen Chase, *What Is the Bible?*

3. **Clarify your definition by stating what the word is not or does not mean.** For instance, the meaning of *mythology* can be clarified by the statement that it is not merely "a story filled with lies." Likewise, *liberty* can be clarified by showing that it does not simply mean "doing anything one wants at any time." In the following paragraph, the term *empirical medicine* is partially defined by what it is not:

By the practice of empirical medicine we mean that conclusions are reached as a result of experience and observation. Diagnoses are made and cures are found as a result of practical experience. Empirical medicine is not the practice of medicine based on scientific theories or knowledge but on what works. Because of its disregard for scientific knowledge, empirical medicine is often considered charlatanry by academicians.

In essays, the overriding aim of a defining paragraph is usually to clarify the meaning of a certain term. Occasionally, however, the technical or dictionary meaning of a word or phrase may not be what the writer is trying to convey. Indeed, some definitions may be philosophical or poetic, as in the following example:

Home is where you hang your hat. Or home is where you spent your childhood, the good years when waking every morning was an excitement, when the round of the day could always produce something to fill your mind, tear your emotions, excite your wonder or awe or delight. Is home that, or is it the place where the people you love live, or the place where you have buried your dead, or the place where you want to be buried yourself? Or is it the place where you come in your last desperation to shoot yourself, choosing the garage or the barn or the woodshed in order not to mess up the house, but coming back anyway to the last sanctuary where you can kill yourself in peace?

—Wallace Stegner, *The Big Rock Candy Mountain*

4. **Expand your definition with examples.** A well-chosen example can add volumes of clarity to your meaning. In the following paragraph, the author tells us what she thinks the word *manhood* means in America:

America has defined the roles to which each individual should subscribe. It has defined "manhood" in terms of its own interests and "femininity" likewise. An individual who has a good job, makes a lot of money and drives a Cadillac is a real man, and conversely, an individual who is lacking in these "qualities" is less of a man. The advertising media in this country continuously inform the American male of his need for indispensable signs of his virility—the brand of cigarettes that cowboys prefer, the whiskey that has a masculine tang or the label of the jock strap that athletes wear.

—Frances M. Beal, *Double Jeopardy: To Be Black and Female*

Whether you agree with this definition, you can at least grasp the author's meaning from her examples.

5. **To define a complex term properly, you may need to practice a combination of techniques: You may have to provide a lexical definition, cite examples, and analyze meaning.** Here is a paragraph in which the writer uses all three devices to define *self-image:*

Lexical definition

         Self-image refers to the conception of worth one has of oneself—sort of like assessing your financial fortune by adding up all of your money and possessions to see in what economic bracket you belong. In this definition of self-image, character traits seem to play the leading role. While everyone agrees that it is important to develop a good self-image, few know how to acquire one. The truth is that you began to form your self-image at a young age. As you related to various important people in your life, you received messages from them about yourself. Over the years these messages imbedded themselves in your subconscious to form your self-image.

Examples

         For example, if your father constantly yelled at you that "you will never amount to a hill of beans because you are stupid," or if your mother kept nagging at you to "quit that hangdog look and sour puss attitude or you'll end up alone in life," these messages will stick to your subconscious like glue. If they are never diluted or scraped away, they turn into beliefs that harden like cement, and they will become part of the way you view yourself. So, if you believe that you are ugly, boring, and too stupid ever to achieve success in life, then, believe it or not, you will defend those beliefs even to yourself.

Practical definition

         Left unchallenged, your self-image will determine what you will and will not accomplish in life because you become what you believe.

—Colette Witt, *What Is Your Self-Image?*

     Remember that your definition is incomplete if it leaves gaps in the meaning of a term or fails to clearly answer the question, "What does this mean?" Keep that question in mind when you write a definition and do your utmost to answer it until your meaning is unmistakably clear to your reader.

     As you write your defining essays, beware of the most common student error— *the circular definition.* To say that "taxation is the act of imposing taxes" is repetitious. Better to say "Taxation is the principle of levying fees to support basic government services." Provide examples and details until you have answered the question "What is it?"

Warming Up to Write a Definition

1. Getting together with three or four of your classmates, sit down and discuss the best definition for each of the following terms. If needed, you may use a dictionary. Once you have agreed on the best definition, write it on a sheet of paper, using only one

sentence. Refine the written definition until it could serve as a thesis statement for an essay.

   a. kleptomania

   b. astrology

   c. insanity

   d. terrorism

   e. deportation

2. In the following paragraph, the word *renaissance* needs to be defined for readers who are not familiar with it. Define the term by using at least three other words in the passage that explain what the word means. Write down your definition so that it could be used as the thesis of an essay about any community experiencing what Harlem is going through.

> Harlem, a community in northern Manhattan that hit bottom in the 1980s when poverty, neglected housing and drug-related crime took their toll, is enjoying a lively second *renaissance.* Some Harlemites dismiss the resurgence as little more than a real estate boom, because the neighborhood's magnificent 19th-century townhouses are being snapped up at a rapid rate. You'll also hear that the cultural scene doesn't compare with Harlem's first flowering, in the 1920s, which was animated by extraordinary creativity in politics, the arts and especially the written word. But if it's true there are no stand-ins today for fiery W. E. B. DuBois, gentle Langston Hughes, or patrician Duke Ellington, the second renaissance is still taking shape . . . Highbrow, mainstream, pop, hiphop, avant-garde—Harlem's cultural and artistic revival is evident on nearly every block.
>
>   —From Peter Hellman, "Coming Up Harlem," *Smithsonian,* November 2002

3. In the blanks provided, check those definitions that are *not* correct; then provide the correct definitions.

   a. ___ *Charismatic* means disgusting.

   b. ___ *Desolation* means a feeling of despair.

   c. ___ A *skeptic* is one who is gullible.

   d. ___ *Suburban* means out in the country.

   e. ___ A *turret* is a tower or steeple.

   f. ___ To *pay homage* means to ridicule.

   g. ___ A *residue* is an evil citizen.

   h. ___ *Genetic* means inherited.

   i. ___ To *scrutinize* means to study or pore over.

   j. ___ *Sovereignty* means debauchery.

4. Rewrite the following definitions to delete the circular meaning.

   a. A *terrorist* is simply a person who tries to terrorize others.

   b. *Prostitution* is the work done by prostitutes.

   c. *Liberty* means to be free like a bird.

   d. *Patriotism* is the act of being patriotic.

   e. Having *popular* appeal means that one appeals to the public.

▧ Examples

Entropy

K.C. COLE

Rhetorical Thumbnail

Purpose: to define and clarify *entropy* so that the average reader can understand the concept

Audience: readers who have time to ponder and enjoy well-written newspaper columns

Language: standard English, written in the kind of casual voice that creates intimacy between writer and audience

Strategy: to define entropy so that readers will not lose hope when they observe the disorder catapulting around them, but will realize that human energy, applied at the right time and place, can prevent the descent into chaos or inertia

K.C. Cole is a writer covering physical science for *The Los Angeles Times,* where she also writes the column "Mind Over Matter." Cole spent her early childhood in Rio de Janeiro and grew up in Port Washington, New York, and Shaker Heights, Ohio. After graduating from Barnard College with a degree in political science, she worked for Radio Free Europe as an editor and subsequently lived in the former Czechoslovakia, the Soviet Union, and Hungary. An article she wrote for *New York Times Magazine* about the Soviet Union's invasion of Czechoslovakia was so well received that she instantly became famous as a news reporter. While working as a writer and editor at the *Saturday Review* in San Francisco, she became intrigued with Frank Oppenheimer's Exploratorium science museum and started writing about science. Cole is the author of numerous national bestsellers. Among her works are the following: *What Only a Mother Can Tell You About Having a Baby* (1982), *Between the Lines* (1984), *The Universe and the Teacup: The Mathematics of Truth and Beauty* (1999), and *First You Build a Cloud: Reflections on Physics as a Way of Life* (1999). The selection below was first published as a "Hers" column in *The New York Times.*

Reading Cole's essay should make you feel grateful for a writer who can explain physics in simple and clear language. While entropy can be made to seem incomprehensible, Cole uses details and examples from ordinary life to describe the concept so that the reader realizes that entropy is nothing more than the normal decay and disintegration we observe all around us—something each of us must confront, explore, and work out.

• • •

1   It was about two months ago when I realized that entropy was getting the better of me. On the same day my car broke down (again), my refrigerator conked out and I learned that I needed root-canal work in my right rear tooth. The windows in the

bedroom were still leaking every time it rained and my son's baby sitter was still failing to show up every time I really needed her. My hair was turning gray and my typewriter was wearing out. The house needed paint and I needed glasses. My son's sneakers were developing holes and I was developing a deep sense of **futility**.

2   After all, what was the point of spending half of Saturday at the Laundromat if the clothes were dirty all over again the following Friday?

3   Disorder, alas, is the natural order of things in the universe. There is even a precise measure of the amount of disorder, called entropy. Unlike almost every other physical property (motion, gravity, energy), entropy does not work both ways. It can only increase. Once it's created it can never be destroyed. The road to disorder is a one-way street.

4   Because of its **unnerving irreversibility**, entropy has been called the arrow of time. We all understand this instinctively. Children's rooms, left on their own, tend to get messy, not neat. Wood rots, metal rusts, people wrinkle and flowers wither. Even mountains wear down; even the **nuclei** of atoms decay. In the city we see entropy in the rundown subways and worn-out sidewalks and torn-down buildings, in the increasing disorder of our lives. We know, without asking, what is old. If we were suddenly to see the paint jump back on an old building, we would know that something was wrong. If we saw an egg unscramble itself and jump back into its shell, we would laugh in the same way we laugh at a movie run backward.

5   Entropy is no laughing matter, however, because with every increase in entropy energy is wasted and opportunity is lost. Water flowing down a mountainside can be made to do some useful work on its way. But once all the water is at the same level it can work no more. That is entropy. When my refrigerator was working, it kept all the cold air ordered in one part of the kitchen and warmer air in another. Once it broke down the warm and cold mixed into a lukewarm mess that allowed my butter to melt, my milk to rot and my frozen vegetables to decay.

6   Of course the energy is not really lost, but it has **diffused** and **dissipated** into a chaotic **caldron** of **randomness** that can do us no possible good. Entropy is chaos. It is loss of purpose.

7   People are often upset by the entropy they seem to see in the haphazardness of their own lives. **Buffeted** about like so many molecules in my **tepid** kitchen, they feel that they have lost their sense of direction, that they are wasting youth and opportunity at every turn. It is easy to see entropy in marriages, when the partners are too preoccupied to patch small things up, almost guaranteeing that they will fall apart. There is much entropy in the state of our country, in the relationships between nations—lost opportunities to stop the avalanche of disorders that seems ready to swallow us all.

8   Entropy is not inevitable everywhere, however. Crystals and snowflakes and galaxies are islands of incredibly ordered beauty in the midst of random events. If it was not for exceptions to entropy, the sky would be black and we would be able to see where the stars spend their days; it is only because air molecules in the atmosphere cluster in ordered groups that the sky is blue.

9   The most profound exception to entropy is the creation of life. A seed soaks up some soil and some carbon and some sunshine and some water and arranges it into a rose. A seed in the womb takes some oxygen and pizza and milk and transforms it into a baby.

10   The catch is that it takes a lot of energy to produce a baby. It also takes energy to make a tree. The road to disorder is all downhill but the road to creation takes work. Though combating entropy is possible, it also has its price. That's why it seems so hard to get ourselves together, so easy to let ourselves fall apart.

11   Worse, creating order in one corner of the universe always creates more disorder somewhere else. We create ordered energy from oil and coal at the price of the entropy of smog.

12   I recently took up playing the flute again after an absence of several months. As the uneven vibrations screeched through the house, my son covered his ears and said, "Mom, what's wrong with your flute?" Nothing was wrong with my flute, of course. It was my ability to play it that had **atrophied**, or entropied, as the case may be. The only way to stop that process was to practice every day, and sure enough my tone improved, though only at the price of constant work. Like anything else, abilities deteriorate when we stop applying our energies to them.

13   That's why entropy is depressing. It seems as if just breaking even is an uphill fight. There's a good reason that this should be so. The mechanics of entropy are a matter of chance. Take any ice-cold air **molecule** milling around my kitchen. The chances that it will wander in the direction of my refrigerator at any point are exactly 50–50. The chances that it will wander away from my refrigerator are also 50–50. But take billions of warm and cold molecules mixed together, and the chances that all the cold ones will wander toward the refrigerator and all the warm ones will wander away from it are virtually nil.

14   Entropy wins not because order is impossible but because there are always so many more paths toward disorder than toward order. There are so many more different ways to do a sloppy job than a good one, so many more ways to make a mess than to clean it up. The obstacles and accidents in our lives almost guarantee that constant collisions will bounce us on to random paths, get us off the track. Disorder is the path of least resistance, the easy but not the inevitable road.

15   Like so many others, I am distressed by the entropy I see around me today. I am afraid of the randomness of international events, of the lack of common purpose in the world; I am terrified that it will lead into the ultimate entropy of nuclear war. I am upset that I could not in the city where I live send my child to a public school; that people are unemployed and inflation is out of control; that tensions between sexes and races seem to be increasing again; that relationships everywhere seem to be falling apart.

16   Social institutions—like atoms and stars—decay if energy is not added to keep them ordered. Friendships and families and economies all fall apart unless we constantly make an effort to keep them working and well oiled. And far too few people, it seems to me, are willing to contribute consistently to those efforts.

17   Of course, the more complex things are, the harder it is. If there were only a dozen or so air molecules in my kitchen, it would be likely—if I waited a year or so—that at some point the six coldest ones would congregate inside the freezer. But the more actors in the equation—the more players in the game—the less likely it is that their paths will coincide in an orderly way. The more pieces in the puzzle, the harder it is to put back together once order is disturbed. "Irreversibility," said a physicist, "is the price we pay for complexity."

THE FACTS

1. What details give us a clue to the time in which the essay was written? Is the time necessary to the main point of the essay? Cite reasons for your answer.

2. Where in the essay is the term *entropy* first defined? What rules pertaining to a proper definition does the author observe? Does the definition clarify the term for you? If it does not, what is it lacking? What better definition can you provide?

3. According to the author, just about everything in our universe is subject to entropy, but what are some exceptions? What noticeable characteristic do these exceptions reveal? Provide some examples from your own experience.

4. Where in your immediate sphere do you most clearly see the workings of entropy? What, if any, steps have you taken to prevent the entropy from descending into total chaos? What foreign countries seem most vulnerable to entropy? Explain your choices.

5. According to the author, why does entropy have a winning edge in the race between disorder and order? Do you agree or disagree with the author's assessment? Give an example from your own experience to support your answer.

THE STRATEGIES

1. Why do you think the author titled his essay "entropy" instead of a more common title like "Disorder?" How does Cole capture the reader's interest with such a scientific concept as *entropy?*

2. What is the thesis of the essay and where is it stated? What does the thesis accomplish for the reader? What problem does the thesis solve?

3. What purpose does the opening sentence of paragraph 5 serve? What would happen to the essay if this sentence were deleted? Try to substitute a sentence of your own and see what happens to the flow of the essay.

4. At which point in the essay does the author focus on what really concerns her the most about the concept of entropy? Is the timing of the focus justified strategically? Explain your answer.

5. What three metaphors does the author use in the final paragraph of her essay? What do they have in common? What point do they stress?

THE ISSUES

1. What ideas contained in this essay really disturbed you or made you think about the order versus disorder around you? Point to two or three passages from the essay and explain your reaction to them.

2. Do you agree or disagree with the author's view (see paragraph 14) that entropy wins because there are so many more paths toward disorder than toward order? Cite examples from your own experience to support or challenge her argument.

3. As you analyze your life style, which kind of person do you tend to be—orderly or disorderly? How has your sense of order affected the way you see yourself? What changes, if any, would you like to make in the way you deal with the order or chaos around you?

4. What relationship exists between entropy and energy? Make a case for what would happen to our society if entropy were to win over energy? Cite an example to clarify your view.

5. From the list of social institutions mentioned in paragraph 16, which one do you consider crucial to the fabric of society? How do you propose to use energy to save it from chaos? Be specific in your prescription.

● SUGGESTIONS FOR WRITING

1. Choosing one of the following terms whose definition depends on who is using it, write what you think it means. Use several appropriate examples and try to persuade your reader that your definition is the correct one:
   a. feminine
   b. pornography
   c. progressive
   d. racist
   e. tolerance

2. Cole claims that "abilities deteriorate when we stop applying our energies to them." Write an essay in which you use this concept as your thesis and try to persuade your reader that it is true. Use statistics, specific examples, quotations, or any other means that will support your thesis.

Invisibly Wounded

DAVID FINKEL

Rhetorical Thumbnail

Purpose: to define *PTSD (post-traumatic stress disorder)* so lay persons can understand the horrors accompanying this disease

Audience: educated readers

Language: standard English, using dramatic examples from the life of a real veteran

Strategy: to use eight years in the life of a veteran—highlighting such events as when he first fell in love with his wife, hellish moments of fighting in the war, and the mental pain suffered during the two years after he returned from the war

David Louis Finkel (b. 1955) is a journalist who in 2006 won a Pulitzer Prize for Explanatory Reporting when he was a staff writer for *The Washington Post*. He has received other awards for his excellence in reporting, among them the Missouri Lifestyle Journalism Award for a story about racial and class conflict (1950), and the Robert F. Kennedy Award for "Invisible Journeys" about illegal immigration (2001). Finkel is best known for his two books about war: *The Good Soldier* (2010), which describes several months where the author was an embedded reporter with the "2-16 Rangers" as they worked to stabilize a portion of Baghdad; and *Thank You for Your Service* (2013), from which the following essay was excerpted. Currently, Finkel is assigned to the national staff of *The Washington Post* as an enterprise reporter.

• • •

1 Adam drops the baby. The baby, who is four days old, is his son, and there is a moment as he is falling that this house he has come home to seems like the most peaceful place in the world. Outside is the cold dead of 3 a.m. on a late-November night in Kansas, but inside is lamplight, the warm smell of a newborn, and Adam's wife, Saskia, beautiful Saskia, who a few minutes before had asked her husband if he could watch the baby so she could get a little sleep. "I got it," he had said. She curled up in the middle of their bed, and the last thing she glimpsed was Adam reclined along the edge, his back against the headboard and the baby in his arms. He was smiling, as if contentment for this wounded man were possible at last, and she believed it enough to shut her eyes, just before he shut his. His arms soon relaxed. His grip loosened. The baby rolled off of his chest and over the edge of the bed, and here came that peaceful moment, the baby in the air. Then the moment is over and everything that will happen is under way.

2 Saskia is the one who hears it. It is not loud, but it is loud enough. Her eyes fly open. She sees Adam closed-eyed and empty-armed, and only when he hears screaming and feels the sharp elbows and knees of someone scrambling across him does he wake up from the sleep he had promised he didn't need. It takes him a second or two. Then he knows what he has done.

3 He says nothing. There is nothing he can say. He is sorry. He is always sorry now. He has been sorry for two years, ever since he slunk home from the war. He dresses and leaves the room. He sits for a while in the dark, listening to her soothe the baby, and then he goes outside, gets into his pickup truck, and positions a shotgun so that it is propped up and pointed at his face. In that way, he starts driving, while back in the house, Saskia is trying to understand what happened. This baby. So **resilient**. Breathing evenly. Not even a mark. Somehow fine. How can that be? But he is. Maybe he is one of the lucky ones, born to be okay.

4 Two years. He is 28 now, is out of the Army, and has gained back some weight. When he left the war as the great Sgt. Schumann, he was **verging** on **gaunt**. Twenty-five pounds later, he is once again solid, at least physically. Mentally, though, it is still the day he headed home. Emory, shot in the head, is still draped across his back, and the blood flowing out of Emory's head is still **rivering** into his mouth. Doster, whom he might have loved the most, is being shredded again and again by a roadside bomb on a mission Adam was supposed to have been on, too, and after Doster is declared dead another soldier is saying to him, "None of this s—would have happened if you were there." It was said as a soldier's compliment—Adam had the sharpest eyes, Adam always found the hidden bombs, everyone relied on Adam—but that wasn't how he heard it then or hears it now. It might as well have been **shrapnel**, the way those words cut him apart. It was his fault. It is his fault. The guilt runs so deep it defines him now. He's always been such a good guy, people say of Adam. He's the one people are drawn to, who they root for, smart, decent, honorable, good instincts, that one. And now? "I feel completely broken," Adam says.

5 "He's still a good guy" is what Saskia says. "He's just a broken good guy."

6   It's not as if he caused this. He didn't. It's not as if he doesn't want to get better. He does. On other days, though, it seems more like an **epitaph**, and not only for Adam. All the soldiers he went to war with—the 30 in his platoon, the 120 in his company, the 800 in his battalion—came home broken in various degrees, even the ones who are fine. "I don't think anyone came back from that deployment without some kind of demons they needed to work out," one of those soldiers who was with Adam says.

7   "Constant nightmares, anger issues, and anytime I go into a public place I have to know what everyone is doing all the time," another of them says.

8   "Depression. Nightmares of my teeth falling out," another says.

9   "Other than that, though," the one who might be in the best shape of all says with an embarrassed laugh, after mentioning that his wife tells him he screams every night as he falls asleep. He sounds **bewildered** by this, as do they all.

10   Two million Americans were sent to fight in Iraq and Afghanistan. Home now, most of them describe themselves as physically and mentally healthy. They move forward. Their war recedes. Some are even stronger for the experience. But then there are the others, for whom the war endures. Of the 2 million, studies suggest that 20 to 30 percent have come home with post-traumatic stress disorder—PTSD—a mental health condition triggered by some type of terror, or traumatic brain injury—TBI—which occurs when a brain is jolted so violently that it collides with the inside of the skull and causes psychological damage. Depression, anxiety, nightmares, memory problems, personality changes, suicidal thoughts: Every war has its after-war, and so it is with the wars of Iraq and Afghanistan, which have created some 500,000 mentally wounded American veterans.

11   He doesn't believe anything is wrong with him. That's part of it. At home, he stares at himself in a mirror, ignores what his red eyes look like except to see with continuing regret that he still has two of them, does the inventory. Two eyes, two ears, two arms, two legs, two hands, two feet. Nothing missing. **Symmetrical** as ever. He is physically unmarked, so how can he be injured? The answer must be that he isn't. So why was he sent home with a diagnosis of severe PTSD? The answer must be that he's weak. So why was that diagnosis confirmed again and again once he was home? Why does he get angry? Why does he forget things? Why is he jittery? Why can't he stay awake, even after 12 hours of sleep? Why is he still tasting Emory's blood? Because he's weak. Because he's a pussy. Because he's a piece of s—.

12   Saskia found the house and bought it during Adam's final deployment, the one that wrecked him. This was where they would claim the life they both had expected to have by his enlisting in the Azrmy: house, kids, dogs, yard, money, stability, predictability. She knew he was coming home ill, but she also knew that he would be better once he was away from the war and back with her, that just by her presence he would heal. "That fairy-tale homecoming" is how she thought of it. "Everybody's happy. Kind of like an it-never-happened kind of thing." When he got home and wasn't happy, she told him she understood, and when he said he wasn't yet ready to be around a lot of people, she understood that, too. Her patience, she had decided, would be bottomless. Saskia decorated the bedroom with a wall stenciling that said "Always Kiss Me Goodnight."

13   He did. Then, dulled by prescriptions for anxiety and depression and jitteriness and exhaustion and headaches, he didn't. And then she didn't, either, not always, and gradually less than that.

14   Now they are on their way to the VA hospital in Topeka, 60 miles to the east, for a doctor's appointment. The war left him with PTSD, depression, nightmares, headaches, **tinnitus**, and mild traumatic brain injury, the result of a mortar round that dropped without warning out of a blue sky and exploded close enough to momentarily knock him silly. Between his government disability check of $800 a month and his $36,000-a-year salary from a job he managed to find, he is pulling in about two thirds of what he made in the Army.

15   It has been eight years since they met. This was in Minot, N.D. She was just out of high school, a girl who never missed curfew and was now on her own in a cheap basement apartment, and one day she emerged from the basement to the sight of a local boy with a rough reputation sitting in the sun without a shirt. What Adam saw was a girl staring at him whose beauty seemed a **counterpoint** to everything in his life so far, and that was that, for both of them. Soon came marriage and now here they are.

16   Sometimes after they fight, she counts his pills to make sure he hasn't swallowed too many and checks on the guns to make sure they're all there. The thought that he might not recover, that this is how it will be, makes her sick with dread sometimes, and the thought that he might kill himself leaves her feeling like her insides are being twisted until she can't breathe.

17   The truth is that he has been thinking about killing himself, more and more. But he hasn't said anything to her, or to anyone, not lately, because what would be the point? How many psychiatrists and therapists has he talked to? How many times has he mentioned it, and where has it gotten him?

18   "You have suicidal thoughts: You reported daily thoughts of suicide with a plan and a means. However, you repeatedly denied intent to harm yourself due to care for your family" was one psychiatrist's report, which went on to note: "You have the ability to maintain minimum personal hygiene."

19   Well, at least there's that, Adam thought when he came across that report. Crazy, but clean. He found it when he was going through papers to see what he might need to bring with him to the VA. His medical file is thick and repetitive and soon bored him, and he turned his attention to several boxes filled with letters that he and Saskia had written to each other while he was overseas, love letters all. They wrote to each other just about every day. That's how they were. He read a few, and when they started making him a little sad over what had been lost between them, he moved on to other boxes.

20   At the hospital now. Adam goes in to the doctor, preceded by all of the previous histories dictated about him over these two years. Saskia waits outside. Sometimes she goes in with him, sometimes not. She is sure she knows what the doctor will say: Adam is wounded. Adam is ill. Adam needs to stay on his medications. Adam deserves the thanks of a grateful **nation**.

● THE FACTS

1. What event sets the essay in motion? In view of what we learn later about Adam Schumann, what significance does this event have?

2. When Saskia found the house in which she and Adam lived, what typical American dream was she pursuing? Which part of the dream was not realized? Why not?

3. How do you know that dropping the baby is not the only blunder Adam has made since returning from the war? What is his reaction to his blunders? What does this reaction indicate?

4. How does Saskia qualify her assessment that Adam is "a good guy"? What does this tell us about Saskia as well as about Adam?

5. What does Saskia sometimes do after a fight has taken place between her and Adam? Is this a wise action, or should she have taken a different approach? Explain your answer.

● THE STRATEGIES

1. How does the author indicate the progress of time? Point to specific passages. Were you able to follow the sequence easily? Why or why not?

2. What purpose do the many questions posed in paragraph 11 serve? What is the answer to these questions? Why is this question-answer section important? If you deleted the section, what, if anything, would be missing?

3. What is the scientific definition of PTSD? Where in the essay is it located? What do the statistics about this disease indicate?

4. How does the author leave the reader in suspense? Is the suspense justified? Explain your answer.

5. What does the final paragraph say about Adam's condition? What irony is involved?

6. What is your opinion of the final paragraph?

● THE ISSUES

1. What is the meaning of the statement made in paragraph 10 that "every war has its after-war"? What example from history can you cite to support this statement?

2. What importance do you ascribe to the question, "He is physically unmarked, so how can he be injured?" What does the question imply? (See paragraph 11.)

3. How do you interpret Saskia's wall stenciling? (See paragraph 12.) Can you suggest another wall stenciling that would be equally appropriate?

4. Based on evidence from the essay, what is the likely outcome of Adam's battle with PTSD? What do you think will happen? Can society affect the outcome of experiences like Adam's?

5. What do you think is the worst collateral damage caused by war? How can it be avoided? What future war do you fear the most? Why? How can it be avoided?

● SUGGESTIONS FOR WRITING

1. Write an essay in which you describe the experience of a wounded veteran whom you know well. Use Finkel's essay as your inspiration.

2. Write a definition of some medical condition with which you are familiar. Use examples to clarify your definition. If you use outside sources, assimilate them according to the guidelines offered in Chapter 3.

Image Gallery for Critical Thinking and Debate: Immigration

Some years ago we took an airplane trip from Atlanta to Zürich, Switzerland, aboard a Swissair jet. During the long crossing, we felt sorry for the poor pilot. The flight attendants spoke to each other in a Swiss dialect. Every time he made an announcement, he had to repeat it in English, French, German, and Swiss German. For most of the eight-hour flight, the pilot quite sensibly remained mute. But his behavior brought to mind one predicted effect of immigration that Americans fear the most—the tendency of new arrivals to settle in communities where they can speak their mother tongue rather than learn English. Miami, and much of Florida, has virtually become a bilingual land, with Spanish as the primary language. California and Texas are in a similar predicament. Countries whose people are polyglot rather than sharing one common language have a tendency to develop profound divisions and differences based on linguistic groupings. One has only to think of Québec and the deep antagonisms that exist between French and English-speaking Canadians. The lack of a common language is one reason the European Union is faltering in its attempt to unite that deeply divided continent.

When it comes to immigrants and immigration, Americans are truly a deeply conflicted people. The vast majority of us are the descendants of immigrants, some with fathers and mothers who came here from other countries, others with foreign great ancestors. It is a rare American whose origin one or two or three generations back does not lie abroad.

One of this book's authors, for example, is a Jamaican immigrant who became a naturalized American citizen many years ago. The other was born to American parents living abroad and grew up speaking French within her immediate family, coming to the United States to attend college as a teenager.

The wife of the male author is the granddaughter of a Polish immigrant who spoke mainly Polish and, even at the end of her life, only badly fractured English. The wife's own mother speaks both Polish and English; the wife herself speaks only English, and has some regrets about not learning her grandmother's language.

In this evolution of language, the family is almost stereotypical, with the experience being repeated throughout millions of American households.

Is immigration good for America? The answer you get depends on whom you ask. In 2004, National Public Radio, collaborating with Harvard's Kennedy School of Government and the Kaiser Family Foundation, undertook a survey of 1,100 native Americans and nearly 800 immigrants and found deep divisions in the opinion of those polled, with 37 percent saying that immigration should be kept the same, 41 percent that it should be decreased, and only 18 percent saying that it should be increased. Those Americans who had direct contact with some immigrant group were, as a whole, less negative about immigrants. Among the strongest fears of the native population was that immigrants would displace Americans from jobs. Another fear was that America would be changed by the influx of immigrants.

Since 9/11, many Americans have expressed the fear that terrorists might exist among immigrants not screened carefully. Yet even the most rabid opponent of immigration has to admit that immigrants do much of the dirty work in our communities, such as digging ditches, cleaning houses, sweeping streets, picking fruit, and other kinds of manual labor that natives do not like to do.

Immigrants bring blessings to America, not the least of which is a variegated cuisine and a unique outlook. What would American cuisine be like without French crème brulee, Italian pizza, Chinese chow mein, Greek gyros, Middle Eastern falafel, or Mexican enchiladas? The infusion of cultural richness into the melting pot is the primary contribution of successive waves of immigrants. There are other benefits as well, one of which is pointed out by writer Eduardo Porter. Immigrants, many of whom are on shaky legal footing, contribute billions of dollars to Social Security, yet they draw no benefits. Without them, Social Security would be in even worse shape than presently reported. As for the charge often made that the country is being overrun by immigrant groups, writer Bill Bryson points out a fact often overlooked: that the vast continent of America is really underpopulated and with far fewer immigrants than European countries such as France and England. It really is an oddity that so many of us, the children and grandchildren of immigrants, would take such a negative attitude toward what is, in effect, a nearly universal common background of immigration roots.

Aside from their contributions of crafts and foods, immigrants bring to the table a fresh perspective of wonderment to the grand experiment that is America. They do not whine as natives are likely to, for they are not used to the manifold opportunities in business and education and the social advancements that are available to the hard-working newcomer, which many natives take for granted. This, of all the immigrant's endowments, is probably the greatest and the least appreciated of all gifts: namely, the gift of fresh eyes to see anew for us and to remind us that no matter what our difficulties or passing worries might be, all in all we have it pretty good.

The Image Gallery gives students the chance to see immigration as it was in the past and how it is today, encouraging them to ponder their heritage as well as their future. The first image is a sinister reminder of the dangers lurking when foreigners try to invade our borders illegally by climbing walls at night or by following some money-hungry mole who promises for a stiff fee to guide them through tangled bushes, over dry prairies, and across the border into the United States. The second is a photograph of early immigrants entering Ellis Island to be processed for the first stage in seeking U.S. citizenship. Last is a modern photo of a blond woman happily embracing the little girl from China she has legally adopted as her own.

Our student essay takes the position that immigration has been good for America. Among the reasons cited is that our country benefits from the brain drain taking place in other countries as we inherit the brains and talents of those driven to our shores as a result of being persecuted in their homelands.

"To the Point" rounds out the issue.

Study the following three images dealing with immigration. Then choose the image that most appeals to you. Answer the questions and do the writing assignment.

 MindTap

For readings, questions, and media on the issue of immigration, visit the *MindTap for Readings for Writers*, 15e online.

AP Images/Dario Lopez-Mills

Studying the Image

1. Which details add a surreal quality to this image?

2. How does the photo preserve the anonymity of the illegal immigrants?

3. How do you personally regard these men? Be specific in whether you view them as a good source of labor, unwanted intruders, or otherwise.

4. Aside from providing the United States with a source of manual labor, what other good do illegal immigrants contribute to American society? Consider intangibles such as a strong work ethic, family loyalty, and religious fervor.

Writing Assignment

Write an essay in which you define "immigrant" and explain the causes that lead certain people to risk their lives to enter the United States. Try to keep your personal biases out of the essay.

Bettmann/Corbis

Studying the Image

1. What general impression of these immigrants does this old photo give?

2. Why do all of the immigrants, even the children, seem glum? Why is there no excitement or frivolity along the line?

3. Contrast the placidity of this scene with the depiction of the illegal immigrants frantically climbing the wall that blocks them from entry into the United States (see previous page). What differences can you see between the people shown here and those climbing over the wall? What part does the society to which they are migrating play in the immigrants' system of getting to the new place?

4. Where is Ellis Island? What historical reputation does it have in its treatment of immigrants?

Writing Assignment

Write an essay comparing and contrasting the Ellis Island immigrants with the illegal immigrants entering our country today. Consider such aspects as the countries' histories, ethnic differences, and levels of poverty.

Inti St. Clair/Photodisc/Getty Images

Studying the Image

1. In recent decades, many American couples looking to adopt a child have traveled to China and found adoptive daughters. However, adopting Chinese girls has become increasingly difficult in recent years. Why do you think most of the Chinese children up for adoption were female? Why has it become more difficult to adopt in China? If you don't know, do some research on the Internet about Chinese laws limiting the number of children legally allowable.

2. Why do some individuals and families travel outside the United States to adopt? What is your opinion of this choice?

3. What advantages or disadvantages do you see in interracial adoptions? How can the adoptive parents make interracial differences become a good fit in a family?

4. What seems to be the relationship between the mother and adopted daughter pictured above?

Writing Assignment

Write an essay in which you state your feelings about parents who choose to adopt children from China, Russia, Africa, Mexico, or other foreign countries. Try to be fair in your evaluation of the hardships or rewards of such an adoption, considering such factors as the biological parents, the future of the child, and the society of origin as well as the adoptive community.

Stumped by ending an essay? Exit on
pages 433–434 at the **Editing Booth!**

Punctuation Workshop

The Apostrophe (')

The apostrophe shows ownership, the omission in a contraction, and certain plurals.

1. Use an apostrophe + *s* to show ownership.

> Pete's baseball bat
>
> Someone's mistake
>
> This bicycle is Katie's. (A possessive can follow the word to which it belongs.)
>
> Venus's beauty
>
> For a plural that ends in *s*, omit an additional *s*.
>
> The Dodgers' baseball camp (rather than *Dodgers's*)

2. Use an apostrophe to show an omission in a contraction.

> don't (for *do not*)
>
> can't (for *cannot*)
>
> High school class of '52

 CAUTION: Don't confuse the contraction *who's* with the pronoun *whose*.

3. Use the apostrophe to form certain plurals.

> He crossed all of his t's and dotted all of his i's.
>
> I love to read about the 1800s (*1800's* is sometimes acceptable).
>
> Her l's are written in bold strokes

 CAUTION: Do not use an apostrophe to form plural nouns that don't show ownership. (The lions were restless—not *lion's*. The Goldmans were out of town—not *Goldman's*.)

Student Corner

Immigrants in America

Dave Herman

Georgia State University

An immigrant is a person whose ancestral roots lie in another country. By that definition nearly all Americans are immigrants or the descendants of immigrants. Even the Native Americans, the so-called American Indians, are immigrants whose ancestors came to the new world via the Bering Straits, which geologists tell us was once connected to the North American continent by a land bridge. Ours, like it or not, is an immigrant society.

One disadvantage of this widespread immigrant influence is an attitude of snobbery that some American citizens have, depending on when their ancestors came to the United States. The most conspicuous example of this is an organization called Daughters of the American Revolution (DAR for short). To be a member of this snobbish group, you have to prove that one of your ancestors fought in the American Revolution. The guidelines for eligibility declare that membership is open to any woman who can prove "lineal, bloodline descent from an ancestor who aided in achieving American independence," adding that the applicant "must provide documentation for each statement of birth, marriage, and death" ("Become a Member").

The children of immigrants sometimes hold a condescending or embarrassed attitude toward their parents, especially if the parents have a strong foreign accent from a language other than English. Often the children make excuses for the way their parents mispronounce words or ignore grammar rules. Once the third generation emerges, the language of the first generation has usually been lost, with only nostalgic scraps of idioms and quaint sayings surviving.

In my own family, for example, my grandmother speaks Spanish, which is her native tongue, and so does my mother. An aunt or two understand a few words. But only my mother has mastered the language, probably because she has a good ear. The third generation, of which I'm a member, speaks no Spanish. One cousin can understand a phrase here and there if the speaker enunciates clearly and slowly. But for the most part, the language is Greek to my generation. Because the cultural emphasis in those days was on instant adaptation to a new society, the children were encouraged to speak English everywhere, even at home. Those who fear that immigrants will introduce and cling to the mother tongue of their parents don't understand the tremendous pressure immigrants and their children are subjected to by American society. Even Miami, which has a majority Hispanic population and where Spanish seems to be the language of the majority, has a bilingual population that speaks both English and Spanish fluently.

I think immigration has been good for America. Wherever there is a brain drain going on in some foreign country of our world, it is likely that the brains leaving their homeland are flowing into America. My uncle, for example, went to school with a boy who later became an astrophysicist for NASA. This boy became so important to the space program that when he came back to the village where my father and he came from, he was in the company of two Secret Service agents as his personal bodyguards.

In my neighborhood are three families from what used to be Armenia. The children have all done well at the University. One is a neurosurgeon, one a gynecologist, and one a successful businessman. Several of the other children are still at the University pursuing advanced degrees. It is impossible to estimate in dollars alone what these three families have or will contribute to the society in which they were born because their parents had migrated to America.

We are a society of immigrants. And we're better off for it. The problems of adjustment to a new culture, or a new culture adjusting to the influx of immigrants, are minor compared to the richness and blessings that immigration bestows on America. There's a reason why the inscription of the base of the Statue of Liberty says,

Give me your tired, your poor,

Your huddled masses yearning to breathe free,

The wretched refuse of your teeming shore,

Send these, the homeless, tempest-tossed to me,

I lift my lamp beside the golden door!

Emma Lazarus, the poet who wrote this jingle, was no fool. She knew a good thing when she saw it.

Work Cited

"Become a Member: Eligibility." *National Society Daughters of the American Revolution*. DAR, 2005. Web. 7 July 2005

How I Write

I write late at night or early in the morning. I cannot write during the day because my thoughts race too fast for writing. I have to be in a slower mode in order to write effectively. Mostly, I rewrite everything over two or three times just to make it smooth.

My Writing Tip

Go over your work again and again. Sometimes when you can't get something just right, an idea will occur to you if you keep going over the material. I know this sounds boring, but it's the technique that works for me.

 To the Point

Some people believe that the anti-immigration movement is a hidden attempt to use racism as a way of keeping certain cultural groups (e.g., Muslims, Jews, blacks, Latinos, gays) from entering our country and reaping the benefits of our treasured resources. Write a tweet in which you condemn racism as a barrier to immigration.

▦ Chapter Writing Assignments

1. In an essay, define *history*. Allow your definition to function as the essay's thesis.

2. Define yourself in an essay, and support your definition with evidence from your life. Here is how one student defined herself: "I am a consummate pessimist because I always expect the darkest of all possible outcomes."

3. Write a definition of *superstition* so that you leave no doubt in the reader's mind as to what the term means.

4. Choose one of the following terms and write an essay in which you first define the term as a dictionary would. Then give an extended definition, using the development most suitable for answering the question, "What is it?"

   curiosity   mercurial

   genetic   pratfall

▦ Writing Assignments for a Specific Audience

1. Define the term *authority* to a seven-year-old child.

2. Write an essay defining *failure* to an audience of your peers.

 Pointer from a Pro

LET YOUR WRITING PERCOLATE

We're horrible judges of the comparative quality of our own work, particularly in the moment. What feels good and what feels bad when we're writing something, isn't always a good indicator of quality.

—Tycho Goren

Usually, if you place a night between writing and checking the product, you will see your writing with renewed clarity because while you were sleeping, your subconscious writer's mind was editing and revising.

CHAPTER 13

Comparison/ Contrast

Road Map to Comparison/Contrast

What Comparison/Contrast Does

To *compare* is to point out how two things are similar; to *contrast* is to stress how they are dissimilar. To say that both John Calvin and Martin Luther were persecuted by the Catholic Church, were opposed to conservative theology, and were personally against materialistic self-indulgence is to make a comparison. A contrast between the two men, however, might stress that Luther wanted the Church to return to the primitive simplicity of the apostles, whereas Calvin heartily supported the advancement of capitalism. The following passage from a student essay draws a contrast, indicated by the use of the bolded contrasting words and expressions, between Egyptian and Greek mythologies.

> A brief consideration of Egyptian mythology contrasted with the mythology of the Greeks is enough to convince us of the revolution in thought that must have taken place from one age to the other. The Egyptian gods had no resemblance to anything in the real world, **whereas** the Greek gods were fashioned after real Greek people. In Egypt, the gods that were typically worshiped consisted of a towering colossus, so immobile and so distorted that no human could imagine it alive; a woman with a cat's head, suggesting inflexible, inhuman cruelty; and a monstrous mysterious sphinx, aloof from anything we might consider human. The Egyptian artists' interpretations of the divine were horrid bestial shapes that combined men's heads with birds' bodies or portrayed lions with eagle wings— creatures that could inhabit only terrifying nightmares. The monstrosities of an invisible world were what the Egyptians worshiped.
>
> The Greek interpretation of divinity stands in **opposition** to this dark picture. The Greeks were preoccupied with the visible world. **Unlike** the Egyptians, they found their desires satisfied in what they could actually see around them. The ancient statues of Apollo, for instance, resemble the strong young bodies of athletes contending in the Olympic games. Homer describes Hermes as if he were a splendid Greek citizen. Generally, the Greek artists found their gods in the idealized beauty or intelligence of actual human counterparts.

In direct contrast to the Egyptians, they had no wish to create some hideous fantasy that they then called God.

On the other hand, the following passage finds similarities between whales and human beings:

> Whales and human beings are like two nations of individuals who have certain characteristics **in common**. As mammals they **both** are warm-blooded, giving milk and breathing air. As social creatures they **both** have basic urges for privacy **as well as** for fraternization. As species bent on reproduction they **both** show **similar** patterns of aggression during courtship, the male trying to gain the female's attention and the female responding. Finally, as mystical beings they **both** are caught in the net of life and time, fellow prisoners of the splendor, travail, and secrets of earth.

Comparisons that take the form of extended analogies are frequently used to clarify abstract or complex ideas. One of the most famous examples of this use comes from the biblical accounts of Jesus's remarks:

> The kingdom of heaven is like unto a grain of mustard seed, which a man took and sowed in his field: which indeed is less than all seeds; but when it is grown, it is greater than the herbs, and becometh a tree, so that the birds of the heaven come and lodge in the branches thereof.
>
> —Matthew 13:31–32

By comparing the kingdom of heaven to a mustard seed, which would have been familiar to his agrarian listeners, Jesus explains the power and the influence that a life dedicated to God can exert.

When to Use Comparison/Contrast

Odds are that you will not get through college without having to write a comparison/contrast, either in an essay exam or in a research paper. An English exam may typically ask for a contrast between the tragic flaws of Oedipus and Othello. A sociology question may call for a comparison between the demands of the feminist and civil rights movements. You may be asked to catalogue the differences between substances of organic and inorganic chemistry, or you may be asked to write an essay contrasting the traits of apes in captivity with those of apes who live in the wild. Comparison/contrast questions, in fact, commonly arise in every imaginable discipline.

How to Use Comparison/Contrast

1. **Use logical bases of contrast.** Suppose you want to develop the key thought "My college experience is teaching me that good instructors are a different breed from bad ones." You must first decide on your bases for contrast. You must ask yourself in which areas of instruction you wish to contrast the activities of good teachers with bad teachers. The following three could be your choice: (1) time spent on lesson preparation; (2) willingness to tolerate dissent; (3) personal relationships with students. Having chosen your bases, write down the three areas

under consideration on the left side of a sheet of paper and then create two columns (one for good instructors, the other for bad instructors) in which you will place comments, as follows:

	Good instructors	Bad instructors
1. **Time spent on lesson preparation**	Good instructors constantly revise lessons, including up-to-date reviews, newspaper clippings, research results, and other relevant material. They refer to more than one source work and give suggestions for further reading. Lectures and discussions are the result of clear objectives.	Bad instructors give the same lectures year in and year out, including the same dead jokes. They do nothing but spell out rudimentary facts, to be memorized verbatim for final tests. They often spend class time on dull workbook assignments. They show as many movies as possible, during which they nap.
2. **Willingness to tolerate dissent**	Good instructors welcome arguments as a way of bringing life into the classroom and of pointing out alternatives. Like Socrates, they believe the classroom dialectic is a valid teaching method.	Bad instructors see dissent or discussion as a threat to discipline and to their authority, so they avoid both. They feel safe only when they are parroting themselves or the textbook.
3. **Personal relationships with students**	Good instructors spend time beyond office hours listening to student questions or complaints. They willingly clarify difficult problems. They never embarrass or patronize students.	Bad instructors are usually too busy off campus to spend time in personal consultation with students. They make students who ask for special help feel inferior.

2. **Use either the alternating or block method of contrast**. Once you have made a preliminary sketch, you can develop it simply by adding a few transitional words and phrases, as has been done in the following passage (transitions are bolded):

My college experience is teaching me that good instructors are a different breed from bad ones. **In terms of time spent on lesson preparation**, good instructors constantly revise their lessons, including such items as up-to-date reviews, newspaper clippings, research results, or any other relevant material. They refer to more than one source work and give suggestions for further reading. Their lectures and discussions are the obvious result of clear objectives. **In contrast**, **bad instructors** give the same lectures year in and year out, including the same dead jokes. Only the rudimentary facts are spelled out in class, to be memorized verbatim and regurgitated on final tests. They often spend classroom time on dull workbook assignments or, as often as possible, a movie, during which they take a nap.

Another big difference between good and bad instructors is in their willingness to tolerate dissent. Good instructors welcome arguments as a way of bringing life into the classroom and of pointing out alternatives. Like Socrates, they believe that the classroom dialectic is a valid learning method. **Bad instructors, however, take the opposite tack**. They see dissent or discussion as a threat to their discipline and to their authority, so they avoid both. They feel safe only when they are parroting themselves or their textbooks.

Good and bad instructors differ markedly in their relationship to students. Good instructors spend time beyond office hours listening to student questions or complaints. They willingly clarify difficult problems, and they never embarrass or patronize students. Bad instructors, **on the other hand**, are usually too busy off campus to spend time in personal consultation with students. They deliver their lectures and disappear. The student who asks for special help is made to feel inferior.

The preceding example demonstrates the *alternating* method of comparison/ contrast. The paragraph is written to alternate back and forth from one side of an issue to the other. Another system—called the *block* method—uses separate paragraphs for each side of the issue, as illustrated in the following passage that contrasts two views of Jewish history:

> On the one hand, the Diaspora Jews can say that this talk of a predestination drama is a lot of nonsense. What has happened is only an interesting constellation of accidental, impersonal events, which some people have distorted out of all pro-portions to reality. We were defeated in war, they could say, we lost our land, we were exiled, and now it is our turn to disappear, just as under similar circumstances the Sumerians, the Hittites, the Babylonians, the Assyrians, the Persians—yes, even the Jews in the Kingdom of Israel—disappeared.
>
> On the other hand, they can say that their ancestors could not have been pur-suing a mere illusion for 2,000 years. They could say that if we are God's Chosen People as our forefathers affirmed, if we have been placed in an exile to accomplish a divine mission as our Prophets predicted, and since we did receive the Torah, then we must survive to fulfill our Covenant with God.
>
> —Max I. Dimont, *The Indestructible Jews*

The alternating and block methods of comparison/contrast are further clarified in the following two outlines contrasting the Toyota Camry and the Volkswagen Jetta on the basis of cost, performance, and looks:

Alternating Outline

First paragraph	I. Cost
	A. Camry
	B. Jetta
Second paragraph	II. Performance
	A. Camry
	B. Jetta

Third paragraph   III. Looks

                                 A. Camry

                                 B. Jetta

Block Outline

First paragraph   I. Camry

                                 A. Cost

                                 B. Performance

                                 C. Looks

Second paragraph   II. Jetta

                                 A. Cost

                                 B. Performance

                                 C. Looks

3. **Make sure that the items to be compared/contrasted belong to the same class.** Some common ground must exist between items in order for a comparison/contrast to be meaningful. For example, a comparison between a hummingbird and a cement mixer or between backgammon and Dutch Cleanser would be silly. On the other hand, some usefulness can be derived from a comparison between the Chinese and Japanese languages or between golf and tennis—pairings that belong to common groups: Asian languages and sports, respectively. Moreover, the expression of the comparison/contrast must be grammatically accurate:

Wrong: Our telephone system is better than Russia.

                    Here, a telephone system is contrasted with all of Russia.

Right: Our telephone system is better than *that* of Russia.

                    or

                    Our telephone system is better than Russia's.

Wrong: Ed's income is less than his wife.

                    Here, Ed's income is contrasted with his wife.

Right: Ed's income is less than that of his wife.

                    or

                    Ed's income is less than his wife's.

4. **Deal with both sides of the question.** All comparisons and contrasts are concerned with two sides, and you must deal equally with both. Do not mention one side and assume that your reader will fill in the other side. If you are contrasting

the summer weather in Death Valley with the summer weather at Donner Pass, you cannot say:

> In Death Valley the heat is so intense that even lizards wilt.

and assume that your reader will fill in "but at Donner Pass the summers remain cool." You must draw the contrast fully, as in the following:

> In Death Valley the heat is so intense that even lizards wilt, whereas at Donner Pass a cool breeze freshens even the hottest day.

5. **Use expressions indicating comparison/contrast.** Although comparison requires less back-and-forth movement than does contrast, you must nevertheless take both sides into account by stating exactly what traits they have in common. For instance, in pointing out that in some ways high schools are *like* prisons, you cannot restrict yourself to discussing the domineering principal, the snoopy truant officer, the pass required to leave campus, or the punitive grading system. You must mention both sides, indicating that the domineering principal in high school is like the stern warden in prison; that the snoopy truant officer who makes sure that students attend school has much *in common with the prison guards* who make sure that inmates stay in prison; that the pass required to leave campus is *similar* to the formal permission required to leave a locked ward; and that the punitive grading system of high schools is *like* the demerit system of prisons. These expressions serve as signposts in your text, telling your reader how your different points relate.

The following expressions indicate comparison:

also	as well as
bears resemblance to both . . .	and in common with
in like manner	like
likewise	neither . . . nor
similar	too

The following expressions indicate contrast:

although this may be true	at the same time
but	for all that
however	in contrast to
in opposition to	nevertheless
on the contrary	on the one hand . . . on the other hand
otherwise	still
unlike	whereas
yet	

Contrast emphasizes the separate sides of an issue by pulling them apart as much as possible in order to clarify their differences. Comparison is less two-sided because it tries to draw together both sides of an issue in order to reveal what they have in common. In short, *contrasts diverge, comparisons converge.* Refer back to the contrast example on page 288, and note how Egyptian mythology and Greek mythology are placed far apart so that their ideological differences stand out. Note also how the bolded expressions indicating contrast clarify the shift from one side to the other.

Warming Up to Write a Comparison/Contrast

Comparing and contrasting are normal ways people think, so you should not have too much difficulty completing these exercises.

1. For the item on the left of each column, write three or four characteristics that describe the item; then write contrasting characteristics for the item at the right.

Example:

Teacher Smith	Teacher Brown
Pleasant	Grouchy
Always prepared	Sometimes disorganized
Fascinating in his presentations	Usually boring

a. Historical romances	Myths
b. Tornadoes	Cyclones
c. Friend with bad ethics	Friend with good ethics
d. Working in a restaurant	Working in a hospital
e. Watching a movie on TV	Watching a movie in a theater

2. Write down three bases of contrast (not comparison) for each of the following subjects.

    a. Two close friends
    b. Two church services
    c. Two holidays
    d. Two sports teams (or persons)
    e. Two attitudes toward work

3. Write down at least three aspects in which each of the following pairs are similar.

    a. A farm and a garden
    b. A storm and a lover's quarrel
    c. An ant hill and city government
    d. Fishing and looking for a wife
    e. An eagle and a lion

Examples

Real Work

RICK BRAGG

Rhetorical Thumbnail

Purpose: to convince the reader that writers have a velvety life compared with laborers who wield sledge hammers and operate bull dozers or front-end loaders

Audience: Anyone who thinks white collar jobs are harder than manual labor involving sweat, dirt, and toil

Language: standard English, occasionally quoting the loose grammar of street talk

Strategy: uses the author's own experience of growing up and helping his uncle with the grueling work of clearing lots for construction sites

---

Rick Bragg (b. 1959) is a Pulitzer Prize–winning author who gained a widespread reputation for writing short stories and essays portraying typical aspects of contemporary America. In addition to writing fiction, Bragg has also taught writing in colleges and in newspaper newsrooms. As a journalist, he is best known for his news reports when he worked for *The New York Times,* covering such subjects as the unrest in Haiti, the Oklahoma bombing, the Jonesboro killings, and the Susan Smith trial. Among the books authored by Bragg are the following: *All Over But the Shoutin'* (1999), *Wooden Churches: A Celebration* (1999), *Somebody Told Me: The Newspaper Stories* (2001), *Avas's Man* (2002), *I Am a Soldier Too: The Jessica Lynch Story* (2003), *The Prince of Frogtown* (2008), and *The Most They Ever Had* (2009). Bragg now works as a writing professor in the journalism program at the University of Alabama.

1   All my life, I believe, I will feel that shock, that force, rush through my hands, feel it travel up my wrists and past my elbows and into the tensed muscles in my neck and face. I even dream about it, decades later, and wake with my hands shaking. I bring them to my face in the gloom of an early morning, fearing the worst, to find them still there, trembling but not twisted or **truncated** or misshapen. Sometimes when I am writing, my fingers freeze above the keys, and I think about it—how even this easy, mechanical thing would be impossible for me if the man in the khaki work clothes had missed even once. But he never missed. I pound home one more key, then another, clumsy fingers searching for the words, and know I will never be half the man he was. He swung that sledge at the end of the chisel I held in my unsteady hands, and he was dead solid perfect a thousand times, ten thousand, more. All I do is tap a damn key, and I rarely get it right the first time.

2   "What if you miss?" I asked him, just once.

3   "I won't miss, son," he replied.

4   I held that chisel for the first time when I was eleven, aiming it at the place where the black rubber of a big, dump truck tire joined the steel wheel. It took the force of a sledge to break that seal on a flat tire, and I did it, among other things, till I was eighteen, till I finally straightened up, dropped that chisel in the dirt, and got myself a necktie job.

5   The man in khakis, my uncle Edward Fair, gave me work all of my young life, but it was hard, dirty, sometimes dangerous work, and I forgot to thank him, across those years, for the money I made. I wasted it on rolling death traps and peroxide blondes, on honky tonks and rum and cokes and snap pearl button shirts—actually, I guess I didn't waste a damn dime. But along the way he gave me some free advice, and I have thanked him, many times, for that.

6   Hang some of those tools on the wall, he told me, some of those chainsaws or chisels or big yard forks that would hold seventy pounds of rock in a single scoop. Hang 'em up high so you can see 'em real good, he told me, after you finally get yourself an easy job, and every time you feel like griping, take a long, hard look.

7   I never did hang a sledge hammer on the wall, but I do think about what he told me, when I start feeling sorry for myself, and sometimes I am a little ashamed and sometimes I laugh out loud.

8   Those of us who write for a living want the rest of the world to think it's real, real hard. We invent **myths** about it, to make it seem like man's work. I have always loved the stories about fighting writers, carousing writers, whiskey drinking, bull fighting, foxhole diving, swordfish catching, senorita romancing, big game hunting, husband defying writers, and tell myself that I belong with them, and not with the fretting, pencil neck writers who need to see their therapist twice a week to con-nect with their inner child. But the toughest writer I ever met, I ever heard of, would have lasted about a week on my Uncle Ed's crew.

9   It makes the fans of such writers angry, to hear that their storied writers would not match up against a plain ol' redneck. But really. How long do you think Hemingway would have lasted against a roofer with a tire iron?

10   I have never considered myself a tough man, within the fraternity of work-ing men, but I know I am one when I stray outside it. I owe my uncle for that toughness, for what there is in me. But mostly what I got from my Uncle Ed was **perspective**, enough of it, one shovel full at a time, to realize how good I have it now, how easy it is—at its hardest—to do what I do.

11   My Uncle Ed was his own boss. He ran a bulldozer and a front-end loader, at the heart of his operation, cutting roads, clearing lots, grading for construction. I have seen him knock the top off a mountain, or dig a lake, in the space of an afternoon.

12   He needed us, my brothers and me, for the pick and shovel work, for the tight places the machines could not get into. We dug water lines, ran chainsaws, loaded **pulpwood** by hand, for minimum wage.

13   The first job I had with the crew, when I was about ten years old, was cleaning the mud and roots from bulldozer tracks. The giant yellow machines would growl and churn through the red clay, unstoppable, until their tracks got all gummed and

choked up with debris. The operators would stop them, impatient, and I would gouge and hack at them, until the tracks were free.

14   It paid nearly nothing, not even minimum wage, but it was my way into that **fraternity**, a circle of men in training where you settled your disagreements with your fists, or a broken-off tree limb, or whatever you could find in the dirt.

15   And the best that could ever happen to you, I once believed, was to be the man on the machine.

16   We would have resented my uncle, sitting up on that big machine, so high and mighty, if he had not on a regular basis crawled down there in the muck and dust with us, and put us to shame. He could do more, faster, than most of the young men on his crew. The shameful part was that he outworked us on damaged legs. A car had crushed him below the waist when he was still a teenager himself, and his legs were held together with steel rods. It was hard to complain, much, when a man with a built-up shoe was kicking your ass, was loading more rock, digging more dirt, piling up more pulpwood.

17   But still, it was hateful work. It did not teach me character, just toughness, taught me that I could stoop lower and strain harder than most people were willing to.

18   The worst of it was the pulpwooding. I had never met a pulpwooder who had all his fingers and toes, but it had to be done, when we cleared land for houses or roads. To leave the pulpwood piled on the land would be like burning money on the ground.

19   We did not fell the trees. The bulldozers did that, knocking the pines down into a morass of stumps, trunks and interlocking limbs. We waded into it the best we could, big chainsaws bucking in our hands, and took off the limbs, then cut the pulpwood into logs.

20   The biggest problem was the footing. The trees were slick with mud, and piled atop one another, limbs twisted back under thousands of pounds of pressure. At best, a tree would just come alive as you straddled or stood on it, bucking, heaving or twisting, rolling you underneath.

21   At worst, a limb as long as a transfer truck and as big around as your waist would just whip free, suddenly, and bash your brains out.

22   I was hit so hard, routinely, that I had to think a minute to remember my name. Once, working near my brother Sam, a limb sent me crashing into him, my saw buzzing, and I came within inches of opening him up like a fish.

23   You worked at a run, because every minute the big machines idled nearby, unable to get at the dirt under your feet and under your trees, money was trickling away. You did not stop except for a few seconds, to wipe the bits of bark from your eyes. You did not even stop for the snakes.

24   Despite what the timber companies want you to believe, not very much lives in a pine barren except rats and snakes. Old growth timber, a true forest, is home to all kinds of living things, but more and more of Alabama is under pines, planted to control erosion after clear-cutting, and nothing warm and fuzzy likes to live in the gummy, sappy, acid-rich world of pines.

25   The rats flee, when the trees come down, but the snakes just get **belligerent**. I don't know how many dozens of rattlers I faced down in that mess of limbs and roots and mud, but usually with the same outcome.

26   The problem is, you can't hear a warning, can't hear them rattle over the noise of your saw. You just see a movement, a limb that writhes more than it should, and you hold out the saw or swing it in a slow arc, and the snake can't resist. It strikes out at the whirring teeth, and its head disappears in a spray of red.

27   Once the pulpwood is cut, you pile and burn the limbs, so the trucks can get into the woods close to you, and you start loading the logs by hand. The skinny ones are light, and you throw them around, and the fat ones—hundreds of pounds apiece—are light, too, because you are tougher than anybody else, and you pick up pine logs that weigh more than you, and heave them onto the trucks.

28   At the end of the day you look barely human, specked head to toe with bark, sap in your hair, grime in every crease of your skin. You don't make enough that day to replace the shirt and pants you ruin in the trees.

29   The next day might be easy. You may just have to haul some dirt, may just have to coax the old Chevy dump truck up the side of a mountain, and hope its bald tires and brakes will last till you get back down again. Or it may be twelve hours on the end of a shovel handle, or pick.

30   I had a friend once who was always after me to go to the weight room with him, and I would laugh out loud every time.

31   The most ridiculous work was on the end of a yard fork. It was about half a man long, with thick iron tines. It looked like a giant salad fork. With it, you scooped up the rocks, roods, and mud clods that were raked or dragged on landscapes, and either piled it into a wheelbarrow or heaved it over the side of a dump truck.

32   It was ridiculous because of the height of the truck. I was not tall enough, and the fork was not long enough, to allow me to heave the load of rocks or clods over the side. I had to get a running start and jump, hoping the sheer force of it would carry me high enough, with my seventy-pound load, to heave it over the side of the truck. If you could leap high enough, your load cleared the lip of the truck and you banged, hard, into the iron bed.

33   If you did not, you banged hard into the iron bed, and seventy pounds of rock and mud clods showered your head. At the end of those days, you felt like you had been drawn and quartered.

34   But this is just whining. It did not kill me, though it killed others.

35   I know that not just any fool can be a writer. But I also know that not just any fool could get that yard fork over the lip of that truck.

36   I know which makes me prouder, now.

● THE FACTS

1. Which memory about the "man in the khaki work clothes" still makes the narrator shudder when he thinks about it? How is the narrator related to this man?

2. What kind of work did the narrator do all of his young life? How does the narrator rate this work? Were the effects good or bad? Give reasons for your evaluation.

3. Why does the author like to hear stories about famous writers who fought, drank, fished or hunted, and caroused? Explain this attraction.

4. The author claims that the most important gift he inherited from his uncle was a sense of "perspective." What is your understanding of this comment? Do you agree with the author? Explain yourself.

5. What does the author mean when he writes, "At the end of those days you felt like you had been drawn and quartered"? Explain the figure of speech.

● THE STRATEGIES

1. How do paragraphs 1–5 support the author's point? What is his point?

2. Why does the author believe that writers invent myths about great writers? Are these really myths or are they biographical truths? If you are in doubt about how to answer this question, Google a famous writer like Ernest Hemingway, William Faulkner, Tennessee Williams, or F. Scott Fitzgerald.

3. Why is the essay titled "Real Work"? What would happen if you retitled it "Dangerous Work"? How would such a change affect the thesis of Bragg's essay?

4. Why does the author use the term "fraternity" in paragraph 14? Would the term "labor union" work as well? Why or why not?

5. What connotation does the term "khakis" convey in this essay? What other word have you used for work clothes?

● THE ISSUES

1. According to the author, the work he did for his uncle did not teach him character—only toughness. What is your response to this insight? Would you be satisfied with a job that taught you only toughness? What danger might be inherent in limiting yourself to such a job?

2. What is your opinion of white collar jobs like lawyer, physician, computer consultant, engineer, or teacher? Do these jobs necessarily turn people into weaklings?

3. How do you define "tough"? Use an example to clarify your definition

4. Have you ever had a "hateful" job? If so, what useful lesson (if any) did it teach you about life? How would you advise a young person to handle a hateful job?

5. Bragg never comes right out and tells us which work makes him feel prouder of himself—writing or dumping debris into a dump truck with a fork lift. Supply an ending to the final sentence that will remove the ambiguity.

● SUGGESTIONS FOR WRITING

1. Using Bragg's "Real Work" as a model, write an essay in which you describe the first job you ever had and what it taught you. Use vivid examples to liven up your writing.

2. Write an essay in which you prove that a white collar job may require mental toughness, and that mental toughness is as valuable as physical toughness.

Grant and Lee: A Study in Contrasts

BRUCE CATTON

Rhetorical Thumbnail

Purpose: to compare/contrast two principals in the Civil War

Audience: history buffs

Language: standard English

Strategy: heaps up details to draw this contrast

Bruce Catton (1899–1978) is regarded as one of the most outstanding Civil War historians of the twentieth century. His books include *Mr. Lincoln's Army* (1951), *Glory Road* (1952), *A Stillness at Appomattox* (1953, Pulitzer Prize), and *This Hallowed Ground* (1956).

The following essay contrasts two famous personalities in American Civil War history: Ulysses S. Grant (1822-1885), commander in chief of the Union army and, later, eighteenth president of the United States (1869-1877), and his principal foe in the Civil War, Robert E. Lee (1807-1870), general in chief of the Confederate armies, who surrendered his forces to Grant in April of 1865. The essay illustrates the development of a comparison/contrast between paragraphs, rather than within a paragraph.

• • •

1   When Ulysses S. Grant and Robert E. Lee met in the parlor of a modest house at Appomattox Court House, Virginia, on April 9, 1865, to work out the terms for the surrender of Lee's Army of Northern Virginia, a great chapter in American life came to a close, and a great new chapter began.

2   These men were bringing the Civil War to its virtual finish. To be sure, other armies had yet to surrender, and for a few days the fugitive Confederate government would struggle desperately and vainly, trying to find some way to go on living now that its chief support was gone. But in effect it was all over when Grant and Lee signed the papers. And the little room where they wrote out the terms was the scene of one of the **poignant**, dramatic contrasts in American history.

3   They were two strong men, these oddly different generals, and they represented the strengths of two conflicting currents that, through them, had come into final collision.

4   Back of Robert E. Lee was the notion that the old aristocratic concept might somehow survive and be dominant in American life.

5   Lee was tidewater Virginia, and in his background were family, culture, and tradition . . . the age of chivalry transplanted to a New World which was making its own legends and its own myths. He embodied a way of life that had come down through the age of knighthood and the English country squire. America was a land

that was beginning all over again, dedicated to nothing much more complicated than the rather hazy belief that all men had equal rights and should have an equal chance in the world. In such a land Lee stood for the feeling that it was somehow of advantage to human society to have a pronounced inequality in the social structure. There should be a leisure class, backed by ownership of land; in turn, society itself should be keyed to the land as the chief source of wealth and influence. It would bring forth (according to this ideal) a class of men with a strong sense of obligation to the community; men who lived not to gain advantage for themselves, but to meet the solemn obligations which had been laid on them by the very fact that they were privileged. From them the country would get its leadership; to them it could look for the higher values—of thought, of conduct, of personal **deportment**—to give it strength and virtue.

6   Lee **embodied** the noblest elements of this aristocratic ideal. Through him, the landed nobility justified itself. For four years, the Southern states had fought a desperate war to uphold the ideals for which Lee stood. In the end, it almost seemed as if the Confederacy fought for Lee; as if he himself was the Confederacy . . . the best thing that the way of life for which the Confederacy stood could ever have to offer. He had passed into legend before Appomattox. Thousands of tired, underfed, poorly clothed Confederate soldiers, long since past the simple enthusiasm of the early days of the struggle, somehow considered Lee the symbol of everything for which they had been willing to die. But they could not quite put this feeling into words. If the Lost Cause, **sanctified** by so much heroism and so many deaths, had a living justification, its justification was General Lee.

7   Grant, the son of a tanner on the Western frontier, was everything Lee was not. He had come up the hard way and embodied nothing in particular except the eternal toughness and sinewy fiber of the men who grew up beyond the mountains. He was one of a body of men who owed reverence and **obeisance** to no one, who were self-reliant to a fault, who cared hardly anything for the past but who had a sharp eye for the future.

8   These frontier men were the precise opposites of the tidewater aristocrats. Back of them, in the great surge that had taken people over the Alleghenies and into the opening Western country, there was a deep, implicit dissatisfaction with a past that had settled into grooves. They stood for democracy, not from any reasoned conclusion about the proper ordering of human society, but simply because they had grown up in the middle of democracy and knew how it worked. Their society might have privileges, but they would be privileges each man had won for himself. Forms and patterns meant nothing. No man was born to anything, except perhaps to a chance to show how far he could rise. Life was competition.

9   Yet along with this feeling had come a deep sense of belonging to a national community. The Westerner who developed a farm, opened a shop, or set up in business as a trader, could hope to prosper only as his own community prospered—and his community ran from the Atlantic to the Pacific and from Canada down to Mexico. If the land was settled, with towns and highways and accessible markets, he could better himself. He saw his fate in terms of the nation's own destiny. As its horizons expanded, so did his. He had, in other words,

an acute dollars-and-cents stake in the continued growth and development of his country.

10   And that, perhaps, is where the contrast between Grant and Lee becomes most striking. The Virginia aristocrat, inevitably, saw himself in relation to his own region. He lived in a static society which could endure almost anything except change. Instinctively, his first loyalty would go to the locality in which that society existed. He would fight to the limit of endurance to defend it, because in defending it he was defending everything that gave his own life its deepest meaning.

11   The Westerner, on the other hand, would fight with an equal **tenacity** for the broader concept of society. He fought so because everything he lived by was tied to growth, expansion, and a constantly widening horizon. What he lived by would survive or fall with the nation itself. He could not possibly stand by unmoved in the face of an attempt to destroy the Union. He would combat it with everything he had, because he could only see it as an effort to cut the ground out from under his feet.

12   So Grant and Lee were in complete contrast, representing two **diametrically** opposed elements in American life. Grant was the modern man emerging; beyond him, ready to come on the stage, was the great age of steel and machinery, of crowded cities and a restless, **burgeoning** vitality. Lee might have ridden down from the old age of chivalry, lance in hand, silken banner fluttering over his head. Each man was the perfect champion of his cause, drawing both his strengths and his weaknesses from the people he led.

13   Yet it was not all contrast, after all. Different as they were—in background, in personality, in underlying aspiration—these two great soldiers had much in common. Under everything else, they were marvelous fighters. Furthermore, their fighting qualities were really very much alike.

14   Each man had, to begin with, the great virtue of utter tenacity and fidelity. Grant fought his way down the Mississippi Valley in spite of acute personal discouragement and profound military handicaps. Lee hung on in the trenches at Petersburg after hope itself had died. In each man there was an indomitable quality . . . the born fighter's refusal to give up as long as he can still remain on his feet and lift his two fists.

15   Daring and resourcefulness they had, too; the ability to think faster and move faster than the enemy. These were the qualities which gave Lee the dazzling campaigns of Second Manassas and Chancellorsville and won Vicksburg for Grant.

16   Lastly, and perhaps greatest of all, there was the ability, at the end, to turn quickly from war to peace once the fighting was over. Out of the way these two men behaved at Appomattox came the possibility of a peace of reconciliation. It was a possibility not wholly realized, in the years to come, but which did, in the end, help the two sections to become one nation again . . . after a war whose bitterness might have seemed to make such a reunion wholly impossible. No part of either man's life became him more than the part he played in their brief meeting in the McLean house at Appomattox. Their behavior there put all succeeding

generations of Americans in their debt. Two great Americans, Grant and Lee—very different, yet under everything very much alike. Their encounter at Appomattox was one of the great moments of American history.

● THE FACTS

1. What was Lee's background? What ideal did he represent?
2. What was Grant's background? What did he represent?
3. What was Grant's view of the past? What was his attitude toward society and democracy?
4. What was the most striking contrast between Grant and Lee?
5. Catton writes that the behavior of Grant and Lee at Appomattox "put all succeeding generations of Americans in their debt" (paragraph 16). Why?

● THE STRATEGIES

1. Although the article is entitled "Grant and Lee: A Study in Contrasts," Catton begins by examining what Lee represented. Why? What logic is there to his order?
2. What function does paragraph 4 serve? Why is this one sentence set off in a separate paragraph?
3. What common contrast phrase does paragraph 11 use?
4. In paragraph 8, the author writes: "These frontier men were the precise opposites of the tidewater aristocrats." What do these types have to do with a contrast between Grant and Lee?
5. What function does paragraph 8 serve?

● THE ISSUES

1. Does an aristocracy still survive in our multicultural United States? If you believe it has survived, describe what and where it is. If you believe it has vanished, then describe what has taken its place.
2. Which kind of citizen do you admire most—the aristocrat or the frontiersman? Which do you believe is needed most for the betterment of our society today? Give reasons for your answers.
3. The aristocrat believes in form and tradition. How important are these ideas, in your view? With which traditions would you be willing to part? Which would you want to keep?
4. What two women from history present an interesting contrast in two cultures? Describe both women and their contrasting cultures.
5. Which U.S. president, besides Ulysses S. Grant, is known for his support of economic growth and expansion? Do you favor continued growth and expansion, or are there other values you cherish more?

⬤ SUGGESTIONS FOR WRITING

1. Examine and analyze the organization of the contrast in this essay. In what various respects are Grant and Lee contrasted? How does Catton order and structure his contrast?

2. Discuss the idea that a society can benefit from the presence of a privileged class. Or, conversely, take the position that a society can benefit from the presence of an underprivileged class.

Image Gallery for Critical Thinking and Debate: Online Dating

People in bygone eras would never have imagined that one day young men and women would have their romantic liaisons arranged by some electronic machine. Back in those days, polite society organized formal coming-out dances where young women could meet proper young men and eventually find an appropriate beau to marry. The matriarchs of the neighborhood made sure that only the best gentlemen in the area had access to the well-bred ladies of the manor. Much bowing, scraping, and card proffering took place before parents would begin the process of evaluating any young man who might send a flirtatious smile toward one of their daughters.

Today, the search for love and marriage partners takes place through the computer. People hungry for a date sign up with one of the popular computer dating services, such as eHarmony.com, Match.com, Perfectmatch.com, Chemistry.com, or Spark.com. After filling out the required papers and paying a fee, they can start emailing the right match.

Research by several universities, including Stanford, indicates clearly that online dating is becoming a growing business and an acceptable way to find a wife or husband. Friends, families, churches, and community functions are still common places where young people meet and connect, but the Internet is rapidly displacing these venues across the social spectrum. Just read the blogs or tweets about popular Internet dating services, and you will realize that a huge tidal wave of romantic activity is taking place in cyberspace. Lonely widows, busy executives, frustrated youth, and even neglected housewives are filling out profiles and selling themselves to some prospective date.

Not long ago, we heard a divorced mother of two teenagers lament that every man she met was either a rogue or a dolt. "I would love to meet a soul mate or even just a good friend, but the men available are culturally deprived and can't carry on a decent conversation. Who wants to sit at a bar and listen to someone whine like a child because so-and-so signed up with such-and-such a league, or watch everyone suddenly roar and scream when Big Bob makes a touchdown? I'd rather stay home and read a good book."

Men can be disillusioned as well. "I love politics," said one male law student, "but I'm a liberal and can't stand to have my date condemn universal healthcare as if it would ultimately usher in an age of Stalinist Communism."

The aim of computer dating is to keep mismatches to a minimum by making sure that all profiles submitted clarify important issues, such as religious commitments, cultural tastes, and educational levels. Accompanying photographs are supposed to give the viewer a correct idea of the potential date's looks (although so far a major complaint is that too many profiles are dishonest or enhanced to make the applicant look more attractive than reality merits).

Online dating magazines suggest that over 120,000 marriages—many of them happy—take place each year as the direct result of meeting online. The forecast is that this number will continue to grow without serious impediment. With that new lens reflecting our future, we might do well to pay attention to what pundits and new-age yentas are saying.

Our image gallery opens with an exaggerated symbolic "vie en rose" envisioned by a love-struck girl who imagines that she will find her prince charming on the Internet as her friends keep raving she will. The second image features one of the most effective and popular dating services—eHarmony—which the romance seeker is asked to evaluate using intelligence and common sense. The last image reveals a married couple who met online and was married two years later. Do they look content? The viewer must be the judge.

Our student essay laments the fact that computer dating, in addition to being risky, also deprives romance seekers of the chance to get to know a person in depth because Internet chatter can never replace the insights gained from face to face encounters.

"To the Point" rounds out the issue.

Study the following three images dealing with online dating. Then choose the image that most appeals to you. Answer the questions and do the writing assignment.

For readings, questions, and media on the issue of online dating, visit the *MindTap for Readings for Writers*, 15e online.

© iStock.com/TheresaTibbetts

Studying the Image

1. Which emotional aspects of online dating does this cartoon capture? What fantasy is at work in this image?

2. If you were single and searching for a companion, would you consider online dating? Why or why not?

3. One common reason given for online dating is that singles who are busy pursuing a career cannot find the time to meet appropriate dates. What is your reaction to this rationale?

4. How has advertising increased the number of people seeking partners online? Is this a good trend? Explain your answer.

Writing Assignment

Write an essay in which you argue for or against the growing trend of online dating. Analyze and synthesize at least two outside sources.

Studying the Image

1. What is this advertisement trying to achieve with its viewers? Consider such matters as trust, enthusiasm, and the promise of romance or companionship.

2. How significant is the physical appearance of the couple portrayed in the ad? How would you describe them to someone who cannot see the ad?

3. What is the meaning of the heading "Free to Review your Matches"? How does that kind of freedom help the success of the service?

4. Has the new trend of computer dating replaced much of the traditional dating through introduction by friends or trusted acquaintances? In what ways is this new trend reshaping society? Is it a blessing or a curse?

Writing Assignment

After interviewing your grandparents or another couple from an older generation, write an essay reflecting their attitudes toward the modern trend of online dating.

William Archie/MCT/Newscom

Studying the Image

1. The middle-aged couple pictured in the preceding image are Larry and Cheryl Bond, who met online in 2007 and married in 2009. As you study their appearance and demeanor, what is your reaction to them as a couple? Do they seem comfortable and confident, or do they seem nervous and worried? What does their clothing reveal about them? Use your imagination to create a word picture of this couple.

2. Larry and Cheryl Bond belong to the 50+ crowd of web daters, who are said to be the fastest growing group of people trying to find companionship and romance online. In fact, the trend has caused "Our Time," a dating service especially for this age group, to be created. What effect does age have on the risk factor for on-line dating? Weigh the advantages and disadvantages of youth versus maturity.

3. What has caused the recent impulse on the part of singles to rush online and trust their entire personality profiles to agents who will match them up with an appropriate partner? Why is this either a good or bad trend?

4. The Internet, newspapers, and magazines are full of admonitions about how to avoid meeting a dangerous partner online. Of all the rules listed, which do you consider crucial to a person's safety—especially that of a vulnerable woman?

Writing Assignment

Write a well-researched essay about online dating as a helpful way to connect with people of your own social class, intellectual interests, and entertainment tastes. If you find no value in online dating, develop an essay clarifying your negative position and supporting it with evidence from your experience or that of experts.

*Stumped by rhetorical questions? Exit on page 427 at the **Editing Booth!***

Punctuation Workshop

The Question Mark (?)

Put a question mark after a direct question, but not after an indirect question, as in the following:

> **DIRECT:** What is keeping the catcher from reading the pitcher's signals?

> **INDIRECT:** We asked what was keeping the catcher from reading the pitcher's signals.

> **DIRECT:** Did you understand the insulting question, "Do you have a low I.Q.?"

(A question within a question contains only one question mark, inside the closing quotation mark.)

> **INDIRECT:** They were asked if they understood the insulting question.

A series of direct questions having the same subject can be treated as follows:

> What on earth is little Freddy doing? Laughing? Crying? Screaming?

Sometimes a declarative sentence contains a direct question that requires a question mark:

> He asked his neighbor, "Have you seen the raccoon?" (The question mark goes inside the quotation mark.)

 CAUTION: Do not write an indirect question as if it were a direct question.

> **WRONG:** He asked her would she join the team?

> **RIGHT:** He asked her if she would join the team.

Student Corner

"OMGILY2!!" Online Dating Is at Your Own Risk

Kindra M. Neuman

Walla Walla University, Washington

Today's world has varied drastically from what it was a century ago. Many aspects have changed, such as transportation, entertainment, communication, and style. Perhaps one of the most startling changes has taken place in the way modern couples date. In the past, couples dated as a result of being introduced by relatives or friends, enrolling in the same college class, or attending events of mutual interest. However, in the last decade dating trends have changed dramatically as more and more dating takes place on the Internet. Despite some people's objections, traditional courting has transformed itself into a lazy, risky, and impatient search for love.

Many reasons make online dating objectionable. One of these reasons is the simple truth that online dating is bogus. The online dating world is full of scams. When you use the computer as your advertising medium, it is not difficult to turn yourself into someone totally different from who you really are and sell yourself as this new person to some gullible victim. While of course you personally would never be that dishonest, there are plenty of people out there who are. Getting involved with online dating is often a straight path toward being painfully deceived. Magazine articles and blog sites reveal numerous cases where young girls meet what appears to be a wonderful guy online and then schedule to meet him, only to find out that he is not the handsome, fascinating, athletic young man he claimed to be in his resume, but rather he turns out to be a boring lout. Moreover, many young girls have found themselves in dangerous situations when they agreed to meet someone they believed they could trust. I live in the dormitory of a private college, where dating is safe, but my roommate and friends are constantly hearing about rape cases that occurred when a girl met a male online, and took the chance of meeting him in person. Meeting people online can be very dangerous. The computer screen you are staring at intently may not be a castle door, leading to your Prince Charming, but in fact may serve as a protective barrier from the vicious monster leering on the other side.

Online Dating magazine offers several good tips for avoiding risky online daters. First of all, it is important never to give away your address or any home information. This is one of the worst things you could do because a stalker can now follow you home. Second, if you insist on meeting an online date, use your own transportation and meet in a public place. If the situation were to take a dangerous turn, you would not want to be in a dark street with no traffic. Third, do not assume that your date is safe. Maintain a skeptical attitude. It is crucial that you stay in touch with the still small voice in your head. If you feel uncomfortable or wary, don't brush those feelings aside. A special tip for women is to pay your part of the expenses of the date. Often men will offer to pay, but expect sexual favors in return. What you thought was to be a friendly get-acquainted dinner turns out to be a skirmish for your body. Last but not least, always tell someone where you are going. That way, if you don't return on time, your contact can check on you and call the police if the situation warrants doing so. *Online Dating* magazine posts these tips because many unpleasant and even dangerous incidents have happened that could have been avoided if these simple rules had been followed.

In addition to being disappointing or unsafe, computer dating deprives you of the opportunity to get to know people in depth. You may waste a large amount of time in aimless and foggy Internet "chatting" when you could have realized after one regular date that you aren't interested in furthering your acquaintance with this person. Interacting with people in person builds social skills that help you judge a person's motives, interests, and lifestyle. Being face to face with people allows you to interpret their thoughts and ideas better than through electronic means because you can engage in follow-up questions that demand evidence for the beliefs they hold.

Blogs, tweets, texting, and emails may be cover-ups for attitudes you wouldn't like if you knew about them. Also, conversing online makes it easy for you to act differently than the way you might act in person. You might discover yourself saying things over the computer that you might never say in person. Research indicates that most people present themselves online in a much better light than they do in reality. Fat people represent themselves as thinner than they are; non readers act as if they read constantly; and males (especially) act as if they were more successful and richer than they really are. It is easy to be someone you aren't when there is a computer screen separating you from the other end of the conversation.

Computer dating also takes a lot less effort, thus making it less special, than old-fashioned dating. Taking the time to go out with someone is far more meaningful than just sending someone a quick text or email. Spending time and effort on individuals shows that you care about them. Internet usage should be kept to a minimum when dealing with relationships. People were made to socialize with one another in flesh and blood—not merely in cyberspace.

Online dating deprives you of one of the greatest joys in life—discovering a soul mate among the crowd of people in your milieu and getting to spend quality time with that person face to face. There is no equal to spending time one on one with another individual whom you know to be part of your world in order to truly get acquainted. In doing so, you experience genuine meaning and feeling as the relationship builds. Don't desperately chase down love by filling out eHarmony resumes to find a match. True love will find you.

How I Write

I use many different approaches to writing a paper. Occasionally I will grab a piece of scratch paper and write down some points I would like to cover. However, most of the time I just sit down at my desk and write the paper. Somehow I think the thoughts in my head and I am able to put them down on paper. I have been blessed with an opinionated attitude and rarely seem short of words. After I write my paper, I go through it to edit any grammar or punctuation issues that I see. Next I adjust any sentences that seem unclear or awkward. When I am done with my paper, I normally send it to my Dad and have him read it through. More often than not, he has a few pointers as far as grammar is concerned. I used to hate it when he would "grade" my papers, but since then I have come to appreciate his constructive criticism. While my strategy for writing may be different than yours, it works for me. And I am able to whip out a paper in a reasonable amount of time!

My Writing Tip

My tip to you is to embrace the opinions you have. Opinions are what make articles interesting. Discover your point of view and then get data to back up your stance. Also, find out what works best for you in order to complete your paper. If you feel the need to create a step-by-step outline, then go with that. Maybe you are a person who uses flash cards to keep track of your data before you begin. Or maybe you are like me and you can just sit down and write. Whatever may get you into the groove, use it! Once you know your pattern, you are set to go. After that, the sky is the limit.

 To the Point

Write a tweet to anyone who is thinking of submitting his or her profile to an online dating service. Offer this person some helpful advice, based on what you know about online dating.

▨ Chapter Writing Assignments

1. Write an essay in which you contrast one of the following pairs of concepts:
   a. Hearing–Listening
   b. Liberty–License
   c. Servant–Slave
   d. Democracy–Demagoguery
   e. Art–Craft
   f. Having an opinion–Being opinionated
   g. Talent–Ability

2. Using the Internet as your research tool, write a paper comparing the levels of job satisfaction in two different professions. Consider such matters as personal growth, financial benefits, future prospects, and relationships with colleagues. Be sure to synthesize outside sources as indicated in Chapter 2 and Chapter 3.

▨ Writing Assignments for a Specific Audience

1. Write a letter to a younger brother or sister—or an imaginary one—contrasting college with high school. Be sure to choose appropriate bases for the contrast, such as academic rigor, social life, relationships with teachers, and independence.

2. With the help of some Internet research, write an essay in which you compare the satisfaction of customers using eHarmony.com with that of customers using Match.com as their online dating service. Be sure that you take a fair and balanced approach to the comparison.

 **Pointer from a Pro**

CONQUER WRITER'S BLOCK

People have writer's block not because they can't write, but because they despair of writing eloquently.

—Anna Quindlen

College students are especially vulnerable to this kind of sudden mental paralysis when they face a deadline for an assignment. Here are three pieces of practical advice:

1. Quit dissing yourself; you aren't the idiot you think you are.
2. Trust yourself because your ideas count.
3. Clear your mind for a while—by taking a walk, listening to music, or chatting with another person.

Then, go back and tackle your writing assignment with a new perspective. Start placing words—random words—on paper. Eventually your mind will unblock, and your writing will flow.

CHAPTER 14

Division/Classification

■ Road Map to Division/Classification

What Division/Classification Does

To write a division/classification essay means to break down a subject into its constituent types. If you write a paragraph on the kinds of books in your library, the types of cars in your miniature-car collection, or the varieties of humor in Mark Twain's works, you are classifying. A prime purpose of division/classification is to discover the nature of a subject by a study of its parts and their relationships to the larger whole. For example, the following paragraph tries to explain and understand people by grouping them together into two primary categories:

> A simple experiment will distinguish two types of human nature. Gather a throng of people and pour them into a ferry-boat. By the time the boat has swung into the river you will find that a certain proportion have taken the trouble to climb upstairs in order to be out on deck and see what is to be seen as they cross over. The rest have settled indoors to think what they will do upon reaching the other side, or perhaps lose themselves in apathy or tobacco smoke. But leaving out those apathetic, or addicted to a single enjoyment, we may divide all the alert passengers on the boat into two classes: those who are interested in crossing the river, and those who are merely interested in getting across. And we may divide all the people on the earth, or all the moods of people, in the same way. Some of them are chiefly occupied with attaining ends, and some with receiving experiences. The distinction of the two will be more marked when we name the first kind practical, and the second poetic, for common knowledge recognizes that a person poetic or in a poetic mood is impractical, and a practical person is intolerant of poetry.
>
> —Max Eastman, *Poetic People*

Division and classification are common to the way we think. We divide and classify the plant and animal kingdoms into phyla, genera, families, and species; we divide the military into the Army, Navy, Air Force, Marines, and Coast Guard. We divide and classify people into kinds and types. When we ask, "What kind of person is he?" we are asking for information developed by division and classification. An assignment asking for an essay developed by division, therefore, is an exercise in this common mode of thinking.

When to Use Division/Classification

Division/classification is especially useful in analyzing big, complex subjects. All of us draw on categories—some accurate, some prejudicial—in our attempts to understand the world around us. We wonder what type of person a certain man or woman is, and when we think we know, we react accordingly. This is not necessarily bad, so long as we do not hold false categories about people that function as prejudices. We speculate on the experiences that happen to us and try to sort them into understandable types. We say that yesterday was that kind of day and that last year was that sort of year. We have theories about kinds of love, types of friends, varieties of personalities. Science, philosophy, and even the practical arts are largely based on classifications. Biology sorts animals and plants into genera and species; medicine organizes diseases into types; chemistry classifies substances; and literature classifies writing. The concept of types rescues us from the tyranny of uniqueness and spares us from having to individually study every event, object, person, or thing. Without categories that tell us that this is like that, experience would have no predictive value and we would be overwhelmed by the uniqueness of every butterfly, thunderstorm, or love affair.

How to Use Division/Classification

1. **All good writing is based on clear thinking, but division/classification most decidedly so.** To classify is to think and analyze, to see relationships between individual items where none are obvious. You are, in a sense, superimposing your mind's filing cabinet onto the world. To classify accurately, then, you must base your typing and sorting on a single principle. This means that your sorting must be done on the basis of one criterion or your scheme will be a muddle. A simple example would be if you were to classify sports by whether or not they involve physical contact and lumped tennis in with football. Obviously, tennis is a noncontact sport, and your sorting would be inaccurate. Likewise, if you were writing a paper on the works written by Samuel Johnson and came up with the following list:

   a. Johnson's poetry

   b. Johnson's prose

   c. Johnson's dictionary

   d. Boswell's Life of Johnson

your division/classification would also be false. Boswell's *Life of Johnson* is not by Johnson but about him and, therefore, does not belong in your list. In a more formal context, we see this error repeated in the following paragraph, whose division/classification is not based on a single principle:

> Mass production in American industry is made up of four distinct elements: division of labor, standardization through precision tooling, assembly line, and consumer public. First is the division of labor, which means that a complicated production process is broken down into specialized individual tasks that are performed by people or machines who concentrate on these tasks only. Second is the standardization of parts as a result of precision tooling. This means that each part can be produced by machines both for interchangeability and for assembly by semiskilled workers. Third is the assembly line, which is a method of moving the work from one person to another in a continual chain of progress until the item is completed. This is a way of moving the work to the person, instead of the person to the work. The last element is the consumer public. Without it mass production would be a futile endeavor, for it is the public that buys up all the mass-produced items as quickly as they roll off the assembly line.

> Clearly, the division/classification is not based on a single principle. Division of labor, standardization through precision tooling, and the use of an assembly line may be part of the mass-production process, but the consumer public plainly is not. Only after production has been completed and an item is ready to be marketed does the consumer enter the picture. As it stands, the paragraph has misrepresented the elements involved in mass production.

2. **Make your division/classification complete.** A complete division/classification is one that includes all the parts of the subject being divided. If you were to classify sports by whether they involve the use of a ball and left out soccer, your division/classification would be incomplete. If you omitted the short story from an essay classifying types of literature, you would likewise be guilty of this error. Similarly, if you were to divide the family of Equidae into its main categories, you would have to include the horse, the ass, and the zebra. Leave out any of these, and your division/classification would be incomplete.

3. **Avoid the overlapping of categories.** Here is an example of an overlapping division in the division/classification of literature according to genres:

   a. Poetry

   b. Short story

   c. Humor

   d. Drama

   e. Novel

   Humor is not a genre but a characteristic of poetry, a short story, a drama, or a novel. Therefore, it does not belong in this list.

Warming Up to Write a Division/Classification

1. Here's a good exercise to get your brain to think in terms of classification—that is, inventing categories into which to divide a subject and then placing items into each category. As quickly as possible, divide each of the following subjects into as many categories as seems sensible. Keep a list of the categories. If, after rereading your list, a category doesn't fit, delete it.

   a. Books

   b. Clothing

   c. Modern inventions

   d. Weather

   e. Computer games

   f. Pets

   g. Music

   h. Meals

2. In the following classifications, check the category that does not fit and write down the reasons why it should be excluded.

   a. Dreams

   _____1. sexual

   _____2. paralyzing

   _____3. imagining

   _____4. replaying the day

   b. Cars

   _____1. SUVs

   _____2. trucks

   _____3. sedans

   _____4. electric cars

   c. Family games

   _____1. card games

   _____2. ping pong

   _____3. domino games

   _____4. board games

   d. Houses in which to live

   _____1. sheds

   _____2. cottages

   _____3. mansions

   _____4. tract homes

   e. Jobs

      _____1. technical

      _____2. waiter

      _____3. professional

      _____4. hard labor

3. Looking back at Exercise 1, choose one of the subjects you classified into categories; then pick one of the categories and place at least three items in it. For instance, if you classified meals into *hors d'oeuvres, main dishes, side dishes,* and *desserts,* you might choose "main dishes" as your category and then list the following items as belonging to it: meat, poultry, fish, and vegetarian substitute. Make sure your items are appropriately related to the category.

Examples

The Six Stages of E-Mail

NORA EPHRON

Rhetorical Thumbnail

Purpose: to write a parody on the disillusionment experienced by a typical email enthusiast

Audience: readers with a sophisticated sense of humor who are also users of email

Language: standard English

Strategy: takes the serious scientific analysis of Elizabeth Kübler-Ross's famous book *The Six Stages of Dying* and turns it into a humorous satire about how the response to receiving email can go from infatuation to death

Nora Ephron (1941–2012) was a journalist, playwright, screenwriter, and novelist much admired for her outlandish sense of humor that lasted all through the devastating cancer that claimed her life. The romantic comedies she wrote for the screen became instant box office hits, attracting large crowds to films like *Silkwood, When Harry Met Sally,* and *Sleepless in Seattle* and winning Ephron three Academy Awards. Among the books she wrote are the following: *Wallflower at the Orgy* (1970), *Scribble, Scribble: Notes on the Media* (1978), *Heartburn* (1983), *I Feel Bad About My Neck: And Other Thoughts On Being a Woman* (2006), and *I Remember Nothing: And Other Reflections* (2010). Ephron came from a Jewish family (who were mostly either writers or in jobs related to filmmaking) and was brought up in Beverly Hills. After graduating from Wellesley College in 1962,

Ephron eventually landed a job at the *New York Post,* where she worked as a reporter for five years. Because her commentaries had a wide impact, she was asked by *Esquire* to write a column on women's issues. Ephron made headline news when it was revealed that her second husband, Carl Bernstein, along with Bob Woodward (both *Washington Post* reporters), broke the notorious Watergate scandal of the 1970s. In 2012, Ephron died of myeloid leukemia, a condition with which she was diagnosed six years earlier but had kept secret.

● ● ●

Stage One: Infatuation

1　I just got e-mail! I can't believe it! It's so great! Here's my handle. Write me! Who said letter writing was dead? Were they ever wrong! I'm writing letters like crazy for the first time in years. I come home and ignore all my loved ones and go straight to the computer to make contact with total strangers. And how great is AOL? It's so easy. It's so friendly. It's a community. Wheeeee! I've got mail!

Stage Two: Clarification

2　O.K., I'm starting to understand—e-mail isn't letter-writing at all, it's something else entirely. It was just invented, it was just born and overnight it turns out to have a form and a set of rules and a language all its own. Not since the printing press. Not since television. It's revolutionary. It's life-*altering*. It's shorthand. Cut to the chase. Get to the point.

3　And it saves so much time. It takes five seconds to accomplish in an e-mail message something that takes five minutes on the telephone. The phone requires you to converse, to say things like hello and goodbye, to pretend to some **semblance** of interest in the person on the other end of the line. Worst of all, the phone occasionally forces you to make actual plans with the people you talk to— to suggest lunch or dinner—even if you have no desire whatsoever to see them. No danger of that with e-mail.

4　E-mail is a whole new way of being friends with people: intimate but not, chatty but not, communicative but not; in short, friends but not. What a breakthrough. How did we ever live without it? I have more to say on this subject, but I have to answer an Instant Message from someone I almost know.

Stage Three: Confusion

5　I have done nothing to deserve any of this:

6　Viagra!!!!! Best Web source for Vioxx. Spend a week in Cancún. Have a rich beautiful lawn. Astrid would like to be added as one of your friends. XXXXXXX-Videos. Add three inches to the length of your penis. The Democratic National Committee needs you. Virus Alert. FW: This will make you laugh. FW: This is funny. FW: This is hilarious. FW: Grapes and raisins toxic for dogs. FW: Gabriel García Márquez's Final Farewell. FW: Kurt Vonnegut's Commencement Address. FW: The Neiman Marcus Chocolate Chip Cookie recipe. AOL Member: We value your opinion. A message from Hillary Clinton. Find low mortgage payments, Nora. Nora, it's your time to shine. Need to fight off bills, Nora? Yvette would like to be added as one of your friends. You have failed to establish a full connection to AOL.

Stage Four: Disenchantment

7   Help! I'm drowning. I have 112 unanswered e-mail messages. I'm a writer—imagine how many unanswered messages I would have if I had a real job. Imagine how much writing I could do if I didn't have to answer all this e-mail. My eyes are dim. I have a mild case of carpal tunnel syndrome. I have a galloping case of attention deficit disorder because every time I start to write something, the e-mail icon starts bobbing up and down and I'm compelled to check whether anything good or interesting has arrived. It hasn't. Still, it might, any second now. And yes it's true—I can do in a few seconds with e-mail what would take much longer on the phone, but most of my messages are from people who don't have my phone number and would never call me in the first place. In the brief time it took me to write this paragraph, three more messages arrived. Now I have 115 unanswered messages. Strike that: 116.

Stage Five: Accommodation

8   Yes. No. No :). No :(. Can't. No way. Maybe. Doubtful. Sorry. So Sorry. Thanks. No thanks. Not my thing. You must be kidding. Out of town. O.O.T. Try me in a month. Try me in the fall. Try me in a year. NoraE@aol.com can now be reached at NoraE81082@gmail.com.

Stage Six: Death

9   Call me.

● THE FACTS

1. What are the six stages this user of email experienced? What is the meaning of the heading assigned to each stage?

2. What is the "handle" to which Ephron refers in the opening paragraph? What other name is commonly used?

3. Why is Stage Three titled "Confusion"? What confuses the author? Do you understand her confusion? Have you experienced similar bewilderment in trying to sort out emails from various sources? Cite examples.

4. What does the final sentence in paragraph 4 indicate? What specifically does it reveal about the author? What sentence or words would you use for the kind of feeling the author describes?

5. In the last stage, what does "death" indicate? Why does the author use such a radical term? What other term can you suggest?

● THE STRATEGIES

1. How does Ephron use the six stages of email to deepen the humor of her essay? Unless you are familiar with the scientific work of Elizabeth Kübler-Ross, a Swiss psychiatrist whose book *On Death and Dying* revolutionized the curriculum in U.S. medical schools to give improved training to doctors dealing with terminally ill patients, you would not see the parody in Ephron's

humorous essay. Before answering the question, do some computer research on Kübler-Ross and her famous acronym DABDA. Then, use it to better understand Ephron's essay.

2. What impression do you have of Stage Three? Why is Hillary Clinton mentioned? What items could you add to the list Ephron provides?

3. How appropriate is the heading "Accommodation" for Stage Five? Is the author adjusting to receiving so much email or does she have something else in mind? Explain the term as it is used in this essay.

4. How does the author hand the *coup de grace* to her email? How do you interpret the word "death" in the context in which Ephron uses it?

5. Why does Ephron use a division-classification rather than a process analysis for her essay about the role of email in her life? Try to explain her reasoning.

● THE ISSUES

1. What in your view is the answer to letting emails dominate one's life? How can one avoid that bulging mailbox, choked with hundreds of emails?

2. If you had the power, would you annihilate email communication in your society? What is your rationale for either keeping or getting rid of the capacity to use email? What are its benefits or detriments? Use examples to support your view.

3. If you are an avid email user or iPhone texter, at what point, if any, do you become disenchanted with your electronic communication? Give specific examples.

4. Email has been around for many years. Since its creation in 1993, have there been other electronic means of communication that have distressed you as much as or more than email? If you see dangers in other areas, what are they? Explain the threat and how it can be solved.

5. What guidelines would you establish in order to keep teenagers from becoming addicted to social networks provided by computers, iPads, smartphones, and other electronic devices? Which of the apps do you consider the most dangerous? Give reasons for your answer.

● SUGGESTIONS FOR WRITING

1. Write an essay in which you strongly defend the marvel of email as a time-saving modern communication device. You might mention such conveniences as not having to use stationery, envelopes, or stamps and never having to mail the letter at a post office.

2. Write a division-classification in which you describe your stages of disillusionment with someone or something that seemed enchanting at its start. Examples to consider are the following: Leaning how to drive a car, falling in love, learning how to cook a delicious breakfast, mastering turns on a steep ski slope, or finding serious character flaws in someone you admired.

Kinds of Discipline

JOHN HOLT

Rhetorical Thumbnail

Purpose: to inform

Audience: education students

Language: academic English

Strategy: to divide discipline into three primary types

John Holt (1923–1985), education theorist, was born in New York. He taught at Harvard University and the University of California, Berkeley. His works include *How Children Fail* (1964), *How Children Learn* (1967), *Freedom and Beyond* (1972), from which this selection was taken, *Escape from Childhood* (1974), *Instead of Education* (1976), and *Teach Your Own* (1981).

Because discipline *is an ambiguous and often misunderstood word, the author attempts to give it a clearer meaning by focusing on three specific kinds of discipline.*

• • •

1   A child, in growing up, may meet and learn from three different kinds of disciplines. The first and most important is what we might call the Discipline of Nature or of Reality. When he is trying to do something real, if he does the wrong thing or doesn't do the right one, he doesn't get the result he wants. If he doesn't pile one block right on top of another, or tries to build on a slanting surface, his tower falls down. If he hits the wrong key, he hears the wrong note. If he doesn't hit the nail squarely on the head, it bends, and he has to pull it out and start with another. If he doesn't measure properly what he is trying to build, it won't open, close, fit, stand up, fly, float, whistle, or do whatever he wants it to do. If he closes his eyes when he swings, he doesn't hit the ball. A child meets this kind of discipline every time he tries to do something, which is why it is so important in school to give children more chances to do things, instead of just reading or listening to someone talk (or pretending to). This discipline is a great teacher. The learner never has to wait long for his answer; it usually comes quickly, often instantly. Also it is clear, and very often points toward the needed correction; from what happened he can not only see that what he did was wrong, but also why, and what he needs to do instead. Finally, and most important, the giver of the answer, call it Nature, is impersonal, impartial, and indifferent. She does not give opinions, or make judgments; she cannot be **wheedled**, bullied, or fooled; she does not get angry or disappointed; she does not praise or blame; she does not remember past failures or hold grudges; with her one always gets a fresh start, this time is the one that counts.

2   The next discipline we might call the Discipline of Culture, of Society, of What People Really Do. Man is a social, a cultural animal. Children sense around them this culture, this network of agreements, customs, habits, and rules binding the adults together. They want to understand it and be a part of it. They watch very carefully what people around them are doing and want to do the same. They want to do right, unless they become convinced they can't do right. Thus children rarely misbehave seriously in church, but sit as quietly as they can. The example of all those grownups is contagious. Some mysterious **ritual** is going on, and children, who like rituals, want to be part of it. In the same way, the little children that I see at concerts or operas, though they may fidget a little, or perhaps take a nap now and then, rarely make any disturbance. With all those grownups sitting there, neither moving nor talking, it is the most natural thing in the world to imitate them. Children who live among adults who are habitually courteous to each other, and to them, will soon learn to be courteous. Children who live surrounded by people who speak a certain way will speak that way, however much we may try to tell them that speaking that way is bad or wrong.

3   The third discipline is the one most people mean when they speak of discipline—the Discipline of Superior Force, of sergeant to private, of "you do what I tell you or I'll make you wish you had." There is bound to be some of this in a child's life. Living as we do surrounded by things that can hurt children, or that children can hurt, we cannot avoid it. We can't afford to let a small child find out from experience the danger of playing in a busy street, or of fooling with the pots on the top of a stove, or of eating up the pills in the medicine cabinet. So, along with other precautions, we say to him, "Don't play in the street, or touch things on the stove, or go into the medicine cabinet, or I'll punish you." Between him and the danger too great for him to imagine we put a lesser danger, but one he can imagine and maybe therefore wants to avoid. He can have no idea of what it would be like to be hit by a car, but he can imagine being shouted at, or spanked, or sent to his room. He avoids these substitutes for the greater danger until he can under-stand it and avoid it for its own sake. But we ought to use this discipline only when it is necessary to protect the life, health, safety, or well-being of people or other liv-ing creatures, or to prevent destruction of things that people care about. We ought not to assume too long, as we usually do, that a child cannot understand the real nature of the danger from which we want to protect him. The sooner he avoids the danger, not to escape our punishment, but as a matter of good sense, the better. He can learn that faster than we think. In Mexico, for example, where people drive their cars with a good deal of spirit, I saw many children no older than five or four walking unattended on the streets. They understood about cars, they knew what to do. A child whose life is full of the threat and fear of punishment is locked into babyhood. There is no way for him to grow up, to learn to take responsibility for his life and acts. Most important of all, we should not assume that having to yield to the threat of our superior force is good for the child's character. It is never good for anyone's character. To bow to superior force makes us feel **impotent** and cowardly for not having had the strength or courage to resist. Worse, it makes us resentful and vengeful. We can hardly wait to make someone pay for our humiliation, yield

to us as we were once made to yield. No, if we cannot always avoid using the Discipline of Superior Force, we should at least use it as seldom as we can.

4   There are places where all three disciplines overlap. Any very demanding human activity combines in it the disciplines of Superior Force, of Culture, and of Nature. The novice will be told, "Do it this way, never mind asking why, just do it that way, that is the way we always do it." But it probably is just the way they always do it, and usually for the very good reason that it is a way that has been found to work. Think, for example, of ballet training. The student in a class is told to do this exercise, or that; to stand so; to do this or that with his head, arms, shoulders, abdomen, hips, legs, feet. He is constantly corrected. There is no argument. But behind these seemingly **autocratic** demands by the teacher lie many decades of custom and tradition, and behind that, the necessities of dancing itself. You cannot make the moves of classical ballet unless over many years you have acquired, and renewed every day, the needed strength and suppleness in scores of muscles and joints. Nor can you do the difficult motions, making them look easy, unless you have learned hundreds of easier ones first. Dance teachers may not always agree on all the details of teaching these strengths and skills. But no novice could learn them all by himself. You could not go for a night or two to watch the ballet and then, without any other knowledge at all, teach yourself how to do it. In the same way, you would be unlikely to learn any complicated and difficult human activity without drawing heavily on the experience of those who know it better. But the point is that the authority of these experts or teachers stems from their greater competence and experience and from the fact that what they do works, not the fact that they happen to be the teacher and as such have the power to kick a student out of the class. And the further point is that children are always and everywhere attracted to that competence, and ready and eager to submit themselves to a discipline that grows out of it. We hear constantly that children will never do anything unless compelled to by bribes or threats. But in their private lives, or in extracurricular activities in school, in sports, music, drama, art, running a newspaper, and so on, they often submit themselves willingly and wholeheartedly to very intense disciplines, simply because they want to learn to do a given thing well. Our Little-Napoleon football coaches, of whom we have too many and hear far too much, blind us to the fact that millions of children work hard every year getting better at sports and games without coaches barking and yelling at them.

● THE FACTS

1. What principle or basis of division does Holt use?
2. How does Holt clarify for the reader what he means by "Discipline of Nature or of Reality"? Is this method of clarification effective? Why?
3. What are the advantages of learning from nature or reality?
4. According to the author, when should the discipline of superior force be used? Do you agree?
5. At the end of his essay, Holt identifies the most successful motivation for discipline. What is it?

● THE STRATEGIES

1. In the last sentence of paragraph 1, the author uses the feminine pronouns *she* and *her* in referring to nature. What is his purpose?

2. What transitional guideposts does the author use to gain coherence and organization?

3. What is the effect of labeling certain football coaches "Little Napoleons"?

● THE ISSUES

1. What additional examples can you supply of the ways in which children submit to the discipline of culture or society?

2. What tips can you provide for someone who has no discipline in studying college courses? What method has worked best for you?

3. Holt warns adults that the use of superior force in order to punish children is never good for the children's characters (see paragraph 3) and should therefore be used as little as possible. What, in your opinion, is the result of never using this superior force in the training of children? Give examples to support your point.

4. Our society is witnessing the self-destruction of many young people through chemical abuse of one kind or another. How is this abuse tied to Holt's idea of discipline?

5. How important is discipline in your life? Do you choose friends who are strongly disciplined, or do you prefer those who are more "laid back"? Give reasons for your answers.

● SUGGESTIONS FOR WRITING

1. Write an essay in which you divide discipline according to the kinds of effects it produces: for example, discipline that results in strong study habits.

2. Develop the following topic sentence into a three-paragraph essay: "To be successful, a person must have three kinds of discipline: of the intellect, of the emotions, and of the body." Use Holt's essay as a model for your organization.

Image Gallery for Critical Thinking and Debate: Racism

Even to the casual observer, racism in America remains a festering problem. Its toxic influence ranges from blatant discrimination in the housing market, where minorities are deliberately steered to specific neighborhoods, to subtle hiring practices wherein deserving employees are denied promotions because of skin color. Blacks live shorter lives than whites, earn less money, and make up over half of U.S. murder victims (94 percent of whom are killed by other blacks). Compared to whites, blacks are also imprisoned more often and are more likely to be executed.

To remedy the inequality between whites and blacks, the U.S. Congress passed the Civil Rights Act of 1964 and set in place laws promoting affirmative action. The effect of this measure was to narrow the educational gap between blacks and whites. Black children today outnumber both white and Hispanic children enrolled in center-based preprimary education. Still, it is sobering to think that nearly one-third of all black families and nearly one-half of all black children still live in poverty. The National Urban League estimated in 2005 that the equality index of blacks stood at 73 percent when measured against whites, little changed from 2004. The League's 2014 Equality Index highlighted the fact that both Latinos and Blacks continued to lag behind their White counterparts in employment rates. 13.1% of Blacks were unemployed, 9.1% of Latinos, but only 6.5% of Whites.

Thus the pesky specter of inequality continues to loom over the top of urban communities in the United States. How this inequality is viewed today depends as much on the viewer's race as on any facts. Predictably, the explanations for the causes of the inequality are divided along liberal/conservative fault lines. Liberals blame white racism and its poisonous legacy, arguing that the remedy for racial inequality is more government intervention. Conservatives argue that the time has come for racially neutral laws, with no affirmative action boost for minorities. Neither side denies the historical effects of racism. But whereas conservatives assert that the past is past and opportunities are now equal, liberals insist that the damage done to black consciousness by past injustices cannot be so casually dismissed.

Our Image Gallery displays two classic images of slavery and its results. The first is an old sketch of the infamous past—a time when slaves were sold on auction blocks and separated from their families. The second is Norman Rockwell's famous painting of Ruby Bridges, the first girl to attend a desegregated elementary school in the South, over the vigorous objections of many Whites. The third image shows an elderly black woman in a wheelchair approaching the security checkpoint of an airport. The question is, Will she be a security threat?

The student essay investigates the special battles African-American college-bound students must face, but it also argues that they should not expect to have college degrees handed to them *gratis,* without the effort expected by Caucasians. The student's main argument is that until the inequality gap is closed, all current college assistance programs and scholarships should remain in place and accessible to minorities, especially Blacks.

"To the Point" rounds out the issue.

Study the following three images dealing with racism. Then choose the image that most appeals to you. Answer the questions and do the writing assignment.

For readings, questions, and media on the issue of racism, visit the *MindTap for Readings for Writers*, 15e online.

Studying the Image

1. How do you think you would react to this picture if you were a member of a race for whom enslavement, as depicted in this scene, was a historical truth? If your ancestors were once slaves, what is your feeling toward this picture?

2. How do you think the woman to whom the child is clinging feels? What does her body language reveal? What message is the artist trying to convey?

3. Many white southern women in the United States insisted that house slaves were often treated like family members. Based on the facts implicit in this picture, what is your opinion of that assertion? Why are there no white women in this sketch?

4. What effect might a history of enslavement have on the descendants of slaves? How do you feel about the proposal that is occasionally brought up in our state legislatures to pay financial reparations to those whose ancestors were once slaves?

Writing Assignment

Write an essay in which you describe the subtle ways in which racism still exists in our society. If you believe racism has been wiped out, then demonstrate proof for your assertion.

Printed by permission of The Norman Rockwell Family Agency, Inc.

Studying the Image

1. This painting, by one of America's most beloved artists, known for his realistic but patriotic depiction of people and events, offended vast numbers of viewers when it was first published. What do you think people, who had formerly admired Rockwell's work, found offensive in this painting?

2. Who are the men accompanying Ruby Bridges? Why are they headless? What point is made by not showing their heads?

3. From her body language, how would you describe the attitude of the little girl? What is special about her looks?

4. Does the painting support, oppose, or remain neutral to desegregation? Depending on your answer to this question, what title would you give the painting?

Writing Assignment

Write an essay analyzing the effects on society of segregated public schools. Do not be afraid to take a stand on the issue. Ask yourself what segregation did to blacks and other minorities, and what advantages are offered by public schools that encourage ethnic variety.

© Ian Shaw/Alamy

Studying the Image

1. When the elderly woman pictured above reaches airport security, how much of a threat will she pose to the safety of other passengers? How much time should the agents spend on checking her baggage or person?

2. Since time often equals money, which passengers at airport security checkpoints should have the closest scrutiny? Describe them in general terms.

3. Because the fear of terrorism has become part of our national mood since 9/11, which characteristics or traits among passengers at airports is worth observing closely—race, behavior, age, clothing, or something else?

4. How do you feel about the security regulations presently in effect at U.S. airports? Do they keep us more secure? Are they worth the taxes spent on them? Why or why not?

Writing Assignment

Write an essay in which you suggest ways to improve the time spent at airport security checkpoints on passengers before they board their planes. You might research how other countries combat the threat of terrorist acts at their airports or border entries. If you believe that our security measures are excellent, then write an essay arguing for their retention.

Punctuation Workshop

The Colon (:)

1. **Put a colon after a complete statement followed by a list or long quotation:**

   These are the reading assignments for next week: Hawthorne's *Scarlet Letter,* two magazine articles about women today, and three books about feminism. This is what Stanley J. Randall said about perfection: "The closest to perfection a person ever comes is when he fills out an application form."

   Use a comma instead of a colon if the quotation is not introduced by a complete statement:

   It was Thomas Jefferson who said, "One generation cannot bind another."

   Do not use a colon between a verb and its object or after *such as:*

   WRONG: The contest winners were: Jerry Meyer, Ani-Hossein, and Franco Sanchez.

   RIGHT: The contest winners were Jerry Meyer, Ani-Hossein, and Franco Sanchez.

   WRONG: People no longer believe in evil spirits, such as: ghosts, witches, and devils.

   RIGHT: People no longer believe in evil spirits, such as ghosts, witches, and devils.

2. **Use a colon between figures that express time:**

   Professor Stern entered the classroom at exactly 2:10 P.M.

3. **Use a colon between titles and subtitles:**

   The Golden Years: Telling the Truth about Aging

4. **Use a colon after the salutation of a formal letter:**

   Dear Mrs. Smith:

   The colon also appears in bibliographic data. (See the student paper on p. 335.)

Student Corner

Color of Their Skin AND Content of Their Character

Carrie Moore

Chamblee Charter High School

Martin Luther King, in his famous speech, declared that he hoped that his children would live in a nation where they "would not be judged by the color of their skin but by the content of their character." But would his opinion change if darker skin could actually be an advantage for college-bound students? Let us ponder this question.

With all of the opportunities for African Americans to obtain a college degree—National Achievement, affirmative action, minority scholarships—it appears to some observers that nonminority students are disadvantaged when it comes to attending college. All of these higher-educational prospects are supposedly "unfairly geared" so as to favor African Americans.

While it is true that a plethora of opportunities exist for African Americans and other minorities to successfully obtain a college degree, these recent gains can hardly be described as biased in favor of African Americans. One could argue that, yes, treatment of college-bound students is *unequal,* but given several circumstances, they are certainly not unjust. I am not arguing that these opportunities encompass some long overdue compensation for slavery. Nor am I arguing that African Americans are dumber than students of other races and therefore need lower standards in order to slide by in life.

As a middle-class National Achievement Semifinalist who technically did not have the PSAT score to qualify for National Merit (though I would like to point out that two African Americans qualified for both this school year), I feel obliged to present an argument regarding an environment rigged against African Americans.

The trouble begins at home. Studies have long shown that whatever influences infants and toddlers are exposed to as they develop affects their progress. For example, younger children have an easier time learning foreign languages or mastering a musical instrument than do adults. Moreover, talking to young children as though they were adults allows them to have better concepts of language and communication. Exposing children to different kinds of music stimulates brain function.

Since many African Americans are first-generation college students or are just now reaching the point where they are second- or third-generation college students (affirmative action began under President Johnson and has allowed the percentage of African Americans holding bachelor degrees to increase gradually over the years), it can be safely inferred that their initial development may not have been as progressive as that of students who have two parents who attended college. This is not to say that African-American parents have failed. They simply lack a fundamental part of education. After all, which parents, who have not earned a college degree, would consider reading Chaucer to their children or playing Mozart for them? Certainly not parents who never attended a college class and never had the faintest idea who Chaucer or Mozart was in the first place.

Consider also that if these parents do not have college degrees, they are probably breaking their backs to make even a small amount of money, meaning that they do not have the time to sit down with their children to discuss Greek philosophy, learn French, or read about the Spanish Civil War. In 2009, 14.3% of Americans were under the poverty line, 25.8% of whom were black, the highest percentage of any racial group (United States 14).

If it has been proven that a college degree can lead to a larger income over the years, it can be safely stated that there is a strong correlation between African Americans' place on the poverty line and their college graduation rate.

While these seemingly small nuances do not affect the overall "intellectual quotient" of first-generation college African-American students, they certainly do affect the results of standardized tests, such as the SAT. In 2009, the average SAT score for African Americans was 1276, the lowest of all racial groups (Marklein).

Even African-American students who are fortunate enough to be born to at least one parent who has a college degree are not *equal* to their white counterparts. If one opts out of attending a historically black college and university, then appreciation of African-American culture is severely limited. It is not so much that today's African Americans are told that they are inferior, though that is true in some cases, but they are certainly not told to celebrate their heritage. History is constantly taught as an appreciation of European and nonblack advancements, and, if there are mentions of achievements by minorities (such as the inventions of the traffic light and air-conditioning unit), then they are often fleeting references.

Moreover, when African-American achievement is discussed, it is usually referred to in terms of "firsts." Toni Morrison was the first African American to win the Nobel Prize in Literature. Hattie McDaniel was the first African American to win an Oscar in the category of Best Supporting Actress in 1940. Barack Obama was the first African American to hold the title of President of the United States. Not that these cannot be marked as advancements, but why can't we acknowledge what African Americans *do* first?

These are just a few of the conflicts that even African Americans who attend college face. True, African Americans can choose to immerse themselves in classes that focus on their culture, but let's face it: What kind of career can you have with a degree in African-American studies?

All of this is not to say that African Americans should be handed everything on a plate until the achievement gap finally closes. National statistics showing that only about 43% of African Americans graduate from college are enough to disprove that. There has to be a clear and comprehensive effort on the part of African-American students to earn a college degree that will make them competitive with other students applying for the best and most lucrative jobs in a variety of markets.

Programs such as National Achievement and minority scholarships with GPA cutoffs set out to reward African Americans and minority students who try to meet them halfway. So yes, the current treatment of African Americans regarding college acceptances and scholarships is fair. Until an African American *can* slack off and get accepted to Harvard with a 2.75 GPA on legacy alone, these programs should stay in place.

Works Cited

Marklein, Mary Beth. "SAT Scores Show Disparities by Race, Gender, Family Income." *USATODAY.com*. USA TODAY, 26 Aug. 2009. Web. 18 May 2011.

United States. Census Bureau. *Income, Poverty, and Health Insurance Coverage in the United States: 2009*. By Carmen DeNavas-Walt, Bernadette D. Proctor, and Jessica C. Smith. Washington: GPO, 2010. Print.

How I Write

When I read a book, my eyes absorb the words on the pages while my imagination translates those words into vivid images, scenes, and details—an easy enough process. When I write, however, that once simple process takes place in a more complicated reverse. The detail will appear first—something as innocuous as an object in front of me or a piece of dialogue leftover from a previous conversation—and my mind will form a story, poem, or essay around it, adding flavor and color and pizzazz the way a chef jazzes up a simple dish before presenting it to others. Perhaps this is even the most fun part of writing—when your mind begins that initial work and you have not yet even realized that the idea you are pondering can become an essay or story or literary piece. It is only when you understand, "Hey! I can do something with this!" that the hard part arrives; you have to put pen to paper and work on converting that envisioned portrait to words that people who may or may not agree with you can understand. Therefore, when I write, I write quickly, using my computer, where the clacking of keys becomes almost hypnotic and I am forced to continue without thinking of losing that initial vision. Without that quick typing, an idea becomes stale and is easily discarded in favor of a fresher one. If I am lucky enough to make it through the first draft in a few sittings, I am no longer a writer but a reviser, molding and remolding until the piece resembles the initial dream that, hopefully, will be apparent to others.

My Writing Tip

Write for yourself, which essentially means write something you'd want to read. By writing something that interests you, you are immediately ensuring audience appeal. There is bound to be someone who will agree with you or find your work interesting simply because you represent a certain population or viewpoint. The work cannot fail. But when writers try to imitate someone else or write something simply because they believe it will be popular, the entire project becomes false.

 **To the Point**

Write a tactful tweet to all of your friends, telling them not to contact you by email or cell phone during a certain period because you will be busy studying for your finals (or for some other reason of your choice).

Chapter Writing Assignments

1. In an essay, divide and classify one of the following subjects:
   a. Your friends
   b. Your relatives
   c. Things or activities that give you pleasure
   d. Classes you like to take
   e. Classes you don't like to take
2. Write an essay dividing and classifying the various techniques you have used over the years to make yourself a better writer.

Writing Assignments for a Specific Audience

1. Pretending that you're writing to a prospective employer, divide and classify your life into various stages leading up to the present.
2. Write a letter to anyone you admire, dividing and classifying into stages the changes you have undergone in your career ambitions since you were young.

 Pointer from a Pro

USE DEFINITE, SPECIFIC, CONCRETE LANGUAGE

If those who have studied the art of writing are in accord on any one point, it is on this: the surest way to arouse and hold the attention of the reader is by being specific, definite, and concrete. The greatest writers—Homer, Dante, Shakespeare—are effective largely because they deal in particulars and report the details that matter. Their words call up pictures.

Note the difference between the examples on the left and those on the right:

A period of unfavorable weather set in.	It rained every day for a week.
He showed satisfaction as he took possession of his well-earned coin.	He grinned as he pocketed the reward.

—William Strunk, Jr., and E. B. White

CHAPTER 15

Causal Analysis

Road Map to Causal Analysis

What Causal Analysis Does

Causal analysis focuses specifically on explanations that show a connection between a situation and its cause or effect. It either answers the question "Why did this happen?" or "What will this do?" An answer to the first question will result in an explanation of cause; an answer to the second, a prediction of effect. An essay based on the controlling idea such as "The lack of tough antipollution laws is the cause of multiple illnesses, including cancer, in the United States" is *analyzing cause*. If the essay was based on the controlling idea that "A law to stiffen penalties against toxic polluters will clear our drinking water from cancer-causing chemicals," it would be *forecasting effect*.

As the diagram illustrates, cause points to past occurrences, whereas effect predicts future consequences.

cause ← situation → effect

Here, for example, is a causal analysis written to answer the question "Why are so many couples unable to discuss their marital problems?"

> Barriers between husbands and wives are often caused by timidity. Many couples are embarrassed to discuss intimate problems, such as sexual maladjustment, personal hygiene, or religious beliefs. They prefer to let their discontent fester rather than confront it openly. A wife says, "I wouldn't hurt my husband by telling him that his dirty hands offend me." A husband says, "I dislike the way my wife compares me to her father in everything I do, from mowing the lawn to smoking my pipe, but I could never tell her so." Guilt feelings can reinforce this sort of timidity. If a wife or husband knows that a frank talk about sex, for instance, will uncover some past indiscretion, he or she will avoid the confrontation either out of personal guilt or fear of knowing about the other partner's past. The longer this silence is kept, the stronger and more destructive it becomes. Many a broken marriage can trace the break back to barriers in communication.

On the other hand, a slight shift in the approach to this topic leads naturally to a discussion of effect. An essay based on the question "What happens when two people no longer discuss their marital problems?" would now focus on the effect, rather than the cause, of no communication in a marriage:

> Barriers between husband and wife result in a tension-filled home. When marriage partners constantly overlook a problem or pretend it does not exist, they eventually become frustrated and angry. They develop feelings of isolation and rejection, as their unfulfilled yearnings become a gnawing hunger. Lacking communication, the marriage is left without an emotional safety valve to let off pent-up frustration. The ensuing strain increases as the angry partners take out hidden, unexpressed resentments on their children, using them as scapegoats for their own great void. In the beginning the tension may show itself only in minor misunderstandings or brief pout sessions, but as the barriers remain, these little hurts turn into large wounds. The husband may become belligerent toward the wife, belittling her in front of friends or ignoring her until she retreats in cold indignation. The wife may feel so rejected and worthless that she seeks another man to comfort her or to treat her with sensitivity. The tension grows. Soon the home has become a place of bitter hostility, where love and warmth are impossible.

When to Use Causal Analysis

Use causal analysis when you are trying to explain why something happened or to predict the likely results if an event does or does not occur. Throughout your college study you will probably be given many assignments that require writing in the causal analysis mode of development. A history paper might ask you to analyze the causes of the Louisiana Purchase in 1803; an astronomy exam, to explain the cause of the aurora borealis. In economics, you might be asked to predict what will happen to the American economy if oil prices surge. A psychology exam might require you to examine three results on the work of Carl Jung caused by his break with Sigmund Freud. Causal analysis is also commonly employed in argumentative papers written in all fields and disciplines.

How to Use Causal Analysis

Know the Differences among Necessary, Sufficient, and Contributory Cause Three kinds of cause can create a given effect:

1. **A necessary cause is one that must be present for the effect to occur, but it alone cannot make the effect occur.** For instance, irrigation is necessary for a crop of good grapes, but irrigation alone will not cause a good crop. Enough sunshine, correct pruning, proper pesticides, and good soil are also required.

2. **A sufficient cause is one that can produce a given effect by itself.** For instance, an empty gasoline tank alone can keep a car from running, even though other problems such as a bad spark plug, a leaking hose, or ignition trouble may also be present.

3. **A contributory cause is one that might help produce an effect but cannot produce the effect by itself.** For instance, vitamin E may help a long-distance runner win a

race but cannot by itself determine the performance of a runner who got a bad start, trained haphazardly, or is not properly conditioned. The runner may also win the race without the help of vitamin E.

Understanding the differences among these three causes will help you in your investigations of cause and effect and keep you from making dogmatic statements such as these:

> A vegetarian diet will prevent cancer.
>
> Acupuncture is the answer to anesthesiology problems in America.
>
> Violence on television is the cause of today's growing criminal violence.

Rather, you will soften your statements by inserting such phrases as "may be," "is a contributing factor," "is one of the reasons," or "is a major cause." A careful study of cause and effect teaches that few causes are sufficient; most are merely necessary or contributory.

Make Your Purpose Clear   The excerpt from Henry Thoreau's book *Walden* opens with this clear statement: "I went to the woods because I wished to live deliberately, to front only the essential facts of life, and see if I could not learn what it had to teach, and not, when I came to die, discover that I had not lived." Thoreau then proceeds to explain the causes that led him to live in the woods. This sort of definiteness early in the piece adds a guiding focus to any explanation of cause.

Be Modest in Your Choice of Subject   It is difficult enough to analyze the causes of simple effects without compounding your problem through the choice of a monstrously large subject. The student who tries to write an essay on the causes of war is already in deep trouble; such a complex phenomenon bristles with thousands of causes. Selecting a more manageable subject for causal analysis will make your task much easier.

Concentrate on Immediate Rather Than Remote Cause   It is easy in analysis of cause to become entangled in the infinite. In a series of causations, the most likely cause is always the nearest. For example, take the case of a student—John Doe—who gets a poor grade on a test. Why? Probably because he failed to study. On the other hand, perhaps John failed to study because he thought he was doomed to fail anyway, and didn't see the point in exerting himself. Why? Probably because the instructor scared him with a lecture on how high her standards were and how hard it was to pass her class. Why did she do that? Probably because of pressure from the Regents, who accused her and her department of grading too easily. Why? The Regents, in turn, may have gotten tough because of an article critical of the department's standards that appeared in a newspaper and was written by a cub reporter who played loose with the facts. This story, in turn, was approved by an editor who had a toothache caused by a badly filled tooth. Yet, in spite of this chain of events, it is a stretch to claim that John Doe failed the test because of sloppy dentistry. Common sense must guide your thinking in this sort of analysis. However, because infinity lies behind even the reason why someone purchases a popsicle, it is safer, as a rule of thumb, to stay with immediate cause and ignore the remote.

Don't Be Dogmatic about Cause   Institutions of learning rigorously demand that students analyze cause with caution and prudence. The reasoning is simple enough:

Colleges and universities are quite determined to impress on their students the complexity of the world. It is advisable, therefore, that you be modest in your claims of causation. You can easily temper a dogmatic statement by interjecting qualifiers into your claims. Instead of writing:

> Violence in America is *caused* by violent television programs.

you could more prudently write:

> Violence in America is *influenced* by television programs.

If a student had written the following paragraph, it would no doubt have drawn the instructor's criticism:

> This brings me to the major cause of unhappiness, which is that most people in America act not on impulse but on some principle, and that principles upon which people act are usually based upon a false psychology and a false ethic. There is a general theory as to what makes for happiness and this theory is false. Life is conceived as a competitive struggle in which felicity consists in getting ahead of your neighbor. The joys which are not competitive are forgotten.

Yet this paragraph is from a Bertrand Russell article, "The Unhappy American Way," which readers have read with much sagacious head-nodding. Bertrand Russell was a Nobel laureate, a mathematician, and a noted philosopher when he wrote this. No doubt it is unfair, but his obvious accomplishments gain for him a temporary suspension of the rules against dogmatizing. Students, however, are not readily granted such license. We advise that, for the time being, anyway, you generalize about cause prudently.

Use Common Sense in Asserting Cause Most writers do not rigidly follow the principles of causal analysis except when they argue a technical question that must be explained according to the rules of logic. The following passage is an example of the free use of the principles of causal analysis:

> The association of love with adultery in much of medieval love poetry has two causes. The first lies in the organization of feudal society. Marriages, being matters of economic or social interest, had nothing whatever to do with erotic love. When a marriage alliance no longer suited the interests of the lord, he got rid of his lady with as much dispatch as he got rid of a horse. Consequently, a lady who might be nothing more than a commodious piece of property to her husband could be passionately desired by her vassal. The second cause lies in the attitude of the medieval Christian church, where the desire for erotic, romantic love was considered wicked and a result of Adam's sin in the Garden of Eden. The general impression left on the medieval mind by the church's official teachers was that all erotic pleasure was wicked. And this impression, in addition to the nature of feudal marriage, produced in the courtly poets the perverse desire to emphasize the very passion they were told to resist.

The student who wrote this paragraph does not demonstrate cause according to precise rules, but rather shows the commonsense result of her research into why medieval poetry emphasized adulterous love.

Warming Up to Write a Causal Analysis

Remember that causes look backward to the source of an event, whereas effects look forward to consequences. Here are some warm-up exercises that will help you focus on cause and effect.

1. List at least three causes for each of the following situations:
   a. Teenage smoking
   b. Recent increase in obesity
   c. Deadlock between executives and strong labor unions
   d. Children's feelings of guilt during a divorce
   e. Grownups not knowing how to use a computer or a cell phone
2. List at least three effects that result from the following situations:
   a. Loss of a parent while one is still young
   b. Having one's car stolen
   c. The fear of further terrorist attacks in the United States and other countries
   d. Listening to classical music
   e. Discovering a rat infestation in one's cellar
3. Write a thesis for each of the answers you gave to Exercise 1. Then, pick the thesis you think would lead to the best essay.
4. Write a thesis for each of the answers you gave to Exercise 2. Then, pick the thesis you think would lead to the best essay.

Examples

A Peaceful Woman Explains Why She Carries a Gun

LINDA M. HASSELSTROM

Rhetorical Thumbnail

Purpose: to justify why the author, a peace-loving woman, carries a gun

Audience: general reader, but especially women who feel vulnerable living alone

Language: standard English

Strategy: projects a reasonable persona while relating tense incidents from which gun ownership has rescued her

Linda M. Hasselstrom (b. 1943) is a writer and teacher who grew up in rural South Dakota. Her works include *Roadkill* (1984), a collection of her poetry, and *Land Circle* (1991), a collection of her essays.

Living alone on an isolated ranch may seem romantic to some who love nature or solitude, but it can be perilous to an unarmed woman. Embedded within the story line is the issue of who, if anyone, should have legal access to a gun.

• • •

1   I am a peace-loving woman. But several events in the past 10 years have convinced me I'm safer when I carry a pistol. This was a personal decision, but because handgun possession is a controversial subject, perhaps my reasoning will interest others.

2   I live in western South Dakota on a ranch 25 miles from the nearest town: for several years I spent winters alone here. As a free-lance writer, I travel alone a lot—more than 100,000 miles by car in the last four years. With women freer than ever before to travel alone, the odds of our encountering trouble seem to have risen. Distances are great, roads are deserted, and the terrain is often too exposed to offer hiding places.

3   A woman who travels alone is advised, usually by men, to protect herself by avoiding bars and other "dangerous situations," by approaching her car like an Indian scout, by locking doors and windows. But these precautions aren't always enough. I spent years following them and still found myself in dangerous situations. I began to resent the idea that just because I am female, I have to be extra careful.

4   A few years ago, with another woman, I camped for several weeks in the West. We discussed self-defense, but neither of us had taken a course in it. She was against firearms, and local police told us Mace was illegal. So we armed ourselves with spray cans of deodorant tucked into our sleeping bags. We never used our **improvised** Mace because we were lucky enough to camp beside people who came to our aid when men harassed us. But on one occasion we visited a national park where our assigned space was less than 15 feet from other campers. When we returned from a walk, we found our closest neighbors were two young men. As we gathered our cooking gear, they drank beer and loudly discussed what they would do to us after dark. Nearby campers, even families, ignored them: rangers strolled past, unconcerned. When we asked the rangers pointblank if they would protect us, one of them patted my shoulder and said, "Don't worry girls. They're just kidding." At dusk we drove out of the park and hid our camp in the woods a few miles away. The illegal spot was lovely, but our enjoyment of that park was ruined. I returned from the trip determined to reconsider the options available for protecting myself.

5   At that time, I lived alone on the ranch and taught night classes in town. Along a city street I often traveled, a woman had a flat tire, called for help on her CB radio, and got a rapist who left her beaten. She was afraid to call for help again and stayed in her car until morning. For that reason, as well as because CBs work

best along line-of-sight, which wouldn't help much in the rolling hills where I live, I ruled out a CB.

6   As I drove home one night, a car followed me. It passed me on a narrow bridge while a passenger flashed a blinding spotlight in my face. I braked sharply. The car stopped, **angled** across the bridge, and four men jumped out. I realized the locked doors were useless if they broke the windows of my pickup. I started forward, hoping to knock their car aside so I could pass. Just then another car appeared, and the men hastily got back in their car. They continued to follow me, passing and repassing. I dared not go home because no one else was there. I passed no lighted houses. Finally they pulled over to the roadside, and I decided to use their tactic: fear. Speeding, the pickup horn blaring, I swerved as close to them as I dared as I roared past. It worked: they turned off the highway. But I was frightened and angry. Even in my vehicle I was too vulnerable.

7   Other incidents occurred over the years. One day I glanced out at a field below my house and saw a man with a shotgun walking toward a pond full of ducks. I drove down and explained that the land was posted. I politely asked him to leave. He stared at me, and the muzzle of the shotgun began to rise. In a moment of utter clarity I realized that I was alone on the ranch, and that he could shoot me and simply drive away. The moment passed: the man left.

8   One night, I returned home from teaching a class to find deep tire ruts in the wet ground of my yard, garbage in the driveway, and a large gas tank empty. A light shone in the house: I couldn't remember leaving it on. I was too embarrassed to drive to a neighboring ranch and wake someone up. An hour of cautious exploration convinced me the house was safe, but once inside, with the doors locked, I was still afraid. I kept thinking of how vulnerable I felt, prowling around my own house in the dark.

9   My first positive step was to take a kung fu class, which teaches **evasive** or protective action when someone enters your space without permission. I learned to move confidently, scanning for possible attackers. I learned how to **assess** danger and techniques for avoiding it without combat.

10   I also learned that one must practice several hours every day to be good at kung fu. By that time I had married George: when I practiced with him, I learned how close you must be to your attacker to use **martial** arts, and decided a 120-pound woman dare not let a six-foot, 220-pound attacker get that close unless she is very, very good at self-defense. I have since read articles by several women who were extremely well trained in the martial arts, but were raped and beaten anyway.

11   I thought back over the times in my life when I had been attacked or threatened and tried to be realistic about my own behavior, searching for anything that had allowed me to become a victim. Overall, I was convinced that I had not been at fault. I don't believe myself to be either **paranoid** or a risk-taker, but I wanted more protection.

12   With some **reluctance** I decided to try carrying a pistol. George had always carried one, despite his size and his training in martial arts. I practiced shooting until I was sure I could hit an attacker who moved close enough to endanger me. Then I bought a license from the county sheriff, making it legal for me to carry the gun concealed.

13   But I was not yet ready to defend myself. George taught me that the most important preparation was mental: convincing myself I could actually shoot a person. Few of us wish to hurt or kill another human being. But there is no point in having a gun; in fact, gun possession might increase your danger unless you know you can use it. I got in the habit of rehearsing, as I drove or walked, the precise conditions that would be required before I would shoot someone.

14   People who have not grown up with the idea that they are capable of protecting themselves—in other words, most women—might have to work hard to convince themselves of their ability, and of the necessity. Handgun ownership need not turn us into gunslingers, but it can be part of believing in, and relying on, ourselves for protection.

15   To be useful, a pistol has to be available. In my car, it's within instant reach. When I enter a deserted rest stop at night, it's in my purse, with my hand on the grip. When I walk from a dark parking lot into a motel, it's in my hand, under a coat. At home, it's on the headboard. In short, I take it with me almost everywhere I go alone.

16   Just carrying a pistol is not protection; avoidance is still the best approach to trouble. Subconsciously watching for signs of danger, I believe I've become more alert. Handgun use, not unlike driving, becomes instinctive. Each time I've drawn my gun—I have never fired it at another human being—I've simply found it in my hand.

17   I was driving the half-mile to the highway mailbox one day when I saw a vehicle parked about midway down the road. Several men were standing in the ditch, relieving themselves. I have no objection to emergency **urination**, but I noticed they'd dumped several dozen beer cans in the road. Besides being ugly, cans can slash a cow's feet or stomach.

18   The men noticed me before they finished and made quite a performance out of zipping their trousers while walking toward me. All four of them gathered around my small foreign car, and one of them demanded what the hell I wanted.

19   "This is private land. I'd appreciate it if you'd pick up the beer cans."

20   "What beer cans?" said the belligerent one, putting both hands on the car door and leaning in my window. His face was inches from mine, and the beer fumes were strong. The others laughed. One tried the passenger door, locked; another put his foot on the hood and rocked the car. They circled, lightly thumping the roof, discussing my good fortune in meeting them and the benefits they were likely to bestow upon me. I felt very small and very trapped and they knew it.

21   "The ones you just threw out," I said politely.

22   "I don't see no beer cans. Why don't you get out here and show them to me, honey?" said the belligerent one, reaching for the handle inside my door.

23   "Right over there," I said, still being polite. "—there, and over there." I pointed with the pistol, which I'd slipped under my thigh. Within one minute the cans and the men were back in the car and headed down the road.

24   I believe this incident illustrates several important principles. The men were **trespassing** and knew it: their judgment may have been impaired by alcohol. Their response to the polite request of a woman alone was to use their size, numbers, and sex to inspire fear. The pistol was a response in the same language. Politeness didn't work: I couldn't match them in size or number. Out of the car, I'd have

been more vulnerable. The pistol just changed the balance of power. It worked again recently when I was driving in a desolate part of Wyoming. A man played cat-and-mouse with me for 30 miles, ultimately trying to run me off the road. When his car passed mine with only two inches to spare, I showed him my pistol, and he disappeared.

25   When I got my pistol, I told my husband, revising the old Colt slogan, "God made men *and women*, but Sam Colt made them equal." Recently I have seen a gunmaker's ad with a similar sentiment. Perhaps this is an idea whose time has come, though the pacifist inside me will be saddened if the only way women can achieve equality is by carrying weapons.

26   We must treat a firearm's power with caution. "Power tends to corrupt, and absolute power corrupts absolutely," as a man (Lord Acton) once said. A pistol is not the only way to avoid being raped or murdered in today's world, but, intelligently wielded, it can shift the balance of power and provide a measure of safety.

From LAND CIRCLE: WRITING COLLECTED FROM THE LAND. Copyright © 1991 by Linda Hasselstrom. Reprinted with permission from Fulcrum Publishing Company.

● THE FACTS

1. How many times did the author actually use her pistol? In each case, what was the pistol's role? How do you feel about her use of a pistol?

2. Why is a woman who travels alone believed to be more vulnerable than a man who does the same? What other precautions besides avoiding bars, approaching her car carefully, and locking doors and windows can a woman traveling alone observe?

3. Why did the author have to go to town at night when she lived on a ranch out in the country? Could she have avoided the regular trips to town?

4. According to the author, why is the martial art of kung fu not an ideal deterrent to anyone with a criminal intent?

5. Why did the author buy a license from the county sheriff after she had practiced shooting and had purchased a gun? Do you think all gun owners should follow her example? Why or why not?

● THE STRATEGIES

1. Where is the thesis of the essay most clearly stated? Evaluate the merits of this particular position.

2. What rhetorical strategy does the author use to convince her readers that she did the appropriate thing by purchasing a pistol that she could easily hide from view? Were you convinced by her argument? Why or why not?

3. At what point in the essay does the author seem to be in the most danger? Explain your answer.

4. Which paragraphs of the essay constitute a fascinating drama with an exciting climax and a happy ending? What technique makes this passage so absorbing?

5. What is the purpose of the famous quotation by Lord Acton? In what context is this quotation usually used? Why does it fit the context of this essay as well?

THE ISSUES

1. How do you interpret the author's revision of the old Colt slogan, "God made men, but Sam Colt made them equal"? What do you think of the notion that carrying a gun is one way for women to achieve equality with men? Why does the author express sorrow at the thought that carrying weapons might be the only way women can achieve equality with men?

2. Do you believe the author was paranoid or an excessive risk taker? Did she in any way contribute to her own insecurity while living at the ranch? What, if anything, could she have done to better protect herself?

3. What are some useful ways in which women in general can learn to protect themselves when they are forced to be in an environment where they could be victims of criminals?

4. What is the most frightening encounter you have ever had? If you were a victim, how did you handle the situation?

5. What is your opinion of gun control? Support your opinion with logic and strong evidence.

SUGGESTIONS FOR WRITING

1. Write an essay in which you propose an effective solution for the crime of rape.

2. Using Hasselstrom's essay as a counterpoint, write an essay entitled *The Dangers of Carrying a Gun.*

Bricklayer's Boy

ALFRED LUBRANO

Rhetorical Thumbnail

Purpose: to define and explore how a boy and his father were affected by the intrusion of class in their relationship

Audience: educated reader

Language: standard English with a journalistic slant

Strategy: is honestly describing how a son and his father became alienated from each other because of their respective jobs

Alfred Lubrano is a journalist on the staff of the *Philadelphia Inquirer.* He has written articles for numerous magazines, such as *Gentleman's Quarterly (GQ),* and he is a regular commentator on public radio. His book *Limbo: Blue-Collar Roots, White-Collar Dreams* (2003) identifies and describes an overlooked and little-understood cultural problem—the internal conflict of individuals raised in blue-collar homes but who work in white-collar jobs.

Imagine the possible gulf between a blue-collar father and a white-collar son. Not only is there a stark difference in what they do and earn, there are also unstated differences in the respect they are given and the way the world expects them to behave. Lubrano raises issues about class in America that many people find uncomfortable.

• • •

1   My father and I were college buddies back in the mid 1970s. While I was in class at Columbia, struggling with the **esoterica** du jour, he was on a bricklayer's scaffold not far up the street, working on a campus building.

2   Sometimes we'd hook up on the subway going home, he with his tools, I with my books. We didn't chat much about what went on during the day. My father wasn't interested in Dante, I wasn't up on arches. We'd share a *New York Post* and talk about the Mets.

3   My dad has built lots of places in New York City he can't get into: colleges, condos, office towers. He makes his living on the outside. Once the walls are up, a place takes on a different feel for him, as if he's not welcome anymore. It doesn't bother him, though. For my father, earning the dough that paid for my entrée into a fancy, bricked-in institution was satisfaction enough, a **vicarious** access.

4   We didn't know it then, but those days were the start of a branching off, a re-defining of what it means to be a workingman in our family. Related by blood, we're separated by class, my father and I. Being the white-collar son of a blue-collar man means being the hinge on the door between two ways of life.

5   It's not so smooth jumping from Italian old-world style to U.S. yuppie in a single generation. Despite the myth of mobility in America, the true rule, experts say, is rags to rags, riches to riches. According to Bucknell University economist and author Charles Sackrey, maybe 10 percent climb from the work-ing to the professional class. My father has had a tough time accepting my decision to become a mere newspaper reporter, a field that pays just a little more than construction does. He wonders why I haven't cashed in on that multi-brick education and taken on some lawyer-**lucrative** job. After bricklaying for thirty years, my father promised himself I'd never pile bricks and blocks into walls for a living. He figured an education—genielike and benevolent—would somehow rocket me into the **consecrated** trajectory of the upwardly mobile, and load some serious loot into my pockets. What he didn't count on was his eldest son breaking blue-collar rule No. 1: Make as much money as you can, to pay for as good a life as you can get.

6   He'd tell me about it when I was nineteen, my collar already fading to white. I was the college boy who handed him the wrong wrench on help-around-the-house Saturdays. "You better make a lot of money," my blue-collar handy dad wryly warned me as we huddled in front of a disassembled dishwasher I had neither the inclination nor the aptitude to fix. "You're gonna need to hire someone to hammer a nail into a wall for you."

7   In 1980, after college and graduate school, I was offered my first job, on a now-dead daily paper in Columbus, Ohio. I broke the news in the kitchen, where all

the family business is discussed. My mother wept as if it were Vietnam. My father had a few questions: "Ohio? Where the hell is Ohio?"

8   I said it's somewhere west of New York City, that it was like Pennsylvania, only more so. I told him I wanted to write, and these were the only people who'd take me.

9   "Why can't you get a good job that pays something, like in advertising in the city, and write on the side?"

10   "Advertising is lying," I said, smug and **sanctimonious**, ever the **unctuous** undergraduate. "I wanna tell the truth."

11   "The truth?" the old man exploded, his face reddening as it does when he's up twenty stories in high wind. "What's truth?" I said it's real life, and writing about it would make me happy. "You're happy with your family," my father said, spilling blue-collar rule No. 2. "That's what makes you happy. After that, it all comes down to dollars and cents. What gives you comfort besides your family? Money, only money."

12   During the two weeks before I moved, he reminded me that newspaper journalism is a dying field, and I could do better. Then he pressed advertising again, though neither of us knew anything about it, except that you could work in Manhattan, the borough with the water-beading high gloss, the island polished clean by money. I couldn't explain myself, so I packed, unpopular and confused. No longer was I the good son who studied hard and fumbled endearingly with tools. I was hacking people off.

13   One night, though, my father brought home some heavy tape and that clear, plastic bubble stuff you pack your mother's second-string dishes in. "You probably couldn't do this right," my father said to me before he sealed the boxes and helped me take them to UPS. "This is what he wants," my father told my mother the day I left for Columbus in my grandfather's eleven-year-old gray Cadillac. "What are you gonna do?" After I said my good-byes, my father took me aside and pressed five $100 bills into my hands. "It's okay," he said over my weak protests. "Don't tell your mother."

14   When I broke the news about what the paper was paying me, my father suggested I get a part-time job to augment the income. "Maybe you could drive a cab." Once, after I was chewed out by the city editor for something trivial, I made the mistake of telling my father during a visit home. "They pay you nothin', and they push you around too much in that business," he told me, the rage building. "Next time, you gotta grab the guy by the throat and tell him he's a big jerk."

15   "Dad, I can't talk to the boss like that."

16   "Tell him. You get results that way. Never take any shit." A few years before, a guy didn't like the retaining wall my father and his partner had built. They tore it down and did it again, but the guy still bitched. My father's partner shoved the guy into the freshly laid bricks. "Pay me off," my father said, and he and his partner took the money and walked. Blue-collar guys have no patience for office politics and corporate bile-swallowing. Just pay me off and I'm gone. Eventually, I moved on to a job in Cleveland, on a paper my father has heard of. I think he

looks on it as a sign of progress, because he hasn't mentioned advertising for a while.

17   When he was my age, my father was already dug in with a trade, a wife, two sons and a house in a neighborhood in Brooklyn not far from where he was born. His workaday, family-centered life has been very much in step with his immigrant father's. I sublet what the real-estate people call a junior one-bedroom in a dormlike condo in a Cleveland suburb. Unmarried and unconnected in an **insouciant**, perpetual-student kind of way, I rent movies during the week and feed single women in restaurants on Saturday nights. My dad asks me about my dates, but he goes crazy over the word "woman." "A girl," he corrects. "You went out with a girl. Don't say 'woman.' It sounds like you're takin' out your grandmother."

18   I've often believed blue-collaring is the more genuine of lives, in greater **proximity** to **primordial** manhood. My father is provider and protector, concerned only with the basics: food and home, love and **progeny**. He's also a generation closer to the heritage—a warmer spot nearer the fire that forged and defined us. Does heat **dissipate** and light fade further from the source? I live for my career, and frequently feel lost and codeless, devoid of the blue-collar rules my father grew up with. With no baby-boomer groomer to show me the way, I've been **choreographing** my own tentative shuffle across the wax-shined dance floor on the edge of the Great Middle Class, a different rhythm in a whole new ballroom.

19   I'm sure it's tough on my father, too, because I don't know much about bricklaying, either, except that it's hell on the body, a daily sacrifice. I idealized my dad as a kind of dawn-rising priest of labor, engaged in holy ritual. Up at five every day, my father has made a religion of responsibility. My younger brother, a Wall Street white-collar guy with the sense to make a decent salary, says he always felt safe when he heard Dad stir before him, as if Pop were taming the day for us. My father, fifty-five years old, but expected to put out as if he were three decades stronger, slips on machine-washable vestments of khaki cotton without waking my mother. He goes into the kitchen and turns on the radio to catch the temperature. Bricklayers have an occupational need to know the weather. And because I am my father's son, I can recite the five-day forecast at any given moment.

20   My father isn't crazy about this life. He wanted to be a singer and actor when he was young, but that was frivolous doodling to his Italian family, who expected money to be coming in, stoking the stove that kept hearth fires ablaze. Dreams simply were not energy-efficient. My dad learned a trade, as he was supposed to, and settled into a life of pre-scripted routing. He says he can't find the black-and-white publicity glossies he once had made.

21   Although I see my dad infrequently, my brother, who lives at home, is with the old man every day. Chris has a lot more blue-collar in him than I do, despite his management-level career; for a short time, he wanted to be a construction worker, but my parents persuaded him to go to Columbia. Once in a while he'll bag a lunch and, in a nice wool suit, meet my father at a construction site and share sandwiches of egg salad and semolina bread.

22   It was Chris who helped my dad most when my father tried to change his life several months ago. My dad wanted a civil-service bricklayer foreman's job that

wouldn't be so physically demanding. There was a written test that included essay questions about construction work. My father hadn't done anything like it in forty years. Why the hell they needed bricklayers to write essays I have no idea, but my father sweated it out. Every morning before sunrise, Chris would be ironing a shirt, bleary-eyed, and my father would sit at the kitchen table and read aloud his practice essays on how to wash down a wall, or how to build a tricky corner. Chris would suggest words and approaches.

23   It was so hard for my dad. He had to take a Stanley Kaplan-like prep course in a junior high school three nights a week after work for six weeks. At class time, the outside men would come in, twenty-five construction workers squeezing themselves into little desks. Tough blue-collar guys armed with No. 2 pencils leaning over and scratching out their practice essays, cement in their hair, tar on their pants, their work boots too big and clumsy to fit under the desks.

24   "Is this what finals felt like?" my father would ask me on the phone when I pitched in to help long-distance. "Were you always this nervous?" I told him yes. I told him writing's always difficult. He thanked Chris and me for the coaching, for putting him through school this time. My father thinks he did okay, but he's still awaiting the test results. In the meantime, he takes life the blue-collar way, one brick at a time.

25   When we see each other these days, my father still asks how the money is. Sometimes he reads my stories; usually he likes them, although he recently criticized one piece as being a bit sentimental: "Too schmaltzy," he said. Some psychologists say that the blue-white-collar gap between fathers and sons leads to alienation, but I tend to agree with Dr. Al Baraff, a clinical psychologist and director of the Men-Center in Washington, D.C. "The core of the relationship is based on emotional and hereditary traits," Baraff says. "Class [distinctions] just get added on. If it's a healthful relationship from when you're a kid, there's a respect back and forth that'll continue."

26   Nice of the doctor to explain, but I suppose I already knew that. Whatever is between my father and me, whatever keeps us talking and keeps us close, has nothing to do with work and economic class.

27   During one of my visits to Brooklyn not long ago, he and I were in the car, on our way to buy toiletries, one of my father's weekly routines. "You know, you're not as successful as you could be," he began, blue-collar blunt as usual. "You paid your dues in school. You deserve better restaurants, better clothes." Here we go, I thought, the same old stuff. I'm sure every family has five or six similar big issues that are replayed like well-worn videotapes. I wanted to fast-forward this thing when we stopped at a red light.

28   Just then my father turned to me, solemn and intense. His knees were aching and his back muscles were throbbing in clockable intervals that registered in his eyes. It was the end of a week of lifting fifty-pound blocks. "I envy you," he said quietly. "For a man to do something he likes and get paid for it—that's fantastic." He smiled at me before the light changed, and we drove on. To thank him for the understanding, I sprang for the deodorant and shampoo. For once, my father let me pay.

● THE FACTS

1. What is the unfair irony about the work accomplished by the author's father?

2. What are the father's two rules about jobs? In what way did the author break these two rules? Do you think the author chose the right path? Explain your answer.

3. How does the father react to the news that his news reporter son was "chewed out" by his city editor? Is the father's reaction justified in your mind? Why or why not?

4. How would you evaluate bricklaying as a trade? What aspects of his father's blue-collar life does the son admire? If you think his admiration is warranted, explain why.

5. Where does the relationship between son and father stand at the end of the essay? What is your forecast for the future? Create some possible scenarios.

● THE STRATEGIES

1. This essay leans heavily on the rhetorical strategy of causal analysis. What cause and what effect are analyzed? What did you as a reader learn from this story?

2. One clear difference between the father and the son is language. How would you define this difference? How inevitable is it?

3. In developing the memories of his father, the author resorts to poetic images, such as in paragraph 19, where he describes his father as "a kind of dawn-rising priest of labor, engaged in holy ritual." How does such an image contrast with the reality of being a bricklayer? How can the image and reality be reconciled?

4. How does the essay explain the difference between a trade and a profession? In your opinion, which deserves more respect? Explain your answer.

5. What is the effect of the final paragraph? Express your personal reaction to it.

● THE ISSUES

1. What is the thesis of this essay? State it in your own words as a single sentence.

2. What is your opinion of the view, often cited, that American mobility is a myth and that the true rule is "rags to rags, riches to riches"? Cite an example from your background or from history that denies the myth.

3. What feelings is the author depicting in paragraph 13? Do his feelings seem genuine or just a pose? Are these feelings typical of students leaving home for college?

4. How much does the author's old-style Italian family contribute to the misunderstanding of values between father and son? Would a story about a Chinese family have the same theme? In other words, do cultural factors affect father–son relationships? Explain your answer.

5. What advice would you give a son whose ambition to attend college is discouraged by his father as a waste of time? How can the son fulfill his desire to earn a college degree but still remain close to his father? Try to give specific advice.

● SUGGESTIONS FOR WRITING

1. Write an analysis of the destructive effects caused by differences in lifestyle between some college students and their parents. Consider such matters as clothing, entertainment, music, hairstyle, and dating. Consider also the effect of religious or political differences.

2. Tell the story of some important lesson you learned from your father. Like Lubrano, use vivid details to enhance your account.

Image Gallery for Critical Thinking and Debate: The Status of Women

Women in the United States are better off today than ever before. We can make that statement boldly on the evidence of statistics and from our own experience. In 1900, women could not vote, could not own property, and derived their legal status from whether they had husbands. Women, who did not win the right to vote until 1920, now vote in larger numbers than men. In a recent poll conducted by *USA Today,* 81 percent of the sampled women predicted the election of a woman president within the next twenty-five years.

Today, women work in as varied a range of occupations as men. Some are senators, CEOs, TV anchors, stockbrokers, and university presidents. Some have made financial fortunes while their husbands took care of the children. As Hillary Clinton proved in 2008, a woman can run for President of the United States with the support of eighty million voters. Only a few decades ago, when a woman's place was thought to be in the home and her job to care for her husband and family, such achievements would have been unthinkable.

In spite of these victories, the war for equality between men and women in the workplace and in society at large continues. One lingering bone of contention is the disparity between the salaries of men and the salaries of women for the same work. The 2005 U.S. census continued to reveal a great disparity between male and female income among all races, with females earning an average of $28,000 contrasted with males earning $40,000. The 2000 census showed that for 1999, the median income of men was $35,922, in contrast to $26,292 for women. In 2010 the median income of FTYR workers was $42,800 for men, compared to $34,700 for women. This inequality has persisted since recordkeeping began.

Anyone with even a scant knowledge of history would have to admit that the significant gains made in the status of woman were mainly won by the feminist movement. It is therefore a paradox that feminism has lost its appeal to many women of the upcoming generation. Daughters who today enjoy the benefits won by yesterday's militants regard feminism as their mother's movement, not theirs. In an ironic way, that attitude is a triumph for feminism, whose central aim has always been the empowerment of the individual to do, say, and think as he or she feels.

The change in the status of women, however, comes at a price. Women now face a world that no longer regards them as delicate and needing protection. If the *Titanic* disaster had happened in our era, the cry heard on deck would not be the chivalrous one that rang out in 1912 aboard the doomed ship, "Women and children first!" It would more likely be, "All persons for themselves!" For some conservative women, this has been too high a price to pay. For many other women, it's a bargain. The cartoon on page 355 addresses with gentle humor the problem of ordaining women to the priesthood or ministry.

The first page of our image gallery brings out black and white photographs of four American women who launched ideas and attitudes that gradually heartened women to compete and rise on the ladder of leadership which in the past had favored only men. The second page presents four Muslim women, covered from head to foot in *burkhas*, exercising their ironic right to vote. The last page features one of the problems many successful career women face—what to do with children during working hours.

"It seems to me that ordination of women might brighten the place up a bit."

   The student essay suggests that women must learn to cherish themselves without becoming slaves to the doll-like aura imposed on them by certain imposters who have a narrow and meager vision of who women should be.

   "To the Point" rounds out the issue.

   Study the following images dealing with the status of women. Then choose the image that most appeals to you. Answer the questions and do the writing assignment.

For readings, questions, and media on the issue of status of women, visit the *MindTap for Readings for Writers*, 15e online.

Susan B. Anthony (1820–1906)

Harriet Tubman (1820–1913)

Eleanor Roosevelt (1884–1962)

Rosa Parks (1913–2005)

Studying the Image

1. Susan B. Anthony was a leader in the woman's suffrage movement. How has the right to vote changed the status of women in the United States?

2. Harriet Tubman was a runaway slave who led more than 300 slaves to freedom during the American Civil War. How much did the abolitionist movement help the civil rights cause?

3. Eleanor Roosevelt, the wife of U.S. President Franklin Delano Roosevelt, was a social activist. Should a first lady remain in the background while her husband is in office or should she as "FLOTUS" (First Lady of the U.S., as often referred to by the press) involve herself in her favorite causes?

4. Rosa Parks inspired the black civil rights movement by refusing to give up her seat to a white man on a bus in 1955, as was the law in Alabama. How much courage did this take? Was the result worth the rebellion?

Writing Assignment

After doing the necessary research, write an essay on some female leaders who through their exemplary performances have opened leadership doors to others of their gender. Follow the guidelines in Chapter 3 to incorporate outside sources into your essay.

Barbara Davidson/Dallas Morning News/CORBIS

Studying the Image

1. What is your reaction to seeing these women voting while covered from head to toe in burkhas?

2. In what country might they live? Why are they wearing burkhas? If you do not already know, look up "burkha" on the Internet and read why certain cultures require that women wear this garb.

3. Imagine what facial expressions the women are revealing under their coverings. Are they showing joy or sadness? Determination or humility? Triumph or despair?

4. How would you respond to a government that forced you to wear clothing like the burkhas even in blistering hot weather? If you discovered that these women were wearing burkhas because of their religious beliefs, and not because they were forced to by a government or religious authority, how would your response change?

Writing Assignment

Write a letter to one of the women in the photo, telling her how you feel about her having to hide her female identity so as not to attract men who might disrespect her for being sordid in appearance.

Myrleen Pearson/PhotoEdit

Studying the Image

1. Under what circumstances do you think it appropriate for a woman to take her baby to work with her? How long should she be allowed to do that? At what point should she find a caregiver for the baby?

2. How would you have reacted if the photo had pictured a father bringing his baby to work with him? Would the photo of a father and baby be more or less appropriate than the photo of a woman? Explain your reaction.

3. What does the woman's appearance tell you about her? What kind of job do you think she has?

4. What alternate plan can women who must work devise to assure good care for their children?

Writing Assignment

Write an essay about the recent explosion of ads for jobs that can be accomplished at a computer in the home. Should more of these jobs be available to women who want to be at home with their children? See what child psychologists have to say on the subject, incorporating their opinions into your essay and documenting each outside source as instructed in Chapter 3.

*Stumped by bad beginnings? Exit on page 424 at the **Editing Booth!***

Punctuation Workshop

The Exclamation Point (!)

1. Use the exclamation point after expressions of strong emotion, such as joy, surprise, disbelief, or anger:

> Hooray! You beat the last record!

> Amazing! The snake is still alive.

> How dark the sky has suddenly become!

> Get out of my sight, you monster!

> "Stop that yelling immediately!" he shouted. (The comma or period that normally follows a direct quotation is omitted when the quotation has an exclamation point.)

2. Use the exclamation point sparingly. Overuse will diminish its impact. Often a comma will suffice after a mild interjection, and a period will suffice after a mild exclamation or command:

> Oh, now I see the difference in their attitude.

> How desperately he tried to please his mother.

> Please sit down and buckle your seat belt.

Student Corner

"Woman" Is a Noun

Paula Rewa

East Tennessee State University

From a local playground, a brave voice yells, "Are you a boy or a girl?" A cluster of children grin as they wait for my answer. They think they've caught me. "I'm a girl," I answer with a forced but friendly smile. I picture myself as they must see me . . . my stubble hair, my chunky black glasses and overloaded backpack. In my standard jeans and plain T-shirt, I'm not the collegiate Barbie they expect. I'm a curious blur as I walk past their games—an oddity.

In a restaurant, an older man at the bar asks me, "What are you, a man or a woman?" I wonder, if he thought I was a man, would he have asked? "I am a woman," I answer as he looks me over. I feel his eyes on me as I leave.

In the mirror, I ask myself, "Who am I?" I know the answer. I am a woman.

No matter what advances women have made in present-day society, we are still restricted by cultural expectations. If we choose to pursue a career, we become women in the workplace. If we have a family and a job, we become working mothers. We are women bankers, women lawyers, and women plumbers.

Today, it seems "woman" is used as an adjective. Defined positively, "woman" means feminine in appearance, even while wearing a suit. A woman person exists in a male world while retaining female qualities. Ideally, she is someone's wife. She is never taken for a "man."

Defined negatively, "woman" also means potentially bossy, overzealous, or emotionally driven (. . . the phrase "woman lawyer" makes more sense now, doesn't it?).

The adjective "woman" confers many, if not all, of these qualities. So where does this leave the woman person who does not fit? She is stripped of her womanhood. Her sexual orientation often is questioned. It may be said that she is trying to be a man. Society pressures her to become the adjectival "woman."

The image of the working woman is simply a modern version of the homemaker dress of the fifties. The codes of womanly appearance dictate what is appropriate. It is acceptable for a woman to have short hair if she wears cosmetics. If she chooses not to wear cosmetics, she should have a naturally pretty face and wear feminine clothing. We may now have access to the world of business, but we are still put in our place as much as ever. Our suit jackets proclaim us as equals, while our skirts hint that we are really just women underneath.

Codes of appearance apply not only in corporate America but also in society in general. The look has changed, but we are still expected to conform. Today, women can wear anything that men wear. In fact, many popular stores carry only clothing that can be worn by both men and women. Yet the expectations persist: when a woman wears it, she must still look "woman."

Our culture must reclaim "woman" as a noun, and recognize that women remain women, regardless of what they wear or what they do. If they are accountants, call them accountants. To say "woman accountant" is unnecessary, and the implications of such a title are not appreciated. If a woman has short hair and prefers suits to skirts, do not assume that she wants to be a man. Instead, consider how secure she must be to feel comfortable without conforming to society's expectations.

Women must learn to cherish themselves without being slaves to femininity. Many women enjoy wearing dresses, and they should be applauded for their own expression of self. But dresses should not be mandatory, and neither should long hair, painted nails, or push-up bras. The true woman is the person inside, not the image she projects.

I have been asked many times if I am a man or a woman. Children ask out of curiosity, men ask with mockery. I answer without hesitation, because I know that "woman" is a noun. I may have very short hair. I may wear cosmetics only occasionally. But I am proud to be a woman, just as I am proud to be myself.

How I Write

When I sit down to write, the most important factor in my productivity is comfort. I do all my writing on a computer, but I don't sit directly in front of the screen, feet flat on the floor, and all that jazz. My high school typing teacher would probably be appalled to see me lounging on my couch with my keyboard on my knees, an extension cord reaching across the living room to my PC. I never have any music playing when I need to concentrate. I used to play my favorite artists as inspiration, but I tended to get carried away. As a result, the flavor of my writing was often influenced by the mood of the music.

I like to do all my writing on a computer, because it is much easier to revise over and over. I tend to revise as I write, and then over again several times as my essay develops. I find that this helps me maintain clarity and stay connected to what I'm writing. I find it frustrating to do first, second, and third drafts, because I feel I should wait for the next official "draft" to change something I don't like. In order to write effectively, it is essential that I give myself permission to change things any time I want. I do save different versions of my paper as it evolves, for reference and in case I decide I like something better the way it was. I also print out my paper several times, in order to make notes for necessary changes.

My Writing Tip

Above all, don't get frustrated when you start writing. I have my bouts with writer's block, but I try to keep writing: Write anything that pops into your head. Don't worry about if it's in the right place.

I tend to have three or four good sentences pushing along ahead of my cursor, just waiting for a good place for me to stick them in.

The trick is to keep going. Eventually, you'll hit on an idea, a sentence, or even a combination of words that say just what you want it to say, and the rest will flow from there.

Good luck!

To the Point

After doing some research on the subject, write a tweet expressing how the 19th Amendment to the U.S. Constitution (approved by Congress on June 4, 1919) has empowered women. Your tweet should indicate your satisfaction or dissatisfaction with the progress made so far.

▥ Chapter Writing Assignments

1. Write a causal analysis for one of the following conditions:
   a. The poor writing habits of today's students
   b. The lack of popular financial support for museums, concerts, and other art forms
   c. The recent growth in prepared meals
   d. The need for prison reform
   e. The worldwide popularity of rock music
   f. The rise in child pornography
   g. The failure of the rapid transit system in most large cities
   h. The need to conserve our beaches
   i. Our tendency to buy throwaway items

2. In a written essay, analyze the causes behind the breakup of a relationship with which you are familiar.

▥ Writing Assignments for a Specific Audience

1. Write a letter to a teacher you once had (but don't send it!) analyzing why you loved or hated his or her class.

2. Write an email to a group of your friends, proposing the formation of a book club that will encourage all of you to read more and better books. The letter should carefully analyze the needs that a book club would fulfill.

 Pointer from a Pro

SCRAP ADVERBS AND ADJECTIVES

Most adverbs and adjectives are not necessary. You will clutter your sentences and annoy the reader if you choose a verb or noun that has a precise meaning and then add an adverb or adjective that carries the same meaning. Don't tell us that the radio "blared loudly" or that someone "clenched his teeth tightly," because "to blare" is to be loud, and there is no other way to clench teeth than "tightly." . . . Most writers sow adjectives almost unconsciously into the soil of their prose to make it more lush and pretty. The sentences become longer and longer as they fill up with "stately elms" and "graceful boughs" and "frisky kittens" and "sleepy lagoons." This is adjective-by-habit, and it's a habit you should stop.

—William Zinsser

If you follow Zinsser's advice, you will be more succinct, which is an additional virtue in writing.

CHAPTER 16

Argumentation and Persuasion

Road Map to Argumentation and Persuasion

What Argumentation and Persuasion Do

Argumentation and persuasion are the fraternal twins of rhetoric. The difference between them is this: An argument appeals strictly by reason and logic; persuasion appeals by both logic and emotion. If you're pleading for more funding for diabetes research and you base your appeal primarily on numbers, you're making an argument. If you supplement the number crunching with testimony from diabetes sufferers who have been horribly affected by the disease, you're being persuasive. The forum in which the argument takes place will determine which tactic you should adopt. A formal paper for a philosophy class should be worded as an argument. An essay or article written for your student newspaper, depending on the topic, should be both logical and persuasive.

Argumentation, unlike the other modes of writing, is a term of rhetorical intent, not of form. It refers to any essay or speech whose aim is to sway or persuade a reader or listener. Because writers resort to many techniques and devices to achieve this aim, the argumentation essay tends to be a mixture of rhetorical forms; that is, you are likely to find the writer defining, describing, narrating, or even dividing during the course of the argument. The tone of the essay can vary from the savage sarcasm of Jonathan Swift's "A Modest Proposal" to the matter-of-fact tone of Gerry Garibaldi's "The Pregnancy Trap." The subject matter can include any topic from the nearly infinite spectrum of issues about which people argue.

When to Use Argumentation and Persuasion

Some people think that all writing is persuasive. Their reasoning is that even if you're describing a scene, what you're really doing is trying to persuade your reader to see through your eyes. If you are comparing two friends, you are hoping to convince your reader that your observations about them are true. Trace elements of the techniques of persuasion are no doubt present in other kinds of writing, but we formally apply the techniques of argumentation and persuasion when we're trying to bring someone around to our opinion or point of view. This may be in a debate or in an essay on a topic that requires you to advocate one side over another.

How to Use Argumentation and Persuasion

What elements are most likely to sway us in an argumentative essay—to make us change our minds and believe a writer's arguments? Research suggests some clues. First, there is our perception of the writer's credentials to hold an opinion on the subject. If we think the writer is competent and qualified on the subject—a medical doctor writing on a medical topic, for example—we are more likely to believe the advocated opinion. If you hold a particular qualification to write on the subject, then mentioning it will probably help. You do not have to blare out your credentials, but you can do it subtly. For example, in his essay on teenage pregnancies, Garibaldi tells us that he is an English teacher in an urban high school and that he became well acquainted with the problem of teenage pregnancies—a revelation that leaves us more likely to accept his views of them. If you are not an expert yourself, quoting an expert can certainly lend weight to your view.

Another element that inclines us to believe an argumentative essay is the quality of its reasoning. If the writer's logic is sound, if the facts and supporting details strike us as reasonable and strong, then we are likely to be swayed by the conclusions. Presenting your facts in all their sharpness while also making the links between the propositions of your argument instantly clear, will make it difficult for anyone to easily dismiss your conclusions.

Finally, arguments are persuasive if they appeal to our self-interests. We are more likely to believe an argument if we think there is something in it for us. This insight explains why arguers huff and puff to portray themselves and their views as if they agreed exactly with our self-interests, even if the correspondence is farfetched. The underlying appeal of Jonathan Swift's ironic proposal, for instance, is to the self-interests of Irish citizens who Swift thinks would be better off in a unified Ireland free from British exploitation.

If your argument is not reasoned logically, it is unlikely to be effective. And if it is not backed with solid evidence, its claims will most likely arouse disbelief. When the issue at stake is a practical one, these two elements—logical reasoning and solid evidence—are basic requirements for any effective argument.

There are, in addition, some common strategies that writers use to make their arguments persuasive. Being persuasive involves more than being strictly logical; it takes in the whole range of writing skills—conciseness, clarity, and the ability to infuse a prose style with a distinctive personality. To write a persuasive argument, then, you should try to use the following techniques:

1. **Begin your argument at the point of contention.** This means that your initial paragraph should immediately focus on the issue being argued. Consider this opening from an argument by Henry Ford's grandson:

   > "We have room for but one language here, and that is the English language, for we intend to see that the crucible turns our people out as Americans and not as dwellers in a polyglot boarding house."
   >
   > —Theodore Roosevelt

In the store windows of Los Angeles, gathering place of the world's aspiring peoples, the signs today ought to read, "English spoken here." Supermarket price tags are often written in Korean, restaurant menus in Chinese, employment-office signs in Spanish. In the new city of dreams, where gold can be earned if not found on the sidewalk, there are laborers and businessmen who have lived five, ten, 20 years in America without learning to speak English. English is not the common denominator for many of these new Americans. Disturbingly, some of them insist it need not be.

—William A. Henry III, *Against a Confusion of Tongues*

As you can see, the writing begins with a quotation from Theodore Roosevelt and a pointed paragraph that makes it immediately clear what he is arguing against: immigrants who refuse to learn English. He wastes no time in pointless preamble or beating around the bush.

Here are two openings from student essays arguing against offshore drilling. One begins with an ominous drift; the other gets immediately to the point.

Unfocused: I oppose offshore drilling for oil. But before I give my reasons for making this statement, I would like to review the various present sources of crude oil in our country . . .

Focused: I oppose offshore drilling for oil because such a project could, in the name of energy, destroy thousands of square miles of our oceans and add to the already staggering amount of pollution on the earth . . .

Your opening sentence or sentences should underscore your stand as well as your preliminary reasoning.

2. **Draw your evidence from multiple sources.** This is a self-evident observation. If your argument is based on a single book or the testimony of one expert, it will be invariably weaker than if it draws support from many sources. Ideally, the direction and force of your research should lead you to different kinds and sources of evidence. However, student papers are often based on the writer's devotion to a single book or the point of view of one expert. This can be a crippling limitation, especially if your one book or one expert hold views that turn out to be wrong. The antidote for overreliance on a single source of evidence is to find a topic you're truly interested in.

3. **Pace your argument with some obvious movement.** Don't allow your argument to become clogged with a dreary recital of evidence or bogged down with pointless hairsplitting. We suggest that you imagine the typical reader's reactions to any argumentative essay or speech:

Reader or Listener	Your Response
Ho hum!	Wake up the reader with a provocative introduction.
Why bring that up?	State your argument in clear, forceful language.
For instance?	Supply evidence and facts.
So what?	Restate the thesis, say what you expect the reader to do.

Responding to these four imagined reader/listener attitudes will give your argument a discernible movement.

4. **Begin your argument with an assumption that is either grounded in evidence or defensible.** You should not attempt to argue the unarguable or prove the unprovable. While the realm of the arguable is constantly expanding before an onslaught of mysticism and fantasy, many instructors would nevertheless find the following theses entirely unacceptable in an argumentative essay:

> Hell exists as a place of punishment for sinners to atone for wrongdoing committed on earth.
> The Great Depression of the 1930s was caused by a destructive astrological conjunction between the planets Venus and Mars.
> Cats and all manner of feline creatures are despicable, nauseating beasts.
> Arthur Conan Doyle, creator of Sherlock Holmes, was the greatest detective-story writer of all times.

All four propositions are based on personal belief and, therefore, unprovable in a strictly logical sense.

5. **Anticipate the opposition.** For instance, if you are arguing that a controversial cancer drug should be legalized, you must not only marshal evidence to show the effectiveness of the drug, you must also answer the arguments of those opposed to its legalization. You might, for instance, introduce these arguments this way:

> Opponents to the legalization of this drug claim that its use will prevent the cancer patient from using other remedies proven effective against cancer. This claim, however, misses the point.

Then, get down to the point that has been missed.

A frequent tactic used in arguments is not only to sum up the opposition's viewpoint but also to point out any inconsistencies in it. Here is an example of this tactic from an argument in favor of using animals in medical research:

> Extremists within the animal-rights movement take the position that animals have rights equal to or greater than those of humans. It follows from this that even if humans might benefit from animal research, the cost to animals is too high. It is ironic that despite this moral position, the same organizations condone—and indeed sponsor—activities that appear to violate the basic rights of animals to live and reproduce. Each year 10,000,000 dogs are destroyed by public pounds, animal shelters and humane societies. Many of these programs are supported and even operated by animal-protectionist groups. Surely there is a strong contradiction when those who profess to believe in animal rights deny animals their right to life. A similar situation exists with regard to programs of pet sterilization, programs that deny animals the right to breed and to bear offspring and are sponsored in many cases by antivivisectionists and animal-rights groups. Evidently, animal-rights advocates sometimes recognize and subscribe to the position that

animals do not have the same rights as humans. However, their public posture leaves little room for examining these subtleties or applying similar standards to animal research.

—Frederick A. King, *Animals in Research: The Case for Experimentation*

Moral logic requires us to practice what we preach; if it can be shown that the opposition is more likely to preach than to practice, that is grounds for calling into question the sincerity of its views.

6. **Supplement your reasoning and evidence with an emotional appeal.** This tactic must, however, be used with discretion and caution—as we said, depending on the topic and the forum. Emotional appeal is no substitute for reasoned argument or solid evidence. However, used in supplementary doses, emotional appeal can be highly persuasive in dramatizing an outcome or condition in a way that evidence and facts alone cannot. Here is an example: A speaker is trying to persuade an audience to donate blood for the benefit of hemophiliacs. A hemophiliac himself, he spends the first half of his speech explaining factually what hemophilia is—reciting statistics about its incidence and discussing its symptoms. Then, to dramatize the awfulness of the disease, he resorts to an emotional appeal, using his own experience with the pain of hemophilia:

> Because medical science had not advanced far enough, and fresh blood was not given often enough, my memories of childhood and adolescence are memories of pain and heartbreak. I remember missing school for weeks and months at a stretch—of being very proud because I attended school once for four whole weeks without missing a single day. I remember the three long years when I couldn't even walk because repeated hemorrhages had twisted my ankles and knees to pretzel-like forms. I remember being pulled to school in a wagon while other boys rode their bikes, and being pushed to my table. I remember sitting in the dark empty classroom by myself during recess while the others went out in the sun to run and play. And I remember the first terrible day at the big high school when I came on crutches and built-up shoes carrying my books in a sack around my neck.
>
> But what I remember most of all is the pain. Medical authorities agree that a hemophilic joint hemorrhage is one of the most excruciating pains known to mankind.
>
> To concentrate a large amount of blood into a small compact area causes a pressure that words can never hope to describe. And how well I remember the endless pounding, squeezing pain. When you seemingly drown in your own perspiration, when your teeth ache from incessant clenching, when your tongue floats in your mouth and bombs explode back of your eyeballs; when darkness and light fuse into one hue of gray; when day becomes night and night becomes day and time stands still—and all that matters is that ugly pain. The scars of pain are not easily erased.

—Ralph Zimmerman, *Mingled Blood*

The appeal is moving and effective and contributes to the persuasiveness of the speaker's plea.

7. **Avoid common logical fallacies.** A logical fallacy occurs when you draw a conclusion that is false or deceptive. Often an argument may seem to be moving in the right direction, but on closer inspection, it has veered off the reasonable course and ends in confusion. Here are the most common logical fallacies to avoid:

Ad hominem (**Latin for "to the man"**) Here the writer mounts a personal attack on an individual rather than dealing with the argument under consideration. **Example:** "Senator X's proposal to cut inflation is nonsensical; however, that should not surprise us since the senator flunked economics in college."

Ad populum (**Latin for "to the public"**) The writer appeals to feelings, passions, or prejudices shared by large segments of the population. **Example:** "The illegal immigrants crossing our borders will bring in gangs, dope, and vile beliefs or habits that will eventually ruin our country." This logical fallacy overlooks the valuable skills and labor provided by many of the illegal immigrants who have entered our country.

False analogy The writer mistakenly compares two situations that have some characteristics in common, treating them as if they were alike in all respects. **Example:** "Since we have legalized cigarettes, we should legalize marijuana, which does not cause lung cancer the way cigarettes do." The writer overlooks a major difference between the two drugs: Marijuana impairs a person's powers of perception and judgment, whereas cigarettes do not.

Begging the question An argument that "begs the question" is one that moves in circles rather than forward. **Example:** "I am against prostitution because it dehumanizes women by having them sell themselves." The writer is saying that prostitution is wrong because it involves women prostituting themselves.

Ignoring the question (also known as the "red herring") This logical fallacy involves shifting the focus of discussion to points that have nothing to do with the basic argument. **Example:** "We must not re-elect Congressman X because he does not believe in subsidizing our farmers during droughts. Moreover, the congressman wants to get rid of Christmas crèches in the lobbies of all City Halls. Do we really want an atheist to represent us in Congress?" Remember that the original argument was about farm subsidies, not religion.

Either-or reasoning Here the writer sees an issue in black or white, with no shades of gray in between. **Example:** "If the administration gets rid of our Music Appreciation and German classes in order to balance the college budget, we shall soon become a technological school rather than a well-balanced undergraduate college." Many colleges with good reputations have had to cut certain nonrequired courses during temporary budget crises.

Hasty generalization It is human to draw conclusions before adequately sampling a situation. But in writing an argument, it is important that your evidence be sufficient and representative. **Example:** "Embryonic stem cell research offers hope to millions of people suffering from diabetes, Parkinson's, and spinal injuries. In the next election, do not vote for those narrow-minded religious fanatics who oppose embryonic stem cell research." Not everyone who is opposed to stem cell research is a narrow-minded religious fanatic.

Non sequitur (**Latin for "it does not follow"**) An argument based on a non sequitur has a faulty premise. **Example:** "All women who have dark skin and wear head scarves hate Americans and support any Jihad that will annihilate us. The counselor of our honor students, Miriam Hussein, has dark skin and always wears a head scarf; therefore, she is to be suspected of disloyalty to the United States." In this example, the major premise ("all women who have dark skin and wear head scarves hate Americans and support any Jihad that will annihilate us") is false; therefore, the conclusion will be false.

All of the logical fallacies just mentioned can crop up when writers do not use solid evidence to support their arguments but instead rely on flimsy hearsay, illogical connections, or improperly tested assumptions to force agreement on their readers.

Warming Up to Write an Argument

1. Write down at least three objections to each of the following propositions:
    a. Women should be drafted into the military.
    b. The United Nations should have its own army.
    c. The euro should now be used in every country of the world.
    d. Every official meeting of Congress should begin with prayer.
    e. "I am not responsible for saving the world."
2. For each of the following areas, list three topics you think you could develop into a persuasive argument:
    a. Something in your personal life you would like to change
    b. A social or political problem that needs solving
    c. An area of education you would like to see improved
3. Sketch out some ideas you would use to support the following quotations:
    a. "Opinions founded on prejudice are always sustained with the greatest violence."
    —Francis Jeffrey
    b. "The most tragic paradox of our time is to be found in the failure of nation-states to recognize the imperatives of internationalism."
    —Chief Justice Earl Warren
    c. "There is no greater lie than a truth misunderstood."
    —William James
    d. "The drive toward complex technical achievement offers a clue to why the U.S. is good at space gadgetry and bad at slum problems."
    —John Kenneth Galbraith

Examples

Why Don't We Complain?

WILLIAM F. BUCKLEY, JR.

Rhetorical Thumbnail

Purpose: to argue against passivity in the face of outrageously poor service

Audience: educated readers

Language: standard English with a snooty touch

Strategy: a variety of examples embedded in a narration

William F. Buckley, Jr. (1925–2008) was an American editor, writer, and television host. Born into a family of wealth and privilege, he was educated in England, France, the Millbrook School in New York, and Yale University. At the age of 25, he became a literary sensation with the publication of his book, *God and Man at Yale* (1950), a stinging indictment of what later would be called "political correctness." His magazine, the *National Review*, reflected his conservative views about politics and society; his television show, *Firing Line*, in which he debated liberals of the day, made him into an American icon during the Ronald Reagan presidency.

Buckley not only analyzes why we are allegedly not a complaining nation, but also he finds a positive side to griping and being more assertive. Today, Buckley's essay—written before the days of blogging, tweeting, and open frustration—probably describes a less complaining America than we observe.

• • •

1   It was the very last coach and the only empty seat on the entire train, so there was no turning back. The problem was to breathe. Outside the temperature was below freezing. Inside the railroad car, the temperature must have been about 85 degrees. I took off my overcoat, and a few minutes later my jacket, and noticed that the car was flecked with the white shirts of passengers. I soon found my hand moving to loosen my tie. From one end of the car to the other, as we rattled through Westchester Country, we sweated; but we did not moan.

2   I watched the train conductor appear at the head of the car. "Tickets, all tickets, please!" In a more virile age, I thought, the passengers would seize the conductor and strap him down on a seat over the radiator to share the fate of his patrons. He shuffled down the aisle, picking up tickets, punching **commutation** cards. *No one addressed a word to him.* He approached my seat, and I drew a deep breath of resolution. "Conductor," I began with a considerable edge to my voice. . . .

Instantly the doleful eyes of my seatmate turned tiredly from his newspaper to fix me with a resentful stare: what question could be so important as to justify my **sibilant** intrusion into his **stupor**? I was shaken by those eyes. I am incapable of making a discreet fuss, so I mumbled a question about what time were we due in Stamford (I didn't even ask whether it would be before or after dehydration could be expected to set in), got my reply, and went back to my newspaper and to wiping my brow.

3   The conductor had nonchalantly walked down the **gauntlet** of eighty sweating American freemen, and not one of them had asked him to explain why the passengers in that car had been **consigned** to suffer. There is nothing to be done when the temperature *outdoors* is 85 degrees, and indoors the air conditioner has broken down; obviously when that happens there is nothing to do, except perhaps curse the day that one was born. But when the temperature outdoors is below freezing, it takes a positive act of will on somebody's part to set the temperature *indoors* at 85. Somewhere a valve was turned too far, a furnace overstoked, a thermostat maladjusted: something that could easily be remedied by turning off the heat and allowing the great outdoors to come indoors. All this is so obvious. What is not obvious is what has happened to the American people.

4   It isn't just the commuters, whom we have come to visualize as a **supine** breed who have got onto the trick of suspending their sensory faculties twice a day while they submit to the creeping **dissolution** of the railroad industry. It isn't just they who have given up trying to rectify irrational **vexations**. It is the American people everywhere.

5   A few weeks ago at a large movie theatre I turned to my wife and said, "The picture is out of focus." "Be quiet," she answered. I obeyed. But a few minutes later I raised the point again, with mounting impatience. "It will be all right in a minute," she said apprehensively. (She would rather lose her eyesight than be around when I make one of my infrequent scenes.) I waited. It was *just* out of focus—not glaringly out, but out. My vision is 20-20, and I assume that is the vision, adjusted, of most people in the movie house. So, after **hectoring** my wife throughout the first reel, I finally prevailed upon her to admit that it *was* off, and very annoying. We then settled down, coming to rest on the presumption that: a) someone connected with the management of the theatre must soon notice the blur and make the correction; or b) that someone seated near the rear of the house would make the complaint in behalf of those of us up front; or c) that—any minute now—the entire house would explode into catcalls and foot stamping, calling dramatic attention to the irksome distortion.

6   What happened was nothing. The movie ended, as it had begun, just out of focus, and as we trooped out, we stretched our faces in a variety of contortions to accustom the eye to the shock of normal focus.

7   I think it is safe to say that everybody suffered on that occasion. And I think it is safe to assume that everyone was expecting someone else to take the initiative in going back to speak to the manager. And it is probably true even that if we had supposed the movie would run right through with the blurred image, someone surely would have summoned up the purposive indignation to get up out of his seat and file his complaint.

8   But notice that no one did. And the reason no one did is because we are all increasingly anxious in America to be **unobtrusive**, we are reluctant to make our voices heard, hesitant about claiming our rights; we are afraid that our cause is unjust, or that if it is not unjust, that it is **ambiguous**; or if not even that, that it is too trivial to justify the horrors of a confrontation with Authority; we will sit in an oven or endure a racking headache before undertaking a head-on, I'm-here-to-tell-you complaint. That tendency to passive compliance, to a **heedless** endurance is something to keep one's eyes on—in sharp focus.

9   I myself can occasionally summon the courage to complain, but I cannot, as I have intimated, complain softly. My own instinct is so strong to let the thing ride, to forget about it—to expect that someone will take the matter up, when the grievance is collective, in my behalf—that it is only when the provocation is at a very special key, whose vibrations touch simultaneously a complexus of nerves, allergies, and passions, that I catch fire and find the reserves of courage and assertiveness to speak up. When that happens, I get quite carried away. My blood gets hot, my brow wet, I become unbearably and unconscionably sarcastic and **bellicose**: I am **girded** for a total showdown.

10   Why should that be? Why could not I (or anyone else) on that railroad coach have said simply to the conductor, "Sir,"—I take that back: that sounds sarcastic—"Conductor, would you be good enough to turn down the heat? I am extremely hot. In fact, I tend to get hot every time the temperature reaches 85 degrees—" Strike that last sentence. Just end it with the simple statement that you are extremely hot, and let the conductor infer the cause.

11   Every New Year's Eve I resolve to do something about the Milquetoast in me and vow to speak up, calmly, for my rights, and for the betterment of our society, on every appropriate occasion. Entering last New Year's Eve I was fortified in my resolve because that morning at breakfast I had had to ask the waitress three times for a glass of milk. She finally brought it—after I had finished my eggs, which is when I don't want it any more. I did not have the manliness to order her to take the milk back, but settled instead for a cowardly sulk, and ostentatiously refused to drink the milk—though I later paid for it—rather than state plainly to the hostess, as I should have, why I had not drunk it, and would not pay for it.

12   So by the time the New Year ushered out the Old, riding in on my morning's indignation and stimulated by the gastric juices of resolution that flow so faithfully on New Year's Eve, I rendered my vow. Henceforward I would conquer my shyness, my despicable disposition to supineness. I would speak out like a man against the unnecessary annoyances of our time.

13   Forty-eight hours later, I was standing in line at the ski-repair store in Pico Peak, Vermont. All I needed, to get on with my skiing, was the loan, for one minute, of a small screwdriver, to tighten a loose binding. Behind the counter in the workshop were two men. One was industriously engaged in servicing the complicated requirements of a young lady at the head of the line, and obviously he would be tied up for quite a while. The other—"Jiggs," his workmate called him—was a middle-aged man, who sat in a chair puffing a pipe, exchanging small talk with his working partner. My pulse began its telltale acceleration. The minutes ticked on. I stared at the idle shopkeeper, hoping to shame him into action, but he was **impervious** to my

telepathic reproof and continued his small talk with his friend, brazenly insensitive to the nervous demands of six good men who were raring to ski.

14   Suddenly my New Year's Eve resolution struck me. It was now or never. I broke from my place in line and marched to the counter. I was going to control myself. I dug my nails into my palms. My effort was only partially successful.

15   "If you are not too busy," I said icily, "would you mind handing me a screwdriver?"

16   Work stopped and everyone turned his eyes on me, and I experienced that **mortification** I always feel when I am the center of **centripetal** shafts of curiosity, resentment, perplexity.

17   But the worst was yet to come. "I am sorry, sir," said Jiggs **deferentially**, moving the pipe from his mouth. "I am not supposed to move. I have just had a heart attack." That was the signal for a great whirring noise that descended from heaven. We looked, stricken, out the window, and it appeared as though a cyclone had suddenly focused on the snowy courtyard between the shop and the ski lift. Suddenly a gigantic Army helicopter materialized, and hovered down to a landing. Two men jumped out of the plane carrying a stretcher, tore into the ski shop, and lifted the shopkeeper onto the stretcher. Jiggs bade his companion good-by, was whisked out the door, into the plane, up to the heavens, down—we learned—to a nearby Army hospital. I looked up manfully—into a score of man-eating eyes. I put the experience down as a reversal.

18   As I write this, on an airplane, I have run out of paper and need to reach into my briefcase under my legs for more. I cannot do this until my empty lunch tray is removed from my lap. I arrested the stewardess as she passed empty-handed down the aisle on the way to the kitchen to fetch the lunch trays for the passengers up forward who haven't been served yet. "Would you please take my tray?" "Just a *moment, sir,*" she said, and marched on sternly. Shall I tell her that since she is headed for the kitchen *anyway,* it cannot delay the feeding of the other passengers by the two seconds necessary to stash away my empty tray? Or remind her that not fifteen minutes ago she spoke **unctuously** into the loudspeaker the words undoubtedly devised by the airline's highly paid public-relations counselor: "If there is anything I or Miss French can do for you to make your trip more enjoyable, *please* let us—" I have run out of paper.

19   I think the observable reluctance of the majority of Americans to assert themselves in minor matters is related to our increased sense of helplessness in an age of technology and centralized political and economic power. For generations, Americans who were too hot, or too cold, got up and did something about it. Now we call the plumber, or the electrician, or the furnace man. The habit of looking after our own needs obviously had something to do with the assertiveness that characterized the American family familiar to readers of American literature. With the **technification** of life goes our direct responsibility for our material environment, and we are conditioned to adopt a position of helplessness not only as regards the broken air conditioner, but as regards the overheated train. It takes an expert to fix the former, but not the latter: yet these distinctions, as we withdraw into helplessness, tend to fade away.

20   Our **notorious** political apathy is a related phenomenon. Every year, whether the Republican or the Democratic Party is in office, more and more power drains away from the individual to feed vast **reservoirs** in far-off places; and we have less and less say about the shape of events which shape our future. From this **aberration** of personal power comes the sense of resignation with which we accept the political **dispensations** of a powerful government whose hold upon us continues to increase.

21   An editor of a national weekly news magazine told me a few years ago that as few as a dozen letters of protest against an editorial stance of his magazine was enough to convene a **plenipotentiary** meeting of the board of editors to review policy. "So few people complain, or make their voices heard," he explained to me, "that we assume a dozen letters represent the **inarticulated** views of thousands of readers." In the past ten years, he said, the volume of mail has noticeably decreased, even though the circulation of his magazine has risen.

22   When our voices are finally mute, when we have finally suppressed the natural instinct to complain, whether the vexation is trivial or grave, we shall have become **automatons**, incapable of feeling. When Premier Khrushchev first came to this country late in 1959 he was primed, we are informed, to experience the bitter resentment of the American people against his tyranny, against his persecutions, against the movement which is responsible for the then great number of American deaths in Korea, for billions in taxes every year, and for life everlasting on the brink of disasters; but Khrushchev was pleasantly surprised, and reported back to the Russian people that he had been met with overwhelming cordiality (read: apathy), except, to be sure, for "a few fascists who followed me around with their wretched posters, and should be . . . horsewhipped."

23   I may be crazy, but I say there would have been lots more posters in a society where train temperatures in the dead of winter are not allowed to climb up to 85 degrees without complaint.

● THE FACTS

1. What illustrations form the backdrop for Buckley's argument? Summarize each in one sentence.

2. Whom does the author blame for being excessively shy about speaking up when something irritating could easily be mended?

3. Basically, what is Buckley's view of the American people? What has happened to them?

4. Why, according to the author, do large groups of people suffer blatant discomforts or even injustices without anyone making a move to rectify them?

5. Why doesn't the author complain about collective inconveniences? Does his reason resonate with you? Why or why not?

● THE STRATEGIES

1. How does the author's language reveal his intellectual level? To whom would this essay appeal? Who would have trouble reading to the end of the essay?

2. How does the title of the essay relate to its content and purpose?

3. Where is the main point of the argument best stated? Does it call for some kind of action or is it merely descriptive?

4. What image does the author use to describe how much his wife hates his infrequent outbursts of temper? (See paragraph 5.) What is your reaction to this image?

5. Why does the author end his essay with such a brief and ambiguous paragraph? Is he praising fascism or communism, or does he have something else in mind? Explain your answer.

● THE ISSUES

1. Do you agree with Buckley's argument that the American people are too passive in their response to conditions that need changing? If you agree, then add a few examples of your own; if you disagree, give some examples of when an individual or a group of people have spoken up and demanded change.

2. Why do you think commuters might be considered a particularly "supine breed"? Explain the term and give reasons for your answer.

3. How does the author relate technology to the lack of initiative he sees in Americans? Do you agree with his observation? What other factors might be responsible?

4. Since the anthologizing of Buckley's essay in 2004, have you seen a change in our national character? For instance, have you noticed an increase in people's resistance to a top-heavy government or to being slaves to machinery?

5. What kind of response do you usually reveal in a situation where many people are uncomfortable yet no one complains? Like the author, do you complain only when your anger reaches the boiling point, or are you assertive enough to complain while you are still calm and collected? What kinds of situations compel you to complain? Are there some situations not important enough to warrant your complaint? Give specific examples of each.

● SUGGESTIONS FOR WRITING

1. Write an essay refuting Buckley's argument by stating that Americans stand up for their individual rights more than most other citizens in the world. Use the guidelines for argumentation offered in this chapter. Be sure to anticipate the opposition, and avoid logical fallacies.

2. Write an argument supporting the thesis that freedom of speech is a mighty privilege that must never be abused. Use the guidelines for argumentation offered in this chapter. Be sure to anticipate the opposition, and avoid logical fallacies.

A Modest Proposal

For Preventing the Children of Poor People from Being a Burden to Their Parents or the Country and for Making Them Beneficial to the Public

JONATHAN SWIFT

Rhetorical Thumbnail

Purpose: to rail against the English for their brutal treatment of the Irish

Audience: eighteenth-century reader of pamphlets

Language: standard eighteenth-century English

Strategy: portrays the landlords as insatiable beasts intent on devouring Irish tenants; affects the pose of a reasonable man anxious to find a solution to the problem

Jonathan Swift (1667–1745) is considered one of the greatest satirists in the English language. He was born in Dublin and educated at Trinity College. His satirical masterpiece, *Gulliver's Travels*, was published in 1726, by which time Swift was already regarded by the Irish as a national hero for his *Drapier's Letters* (1724). Originally published as a pamphlet, "A Modest Proposal" first appeared in 1729.

In this famous satire, Swift proposes a savage solution to Irish poverty and the historical indifference of the English to it.

• • •

1   It is a melancholy object to those who walk through this great town, or travel in the country, when they see the streets, the roads, and cabin doors crowded with beggars of the female sex followed by three, four, or six children, all in rags and **importuning** every passenger for an alms. These mothers, instead of being able to work for their honest livelihood, are forced to employ all their time in strolling, to beg **sustenance** for their helpless infants, who, as they grow up, either turn thieves for want of work or leave their dear native country to fight for the Pretender in Spain or sell themselves to the Barbadoes.[1]

2   I think it is agreed by all parties that this **prodigious** number of children, in the arms or on the backs or at the heels of their mothers and frequently of their fathers, is in the present deplorable state of the kingdom a very great additional grievance, and therefore whoever could find out a fair, cheap, and easy method of making these children sound and useful members of the commonwealth would deserve so well of the public as to have his statue set up for a preserver of the nation.

[1] Swift refers to the exiled Stuart claimant of the English throne, and to the custom of poor emigrants to commit themselves to work for a number of years to pay off their transportation to a colony.

3   But my intention is very far from being confined to provide only for the children of professed beggars; it is of a much greater extent, and shall take in the whole number of infants at a certain age who are born of parents in effect as little able to support them as those who demand our charity in the streets.

4   As to my own part, having turned my thoughts for many years upon this important subject and maturely weighed the several schemes of other projectors, I have always found them grossly mistaken in their computation. It is true, a child just dropped from its dam may be supported by her milk for a solar year, with little other nourishment, at the most not above the value of two shillings, which the mother may certainly get, or the value in scraps, by her lawful occupation of begging; and it is exactly at one year old that I propose to provide for them in such a manner as, instead of being a charge upon their parents or the parish or wanting food and raiment for the rest of their lives, they shall on the contrary contribute to the feeding, and partly to the clothing, of many thousands.

5   There is likewise another great advantage in my scheme, that it will prevent those voluntary abortions and that horrid practice of women murdering their bastard children, alas! too frequent among us, sacrificing the poor innocent babes, I doubt more to avoid the expense than the shame, which would move tears and pity in the most savage and inhuman breast.

6   The number of souls in this kingdom being usually reckoned one million and a half, of these I calculate there may be about two hundred thousand couples whose wives are breeders, from which number I subtract thirty thousand couples who are able to maintain their own children (although I apprehend there cannot be so many, under the present distresses of the kingdom); but this being granted, there will remain a hundred and seventy thousand breeders. I again subtract fifty thousand for those women who miscarry or whose children die by accident or disease within the year. There only remain a hundred and twenty thousand children of poor parents annually born. The question therefore is how this number shall be reared and provided for, which, as I have already said, under the present situation of affairs is utterly impossible by all the methods hitherto proposed. For we can neither employ them in handicraft or agriculture; we neither build houses (I mean in the country) nor cultivate land; they can very seldom pick up a livelihood by stealing, till they arrive at six years old, except where they are of towardly parts, although I confess they learn the rudiments much earlier, during which time they can, however, be properly looked upon only as probationers; as I have been informed by a principal gentleman in the County of Cavan who protested to me that he never knew above one or two instances under the age of six, even in a part of the kingdom so renowned for the quickest **proficiency** in that art.

7   I am assured by our merchants that a boy or a girl before twelve years old is no saleable commodity, and even when they come to this age they will not yield above three pounds or three pounds and a half a crown at most on the exchange, which cannot turn to account either to the parents or the kingdom, the charge of nutriment and rags having been at least four times that value.

8   I shall now, therefore, humbly propose my own thoughts, which I hope will not be liable to the least objection.

9   I have been assured by a very knowing American of my acquaintance in London that a young, healthy child well nursed is, at a year old, a most delicious, nourishing, and wholesome food, whether stewed, roasted, baked, or boiled; and I make no doubt that it will equally serve in a fricassee or a ragout.

10   I do therefore humbly offer it to public consideration that of the hundred and twenty thousand children already computed, twenty thousand may be reserved for breed, whereof only one fourth part to be males, which is more than we allow to sheep, black cattle, or swine; and my reason is that these children are seldom the fruits of marriage, a circumstance not much regarded by our savages; therefore one male will be sufficient to serve four females. That the remaining hundred thousand may, at a year old, be offered in sale to the persons of quality and fortune through the kingdom, always advising the mother to let them suck plentifully in the last month, so as to render them plump and fat for a good table. A child will make two dishes at an entertainment for friends; and when the family dines alone, the fore-or hind-quarter will make a reasonable dish, and seasoned with a little pepper or salt, will be very good boiled on the fourth day, especially in winter. I have reckoned, upon a medium, that a child just born will weigh twelve pounds, and in a solar year, if tolerably nursed, will increase to twenty-eight pounds.

11   I grant this food will be somewhat dear, and therefore very proper for the landlords, who, as they have already devoured most of the parents, seem to have the best title to the children.

12   Infant's flesh will be in season throughout the year, but more plentifully in March and a little before and after; for we are told by a grave author, an eminent French physician, that fish being a prolific diet, there are more children born in Roman Catholic countries about nine months after Lent than at any other season; therefore, reckoning a year after Lent, the markets will be more glutted than usual, because the number of Popish infants is at least three to one in this kingdom; and therefore it will have one other **collateral** advantage, by lessening the number of Papists among us. I have already computed the charge of nursing a beggar's child (in which list I reckon all cottagers, laborers, and four fifths of the farmers) to be about two shillings per annum, rags included; and I believe no gentleman would repine to give ten shillings for the carcass of a good fat child, which, as I have said, will make four dishes for excellent nutritive meat, when he has only some particular friend or his own family to dine with him. Thus the squire will learn to be a good landlord and grow popular among his tenants; the mother will have eight shillings net profit and be fit for work till she produces another child.

13   Those who are more thrifty (as I must confess the times require) may flay the carcass, the skin of which, artificially dressed, will make admirable gloves for ladies and summer boots for fine gentlemen.

14   As to our city of Dublin, shambles[2] may be appointed for this purpose in the most convenient parts of it; and butchers, we may be assured, will not be wanting,

[2]Slaughterhouses.

although I rather recommend buying the children alive than dressing them hot from the knife as we do roasting pigs.

15   A very worthy person, a true lover of his country, and whose virtues I highly esteem, was lately pleased in discoursing on this matter to offer a refinement upon my scheme. He said that many gentlemen of his kingdom having of late destroyed their deer, he conceived that the want of venison might be well supplied by the bodies of young lads and maidens, not exceeding fourteen years of age nor under twelve, so great a number of both sexes in every country being now ready to starve for want of work and service; and these to be disposed of by their parents if alive, or otherwise by their nearest relations. But with due deference to so excellent a friend and so deserving a patriot, I cannot be altogether in his sentiments; for as to the males, my American acquaintance assured me, from frequent experience, that their flesh was generally tough and lean, like that of our schoolboys, by continual exercise, and their taste disagreeable; and to fatten them would not answer the charge. Then as to the females, it would, I think, with humble submission, be a loss to the public, because they would soon become breeders themselves, and besides, it is not improbable that some scrupulous people might be apt to **censure** such a practice (although indeed very unjustly) as a little bordering upon cruelty, which, I confess, has always been with me the strongest objection against any project, however so well intended.

16   But in order to justify my friend, he confessed that this expedient was put into his head by the famous Psalmanazar, a native of the island Formosa, who came from thence to London above twenty years ago and in conversation told my friend that in his country, when any young person happened to be put to death, the executioner sold the carcass to persons of quality as a prime dainty and that in his time the body of a plump girl of fifteen, who was crucified for an attempt to poison the emperor, was sold to his imperial Majesty's prime minister of state and other great mandarins of the court in joints from the **gibbet** at four hundred crowns. Neither, indeed, can I deny that if the same use were made of several plump young girls in this town who, without one single groat to their fortunes, cannot stir abroad without a chair, and appear at playhouse and assemblies in foreign fineries which they never will pay for, the kingdom would not be the worse.

17   Some persons of a desponding spirit are in great concern about that vast number of poor people who are aged, diseased, or maimed, and I have been desired to employ my thoughts what course may be taken to ease the nation of so grievous an **encumbrance**. But I am not in the least pain upon the matter, because it is very well known that they are every day dying and rotting by cold, and famine, and filth, and vermin, as fast as can be reasonably expected. And as to the young laborers, they are now in almost as hopeful a condition; they cannot get work and consequently pine away for want of nourishment to a degree that if at any time they are accidentally hired to common labor, they have not strength to perform it; and thus the country and themselves are happily delivered from the evils to come.

18   I have too long **digressed** and therefore shall return to my subject. I think the advantages by the proposal which I have made are obvious and many, as well as of the highest importance.

19   For first, as I have already observed, it would greatly lessen the number of Papists, with whom we are yearly overrun, being the principal breeders of the nation as well as our most dangerous enemies, and who stay at home on purpose to deliver the kingdom to the Pretender, hoping to take their advantage by the absence of so many good Protestants, who have chosen rather to leave their country than stay at home and pay tithes, against their conscience, to an Episcopal curate.

20   Secondly, the poorer tenants will have something valuable of their own which by law may be made liable to distress and help to pay their landlord's rent, their corn and cattle being already seized and money a thing unknown.

21   Thirdly, whereas the maintenance of a hundred thousand children from two years old and upward cannot be computed at less than ten shillings apiece per annum, the nation's stock will thereby be increased fifty thousand pounds per annum, beside the profit of a new dish introduced to the tables of all gentle-men of fortune in the kingdom who have any refinement in taste. And the money will circulate among ourselves, the goods being entirely of our own growth and manufacture.

22   Fourthly, the constant breeders, beside the gain of eight shillings sterling per annum by the sale of their children, will be rid of the charge of maintaining them after the first year.

23   Fifthly, this food would likewise bring great custom to taverns, where the vintners will certainly be so prudent as to procure the best receipt for dressing it to perfection and consequently have their houses frequented by all the fine gentlemen who justly value themselves upon their knowledge in good eating; and a skillful cook who understands how to oblige his guests will contrive to make it as expensive as they please.

24   Sixthly, this would be a great inducement to marriage, which all wise nations have either encouraged by rewards or enforced by laws and penalties. It would increase the care and tenderness of mothers toward their children when they were sure of a settlement for life to the poor babes, provided in some sort by the public, to their annual profit or expense. We could see an honest emulation among the married women, which of them could bring the fattest child to the market. Men would become as fond of their wives during the time of their pregnancy as they are now of their mares in foal, their cows in calf, or sows when they are ready to farrow, nor offer to beat or kick them (as is too frequent a practice) for fear of a miscarriage.

25   Many other advantages might be enumerated. For instance, the addition of some thousand carcasses in our exportation of barreled beef; the **propagation** of swine's flesh and improvement in the art of making good bacon, so much wanted among us by the great destruction of pigs, too frequent at our table, which are no way comparable in taste or magnificence to a well-grown fat year-ling child, which, roasted whole, will make a considerable figure at a lord mayor's

feast or any other public entertainment. But this and many others I omit, being studious of brevity.

26   Supposing that one thousand families in this city would be constant customers for infant's flesh, beside others who might have it at merry-meetings, particularly at weddings and christenings, I compute that Dublin would take off annually about twenty thousand carcasses and the rest of the kingdom (where probably they will be sold somewhat cheaper) the remaining eighty thousand.

27   I can think of no one objection that will possibly be raised against this proposal unless it should be urged that the number of people will be thereby much lessened in the kingdom. This I freely own, and it was indeed one principal design in offering it to the world. I desire the reader will observe that I calculate my remedy for this one individual kingdom of Ireland and for no other that ever was, is, or I think ever can be, upon earth. Therefore let no man talk to me of other expedients; of taxing our absentees at five shillings a pound; of using neither clothes nor household furniture except what is of our own growth and manufacture; of utterly rejecting the materials and instruments that promote foreign luxury; of curing the expensiveness of pride, vanity, idleness, and gaming in our women; of introducing a vein of **parsimony**, prudence, and temperance; of learning to love our country, in the want of which we differ even from Laplanders and the inhabitants of Tupinamba; of quitting our animosities and factions, nor acting any longer like the Jews, who were murdering one another at the very moment their city was taken; of being a little cautious not to sell our country and conscience for nothing; of teaching landlords to have at least one degree of mercy toward their tenants; lastly, of putting a spirit of honesty, industry, and skill into our shop-keepers, who, if a resolution could now be taken to buy only our native goods, would immediately unite to cheat and exact upon us in the price, the measure, and the goodness, nor could ever yet be brought to make one fair proposal of just dealing, though often and earnestly invited to it.

28   Therefore, I repeat, let no man talk to me of these and the like expedients till he has at least some glimpse of hope that there will be ever some hearty and sincere attempt to put them in practice.

29   But as to myself, having been wearied out for many years with offering vain, idle, visionary thoughts and at length utterly despairing of success, I fortunately fell upon this proposal, which, as it is wholly new, so it has something solid and real, of no expense and little trouble, full in our own power, and whereby we can incur no danger in disobliging England. For this kind of commodity will not bear exportation, the flesh being of too tender a consistence to admit a long continuance in salt, although perhaps I could name a country which would be glad to eat up our whole nation without it.

30   After all, I am not so violently bent upon my own opinion as to reject any offer proposed by wise men which shall be found equally innocent, cheap, easy, and effectual. But before some thing of that kind shall be advanced in contradiction to my scheme and offering a better, I desire the author or authors will be pleased maturely to consider two points: first, as things now stand, how they will be able to find food and raiment for a hundred thousand useless mouths and

backs; and secondly, there being a round million of creatures in human figure throughout this kingdom whose whole subsistence, put into a common stock, would leave them in debt two millions of pounds sterling, adding those who are beggars by profession to the bulk of farmers, cottagers, and laborers, with the wives and children who are beggars in effect, I desire those politicians who dislike my **overture**, and may perhaps be so bold as to attempt an answer, that they will first ask the parents of these mortals whether they would not at this day think it a great happiness to have been sold for food at a year old in the manner I prescribe, and thereby have avoided such a perpetual scene of misfortunes as they have since gone through by the oppression of landlords, the impossibility of paying rent without money or trade, the want of common sustenance, with neither house nor clothes to cover them from the **inclemencies** of the weather, and the most inevitable prospect of entailing the like of greater miseries upon their breed forever.

31   I profess in the sincerity of my heart that I have not the least personal interest in endeavoring to promote this necessary work, having no other motive than the public good of my country, by advancing our trade, providing for infants, relieving the poor, and giving some pleasure to the rich. I have no children by which I can propose to get a single penny, the youngest being nine years old and my wife past childbearing.

● THE FACTS

1. On what premise is "A Modest Proposal" based? What is the chief assumption of its argument?
2. Reread paragraph 11. Why do the landlords have "the best title to the children"?
3. Swift's satire redefines children in economic terms. What does this say about his view of the society in which he lived?
4. What does the satire imply about religious feelings in Ireland during Swift's time?
5. Given the state of affairs as the author describes them, is his argument logical? Explain.

● THE STRATEGIES

1. What is the effect of the word *Modest* in the title?
2. Swift describes people with words like breeder, dam, carcass, and yearling child. What are the effects of these words?
3. Satire usually provides hints of the true state of things as it proposes its own alternatives. How does Swift hint at the true state of things? Give examples.
4. How would you characterize the tone of this piece?
5. Reread the final paragraph. What is its purpose?

● THE ISSUES

1. Do you consider satire an effective way to call attention to social ills? Why or why not?

2. Which paragraphs reveal Swift's real suggestions for improving the economic condition of the Irish? How do these paragraphs fit into the general scheme of Swift's essay?

3. How persuasive do you consider this essay? Would a straightforward essay be more effective? Why or why not?

4. Is Swift's essay simply a literary masterpiece to be studied within its context, or does it have a message for us today?

5. What condition existing in our country today would make an excellent subject for the kind of satire used by Swift? What satirical proposal can you suggest?

● SUGGESTIONS FOR WRITING

1. Infer from "A Modest Proposal" the state of life in Ireland during Swift's time. Do some additional research online if needed and write an essay about the treatment of the poor in Swift's day. Make specific references to the article to justify your inferences and give proper credit for any other source you use.

2. Using your answer to question 5, under the Issues, write a satirical proposal for curing some aspect of today's society.

Image Gallery for Critical Thinking and Debate: Homelessness

Homelessness would seem to be a nondebatable issue. Everyone is against it, at least in principle. The spotlight of the debate does not focus on whether or not homelessness is terrible—everyone agrees that it is—but on its causes. The division of opinion is predictably political: Conservatives, as a whole, blame homelessness on lapses and addictions in the individual; liberals tend to blame economic causes.

Adding to the muddle is the blurry definition of homelessness. Is a person who lives in a government-funded shelter, such as a hotel that houses the poor through a system of voucher payments from the state, homeless? Or is the homeless person one with no permanent residence, who sleeps on the street, in a car, or in a bus station? Most government statistics count both groups among the homeless. Yet, government-funded housing, as some critics point out, may be drawing people who had been doubling up with family members into the ranks of the counted homeless. The result is that the more the government funds shelters for the homeless, the greater the homeless population seems to grow.

How many people are homeless in America? No one knows for sure. Homelessness advocates say there are three million. Other studies have put the figure at around 400,000. A recent study indicated that every night in the United States about 760,000 people experience homelessness. In its 2008 Report to Congress, the U.S. Department of Housing and Urban Development (HUD) indicated that on a single night 56 percent of homeless people were sheltered and 44 percent were unsheltered. Of the unsheltered homeless, a staggering 30 percent were persons in households with children. Thanks to HUD's ongoing efforts to address the special needs of the chronically homeless, the number of this subpopulation has declined since this report was issued. Despite such hopeful signs, the speculation is that nearly 1 percent of American families, even in a robust economy, will go through episodes of homelessness within a year. Most figures—whether high or low—are difficult to trust because they are always based on different methods of counting. Added to the roster of the uncountable are the so-called "invisible homeless," who have no residence of their own but live in makeshift arrangements with relatives.

What causes homelessness? Some argue that the people living on city streets are mentally ill. Others claim that unpredictable financial disasters or rigid rent control is to blame. Certainly, one can imagine a scenario where an individual, even a family, can fall on hard times that result in homelessness. Yet anyone who lives in a city also knows from plain observation that many dysfunctional, tormented souls haunt the streets. Why homelessness exists in such an affluent country as ours may be impossible to explain, but one thing is certain: It should not exist.

On the first page of our image gallery, you will recognize a tragic scene played out in most of our large cities—human beings huddled in blankets or inside cardboard boxes—spending the daylight hours with a cup or hat at their side, begging for cash to keep them from starving. The second page reveals another kind of homelessness— the kind that strikes unannounced and with monstrous vengeance—in the form of a natural disaster like Typhoon Haiyan that devastated the Philippines on November 8, 2013, and left entire communities homeless and hopeless. The last image portrays a third kind of homelessness—often observed in small towns, but rarely fully supported by the townspeople—that is, couples with pets or children sitting curbside, holding a sign soliciting money to keep the family afloat.

The student essay asks readers not to sit in judgment on those who are homeless, but instead to whisper a message of gratitude: "There but for the love of my family, go I!"

"To the Point" rounds out the issue.

Study the following three images dealing with homelessness. Then choose the image that most appeals to you. Answer the questions and do the writing assignment.

For readings, questions, and media on the issue of homelessness, visit the *MindTap for Readings for Writers*, 15e online.

Viviane Moos/CORBIS

Studying the Image

1. What title would you give this photo if it were to appear on a city poster?

2. What are some contrasts between the beggar and the passersby? How would you describe the expression on the face of the first woman passing by?

3. In what geographic areas are scenes like this one typical? What are the conditions that usually lead to such a scene?

4. What is the gender of the homeless beggar? Does knowing the gender affect your response to the image? If yes, in what ways? If no, why not?

Writing Assignment

Nearly all of us have either passed, or had casual encounters with, homeless people. Write an essay arguing for better facilities in which to house homeless people in order to keep them off the main thoroughfares of populated cities. Keep in mind that many of these homeless beggars are mentally ill or addicted to drugs.

Erik De Castro/REUTERS

Studying the Image

1. As you study the image of a Japanese woman standing in front of a collapsed house, what strikes you as the worst aspect of this catastrophe?

2. What do you think is going through the victim's mind? What is she thinking as she stares stoically at her surroundings? Describe her desolation in your own words.

3. What is your definition of nature and the power it exerts? Is this force obeying orders from a higher being, or is it simply an indifferent reaction to meteorological convergences?

4. What steps need to be taken to rebuild the destroyed area? Who must take on the responsibility of restoring the houses, the streets, and the general order of affected neighborhoods? How long will the restoration take?

Writing Assignment

Write an essay about what you think citizens in areas where typhoons, tornadoes, earthquakes, or other destructive forces of nature are common can do to protect themselves from instant calamity. Choose one particular force and give specific instructions to the citizens within its sphere.

Tony Freeman/PhotoEdit

Studying the Image

1. How can a sympathetic bystander tell whether this family is really in financial distress or simply trying to make some easy money?

2. What economic and social problems could cause a family to become destitute and unable to cope?

3. How do you feel about the child in the photo? Why would some authorities interpret the boy's presence as a form of abuse?

4. Does the fact that the family isn't completely deprived of all material goods make you less sympathetic to them? What arguments can you give to urge someone to help this family? What arguments can you give to convince a reader that the family doesn't need help?

Writing Assignment

Write an essay in which you propose a way other than legislation bolstered by taxes to assure that no family in our country is forced to sit outdoors and beg for food in order to survive. Consider the backing of personal charities, churches, community clubs, and the like. If you do not believe in helping the poor, then explain your position.

Punctuation Workshop

Quotation Marks ("")

1. **Put quotation marks around the exact words of a speaker:**

   He said, "I'll buy the house."

2. **Begin every full quotation with a capital letter. If a quotation is broken, the second part does not begin with a capital letter unless it is a new sentence:**

   "You are an angel," Guido whispered, "and I want to marry you."

   "Some people feel," said the woman. "Others think."

   Set off with a comma the identification of the person who is speaking unless a question mark or exclamation mark is needed:

   "You need to learn how to use a computer," he told his grandfather.

   "Are you satisfied with your life?" she asked.

3. **When you are writing a dialogue, begin a new paragraph with each change of speaker:**

   "It never occurred to me that I might have a half-brother," he muttered.

   "Why not? It seemed so obvious to us," she said.

   If a speaker takes up more than one paragraph, put quotation marks at the beginning of each new paragraph. Use one set of quotation marks at the end of the last paragraph.

Student Corner

People Out on a Limb
Antoinette Poodt
Furman University

Homelessness is an epidemic in our country, but just how many people are homeless is unclear. One estimate says that 600,000 people are chronically homeless and another 700,000 sometimes homeless. A large number of the homeless are blacks and some 40 percent are veterans. The homeless are not lazy as some people think. Ninety percent of them once held jobs, and 15 to 20 percent of them are currently employed but unable to afford a home. In another chilling statistic, it was found that 40 percent of the homeless are entire families ("Ending Homelessness").

So what is the cause of homelessness? Some of the explanations suggest it is economic, and some suggest it is individual circumstances. But one cause of homelessness is almost certainly deinstitutionalization, or the releasing of patients from mental hospitals. In the early '70s, with the emergence of psychoactive drugs, deinstitutionalizing the homeless appeared to be a good way to save money and a way of giving freedom to people whose mental illnesses had trapped them in institutions such as asylums. Unfortunately, releasing the mentally ill into the streets and expecting them to function as responsible citizens turned out to be a pipe dream. Many of the mentally ill had developed "institutionalism," which means they had become used to living a life that had been over-regulated (Lamb). In a nutshell, people who were released on the streets were incapable of taking care of themselves.

As a society, many of us are unsure what we think about the homeless. The typical reaction is either one of pity or of condemnation. Yet, if we live in an urban area, the likelihood is great that our lives will intersect with the homeless people who hang out around our neighborhood. For the past year, for example, an elderly woman who was obviously mentally ill had been sleeping in a public garage near where I park. Some of my coworkers were so familiar with her that they would greet her by name. Some brought her food; some gave her money. When I worked late, I often saw her curled up asleep on pieces of cardboard laid out on the floor. One morning she was found dead in the same spot where she had always slept.

The attitude of my town towards the homeless is mixed. Because many of the homeless are dirty and smell from living outdoors, and because many of them are aggressive panhandlers, the city council often instructs the police to jail the homeless for vagrancy and keep them out of sight of the tourists. The police, themselves, are inconsistent in their treatment of the homeless. For example, there's a post office near work with two rooms filled with only post boxes. A homeless man sleeps in one of the rooms when the weather is bad. An older police officer cruising past will often turn a blind eye, but will make certain that the man is gone before daybreak. On the other hand, when the older police officer is off duty, other police officers drive the homeless man away from this make-shift shelter.

Not so long ago Americans had extended families who acted as a safety net against homelessness. If a family member fell on bad times, the unfortunate one would be welcomed into the home of an aunt or uncle or cousin and given shelter until he or she got on his or her feet. That sense of obligation to the extended family is rarely practiced any-more. Today's family generally consists of mom, pop, and children. We do not always feel a sense of obligation or responsibility for anyone else in the family. This shift has made the government a last resort. But govern-ment benefits have taken more cuts in the past three years than in the past twenty-five years. Rent has also risen substantially in the past few years, making the issue hit closer to home than many ever imagined. As a college student, who is earning below the poverty line, who cannot afford housing on her own, and who receives little or no government benefits, I can empathize with the homeless. When it comes right down to it, the only difference between me and a homeless person is that I have a family who cares.

It is easy for me to sit in judgment when I see a "bum" on the side of the street and think to myself that he should get a job, because I am not

Poodt 3

in his position. Usually as I walk past this helpless-looking unkempt creature, whose possessions are bundled in crude wrapping, I mutter to myself, "There, but for the grace of God, go I." And I sometimes even add a
more secular thanksgiving, "There, but for the love of my family, go I."

Works Cited

"Ending Homelessness in America." *Mental Health Association*. Mental
Health Assn., 2005. Web. 22 June 2005.

Lamb, H. Richard. "Deinstitutionalization and the Homeless Mentally Ill."
Interactivist. N.p., June 2005. Web. 22 June 2005.

How I Write

Writing has always been a challenge for me, and it is usually very difficult for me
to get started. Once I get the introduction down, however, the rest of the paper
usually flows. Before I begin writing, I gather information about my topic, which
I get from the Internet or the library. Then I go to my computer and begin typing.
I cannot write in pen or pencil, and then type a paper. Instead, I type as I write.
This is easier for me because it is simple to make corrections as I go along.
When writing a paper or essay, I usually begin with a story, quote, or statement
that will grab the reader's attention. Then, taking into account the audience and
depending on the type of writing I am to do, I follow with an outline covering
specific points. If the paper is a story about me, or something I am very familiar
with, I do not follow an outline.

   After I write the first draft, I begin with a spell check followed by a computer
grammar check. Then I print out the paper and do at least three to five revisions.
Once I think the paper is good, I give it to someone else to read. I feel that I do
much better on a paper when I spend a few days revising it instead of writing,
revising, and turning it in all in one day. When I leave a paper for a while, and
then go back to look at it, I see new things that I can do to improve it. Once
I have made all the revisions, I read it over one more time and then turn it in.

My Writing Tip

One word of wisdom I can give to fellow writers is to learn to type on a computer as they write. Being a college student, I do not know where I would find the time if I had to write, say, in pen or pencil, and then type. Corrections are so much quicker and easier to make when you can see them on the computer screen. It saves so much time, leading to less stress and hence better writing.

Another tip I would give is not to follow a cookie-cutter style of writing. Find your style, become comfortable with it, and use it whenever you write. Do not let one teacher discourage your writing ability because he or she doesn't like your style. We all have our own style. Write in your own style and your paper will turn out better than if you try to write like everyone else. In other words, trust your own personality.

To the Point

You have loyally followed the famous singer, Beyoncé Knowles, on Twitter, but recently you have become disillusioned with what you perceive as her indifference to social ills, especially homelessness. Send her a tweet expressing your view that celebrities must lead in the effort to help the poorest of the poor, who are forced to sleep in the streets.

▦ Chapter Writing Assignments

1. Write an essay arguing the point that religion is a conditioned reflex.
2. Write an argument opposing or supporting a recent legislative action imposed by our government.
3. Write an argument pointing out the benefits or the dangers of our political parties becoming more and more polarized.
4. Should a belief in intelligent creation be taught along with Darwin's theory of evolution? Write an argument answering this question.
5. Write an essay suggesting ways of achieving sexual equality.

▦ Term Paper Suggestions

Investigate the major arguments related to any one of the following subjects:

a. The influence of the church in our country today
b. Animal experimentation

    c. Better care for the poor

    d. Increased emphasis on physical fitness

    e. Careful monitoring of the ecosystems on our planet

    f. Equal rights for women (or some other population group)

    g. Maintaining ethnic identities in a pluralistic environment

    h. Improved local and federal response to natural disasters

    i. The need for a national health program that provides funding for long-term health care

Writing Assignments for a Specific Audience

1. Write an essay arguing for a campus completely free of smoking. Your audience consists of the readers of your college paper. State your proposition clearly and support it with convincing evidence about the hazards of second-hand smoke.

2. Write an essay in which you argue that movies often portray minorities inaccurately or offensively. Be specific with your facts and examples.

 Pointer from a Pro

READ WELL, WRITE WELL

Back in the '20s there was no rivalry between people who watched movies and those who read. Technology was an art form. We watched movies, but we also read. No one supervised our reading. We were on our own. We civilized ourselves. We found or made a mental and imaginative life. Because we could read, we learned also to write. From watching Charlie Chaplin in The Gold Rush *to reading Jack London's stories was a short step. If the woods were filled with readers gone astray, among those readers there were probably writers as well.*

—Saul Bellow

The parallel today is our present world of technology. If you can watch TV, your computer, your iPad, or any other modern electronic device and then segue from there to a book or an article, you can probably become part of the minority of "highbrows" who write well, for research continues to draw a close connection between people who read and people who write.

CHAPTER 17

Combining the Modes

▌ Road Map to the Modes

What Combining the Modes Does

The rhetorical modes are an idealization. In the rough-and-tumble writing of the everyday world, they exist only in hit-or-miss practice. It is possible to find a paragraph or even an entire essay that is written strictly in one mode; it is far more typical to find essays that blend the modes rather than observe them faithfully. Writing, a creative art, is nothing if not unpredictable.

Here are two examples that illustrate what we mean. The first is a paragraph that we would say was developed by *illustration*. It opens with the traditional topic sentence (**bolded**), which it then supports with a series of examples.

> **Considerations of what makes for good English or bad English are to an uncomfortably large extent matters of prejudice and conditioning.** Until the eighteenth century it was correct to say "you was" if you were referring to one person. It sounds odd today, but the logic is impeccable. *Was* is a singular verb and *were* a plural one. Why should *you* take a plural verb when the sense is clearly singular? The answer—surprise, surprise—is that Robert Lowth[1] didn't like it. "I'm hurrying, are I not?" is hopelessly ungrammatical, but "I'm hurrying, aren't I?"—merely a contraction of the same words—is perfect English. *Many* is almost always a plural (as in "Many people were there"), but not when it is followed by *a*, as in "Many a man was there." There's no inherent reason why these things should be so. They are not defensible in terms of grammar. They are because they are.
>
> —Bill Bryson, *The Mother Tongue: English and How It Got That Way*

---

[1] An amateur grammarian whose influential book, *A Short Introduction to English Grammar* (1762), enshrined many of the stupid rules of English usage still observed today.

Here, however, is an example of a mixed-mode paragraph that is even more typical of everyday writing:

causal
analysis
illustration

    English grammar is so complex and confusing for the one very simple reason that its rules and terminology are based on Latin—a language with which it has precious little in common. In Latin, to take one example, it is not possible to split an infinitive. So in English, the early authorities decided, it should not be possible to split an infinitive either. But there is no reason why we shouldn't, any more than we should forsake instant coffee and air travel because they weren't available to the Romans. Making

comparison
argument

English grammar conform to Latin rules is like asking people to play baseball using the rules of football. It is a patent absurdity. But once this insane notion became established grammarians found themselves having to draw up ever more complicated and circular arguments to accommodate the inconsistencies. As Burchfield notes in *The English Language,* one authority, F. Th. Visser, found it necessary to devote 200 pages to discussing just one aspect of the present participle. That is as crazy as it is amazing.

—Bill Bryson, *The Mother Tongue: English and How It Got That Way*

The writer begins with a causal analysis, gives an illustration, makes a comparison, and then develops an argument.

This is exactly how writers actually write. They treat the rhetorical modes the way a baker might treat a cookie cutter. The object is to produce cookies, not exalt the cutter. It is the same with the rhetorical modes—they exist to make writing easier for beginners. When you're no longer a beginner, you will discard them.

When to Combine the Modes

Combining modes is a tactic many writers follow, especially for long and complex subjects. You should use a combination of modes only when you feel comfortable with it and when your subject is a particularly demanding one that requires a complex form. If you're ranging far afield on an unfamiliar topic, you may not wish to follow any strict pattern and might prefer to improvise as you go along. This is the ideal time to combine the rhetorical modes.

How to Use Combined Modes

The key in writing a mixed-mode essay is to stick to the point and use ample transitions. Essays that are written in a combination of modes have a tendency to either drift from the point or to be herky-jerky rather than smooth. Writers overcome these tendencies by using the techniques of paragraph writing covered in Chapter 7 (now would be a good time to review this material). If you use transitions to guide the reader from one point to the next and if you faithfully stick to your announced topic, your mixed-mode essays will read as smoothly as anything you've ever written in any single pattern. Here is an example of a mixed-mode paragraph that sticks to the point. The writer is discussing the implements that the Arawak Indians, who lived in Jamaica at the time of Columbus, used in their daily lives. He begins with a description, moves to a process, and ends with a definition. He is able to do all of these things without losing the reader because his focus is so tight and his transitions skillful.

> Apart from earthen pots and other utensils, the main items of furniture were hammocks and wooden stools. The hammock was an Indian invention (even the original name, which was *hamac*), one which was not known in Europe before the discovery of the West Indies. These hammocks were made either of cotton string "open-work," or of a length of woven cotton cloth, sometimes dyed in bright colours. Jamaica was well known at that period for the cultivation of cotton, and much of the women's time was spent spinning and weaving it. In fact Jamaica supplied hammocks and cotton cloth to Cuba and Haiti for some time after those islands had been occupied by Spain, and the Spaniards themselves had sail-cloth made in Jamaica. Because of this, one of the many suggested origins of the name *Jamaica* attempts to link it with the Indian word for hammock and to prove that it means "land of cotton." The name Jamaica is of great interest. Some of the early Spanish historians, substituting X for J as they often did, write the name *Xaymaca,* but it also appears in its present form in a work published as early as 1511. Columbus called the island *St. Jago* (Santiago), but as with the other islands of the Greater Antilles, the Indian name has survived the Spanish. It is commonly thought that Xaymaca in the Arawak language meant "land of springs," but since the discoverers do not give the meaning of the name (as they do in the case of various place-names in Haiti) it is possible that the meaning had already been forgotten by the Indians themselves.
>
> —Clinton V. Black, *The Story of Jamaica*

Notice the repetition of the word *hammocks,* the variant forms of *Jamaica,* and the writer's use of the transitional sentence "The name Jamaica is of great interest." These little transitional touches are designed to nudge the reader along the writer's line of thought.

To sum up, if you do not now do it, eventually you will find yourself commonly writing essays that conform more to the mixed-mode pattern than to any other. The rhetorical modes are useful tools for the beginning writer, but less so for the veteran. As you make your way through school, you, too, will become a practiced writer who has outgrown them.

Examples

Shrew—The Littlest Mammal

ALAN DEVOE

Rhetorical Thumbnail

Purpose: to inform us about the life habits of the littlest mammal

Audience: educated readers

Language: academic English

Strategy: Covers The Life Cycle Of The Shrew From Birth To Death

---

Alan DeVoe (1909–1955) wrote many naturalist essays that were much admired by his readers. He also contributed widely to numerous magazines, among them the *American Mercury, Audubon,* and *Readers' Digest.* Additionally, he was the author of numerous books, including *Phudd Hill* (1937), *Down to Earth* (1940), and *This Fascinating Animal World* (1951).

DeVoe's description of the tiniest mammal, the shrew, tells us how this frenzied little beast got its reputation for ferocity. The shrew, having features similar to those of a mouse, is so rabid about pursuing its one mission in life—to eat—that it will attack animals twice its size. DeVoe uses paragraphs of different modes to portray the life cycle of this tiny creature whose nature is driven by a giant appetite.

• • •

1 "The zoological Class to which we human beings belong is the Mammalia. There has been some dispute as to whether we possess immortal souls and the capacity for a unique kind of intellection, but we do possess unquestionably the ". . . four-chambered heart, double circulatory system, thoracic cavity separated from abdominal cavity by muscular diaphragm, and habit of bearing the young alive and nursing them at the breast" which classically establish our membership in that group of warm-blooded animals which are guessed to have come into being on the planet some hundred-odd million years ago.

2   It is today a large and various group, this mammalian kindred. With some of our fellow-mammals it is not hard to feel relationship: with apes, for instance, or with the small sad-eyed monkeys that we keep for our **beguilement** as flea-bitten captives in our pet shops. But with others of the group our tie is less apparent; and the reason, often enough, is **disparity** of size and shape. It is such disparity, no doubt, that prevents our having much fellow-feeling for the hundred-ton sulphur-bottomed whales that plunge through the deep waters of both Pacific and Atlantic, though whales' blood is warmed as ours is, and the females of their kind have

milky teats; and likewise it is doubtless in part because we have two legs and attain to some seventy inches of height that we do not take as much account as otherwise we might of the little animal that is at the opposite end of the mammal size-scale: the little four-footed mammal that is rather smaller than a milkweed pod and not as heavy as a cecropia cocoon.

3   This tiniest of mammals is the minute beast called a shrew. A man need go to no great trouble to look at it, as he must to see a whale; he can find it now in the nearest country woodlot. Despite its tininess a shrew is still after a fashion a relative of ours; and on that account, even if on no other, should merit a little knowing.

4   In the narrow twisting earth-burrow dug by a mouse or a mole the least of the mammals is usually born. Its fellows in the litter may number four or five, and they lie together in the warm subterranean darkness of their tiny nest chamber in a little group whose whole bulk is scarcely that of a walnut. The infant shrew, relative of whales and elephants and us, is no more than a squirming pink speck of warm-fleshed animal aliveness. Totally defenseless and unequipped for life, it can only nuzzle the tiny dugs of its mother, wriggle tightly against its brothers to feel the warmth of the litter, and for many hours of the twenty-four lie asleep in the curled head-to-toes position of a **minuscule** foetus.

5   The baby shrew remains a long time in the birth-chamber. The size of even an adult shrew is very nearly the smallest possible for mammalian existence, and the young one cannot venture out into the world of adult activity until it has almost completely matured. Until then, therefore, it stays in the warm darkness of the burrow, knowing the universe only as a heat of other little bodies, a pungence of roots and grasses, a periodic sound of tiny chittering squeakings when its mother enters the burrow after foraging-trips, bringing food. She brings in mostly insects—small lady-beetles whose brittle spotted wing-covers must be removed before they can be eaten, soft-bodied caterpillars, ants, and worms. The young shrew, after its weaning has come about, acquires the way of taking this new food between its slim delicate forepaws, fingered like little hands, and in the under-earth darkness nibbles away the wing-covers and **chitinous** body-shells as **adroitly** as a squirrel removes the husk from a nut.

6   When at last the time comes for the young shrew to leave its birthplace, it has grown very nearly as large as its mother and has developed all the adult shrew-endowments. It looks, now, not unlike a mouse, save that its muzzle is more sharply pointed, but a mouse reduced in size to extreme miniature. The whole length of its soft-furred little body is only a fraction more than two inches, compared to the four-inch length of even the smallest of the whitefooted woods-mice; its tail is less than half as long as a mouse's. The uniquely little body is covered with dense soft hair, sepia above and a paler buffy color underneath—a covering of fur so fine and close that the shrew's ears are nearly invisible in it, and the **infinitesimal** eyes are scarcely to be **discerned**. The shrew's hands and feet are white, smaller and more delicate than any other beast's; white also is the underside of the minute furry tail. The whole body, by its softness of coat and coloring and its tininess of bulk, seems far from kinship with the tough strong bodies of the greater mammals. But it is blood-brother to these, all the same; warm

blood courses in it; the shrew is as much mammal as a wolf. It sets forth, with its unparalleledly tiny physical equipments, to live as adventurous a life as any of its greater warm-blooded relatives.

7   The life-adventure of Man, "the medium-sized mammal," is shaped by such **diverse** motives and **impulsions** that it is difficult to say what may be the most powerful of the driving urges that direct it. In the life-adventure of the littlest mammal, the shrew, the driving urge is very plain and single: it is hunger. Like hummingbirds, smallest of the aves, this smallest of the mammals lives at a tremendous pitch of nervous intensity. The shrew's little body quite literally quivers with the vibrance of life-force that is in it; from tiny pointed snout to tailtip the shrew is ever in a taut furor of aliveness. Its body-surface, like a hummingbird's, is maximally **extensive** in relation to its minimal weight; its metabolism must proceed with immense rapidity; to sustain the quivering nervous aliveness of its mite of warm flesh it must **contrive** a food-intake that is almost constant. It is possible on that account to tell the shrew's life-story almost wholly in terms of its feeding. The shrew's life has other ingredients, of course—the seeking of its small mate, the various rituals of copulating and sleeping and dung-dropping and the rest, that are common to all mammal lives—but it is the process of feeding that is central and primary, and that is the distinguishing preoccupation of the littlest mammal all its days.

8   The shrew haunts mostly moist thick-growing places, the banks of streams and the undergrowth of damp woods, and it hunts particularly actively at night. Scuttling on its pattery little feet among the fallen leaves, scrabbling in the leaf-mould in a frenzy of tiny investigation, it looks ceaselessly for food. Not a rodent, like a mouse, but an insectivore, it seizes chiefly on such creatures as crickets, grasshoppers, moths, and ants, devouring each victim with nervous eagerness and at once rushing on with quivering haste, tiny muzzle incessantly a-twitch, to look for further **provender**.

9   Not infrequently the insects discoverable in the shrew's quick scampering little sallies through the darkness are inadequate to nourish it, so quick is its digestion and so intense the nervous energy it must sustain. When this is the case, the shrew widens its diet-range, to include seeds or berries or earthworms or any other sustenance that it can stuff with its little shivering forepaws into its tiny muzzle. It widens its diet to include meat; it becomes a furious and desperate carnivore. It patters through the grass-runways of the meadow-mice, sniffing and quivering; it darts to the nest of a deer-mouse. And presently, finding deer-mouse or meadowmouse, it plunges into a wild attack on this "prey" that is twice its size. The shrew fights with a kind of mad recklessness; it becomes a leaping, twisting, chittering, squeaking speck of hungering fury. Quite generally, when the battle is over, the shrew has won. Its thirty-two pinpoint teeth are sharp and strong, and the wild fury of its attack takes the victim by surprise. For a little while, after victory, the shrew's relentless body-needs are appeased. For a little while, but only a little; and then the furry speck must go pattering and scuttling forth into the night again, sniffing for food and quivering with need.

10   That is the pattern of shrew-life: a hunting and a hungering that never stops, an endless preoccupied catering to the demands of the kind of metabolism which

unique mammalian smallness necessitates. The littlest mammal is a mammal in all ways; it breathes and sleeps and mates and possibly **exults**, as others do; but chiefly, as the price of unique tininess, it engages in restless never-ending search for something to eat.

11   The way of a shrew's dying is sometimes curious. Sometimes, of course, it dies in battle, when the larger prey which it has tackled proves too strong. Sometimes it dies of starvation; it can starve in a matter of hours. But often it is set upon by one of the big predators—some fox or lynx or man. When that happens, it is usually not the clutch of fingers or the snap of the carnivorous jaws that kills the shrew. The shrew is usually dead before that. At the first instant of a lynx's pounce—at the first touch of a human hand against the shrew's tiny quivering body—the shrew is apt to shiver in a quick violent spasm, and then lie still in death. The littlest of the mammals dies, as often as not, of simple nervous shock.

From THIS FASCINATING ANIMAL WORLD, 1951

● THE FACTS

1. About which zoological fact is the author sure? About which element is he less sure? Why is he so much more sure about one than the other?
2. Where is the shrew usually born? What does this tell us about shrew parents?
3. In terms of its impulses, how does the shrew differ from its other mammal relatives? What causes this difference?
4. If the shrew can't find enough insects to feed its hunger, what will it do?
5. If insects and vegetation are not available, what will the shrew do to get the food it so badly needs to stay alive? What attitude does the shrew convey? How do you view this attitude?

● THE STRATEGIES

1. This essay reveals the use of more than one rhetorical mode. What modes other than description are used? Try to name these modes paragraph by paragraph.
2. What dominant impression of the shrew did you receive from this essay?
3. What is the purpose of the quotation in the opening paragraph? What, if anything, does it add to the essay?
4. Of what help is paragraph 10 as you learn about the shrew?
5. Why does the author sprinkle specialized terms throughout the essay (e.g., *cecropia, cocoon, chitinous body shells*)? How do these terms affect the author's style?

● THE ISSUES

1. The author declares a kinship among whales, monkeys, shrews, and humans. Of the nonhuman mammals, which do you feel closest to? Why? Of all animals, which one would you prefer to have as a pet? Why?
2. Do you agree with the author that because the shrew is related to us, we should know something about this mammal? Give reasons for your answer. What other reasons are there to encourage us to learn more about animals?

3. If a woman is called a "shrew," what is meant by the label? What connection can you see between this metaphor and the tiniest mammal?

4. Do you think that laboratory experiments on the mammalian shrew would be justified if the purpose were to benefit humans?

5. What is the largest mammal? Where have you seen this mammal other than in pictures? How do you react toward it?

● SUGGESTIONS FOR WRITING

1. Describe the most interesting animal you have ever observed. If needed, use more than one rhetorical mode for this assignment.

2. Choose one of the following creatures and write an essay describing in what ways it is superior to human beings: lion, tiger, cat, dog, eagle, snake, or ant.

Once More to the Lake

E. B. WHITE

Rhetorical Thumbnail

Purpose: on the face of it, to relate a traditional family holiday

Audience: educated readers

Language: standard English, written in an elegant style

Strategy: lulls the reader into a mood of quiet reminiscence—and then drops the bombshell

Elwyn Brooks White (1899–1985) was one of the wittiest and most admired observers of contemporary American society. As a member of *The New Yorker* magazine staff, he wrote a number of essays for the section called "Talk of the Town"; some of these essays have been collected in *The Wild Flag* (1946) and *Writings from* The New Yorker (1991). With James Thurber, White wrote *Is Sex Necessary?* (1929). His other well-known works include *One Man's Meat* (1942), *Here Is New York* (1949), and two beloved children's books, *Stuart Little* (1945) and *Charlotte's Web* (1952).

This essay ends with a bang, not a whimper. The writer tackles what might seem at first glance a humdrum subject—an annual vacation trip to a lake—and describes in evocative and lovely prose the carefree summer days he spent hiking and fishing with his son. Then, at the very end, the true meaning of the essay is revealed.

• • •

August 1941

1   One summer, along about 1904, my father rented a camp on a lake in Maine and took us all there for the month of August. We all got ringworm from some kittens and had to rub Pond's Extract on our arms and legs night and morning, and my father rolled over in a canoe with all his clothes on; but outside of that the vacation was a success and from then on none of us ever thought there was any place in the world like that lake in Maine. We returned summer after summer—always on August 1 for one month. I have since become a salt-water man, but sometimes in summer there are days when the restlessness of the tides and the fearful cold of the sea water and the **incessant** wind that blows across the afternoon and into the evening make me wish for the placidity of a lake in the woods. A few weeks ago this feeling got so strong I bought myself a couple of bass hooks and a spinner and returned to the lake where we used to go, for a week's fishing and to revisit old haunts.

2   I took along my son, who had never had any fresh water up his nose and who had seen lily pads only from train windows. On the journey over to the lake I began to wonder what it would be like. I wondered how time would have marred this unique, this holy spot—the coves and streams, the hills that the sun set behind, the camps and the paths behind the camps. I was sure that the tarred road would have found it out, and I wondered in what other ways it would be **desolated**. It is strange how much you can remember about places like that once you allow your mind to return into the grooves that lead back. You remember one thing, and that suddenly reminds you of another thing. I guess I remembered clearest of all the early mornings, when the lake was cool and motionless, remembered how the bedroom smelled of the lumber it was made of and of the wet woods whose scent entered through the screen. The partitions in the camp were thin and did not extend clear to the top of the rooms, and as I was always the first up I would dress softly so as not to wake the others, and sneak out into the sweet outdoors and start out in the canoe, keeping close along the shore in the long shadows of the pines. I remembered being very careful never to rub my paddle against the gunwale for fear of disturbing the stillness of the cathedral.

3   The lake had never been what you would call a wild lake. There were cottages sprinkled around the shores, and it was in farming country although the shores of the lake were quite heavily wooded. Some of the cottages were owned by nearby farmers, and you would live at the shore and eat your meals at the farmhouse. That's what our family did. But although it wasn't wild, it was a fairly large and undisturbed lake and there were places in it that, to a child at least, seemed infinitely remote and **primeval**.

4   I was right about the tar: it led to within half a mile of the shore. But when I got back there, with my boy, and we settled into a camp near a farmhouse and into the kind of summertime I had known, I could tell that it was going to be pretty much the same as it had been before—I knew it, lying in bed the first morning smelling the bedroom and hearing the boy sneak quietly out and go off along the shore in a boat. I began to sustain the illusion that he was I, and therefore, by simple **transposition**, that I was my father. This sensation persisted, kept cropping

up all the time we were there. It was not an entirely new feeling, but in this setting it grew much stronger. I seemed to be living a dual existence. I would be in the middle of some simple act, I would be picking up a bait box or laying down a table fork, or I would be saying something and suddenly it would be not I but my father who was saying the words or making the gesture. It gave me a creepy sensation.

5 We went fishing the first morning. I felt the same damp moss covering the worms in the bait can, and saw the dragonfly alight on the tip of my rod as it hovered a few inches from the surface of the water. It was the arrival of this fly that convinced me beyond any doubt that everything was as it always had been, that the years were a mirage and that there had been no years. The small waves were the same, chucking the rowboat under the chin as we fished at anchor, and the boat was the same boat, the same color green and the ribs broken in the same places, and under the floorboards the same fresh water leavings and débris—the dead helgramite, the wisps of moss, the rusty discarded fishhook, the dried blood from yesterday's catch. We stared silently at the tips of our rods, at the dragonflies that came and went. I lowered the tip of mine into the water, **tentatively**, **pensively** dislodging the fly, which darted two feet away, poised, darted two feet back, and came to rest again a little farther up the rod. There had been no years between the ducking of this dragonfly and the other one—the one that was part of memory. I looked at the boy, who was silently watching his fly, and it was my hands that held his rod, my eyes watching. I felt dizzy and didn't know which rod I was at the end of.

6 We caught two bass, hauling them in briskly as though they were mackerel, pulling them over the side of the boat in a businesslike manner without any landing net, and stunning them with a blow on the back of the head. When we got back for a swim before lunch, the lake was exactly where we had left it, the same number of inches from the dock, and there was only the merest suggestion of a breeze. This seemed an utterly enchanted sea, this lake you could leave to its own devices for a few hours and come back to, and find that it had not stirred, this constant and trustworthy body of water. In the shallows, the dark, water-soaked sticks and twigs, smooth and old, were **undulating** in clusters on the bottom against the clean ribbed sand, and the track of the mussel was plain. A school of minnows swam by, each minnow with its small individual shadow, doubling the attendance, so clear and sharp in the sunlight. Some of the other campers were in swimming, along the shore, one of them with a cake of soap, and the water felt thin and clear and **unsubstantial**. Over the years there had been this person with the cake of soap, this **cultist**, and here he was. There had been no years.

7 Up to the farmhouse to dinner through the teeming dusty field, the road under our sneakers was only a two-track road. The middle track was missing, the one with the marks of the hooves and the splotches of dried, flaky manure. There had always been three tracks to choose from in choosing which track to walk in; now the choice was narrowed down to two. For a moment I missed terribly the middle alternative. But the way led past the tennis court, and something about the way it lay there in the sun reassured me; the tape had loosened along the backline, the alleys were green with plantains and other weeds, and the net (installed in June and removed in September) sagged in the dry noon, and the whole place steamed with midday heat and hunger and emptiness. There was a choice of pie

for dessert, and one was blueberry and one was apple, and the waitresses were the same country girls, there having been no passage of time, only the illusion of it as in a dropped curtain—the waitresses were still fifteen; their hair had been washed, that was the only difference—they had been to the movies and seen the pretty girls with the clean hair.

8   Summertime, oh, summertime, pattern of life **indelible** with fade-proof lake, the wood unshatterable, the pasture with the sweetfern and the juniper forever and ever, summer without end; this was the background, and the life along the shore was the design, the cottages with their innocent and tranquil design, their tiny docks with the flagpole and the American flag floating against the white clouds in the blue sky, the little paths over the roots of the trees leading from camp to camp and the paths leading back to the outhouses and the can of lime for sprinkling, and at the souvenir counters at the store the miniature birch-bark canoes and the postcards that showed things looking a little better than they looked. This was the American family at play, escaping the city heat, wondering whether the newcomers in the camp at the head of the cove were "common" or "nice," wondering whether it was true that the people who drove up for Sunday dinner at the farmhouse were turned away because there wasn't enough chicken.

9   It seemed to me, as I kept remembering all this, that those times and those summers had been infinitely precious and worth saving. There had been jollity and peace and goodness. The arriving (at the beginning of August) had been so big a business in itself, at the railway station the farm wagon drawn up, the first smell of the pine-laden air, the first glimpse of the smiling farmer, and the great importance of the trunks and your father's enormous authority in such matters and the feel of the wagon under you for the long ten-mile haul, and at the top of the last long hill catching the first view of the lake after eleven months of not seeing this cherished body of water. The shouts and cries of the other campers when they saw you, and the trunks to be unpacked, to give up their rich burden. (Arriving was less exciting nowadays, when you sneaked up in your car and parked it under a tree near the camp and took out the bags and in five minutes it was all over, no fuss, no loud wonderful fuss about trunks.)

10   Peace and goodness and jollity. The only thing that was wrong now, really, was the sound of the place, an unfamiliar nervous sound of the outboard motors. This was the note that jarred, the one thing that would sometimes break the illusion and set the years moving. In those other summertimes all motors were inboard; and when they were at a little distance, the noise they made was a **sedative**, an ingredient of summer sleep. They were one-cylinder and two-cylinder engines, and some were make-and-break and some were jumpspark, but they all made a sleepy sound across the lake. The one-lungers throbbed and fluttered, and the twin-cylinder ones purred and purred, and that was a quiet sound, too. But now the campers all had outboards. In the daytime, in the hot mornings, these motors made a petulant, irritable sound; at night in the still evening when the afterglow lit the water, they whined about one's ears like mosquitoes. My boy loved our rented outboard, and his great desire was to achieve single-handed mastery over it, and authority, and he soon learned the trick of choking it a little (but not too much), and the adjustment of the needle valve. Watching him I would remember

the things you could do with the old one-cylinder engine with the heavy flywheel, how you could have it eating out of your hand if you got really close to it spiritually. Motorboats in those days didn't have clutches, and you would make a landing by shutting off the motor at the proper time and coasting in with a dead rudder. But there was a way of reversing them, if you learned the trick, by cutting the switch and putting it on again exactly on the final dying revolution of the flywheel, so that it would kick back against compression and begin reversing. Approaching a dock in a strong following breeze, it was difficult to slow up sufficiently by the ordinary coasting method, and if a boy felt he had complete mastery over his motor, he was tempted to keep it running beyond its time and then reverse it a few feet from the dock. It took a cool nerve, because if you threw the switch a twentieth of a second too soon you would catch the flywheel when it still had speed enough to go up past center, and the boat would leap ahead, charging bull-fashion at the dock.

11   We had a good week at the camp. The bass were biting well and the sun shone endlessly, day after day. We would be tired at night and lie down in the accumulated heat of the little bedrooms after the long hot day and the breeze would stir almost **imperceptibly** outside and the smell of the swamp drift in through the rusty screens. Sleep would come easily and in the morning the red squirrel would be on the roof, tapping out his gay routine. I kept remembering everything, lying in bed in the mornings—the small steamboat that had a long rounded stern like the lip of a Ubangi, and how quietly she ran on the moonlight sails, when the older boys played their mandolins and the girls sang and we ate doughnuts dipped in sugar, and how sweet the music was on the water in the shining night, and what it had felt like to think about girls then. After breakfast we would go up to the store and the things were in the same place—the minnows in a bottle, the plugs and spinners disarranged and pawed over by the youngsters from the boys' camp, the Fig Newtons and the Beeman's gum. Outside, the road was tarred and cars stood in front of the store. Inside, all was just as it had always been, except there was more Coca-Cola and not so much Moxie and root beer and birch beer and sarsaparilla. We would walk out with the bottle of pop apiece and sometimes the pop would backfire up our noses and hurt. We explored the streams, quietly, where the turtles slid off the sunny logs and dug their way into the soft bottom; and we lay on the town wharf and fed worms to the tame bass. Everywhere we went I had trouble making out which was I, the one walking at my side, the one walking in my pants.

12   One afternoon while we were at that lake a thunderstorm came up. It was like the revival of an old melodrama that I had seen long ago with childish awe. The second-act climax of the drama of the electrical disturbance over a lake in America had not changed in any important respect. This was the big scene, still the big scene. The whole thing was so familiar, the first feeling of oppression and heat and a general air around camp of not wanting to go very far away. In midafternoon (it was all the same) a curious darkening of the sky, and a lull in everything that had made life tick; and then the way the boats suddenly swung the other way at their moorings with the coming of a breeze out of the new quarter, and the **premonitory** rumble. Then the kettle drum, then the snare, then the bass

drum and cymbals, then crackling light against the dark, and the gods grinning and licking their chops in the hills. Afterward the calm, the rain steadily rustling in the calm lake, the return of light and hope and spirits, and the campers running out in joy and relief to go swimming in the rain, their bright cries perpetuating the deathless joke about how they were getting simply drenched, and the children screaming with delight at the new sensation of bathing in the rain, and the joke about getting drenched linking the generations in a strong indestructible chain. And the comedian who waded in carrying an umbrella.

13   When the others went swimming my son said he was going in, too. He pulled his dripping trunks from the line where they had hung all through the shower and wrung them out. Languidly, and with no thought of going in, I watched him, his hard little body, skinny and bare, saw him wince slightly as he pulled up around his vitals the small, soggy, icy garment. As he buckled the swollen belt, suddenly my groin felt the chill of death.

● THE FACTS

1. How old was White when he first went to the lake with his father? How old was he when he took his own son there?

2. What illusion did White begin to sustain on hearing his own son sneaking out to go down to the boat on the lake?

3. What changes did the author notice in the road leading from the lake to the farmhouse? What did these changes say about the passing of time?

4. What difference did the author note between the way guests arrived at the lake in his own boyhood days and their arrival now?

5. What experience precipitated White's realization that time had passed, that he was no longer young, that he was mortal?

● THE STRATEGIES

1. Aside from description, what other mode of development is implicitly part of the structure of this essay? What is the purpose of holding back the true meaning of the essay until the final paragraph?

2. In paragraph 2, White writes that he "was sure that the tarred road would have found it [the lake] out." What is odd about the phrasing of this sentence? What do you think White was trying to achieve in phrasing it that way?

3. Examine the author's boyhood recollections of the lake (paragraph 2). To which of our senses do his details and images appeal?

4. Examine the description of the fishing boat in paragraph 5. How does White manage to convey such a vivid picture of the boat?

5. In what part of his body did White feel the chill of death? In the context of the essay, why is this such an appropriate place?

● THE ISSUES

1. In paragraph 2, why does White refer to the lake as a "holy spot"? What is the connotation of this term, given that the place was not a religious shrine? What, in your life, would be a similar spot? Give reasons for your choice.

2. The author states that he missed the "middle track" of the road leading up to the farmhouse for dinner. Try to imagine yourself in a similar situation forty years hence. What vehicles of transportation, not yet commonly used, might invade your road then?

3. What is the social implication of the words *common* and *nice* in paragraph 8? Have times changed, or are these distinctions still made?

4. Not everyone would have reacted in the way the author describes his own reaction in the final sentence of the essay. What might be another realistic reaction?

5. What are some clear signs in your life to indicate that you are not immortal? What are your feelings about these signs?

● SUGGESTIONS FOR WRITING

1. Write a mixed-pattern essay about some aspect of life that troubles you. Feel free to describe, narrate, give examples, cite causes, or use any other rhetorical pattern that would support your main point.

2. Write an essay in any rhetorical pattern about which aspect of life gives you the most hope for a decent future. Consider such aspects as global security, cultural advances, personal relationships, and a purpose-driven life.

Image Gallery for Critical Thinking and Debate: The New Technology

Every era of human history is characterized by its own technology. Even primitive peoples with nothing but simple tools are capable of evolving a technology for coping with their environment. Take the example of the Arawak Indians, a Stone Age people who once inhabited Central America and the West Indies. They had no metal for making fishhooks, but they still came up with a unique way of fishing, using the remora or sucker fish, which uses its suckers to fasten itself to other fish and suck out their nutrients. The remora was kept hungry in captivity and taken to sea, where it was released with a string tied around its tail. As soon as it had fastened itself to another fish, the remora was pulled to the surface, the fish pried from its suckers, and the still-hungry hunter thrown overboard to seek more prey. One can imagine the shrieks of something like "Eureka!" the first time this technology was used successfully.

Technology today is a complex mesh of mathematics, engineering, computer chips, and old-fashioned ingenuity. For the most part, it feeds us and clothes us and allows us to live in relative comfort. But there is a penalty attached to many kinds of technology. The technology of atomic power, for example, while generating electricity for millions, leaves behind radioactive waste that will continue to be deadly to life for hundreds, even thousands, of years. The stuff keeps piling up, usually in secluded caves until one day we shall run out of room—then what will we do? Who can forget the horrendous accident at the Chernobyl nuclear plant in Russia on April 26, 1986, which came within a hairsbreadth of core meltdown and required the evacuation of over 60,000 people, many of whom had to permanently abandon their homes? And what of the frightening explosions in various plants at Yamuguchi Daiichi, Japan, when several nuclear plants exploded after a 9.9 earthquake (followed by a demonic tsunami) hit Japan on March 18, 2011? It took months to calculate the range of damage that might occur globally.

The invention of the internal combustion engine equipped humankind with the splendid vehicles we see today on the roads. But we have paid a heavy price in air pollution and motor vehicle accident mortality. Even with 100,000 horses passing in and out of the cramped roads of nineteenth-century London, depositing tons of manure on the streets daily, the environment was still cleaner than it is today.

The speed at which new technology increases is downright bewildering. We are warned that by the time students seeking a degree in electronics finish their first two years of college, half of the information they acquired will already be outdated. According to a Sony video produced in 2011, more than a trillion Internet devices existed at that time, with the number growing exponentially. To contemplate the future is inconceivable. Here are some further statistics provided by Sony:

70 million people use MySpace every month.

1 out of every 8 married couples met online.

174 million users visit Facebook every day.

YouTube is the most popular website for video watching in the world.

The total number of text messages sent daily exceeds the number of people on our planet. To contemplate the future is inconceivable.

Young people exult in the new technology whereas old people shake their heads, wondering if this mad rush to acquire the latest gadget is not a sign of cultural decline as they observe reading skills and interaction with people being corroded.

The technology of communication has evolved in a special way. Some people call it social networking; others call it the Apps, short for applications. Whatever the label used, the reference is to computer software that can run on the Internet, computer, cell phone, or other computer device. We recognize this software by names like Facebook, MySpace, Twitter, iPhone, iPad, Kindle, YouTube, GPS, and many other descriptive brands.

Over the centuries, technology has had its enemies, who insist that its price is too high. Probably the best example from history is the movement of the Luddites from 1811 to 1816. The Luddites were artisans who objected to the technological improvements in the English textile industry because they thought their way of life was threatened by the new super-efficient looms. Mobs of them roamed the English countryside destroying textile manufacturing facilities and machinery. The movement was violently suppressed by 12,000 troops sent by Parliament, its ringleaders captured and either hanged or deported to Australia. Still, even today the Luddite spirit lingers in our attitude toward new technology. With the evidence before our own eyes, these misgivings are understandable.

To encourage students to view the current age of new technology with an objective critical eye, we present three of the most influential applications in vogue. Our first page shows an adoring crowd of fans training their iPhones and other photographic lenses on the Duke and Duchess of Cambridge on July 23 of 2013, as they stand in front of London's St. Mary's Hospital, where the royal parents present the newly born Prince George to the public. The scene reminds us that smart phones have revolutionized the way ordinary people record their lives in photographs. The second image captures President Barack Obama holding a Townhall video on his Facebook page. Never before have U.S. presidents been able to interact more closely with the voters who put them in office than is possible today. The last image is a cartoon showing the smug look on a woman's face as she announces that she has found the ultimate revenge for a man who riled her—placing him at the mercy of those unrelenting telemarketers that bother people day and night.

The student essay was written by a Harvard student who praises the Internet for its limitless capacity to help him find obscure information in the blink of an eye.

"To the Point" rounds out the issue.

Study the following three images dealing with new technology. Then choose the image that most appeals to you. Answer the questions and do the writing assignment.

For readings, questions, and media on the issue of new technology, visit the *MindTap for Readings for Writers*, 15e online.

Michael Tubi/Demotix/Corbis

Studying the Image

1. What difference exists in the public's ability to capture the news today compared with fifty years ago? Consider what kind of photography was used at your last family gathering and ask your parents or grandparents to remember what photography was used at family gatherings when they were young.

2. Kate and William, the Duke and Duchess of Cambridge, are popular high-profile celebrities. Judging from the preceding photo, what is part of their attraction? Why do you think they fascinate both the British public and people around the world?

3. What do you think would happen to the British Throne if the king or queen of England were to behave with the same ostentation that did the first Queen Elizabeth and other royal descendants? Why have most countries revolted against royalty?

4. What role, if any, has the new technology played in reining in dictatorships and totalitarian regimes?

Writing Assignment

Write an essay either praising or criticizing smartphones, tablets, and laptops. If you believe they have both advantages and disadvantages, then balance the good against the bad. Begin your essay with a clear thesis.

ICP-Tech/incamerastock/Alamy

Studying the Image

1. Most Facebook participants place an action photo of themselves (which they change often for variety) on their home pages, but Barack Obama's White House page shows the President in a dignified portrait. How would a snapshot of the President playing golf or basketball affect his image as President? Would it be more or less effective than a serious portrait?

2. If you could be a Facebook friend to anyone you choose, whom would you select? Why?

3. What problem does befriending huge numbers of people on Facebook present? What happens when a person becomes addicted to Facebook? How can you avoid being overpowered by Facebook?

4. How can social networking be used to improve world conditions? Cite one specific possibility.

Writing Assignment

After researching the subject, write an essay on how social networking became part of the Arab Spring Revolution in Egypt (2011). If you use outside sources to support your essay, be sure to document them.

William Haefeli/The New Yorker Collection/The Cartoon Bank

"I sold his unlisted phone number to telemarketers."

Studying the Image

1. What ironic humor is involved in this cartoon? What is the meaning of the speaker's confession? Explain it as you imagine it to be. In brief, what do you think caused the speaker to pull this trick on "him"?

2. What importance does the technology of telemarketing bring to the satire of this cartoon?

3. What is your personal reaction to today's aggressive telemarketing to raise funds or to sell products? How do you think most people react to this strategy? How can it be controlled so as not to antagonize people who feel that telemarketing invades their privacy?

4. Under which circumstances would you consider telemarketing a useful and appropriate tool?

Writing Assignment

Write a letter of complaint to some imaginary company that has bothered you with repeated automated phone calls, asking for money in support of their cause. Try to keep the tone of your letter civil, yet firm.

Stumped by monotonous sentences? Exit on page 432 at the **Editing Booth!**

Punctuation Workshop

Using Other Punctuation with Quotation Marks

1. **Periods and commas go inside quotations marks; semicolons and colons go outside.**

   "Gilberto," she insisted, "let's do some rope climbing."

   He lectured on "Terrorism in Spain"; I immediately thought of the story "Flight 66": It seemed to follow the lecturer's claims.

2. **Question marks, exclamation points, or dashes that apply only to the quoted material go inside the quotation marks. Otherwise, they go outside:**

   INSIDE: The Senator asked, "Who will pay for it?"

   OUTSIDE: Which of the senators asked, "Who will pay for it"? (Do not use double quotation marks for questions within questions.)

   INSIDE: The crowd shouted, "No more lies!"

   OUTSIDE: Stop playing Bob Marley's "Crazy Baldhead"!

   INSIDE: "Materialism—the greed for things—" insists my father, "is bad."

   OUTSIDE: The article said, "You may be at risk for cancer"— something to think about.

3. **Put quotation marks around titles of small works, such as stories, essays, newspaper or magazine articles, poems, songs, and book chapters.**

   "Design" (poem by Robert Frost)

   "The Annihilation of Fish" is a short story that became a cult movie.

   "My Brown-eyed Girl" was a big hit for Van Morrison.

   "The Rainbow Coalition" (Chapter 20) discusses blended families.

4. **Either quotation marks or italics can be used in definitions:**

   The word "aquiline" means "related to eagles."

   or

   The word *aquiline* means related to *eagles*.

Student Corner

Thoughts about the Internet

Charlie Sorensen

Harvard University

I'm worried I waste too much time. Like many of you reading this, I'm a student. I'm a college freshman to be precise, and I've had my share of trouble managing on my own for the very first time. The intensity of the pressure to do well at school is insane. Unless I'm spending every waking second buried in a textbook or writing an essay, I feel like a lackluster student. I feel like I'm doing something wrong. Or bad. I can tell myself that this is an unreasonable way to think. And I know that it is. But I can't shake the feeling.

Virtually every student I know suffers the same feeling. In a way, we feel torn. On the one hand, we never work as much or as hard as we are telling ourselves we should; yet, on the other hand, we crave time without obligation—"free time" to ourselves. I'm a part of this ambivalent crowd, and as such, I am particularly susceptible to the seduction of the Internet. I'm going to go ahead and say that I waste 80% of my time on the Internet.

A lot has been said about the distracted nature of my generation. And while I won't disagree that many of us, myself included, have issues holding our concentration from time to time, I don't think exploring the Internet should be considered a social problem. The Internet is an incredible tool with an enormous capacity to help one learn. It's been a great benefit in my life. In other words, the pros outweigh the cons.

Just think about everything that we can do now that just a generation ago was science fiction. As a student, the Internet is my number one resource tool. Sure, I'm distracted from time to time, but I can't imagine being a student twenty years ago. How slow must it have been doing research in those days! When I use the Internet, a search query can turn up hundreds of results from authentic sources on any topic imaginable. For example, this semester I'm taking a course on Albert Einstein and twentieth-century physics, a topic about which I know next to nothing. In my readings I came across references to a group known as the "Vienna Circle." A quick search on Google, and in only a couple of minutes I have sources to tell me who these philosophers like Moritz Schlick were, and why they are important. The Internet is also the best tool I have for staying in touch with all the friends and family who make it easier for me to be away from home and face a brave new world. E-mail and social networking Web sites help me maintain friendships that I'm afraid I might otherwise lose.

When I mull over the role of the Internet, it's hard not to be in awe of the volumes of information available to anyone with a computer and an Internet connection. The entire world opens up to you. I can share my experiences with someone on the other side of the globe, and get a glimpse into a life I never otherwise would see. I work hard in the classroom, of course. There's nothing more valuable than a good education that includes stimulating lectures or rousing classroom discussions. But I value what I learn everyday searching through the Web just as much as what I learn in a classroom. The Internet is the home to the world's most astonishing communities, and if you know where to look, you can learn more online than anywhere else. If there is such a thing as "Internet addiction," then maybe I'm an addict. The Internet is rounding out the best education I could hope to get.

How I Write

It always helps to create an outline first—even if it's the roughest of sketches, as mine usually is. I used to be a writer who sat down and wrote without sketch or design. My first instinct is still to sit down and write the first thoughts that come to mind. But I've learned that taking a couple of minutes to organize ideas and get the focus of my essay down on paper improves my essay.

My Writing Tip

The most difficult part of writing, in my experience, is getting that first sentence down. The best lesson I ever learned was how important it is to simply start. Get it down on paper. Write, write, and write! After I get that first draft down, then the essay writing really begins. Until then, the most important thing to do is place your ideas down on paper. Once you've done that, it is much easier to rewrite your sentences and reform your essay into the one you want.

 To the Point

You believe that smartphones are saving humanity by helping out during roadside emergencies, communicating important messages instantly, allowing immediate Google searches, and connecting people all over the world. You have a Twitter account, so you decide to mount a tweet attack on the "flat-earth cranks" who dare to imply that young people are becoming dangerously addicted to their cell phones. Remember to formulate your tweet in 140 characters or less.

▧ Chapter Writing Assignments

1. Write an essay about your favorite Internet site.
2. Write an imaginative essay that predicts and describes useful gadgets yet to be invented.
3. Who is your favorite actor for playing the "heavy" or a villain in movies? Write an essay that vividly describes the skills that make this actor dominate the screen as an ill-famed scoundrel.
4. Write an essay about the job you would least like to have. Make this job unappealing to your reader.
5. Write an essay in which you argue that the latest new technology has opened the door into an entirely new world that would seem like outer space to our ancestors.
6. Write an essay about your favorite board game, emphasizing the lure or excitement of this particular pastime.

▧ Writing Assignments for a Specific Audience

1. Write to the Internal Revenue Service, outlining your expenses for a semester of school. Make these expenses seem indispensable and therefore nontaxable.
2. Explain baseball to a foreigner who has never heard of the game.

Pointer from a Pro

AVOID NOUN CLUSTERS (NOUN+NOUN+NOUN)

Never use a series of nouns to modify another noun. If you do, your writing will fade into deadly haziness. Note these examples that should make any reader cringe:

Medication maintenance level evaluation procedures

Automobile tire durability guidelines

Training needs assessment review

—Joseph P. Williams

PART THREE

Rewriting Your Writing
The Editing Booth

Inside the Editing Booth, you will find information on the following topics:

Revising
Editing

Revising is part of writing. Few writers are so expert that they can produce what they are after on the first try.

—William Strunk, Jr., and E. B. White

Rewriting is a necessary part of the composing process. That a writer's best comes gushing out spontaneously at the first and only sitting is true only in some rare instances. Most of the time, it must be coaxed out of the pen, drop by drop (or from the computer, keystroke by keystroke), by labored rereading and rewriting. Rewriting means reviewing what you have written and making changes to your text. These steps may be broadly classified as revising and editing.

Revising literally means "seeing again." You take a second look at your paragraphs, sentences, and words and change them until they express your intended meaning. You make major changes to the essay's structure, sentences, and paragraphs. You are trying to stick to a thesis, present evidence in a logical order, and project a tone appropriate to your audience. Accomplishing any of these three tasks may require you to move or insert paragraphs, cut out sentences, add transitions, rewrite your essay's beginning or ending, or even do more research.

Editing, on the other hand, means focusing your rewriting efforts mainly on individual words and sentences. It entails making small changes to the text, often with an eye to improving syntax and overall smoothness. It means choosing a better synonym, correcting a misspelling, inventing a sharper image, improving punctuation, conforming to a specific format, and pruning unnecessary words or phrases.

Both revising and editing are important parts of any rewriting effort. And although it is true that revising usually comes before editing, even this sequence does not necessarily always apply. You may find yourself making small changes to individual words and sentences when you go over your text the first time. On a second reading, you may find an obvious defect missed earlier, causing you to make major changes in the material. As with writing, rewriting is hard to segment into absolute steps.

Both revising and editing are important parts of any rewriting effort. And although it is true that revising usually comes before editing, even this sequence does not necessarily always apply. You may find yourself making small changes to individual words and sentences when you go over your text the first time. On a second reading, you may find an obvious defect missed earlier, causing you to make major changes in the material. As with writing, rewriting is hard to segment into absolute steps.

▪ Revising

Essential to all rewriting is careful and purposeful rereading. You reread your work with an eye on its intended audience and overall purpose. As you reread what you have written, you ask yourself whether your audience is likely to understand it. You ask yourself whether this paragraph, sentence, or word is appropriate, whether this passage makes your views emphatic and plain. You read with pen in hand or fingers on the keyboard, slashing away here and there, scribbling in the margins, striking out and rewriting some sentences. And as you progress through multiple rereadings, your text will gradually begin to get better.

But the key is rereading, and its importance to a writer cannot be overstated. If you wish to write well, you must be willing to reread your work constantly. You must reread it not only when it is done, but also while you are doing it. If you should even become temporarily stuck—and virtually every writer occasionally does—don't stare vacantly into space or at the ceiling. Reread your work from the beginning. If no new ideas occur to you and you're still stuck, reread your work again. Sooner or later you will see where your text made a lurch in the wrong direction and be able to correct it.

Writing and rewriting are part of the recursive pattern of composing. Some revising to your rough plan or purpose will take place in your head even before you have scribbled a first draft. But most will occur immediately after or during the act of composition. You will set down a sentence or two on the page, glance at it, and see a way to make it better. Or you will write a paragraph, begin another and become stuck, then go back to the first and insert some details or transitional material. Regardless of your personal method of composing, once you have finished your first draft, you should begin the formal process of revising by rereading it. As an example of what we mean by revising, consider the following student paper in its first draft. The writer was asked to indicate through marginal comments the changes she proposed to make. Since this section emphasizes revising, as opposed to editing, we have corrected the errors that would have been caught in the editing process and have left only those that could be improved through revising. In the next part of this chapter, we shall stress editing.

The Exploitation of Endangered Wildlife

The fascination with endangered wildlife within the affluent nations of the world increases the market for illegal poaching and exporting of wildlife goods. Wildlife is big business. Exotic-bird collectors will pay as much as $10,000 for a hyacinth macaw. At Saks Fifth Avenue in New York a pair of cowboy boots, trimmed in lizard skin, will sell for $900. A Christian Dior coat, made from only the belly fur of seventeen lynx cats, will cost a staggering $100,000. These are rather mild examples of what is being done with animals stolen from wildlife retreats across the world.

Move to end of paragraph

For stronger opening, begin here.

Of course, it's not that anyone cares if people spend their thousands on nonessentials. Instead, the act of murdering innocent and lovely animals for vanity's sake is an irreversible and despicable crime. For example, the baby seals, so prized for their exquisitely soft furs, are repeatedly beaten over the head with heavy clubs until they lie spread out on the ground, unconscious. To the poachers who routinely do the butchering, death is not relevant to this ugly scenario, nor are humane methods of killing. All they care about is the blood money extracted from the skins of these helpless little creatures. Another example is the thousands of wild birds imported live from Brazil and Australia. Since these countries have laws banning such exports, each cage of birds is smuggled aboard the smugglers' boat and has a weight attached to it. In case of being spotted by some police official, the cages can easily be thrown overboard, and no implicating evidence will remain. Still another species of endangered wildlife being exploited is the elephant. Investigators have found as many as twenty of these enormous pachyderms,

Delete: adds nothing. Is too informal.

More commentary needed here. Add a transition.

of...

How often? For what purpose?

Where? Add detail.

gunned down with automatic weapons or shot with poison darts, lying close together as if they were victims of some cruel genocide. Their tusks have been carved from their heads and carried away, leaving the bloody carcasses to rot and waste away on the plains.

The irreversible effect of this illegal murdering could <u>mean</u> the

Be more direct.

extinction of many exotic wildlife species. In the seventeenth century,

Add a transition.

13,200 species of mammals and birds were known, but today more than 130 species have gone. An estimated 240 more are considered seriously endangered. Almost all of the cases can be traced to human activity.

Rewrite to make stronger appeal to reader's sense of fair play. Make more coherent.

It's not because we needed these animals for food, nor because their unique traits could help us find cures for diseases, nor because killing them taught us anything relevant, except that perhaps when they are gone forever, taking with them their natural mystery, beauty, and grace, then we may learn how ignorant we have been.

Following is the revised version of the first draft:

The Exploitation of Endangered Wildlife

Wildlife is big business. Exotic-bird collectors will pay as much as $10,000 for a hyacinth macaw. At Saks Fifth Avenue in New York a pair of cowboy boots, trimmed in lizard skin, will sell for $900. A Christian Dior coat, made from only the belly fur of seventeen lynx cats, will cost a staggering $100,000. These are rather mild examples of what is being done with animals stolen from wildlife retreats across the world. The fascination with endangered wildlife within the affluent nations of the world increases the market for illegal poaching and exporting of wildlife goods.

The act of murdering innocent and lovely animals for vanity's sake is an irreversible and despicable crime. It is a way of saying that animals have no feelings and that human beings have the right to plunder and kill the lower orders if doing so will enhance the human lifestyle. For example, the baby seals, so prized for their exquisitely soft furs, are repeatedly beaten over the head with heavy clubs until they lie spread out on the ground, unconscious. To the poachers who routinely do the butchering, death is not relevant to this ugly scenario, nor are humane methods of killing. All they care about is the blood money extracted from the skins of these helpless little creatures. Another example of this savage and unnecessary rape is the thousands of wild birds imported yearly live from Brazil and Australia—to end up either in cages gracing the living rooms of tycoons who like to collect birds, or as ornaments on sweaters and hats of rich and fashion-conscious women. But since most countries have laws banning such exports, each cage of birds is smuggled aboard the smugglers' boat and has a weight attached to it. In case of being spotted by some police official, the cages can easily be thrown overboard, and no implicating evidence will remain. Still another species of endangered wildlife being exploited is the elephant. Investigators in West Africa have found as many as twenty of these enormous pachyderms, gunned down with automatic weapons or shot with poison darts, lying close together as if they were victims of some cruel genocide. Their tusks have been carved from their heads and carried away, leaving the bloody carcasses to rot and waste away on the plains.

The irreversible effect of this illegal murdering will certainly eventually lead to the extinction of many exotic wildlife species. Already time has witnessed the demise of many exotic animals. In the seventeenth century, 13,200 species of mammals and birds were known, but today more than 130 species are extinct. An estimated 240 more are considered seriously endangered. In almost all cases, the extinction can be traced to greedy plunder by human beings. And the tragic part is that we did not commit the plunder because we needed these animals for food, nor because their unique traits could help us find cures for diseases, nor because killing them taught us anything useful. But perhaps when they are gone forever—taking with them their natural mystery, beauty, and grace—then we may see how ignorant and foolish we were. Then we will realize, much too late, that we sold our birthright for a mess of pottage.

Editing

After revising—in most cases—comes editing. You now concentrate on the smaller elements of your writing—on individual words and sentences—with the goal of improving them. Again, careful editing begins with close rereading. You remember whom you are writing for and why, and you use your intended audience and purpose to judge the suitability of both your syntax and diction.

What follows is a checklist of some fundamental rules of editing. Have your own work in front of you as you go over this list. If your writing suffers from mechanical problems, such as fragments, comma splices, and dangling modifiers, you should consult a good grammar handbook.

Rule 1: Make Your Title Descriptive

The title of a paper should describe its content. Avoid puffy, exotic titles like this one on a paper dealing with the use of fantasy in Keats's poetry:

Poor: Keats: The High Priest of Poetry

Rewrite: The Use of Fantasy in Keats's Poetry

Rule 2: Begin with a Simple Sentence

It is stylistically good sense to open your paper with a short and simple sentence. A long and involved opening will repel, rather than attract, a reader:

Poor: The problem that has come up again and again before various workers in the social sciences, and especially before sociologists and anthropologists, and one that has been debated at length in the journals of both disciplines as well as in the classrooms of various universities and colleges across the country, and one to which various answers, none satisfactory, have been proposed, is this: Are social scientists politically neutral, or are they *ipso facto* committed by their research?

To open with such a cumbersome sentence is like compelling a friend to view a landscape through a dirty windowpane. It is better to begin with an easily grasped sentence:

Rewrite: The question is this: Are social scientists politically neutral, or are they committed by their research?

Rule 3: Prune Deadwood

Deadwood refers to any word, phrase, or sentence that adds bulk without meaning. It accumulates wherever the writing is roundabout and indistinct. Some styles of writing are so vested in wordiness that it is impossible to assign blame to any single word or phrase:

Poor: There are many factors contributing to the deficiencies of my writing, the most outstanding being my unwillingness to work.

Rewrite: I write badly mainly because I am lazy.

Poor: Anthropologists carrying their studies of primate behavior deep into the tropical forests of Malaysia contribute, through the pursuit of their specialized interest, to the one field that in fact gives us our broadest perspective of human beings.

Rewrite: Anthropologists add to our knowledge of human beings by studying primate behavior in the forests of Malaysia.

The solution to wordiness is to be plain and direct—to state your ideas without fluff or pretension.

Aside from wordiness there are other, more specific kinds of deadwood:

a. Cut *there are* and *there is* whenever possible, thereby tightening a sentence.

Poor: There are many reasons why businesses fail.

Rewrite: Businesses fail for many reasons.

Poor: There is a cause for every effect.

Rewrite: Every effect has a cause.

b. Cut *I think, I believe,* and *in my opinion.* Such phrases make the writer sound insecure.

Poor: I think that Freud's approach to psychology is too dominated by sex.

Rewrite: Freud's approach to psychology is too dominated by sex.

Poor: I believe that women should be paid as much as men for the same work.

Rewrite: Women should be paid as much as men for the same work.

Poor: In my opinion, marriage is a dying institution.

Rewrite: Marriage is a dying institution.

c. Cut all euphemistic expressions.

Poor: He went to Vietnam and paid the supreme sacrifice.

Rewrite: He was killed in Vietnam.

Poor: Last year for the first time I exercised the right of citizens on Election Day.

Rewrite: Last year I voted for the first time.

d. Cut *-wise, -ly,* and *-type* word endings. Such words, easily concocted from adverbs and adjectives, have become popular in college writing, but they add bulk, not meaning.

Poor: Moneywise, she just didn't know how to be careful.

Rewrite: She didn't know how to be careful with her money.

Poor: Firstly, let me point out some economic problems.

Rewrite: First, let me point out some economic problems.

Poor: A jealous-type man annoys me.

Rewrite: A jealous man annoys me.

e. Eliminate all redundant phrases or expressions. Here are some typical examples, followed by possible substitutes:

Redundancy	*Rewrite*
bright in color	bright
large in size	large
old in age	old
shiny appearance	shiny
in this day and age	today
true and accurate	accurate (*or* true)
important essentials	essentials
end result	result
terrible tragedy	tragedy
free gift	gift
unexpected surprise	surprise
each and every	each (*or* every)
beginning preparation	preparation
basic and fundamental	basic (*or* fundamental)

In the preceding cases, all you have to do is cross out the words that *do not add* any meaning.

Another kind of redundancy is the use of ready-made phrases that could be replaced by a single word:

Ready-Made Phrase	*Rewrite*
owing to the fact that	because
plus the fact that	and
regardless of the fact that	although
in the event that	if
in a situation in which	when
concerning the matter of	about

Ready-Made Phrase	*Rewrite*
it is necessary that	must
has the capacity for	can
it could happen that	may, can, could, might
prior to	before
at the present time	now (*or* today)
at this point in time	now (*or* today)
as of this date	today
in this day and age	nowadays
in an accurate manner	accurately
in a satisfactory manner	satisfactorily
subsequent to	after
along the lines of	like

Unfortunately, we cannot give you an exhaustive list of all unnecessary phrases. Only by a thorough rereading of your text can you spot these redundancies.

However, some chronic redundancies are caused by such words as *process, field, area, systems,* and *subject* being unnecessarily attached by the preposition *of* to certain nouns. Usually these words and the preposition can be eliminated with no damage whatsoever to your meaning and a considerable lightening of your style. Here are some examples:

The *process of law* is not free of faults.

The *field of education* needs creative minds.

Some incompetence exists in the *area of medicine.*

People employed in *systems of management* make good salaries.

They know little about the *subject of mathematics.*

In each case, if you delete the "of" phrase, the redundancy disappears:

The law is not free of faults.

Education needs creative minds.

Some incompetence exists in medicine.

People employed in management make good salaries.

They know little about mathematics.

Context, activity, concept, factor, and *problem* are similar offenders.

f. Cut all preamble phrases such as *the reason why . . . is that.*

Poor: The reason why wars are fought is that nations are not equally rich.

Rewrite: Wars are fought because nations are not equally rich.

Poor: The thing I wanted to say is that history has shown the human being to be a social predator.

Rewrite: History has shown the human being to be a social predator.

Poor: The point I was trying to make is that reality is sometimes confused with fantasy in Keats's poetry.

Rewrite: Reality is sometimes confused with fantasy in Keats's poetry.

In all such cases the rewrite principle is the same: lift out the heart of the idea and state it plainly.

g.   Cut most rhetorical questions.

Poor: That illusion, though deceptive, is more consoling and less hostile to human needs than reality appears to be a central theme in Keats's poetry. Why would anyone feel this way? Why did Keats himself feel this way? Possibly because he had tuberculosis and knew he was going to waste away and die.

Rewrite: That illusion, though deceptive, is more consoling and less hostile to human needs than reality appears to be a central theme in Keats's poetry. Keats possibly felt this way because he had tuberculosis and knew he was going to waste away and die.

Rule 4: Do Not Overexplain

Poor: Some critics sneered at Keats for being an apothecary-surgeon, which is what he was trained for.

Rewrite: Some critics sneered at Keats for being an apothecary-surgeon.

If Keats was an apothecary-surgeon, then that is obviously what he was trained to be.

Poor: As president of the company, which is an executive-type position, he never scheduled work for himself during April.

Rewrite: As president of the company, he never scheduled work for himself during April.

The term *president* already lets the reader know that the position is an executive one.

Poor: The car is blue in color and costs $18,000 in price.

Rewrite: The car is blue and costs $18,000.

That blue is a color and that $18,000 is the price are self-evident.

Rule 5: Be Specific

Lack of specific detail will infect your prose with a pallid vagueness.

Poor: The effect of the scenery was lovely and added a charming touch to the play.

Rewrite: The scenery, which consisted of an autumn country landscape painted on four flats extended to cover the entire background of the stage, added a charming touch to the play.

Being specific is simply calling things by their proper names. In speech, it might pass as cute to call things *thingamajigs* or *thingamabobs* or *widgets,* but in prose, any sort of vagueness caused by the writer's not calling things by their proper names will leave a bad impression. Consider the following examples:

Poor: James Boswell, the famous writer, died from living badly.

Rewrite: James Boswell, the famous biographer, died of uremia following a gonorrheal infection.

The writer of the second sentence, who has simply named Boswell's terminal infection, appears more competent than the writer of the first.

Poor: Browning wrote poetry in which a speaker talked either to himself or to someone else.

Rewrite: Browning wrote *dramatic monologues.*

In the first sentence, for want of a name, the writer is forced into a roundabout description of the kind of poetry Browning wrote. A little research on Browning would have yielded the term *dramatic monologue.*

Rule 6: Avoid Trite Expressions

Some words, phrases, or expressions through overuse have become unbearably hackneyed and should be avoided. Following are some of the most glaring offenders.

in conclusion, I wish to say

last, but by no means least

slowly but surely

to the bitter end

it goes without saying

by leaps and bounds

few and far between

in the final analysis

Rule 7: Use the Active Voice

The active voice is more vigorous and understandable than the passive because it allows the subject of a sentence to stand in its familiar position in front of the verb: for example, "I took a walk." The subject *I* occupies the position immediately in front of the verb *took.* The same sentence in the passive voice denies this familiar immediacy between subject and verb, "A walk was taken by me." The subject and verb stand at opposite ends of the sentence, with *by* intervening between them. In some passive constructions, the subject is even dropped:

Information about the suspect could not be obtained.

By whom, you might ask. The answer is not evident in this sentence. Because of this tendency to implicate no one as the doer of an action, the passive voice enjoys widespread use among bureaucratic writers. Notice how converting the earlier sentence to the active voice not only makes the sentence more vigorous, but also makes some agency or person its subject and, therefore, responsible:

> The police could not obtain any information about the suspect.

The strongest argument to be given for using the active instead of the passive voice, however, is the simplest one: the active voice is easier to read and understand. Here are some more examples of the passive voice, followed by appropriate revisions:

> **Passive:** Her makeup was applied in thick, daubing strokes by her.
>
> **Active:** She applied her makeup in thick, daubing strokes.
>
> **Passive:** To see their hero in person was the fans' most cherished dream.
>
> **Active:** The fans' most cherished dream was to see their hero in person.
>
> **Passive:** It was determined by the committee that the new tax law would benefit middle-income people.
>
> **Active:** The committee determined that the new tax law would benefit middle-income people.
>
> **Passive:** My last trip to Jamaica will always be remembered.
>
> **Active:** I shall always remember my last trip to Jamaica.

The use of the passive voice is stylistically justified only when an action or the object of an action is more important than the subject:

> There, before our eyes, two human beings were burned alive by gasoline flames.

In this case the object, *human beings,* is more important than the subject, *gasoline flames,* and the passive voice is therefore effective. Here are two more examples of the passive voice appropriately used:

> Cancer-producing particles are released into the atmosphere by spray guns applying asbestos during building construction.

In this context, cancer-producing particles are more important than spray guns.

> Widespread death and injury were caused when 20,000 tons of TNT were dropped on Hiroshima in an atomic bomb.

Obviously the human dead and injured are more important than the atomic bomb.

Rule 8: Make Your Statements Positive

Statements that hedge, hesitate, or falter in the way they are worded tend to infuse your style with indecision. Whenever possible, word your statements positively:

> **Poor:** He was not at all a rich man.
>
> **Rewrite:** He was a poor man.

Poor: *The Cherry Orchard* is not a strong play; it does not usually sweep the audience along.

Rewrite: *The Cherry Orchard* is a weak play that usually bores its audience.

Poor: A not uncommon occurrence is for rain to fall this time of the year.

Rewrite: It commonly rains this time of the year.

Rule 9: Keep to One Tense

Once you have decided to summarize an action or event in one tense, you must thereafter stick to that tense. Don't start in the past and shift to the present, nor start in the present and shift to the past. Notice the corrections in the following passage.

Here is what I saw: For two acts the ballerina pirouetted, leapt, and floated

fell

like a silver swallow; then suddenly, she ~~falls~~ to the ground like a heavy

was

boulder. Her leg ~~is~~ fractured. For years before I observed this spectacular

had   *was*

drama, I∧often heard of this artist's brilliant career. Now I ~~am~~ watching her final performance.

Rule 10: Place Key Words at the Beginning or End of a Sentence

Poor: Workers today have forgotten the meaning of the word *quality,* so most craftsmen tell us.

Rewrite: Workers today, so most craftsmen tell us, have forgotten the meaning of the word *quality.*

Poor: Generally speaking, *wars* turn civilized nations into barbaric tribes.

Rewrite: *Wars,* generally speaking, turn civilized nations into barbaric tribes.

Rule 11: Prune Multiple *Of*s

A double *of* construction is tolerable; a triple *of* construction is not.

Poor: The opinions *of* the members *of* this panel *of* students are their own.

Rewrite: The opinions expressed by this panel of students are their own.

A good way to break up an *of* construction is to add another verb. In the preceding example, the verb *expressed* is inserted in the sentence.

Rule 12: Break Up Noun Clusters

A noun cluster is any string of noun + adjective combinations occurring at length without a verb. The cluster is usually preceded by either *the* or *a*. Noun clusters contribute a tone of unarguable objectivity to prose and have consequently found favor in the writing styles of textbooks, the government, and the social sciences. Note the italicized noun clusters in the following:

Poor: We therefore recommend *the use of local authorities for the collection of information on this issue.*

Poor: *The increased specialization and complexity of multicellular organisms* resulted from evolution *according to the principles of random variation and natural selection.*

Poor: *The general lessening of the work role in our society* does not mean that we have abandoned the work basis for many of our values.

Poor: One cannot doubt *the existence of polarized groups in America.*

The test for a noun cluster is whether or not it can be replaced by a single pronoun. Each of the preceding examples can be.

To rewrite noun clusters, convert one or more of the nouns to an equivalent verb form:

Better: We therefore recommend *using* local authorities *to collect* information on this issue.

Better: Multicellular organisms *specialized and evolved* in complexity by the principles of random variation and natural selection.

Better: Because people today *work* less than they used to is no reason to believe that we have abandoned work as a basis for many of our values.

Better: One cannot doubt that polarized groups *exist* in America.

Noun clusters clot the flow of a sentence. Avoid them by being generous in your use of verbs.

Rule 13: Use Exclamation Points Sparingly

The exclamation point should be used rarely and only when urgency or strong emotion is being expressed, as in the following:

This is what we fought our wars for!

Hooray! They found the prize!

Otherwise, it adds a forced breeziness to your prose.

We must have urban renewal; and we must have it now!

One cannot construct a science with unreliable instruments!

Rule 14: Vary Your Sentences

Do not begin two sentences in a row with the same word or phrase unless you are deliberately aiming for an effect.

> **Poor:** The true Keats scholar is as familiar with the poet's life as with his poetry and can instantly relate any stage of the two. The true Keats scholar has a tendency to use Keats's poetry to explicate his life, and to use his life to explicate his poetry.

> **Rewrite:** Scholars of Keats know the poet's life as well as they know his poetry and can instantly relate any stage of the two. They use Keats's poetry to explain his life, and his life to explain his poetry.

In addition to varying the words, vary the length of your sentences.

> **Poor:** The man was angry and wanted his money back. But the officer would not give it back and told him to leave. That made the man angrier, and he threatened to call the police.

> **Rewrite:** The man was angry; he wanted his money back. But the officer would not give it back to him, and told him to leave, which made the man angrier. He threatened to call the police.

The rewrite is more effective because the sentences have a greater variety in length and style.

Rule 15: Keep Your Point of View Consistent

If you begin a sentence by referring to yourself first as "I" and then as "one," you have made the error known as shift in point of view. Such shifts can occur because of the several ways in which you can refer to yourself, your audience, and people in general. You can refer to yourself as *the writer, I,* or *we.* You can refer to your audience as *you, we,* or *all of us.* You can refer to people in general as *people, one,* and *they.* The rule is that once you have chosen your point of view, it must remain consistent:

> **Poor:** Do not buy Oriental rugs at an auction, because if we do, we may get cheated.

> **Better:** Do not buy Oriental rugs at an auction, because if you do, you may get cheated.

> **Poor:** I try to take good care of my car, for when one does not, they usually pay a big price.

> **Better:** I try to take good care of my car, for when I do not, I usually pay a big price.

> **Poor:** Everyone stood aghast when I told them about the accident.

> **Better:** They all stood aghast when I told them about the accident.

Rule 16: Use Standard Words

College students can be unrelenting in their invention of newfangled vocabulary and often fall prey to the excesses of neologisms—new or coined words. Voguish words fade as quickly as they appear. By the time this book sees print, such words as *tight, trippin', skeezy, cool,* and *"sweet"* (for *"perfect"*) will have begun to sound dated and old-fashioned. You should use neologisms sparingly—if at all—in your writing. Instead, draw your primary stock of words from the vocabulary established over the centuries. Remember, too, standard words must be written in standard spelling. Double-check any doubtful spelling in a dictionary.

We also warn against using the capitalized acronyms so popular in texting nowadays. Abbreviations such as LOL (Laughing Out Loud), IMHO (In My Humble Opinion), OMG (Oh My God), FYEO (For Your Eyes Only) or JK (Just Kidding) should be avoided because they are ever-changing and therefore can quickly become meaningless to any reader. Limit your texting dictionary of acronyms to the intimate circle of your smartphone correspondents. For your public writing, stick to standard English.

Rule 17: End with Impact

The ending of your essay should clinch your argument, summarize your main point, reassert your thesis, urge some kind of action, or suggest a solution. Avoid committing the following common errors in your ending:

a. Endings that are trite:

In conclusion I wish to say . . .

And now to summarize . . .

Such endings are too obvious. If your essay has been properly developed, no special announcement of the conclusion is necessary.

b. Endings that introduce a new idea:

Wealth, position, and friends, then, made him what he is today, although his father's death may also have influenced him.

If an idea has not been covered earlier, do not give in to the temptation to introduce it as a novelty item in the final paragraph.

c. Endings that are superfluous:

And so these are my thoughts on the subject.

As you can see, my essay proves that carbohydrates are bad for our health.

From these thoughts you will clearly see that Diaghilev was a dominant figure in modern ballet.

These endings do not reflect thoughtfulness on the part of the writer; they are useless in an essay.

◼ Editing an Actual Essay

Following is the first draft of a student paper, with revisions marked in boldface. In the left margin is the corresponding number of the rule in this section that has been broken.

Rule 1

The Loss of Horror in Horror Movies
~~Goose Pimples, Where Are You?~~

Rule 6

Audiences
~~For various and sundry reasons,~~ ‸udiences are no longer

scared as they once were by the old-fashioned horror

movies. Over the years people have been exposed to

Rule 5

vampires, werewolves, zombies, and mummies
so many ~~monsters~~ that such creatures have lost their

Rule 3g

effectiveness as objects of terror. ~~Why do you think this~~

~~happened?~~

Lack of novelty has produced indifference. Originally, a

movie monster, such as the one created by Frankenstein,

terrified audiences simply because the concept of a man

Rule 9/3e

was
creating human life ~~is~~ new. ~~Plus the fact that~~ Frankenstein's

monster had a sinister plausibility that people of the 1930s

had not experienced. But then the public was inundated by

a deluge of other film monsters as studios tried to capital-

ize on the success of the original. Gradually audiences grew

bored as these creations became trite and shopworn.

Fearing loss of business, ambitious movie producers

Rule 3d   tried to invent fresh ~~type~~, grisly shapes that would lure mov-

iegoers back into the theaters. But their attempts had no

effect on a public surfeited with horror, so Frankenstein's

monster, Wolfman, and Dracula eventually became comic

creatures in Abbott and Costello films.

Rule 3e   Most modern horror films fail *to produce* ~~in the production of~~

genuine, goose-pimply terror in their audiences. Of course,

it may be argued that films like *The Exorcist* and *Jaws*

Rule 5   scared many people—even to the point of ~~great fear~~ *hysterical screams*. But

these films relied heavily on shock rather than on fear.

Rule 8   Shock ~~and fear are not the same~~ *differs from fear.* . Genuine fear involves

the unknown or the un-seen. ~~Genuine fear~~ *It* seduces the

Rule 14   imagination into fantastic realms. ~~Genuine fear appeals~~ *and appeals*

to our innate store of nightmares. But shock is merely

synonymous with repulsion. People are shocked when

they see something they don't want to see. For example,

the scene of a man being devoured by a shark will shock.

The flaw here is that the shock value of such a scene

Rule 16   serves more to ~~give the creeps or the heebie-jeebies~~ *repulse or offend* than

to frighten.

Today, shock devices are used far too frequently in

motion pictures; yet, the sad truth is that these graphic

displays of blood and gore lack imagination. In older horror

movies, the audience was not privy to the horrible details

Rule 7   of murder. Scenes ~~which~~ merely suggested evil ~~were used~~
                        audience's imagination supplied the details.
          instead, and the ~~details were supplied by the audience's~~

Rule 4   ~~imagination.~~ This approach is more effective ~~in its results~~

than shock because it spurs the viewers to conjure up their

own images of the unseen. The old movie formulas did

not have to use shock devices, such as bloody murders,

to achieve a pinnacle of horror. Unfortunately, today's audi-

ences have become "shockproof" in the
                        bigger and more bizarre doses of horror
Rule 5   sense that it takes ~~more and more~~ to scare them.
          One wonders what the ultimate horror movie will be.
Rule 17a ~~In conclusion, horror movies have truly lost their effect.~~

Here is the polished version of the paper, ready to be submitted to the instructor.

The Loss of Horror in Horror Movies

Audiences are no longer scared as they once were by the old-

fashioned horror movies. Over the years, people have been exposed

to so many vampires, werewolves, zombies, and mummies that such

creatures have lost their effectiveness as objects of terror.

Lack of novelty has produced indifference. Originally, a movie

monster, such as the one created by Frankenstein, terrified audi-

ences simply because the concept of a man creating a human

life was new. Frankenstein's monster had a sinister plausibility that people of the 1930s had not experienced. But then the public was inundated by a deluge of other film monsters as studios tried to capitalize on the success of the original. Gradually audiences grew bored as these creations became trite and shopworn. Fearing loss of business, ambitious movie producers tried to invent fresh, grisly shapes that would lure moviegoers back into the theaters. But their attempts had no effect on a public surfeited with horror, so Frankenstein's monster, Wolfman, and Dracula eventually became comic creatures in Abbott and Costello films.

Most modern horror films fail to produce genuine, goose-pimply terror in their audiences. Of course, it may be argued that films like *The Exorcist* and *Jaws* scared many people—even to the point of hysterical screams. But these films relied heavily on shock rather than on fear. Shock differs from fear. Genuine fear involves the unknown or the unseen. It seduces the imagination into fantastic realms and appeals to our innate store of nightmares. But shock is merely synonymous with repulsion. People are shocked when they see something they don't want to see. For example, the scene of a man being devoured by a shark will shock. The flaw here is that the shock value of such a scene serves more to repulse or offend than to frighten.

Today, shock devices are used far too frequently in motion pictures; yet, the sad truth is that these graphic displays of blood and gore lack imagination. In older horror movies, the audience was not privy to the horrible details of murder. Scenes merely suggested evil instead, and the audience's imagination supplied the details. This approach is more effective than shock because it spurs the viewers to conjure up their own images of the unseen. The old movie formulas did not have to use shock devices, such as bloody murders, to achieve a pinnacle of horror. Unfortunately, today's audiences have become "shockproof" in the sense that it takes bigger and more bizarre doses of horror to scare them. One wonders what the ultimate horror movie will be.

● EXERCISES

1. What follows is the opening paragraph of a student essay. Revise it to improve its effectiveness. Remember that your lead sentence should captivate your audience.

   Wars are always destructive and rarely worth the devastation they cause. Today, Europe is still recuperating from World War II. Endless statistics attempt to project what would happen if a nuclear war were to break out today; yet, nobody really knows the actual effects. The most accurate picture to date was provided by the bombing of Hiroshima in 1945. This terrible historical event provided actual evidence of what a super weapon has the capability of accomplishing. For the first time, the world saw the greatest disaster ever created by man. The effects were unforgettably horrifying and disastrous. No one had bargained for the ensuing nightmare.

2. From the following pairs, choose the more descriptive title.
   a. (1) The Dreadful Nightmare of 1945
      (2) The Crippling Effects of the Atom Bomb on Hiroshima
   b. (1) Whence Did We Come and Why Are We Here?
      (2) What Is Philosophy?
   c. (1) China and Europe: Two Different Cultures
      (2) Dynamic Growth versus Static Social Principles
   d. (1) The People of the Black Moccasin
      (2) The Plains Culture of the Blackfoot Indians
   e. (1) Francisco Pizarro, Conqueror of Peru
      (2) Mighty Conquistador of the New World

3. Rid the following sentences of all deadwood:
   a. There are many ways in which light can be diffracted.
   b. No one has the right, in my opinion, to dictate to another human being whom to worship.
   c. Educationwise Will Rogers never did go to college.
   d. It has been said many times that power corrupts.
   e. There were thousands of teachers who attended the conference.
   f. The attitude-adjustment hour will begin at 5:00 P.M. and will be "no host."

4. Eliminate all redundant or imprecise phrases from the following sentences. Rewrite passages if necessary.
   a. Owing to the fact that it rained, Napoleon was defeated at Waterloo.
   b. We asked for a full and complete list of the passengers.
   c. One-man-one-vote should be a basic and fundamental reality of any political system.
   d. The room is square in shape, pale blue in color, and cheerful in appearance.
   e. The custodian was fired on the grounds that he slept on the job.
   f. A huge celebration marked the occasion of Martin Luther King's birthday.
   g. Those engaged in the profession of writing should be the guardians of grammar.

5. Rewrite the following sentences in the active voice:

    a. From early times on, stucco was used by the Romans as a finish for important buildings.

    b. Immortality was not believed in by the Sadducees of Jerusalem.

    c. The *Brahmanas,* originally written in Sanskrit, were produced by Indian priests.

    d. Chewing mouths are used by termites to eat wood.

    e. A good time was had by all of us.

    f. Sometimes no symptoms are exhibited by victims of trichinosis.

6. Rewrite the following sentences to break up the noun clusters:

    a. The way to avoid a worsening future fuel crisis is the construction of a mass transportation system and the investing in quality insulation.

    b. The inspecting of the chemical-disposal plant was never accomplished.

    c. One can hope for the existence of an afterlife.

    d. The making of great strides by medical technology gives hope to people with incurable heart diseases.

    e. The development of a good ear is necessary to the writing of effective prose.

7. Rewrite the following sentences to correct an inconsistent point of view or shift in tense:

    a. They left early for the big city of San Francisco. Once there, they take the cable car to the top of Nob Hill. At five in the evening, they eat at a restaurant on the wharf.

    b. One must have respect for the flag of our country. If you don't, how can we expect others to respect it?

    c. Swarms of bees attacked him, so he quickly hides his face inside his heavy wool jacket.

    d. If one has ever lived by the sea, you always tend to miss the roar of the waves and the sound of seagulls.

PART FOUR

Special Writing Projects
Why English Instructors Assign Research Papers

Students rarely greet the research paper with joy, but it still remains one of the most important college assignments. Writing one entails thinking critically about a subject, tracking down and evaluating facts for relevance and truth, organizing materials in support of a thesis, and cultivating a readable style. Success in college depends largely on the acquisition of these skills, which are also essential for accomplishment in business, the major professions, and even in private life. Salespeople often research a market and analyze it for trends; lawyers track down facts and organize them when preparing briefs and contracts; journalists depend on investigative research to gather material for stories. Engineers, nurses, secretaries, actors, architects, insurance agents—members of virtually all the professions—rely on the research techniques exemplified in this chapter.

How to Choose Your Topic

Typically, English instructors grant students the freedom to choose their own research topics, thus promoting exploration and self-discovery. If such a choice is indeed available to you, we recommend some preliminary browsing through the library until you come across a subject that arouses your curiosity—be it primitive Indians, the reign of the last empress of China, some influential sports figure, the complexities of the New York Stock Exchange, children's psychological problems, or the fiction or poetry of a modern writer. Here are some tips on finding a suitable topic:

1. Work with a familiar subject. For instance, you may have been fascinated by historical attempts of the super-rich to manipulate the U.S. economy, such as the Gould-Fisk scheme to corner gold in 1869, with the consequent Black Friday market panic. Now you must find out more about Jay Gould, who became symbolic of autocratic business practices and was hated by most American businesspeople. Research will supply the necessary information.

2. If familiarity fails, try an entirely new area. Perhaps you have always wanted to learn about Lenin's philosophy of government, genetic engineering, stem cell

441

technology, evolution in the Paleozoic era, the Roman empress Galla Placidia, the causes of earthquakes, pre-Columbian art, or the historical causes for the political unrest in the Middle East. A research paper finally gives you the opportunity to do so.

3. Books, magazines, newspapers, and the Internet can suggest possible topics. The library is a gold mine of hidden information. Browse through books, magazines, and newspapers. Some topic of interest is bound to leap out at you. Looking at secondary sources online is probably today's most popular way of finding research material. However, since anyone—from a well-known writer to a smart elementary school student—can place material on the Web, it is best to base your research on databases that are maintained by professionals. Some of these databases may even contain indexes that will allow you to download interesting material at no charge. The process of finding information on the Internet is always the same: access a search engine such as Google and enter a topic in the search slot. The computer will then search databases and Web sites on your topic and present a list of matching items. For example, we did a Google search on "illegal immigrants" and in less than a second got 2,380,000 hits. If you are new to computer research, ask for assistance from the librarian.

Avoid topics for which a single source can provide all the needed information; those that require no development but end as soon as started; those so popular that virtually everything about them has already been written and said; those so controversial that you have only fresh fuel to add to the already raging fire; or those decidedly unsuited to your audience, such as a paper advocating radical revision of the U.S. Constitution written for an instructor who is a conservative Republican.

How to Narrow Your Subject

Good research papers deal with topics of modest and workable proportions. To attempt a paper on the galaxies of the universe or on World War II is to attempt the impossible. A simple but practical way to narrow your subject is to subdivide it into progressively smaller units until you reach a topic specific enough for a paper. The following diagram on the sport of fencing illustrates what we mean:

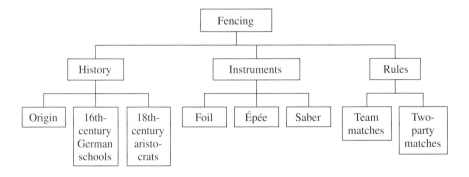

Any of the entries found on the lowest subdivision are properly narrowed subjects. For instance, you could write a useful paper on the sixteenth-century German schools that taught fencing to European gentlemen, on the use of the saber in fencing, or on the rules of modern team fencing. But a paper just on fencing would be overambitious and tricky to write.

Another point to bear in mind is that unlike the typical class-written paper, in which you must first formulate a thesis and then write the text, in the research paper you gather evidence, study it, and only then deduce a thesis. The assembled facts, statistics, graphs, schematics, arguments, expert testimony, and so on will suggest a topic that will be your thesis. What you learn in this process of writing the research paper is not only how to write but also how to infer a reasonable conclusion from a body of evidence.

The Process of Writing the Paper

You have narrowed your subject. You do not yet have a thesis or a definite topic, but you have a likely subject area to explore. You can do it in these simple steps:

1. **Find and Evaluate Sources** To do this, you must spend time in a library, which is your systematized retrieval network. Materials for your subject will most likely be found in electronic databases that have replaced the card catalog and are instantaneously linked to other sources that may be a thousand miles away. Most library storage systems are straightforward and easy to use—if there's something about the one at your school that you don't understand, ask your friendly librarian. You evaluate each source by scanning titles, tables of contents, chapter headings, or article summaries. Check the date of publication to make sure the information in the source is still valid. As you work, write down information on a possible source on its own bibliography card, providing the information necessary for easy retrieval. Some students prefer to record this information on a laptop but we still recommend that you use bibliography cards such as the one shown below.

   The most important part of Internet research is to evaluate the accuracy and dependability of sources. Here are some guidelines for evaluating Internet sources:

813.409   *College Library*

Sch.

Schneider, Robert W. *Five Novelists of the*

    Progressive Era.

    New York: Columbia University Press, 1965

Chapter 5 evaluates the novels of Winston Churchill, stating why

they were loved by contemporaries but scorned by succeeding generations.

- Check the reliability of the source. Since the World Wide Web grows bigger and more complex daily, some of the sources are bogus. We suggest that you stick to Web sites that end in *.org* (nonprofit organization), *.gov* (government entity), or *.edu* (educational body), since they are usually reliable.

- Check the dates of the sources to make sure that the information is not outdated.

- Check the authors of the material you have found by logging in their names on the Internet. Their biographies will tell you about their credentials, contributions, and reputations. For instance, if the author is a seasoned journalist reporting for the *New York Times* or the *Wall Street Journal,* you can be reassured that he or she is most likely a credible source.

2. **Take Notes** Using your electronic notebook or pile of bibliography cards, retrieve the books, magazines, pamphlets, and other identified sources and place them in front of you. Skim each source to get the drift of its content. Decide if it contains material relevant enough to warrant a more detailed reading. Once you have skimmed your sources, you can start taking four basic kinds of notes:

   a. **summary**—record the gist of a passage

   b. **paraphrase**—restate in your own words what the source says

   c. **direct quotation**—copy the exact words of a source

   d. **personal comments**—express your own views on the subject or source

Handwrite your notes on cards or type them on your computer and print them out on sheets of paper, which can be easily shuffled or discarded when you get down to the business of writing the paper. For easier reorganization of your notes, restrict each card or page to a single idea. To guard against unintentional plagiarism, copy down only exact quotations from your sources, and note these direct quotations as such, while digesting and expressing all other ideas in your own words. At some point in this stage (it varies from paper to paper), a thesis will occur to you. When it does, write it down for permanent reference. This will be the starting point for your paper.

Plagiarism Plagiarism is the willful or accidental stealing of someone else's writing. To help you understand the ins and outs of plagiarism, here are first the original source passage and then three passages about the American poet Walt Whitman, two of them plagiarized and one of them not.

Original Passage

Even when Whitman was working at his career as a newspaperman, his casualness threatened his advancement. As the owners of the New York *Aurora* fired him from the editorial staff, they accused him in print of "loaferism," describing him as "the laziest fellow who ever undertook to edit a city paper." Whitman never reformed. It remained his custom as editor to have the paper made up and ready for printing by noon, then to be off for a swim, a stroll, or a ride down Broadway on a horse-car. Even when working at that leisurely pace, he was complaining in the columns of the Brooklyn *Daily Eagle* that "most editors have far, far too much to do."

Plagiarized (Version 1)

During his career as a newspaperman, Walt Whitman was considered a loafer because his bosses felt that he didn't spend enough time in the newspaper office. In fact, he was fired from the editorial staff of the *Aurora* and labeled "the laziest fellow who ever undertook to edit a city paper." Being fired did not change Whitman, who always felt that editors worked much too hard. It remained his custom as editor to have the paper made up and ready for printing by noon, then to be off for a swim, a stroll, or a ride down Broadway on a horse car.

This is blatant plagiarism. The student has not acknowledged any source for the comments made about Whitman, in effect taking credit for them himself. Even the quotation is not documented.

Plagiarized (Version 2)

Whitman was considered a lazy loafer by the owners of the New York *Aurora* who employed him. They even fired him from their editorial staff and called him "the laziest fellow who ever undertook to edit a city paper." Whitman never reformed. He continued his habit of having the newspaper ready for printing by noon so that he could be off on some adventure of his own—a swim, a stroll, or a ride down Broadway in a horse carriage (Bridgman vii, viii).

This is the "Works Cited" information:

> Bridgman, Richard. Introduction. *Leaves of Grass*. By Walt Whitman. San Francisco: Chandler, 1968. Print.

Despite correct documentation, this passage is still plagiarized because the student has retained too much of the original source's wording, leaving the impression that it is his own.

Not Plagiarized

According to most of Walt Whitman's biographers, the poet did not have a compulsive or ambitious personality as far as his career as a journalist was concerned. In fact, "as the owners of the New York *Aurora* fired him from the editorial staff, they accused him in print of 'loaferism,' describing him as 'the laziest fellow who ever undertook to edit a city paper'" (Bridgman vii, viii).

Reading Whitman's own letters to friends or studying his poetry makes one aware that part of Whitman's philosophy was that a worthwhile life included both partying and working.

The "Works Cited" page then contains this entry:

> Bridgman, Richard. Introduction. *Leaves of Grass*. By Walt Whitman. San Francisco: Chandler, 1968. Print.

This passage is not plagiarized. The documentation is accurate and the ideas found in the original source are properly paraphrased. Remember that it is not enough to simply cite a source. If you're quoting from it, you should use quotation marks. If you're paraphrasing its material, you must do a true paraphrase. Whether you find material on the Internet or in a library book, you should never plagiarize. To avoid plagiarism, follow these rules meticulously:

- Acknowledge any idea taken from another source.
- Place quoted passages inside quotation marks.
- Provide a bibliographic entry at the end of the paper for every source used in your text.

You do not, however, have to document everything. Facts that are common knowledge need no documentation (example: "Abraham Lincoln was shot by John Wilkes Booth"). As a rule, a piece of information that has appeared in five standard sources can be considered common knowledge and needs no documentation.

3. **Write the First Draft** With a jumble of notes strewn on your desk, you may feel bewildered about what to include or exclude as you tackle your first draft. This may be the time for an outline, which can be adjusted later to fit your paper, or your paper can subsequently be adjusted to fit your outline.

   In any case, by now you should have become something of an expert on your subject. Using your outline, start composing your first draft. As you write, you will be backing up your own opinions and views with source material uncovered by your research and recorded in your notes.

4. **Use Proper Documentation** Except for statements that are common knowledge, all information taken from your sources—whether quoted, paraphrased, or summarized—must be accompanied by a source citation given in parentheses and conforming to the proper format. We provide two sample papers in this chapter—one in the Modern Language Association (MLA) format, the other in the American Psychological Association (APA) format. Use the MLA author-work format if your instructor tells you to do so or if your paper is on a subject in the liberal arts or humanities, such as literature, philosophy, history, religion, or fine arts. For a paper in a more scientific field, such as psychology, sociology, or anthropology, the APA author-date format should be used. Always check with your instructor about the documentation format that is expected and appropriate. One caution: Do *not* mix styles.

The two annotated student papers represented in this part serve as general models and illustrate many of the documenting problems you are likely to encounter. For more complex citations, we recommend that you consult a style sheet or a research paper handbook. Both MLA and APA have gone to a system of parenthetical documentation, which gives brief but specific information about the sources within the text itself. The MLA style cites the author's surname or the title of a work, followed by a page number;

the APA style cites the author's surname, followed by a date and a page number. In both styles, the author's name, work, and date can be omitted from the parentheses if they have already been supplied within the text. The rule of thumb is this: If the citation cannot be smoothly worked into the text, it should be supplied within parentheses. This kind of parenthetical documentation is obviously simpler than footnotes or endnotes because the citation can be given as the paper is being written rather than being tediously repeated in the text, the note, and the bibliography.

Flexibility in citations is a characteristic of both the MLA and APA styles. For example, you might choose to cite the author's name in the text while putting the page (MLA) or year and page (APA) in parentheses:

MLA Example

In her autobiography, Agatha Christie admits that often she felt the physical presence of Hercule Poirot (263).

APA Example

According to *800-Cocaine* by Mark S. Gold (1985, p. 21), cocaine has exploded into a business with brand names.

Or you might choose to include the title or author(s) of the citation in the parentheses:

MLA Example

The author began to realize how much she liked Poirot and how much a part of her life he had become (Christie 263).

APA Example

During the airing of ABC's *Good Morning, America* (Ross & Bronkowski, 1986), case histories were analyzed in an extremely serious tone.

In any case, the overriding aim should be to cite the necessary information without interrupting the flow of the text. What cannot be worked elegantly into the text is cited within parentheses.

This textbook does not have the space to pack in examples of every possible source you might use in your research. Aside from common sources, such as a periodical article or a book by one author, your investigation may lead you to include periodicals or books by multiple authors, edited volumes, scholarly journals, anthologies, translations, government documents, legal works, organizational papers, graphics, emails, blogs, tweets, anonymous works, published or personal interviews, and a whole stack of other sources that require meticulous citations. We offer only the most common variations. The following two guide books, for purchase online or in college bookstores, offer precise answers to most questions students have concerning citation or documentation formats:

Tensen, Bonnie. *Research Strategies for a Digital Age,* 4th ed. Boston: Cengage, 2013.

Winkler, Anthony C., and Jo Ray McCuen-Metherell. *Writing the Research Paper: A Handbook,* 8th ed. Boston: Cengage, 2012.

By typing "MLA Style" or "APA Style" into your Web browser, you can also receive free help from several online sources. One of the most helpful comes from the Online Writing Lab at Purdue University, which offers extensive advice on how to use the MLA style or APA style for properly formatted college research papers. To date, Purdue has allowed students to download their guidelines without paying a fee.

Preparing "Works Cited" or "References"

The sources cited in your text must be alphabetically listed in full at the end of your paper. In the MLA style of documentation, the list is titled "Works Cited"; in the APA style, it is titled "References." Both styles require the same general information, but differ slightly in details of capitalization and order. MLA entries, for example, begin with a surname, followed by the author's full (first) name; on the other hand, APA requires a surname, followed only by the initial letters of the author's first and middle names. In MLA entries, the author's name is followed by the title of the work, whereas in APA entries, the author's name is followed by the date. Both APA and MLA entries use hanging indentations (second and subsequent lines are indented one-half inch). Other differences are also minor: MLA requires titles of periodicals or books to be italicized, articles or chapters to be placed within quotation marks, and all principal words of a title to be capitalized (articles, prepositions, coordinating conjunctions, and the "to" in infinitives are not capitalized if they fall in the middle of a title). On the other hand, APA italicizes the titles of magazines and books but uses no quotation marks around the titles of chapters or articles within these longer works. APA capitalizes only the first word of an article or book title, the first word of a subtitle (if there is one), and any proper nouns; all other words are lowercase. For titles of periodicals, MLA capitalizes all principal words. See the sample student papers for specific examples of how to handle various bibliographic matters. Here are two typical examples that will allow you to see the difference between MLA and APA bibliographic listings for an article in a periodical:

MLA: Leonard, Christopher. "The Ugly Economics of Chicken." *The Week* 18 Apr. 2014: 36–37. Print.

Note that the MLA style now requires all "Works Cited" entries to include the medium of publication used. Most entries will be listed as **Print** or **Web** sources; however, other possibilities are **Film, CD-ROM,** or **DVD.** The MLA style no longer requires writers to provide URLs for Web entries. Nonetheless, if your instructor insists on them, provide them in angle brackets at the end of the entry, and end with a period, as follows: <http://classics.mit.edu/>.

APA: Dixit, J. (2010, January). Heartbreak and home runs: The power of first experiences. *Psychology Today, 43,* 61–69.

Here are two further examples to indicate the difference between MLA and APA when listing a book:

MLA: Martel, Yann. *Beatrice and Virgil.* New York: Spiegel, 2011. Print.

APA: Moyers, W. C. (2006). *Broken: My story of addiction and redemption.* New York, NY: Viking.

Online sources require a special format. In MLA style, the "Works Cited" reference for a Web page should include the following elements: name of the author or editor of the project or database, if available; italicized title of the project or database; electronic publication information, including version number (if relevant and not part of the title); publisher of the project or database; date of electronic publication or of the latest update; medium (Web); and date of access. MLA no longer requires the use of URLs in "Works Cited" entries. Because Web addresses can change often and because documents sometimes appear in multiple places on the Web, MLA explains that most readers can find electronic sources through title or author searches via Internet search engines. If your instructor does require the URL, place it within angle brackets (<>) after the date of access.

APA style for online sources requires a retrieval statement at the end of the reference item—with a date, if the information is likely to change, as with Wikis—such as the following: "Retrieved January 23, 2014, from http://www.apa.org/pubs/databases/psycarticles/index.aspx." If an article has a DOI (Digital Object Identifier), include it in your citation rather than the URL: doi:0000000/000111111101.

When using electronic sources, it is always a good idea to keep personal copies of information. Get in the habit of printing out or saving Web pages and articles in PDF format for future reference. Also, you might use the Bookmark function on your Web browser in order to return to documents more easily.

Writing the Final Copy

Revising and editing your paper is the final step. Do not be easy on yourself. Pretend that the paper is someone else's and badly in need of work. Check for logical progression, completeness of development, and mechanical correctness. The only way to produce an excellent paper is to pore over it paragraph by paragraph looking for weaknesses or faults. After careful review and editing, prepare the final copy using one of the formats exemplified by the two student papers. If you are following the APA format, you will also need to write an abstract summarizing your findings (see student sample, pp. 473–505). Remember that the appearance of a paper can add to or detract from its quality. Here are some important tips on manuscript appearance:

1. Use 8.5″ × 11″ white paper. Double-space throughout the paper.
2. Except for page numbers, use one-inch margins at the top, bottom, and sides of the paper. (For page numbers, see item 6.)
3. Avoid fancy fonts such as script. Times New Roman 12 pt. is preferred.
4. If required, place a balanced and uncluttered outline before the text of the paper. Double-space throughout the outline.
5. APA papers require a title page. For MLA papers do not use a title page unless your instructor requires one. Instead, put your name, instructor's name, course number, and date on the first page of the outline, repeating this information in the upper left-hand corner of the first page of the text. The title should be centered and double-spaced below the date. (See sample papers.)
6. Number pages consecutively throughout the paper itself (see item 1 below, regarding the outline for an MLA paper) in the upper right-hand corner, ½ inch from the top

border. Do not follow page numbers with hyphens, parentheses, periods, or other characters. Number the first page of the paper with an Arabic "1", and continue numbering pages consecutively throughout the paper, including "Works Cited" or "References" list.

7. Double-check the appropriate format (MLA or APA) for citing and documenting. Once again, we point out that you can use the online writing lab at Purdue University free of charge to find listings of all possible citations—both within your text and in "Works Cited" or "References."

8. Note that APA papers feature an abstract and a running header. (See sample paper.)

ANNOTATED STUDENT
RESEARCH PAPER

Modern Language Association (MLA) Style

(1) *The first page seen by your reader is usually the first page of your paper; however, some teachers require an outline to precede the first page. If so, paginate the outline with small Roman numerals (i, ii, iii . . .). Place your name in the top left-hand margin, followed by your instructor's name, the course number, and the date the paper is due.

See the sample outline on the next page. If you are using an outline, begin with a thesis, consisting of a single declarative sentence preceded by the word *Thesis.* The rest of the outline follows the rules for correct sentence outlining. Some instructors allow topic outlines, which consist of phrases rather than full sentences. Do not make the outline too long. A sound rule is to have one page of outline for every five pages of writing. The outline leaves out the details of the paper, mentioning only major points.

(2) Center the title (as well as the subtitle) of your paper. A good title should tell the reader what the paper is about. Double-space throughout the entire paper.

---

*The Arabic numerals in the left margin of the student paper correspond to the comments on the facing page.

1 → Stephanie Hollingsworth

Professor Dekker

English 101

30 September 2014

2 →   Choosing Single Motherhood: A Sign of Modern Times?

Thesis: Increases in educational and career opportunities for women, advances in medical technology, and diminishing social stigma all contribute to the rising number of women who are choosing to become single mothers.

I. Women are waiting longer to start families.

   A. A CA shift in women's consciousness has occurred since the 1960s.

      1. Marriage is no longer a necessary component to childbearing.

      2. The use of birth control gave women more choices over when or even if to get pregnant.

   B. There are more opportunities for women today.

      1. More women are taking advantage of higher education.

      2. The number of career opportunities for women has increased.

   C. Women are more willing to wait for the right partner.

      1. Personal fulfillment plays a higher role in the consciousness of today's woman.

      2. Many of today's women are children of divorce and would like to avoid that situation in their own marriages.

   D. Waiting longer creates concern for some women who fear the biological clock's ticking.

II. Advances in fertility technology are providing women with more options as to when and how to have a child.

   A. Women can have children later in life.

   B. Single women have the option of conceiving a child through donor insemination.

III. The social stigma of a single woman having a child has diminished.

   A. More adults today are children of divorce and therefore more tolerant of single parenting.

   B. The formation of support groups for single mothers has given single parenting a boost.

IV. Although many critics argue that single mothering by choice represents a breakdown of traditional family values, some studies indicate otherwise.

   A. Critics fear that the traditional nuclear family is quickly becoming the exception.

   B. Some studies argue that a father is not necessary for the healthy upbringing of a child.

      1. These studies show that children do not necessarily fare better when a father is present.

      2. Many fathers spend less than two and a half hours a day with their children.

1. Place your last name and page # in the upper right corner of each page, ½ inch from the top border.

2. Use Times New Roman 12 pt. or a similar font that is easy to read.

3. Give your name, instructor's name, course number, and date.

4. Center the title of your paper.

5. Double space throughout the entire paper.

6. Margins are 1 inch left, right, and bottom.

7. Margins are 1 inch left, right, and bottom.

8. You may use figures when the paper features many numbers. Very large numbers can be expressed by a combination of words and figures (11 million bricks), but be consistent.

9. In-text citation to a specific source in "Works Cited."

10. The thesis statement appears in its conventional position, at the end of the first paragraph.

11. In-text citation for two separate works.

12. Throughout this paragraph, the student does not use any direct quotation, but simply synthesizes Band, Bailey, and Jeweler's ideas and restates them in his own words, keeping the rhetorical style consistent.

Penaranda 1

Nick Penaranda

Professor Burnham

English 302

2 December 2013

A Victory for Readers?

Copyright Law and Google Book Search

Imagine being able to do months of meticulous research in only a matter of minutes. Actually, you don't have to imagine; a service already exists that allows a person to perform a full-text search of over 7 million books from any Internet-enabled computer (Google). An ambitious project by Internet giant Google is digitizing the libraries of the world, using image scanners and optical character recognition software. Entire books are being saved in Google's databases as both raw images and text data, enabling users not only to search books, but also view, copy, paste, and print them. The aptly named Google Book Search (GBS) project, which promises to provide an unprecedented level of access to millions of books for millions of people worldwide, sounds like great news to many students and researchers, but not everyone shares their enthusiasm (Google; Wiese).

In late 2004, Google announced that it had entered into partnership with several university libraries in the United States lo begin digitizing their collections. In exchange for the right to save digital copies of books into its own databases, Google would provide the libraries with one or more copies of each work for their own use. Conspicuously unrepresented in this transaction were the rights holders to the books still under copyright in those libraries. It wasn't long until publishers and authors everywhere were accusing Google of blatant, large-scale theft

13 In-text citation for three works. The Jeweler citation has a page reference because it is a print document. Whenever you cite authors from different works, provide enough information to direct the reader to the correct source.

14 Italicize names of books, plays, long poems, television shows, newspapers, magazines, Web sites, databases, art, films, and record albums.

15 Use ellipsis points (three equally spaced periods) to indicate an omission within a quotation.

16 Use the phrase "qtd. in" when quoting an author from another source. In this case, Verba is quoted in Hafner's work.

17 Use brackets to indicate explanatory interpolations within quotations.

18 Notice how the student smoothly integrates quotation, paraphrase, and personal commentary throughout this entire paragraph—proving that he has synthesized the original material and understands it.

19 Leave a 1-inch margin from the bottom of page.

Penaranda 2

13 ▸ of their intellectual property. Google's 2004 announcement would spark one of the largest copyright and fair-use debates that the Internet era has ever seen (Band; Bailey; Jeweler 95–96).

Sidney Verba, former director of the Harvard University Library,
14 ▸ has a unique perspective on GBS. In an interview for *The New York Times* in 2005, he discussed the concerns of publishers regarding
15 ▸ GBS: "Scanning the whole text |makes publishers very nervous. . . . They have to be assured that there will be security, that no one will
16 ▸ hack in and steal contents, or sell it to someone" (qtd. in Hafner). In addition, because some of his books are still in print, he says that he understands writers' concerns that GBS may disrupt their books' markets. Despite this, he believes that GBS will ultimately do more good than harm, and eventually agreed to give Google access to Harvard University Library's seven million volumes (Hafner).

On the other hand, one publisher, Rowman & Littlefield, opted out of GBS entirely. Jed Lyons, president and CEO of the publishing
17 ▸ company, called Google's project "an outrageous rip-off," and added, "[Google is] flagrantly violating U.S. copyright law" (qtd. in Albanese).
18 ▸ More specifically, Lyons was referring to Google's backwards method of obtaining permission. Traditionally, the burden of obtaining permission is the user's. Google, on the other hand, has assumed that it has permission and has given publishers and other rights holders a chance to opt out. He, like many other publishers and authors, felt that Google was going too far with GBS (Albanese).

And so, approximately one year after Google first announced its then-named Google Print project, two major lawsuits were filed against it. The first was a class action lawsuit filed by the Author's Guild and a
19 ▸ handful of authors, representing individual rights holders. McGraw-Hill

(20) The word *except* is italicized for emphasis.

(21) In-text citation for a U.S. government code.

(22) Here the student uses both quotation and paraphrase in a passage that requires accurate reflections from a legal code. For clarity, the guidelines are numbered, but only the first is directly quoted, presumably because it is the most important.

Penaranda 3

and several other publishers filed a second lawsuit a month later to represent publishers' interests. Both lawsuits claimed that Google, in creating and retaining digital copies of works to which the plaintiffs held rights, infringed on their copyrights. The plaintiffs of these two lawsuits believed that Google was committed only to increasing its revenue, regardless of copyright laws. In addition, they claimed that GBS would devalue their product or otherwise harm their market. They wanted the courts to order Google to destroy its collection and to declare such activity illegal ("Author's Guild"; "McGraw-Hill").

In response, Google claimed that their right to provide GBS is first and foremost protected under the First Amendment. Specifically, it claimed that its searchable digital library constitutes fair use and that no express permission was required from the rights holders. Further, it also claimed that only a portion of works are protected by copyright, and even that some works are unprotectable under U.S. copyright law. Google also fired back at some of the rights holders, claiming that some of them "have engaged in copyright misuse and have unclean hands" ("Author's Guild"). It also felt that GBS, by providing links to places where book search results could be purchased, could only benefit book markets. Predictably, Google wanted the courts to reward the plaintiffs nothing and declare that GBS was within copyright laws ("Author's Guild").

Il should be noted that Google's defense relied almost exclusively on the notion of "fair use." According to copyright law, all manner of reproduction, distribution, or displaying of intellectual property are the

20 → exclusive rights of the owner, except when its use falls within a set of guidelines set forth in the United States Code. When a party is accused of copyright infringement, courts are specifically instructed to

21 → consider (1) "the purpose and character of the use" (USC 107); (2) what the copyrighted material is, e.g., textbook or painting; (3) how much

22 → of the work was used; and (4) how the use will affect the copyrighted material's market or value. Beyond these four guidelines, courts have

(23) Names of legal cases are italicized.

(24) If a quotation runs more than four lines, indent an additional 1/2 inch with no quotation marks except for a quotation within the quotation (note "for the public good?").

(25) This long paragraph serves as a fine example of how to alternate between quoting, paraphrasing, and using personal commentary. By fully synthesizing the background material and making it his own, the student has avoided a choppy style and has maintained the integrity of his research.

Penaranda 4

little else on which to base their decisions. One can quickly see how the charges brought against Google are difficult and highly subjective matters to arbitrate (USC 106–107; Jeweler, 97).

Should publishers and authors have to give up their copyrights for Google's and, by extension, students and researchers' benefit? Or should Google be required to compensate rights holders for its digital copies? To date, there is no clear-cut answer. Like many other issues, this one is subject to "case law" or legal precedents created by past court decisions which guide future rulings. Unfortunately, there have never been disputes of this type, scale, or scope until now (Kohler). A few cases in the past have been only slightly similar—for instance, *Kelly v. Arriba Soft Corp.,* in which the court ruled that "Internet search engines' indexing activities constitute a fair use" (Jeweler 97). Thus, both the court and the litigants have a very limited historical guide to rely on. Perhaps this is the reason that, at the time of this writing, neither lawsuit has been settled in court ("Author's Guild"; "McGraw-Hill"). The case was not settled until 2013 when a judge sided with Google on the matter. (*The New York Times,* 15 Nov. 2013, Business).

The murky book settlement has caused hundreds of blogs, tweets, and other comments to be posted in cyberspace. One typical blogger's reaction is in the form of a question:

> Why can't the public just buy in-print books outside the Settlement, and buy out-of-print books from used booksellers or take them out of the library? The libraries who lent the books for scanning will also lend them for inter-library loan. Why is it that the creators of the works are not supposed to have any say in what is done "for the public good?" (Grimble)

Legal matters aside, Google states that one of its motivations behind GBS is to "ensure the ongoing accessibility of out-of-print books . . . to protect mankind's cultural history" (Google). At least to some extent, publishers and authors agree with this end, and their agreement has

23

24

25

26 Use parentheses to enclose nonessential or supplementary material within the text.

Penaranda 5

allowed the parties to negotiate a settlement out-of-court. This settlement includes, among other things, provisions for rights holders to exclude their work from CBS and for the establishment of a non-profit organization to guarantee the rights of authors, publishers, and others whose work is indexed. Perhaps most significantly, it outlines how rights holders will be able to profit from the inclusion of their works in GBS. The settlement distinguishes books into three categories: Books that

26 → are in print and under copyright, out-of-print but still under copyright, and those that are out-of-copyright (i.e., public domain). The first two types of books will have limited previews, enabling users to flip through them "just like you'd browse them at a bookstore or library" (Google). In addition, GBS will provide a means to purchase full versions of copyrighted books, while full versions of out-of-copyright books will be available free of charge. Lastly, GBS also intends to make physical copies of books more accessible, by pointing users to where they can get their hands on actual print versions of search results. Rights holders are poised to reach a bigger market for books that are in print and to rediscover markets for out-of-print books. Libraries and bookstores will enjoy greater patronage and advertisement, respectively. Lastly, Google will undoubtedly see increased traffic and thus increased revenue (Google; Kohler).

But what does it all mean for those not immediately invested in GBS? For starters, it means that anyone in search of an old, out-of-print book won't have to dig through used book stores or dusty library shelves, provided, of course, that the author didn't opt to turn his or her book's listing off in GBS. It means that students who are lucky enough to attend a university that purchases a GBS subscription, or anyone who happens to live near a subscribing library, will have access to full versions of millions of books, new and old. It means that some books that,

27   The paper ends by restating the thesis. It also includes a quotation, which at first glance might seem to diminish some of the student author's sway; however, the quotation happens to come from the co-founder of Google; thus, it lends a sense of final authority to the paper.

Penaranda 6

until recently, could only be found in a handful of libraries in the world, are now accessible to anyone with an Internet connection (Google).

Like the legal struggle that its inception sparked, GBS's contribution to the accessibility of knowledge is unprecedented. It's hard to imagine what the Internet would be like without search engines like Google, and soon it may be just as hard to imagine what doing research would be like without digital libraries like GBS. In sum, the GBS settlement stands to usher in a new era in publishing. In much the same way that iTunes changed the music industry for artists and record companies, GBS could potentially rock the literary world for publishers and authors. But perhaps most exciting of all, "the real victors are all the readers," said Sergey Brin, co-founder of Google. "The tremendous wealth of knowledge that lies within the books of the world will now be at their fingertips" (qtd. in Google).

28   The "Works Cited" list follows the MLA rules for citing references. Most of the references are to works from a database or a Web site. The date following the word "Web" is when the student retrieved the article from the website. The other date is the date of publication.

29   Center the title "Works Cited."

30   Arrange sources alphabetically by the author's last name, or if there is no author, by the first word in the citation.

31   Indent each source 1 inch from the border, double space, and indent the second and consecutive lines ½ inch.

32   Include the medium of each source: print, Web, CD, DVD, television, radio, film, email, performance, etc.

Penaranda 7

28 29 ────────────────────────→ Works Cited

30 31 ──→ Albanese, Andrew. "Publisher: No Thanks, Google," *Library Journal.*
32   Libraryjoumal.com, 1 Nov. 2005: n.p. Web. 21 Nov. 2013.

"Author's Guild et al. v. Google Inc." *Justia.com*. Justia, 2009. Web. 12
         Nov. 2013.

Bailey, Charles W., Jr. "Google Book Search Bibliography." *Digital-
         scholarship.org,* Digital Scholarship. 14 Sep. 2009. Web. 6 Nov.
         2013.

Band, J. "The Google Library Project: Both Sides of the Story." *Plagiary:
         Cross-Disciplinary Studies in Plagiarism, Fabrication, and Falsification*, 1
         (2006): 1–17. Web. 12 Nov. 2013.

Google, Inc. "Google Books Settlement Agreement." *Google.com.*
         Google, 2009. Web. 12 Nov. 2013.

Grimble, Frances. Blog. *The Laboratorium* Web. 22 Nov. 2013.

Hafner, Katie. "At Harvard, a Man, a Plan, and a Scanner." *The New York
         Times,* 21 Nov. 2005: n.p. *Nytimes.com.* Web. 21 Nov. 2013.

Jeweler, Robin. "The Google Book Search Project: Is Online Indexing a
         Fair Use Under Copyright Law?" *Focus on the Internet.* Ed. B. G.
         Kutais. New York: Nova Science Publishers, 2006. 95–100. Print.

Kohler, David. "This Town Ain't Big Enough for the Both of Us—Or Is It?
         Reflections on Copyright, the First Amendment and Google's Use of
         Others' Content." *Duke Law & Technology Review* 5, (2007): n.p.
         Social Science Research Network. Web. 8 Nov. 2013.

"McGraw-Hill et al. v. Google Inc." *Justia.com.* Justia, 2009. Web. 12
         Nov. 2013.

33 Include the URL only if the instructor requires it, or if the source is difficult to find without it.

Penaranda 8

Peritz, Rudolph J.R. and Marc Miller. "GBS: An Introduction to
    Competition Concerns in the Google Books Settlement." *The
    Laboratorium.* Web. 21 Nov. 2013. <http://laboratorium.net/
    archive/2010/03/21/gbs_an_introduction_to_competition_
    concerns . . . >

United States Copyright Law, Section 106: Exclusive Rights in
    Copyrighted Works. Amended 1990.

United States Copyright Law, Section 107: Limitations on Exclusive Rights:
    Fair Use. Amended 1990.

Wiese, Katie. "The Pens and the Keys: Controversy over Google Books
    and Scholar." *Echoditto.* 31 July 2009: n.p. Web. 6 Nov. 2013.

ANNOTATED STUDENT RESEARCH PAPER

American Psychological Association (APA) Style

Running Head: Development of a Scale 1

Development of a Scale to
Detect Sexual Harassers:
The Potential Harasser Scale (PHS)
Leanne M. Masden
and
Rebecca B. Winkler
DePaul University

(1) The Abstract should not exceed 120 words. Any numbers present in the Abstract should appear as Arabic numerals (except a number that begins a sentence).

DEVELOPMENT OF A SCALE 2

1 —————————————————————→ Abstract

The current study was an attempt to design a scale to detect one's propensity to sexually harass women. The Likelihood to Sexually Harass (LSH) scale designed by Pryor (1987) was used as a starting point in probing the characteristics held by men who sexually harass women. Using existing research, an initial scale was designed and tested on a pilot sample of men known to the authors. After the scale was completed by the participants, statistics were calculated and explored to determine which items needed to be retained and which needed to be dropped. Following these analyses, the Potential Harasser Scale (PHS) was determined to be statistically sound and ready for future use.

(2) This is a typical citation, appearing at the sentence's conclusion and followed by a period. This work has three authors.

(3) Because the information mentioned in this sentence is derived from three different sources, the paper's authors have chosen to place each citation adjacent to the corresponding element. Note that the first citation identifies a source with two authors, the second citation has three authors, and the third citation has one author.

Development of a Scale to Detect Sexual Harassers: The Potential
Harasser Scale (PHS)

Our interest in the current topic was first sparked as a result of sexual
harassment being the focus of one team member's master's thesis.
Current estimates state that approximately one out of every two women
will be sexually harassed at least once during her working or educational
life (Fitzgerald, Swan, & Magley, 1997). But why do so many women
experience sexual harassment? Researchers have found evidence to
support a power threat motive for offenders, whereby women who
possess certain characteristics that would put them in direct competition
with men for resources are more likely to be harassed, apparently
in an attempt to dissuade them from entering the male-dominated
sphere of privilege and power. Some such female characteristics are
having egalitarian sex-role attitudes (Dall'Ara & Maass, 1999), being
single, having more education and longer tenure within the organization
(DeCoster, Estes, & Mueller, 1999), and being young (Gruber, 1998).
However, there is not pure consensus in the field regarding the effect of
age on the risk of being sexually harassed (O'Connell & Korabik, 2000).
Because men are more likely than women to be perpetrators of sexual
harassment (Fitzgerald, Magley, Drasgow, & Waldo, 1999), this particular
population will be the focus of the present study.

During the initial research process, we discovered the Likelihood
to Sexually Harass (LSH) scale, originally developed by Pryor (1987).
This scale was designed to measure one's propensity to sexually harass
based on the possession of certain characteristics that perpetrators of
sexual harassment tend to have.

4 Because the authors are mentioned in the sentence, a citation is not necessary at the sentence's conclusion.

5 The paper's first-level internal heading appears centered, using bold uppercase and lowercase.

6 The paper's second-level internal heading appears flush with the left margin, using bold uppercase and lowercase.

This scale gave us the direction we needed to conduct further research in order to identify the relevant constructs this topic contained. Luckily, the LSH scale has generated a fair amount of research as a result of

4 → others attempting to find exactly what constructs this scale measures. For example, Driscoll, Kelly, and Henderson (1998) found that men who scored high on the LSH also held more traditional views toward women, more negative views toward women, and had a more masculine personality. Other researchers also found that aggression, acceptance of interpersonal violence, fraternity affiliation, and sex-role stereotyping were related to scoring high on the LSH (Lackie & de Man, 1997). In addition, Pryor (1987) showed that men scoring high on the LSH found it more difficult to view things from another's perspective and had higher authoritarian beliefs. As a result of this research, we now knew what we needed to include when we started to develop our own Potential Harasser Scale (PHS).

5 ————————————————→ **Method**

6 → **Item and Scale Development**

After reading the relevant research on our topic, we decided that our scale should include eight dimensions plus a few demographic questions. We also decided that each dimension should have four items. Our eight dimensions were as follows: aggression, sex role stereotyping (i.e., holding traditional views toward women), egalitarianism/negative views toward women, masculinity, acceptance of interpersonal violence, lack of empathy, authoritarianism, and hostile environment behaviors.

DEVELOPMENT OF A SCALE 5

The first seven dimensions were derived from the current literature on the topic of sexual harassment and related concepts. However, the last dimension was developed to fill a gap in the existing LSH scale. The LSH scale is designed to detect sexual harassers who exhibit *quid pro quo* behaviors, meaning those who attempt to exchange sexual favors for work-related promotions or other advantages (Pryor, 1987). However, this focus fails to address other forms of sexual harassment, such as hostile environment behaviors. This type of sexual harassment is considered to be less severe but even more pervasive (Fitzgerald, Gelfand, & Drasgow, 1995). Therefore, we thought it would be important to attempt to capture this dimension in our PHS instrument.

We also included a few demographic questions to see if age, race, or marital status were related to one's potential to sexually harass. In addition, a short section about fraternity membership and extent of one's involvement were included as a result of this affiliation being significantly related in previous research (Lackie & de Man, 1997). Therefore, our total scale had 37 items, 32 in the actual scale and 5 demographic questions. Furthermore, we renamed our instrument the *Personal Beliefs Questionnaire* so that those who completed our instrument would not be alerted to what it was attempting to measure.

Characteristics of the Pilot Sample

We recruited male classmates, co-workers, fathers, and significant others to complete our scale. As a result of our efforts, we had 14 respondents. All of them were Caucasian with the exception of one Hispanic. In addition, three individuals in our sample were married, five were single, and six currently lived with a partner.

DEVELOPMENT OF A SCALE 6

Our respondents ranged in age from 23 to 60, with a mean age of 30.28. Concerning fraternity affiliation, 35.7 percent of our sample were members of a fraternity, and 40 percent reported being "very involved."

Results

Results of Preliminary Item Analyses

First, we cleaned the data by looking at the frequencies and descriptive statistics. All values were within the expected range, so we considered our data to be clean. By taking a closer look at our means and standard deviations, we immediately noticed some items had extremely low standard deviations. For example, item 11 asks about one's acceptance of domestic violence. Whether the answers reflected socially desirable responses due to lack of anonymity with only 14 respondents or true beliefs, everyone in our sample strongly disagreed with the appropriateness of hitting one's spouse.

We scanned the correlation matrix including all of our items, and with the exception of item 11, which had no correlations due to its lack of variance, every other item exhibited at least one theoretically meaningful correlation with another item. For example, two items relating to aggression were significantly correlated (i.e., "I am an aggressive driver" and "I enjoy playing sports with a lot of physical contact"). The only items that were not significantly correlated with anything else on the scale were those that tapped into fraternity affiliation and involvement.

We also ran an intraclass correlation analysis to determine our scale's internal consistency. As a result, our Cronbach's alpha was $r = .8069$, which shows that our scale had high internal consistency.

7   The authors refer the reader to the Appendix, which appears at the paper's conclusion and following the References.

Final Scale Revision

Based on our initial item analyses, we determined that a few changes could be made that would improve our scale's psychometric properties. Therefore, we removed the items on fraternity affiliation and involvement. Although previous research has shown these constructs to be related to one's likelihood to sexually harass (Lackie & de Man, 1997), our analyses showed that these items were the only ones that were not significantly correlated to any other item in our scale. Since these items were in the demographics section, they were not included in the intraclass correlation analysis. Therefore, this analysis was not re-run, because no improvement would have been noted here.

Although traditional scale construction theory would normally guide us to remove a few other items due to their low standard deviations, we decided that the low variance on these items was most likely due to the restrictions placed on us by our small sample. If we were to administer our scale to a greater number of people in a more anonymous setting, perhaps we would not see the same restricted variance due to the greater chance of people answering truthfully. In our small and familiar sample, we found many answers that may have been driven by a socially desirable and appropriate manner of responding. See the Appendix for the final version of the PHS.

7 ▸

Discussion

This project taught us many valuable lessons. To begin with, we were pleased with the fact that we were able to construct a theoretically meaningful instrument that also displayed desirable psychometric properties, such as our high Cronbach's alpha. In addition, it was

an interesting experience to design items that fit into our proposed dimensions. We also had a fun time piloting it on our sample and gathering the reactions from our participants, in addition to analyzing their answers to draw the relevant conclusions on our new tool. However, there are also many things we would have done differently had this been a "real world" project.

First, merely masking our scale's true intent by designing a new label did not do much to mask the content and what we were trying to measure. Our participants (especially our classmates) could tell by the transparency of many of our items what we were aiming for. In addition, although we believe our sample to be well-educated and fairly liberal overall in their views toward women, they all still knew that we would be analyzing their responses and would probably be able to tell who was who if we really wanted to. Therefore, there may have been some socially desirable responding that caused many of our items to have low variances.

Some improvements in methodology could prevent this type of responding from occurring. For example, administering this scale in a more anonymous format with many other respondents (e.g., in an auditorium setting) would probably allow more truthful answers to emerge. Furthermore, if the scale items could be embedded within a larger instrument, the aim of the Potential Harasser Scale would also be less obvious. Overall, however, we were pleased with both the process and the results.

During the course of this project, we each also attempted to contact a publisher who had designed a relevant scale. One person contacted the company Risk and Needs Assessment, Inc., to obtain their Sexual Adjustment Inventory. The other person contacted Sigma Assessment Systems to obtain their Sex-Role Egalitarianism Scale.

DEVELOPMENT OF A SCALE 9

Both of us were successful in our endeavors and did not have to endure any trouble at all. One team member simply called the publisher and received a sample packet in a matter of days that included one test book, two answer sheets, one training manual, one example report, and a computer disk that provided the scoring key program. The other person emailed the publisher and received a sample brochure in the mail a few days later. Therefore, the ease in contacting the publishers was about equal between the two team members, but the amount of scale information given varied greatly.

In summary, working on this project allowed us to put into action much of the theory that we have spent the past ten weeks learning. It was interesting to us to experience the process of developing a scale as well as learning to deal with some of the pitfalls that inevitably occur with not having a large group of people we don't know to pilot our instrument on.

However, all in all, we think we will be better survey and test developers in the future as a result of constructing the Potential Harasser Scale.

8　The list of references appears on a separate page (or pages), with the heading "References" centered at the top of the page. All references cited in the text must appear in the Reference list; and each entry in the Reference list must be cited in the text of the paper. Note that APA prefers italicizing titles of books, magazines, and journals over underlining.

9　References with the same first author and different second, third, or fourth authors are alphabetized by the surname of the second author (or, if the second author is the same in the two references, the surname of the third).

DEVELOPMENT OF A SCALE 10

8 →　　　　　　　　References

Dall'Ara, E., & Maass, A. (1999). Studying sexual harassment in the
　　laboratory: Are egalitarian women at higher risk? *Sex Roles, 41*(9/10),
　　681–704. Retrieved December 9, 2011, from Proquest Education
　　Complete database.

DeCoster, S., Estes, S. B., & Mueller, C.W. (1999). Routine activities and
　　sexual harassment in the workplace. *Work and Occupations, 26*(1),
　　21–49.

Driscoll, D. M., Kelly, J. R., & Henderson, W. L. (1998). Can perceivers
　　identify likelihood to sexually harass? *Sex Roles, 38*(7/8), 557–588.

9 → Fitzgerald, L. F., Gelfand, M. J., & Drasgow, F. (1995). Measuring sexual
　　harassment: Theoretical and psychometric advances. *Basic and
　　Applied Social Psychology, 17,* 425–427.

Fitzgerald, L. F., Magley, V. J., Drasgow, F., & Waldo, C. R. (1999).
　　Measuring sexual harassment in the military: The sexual experiences
　　questionnaire (SEQ-DoD). *Military Psychology, 11*(3), 243–263.
　　Retrieved December 9, 2011, from Academic Search Elite database.

Fitzgerald, L. F., Swan, S., & Magley, V. J. (1997). But was it really
　　sexual harassment? Legal, behavioral, and psychological definitions
　　of the workplace victimization of women. W. O'Donohue (Ed.),
　　Sexual harassment: Theory, research, and treatment (pp. 5–28).
　　Boston: Allyn & Bacon.

Gruber, J. E. (1998). The impact of male work environments and
　　organizational policies on women's experiences of sexual
　　harassment. *Gender and Society, 12*(3), 301–320.

DEVELOPMENT OF A SCALE 11

Lackie, L., & de Man, A. F. (1997). Correlates of sexual aggression among male university students. *Sex Roles, 37*(5/6), 451–457.

O'Connell, C. E., & Korabik, K. (2000). Sexual harassment: The relationship of personal vulnerability, work context, perpetrator status, and type of harassment to outcomes. *Journal of Vocational Behavior, 56,* 299–329.

Pryor, J. B. (1987). Sexual harassment proclivities in men. *Sex Roles, 17*(5/6), 269–290.

10   If the paper has only one appendix, label it "Appendix." If your paper has more than one appendix, label each one with a capital letter (e.g., "Appendix A," "Appendix B"). Provide a title for each appendix.

10 ────────────────────────▶   Appendix

Personal Beliefs Questionnaire

Please rate how strongly you agree or disagree with the following statements using the scale provided below. Please answer all questions honestly; note that all of your answers will remain anonymous.

1 = Strongly Disagree

2 = Disagree

3 = Neither Agree nor Disagree

4 = Agree

5 = Strongly Agree

1. Being around strong women makes me   1   2   3   4   5
   uncomfortable.
2. I am an aggressive driver (e.g., I cut   1   2   3   4   5
   people off, honk the horn often).
3. I believe some women are to blame   1   2   3   4   5
   for being raped (e.g., by wearing sexy
   clothes, flirting, etc.).
4. I believe that every citizen should have   1   2   3   4   5
   the right to carry a gun.
5. I believe that it is important for a woman   1   2   3   4   5
   to take care of her body so that she looks
   good for her man.
6. I believe that it is important to volunteer   1   2   3   4   5
   time or donate money to help others in
   need.

1 = Strongly Disagree

2 = Disagree

3 = Neither Agree nor Disagree

4 = Agree

5 = Strongly Agree

7. I believe that men should be the primary breadwinners for their families. 1 2 3 4 5

8. I believe that most homeless people are still homeless because they are lazy. 1 2 3 4 5

9. I believe that people should respect their place within an organizational hierarchy. 1 2 3 4 5

10. I believe that some women are still paid less than men for doing the same work. 1 2 3 4 5

11. I believe that sometimes it is OK for a husband to hit his wife. 1 2 3 4 5

12. I believe that too many women are focusing too much on their careers, to the detriment of their families. 1 2 3 4 5

13. I believe that too many women are trying to enter occupations that are better suited for men. 1 2 3 4 5

14. I believe that women should be primarily responsible for taking care of children. 1 2 3 4 5

15. I believe that women should not play sports with a lot of physical contact (e.g., football). 1 2 3 4 5

DEVELOPMENT OF A SCALE 14

1 = Strongly Disagree

2 = Disagree

3 = Neither Agree nor Disagree

4 = Agree

5 = Strongly Agree

16. I display pictures of naked/near naked women at work/school.	1	2	3	4	5
17. I do not question the decisions made by the President.	1	2	3	4	5
18. I enjoy cooking for others.	1	2	3	4	5
19. I enjoy magazines that display pictures of scantily clad women.	1	2	3	4	5
20. I enjoy participating in cultural events (e.g., attending dramatic plays, museums, poetry readings).	1	2	3	4	5
21. I enjoy playing sports with a lot of physical contact.	1	2	3	4	5
22. I enjoy playing video games that allow you to fight and kill others.	1	2	3	4	5
23. I enjoy watching action movies with scenes involving car crashes, fights, and guns.	1	2	3	4	5
24. I flirt with women at my place of work/school.	1	2	3	4	5
25. I often get into fights.	1	2	3	4	5
26. I tell lewd jokes at work/school.	1	2	3	4	5

DEVELOPMENT OF A SCALE 15

1 = Strongly Disagree

2 = Disagree

3 = Neither Agree nor Disagree

4 = Agree

5 = Strongly Agree

27. I tend to raise my voice when I am upset.	1	2	3	4	5
28. I think it is important to obey authority figures.	1	2	3	4	5
29. I try to put myself in others' shoes to help me understand their situation.	1	2	3	4	5
30. In spousal disagreements, I believe that the man should have the final say.	1	2	3	4	5
31. Watching the nightly news can be depressing.	1	2	3	4	5
32. When it comes to asking a girl for a date, I don't take no for an answer.	1	2	3	4	5

DEVELOPMENT OF A SCALE 16

Demographics

33. How old are you?___

34. What is your race? Check one.

☐ Caucasian   ☐ African American   ☐ Hispanic

☐ Asian   ☐ Native American   Other_____

35. Please indicate your marital status. Check one.

☐ Married   ☐ Single   ☐ Divorced

☐ Widowed   ☐ Living with partner

36. Did you belong to a fraternity? Circle one.   Yes   No

If so, how involved were you? Circle one.

Not at all involved   Somewhat involved   Very involved

EXERCISES TO HELP YOU LEARN HOW TO SYNTHESIZE SOMEONE ELSE'S WORK INTO YOUR OWN WRITING.

The purpose of each exercise is to merge someone else's expression into your own writing without having your style lurch or stagger. While the smoothness we seek is not always easy to achieve, practice helps you improve.

1. On the Internet, find some biographical information on Jawaharlal Nehru, the first Prime Minister of India following its independence from England in 1947. After reading some of Nehru's public statements, write a passage in which you declare in your own words what Nehru's primary goals were for India. Since Nehru's words are in the public domain, you will not need to attribute a secondary source to them.

2. Read "kinds of Discipline" by John Holt (pp. 324–326) and restate the three kinds of disciplines he proposed by using them in the introduction to a paper about the lack of discipline in children today. Give Holt credit for his classification, but synthesize his ideas and reflect them rather than quote him. Then use your own evidence to support your thesis.

3. Through some Internet sleuthing, find out what Libya was like before Moammar Kadafi took over. Then, write a paragraph pointing out the upheaval and violence that preceded his rule and his subsequent death. Cite one or two experts on Libya, but summarize their words, turning them into a natural part of your own writing rather than quoting them verbatim.

4. In preparation for a research paper on stuttering, study paragraphs 16 and 17 of "My Strangled Speech" by Dan Slater on page 221. Then, compare the ancient explanations of stuttering with modern ones. You may refer to Slater by quoting him directly or by absorbing his ideas and then stating them in your own words, but either way, give him credit where credit is due.

5. For an APA-style paper on how the high school grades of athletes compare with the grades of nonathletes, assimilate the following statistics into a smooth sentence that indicates your understanding of the statistics. Use those statistics that strike you as the most reliable and least biased.

   • High school students who participate in sports have an average 2.61 GPA compared with an average 2.39 GPA for those who do not participate (from the Iowa High School Athletic Association, n.d.).

   • According to a recent Indiana University study, high school athletes have a 3.05 average GPA, whereas high school nonathletes have a 2.54 average GPA.

   • High school athletes have higher grades, lower drop-out rates, and attend college more often than nonathletes (from a recent survey by the Women's Sports Foundation).

   • A study of 22,000 students conducted at the University of Colorado in 1999 indicates that students who participate in sports have an overall significantly higher grade-point average than those who do not.

6. Review paragraphs 5 and 6 of "Grant and Lee: A Study in Contrasts" on page 300–301 and quote from them in order to establish Lee's cultural background. Use only those words or phrases that reveal his aristocratic way of life.

7. For a paper on the future of computer dating, go to MindTap and study the two papers dealing with that issue. The first is "The Truth About Online Dating" by Robert Epstein. The second is "Dating in Cyberspace" by Julius Lewis. Track down some other ideas offered by experts on computer dating. Quote or summarize, but make sure that you have digested the writer's statements so you can present them smoothly in your own words. Follow the guidelines offered in Chapter 3 for incorporating outside sources into your own work.

8. In preparation for a research paper on bullying, surf the Internet for recent cases in which bullying caused serious consequences, including death. Summarize in your own words the essence of what happened in each case. Then, write an introduction leading up to your thesis statement. If a direct quotation strengthens your thesis, use it, but do not pawn it off as your own or quote it out of context.

9. Integrate the following quotation into a paragraph about our modern world: "The picture of a meaningless world, and a meaningless human life, is, I think the basic theme of much modern art and literature" (W. T. Stace, p. 158). You may support, challenge, or qualify this quotation, but use it as the nub of your paragraph—knitting it into your writing so it fits there naturally.

10. Paraphrase the following quotation, preserving the tone and mood of the original. Retain exceptional words or phrases of the original by enclosing them in quotation marks. Use approximately the same number of words as the original and be sure to give credit to the original source:

The shrew haunts mostly moist thick-growing places, the banks of streams and the undergrowth of damp woods, and it hunts particularly actively at night. Scuttling on its pattery little feet among the fallen leaves, scrabbling in the leaf-mould in a frenzy of tiny investigation, it looks ceaselessly for food. Not a rodent, like a mouse, but an insectivore, it seizes chiefly on such creatures as crickets, grasshoppers, moths, and ants, devouring each victim with nervous eagerness and at once rushing on with quivering haste, tiny muzzle incessantly a-twitch, to look for further provender (from "Shrew—the Littlest Mammal," *This Fascinating Animal World* by Alan DeVoe, McGraw-Hill, 2005)

● SUGGESTIONS FOR WRITING

The following topics are not meant to be used as compulsory assignments, but to spark some ideas of your own. Use the suggestions only if they appeal to you or your instructor.

1. Using the MLA style, write a five- to eight-page research paper on one of the following topics: Pay attention to the advice put forward in this chapter.
   a. The importance of studying the classics in literature
   b. Katniss Everdeen, Harry Potter, or some other contemporary literary character as an emerging hero.
   c. The treatment of women in Muslim countries
   d. Mandatory sentencing—fair or unfair?
   e. How altruism can shape character
   f. The need for government-funded stem cell research

    g. Analyzing the relationship between plot and character in a favorite novel

    h. The rise of social networking (e.g., Facebook, YouTube)

    i. Religious faith and politics

    j. A critical analysis of one of the following influential female writers: Maya Angelou, Pearl S. Buck, Kate Chopin, Sandra Cisneros, Willa Cather, Isak Dinesen, Shirley Jackson, Harper Lee, Doris Lessing, Mary McCarthy, Carson McCullers, Flannery O'Connor, Tillie Olson, Katherine Anne Porter, Gertrude Stein, Alice Walker, Eudora Welty, Virginia Woolf

2. Using the APA style, write a five- to eight-page paper on one of the following topics. Pay attention to the advice put forward in this chapter:

    a. Eating disorders among teenagers

    b. The effects of loneliness and purposelessness on the elderly

    c. The growing rate of divorce in our society

    d. Gender roles in the United States or a foreign country

    e. Climate experimentation

    f. The need for anger management

    g. Exploring one of the latest anthropological findings (e.g., leeches in Rwanda, the Japanese Ainu, continued search for the Abominable Snowman, Ghengis Khan's tomb, prehuman tools, female infidelity in anthropology, fossil finds that trace our ancestry)

    h. Facilitating death in the universal health care system

    i. Dealing with addictions

    j. The psychology of cartoons

● SUGGESTIONS FOR A THESIS-DRIVEN RESEARCH PAPER

1. Write a research paper, following the format suggested by your instructor. Above all, choose a topic in which you have a genuine interest. The following titles and restricted theses are presented to stimulate your own investigation.

Title	Thesis
"A Look at Thomas Wolfe"	The inconsistencies in Thomas Wolfe's writing can be directly attributed to constant family conflicts, to his doubts concerning his country's economic stability, and to his fear of not being accepted by his reading public.
"American Architectural Development"	The development of American architecture was greatly attenuated until the eighteenth century because of the lack of adequate transportation and manufacturing facilities, and because city life had not formed prior to that century.
"Wordsworth and Coleridge: Their Diverse Philosophies"	Although Wordsworth and Coleridge were both Romantic poets, they believed in two completely different philosophies of nature.

"Why Jazz Was What We Wanted"	Various trends led to the rise, development, and recognition of jazz as an important part of American musical culture during the nineteenth and twentieth centuries.
"The Influence of Imagism on Twentieth-Century Poetry"	Imagism, a self-restricted movement, has greatly influenced twentieth-century poetry.
"Automation and Employment"	The current fear of humans being displaced by machines, or what alarmists term the "automa-tion hysteria," is based on insubstantial reports.
"Needed: A New Definition of Insanity"	Our courts need a better definition of insanity because neither the M'Naghten Rule nor the psychological definition is adequate.
"The Proud Sioux"	The Sioux Indians, although confined to a shabby reservation, still fought on stubbornly against their captors—the white man and his hard-to-accept peace terms.
"Women's Fashions after the World Wars"	The First and the Second World Wars had signifi-cant effects on women's fashions in America.
"Charlie Chaplin"	Various factors made Charlie Chaplin the master of silent movies.
"The Funnies"	Today's funnies reflect a change in America's attitude toward violence, ethnic minorities, and ecology.
"The Decline of the Mayans"	The four most popular theories that have been advanced to explain the abrupt end of the Mayan civilization are the effects of natural disaster, physical weaknesses, detrimental social changes, and foreign influence.
"Relief Paintings in Egyptian Mastabas"	The relief paintings found in the mastabas depict the everyday life of the Egyptian people.
"Athena"	The goddess Athena bestowed her favors not on those who worshipped her, but on those who fought for their own beliefs.
"Goldfish"	Originally from China, goldfish have been bred into one of the most beautiful and marketable species of fish.

2. Choosing any poem or short story in this book, write a literary analysis focusing on theme, character, action, or form.

Glossary

abstract   Said of words or phrases denoting ideas, qualities, and conditions that exist but cannot be seen. *Love,* for example, is an abstract term; so are *happiness, beauty,* and *patriotism.* The opposites of abstract terms are concrete ones—words that refer to things that are tangible, visible, or otherwise physically evident. *Hunger* is abstract, but *hamburger* is concrete. The best writing blends the abstract with the concrete, with concrete terms used in greater proportion to clarify abstract ones. Writing that is too steeped in abstract words or terms tends to be vague and unfocused.

ad hominem argument   A fallacious argument that attacks the integrity or character of an opponent rather than the merits of an issue. (*Ad hominem* is Latin for "to the man.") It is also informally known as "mud-slinging."

ad populum argument   A fallacious argument that appeals to the passions and prejudices of a group rather than to its reason. (*Ad populum* is Latin for "to the people.") An appeal, for instance, to support an issue because it's "the American Way" is an *ad populum* argument.

allusion   A casual reference to some famous literary work, historical figure, or event. For example, to say that a friend "has the patience of Job" means that he is as enduring as the biblical figure of that name. Allusions must be used with care lest the audience miss their meaning.

ambiguity   A word or an expression having two or more possible meanings is said to be ambiguous. Ambiguity is a characteristic of some of the best poetry, but it is not a desired trait of expository writing, which should clearly state what the writer means.

analogy   A comparison that attempts to explain one idea or thing by likening it to another. Analogy is useful if handled properly, but it can be a source of confusion if the compared items are basically unlike.

argumentation   A writer's attempt to convince the reader of a point. It is based on appeals to reason, evidence proving the argument, and sometimes emotion to persuade. Some arguments attempt merely to prove a point, but others go beyond proving to inciting the reader to action. At the heart of all argumentation lies a debatable issue.

audience   The group for whom a work is intended. For a writer, the audience is the reader whom the writer desires to persuade, inform, or entertain. Common sense tells us that a writer should always write to the level and needs of the particular audience for whom the writing is meant. For example, if you are writing for an unlettered audience, it is pointless to cram your writing with many literary allusions whose meanings will likely be misunderstood.

balance   In a sentence, a characteristic of symmetry between phrases, clauses, and other grammatical parts. For example, the sentence "I love Jamaica for its weather, its lovely scenery, and its people" is balanced. This sentence—"I love Jamaica for its weather, its lovely scenery, and because its people are friendly"—is not. See also **parallelism**.

causal analysis   A mode of developing an essay in which the writer's chief aim is to analyze cause or predict effect.

cliché   A stale image or expression, and the bane of good expository writing. "White as a ghost" is a cliché; so is "busy as a bee." Some clever writers can produce an effect by occasionally inserting a cliché in their prose, but most simply invent a fresh image rather than cull one from the public stock.

coherence   The principle of clarity and logical adherence to a topic that binds together all parts of a composition. A coherent essay is one whose parts—sentences, paragraphs, pages—are logically fused into a whole. Its opposite is an incoherent essay—one that is jumbled, illogical, and unclear.

colloquialism   A word or expression acceptable in informal usage but inappropriate in formal discourse. A given word may have a standard as well as a colloquial meaning. *Bug,* for example, is standard when used to refer to an insect, but when it is used to designate a virus—for example, "She's at home recovering from a bug"—the word is a colloquialism.

comparison/contrast   A rhetorical mode used to develop essays that systematically match two items for similarities and differences. See the comparison/contrast essay examples in Chapter 13.

conclusion   The final paragraph or paragraphs that sum up an essay and bring it to a close. Effective conclusions vary widely, but common tacks used by writers to end their essays include summing up what has been said, suggesting what ought to be done, specifying consequences that are likely to occur, restating the beginning, and taking the reader by surprise with an unexpected ending. Most important of all, however, is to end the essay artfully and quietly in a way that emphasizes your main point without staging a grand show for the reader's benefit.

concrete   Said of words or terms denoting objects or conditions that are palpable, visible, or otherwise evident to the senses. *Concrete* is the opposite of *abstract.* The difference between the two is a matter of degree. *Illness,* for example, is abstract; *ulcer* is concrete; "sick in the stomach" falls somewhere between the two. The best writing usually expresses abstract propositions in concrete terms.

connotation   The implication or emotional overtones of a word rather than its literal meaning. *Lion,* used in a literal sense, denotes a beast (see **denotation**). But to say that Winston Churchill had "the heart of a lion" is to use the connotative or implied meaning of *lion.*

critical thinking (or reading)   The attempt to understand and judge the underlying assumptions of a claim. It involves the following steps: (1) *analysis*—looking at the components that support a claim; (2) *synthesis*—blending the components analyzed into a new, original claim; (3) *evaluation*—judging or assessing a claim.

deduction   Something inferred or concluded. Deductive reasoning moves from the general to the specific.

denotation   The specific and literal meaning of a word, as found in the dictionary. The opposite of *connotation.*

description   A rhetorical mode used to develop an essay whose primary aim is to depict a scene, person, thing, or idea. Descriptive writing evokes the look, feel, sound, and sense of events, people, or things. See Chapter 9 for instructions on writing a descriptive essay.

diction   The choice of words a writer uses in an essay or other writing. Implicit in the idea of diction is a vast vocabulary of synonyms—words that have more or less equivalent meanings. If only one word existed for every idea or condition, diction would not exist. But because we have a choice of words with various shades of meaning, a writer can and does choose among words to express ideas. The diction of skilled writers is determined by the audience and occasion of their writing.

division and classification   A rhetorical mode for developing an essay whose chief aim is to identify the parts of a whole. A division and classification essay is often an exercise in logical thinking. See, for example, "Thinking as a Hobby" by William Golding in Chapter 14.

documentation   In a research paper, the support provided for an assertion, theory, or idea, consisting of references to the works of other writers. Different styles of documentation exist. Most disciplines now use the parenthetical style of documentation—see the sample research paper, "Choosing Single Motherhood: A Sign of Modern Times," in Part Four—where citations are made within the text of the paper rather than in footnotes or endnotes.

dominant impression   The central theme around which a descriptive passage is organized. For example, a description of an airport lobby would most likely use the dominant impression of rush and bustle, which it would support with specific detail, even though the lobby may contain pockets of peace and tranquility. Likewise, a description of Cyrano de Bergerac—the famous dramatic lover whose nose was horrendously long—would focus on his nose rather than on an inconspicuous part of his face.

emotion, appeal to   An appeal to feelings rather than to strict reason; a legitimate ploy in an argument, as long as it is not excessively and exclusively used.

emphasis   A rhetorical principle that requires stress to be given to important elements in an essay. Emphasis may be given to an idea in various parts of a composition. In a sentence, words may be emphasized by placing them at the beginning or end or by judiciously italicizing them. In a paragraph, ideas may be emphasized by repetition or by the accumulation of specific detail.

essay   From the French word *essai,* or "attempt," the essay is a short prose discussion of a single topic. Essays are sometimes classified as formal or informal. A formal essay is aphoristic, structured, and serious. An informal essay is personal, revelatory, humorous, and somewhat loosely structured.

evidence   The logical bases or supports for an assertion or idea. Logical arguments consist of at least three elements: propositions, reasoning, and evidence. The first of these consists of the ideas that the writer advocates or defends. The logical links by which the argument is advanced make up the second. The statistics, facts, anecdotes, and testimonial support provided by the writer in defense of the idea constitute the evidence. In a research paper, evidence consisting of paraphrases or quotations from the works of other writers must be documented in a footnote, endnote, or parenthetical reference. See also **argumentation** and/or **documentation**.

example   An instance that is representative of an idea or claim or that otherwise illustrates it. The example mode of development is used in essays that make a claim and then prove it by citing similar and supporting cases. See, for example, the essays in Chapter 11.

exposition   Writing whose chief aim is to explain. Most college composition assignments are expository.

figurative   Said of a word or expression used in a nonliteral way. For example, the expression "to go the last mile" may have nothing at all to do with geographical distance, but may mean to complete a task or job.

focus   In an essay, the concentration or emphasis on a certain subject or topic.

generalization   A statement that asserts some broad truth based on a knowledge of specific cases. For instance, the statement "big cars are gas guzzlers" is a generalization about individual cars. Generalizations are the products of inductive reasoning, whereby a basic truth may be inferred about a class after experience with a representative number of its members. However, one should beware of rash or faulty generalizations—those made on insufficient experience or evidence. It was once thought, for example, that scurvy sufferers were malingerers, which led the British navy to the policy of flogging the victims of scurvy aboard its ships. Later, medical research showed that the lethargy of scurvy victims was an effect rather than the cause of the disease. The real cause was found to be a lack of vitamin C in their diet.

image   A phrase or expression that evokes a picture or describes a scene. An image may be either literal, in which case it depicts what something looks like, or figurative, in which case an expression is used that likens the thing described to something else (e.g., "My love is like a red, red rose").

induction   A form of reasoning that proceeds from specific instances to a general inference or conclusion. Inductive reasoning is the cornerstone of the scientific method, which begins by examining representative cases and then infers some law or theory to explain them as a whole. See Chapter 14.

interparagraph   Between paragraphs. A comparison/contrast, for example, may be drawn between several paragraphs rather than within a single paragraph. For an example of an interparagraph comparison/contrast, see Chapter 7.

intraparagraph   Within a single paragraph. For an example of an intraparagraph comparison/contrast, see Chapter 7.

inversion   The reversal of the normal order of words in a sentence to achieve some desired effect, usually emphasis. Inversion is a technique long used in poetry, although most modern poets shun it as too artificial. For examples of inversion, see Shakespeare's "That Time of Year" (Sonnet 73) in Chapter 6.

irony   The use of language in such a way that apparent meaning contrasts sharply with real meaning. One famous example (in Shakespeare's *Julius Caesar*) is Antony's description of Brutus as "an honorable man." Because Brutus was one of Caesar's assassins, Antony meant just the opposite. Irony is a softer form of sarcasm and shares with it the same contrast between apparent and real meaning.

jargon The specialized or technical language of a trade, profession, class, or other group of people. Jargon is sometimes useful, but when used thoughtlessly it can become meaningless expression bordering on gibberish, as in the following sentence from a psychology text: "Her male sibling's excessive psychogenic outbursts were instrumental in causing her to decompensate emotionally." A clearer statement would be the following: "Her brother's temper eventually caused her to have a nervous breakdown."

literal *Literal* and *figurative* are two opposing characteristics of language. Literal meaning is a statement about something rendered in common, factual terms: "Good writers must be aggressive and daring." Figurative meaning is clouded in an image: "Good writers must stick out their necks." See **figurative**.

logical fallacies Errors in reasoning used by speakers or writers, sometimes in order to dupe their audiences. Most logical fallacies are based on insufficient evidence ("All redheads are passionate lovers") or on irrelevant information ("Don't let him do the surgery; he cheats on his wife") or on faulty reasoning ("If you don't quit smoking, you'll die of lung cancer").

metaphor A figurative image that implies a similarity between things otherwise dissimilar, such as the poet Robert Frost's statement "I have been acquainted with the night," meaning that he has suffered despair.

mood of a story The pervading impression made on the feelings of the reader. For instance, Edgar Allan Poe often created a mood of horror in his short stories. A mood can be gloomy, sad, joyful, bitter, frightening, and so forth.

mood of verbs A verb form expressing the manner or condition of the action. The moods of verbs are *indicative* (statements or questions), *imperative* (requests or commands), and *subjunctive* (expressions of doubt, wishes, probabilities, and conditions contrary to fact).

narrative An account of events that happened. A narrative organizes material on the basis of chronological order or pattern, stressing the sequence of events and pacing these events according to the emphasis desired. Narration is often distinguished from three other modes of writing: argumentation, description, and

exposition. See "How to Write a Narrative" in Chapter 8.

objective and subjective Two attitudes toward writing. In *objective* writing, the author tries to present the material fairly and without bias; in *subjective* writing, the author stresses personal responses and interpretations. For instance, news reporting should be objective, whereas poetry can be subjective.

pacing The speed at which a piece of writing moves along. Pacing depends on the balance between summarizing action and representing the action in detail. See "How to Write a Narrative" in Chapter 8.

parallelism The principle of coherent writing requiring that coordinate elements be given the same grammatical form, as in Daniel Webster's dictum, "I was born an American; I will live an American; I will die an American."

paraphrase A restatement of a text or passage in another form or in other words, often to clarify the meaning. Paraphrase is commonly used in research papers to assimilate the research into a single style of writing and thereby avoid a choppy effect. See also **plagiarism**.

personification Attributing human qualities to objects, abstractions, or animals: "'Tis beauty calls and glory leads the way."

plagiarism Copying words from a source and then passing them off as one's own. Plagiarism is considered dishonest scholarship. Every writer is obligated to acknowledge ideas or concepts that represent someone else's thinking.

point of view The perspective from which a piece of writing is developed. In nonfiction, the point of view is usually the author's. In fiction, the point of view can be first- or third-person. In the first-person point of view, the author becomes part of the narrative and refers to him- or herself as "I." In the third-person point of view, the narrator simply observes the action of the story. Third-person narration is either *omniscient* (the narrator knows everything about all of the characters) or *limited* (the narrator knows only those things that might be apparent to a sensitive observer).

premise An assertion or statement that is the basis for an argument. See **syllogism**.

process A type of development in writing that stresses how a sequence of steps produces a certain effect. For instance, explaining to the reader all of the steps involved in balancing a checkbook would be a *process* essay. See Chapter 10 for examples of process writing.

purpose The commitment on the part of authors to explain what they plan to write about. Purpose is an essential part of unity and coherence. Most teachers require students to write a statement of purpose, also called a *thesis*: "I intend to argue that our Federal Post Office needs a complete overhaul."

red herring A side issue introduced into an argument to distract from the main argument. It is a common device of politicians: "Abortion may be a woman's individual right, but have you considered the danger of the many germ-infested abortion clinics?" Here the side issue of dirty clinics clouds the ethical issue of having an abortion.

repetition A final review of all of the main points in a piece of writing; also known as *recapitulation*. In skillful writing, repetition is a means of emphasizing important words and ideas, of binding together the sentences in a passage, and of creating an effective conclusion. Its purpose is to accumulate a climactic impact or to cast new light on the material being presented.

rhetoric The art of using persuasive language. This is accomplished through the author's diction and sentence structure.

rhetorical question A question posed with no expectation of receiving an answer. This device is often used in public speaking to launch or further discussion. For example, a speaker might say, "What is the meaning of life, anyway?" as a way of nudging a talk toward a discussion of ethics.

satire Often an attack on a person. Also the use of wit and humor to ridicule society's weaknesses so as to correct them. In literature, two types of satire have been recognized: *Horatian satire,* which is gentle and smiling, and *Juvenalian satire,* which is sharp and biting.

simile A figure of speech that, like the metaphor, implies a similarity between things otherwise dissimilar. The simile, however, always uses *like, as,* or *so* to introduce the comparison: "My word is like a steel plate, never to be broken."

slang The casual vocabulary used by specific groups or cultures, especially students—usually considered inappropriate for formal writing. In today's technological culture of text messaging, chat speak has developed as a particular kind of slang. Examples are LOL (laughing out loud), IMHO (in my humble opinion), or OMG (oh, my god).

slanting The characteristic of selecting facts, words, or emphasis to achieve a preconceived intent:

favorable intent: "Although the Senator looks bored, when it comes time to vote, she is on the right side of the issue."

unfavorable intent: "The Senator may vote on the right side of issues, but she always looks bored."

social networking The use of websites and applications that create an online system of written communication among persons of similar interests. The most popular social networking websites today are Facebook, Twitter, LinkedIn, Pinterest, Google Plus, Tumblr, and various dating sites, such as eHarmony.com. People who communicate on social networks do so through blogs, emails, texts, tweets, or posts.

specific A way of referring to the level of abstraction in words; the opposite of *general.* A *general* word refers to a group or class, whereas a *specific* word refers to a member of a group or class. Thus, the word *nature* is general, the word *tree* more specific, and the word *oak* even more specific. The thesis of an essay is general, but the details supporting that thesis are specific. See also **abstract** and **concrete**.

Standard English The English of educated speakers and writers. Any attempt to define Standard English is controversial because no two speakers of English speak exactly alike. What is usually meant by "Standard English" is what one's grammar book dictates.

statement of purpose What an author is trying to tell an audience; the main idea of an essay. Traditionally, what distinguishes a statement of purpose from a *thesis* is wording, not content. A statement of purpose includes words such as "My purpose is . . ." and "In this paper, I intend to . . ." A statement of purpose is often the lead sentence of an essay. See Chapter 5.

straw man An opposing point of view, set up so it can easily be refuted. This is a common strategy used in debate.

style   The expression of an author's individuality through the use of words, sentence patterns, and selection of details. Our advice to fledgling writers is to develop a style that combines sincerity with clarity.

subordination   Expressing in a dependent clause, phrase, or single word any idea that is not significant enough to be expressed in a main clause or an independent sentence:

lacking subordination: John wrote his research paper on Thomas Jefferson; he was interested in this great statesman.

with subordination: Because John was interested in Thomas Jefferson, he wrote his research paper on this great statesman.

syllogism   In formal logic, the pattern by which a deductive argument is expressed:

All men are mortal. (major premise)

John Smith is a man. (minor premise)

Therefore John Smith is mortal. (conclusion)

symbol   An object or action that in its particular context represents something else. For instance, in Ernest Hemingway's novel *A Farewell to Arms,* the rain represents impending disaster because when it rains something terrible happens.

synonym   A word or phrase that has the same meaning as another. For instance, the words *imprisonment* and *incarceration* are synonyms. The phrases "fall short" and "miss the mark" are synonymous.

syntax   The order of words in a sentence and their relationships to each other. Good syntax requires correct grammar as well as effective sentence patterns, including unity, coherence, and emphasis.

theme   See **thesis**.

thesis   The basic idea of an essay, usually stated in a single sentence. In expository and argumentative writing, the thesis (or *theme*) is the unifying force that every word, sentence, and paragraph of the essay must support.

tone   The reflection of the writer's attitude toward subject and audience. The tone can be personal or impersonal, formal or informal, objective or subjective, or expressed in irony, sarcasm, anger, humor, satire, hyperbole, or understatement.

topic sentence   The *topic sentence* is to a paragraph what the *thesis* or *theme* is to the entire essay—that is, it expresses the paragraph's central idea.

transition   Words, phrases, sentences, or even paragraphs that indicate connections between the writer's ideas. These transitions provide landmarks to guide readers from one idea to the next. The following are some standard transitional devices:

time: soon, immediately, afterward, later, meanwhile, in the meantime

place: nearby, on the opposite side, further back, beyond

result: as a result, therefore, thus, as a consequence

comparison: similarly, likewise, also

contrast: on the other hand, in contrast, nevertheless, but, yet, otherwise

addition: furthermore, moreover, in addition, and, first, second, third, finally

example: for example, for instance, to illustrate, as a matter of fact, on the whole, in other words.

understatement   Deliberately representing something as less than it is in order to stress its magnitude. Also called *litotes.* A good writer will restrain the impulse to hammer home a point and will use understatement instead. An example is the following line from Oscar Wilde's play *The Importance of Being Earnest:* "To lose one parent, Mr. Worthing, may be regarded as a misfortune; to lose both looks like carelessness."

unity   The characteristic in writing of having all parts contribute to an overall effect. An essay or paragraph is described as having *unity* when all of its sentences develop one central idea. The worst enemy of unity is irrelevant material. A good rule is to delete all sentences that do not advance or prove the thesis or topic sentence of an essay.

voice   The presence or the sound of self chosen by an author. Most good writing sounds like someone delivering a message. The aim in good student writing is to sound natural. Of course, the voice will be affected by the audience and occasion for writing. See Chapter 4, "What Is a Writer's Voice?"

Index

(Page number in bold indicates images)